OB Skills Workbook

Self-Assessments

1. Managerial Assumptions
2. A Twenty-First-Century Manager
3. Turbulence Tolerance Test
4. Global Readiness Index
5. Personal Values
6. Intolerance for Ambiguity
7. Two-Factor Profile
8. Are You Cosmopolitan?
9. Group Effectiveness
10. Least Preferred Co-Worker Scale
11. Leadership Style
12. "TT" Leadership Style
13. Empowering Others
14. Machiavellianism
15. Personal Power Profile
16. Your Intuitive Ability
17. Decision-Making Biases
18. Conflict Management Strategies
19. Your Personality Type
20. Time Management Profile
21. Organizational Design Preference
22. Which Culture Fits You?

Team and Experiential Exercises

1. My Best Manager
2. Graffiti Needs Assessment
3. My Best Job
4. What Do You Value in Work?
5. My Asset Base
6. Expatriate Assignments
7. Cultural Cues
8. Prejudice in Our Lives
9. How We View Differences
10. Alligator River Story
11. Teamwork & Motivation
12. The Downside of Punishment
13. Tinkertoys
14. Job Design Preferences
15. My Fantasy Job
16. Motivation by Job Enrichment
17. Annual Pay Raises
18. Serving on the Boundary
19. Eggsperiential Exercise
20. Scavenger Hunt—Team Building
21. Work Team Dynamics
22. Identifying Team Norms
23. Workgroup Culture
24. The Hot Seat
25. Interview a Leader
26. Leadership Skills Inventories
27. Leadership and Participation in Decision Making
28. My Best Manager—Revisited
29. Active Listening
30. Upward Appraisal
31. 360° Feedback
32. Role Analysis Negotiation
33. Lost at Sea
34. Entering the Unknown
35. Vacation Puzzle
36. The Ugli Orange
37. Conflict Dialogues
38. Force-Field Analysis
39. Organizations Alive!
40. Fast-Food Technology
41. Alien Invasion
42. Power Circles

A. Sweet Tooth
B. Interrogatories
C. Decode
D. Choices
E. Internal/External Motivators
F. Quick Hitter

Cases for Critical Thinking

Trader Joe's Keeps Things Fresh
Getting the Evidence: Leadership Training Dilemma
Diversity Leads the Way
OB Classic: The Jim Donovan Case
Tough Situation at MagRec, Inc.
"It Isn't Fair..."
Perfect Pizzeria, or Not?
OB Classic: Hovey and Beard Company
The Forgotten Group Member
Teams Drive the Fast Cars
Decisions, Decisions, Decisions
The Case of the Missing Raise
The Poorly Informed Walrus
Political Behavior Analysis
Selecting a New Vice President
Zappos Does it with Humor
Never on a Sunday
First Community Financial

WileyPLUS

Now with: **ORION**, An Adaptive Experience

WileyPLUS is a research-based, online environment for effective teaching and learning.

WileyPLUS builds students' confidence because it takes the guesswork out of studying by providing students with a clear roadmap:

- **what to do**
- **how to do it**
- **if they did it right**

It offers interactive resources along with a complete digital textbook that help students learn more. With *WileyPLUS*, students take more initiative so you'll have greater impact on their achievement in the classroom and beyond.

Now available for **Bb** Blackboard

For more information, visit www.wileyplus.com

WileyPLUS with ORION

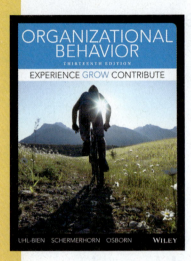

Based on cognitive science, *WileyPLUS* with ORION provides students with a personal, adaptive learning experience so they can build their proficiency on topics and use their study time most effectively.

BEGIN

Unique to ORION, students **BEGIN** by taking a quick diagnostic for any chapter. This will determine each student's baseline proficiency on each topic in the chapter. Students see their individual diagnostic report to help them decide what to do next with the help of ORION's recommendations.

PRACTICE

For each topic, students can either **STUDY**, or **PRACTICE**. Study directs students to the specific topic they choose in *WileyPLUS*, where they can read from the e-textbook or use the variety of relevant resources available there. Students can also practice, using questions and feedback powered by ORION's adaptive learning engine. Based on the results of their diagnostic and ongoing practice, ORION will present students with questions appropriate for their current level of understanding, and will continuously adapt to each student to help build proficiency.

MAINTAIN

ORION includes a number of reports and ongoing recommendations for students to help them **MAINTAIN** their proficiency over time for each topic.

Students can easily access ORION from multiple places within *WileyPLUS*. It does not require any additional registration, and there will not be any additional charge for students using this adaptive learning system.

ABOUT THE ADAPTIVE ENGINE

ORION includes a powerful algorithm that feeds questions to students based on their responses to the diagnostic and to the practice questions. Students who answer questions correctly at one difficulty level will soon be given questions at the next difficulty level. If students start to answer some of those questions incorrectly, the system will present questions of lower difficulty. The adaptive engine also takes into account other factors, such as reported confidence levels, time spent on each question, and changes in response options before submitting answers.

The questions used for the adaptive practice are numerous and are not found in the *WileyPLUS* assignment area. This ensures that students will not be encountering questions in ORION that they may also encounter in their *WileyPLUS* assessments.

ORION also offers a number of reporting options available for instructors, so that instructors can easily monitor student usage and performance.

WileyPLUS with ORION helps students learn by learning about them.™

Organizational Behavior

13TH EDITION

Mary Uhl-Bien
University of Nebraska

John R. Schermerhorn, Jr.
Ohio University

Richard N. Osborn
Wayne State University

VICE PRESIDENT & EXECUTIVE PUBLISHER	George Hoffman
EXECUTIVE EDITOR	Lisé Johnson
CONTENT EDITOR	Jennifer Manias
EDITORIAL ASSISTANT	Jacqueline Hughes
DIRECTOR OF MARKETING	Amy Scholz
SENIOR MARKETING MANAGER	Kelly Simmons
MARKETING ASSISTANT	Juliette San Fillipo
DESIGN DIRECTOR	Harry Nolan
SENIOR CONTENT MANAGER	Dorothy Sinclair
SENIOR PRODUCTION EDITOR	Erin Ault
SENIOR PRODUCT DESIGNER	Allison Morris
MEDIA SPECIALIST	Elena Santa Maria
SENIOR PHOTO EDITOR	Mary Ann Price
PHOTO RESEARCHER	Susan McLaughlin
SENIOR DESIGNER	Thomas Nery
COVER PHOTO	©Philip and Karen Smith/Iconica/Getty Images
UMBRELLA ICON	©Monti26/Shutterstock

This book was typeset in 10/12 Kepler Std Light at Aptara®, Inc. and printed and bound by Quad Graphics/Versailles. The cover was printed by Quad Graphics/Versailles.

This book is printed on acid free paper. ∞

Founded in 1807, John Wiley & Sons, Inc. has been a valued source of knowledge and understanding for more than 200 years, helping people around the world meet their needs and fulfill their aspirations. Our company is built on a foundation of principles that include responsibility to the communities we serve and where we live and work. In 2008, we launched a Corporate Citizenship Initiative, a global effort to address the environmental, social, economic, and ethical challenges we face in our business. Among the issues we are addressing are carbon impact, paper specifications and procurement, ethical conduct within our business and among our vendors, and community and charitable support. For more information, please visit our website: www.wiley.com/go/citizenship.

Copyright ©2014, 2012, 2010, 2008, 2005, John Wiley & Sons, Inc. All rights reserved. No part of this publication may be reproduced, stored in a retrieval system or transmitted in any form or by any means, electronic, mechanical, photocopying, recording, scanning or otherwise, except as permitted under Sections 107 or 108 of the 1976 United States Copyright Act, without either the prior written permission of the Publisher, or authorization through payment of the appropriate per-copy fee to the Copyright Clearance Center, Inc., 222 Rosewood Drive, Danvers, MA 01923, website www.copyright.com. Requests to the Publisher for permission should be addressed to the Permissions Department, John Wiley & Sons, Inc., 111 River Street, Hoboken, NJ 07030-5774, (201)748-6011, fax (201)748-6008, website http://www.wiley.com/go/permissions.

Evaluation copies are provided to qualified academics and professionals for review purposes only, for use in their courses during the next academic year. These copies are licensed and may not be sold or transferred to a third party. Upon completion of the review period, please return the evaluation copy to Wiley. Return instructions and a free of charge return shipping label are available at www.wiley.com/go/returnlabel. If you have chosen to adopt this textbook for use in your course, please accept this book as your complimentary desk copy. Outside of the United States, please contact your local representative.

ISBN 13 978-1-118-45632-3

Printed in the United States of America.

10 9 8 7 6 5 4 3 2 1

About the Authors

Dr. Mary Uhl-Bien

DR. MARY UHL-BIEN is the Howard Hawks Chair in Business Ethics and Leadership at the University of Nebraska. She earned her Ph.D. and M.B.A. in organizational behavior at the University of Cincinnati after completing an undergraduate degree with a focus in International Business and Spanish. She teaches organizational behavior, leadership, and ethics courses at the undergraduate and graduate (MBA and doctoral) levels, and has been heavily involved in executive education around the world. She has been a visiting professor/scholar at Queensland University of Technology (QUT) in Australia, Lund University in Sweden, Pablo de Olavide University in Seville, Spain, and the Universidade Nova de Lisboa/Catolica Portuguesa in Lisbon, Portugal.

Dr. Uhl-Bien's research interests are in leadership, followership, and ethics. In addition to her conceptual work on complexity and relational leadership, some of the empirical projects she is currently involved in include investigations of "Leadership and Adaptability in the Healthcare Industry" (a $300,000 grant from Booz Allen Hamilton), "Adaptive Leadership and Innovation: A Focus on Idea Generation and Flow" (at a major financial institution in the U.S.), and "Social Constructions of Followership and Leading Up." She has published in such journals as *The Academy of Management Journal*, the *Journal of Applied Psychology*, *The Leadership Quarterly*, the *Journal of Management*, and *Human Relations*. She won the Best Paper Award in *The Leadership Quarterly* in 2001 for her co-authored article on Complex Leadership. She has been on the editorial boards of *The Academy of Management Journal*, *The Academy of Management Review*, *The Leadership Quarterly*, *Leadership*, and *The International Journal of Complexity in Leadership* and Management, and is senior editor of the Leadership Horizons series (Information Age Publishers). Dr. Uhl-Bien has consulted with Disney, the U.S. Fish and Wildlife Service, British Petroleum, and the General Accounting Office, and served as the executive consultant for State Farm Insurance Co. from 1998–2004. She has been a Visiting Scholar in Spain, Portugal, and Sweden. Dr. Uhl-Bien has trained Russian businesspeople for the American Russian Center at the University of Alaska Anchorage from 1993–1996, worked on a USAID grant at the Magadan Pedagogical Institute in Magadan, Russia from 1995–1996, and participated in a Fulbright-Hays grant to Mexico during the summer of 2003.

Dr. John R. Schermerhorn, Jr.

DR. JOHN R. SCHERMERHORN JR. is the Charles G. O'Bleness Emeritus Professor of Management in the College of Business at Ohio University where he teaches undergraduate and MBA courses in management, organizational behavior, and Asian business. He earned a PhD degree in organizational behavior from Northwestern University, after receiving an MBA degree (with distinction) in management and international business from New York University, and a BS degree in business administration from the State University of New York at Buffalo.

Dr. Schermerhorn focuses his teaching and textbooks on bridging the gap between the theory and practice of management. He has won awards for teaching excellence at Tulane University, The University of Vermont, and Ohio University, where he was named a *University Professor*, the university's leading campus-wide award for undergraduate teaching. He also received the excellence in leadership award for his service as Chair of the Management Education and Development Division of the Academy of Management.

Dr. Schermerhorn's international experience adds a unique global dimension to his teaching and writing. He holds an honorary doctorate from the University of Pécs in Hungary, awarded for his international scholarly contributions to management research and education. He has also served as a Visiting Fulbright Professor at the University of Botswana, Visiting Professor of Management at the Chinese University of Hong Kong, on-site Coordinator of the Ohio University MBA and Executive MBA programs in Malaysia, and Kohei Miura Visiting Professor at the Chubu University of Japan. Presently he is Adjunct Professor at the National University of Ireland at Galway, a member of the graduate faculty at Bangkok University in Thailand, and Permanent Lecturer in the PhD program at the University of Pécs in Hungary.

An enthusiastic scholar, Dr. Schermerhorn is a member of the Academy of Management, where he served as chairperson of the Management Education and Development Division. Educators and students alike know him as author of *Exploring Management* (2014) *and Management 12e* (Wiley, 2013). His many books are available in Chinese, Dutch, French, Indonesian, Portuguese, Russian, and Spanish language editions. Dr. Schermerhorn has also published numerous articles in publications such as the Academy of Management Journal, *Academy of Management Review, Academy of Management Executive, Organizational Dynamics, Journal of Management Education, and the Journal of Management Development*.

Dr. Schermerhorn is a popular guest speaker at colleges and universities. His recent student and faculty workshop topics include innovations in business education, teaching the millennial generation, global perspectives in management, and textbook writing and scholarly manuscript development.

Dr. Richard N. Osborn

Dr. Richard N. Osborn is a Wayne State University Distinguished Professor, Professor of Management Emeritus, and former Board of Governors Faculty Fellow. He has received teaching awards at Southern Illinois University at Carbondale and Wayne State University, and he has also taught at Arizona State University, Monash University (Australia), Tulane University, University of Munich, and the University of Washington. He received a DBA from Kent State University after earning an MBA at Washington State University and a B.S. from Indiana University. With over 200 presentations and publications, he is a charter member of the Academy of Management Journals Hall of Fame. Dr. Osborn is a leading authority on international alliances in technology-intensive industries and is co-author of an organization theory text as well as *Basic Organizational Behavior* (John Wiley & Sons, 1995, 1998). He has served as editor of international strategy for the *Journal of World Business* and Special Issue Editor for *The Academy of Management Journal*. He serves or has served as a member of the editorial boards for *The Academy of Management Journal, The Academy of Management Review, Journal of High Technology Management, The Journal of Management, Leadership Quarterly*, and *Technology Studies*, among others. He is very active in the Academy of Management, having served as divisional program chair and president, as well as the Academy representative for the International Federation of Scholarly Associations of Management. Dr. Osborn's research has been sponsored by the Department of Defense, Ford Motor Company, National Science Foundation, Nissan, and the Nuclear Regulatory Commission, among others. In addition to teaching, Dr. Osborn spent a number of years in private industry, including a position as a senior research scientist with the Battelle Memorial Institute in Seattle, where he worked on improving the safety of commercial nuclear power.

From the Authors

Global warming, economic uncertainty, poverty, discrimination, unemployment, illiteracy—these are among the many issues and problems we now face. But how often do we stop and accept responsibility for problem solving and positive action in an increasingly complex world? What we do today will have a lasting impact on future generations. And whether we are talking about families, communities, nations, or the organizations in which we work and volunteer, the core question remains: How can we join together to best serve society?

Look at the cover and think about people with goals and aspirations. Think about people working together and collaborating around the world. Think about how people can expand the positive impact of society's institutions when their ideas and talents come together in supportive and nurturing work settings. And think about the delicate balances—between work and family, between individuals and teams, and between organizations and society—that must be mastered in the quest for future prosperity.

Yes, our students do have a lot to consider in the complex and ever-shifting world of today. But, we believe they are up to the challenge. And, we believe that courses in organizational behavior have strong roles to play in building their capabilities to make good judgments and move organizational performance forward in positive and responsible ways.

That message is a fitting place to begin *Organizational Behavior*, 13th Edition. Everyone wants to have a useful and satisfying job and career; everyone wants all the organizations of society—small and large businesses, hospitals, schools, governments, nonprofits, and more—to perform well; everyone seeks a healthy and sustainable environment. In this context the lessons of our discipline are strong and applicable. Armed with an understanding of organizational behavior, great things are possible as people work, pursue careers, and contribute to society through positive personal and organizational accomplishments.

Organizational behavior is rich with insights for career and life skills. As educators, our job is to engage students and share with them the great power of knowledge, understanding, and inquiry that characterizes our discipline. What our students do with their talents will not only shape how organizations perform, but also fundamentally contribute to society and alter lives around the globe. Our job is to help them gain the understanding and confidence to become leaders of tomorrow's organizations.

MARY UHL-BIEN
University of Nebraska

JOHN R. SCHERMERHORN, JR.
Ohio University

RICHARD N. OSBORN
Wayne State University

Welcome to *Organizational Behavior*, 13th Edition

New Edition at a Glance

OB 13/e has a new author team.

We are pleased to feature in this edition the ideas, insights, and scholarly expertise of **Mary Uhl-Bien**. Mary brings extensive knowledge of leadership and relational processes in OB. She has received awards for her research, and is currently serving in the OB Division Chair track in the Academy of Management. She places deep value on rigor *and* relevance in OB, which she accomplishes by engaging in cutting edge research conducted through strong partnerships between scholars and practitioners. Along with Mary, **John Schermerhorn** continues to play a senior role in content, design, and pedagogy, while **Dick Osborn** focuses his attention on updating macro themes.

OB 13/e offers flexible, topic-specific presentation of OB topics.

Topics in the book are easily assigned in any order based on instructor preferences. There are many options available for courses of different types, lengths, and meeting schedules, including online and distance learning formats. It all depends on what fits best with your course design, learning approaches, and class session objectives. There is no complicated "model" that requires a structured content approach. Instructors can select core OB topics and themes while moving among chapters organized in four parts—Individual Behavior and Performance, Teams and Teamwork, Influence Processes and Leadership, and Organizational Context.

In this edition you will see timely updates to all chapters as well as extensive revisions to enhance the discussion of interpersonal and relational processes and streamline the macro treatment. Look for the following updates and special themes in *Organizational Behavior, 13th edition.*

- *Context.* We place context front and center as a key theme throughout the book. Students are continually reminded to think about organizational behavior as it occurs in a dynamic and ever changing world.
- *Relationships.* Positive relationships are essential building blocks for effective organizations, but this topic is often missed in OB texts. We draw from research to describe the importance of interpersonal relationships in OB, while giving special emphasis to relationship-building processes relative to communication, power, and leadership.
- *Collaboration.* Along with expanded focus on relationships, this edition pushes beyond the limits of hierarchical thinking and recognizes we live in an increasingly interconnected and collaborative world. The changing nature of organizational

life requires everyone, not just managers, to embrace shared responsibility and collaborative thinking. Making sense of and building skills to succeed in this collaborative context are mainstream themes for the book.

- *Communication.* Organizations need effective communicators. The discussion of communication has been refreshed to incorporate research on voice, silence, feedback-giving and feedback-seeking. We also expand coverage of supportive communication principles and how to use communication to build and maintain effective relationships. A key goal is helping students understand how they can overcome problems of avoidance in communication.

- *Leadership.* Our approach to the leadership process material has been substantially updated to reflect emerging trends in leadership research in reaction to changing leadership environments. We recognize leadership as a process and not just a position or an individual behavior. We bring in the latest research on identity, followership, relational leadership, and collective leadership. And, the overview of trait, behavioral, and contingency approaches to leadership is extended to include a discussion of complexity leadership and ethics.

- *Power and politics.* Power and politics are essential in organizational functioning, and many employers indicate that new graduates are naïve when it comes to these issues. We provide a more balanced view of both positive and negative aspects of power and politics. New findings from network theory, research on perceptions of politics and political skills, and the nature of political climates provide students with a broad-based and practical understanding of how power and politics issues matter to them.

OB 13/e uses an integrated learning design.

Every chapter opens with a subtitle and photograph that help students identify with the content right from the beginning. This is followed by the **Key Point** conveyed in a short smart-phone sized message. Major chapter headings are listed in **Chapter At a Glance**. And, **What's Inside** directs student attention to major chapter features or learning accents—*Bringing OB to Life, Worth Considering… Or Best Avoided? Checking Ethics in OB, Finding the Leader in You, OB in Popular Culture,* and *Research Insight.*

Chapter content begins with each major heading linked with a Learning Roadmap which identifies major subheads for the section. The end-of-chapter **Study Guide** includes a summary of **Key Questions and Answers, Terms to Know,** a **Chapter Self-Test,** and suggested active learning activities found in the end-of-book **OB Skills Workbook**—a selection of *Cases for Critical Thinking, Team and Experiential Exercises,* and *Self-Assessments.*

OB 13/e makes "flipping" the classroom easy.

"Flipped" classrooms shift the focus from instructors lecturing and students listening, to instructors guiding and students engaging. The first step to making that possible is for students to read and study assigned materials outside of class. When they come to class prepared, the instructor has many more options for engagement. The organization and content of *Organizational Behavior, 13th Edition,* coupled with the power of the *WileyPLUS* online learning environment help greatly in this regard.

Success in flipping the classroom also requires a variety of discussion activities, projects, and quick-hitting experiences that turn class time into engaged learning time. You will find that this book is "packed" with such opportunities. The following chapter features are not only interesting to readers; they are also prompts and frames that can be used for flipped classroom activities and discussions, and for individual and team assignments.

Welcome to *Organizational Behavior*, 13th Edition

OB 13/e is full of timely and engaging application and discussion features.

- **Bringing OB to Life**—Timely, even controversial issues from real life, are framed for student thought and discussion. Examples include "Building Skills to Succeed in a Collaboration Economy," "Taking Steps to Curb Bias in Performance Assessment," "Welcoming the Elephant to the Conference Room," and "Paying or Not Paying for Kid's Grades."

- **Worth Considering... Or Best Avoided?**—Briefly summarizes a recent trend or decision from practice with pro and con aspects that can be analyzed from an OB perspective, and asks students to take a position on its efficacy. Examples include "Want Vacation? No Problem, Take as Much as You Want," "Not Enough Women on Board? Europe Considers Setting Quotas," "Own a Yoga Mat? Meditation Can be Good for You and Your Job," and "Software Makes Online Meetings Easy. Is It Time to Kill Face-to-Face Sit Downs?"

- **Finding the Leader in You**—Introduces a real person's leadership experience and asks students to use it to inquire into their personal leadership capacities. Examples include: Michelle Greenfield, sustainability entrepreneur, Ursula Burns, CEO of Xerox and the first African American woman to head a *Fortune* 500 firm; Gary Hirshberg, social entrepreneur and co-founder of Stonyfield Farms; and, Sarah Blakely, founder of Spanx.

- **Checking Ethics in OB**—Poses a situation or dilemma and asks students to answer the ethics questions. Examples include: "Social Loafing May Be Closer than You Think," "Privacy in an Age of Social Networking," "Workers Share their Salary Secrets," "Cheat Now . . . Cheat Later," "Blogging Can be Fun, but Bloggers Beware," and "Furlough or Fire? Weighing Alternative Interests."

- **OB in Popular Culture**—A short vignette that links chapter topics with popular culture examples from movies and television. Examples include "Ambition and the *Social Network*," "Self-Management and *Slumdog Millionaire*," "Conflict and the Devil *Wears Prada*," and "Critical Thinking and *Tron Legacy*."

- **Research Insight**—Highlights an article from a respected journal such as the *Academy of Management Journal* and the *Journal of Applied Psychology*. Sample topics include—interactional justice, racial bias, social loafing, demographic faultlines, and workplace identities.

OB 13/e once again includes the popular all-in-one teaching resource—The OB Skills Workbook.

The end-of-text *OB Skills Workbook* has become a hallmark feature of the textbook, and it has been updated and expanded for the new edition. The four sections in the new updated workbook that offer many ways to extend the OB learning experience in creative and helpful ways. All items have chapter assignment recommendations.

- **Cases for Critical Thinking**—20 cases selected for topical content and matched with recommended chapters.
- **Student Leadership Practices Inventory**—The popular Kouzes/Posner instrument ready for class use.
- **Team and Experiential Exercises**—52 exercises useful for teamwork and in-class experiential activities.
- **Self-Assessment Portfolio**—22 self assessment instruments for students' personal reflection.

Student and Instructor Support

Organizational Behavior, 13th Edition, is supported by a comprehensive learning package that assists the instructor in creating a motivating and enthusiastic environment.

We are pleased to provide you with an instructor's hardback copy of *Organizational Behavior, 13th Edition* by Uhl-Bien, Schermerhorn, and Osborn. Thank you for considering this text for adoption. As Wiley strives to provide products of high value and low cost to students, listed on the back cover of this book are the value-priced student versions of the text that you can select from to order for your class.

The student version of the text is in the Wiley Binder Version format; if you would like to adopt the text in another format, please contact your Wiley representative for additional ordering options. Wiley Binder Versions provide an alternative to the traditional hardback version at a lower cost. Delivered in a three-hole punched, loose-leaf format; students carry only the content they need, insert class notes and hand-outs, all in one place.

For the student-on-the-go, Wiley also offers digital textbooks allowing students to access a complete version of the text online and offline on their desktop, laptop, and mobile devices at a discounted price.

Uhl-Bien, Schermerhorn, Osborn, *Organizational Behavior, 13th Edition* Binder Version
ISBN for ordering: 978-1-118-51737-6

Annotated Instructor's Edition With teaching notes prepared by the authors, the Annotated Instructor's Edition includes a Teaching Note for each section of the book. These notes are designed to spark discussion and thought among students and to stimulate deeper discussion, energize the class, and improve learning through reinforcement and application.

Companion Web Site The text's Web site at http://www.wiley.com/college/schermerhorn contains myriad tools and links to aid both teaching and learning, including nearly all of the student and instructor resources.

Instructor's Resource Guide The Instructor's Resource Guide offers helpful teaching ideas, advice on course development, sample assignments, and chapter-by-chapter text highlights, learning objectives, lecture outlines, class exercises, lecture notes, answers to end-of-chapter material, and tips on using cases.

Test Bank This comprehensive Test Bank is available on the instructor portion of the Web site and consists of over 200 questions per chapter. Each chapter has true/false, multiple choice, and short answer questions. The questions are designed to vary in degree of difficulty to challenge your OB students. The *Computerized Test Bank* contains content from the Test Bank provided within a test-generating program that allows instructors to customize their exams.

PowerPoint This robust set of lecture/interactive PowerPoints is provided for each chapter to enhance your students' overall experience in the OB classroom. The PowerPoint slides can be accessed on the instructor portion of the Web site and include lecture notes to accompany each slide. An *Image Gallery*, containing jpg files for all of the figures in the text, is also provided for instructor convenience.

Web Quizzes This set of online quizzes is written to match the Test Bank and varies in level of difficulty. It is designed to help your students evaluate their individual progress through a chapter. Web quizzes are available on the student portion of the Web site. Here students will have the ability to test themselves with 15–25 multiple choice and true-false questions per chapter.

Organizational Behavior Video Series and Teaching Guide   Short news clips tied to the major topics in organizational behavior are available. These clips provide an excellent starting point for lectures or for general class discussion. Teaching notes for using the video clips are available on the instructor's portion of the Web site.

Darden Business Cases   Through the Wiley Custom Select website, you can choose from thousands of cases from Darden Business Publishing to create a book with any combination of cases, Wiley textbook chapters and original material. Visit http://www.customselect.wiley.com/collection/dardencases for more information.

Organizational Behavior All Access Pack   The All Access Pack is perfect for today's students who want all of their course materials to be accessible anytime, anywhere. The All Access Pack includes the *WileyPLUS* online learning environment, a Wiley E-Text, downloadable to any device, and the printed OB Skills Workbook, which contains Self-Assessments, Team and Experiential Exercises, and Cases for Critical Thinking.

WileyPLUS

WileyPLUS is an innovative, research-based, online environment for effective teaching and learning.

WileyPLUS builds students' confidence because it takes the guesswork out of studying by providing students with a clear roadmap: **what to do, how to do it, if they did it right.** This interactive approach focuses on:

CONFIDENCE—Research shows that students experience a great deal of anxiety over studying. That's why we provide a structured learning environment that helps students focus on **what to do**, along with the support of immediate resources.

MOTIVATION—To increase and sustain motivation throughout the semester, *WileyPLUS* helps students learn **how to do it** at a pace that's right for them. Our integrated resources—available 24/7—function like a personal tutor, directly addressing each student's demonstrated needs with specific problem-solving techniques.

SUCCESS—*WileyPLUS* helps to assure that each study session has a positive outcome by putting students in control. Through instant feedback and study objective reports, students know *if they did it right*, and where to focus next, so they achieve the strongest results.

With *WileyPLUS*, our efficacy research shows that students improve their outcomes by as much as one letter grade. *WileyPLUS* helps students take more initiative, so you'll have greater impact on their achievement in the classroom and beyond.

What do students receive with WileyPLUS?

- The complete digital textbook, saving students up to 60% off the cost of a printed text.
- Question assistance, including links to relevant sections in the online digital textbook.
- Immediate feedback and proof of progress, 24/7.
- Integrated, multi-media resources including the following resources and many more that provide multiple study paths and encourage more active learning.
- CBS/BBC videos
- Self-Assessments quizzes students can use to test themselves on topics such as emotional intelligence, diversity awareness, and intuitive ability.
- Flash Cards
- Hot Topic Modules
- Crossword Puzzles
- Self-Study Questions

What do instructors receive with WileyPLUS?

Customizable Course Plan: *WileyPLUS* comes with a pre-created Course Plan designed by a subject matter expert uniquely for this course. Simple drag-and-drop tools make it easy to assign the course plan as-is or modify it to reflect your course syllabus.

Pre-created Activity Types Include:

- Questions
- Readings and resources
- Presentations
- Print Tests
- Concept Mastery
- Projects

Course Materials and Assessment Content:

- PowerPoint Slides
- Image Gallery
- Instructor's Resource Guide
- Gradable Reading Assignment Questions (embedded with online text)
- Question Assignments: all end-of-chapter questions
- Test Bank
- Web Quizzes
- Video Teaching Notes—includes questions geared towards applying text concepts to current videos

www.wileyplus.com

WileyPLUS inside Blackboard Learn™

Discover the advantage of integrating all your course materials in one place with WileyPLUS and Blackboard.

Digital content in higher education is advancing rapidly—moving from static content to dynamic digital assets that provide for personalized, interactive learning. That's why Blackboard and Wiley have partnered to deliver all the benefits of WileyPLUS within the familiar Blackboard Learn™ experience. Tested by instructors and students, this best-in-class integration is designed to meet varying levels of digital usage.

With direct access to WileyPLUS inside Blackboard Learn™, you can create a unified learning experience for your students. You'll have everything you need for teaching and learning all in one place:

- Single sign-on provides faculty and students with direct access to all WileyPLUS content with the convenience of one login.
- Direct links to WileyPLUS readings and assignments give faculty greater control over how they deliver information and allow students to conveniently access their course work.
- Gradebook synchronization ensures all grades appear in the Blackboard Grade Center, saving instructors time and increasing student accountability.
- Student data privacy compliance means student data is always protected and secure.

It's easy to get Started with WileyPLUS and Blackboard. The free WileyPLUS Building Block is available now on Behind the Blackboard for U.S. and international higher education institutions that license Blackboard Learn 9.1, Service Pack 5 and higher. Download the Building Block today.

WileyPLUS with ORION

Helping you learn by learning about you™.

***WileyPLUS* with ORION** is an adaptive, personal learning experience that helps students find their way as they make new discoveries about how they learn. Highlighting both strengths and problem areas, ***WileyPLUS* with ORION** is the guide that helps all types of learners navigate through their studies to get optimal results in the most efficient amount of time.

WileyPLUS with ORION provides students with a personal, adaptive learning experience so they can build their proficiency on topics and use their study time most effectively. ORION helps students learn by learning about them.

- Unique to ORION, students **begin** by taking a quick diagnostic for any chapter. This will determine each student's baseline proficiency on each topic in the chapter. Students see their individual diagnostic report to help them decide what to do next with the help of ORION's recommendations.

- For each topic, students can either **Study** or **Practice**. Study directs students to the specific topic they choose in *WileyPLUS*, where they can read from the e-textbook or use the variety of relevant resources available there. Students can also practice, using questions and feedback powered by ORION's adaptive learning engine. Based on the results of their diagnostic and ongoing practice, ORION presents students with questions appropriate for their current level of understanding. The system continuously adapts to each student so that he or she can build proficiency.

- *WileyPLUS* with ORION includes a number of reports and ongoing recommendations for students to help them **maintain** their proficiency over time for each topic.

Contributors

Cases for Critical Thinking

Barry R. Armandi, *State University of New York*, David S. Chappell, *Ohio University*, Bernardo M. Ferdman, *Alliant International University*, Placido L. Gallegos, *Southwest Communications Resources, Inc.* and the *Kaleel Jamison Consulting Group. Inc.*, Carol Harvey, *Assumption College*, Ellen Ernst Kossek, *Michigan State University*, Barbara McCain, *Oklahoma City University*, Mary McGarry, *Empire State College*, Marc Osborn, *Kutak Rock LLP, Phoenix*, Franklin Ramsoomair, *Wilfrid Laurier University*, Hal Babson and John Bowen of *Columbus State Community College*.

Experiential Exercises and Self-Assessment Inventories

Barry R. Armandi, *State University of New York, Old Westbury*, Ariel Fishman, *The Wharton School, University of Pennsylvania*, Barbara K. Goza, *University of California, Santa Cruz*, D.T. Hall, *Boston University*, F.S. Hall, *University of New Hampshire*, Lady Hanson, *California State Polytechnic University, Pomona*, Conrad N. Jackson, *MPC, Inc.*, Mary Khalili, *Oklahoma City University*, Robert Ledman, *Morehouse College*, Paul Lyons, *Frostburg State University*, J. Marcus Maier, *Chapman University*, Michael R. Manning, *New Mexico State University*, Barbara McCain, *Oklahoma City University*, Annie McKee, *The Wharton School, University of Pennsylvania*, Bonnie McNeely, *Murray State University*, W. Alan Randolph, *University of Baltimore*, Joseph Raelin, *Boston College*, Paula J. Schmidt, *New Mexico State University*, Susan Schor, *Pace University*, Timothy T. Serey, *Northern Kentucky University*, Barbara Walker, *Diversity Consultant*, Paula S. Weber, *New Mexico Highlands University*, Susan Rawson Zacur, *University of Baltimore*.

Acknowledgments

Organizational Behavior, 13th Edition, benefits from insights provided by a dedicated group of management educators from around the globe who carefully read and critiqued draft chapters of this and previous editions. We are pleased to express our appreciation to the following colleagues for their contributions:

Merle Ace	Ann Cowden	Don Hantula
Chi Anyansi-Archibong	Suzanne Crampton	Kristi Harrison
Terry Armstrong	Deborah Crown	William Hart
Leanne Atwater	Roger A. Dean	Nell Hartley
Forrest Aven	Robert Delprino	Neil J. Humphreys
Steve Axley	Emmeline De Pillis	David Hunt
Abdul Aziz	Pam Dobies	Eugene Hunt
Richard Babcock	Delf Dodge	Howard Kahn
David Baldridge	Dennis Duchon	Harriet Kandelman
Michael Banutu-Gomez	Michael Dumler	Edward Kass
Robert Barbato	Ken Eastman	Barcley Johnson
Heidi Barclay	Norb Elbert	Paul N. Keaton
Richard Barrett	Gary J. Falcone	Andrew Klein
Nancy Bartell	Theresa Feener	Leslie Korb
Anna Bavetta	Janice M. Feldbauer	Peter Kreiner
Robb Bay	Claudia Ferrante	Eric Lamm
Hrach Bedrosian	Mark Fichman	Donald Lantham
Bonnie Betters-Reed	Dalmar Fisher	Jim Lessner
Gerald Biberman	J. Benjamin Forbes	Les Lewchuk
Melinda Blackman	Dean Frear	Kristi M. Lewis
Robert Blanchard	Nancy Fredericks	Robert Liden
Lisa Bleich	Cynthia V. Fukami	Beverly Linnell
Mauritz Blonder	Normandie Gaitley	Kathy Lippert
Dale Blount	Daniel Ganster	Michael London
G. B. Bohn	Joe Garcia	Michael Lounsbury
William Bommer	Cindy Geppert	Carol Lucchesi
H. Michal Boyd	Virginia Geurin	David Luther
Pat Buhler	Robert Giambatista	Jim Maddox
Gene E. Burton	Manton Gibbs	Marcia Marriott
Roosevelt Butler	Eugene Gomolka	Lorna Martin
Ken Butterfield	Barbara Goodman	Tom Mayes
Joseph F. Byrnes	Stephen Gourlay	Daniel McAllister
Michal Cakrt	Frederick Greene	Douglas McCabe
Tom Callahan	Richard Grover	Randy McCamey
Daniel R. Cillis	Bengt Gustafsson	James McFillen
Nina Cole	Peter Gustavson	Jeanne McNett
Paul Collins	Lady Alice Hanson	Charles Milton

Acknowledgments

Herff L. Moore	Robert Salitore	Ed Tomlinson
David Morand	Terri Scandura	Sharon Tucker
David Morean	Mel Schnake	Nicholas Twigg
Sandra Morgan	Holly Schroth	Tony Urban
Paula Morrow	L. David Schuelke	Ted Valvoda
Richard Mowday	Richard J. Sebastian	Joyce Vincelette
Christopher Neck	Anson Seers	David Vollrath
Linda Neider	William Sharbrough	Andy Wagstaff
Lam Nguyen	R. Murray Sharp	W. Fran Waller
Judy C. Nixon	Ted Shore	Charles Wankel
Regina O'Neill	Allen N. Shub	Edward Ward
Dennis Pappas	Sidney Siegal	Fred A. Ware, Jr.
Edward B. Parks	Dayle Smith	Andrea F. Warfield
Robert F. Pearse	Mary Alice Smith	Harry Waters, Jr.
Lawrence Peters	Wendy Smith	Joseph W. Weiss
Prudence Pollard	Walter W. Smock	Deborah Wells
Joseph Porac	Pat Sniderman	Robert Whitcomb
Samuel Rabinowitz	Ritch L. Sorenson	Donald White
Franklin Ramsoomair	Shanthi Srinivas	Bobbie Williams
Clint Relyea	Paul L. Starkey	Barry L. Wisdom
Bobby Remington	Robert Steel	Wayne Wormley
Charles L. Roegiers	Ronni Stephens	Barry Wright
Steven Ross	Ron Stone	Kimberly Young
Joel Rudin	Tom Thompson	Raymond Zammuto
Michael Rush	Jody Tolan	

We are grateful for all the hard work of the supplements authors who worked to develop the comprehensive ancillary package described above. We thank Amit Shah, Shelley Smith, Robert (Lenie) Holbrook, and many others who have contributed over several editions.

As always, the support staff at John Wiley & Sons was most helpful in the various stages of developing and producing this edition. We would especially like to thank Lisé Johnson (Executive Editor), George Hoffman (Publisher), Jennifer Manias (Content Editor), and Jacqueline Hughes (Editorial Assistant) for their extraordinary efforts in support of this project. They took OB to heart and did their very best to build a high-performance team in support of this book. We thank everyone at Wiley for maintaining the quest for quality and timeliness in all aspects of the book's content and design. Special gratitude goes to Tom Nery as the creative force behind the new design. We also thank Erin Ault and Jackie Henry for their excellent production assistance, Allie Morris for overseeing the media development, and Kelly Simmons for leading the marketing campaign. Thank you everyone!!

Brief Contents

PART 1 **Organizational Behavior Today**
    1 Introducing Organizational Behavior   3

PART 2 **Individual Behavior and Performance**
    2 Diversity, Personality, and Values   27
    3 Perception, Attribution, and Learning   51
    4 Emotions, Attitudes, and Job Satisfaction   75
    5 Motivation   99
    6 Motivation and Performance   119

PART 3 **Teams and Teamwork**
    7 The Nature of Teams   141
    8 Teamwork and Team Performance   163
    9 Decision Making and Creativity   189
    10 Conflict and Negotiation   213

PART 4 **Influence Processes and Leadership**
    11 Communication   235
    12 Power and Politics   259
    13 The Leadership Process   281
    14 Leader Traits and Behavioral Styles   301

PART 5 **Organizational Context**
    15 Organizational Culture and Innovation   327
    16 Organizational Structure and Design   353

OB Skills Workbook

OB Modules Online

Contents

PART 1
Organizational Behavior Today

1 Introducing Organizational Behavior 3

Introducing Organizational Behavior 4
  What Is Organizational Behavior? 4
  Importance of Organizational Behavior 4

Organizational Behavior as a Science 6
  Scientific Foundations of Organizational Behavior 6
  Learning about Organizational Behavior 9

The Context of Organizational Behavior 11
  Organizations and the External Environment 11
  The Internal Environment of Organizations 13
  Diversity and Multiculturalism in Organizations 13

Management and Organizational Behavior 14
  Effective Managers 14
  The Management Process 15
  Essential Managerial Skills 16
  Ethical Management 18

Leadership and Organizational Behavior 19
  The Leadership Process 19
  Effective Leaders 20
  Effective Followers 21

Study Guide 22

PART 2
Individual Behavior and Performance

2 Diversity, Personality, and Values 27

Individual Differences and Diversity 28
  Self-Concept, Self-Awareness, and Awareness of Others 28
  Valuing-or Not Valuing-Diversity 29
  Diversity Issues in the Workplace 30
  Diversity and Social Identity 33

Personality 34
  Big Five Personality Traits 34
  Social Traits 35
  Personal Conception Traits 37

Personality and Stress 40
  Type A Orientation and Stress 40
  Work and Life Stressors 40
  Outcomes of Stress 41
  Approaches to Managing Stress 42

Values 43
  Sources of Values 43
  Personal Values 43
  Cultural Values 44

Study Guide 46

3 Perception, Attribution, and Learning 51

The Perception Process 52
  Factors Influencing Perception 52
  Information Processing and the Perception Process 53
  Perception, Impression Management, and Social Media 56

Common Perceptual Distortions 57
  Stereotypes 57
  Halo Effects 58
  Selective Perception 58
  Projection 59
  Contrast Effects 60
  Self-Fulfilling Prophecies 60

Perception, Attribution, and Social Learning 61
  Importance of Attributions 61
  Attribution Errors 62
  Attribution and Social Learning 62

Learning by Reinforcement 64
    Classical Conditioning 64
    Operant Conditioning and the Law of Effect 64
    Positive Reinforcement 65
    Negative Reinforcement 68
    Punishment 68
    Extinction 69
    Reinforcement Pros and Cons 69
Study Guide 69

4 Emotions, Attitudes, and Job Satisfaction 75

Understanding Emotions and Moods 76
    The Nature of Emotions 76
    Emotional Intelligence 76
    Types of Emotions 77
    The Nature of Moods 78
How Emotions and Moods Influence Behavior 79
    Emotion and Mood Contagion 79
    Emotional Labor 80
    Emotional Empathy 81
    Cultural Aspects of Emotions and Moods 81
    Emotions and Moods as Affective Events 82
How Attitudes Influence Behavior 83
    What Is an Attitude? 83
    Components of Attitudes 83
    Attitudes and Cognitive Consistency 84
    Attitudes and the Workplace 84
Job Satisfaction Trends and Issues 87
    Components of Job Satisfaction 87
    Job Satisfaction Trends 87
    How Job Satisfaction Influences Work Behavior 89
    Linking Job Satisfaction and Job Performance 91
Study Guide 93

5 Motivation 99

What Is Motivation? 100
    Motivation Defined 100
    Motivation Theories 100
Motivation and Human Needs 101
    Hierarchy of Needs Theory 101
    ERG Theory 102
    Acquired Needs Theory 102
    Two-Factor Theory 103
    Emotional Drives or Needs Model 105
Motivation and Equity 105
    Equity and Social Comparisons 105
    Equity Theory Predictions and Findings 106
    Equity and Organizational Justice 107

Motivation and Expectancy 109
    Expectancy Terms and Concepts 109
    Expectancy Theory Predictions 110
    Expectancy Theory Implications and Research 110
Motivation and Goals 111
    Motivational Properties of Goals 112
    Goal-Setting Guidelines 112
    Goal Setting and the Management Process 113
Study Guide 114

6 Motivation and Performance 119

Motivation, Rewards, and Performance 120
    Employee Value Proposition and Fit 120
    Integrated Model of Motivation 120
    Intrinsic and Extrinsic Rewards 121
    Pay for Performance 121
Motivation and Performance Management 125
    Performance Management Process 125
    Performance Measurement Approaches and Errors 125
    Performance Assessment Methods 126
Motivation and Job Design 129
    Scientific Management 129
    Job Enlargement and Job Rotation 130
    Job Enrichment 131
    Job Characteristics Model 131
Alternative Work Schedules 133
    Compressed Workweeks 134
    Flexible Working Hours 134
    Job Sharing 134
    Telecommuting 134
    Part-Time Work 136
Study Guide 136

PART 3
Teams and Teamwork

7 The Nature of Teams 141

Teams in Organizations 142
    Teams and Teamwork 142
    What Teams Do 142
    Organizations as Networks of Teams 143
    Cross-Functional and Problem-Solving Teams 144
    Self-Managing Teams 145
    Virtual Teams 146
Team Effectiveness 147
    Criteria of an Effective Team 147
    Synergy and Team Benefits 148

Social Facilitation 148
Social Loafing and Team Problems 149

Stages of Team Development 151
Forming Stage 151
Storming Stage 151
Norming Stage 151
Performing Stage 152
Adjourning Stage 152

Input Foundations for Teamwork 152
Team Resources and Setting 153
Team Task 154
Team Size 154
Team Composition 155
Membership Diversity and Team Performance 156

Study Guide 158

8 Teamwork and Team Performance 163

High-Performance Teams 164
Characteristics of High-Performance Teams 164
The Team-Building Process 165
Team-Building Alternatives 166

Improving Team Processes 167
Entry of New Members 167
Roles and Role Dynamics 168
Task and Maintenance Leadership 169
Team Norms 170
Team Cohesiveness 174
Inter-Team Dynamics 175

Improving Team Communications 176
Interaction Patterns and Communication Networks 176
Proxemics and Use of Space 178
Communication Technologies 178

Improving Team Decisions 179
Ways Teams Make Decisions 179
Assets and Liabilities of Team Decisions 180
Groupthink Symptoms and Remedies 181
Team Decision Techniques 182

Study Guide 184

9 Decision Making and Creativity 189

The Decision-Making Process 190
Steps in the Decision-Making Process 190
The Decision to Decide 191
Ethical Reasoning and Decision Making 191
Alternative Decision Environments 193
Decisions with Extreme Consequences 195

Decision-Making Models 196
Classical Decision Model 197
Behavioral Decision Model 197
Systematic and Intuitive Thinking 198

Decision-Making Traps and Issues 200
Judgmental Heuristics 201
Decision Biases 201
Knowing When to Quit 202
Knowing Who to Involve 203

Creativity in Decision Making 205
Personal Creativity Drivers 205
Team Creativity Drivers 206

Study Guide 208

10 Conflict and Negotiation 213

Conflict in Organizations 214
Types of Conflict 214
Levels of Conflict 214
Functional and Dysfunctional Conflict 215
Culture and Conflict 217

Conflict Management 218
Stages of Conflict 218
Hierarchical Causes of Conflict 218
Contextual Causes of Conflict 219
Indirect Conflict Management Strategies 220
Direct Conflict Management Strategies 222

Negotiation 224
Organizational Settings for Negotiation 224
Negotiation Goals and Outcomes 224
Ethical Aspects of Negotiation 224

Negotiation Strategies 226
Approaches to Distributive Negotiation 226
How to Gain Integrative Agreements 227
Common Negotiation Pitfalls 228
Third-Party Roles in Negotiation 230

Study Guide 230

PART 4
Influence Processes and Leadership

11 Communication 235

The Nature of Communication 236
Importance of Communication 236
The Communication Process 236
Nonverbal Communication 238

Communication Barriers 239
Interpersonal Barriers 239
Physical Barriers 240

Semantic Barriers 240
Cultural Barriers 241

Communication in Organizational Contexts 242
Communication Channels 242
Communication Flows 243
Voice and Silence 245

Communication in Relational Contexts 246
Relationship Development 246
Relationship Maintenance 247
Supportive Communication Principles 248
Active Listening 250

Developmental Feedback 251
Feedback Giving 251
Feedback Seeking 252
Feedback Orientation 252

Study Guide 254

12 Power and Politics 259

Understanding Power 260
What Is Power and Why Is It Important? 260
Power and Dependence 260
The Problem of Powerlessness 261
Power as an Expanding Pie 262

Sources of Power and Influence 263
Position Power 263
Personal Power 265
Information Power 266
Connection Power 266

Responses to Power and Influence 267
Conformity 267
Resistance 268
How Power Corrupts 268

Understanding Organizational Politics 270
Why Do We Have Organizational Politics? 270
The Role of Self-Interest 270
Political Climates 270

Navigating the Political Landscape 272
Building Power Bases 273
Developing Political Skills 274
Networking 275

Study Guide 276

13 The Leadership Process 281

Leadership 282
Formal and Informal Leadership 282
Leadership as Social Construction 284
Implicit Leadership Theories 286

Followership 287
What Is Followership? 288
How Do Followers See Their Roles? 288
How Do Leaders See Follower Roles? 290

The Leader–Follower Relationship 292
Leader–Member Exchange (LMX) Theory 292
Social Exchange Theory 293
Hollander's Idiosyncrasy Credits 294

Collective Leadership 294
Distributed Leadership 294
Co-Leadership 295
Shared Leadership 296

Study Guide 296

14 Leader Traits and Behavioral Styles 301

Leader Traits and Behaviors 302
Early Trait Approaches 302
Later Trait Approaches 302
Behavioral Leadership Approaches 303
Are Leaders Born or Made? 305

Contingency Theories 305
The Contingency Model 306
Findings from Contingency Theories 307
Fiedler's Leader-Match 307
Problems with Contingency Approaches 307

Charismatic/Transformational Views 309
Charismatic Leadership 309
Burns's Transforming Leadership Theory 310
Bass's Transactional/Transformational Leadership Theory 312
Problems of "Heroic" Leadership Views 313

Complexity Leadership Views 315
Today's Complex Environments 315
Complexity Leadership Theory 316
Challenges of Complexity Leadership Approaches 317

Leadership Ethics 318
Shared Value View 319
Servant Leadership 319
Empowering Leadership 320
Ethical Leadership Theory 321

Study Guide 321

PART 5
Organizational Context

15 Organizational Culture and Innovation 327

Organizational Culture 328
- Functions of Organizational Culture 328
- Subcultures and Countercultures 330
- National Culture and Corporate Culture 332

Understanding Organizational Cultures 333
- Layers of Cultural Analysis 334
- Stories, Rites, Rituals, and Symbols 334
- Cultural Rules and Roles 335
- Shared Values, Meanings, and Organizational Myths 336

Managing Organizational Culture 337
- Direct Attempts to Change Values 337
- Developing Shared Goals 338
- Modifying Visible Aspects of Culture 340

Innovation in Organizations 341
- The Process of Innovation 342
- Product and Process Innovations 343
- Balancing Exploration and Exploitation 345
- Managing Tensions between Cultural Stability and Innovation 345

Study Guide 347

16 Organizational Structure and Design 353

Formal Organizational Structure 354
- Organizations as Hierarchies 354
- Controls as a Basic Feature 356

Organizing and Coordinating Work 359
- Traditional Types of Departments 359
- Coordination 362

Organizational Design 364
- Size and the Simple Design 364
- Technology and Organizational Design 365
- Environment and Organizational Design 368

Bureaucracy and Beyond 370
- Mechanistic Structures and the Machine Bureaucracy 371
- Organic Structures and the Professional Bureaucracy 372
- Hybrid Structures 372

Study Guide 373

OB Skills Workbook W-1

Student Leadership Practices Inventory W-8
Learning Style Inventory W-29
Self-Assessment Portfolio W-33
Team and Experiential Exercises W-54
Cases for Critical Thinking W-96

Glossary G-1

Self-Test Answers ST-1

Notes N-1

Name Index NI-1

Organization Index OI-1

Subject Index SI-1

Online Module

Research Methods in OB
Human Resource Management
Organizational Development

People make the difference

1

Introducing Organizational Behavior

The Key Point

People in all of their rich diversity are the basic building blocks of organizations. Everyone deserves to be respected at work and to be satisfied with their jobs and accomplishments. The field of organizational behavior offers many insights into managing individuals and teams for high performance in today's complex workplace. ■

What's Inside

- **Bringing OB to LIFE**
  BUILDING SKILLS TO SUCCEED IN A COLLABORATION ECONOMY
- **Worth Considering . . . or Best Avoided?**
  TROUBLE BALANCING WORK AND HOME? HOME WORKING MAY BE THE ANSWER
- **Checking Ethics in OB**
  IS MANAGEMENT A PROFESSION?
- **Finding the Leader in You**
  MICHELLE GREENFIELD LEADS WITH A SUSTAINABILITY VISION
- **OB in Popular Culture**
  MORAL MANAGEMENT AND *JOHN Q*
- **Research Insight**
  WOMEN MIGHT MAKE BETTER LEADERS

Chapter at a Glance

- What Is Organizational Behavior, and Why Is It Important?
- How Do We Learn about Organizational Behavior?
- What Is the Context of Organizational Behavior?
- What Are the Challenges of Management in Organizations?
- What Are the Challenges of Leadership in Organizations?

Introducing Organizational Behavior

> **TEACHING NOTE:** Start a discussion that pushes students to personalize organizational behavior issues. Ask: What you are worried about in terms of trends, issues, and uncertainties that could limit your career opportunities? Choose two or three answers and ask: What can be done about them, starting now?

LEARNING ROADMAP WHAT IS ORGANIZATIONAL BEHAVIOR? / IMPORTANCE OF ORGANIZATIONAL BEHAVIOR

■ What Is Organizational Behavior?

If you pause to consider the vast effects of our recent economic and social turmoil, there shouldn't be any doubt that organizations and their members face huge challenges. Talk to friends and follow the news headlines. Preferred jobs are still hard to come by for new college graduates, and unemployment remains high, especially for candidates without strong career skills. Those with jobs often struggle to support a desired lifestyle while balancing conflicting demands of work and family responsibilities. Like it or not, this is your world. It's the one you'll have to master for both career and personal success.

In this challenging era, the body of knowledge we call organizational behavior offers many insights of great value. **Organizational behavior (OB)** is the study of human behavior in organizations. It is an academic discipline devoted to understanding individuals, teams, interpersonal processes, and organizational dynamics. Learning about OB can help you build solid job skills and expand your potential for career success in the dynamic, shifting, and complex workplaces of today . . . and tomorrow.

> **Organizational behavior** is the study of human behavior in organizations.

■ Importance of Organizational Behavior

Think OB and great jobs! Think OB and career success! Think OB and overall life satisfaction! Don't think—OB and another course completed for my degree!

The real importance of OB boils down to how it helps you develop the skills needed for a successful career in our ever-changing world. This is a time in which the normal complexities of human behavior in organizations are ramped up by an environment of constant change and the growing influence of social technology. Take the OB relevance test. How prepared are you to excel in jobs with fashion-forward titles like these?[1]

- Relationship champion • Logistics ringmaster • Innovation game changer
- Collaboration pioneer • Market trends virtuoso

If you can describe in your own words what these job holders would be doing, you're already moving in the right direction. You're starting to get a real sense of what it takes to succeed in this emerging new workplace and why it pays to learn what OB can teach us about human behavior in organizations.

Behind each of the prior job titles is a common foundation that comes to life as "networking," "connecting," "ideating," "collaborating," "helping," "linking," "supporting," "seeking," and "performing." These and other similar behaviors drive what can be called a **smart workforce**, one in which you must be prepared to excel.[2] Smart workforces are communities of action whose members tackle constantly shifting projects while sharing knowledge and skills to solve real and often complex problems. Smart workforces are built through connections activated by relational skills and social technologies and used to forge a powerful collective brain that keeps growing and adapting over time.

> Members of a **smart workforce** work in shifting communities of action in which knowledge and skills are shared to solve real and complex problems.

This text helps you bridge the gap between OB as a body of knowledge and OB as a pathway to career and life success. Our book is about people, everyday people like you and like us, who work and pursue careers in today's demanding settings. It's about people who seek fulfillment in their lives and jobs in a variety of ways and in uncertain times. It's about

Introducing Organizational Behavior

BRINGING OB TO LIFE

> "Collaboration leaders help make the people-to-people connections that give life to collaborative organizations."

Building Skills to Succeed in a Collaboration Economy

Every time you log onto Facebook or LinkedIn, join a multiplayer online game, or check Yelp for advice on a good restaurant, you are part of a fast-moving technology-driven, and very social world. But, are you taking the skills honed in these everyday experiences and developing them for career success in a new "collaboration economy?" It's a setting where work gets done, customers get served, and ideas and information get shared 24/7.

Dean Sally Blount of Northwestern's Kellogg School says that success is earned in our collaboration economy by "people and companies who connect and collaborate more effectively." Jacob Morgan, author of *The Collaborative Organization* (McGraw-Hill, 2012), says that there is a great opportunity for "collaboration leaders" who value and respect others as the most important assets of organizations.

Collaboration leaders aren't figureheads with formal titles. They are everyday leaders who are exceptionally good at teamwork, information sharing, giving and receiving feedback, providing peer support, and recognizing the contributions of others. In other words, collaboration leaders help make the people-to-people connections that give life to collaborative organizations. They bring social technology together with face-to-face interactions to harness the powers of knowledge, creativity, and teamwork.

© Anatolii Babii/Alamy Limited

The collaboration economy presents a pretty stiff career test. It calls for "hard" technology skills and real job expertise to be combined with "soft" people skills and a genuine personal presence. But that's the great opportunity of your course in organizational behavior—a chance to learn more about yourself and how people work together in organizations. The question is this: Are you ready to jump in and let OB help build your skills for success in a collaboration economy?

---

the challenges of leadership, ethics, globalization, technology, diversity, work–life balance, and many social issues. And it is about how our complex ever-changing environment requires people and organizations to continuously adapt and improve in the quest for promising futures.

There is no doubt that success with our life and career goals requires ongoing learning and continuous attention to new trends, practices, and opportunities. The following changes in what people expect and value in terms of human behavior in organizations are of special interest in the study of OB.[3]

- ■ *Importance of connections and networks.* Work is increasingly being done through personal connections and networks. In this environment, building effective relationships face to face and online is a must-have career skill.

- ■ *Commitment to ethical behavior.* Highly publicized scandals involving unethical and illegal practices prompt concerns for ethical behavior in the workplace; growing intolerance for breaches of public faith by organizations and those who run them are drawing new attention to business ethics.

◀ Trends with human behavior in organizations

- *Broader views of leadership.* New pressures and demands mean organizations can no longer rely on just managers for leadership. Leadership is valued from all members, found at all levels, and flows in all directions—not just top-down.
- *Emphasis on human capital and teamwork.* Success is earned through knowledge, experience, and commitments to people as valuable human assets; work is increasingly team based with a focus on peer contributions.
- *Demise of command-and-control.* Traditional hierarchical structures and practices are being replaced by shared leadership, flexible structures, and participatory work settings that engage human and social capital.
- *Influence of information technology.* As new technologies—including social media—penetrate the workplace, implications for work arrangements, organizational systems and processes, and individual behavior are continuously evolving.
- *Respect for new workforce expectations.* The new generation is less tolerant of hierarchy, more high tech, and less concerned about status. Balance of work and nonwork responsibilities is a top-priority value.
- *Changing concept of careers.* New economy jobs require special skill sets and a continuous development. More people now work as independent contractors and freelancers who shift among employers rather than hold full-time jobs.
- *Concern for sustainability.* Issues of sustainability are top priorities. Decision making and goal setting increasingly give attention to the environment, climate justice, and preservation of resources for future generations.

Organizational Behavior as a Science

LEARNING ROADMAP SCIENTIFIC FOUNDATIONS OF ORGANIZATIONAL BEHAVIOR / HOW WE LEARN ABOUT ORGANIZATIONAL BEHAVIOR

> TEACHING NOTE: Ask student teams to build an OB model that they would like to research. Have them select a dependent variable and at least two independent variables. Choose two or three of the models to discuss in relationship to the course direction and objectives.

How do we find out what a new generation of graduates really wants and needs from work and in careers? How do we learn how to integrate multigenerational workforces around common goals and high performance expectations? How do we gain solid insights into how these and other important issues of human behavior play out in day-to-day organizational practice? The answer is found in one word: *science*.

Scientific Foundations of Organizational Behavior

More than a century ago, consultants and scholars were already giving attention to the systematic study of management and organizational practices. Although the early focus was on physical working conditions, principles of administration, and industrial engineering, interest soon broadened to include the human factor. This led to research dealing with individual attitudes, group dynamics, and the relationships between managers and workers. Organizational behavior then emerged as a scholarly discipline devoted to scientific understanding of individuals and groups in organizations, and of the performance implications of organizational processes, systems, and structures.[4]

Interdisciplinary Body of Knowledge Organizational behavior is an interdisciplinary body of knowledge with strong ties to the behavioral sciences—psychology, sociology, and anthropology—as well as to allied social sciences such as economics and political science. What makes OB unique is its desire to integrate the diverse insights of these other disciplines and apply them to real-world organizational problems and opportunities. The ultimate goal of OB is to improve the performance of people, groups, and organizations, and to improve the quality of work life overall.

Use of Scientific Methods The field of organizational behavior uses scientific methods to develop and empirically test generalizations about behavior in organizations. OB scholars often propose and test **models**—simplified views of reality that attempt to identify major factors and forces underlying real-world phenomena. These models link **independent variables**—presumed causes—with **dependent variables**—outcomes of practical value and interest. For example, the following model describes one of the findings of OB research: Job satisfaction (independent variable) influences, absenteeism (dependent variable). The "+" and "−" signs indicate that as job satisfaction increases absenteeism is expected to go down, and as job satisfaction decreases, absenteeism should go up.

> **Models** are simplified views of reality that attempt to explain real-world phenomena.
>
> **Independent variables** are presumed causes that influence dependent variables.
>
> **Dependent variables** are outcomes of practical value and interest that are influenced by independent variables.

As you look at the above model, you might ask what dependent variables other than absenteeism are also important to study in OB—perhaps things like task performance, ethical behavior, work stress, incivility, team cohesion, and leadership effectiveness. Think also about job satisfaction as a dependent variable in its own right. What independent variables do you believe might explain whether satisfaction will be high or low for someone doing a service job, such as an airline flight attendant, or a managerial job, such as a school principal?

Figure 1.1 describes methods commonly used by OB researchers to study models and the relationships among variables. These research methods are based on scientific thinking. This means (1) the process of data collection is controlled and systematic, (2) proposed explanations are carefully tested, and (3) only explanations that can be rigorously verified are accepted.

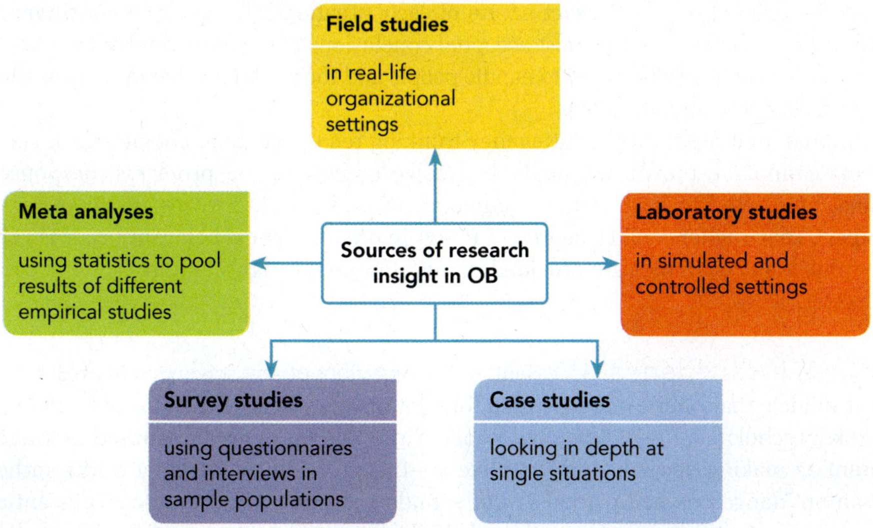

Sources of research insight in OB

- **Field studies** — in real-life organizational settings
- **Laboratory studies** — in simulated and controlled settings
- **Meta analyses** — using statistics to pool results of different empirical studies
- **Survey studies** — using questionnaires and interviews in sample populations
- **Case studies** — looking in depth at single situations

FIGURE 1.1 Common scientific research methods in organizational behavior.

Something to Read—*The Shift: The Future of Work Is Already Here*

As professor of management at the London Business School, Lynda Gratton worries that students fail to understand the nature, pace, and complexity of forces shaping the future of work. Her book, *The Shift* (HarperBusiness UK, 2011) describes five key forces: technology (helpful but time consuming), globalization (workers from everywhere compete for the same jobs), demography (more people, less space), society (traditional communities under threat), and energy resources (too few and shrinking). So "What's the worker to do?" she asks. Her answer is that we can default and accept a bleak future, or craft for ourselves a bright one. To work on the bright side we have to shift from "shallow generalist to serial master" of things; from "isolated competitor to innovative connector" in vast networks; and from "voracious consumer to impassioned producer" more focused on creating things than buying them.

Eamonn McCabe/Camera Press/Redux Pictures

Focus on Application
The science of organizational behavior focuses on applications that can make a real difference in how organizations and people in them perform. Some examples of the many practical research questions addressed by the discipline of OB and reviewed in this book are:

What causes unethical and socially irresponsible behavior by people in organizations? • How should rewards such as pay raises be allocated? • How can jobs be designed for both job satisfaction and high performance? • What are the ingredients of successful teamwork? • How can a manager deal with resistance to change? • Should leaders make decisions by individual, consultative, or group methods? • How can win–win outcomes be achieved in negotiations?

Contingency Thinking
Rather than assuming that there is one best or universal answer to questions such as those just posed, OB recognizes that behavior and practices must be tailored to fit the exact nature of each situation—this is called **contingency thinking**. In fact, one of the most accepted conclusions of scientific research to date is that there is no single best way to handle people and the situations that develop as they work together in organizations.

Contingency thinking seeks ways to meet the needs of different management situations.

Stated a bit differently, contingency thinking recognizes that cookie-cutter solutions cannot be universally applied to solve organizational problems. Responses must be crafted to best fit the circumstances and people involved. As you might expect, this is where solid scientific findings in organizational behavior become very helpful. Many examples are provided in the "Research Insight" feature found in each chapter.

Quest for Evidence
An essential responsibility of any science is to create and test models that offer evidence-based foundations for decision making and action. A book by scholars Jeffrey Pfeffer and Robert Sutton defines **evidence-based management** as making decisions on "hard facts"—that is, about what really works, rather than on "dangerous half-truths"—what sounds good but lacks empirical substantiation.[5] One of the ways evidence-based thinking manifests itself in OB is through a

Evidence-based management uses hard facts and empirical evidence to make decisions.

Research Insight

Women Might Make Better Leaders

No one doubts there are good and bad leaders of both genders. But research by Alice Eagley and her colleagues at Northwestern University suggests that women are often perceived as more likely than men to use leadership styles that result in high performance by followers.

In a meta-analysis that statistically compared the results of forty-five research studies dealing with male and female leadership styles, Eagley and her team concluded that women are frequently described as leading by inspiring, exciting, mentoring, and stimulating creativity. They point out that these behaviors have "transformational" qualities that build stronger organizations through innovation and teamwork. Women also score higher on rewarding positive performance, while men score higher in punishing and correcting mistakes.

Eagley and her colleagues explain the findings in part by the fact that followers are more accepting of a transformational style when the leader is female, and that the style comes more naturally to women because of its emphasis on nurturing. They also suggest that because women may have to work harder than men to succeed, their leadership skills get tough tests and end up being better developed.

Possible Leadership Strengths of Women
- Transformational
- Good at mentoring
- Very inspiring
- Encourage creativity
- Show excitement about goals
- Reward positive performance

Do the Research What do you think: Is this study on track? Conduct an interview study of people working for female and male managers. Ask this question: Do women lead differently from men? Organize the responses, and prepare an analysis that answers your research question. Although not scientific, your study could prove quite insightful.

Source: Alice H. Eagley, Mary C. Johannesen-Smith, and Marloes I. van Engen, "Transformational, Transactional and Laissez-Faire Leadership: A Meta-Analysis of Women and Men," *Psychological Bulletin* 24.4 (2003), pp. 569–591.

---

contingency approach in which researchers identify how different situations can best be understood and handled.

Cross-Cultural Awareness

In a time of complex globalization, it's important for everyone, from managers and employees to government leaders, to understand how OB theories and concepts apply in different countries.[6] Although it is relatively easy to conclude that what works in one culture may not work as well in another, it is far more difficult to describe how specific cultural differences can affect such things as ethical behavior, motivation, job satisfaction, leadership style, and negotiating tendencies. OB is now rich with empirically based insights into cross-cultural issues.

▣ Learning about Organizational Behavior

Today's knowledge-based world and smart workforces place a great premium on learning. Only the learners, so to speak, will be able to keep the pace and succeed in a connected, high-tech, global, and constantly changing environment. But just what are we talking about here?

Think of **learning** as an enduring change of behavior that results from experience. Think also of **lifelong learning** as a process of learning continuously from day-to-day experiences. When it comes to learning about OB, this book and your course are starting points and launch platforms to make your experiences more meaningful. There also is a rich and ever-expanding pool of learning experiences available in the work events and

Learning is an enduring change in behavior that results from experience.

Lifelong learning is continuous learning from everyday experiences.

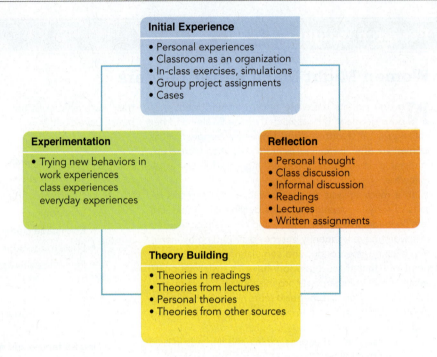

FIGURE 1.2 Experiential learning in an OB course.

activities, conversations with colleagues and friends, counseling and advice provided by mentors, success models, training seminars and workshops, and other daily opportunities that consume your time. What is learned from all such experiences—now and in the future—will in many ways be the key to your personal and career success. The "Bringing OB to Life" feature helps you make these connections between OB and our everyday experiences.

Figure 1.2 shows how the content and activities of the typical OB course fit together in an experiential learning cycle.[7] The learning sequence begins with initial experience and subsequent reflection. It grows as theory building takes place to try to explain what has happened. Theory is then tested in behavior. Textbooks, readings, class discussions, and other course assignments and activities should help you practice the phases of the learning cycle.

Notice that Figure 1.2 assigns to you a substantial responsibility for learning. Along with your instructor, our author team can offer examples, cases, and exercises to provide you with initial experience. We can even stimulate your reflection and theory building by presenting concepts and discussing their research and practical implications. Sooner or later, however, you must become an active participant in the process; you and only you can do the work required to take full advantage of the learning cycle.

At the end of this book you'll find the rich and useful *OB Skills Workbook*. It provides a variety of active learning opportunities that can help you better understand the practical applications of OB concepts, models, and theories. The workbook contains cases for analysis, team and experiential exercises, and a portfolio of self-assessments that includes the popular Kouzes and Posner "Student Leadership Practices Inventory."

Finally, don't forget that opportunities to learn more about OB and yourself abound in everyday living. Every team project, part-time work experience, student co-curricular activity, or visit to the store is rich in learning potential. Even our leisure pastimes from sports to social interactions to television, movies, and online games offer learning insights—if we tune in. The "OB in Popular Culture" feature in each chapter is a reminder to keep your learning dialed in all the time.

OB IN POPULAR CULTURE

Moral Management and *John Q*

New Line Cinema/Photofest

Moral managers try to act with ethical principles while immoral managers make decisions primarily on self-interest. To be sure, many decisions in organizations are quite complicated, and their ethical components may be hard to sort out.

The film *John Q* depicts the story of a desperate father's attempt to save his dying child. John Archibald (Denzel Washington) learns that his son, Mike, needs a heart transplant and he does not have sufficient insurance coverage. He decides to take the heart surgeon hostage in the hospital's emergency room. During a lull, the hostages and medical staff discuss how managed care insurance practices and hospital policies result in treatment decisions that are not always in the best interests of the patient. One hostage questions these practices in light of the medical profession's Hippocratic Oath.

When Mike's (Daniel Smith) condition worsens, John decides to commit suicide so that a heart will be available. The heart surgeon initially balks for ethical reasons, then agrees to do the surgery. In the end, the sacrifice is not necessary. The hospital gets word that a donor heart is available and on its way.

This movie is worth watching as a study in organizational behavior. It illustrates that ethical lines can sometimes be blurry. What's "right" or "wrong" isn't always clear or agreed upon. If an insurance company refuses to pay for preventive health screening, should the doctor order it? If someone can't pay, should doctors and hospitals still provide medical care? Should a doctor adhere to hospital policies if they jeopardize the health of a patient?

Get to Know Yourself Better Take Assessment 5, Personal Values, in the *OB Skills Workbook*. The values we hold influence our ethical views. This is a good time to check yours by taking the assessment and asking yourself these questions: What did I learn about my values? Are they balanced? Do the results suggest anything about how I might approach situations with ethical components? Can the emphasis I place on certain values create pressures to act unethically?

The Context of Organizational Behavior

LEARNING ROADMAP
ORGANIZATIONS AND THE EXTERNAL ENVIRONMENT
THE INTERNAL ENVIRONMENT OF ORGANIZATIONS
DIVERSITY AND MULTICULTURALISM IN ORGANIZATIONS

> TEACHING NOTE: Choose an organization. Ask students to map the key stakeholders of this organization and identify their respective interests. Have them look for conflicts of interest and discuss the implications.

■ Organizations and the External Environment

In order to understand the complex forces that influence human behavior in organizations, we need to begin with the nature of the "organization" itself. Simply stated, an **organization** is a collection of people working together in a division of labor to achieve a common purpose. This definition describes everything from clubs, voluntary

An **organization** is a collection of people working together to achieve a common purpose.

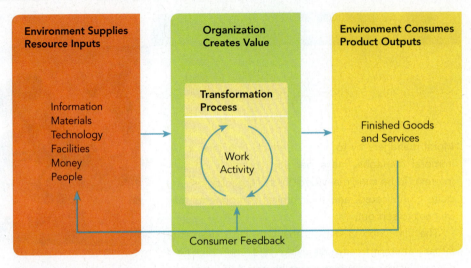

FIGURE 1.3 Organizations are open systems that create value while interacting with their environments.

organizations, and religious bodies to entities such as small and large businesses, schools, hospitals, and government agencies.

Figure 1.3 shows that organizations are dynamic **open systems**. They obtain resource inputs from the environment and transform them into finished goods or services that are returned to the environment as product outputs. If everything works right, suppliers value the organization and continue to provide needed resources, employees infuse work activities with their energies and intellects, and customers and clients value the organization's outputs enough to create a continuing demand for them.

Organizations are also **complex adaptive systems**. Because the environments they interact with are constantly evolving and changing, organizations must adapt to survive. And in a world that is increasingly complicated—socially, politically, and economically—this process of adaptation is never ending. Organizations today are embedded in environments whose components are so highly interconnected that changes in one have consequences—sometimes unpredictable and even uncontrollable—for other parts. A recent IBM Global Chief Executive Officer Study identifies this rise of complexity as the biggest challenge facing world leaders today. One CEO says: "The time available to capture, interpret and act on information is getting shorter and shorter."[8]

It can be useful to describe and analyze the external environments of organizations in terms of **stakeholders**—people, groups, and institutions that are affected by and thus have an interest or stake in an organization's performance. Key stakeholders from an OB perspective include an organization's customers, owners, employees, suppliers, regulators, and local communities, as well as future generations.

Although an organization should ideally operate in ways that best serve all stakeholders, the realities are that conflicting interests add to the complexity faced by decision makers. Consider possibilities such as these. Customers want value pricing and high-quality products, owners want profits and returns on investments. Employees want secure jobs with good pay and benefits, suppliers want reliable contracts and on-time payments. Regulators want compliance with laws, local communities want good organizational citizenship and community support. Present generations want the benefits of available natural resources, future generations want preserved and protected for long-term sustainability.

Open systems transform human and material resource inputs into finished goods and services.

Complex adaptive systems interact and adapt with their environments to survive.

Stakeholders are people and groups with an interest or stake in the performance of the organization.

The Internal Environment of Organizations

The internal environment of organizations also creates an important context for human behavior. Think about it. Do you act differently when you are with your friends, at school, or at work? In many cases the answer is probably "yes," and the question then becomes "Why?" The answer is that the context is different. To understand behavior in any setting, we must always ask how contextual factors influence it and in what ways. And, we must also consider how we or other people are affecting the context. The question in this respect is: How do our behaviors contribute to what is happening to us and around us, and in both positive and negative ways?

One of the strongest contextual influences on human behavior is **organizational culture**—the shared beliefs and values that influence the behavior of organizational members. Former eBay CEO Meg Whitman calls it the "character" of the organization. She says organization culture is "the set of values and principles by which you run a company" and becomes the "moral center" that helps every member understand what is right and wrong in terms of personal behavior.[9]

Organizational cultures influence the way we feel and act as members. In more authoritarian and hierarchical cultures, people are hesitant to make decisions and take action on their own. So, they withhold initiative and wait for approval. In competitive cultures, people can be extremely aggressive in the quest for rewards. Still other cultures are known for their emphasis on speed and agility in dealing with markets and environments, and in generating new ideas and innovations.

There is also something called **organizational climate**—the shared perceptions among members regarding what the organization is like in terms of management policies and practices. You have probably noticed that relations among managers and employees are relaxed and communication is free-flowing in some climates. But in others, managers act distant and communication is restricted.

Just how an organization's culture and climate affect members depends on something called "fit"—the match of internal environment and individual characteristics. People who find a good fit tend to experience confidence and satisfaction. Those with a bad fit may be prone to withdraw, experience stress, and even become angry and aggressive due to dissatisfaction. The sidebar suggests possible fit preferences for today's graduates.

Organizational culture is a shared set of beliefs and values within an organization.

Organizational climate represents shared perceptions of members regarding what the organization is like in terms of management policies and practices.

Workforce diversity describes how people differ on attributes such as age, race, ethnicity, gender, physical ability, and sexual orientation.

Diversity and Multiculturalism in Organizations

People are an important aspect of the internal environment of any organization. Consultant R. Roosevelt Thomas makes the point that positive organizational cultures tap the talents, ideas, and creative potential of *all* members.[10] This focuses attention on **workforce diversity**, the presence of individual differences based on gender, race and ethnicity, age, able-bodiedness, and sexual orientation.[11] It also highlights

Today's Grads Take Values to Work

They're called "Generation F," short for the Facebook Generation. Management scholar and consultant Gary Hamel says they are bringing new expectations to the workplace.

- All ideas deserve a hearing.
- Contributions overrule credentials.
- Authority is earned, not given.
- Leaders are chosen, not assigned.
- Power comes from information sharing.
- Wisdom lies within the crowd.
- Teams are self organizing.
- Community grows from shared decision making.
- Recognition and joy count along with money as motivators.
- Rabble rousing is embraced, not discouraged.

Multiculturalism refers to pluralism and respect for diversity in the workplace.

multiculturalism as an attribute of organizations that emphasize pluralism, and genuine respect for diversity and individual differences.[12] And in respect to Thomas's point again, organizations benefit when the variety of ideas and perspectives of a diverse workforce help them deal with complexity through innovation and adaptability.

Demographic trends driving workforce diversity in American society are well recognized. There are more women working than ever before. They earn 60 percent of college degrees and fill a bit more than half of managerial jobs.[13] The proportion of African Americans, Hispanics, and Asians in the population is now above 43 percent and increasing. By the year 2060, six out of every 10 Americans will be a person of color, and close to 30 percent of the population overall will be Hispanic.[14]

Inclusion is the degree to which an organization's culture respects and values diversity.

A key issue in any organization is **inclusion**—the degree to which the culture embraces diversity and is open to anyone who can perform a job, regardless of their diversity attributes.[15] In practice, however, valuing diversity must still be considered a work in progress. Women still earn only about 75 cents per dollar earned by men; female CEOs earn 85 cents per dollar earned by males. At *Fortune* 500 companies women hold only 15 CEO jobs and 6.2 percent of top-paying positions; women of color hold only 1.7 percent of corporate officer positions and 1 percent of top-paying jobs.[16] Indeed, when Ursula Burns was named CEO of Xerox, she became the first African-American woman to head a Fortune 500 firm.[17]

TEACHING NOTE: This is a great place for the exercise My Best Manager. Use teams and make a master list when they report. Add to the exercise by asking teams to also identify their "worst" managers. Push them for specifics on what these managers did to quality for the title.

Management and Organizational Behavior

LEARNING ROADMAP   EFFECTIVE MANAGERS • THE MANAGEMENT PROCESS
ESSENTIAL MANAGERIAL SKILLS • ETHICAL MANAGEMENT

Effective Managers

A **manager** is a person who supports the work efforts of other people.

A **manager** is someone whose job it is to directly support the work efforts of others. Being a manager is a unique challenge with responsibilities that link closely with the field of organizational behavior. At the heart of the matter, managers help other people get important things done in timely, high-quality, and personally satisfying ways. And in the workplaces of today, this is accomplished more through "helping" and "supporting" than through traditional notions of "directing" and "controlling." You'll find that the word *manager* is increasingly being replaced in conversations by such terms as *coordinator*, *coach*, or *team leader*.

Technology Makes Crowdsourcing Grades Easy, But Is It a Step Too Far?

As colleges and universities face financial and political pressures to increase "productivity" in academic programs, online course offerings are proliferating. Instructors are experimenting with new ways to deliver and grade online content.

One innovation is to take grading away from the instructor and give it to the "crowd." An assignment is graded by averaging scores assigned by the online students reading each other's work.

It's an attractive option since productivity goes up as instructors can easily handle more student enrollments. But critics view it as an unfortunate change in the instructor's role. Professor Adam Falk of Williams College asks if the educational outcome is the "equivalent of a highly trained professor providing thoughtful evaluation and detailed response?"

© Chris Schmidt/iStockphoto

Whatever the label used, someone who is an **effective manager** helps other people achieve both high performance and job satisfaction. This definition focuses attention on two key outcomes, or dependent variables, that are important in OB. The first is **task performance**. Think of this as the quality and quantity of the work produced or the services provided by an individual, team or work unit, or organization as a whole. The second is **job satisfaction**. It indicates how people feel about their work and the work setting.

OB is quite clear that managers and team leaders should be held accountable for both task performance and job satisfaction. Performance pretty much speaks for itself. Satisfaction might give you some pause for thought. But just as a valuable machine should not be allowed to break down for lack of proper maintenance, the talents and enthusiasm of an organization's workforce should never be lost or compromised for lack of proper care. In this sense, taking care of job satisfaction today can be considered an investment in tomorrow's performance potential.

An **effective manager** helps others achieve high levels of both performance and satisfaction.

Task performance is the quantity and quality of work produced.

Job satisfaction is a positive feeling about one's work and work setting.

The Management Process

Anyone serving as a manager or team leader faces a challenging and complicated job. The nature of managerial work is often described and taught through the four functions shown in Figure 1.4—planning, organizing, leading, and controlling. These functions make up the **management process** and involve the following responsibilities.

Four functions of management
- **Planning.** Defining goals, setting specific performance objectives, and identifying the actions needed to achieve them.
- **Organizing.** Creating work structures and systems, and arranging resources to accomplish goals and objectives.
- **Leading.** Instilling enthusiasm by communicating with others, motivating them to work hard, and maintaining good interpersonal relations.
- **Controlling.** Ensuring that things go well by monitoring performance and taking corrective action as necessary.

In what has become a classic study, Henry Mintzberg described how managers enact the management process in a busy, hectic, and challenging work context where they are move among many tasks and face many interruptions.[18] He went on to point out that the

The **management process** involves fulfilling the four responsibilities of planning, organizing, leading, and controlling.

Planning sets objectives and identifies the actions needed to achieve them.

Organizing divides up tasks and arranges resources to accomplish them.

Leading creates enthusiasm to work hard to accomplish tasks successfully.

Controlling monitors performance and takes any needed corrective action.

FIGURE 1.4 The management process of planning, organizing, leading, and controlling.

CHAPTER 1 ■ Introducing Organizational Behavior

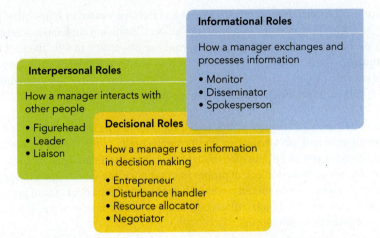

FIGURE 1.5 Mintzberg's ten roles of effective managers.

four management functions are fulfilled more simultaneously than step-by-step. They are also accomplished while a manager acts out the set of ten managerial roles shown in Figure 1.5.

A manager's *interpersonal roles* involve working directly with other people, hosting and attending official ceremonies (figurehead), creating enthusiasm and serving people's needs (leader), and maintaining contacts with important people and groups (liaison). The *informational roles* involve managers exchanging information with other people, seeking relevant information (monitor), sharing it with insiders (disseminator), and sharing it with outsiders (spokesperson). A manager's *decisional roles* involve making decisions that affect other people, seeking problems to solve and opportunities to explore (entrepreneur), helping to resolve conflicts (disturbance handler), allocating resources to various uses (resource allocator), and negotiating with other parties (negotiator).

■ Essential Managerial Skills

A **skill** is an ability to turn knowledge into effective action.

We all need skills to do well in work and life. It's no different for managers and team leaders—it takes skill to perform well. Formally stated, a **skill** is an ability to translate knowledge into action that results in a desired performance. Robert Katz divides the essential managerial skills into three categories: technical, human, and conceptual.[19]

Technical skill is an ability to perform specialized tasks.

Technical Skills
A **technical skill** is an ability to perform specialized tasks using knowledge or expertise gained from education or experience. A good example is skill in using the latest communication and information technologies. In the high-tech workplaces of today, technical proficiency in database management, spreadsheet analysis, presentation software, video chats and conferencing, and social media is often a hiring prerequisite. It's also helpful to think "skills" in respect to your college major. Recruiters today don't just want to know that you are a marketing or finance or MIS major with high grades. They want to know what skills in the major you are going to bring with you to the job.

Human skills comprise the ability to work well with other people.

Human Skills
Central to all aspects of managerial work and team leadership are **human skills**, or the ability to work well with other people. They show up as a spirit of trust, enthusiasm, and genuine involvement in interpersonal relationships. A person with good human skills will have a high degree of self-awareness and a capacity for understanding or empathizing with the feelings of others. People with this skill are able to interact well with others, engage in persuasive communications, and deal successfully with disagreements and conflicts.

Emotional intelligence is the ability to manage oneself and one's relationships effectively.

A manager or team leader's human skills should contain a strong base of **emotional intelligence** (EI). As defined by Daniel Goleman, EI is the ability to understand and

WORTH CONSIDERING ...OR BEST AVOIDED?

Trouble Balancing Work and Home? Home Working May Be the Answer

A group of Stanford University researchers wondered if allowing work to be done at home was really worth it to employers. Seeking real facts upon which to base a conclusion, they set up a field experiment using call center workers at a large Chinese travel agency.

Using odd or even birth dates, 255 volunteers were randomly assigned to "at home" or "in the office" work shifts for 9 months. Their performance was monitored and an overall evaluation made at the end of the research period. Results showed that telecommuters were online for more minutes, took more calls per hour, and were less likely to quit. They also reported more positive moods and greater job satisfaction than did the office workers. working at home also resulted in fewer break times while on shift and fewer days of sick leave.

When productivity gains, reduced training and hiring costs, and office rentals were tallied, the company calculated it saved $2,000 for every $3,000 spent on telecommuter salaries. And when the experiment was over and workers were given the chance to switch groups if they wished, those that ended up in the telecommuter group became even more productive.

© Blend Images/iStockphoto

Do the Analysis

What's your take? Do the findings make sense in terms of your impressions and experience? Does this study suggest that everyone should be given the option to work from home at least part of the time? What conditions might you set on the types of jobs and job holders that qualify for work from home? Is the evidence from this study good enough to make real-world decisions about the use of telecommuting?

---

manage emotions well, both personally and in relationships with others.[20] The building blocks for emotional intelligence are:

- *Self-awareness*—ability to understand your own moods and emotions
- *Self-regulation*—ability to think before acting and to control bad impulses
- *Motivation*—ability to work hard and persevere
- *Empathy*—ability to understand the emotions of others
- *Social skill*—ability to gain rapport with others and build good relationships

◀ Core building blocks of emotional intelligence

Human skills in emotional intelligence and interpersonal relationships are essential to success in each of the managerial activities and roles previously discussed. If you don't have the human skills you can't connect with other people in a positive way. Managers and team leaders need these skills to develop, maintain, and work well with a wide variety of people, both inside and outside the organization.[21] These include *task networks* of specific job-related contacts, *career networks* of career guidance and opportunity resources, and *social networks* of trustworthy friends and peers.[22] It can be said in this sense that strong human skills are the pathways to obtain **social capital** in the form of relationships and networks that can be called upon as needed to get work done through other people.

Social capital is a capacity to get things done due to relationships with other people.

Conceptual Skills
In addition to technical and human skills, managers should be able to view the organization or situation as a whole so that problems are always solved

Conceptual skill is the ability to analyze and solve complex problems.

for the benefit of everyone concerned. This capacity to think analytically and solve complex and sometimes ambiguous problems is a **conceptual skill**. It involves the ability to see and understand how systems work and how their parts are interrelated, including human dynamics. Conceptual skill is used to identify problems and opportunities, gather and interpret relevant information, and make good problem-solving decisions.

One final point about Katz's model of essential managerial skills is worth thinking about. He suggests that the relative importance of these skills varies across the different levels of management. Technical skills are considered more important at entry levels, where supervisors and team leaders must deal with job-specific problems. Senior executives require more conceptual skills as they face more complex problems and deal with strategic issues related to organizational mission and fitness. Human skills, which are strongly grounded in the foundations of organizational behavior, are consistently important across all managerial levels.

■ Ethical Management

Having managerial and leadership skills is one thing; using them correctly to get things done in organizations is quite another. And when it comes to ethics and morality, scholar Archie B. Carroll draws a distinction between immoral managers, amoral managers, and moral managers.[23]

An **immoral manager** chooses to behave unethically.

The **immoral manager** essentially chooses to behave unethically. She or he doesn't subscribe to any ethical principles, making decisions and acting to gain best personal

---

CHECKING ETHICS IN OB

Is Management a Profession?

Does it surprise you that a *Harvard Business Review* article claims managers are losing the public trust? To help change things for the better, the authors call for business schools to address management as a "profession" that is governed by codes of conduct that "forge an implicit social contract with society." One response to their call is MBA Oath, a nonprofit organization. Its goal is to create a community of graduating MBA students from any university that voluntarily sign an oath that pledges them to "create value responsibly and ethically." So far over 250 schools are represented in the community. A student signing the MBA Oath accepts statements such as these:

"I will manage my enterprise with loyalty and care, and will not advance my personal interests at the expense of my enterprise or society."

Jin Lee/Bloomberg/Getty Images, Inc.

"I will refrain from corruption, unfair competition, or business practices harmful to society."

"I will protect the human rights and dignity of all people affected by my enterprise, and I will oppose discrimination and exploitation."

Make Ethics Personal
What is your position on the MBA Oath? Would you take it, and sincerely try to live up to it in day-to-day practice? How about the whole concept of management being a profession like medicine and law? Can professionalizing management really make a difference in terms of ethical accountability and everyday managerial behavior?

FIGURE 1.6 Moral leadership, ethics mindfulness, and the virtuous shift.
Source: Developed from Terry Thomas, John R. Schermerhorn Jr., and John W. Dinehart, "Strategic Leadership of Ethical Behavior in Business," *Academy of Management Executive* 18 (May 2004), pp. 56–66.]

advantage. Perhaps the best examples are disgraced executives such as Bernard Madoff, whose unethical acts made national and world headlines. The **amoral manager**, by contrast, acts unethically at times but does so unintentionally. This manager fails to consider the ethics of a decision or behavior. Unintentional ethical lapses that we all must guard against include prejudice from unconscious stereotypes and attitudes, showing bias based on in-group favoritism, and claiming too much personal credit for performance accomplishments.[24] The **moral manager** incorporates ethical principles and goals into his or her personal behavior. Ethical behavior is a goal, a standard, and even a matter of routine; ethical reasoning is part of every decision, not just an occasional afterthought.

Carroll believes that the majority of managers tend to act amorally. If this is true, and because we also know immoral managers are around, it is very important to understand personal responsibilities for everyday ethical behavior and leadership. All organization members can and should be ethical leaders. This includes always acting as ethical role models and being willing to take stands in the face of unethical behavior by those above, below, and around them.

A review article by Terry Thomas and his colleagues describes how the "ethics center of gravity" shown in Figure 1.6 can be moved positively through moral leadership or negatively through amoral leadership.[25] In this view, a moral manager or moral leader always sets an ethics example, communicates ethics values, and champions **ethics mindfulness**. This is defined as an "enriched awareness" that causes one to behave with an ethical consciousness from one decision or behavioral event to another.

Moral managers and moral leaders contribute to the "virtuous shift" shown in Figure 1.6. They help create an organizational culture in which people encourage one another to act ethically as a matter of routine. One of the themes of this book, as reflected in the "Ethics in OB" feature in each chapter, is that ethics is the responsibility of everyone in the organization.

An **amoral manager** fails to consider the ethics of a decision or behavior.

A **moral manager** makes ethical behavior a personal goal.

Ethics mindfulness is an enriched awareness that causes one to consistently behave with ethical consciousness.

Leadership and Organizational Behavior

 THE LEADERSHIP PROCESS • EFFECTIVE LEADERS • EFFECTIVE FOLLOWERS

▸ The Leadership Process

The job of a manager or team leader has never been more demanding than it is in today's dynamic and hypercompetitive work environments. But the fact is, not all managers are

TEACHING NOTE: Open a discussion about the interchangeability of leadership skills and life skills. Ask: What life skills can a person draw upon to be a better leader? Ask: What leadership skills can a person draw upon to better deal with life's problems and opportunities?

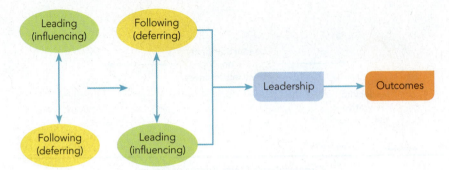

FIGURE 1.7 The leadership process.

good leaders. And even if they were, the challenges facing organizations are too complex for managers alone to resolve. Organizations today require leadership at all levels, not just from those holding the formal titles.

Leadership occurs when leaders and followers work together to advance change that benefits the mission and vision of the organization. Leadership is a *process*, not just the leader's behavior. As shown in Figure 1.7, it requires leaders and followers to partner in jointly producing leadership outcomes. Effective following is an essential—perhaps the most important part—of the **leadership process**. Without followers there can be no leaders.

Interestingly, leadership doesn't always have to be intentional. Sometimes others follow because they see leadership potential in someone, or they like what a person says and how they say it. This means that leadership is not only downward influence, it also involves influencing upward and side to side. You can be a leader by convincing higher management to adopt new practices suggested from your level. You can be a leader among your peers by becoming the person people turn to for advice, support, or direction. And, remember the notion of the manager as "coach" and "coordinator"? Every time you act in ways that fit these descriptions, there's no doubt you're being a leader.

> The **leadership process** involves leaders and followers jointly producing leadership outcomes.

Effective Leaders

Effective leaders contribute to the leadership process by using their influence to advance positive outcomes. Leaders are those who are willing to proactively envision new ways of doing things and take initiative in promoting needed changes in organizations. Organizations are full of leaders, managers and non-managers alike. These are people who get listened to by their peers, their bosses, and people below and higher up in the organization.

Leaders know that competence and reputation, being an effective communicator, and developing relationships and influence are vital to their success. Therefore they work to develop these skills. Effective leaders, for example, frame communication in ways that others will listen. **Framing** in this setting means tailoring communication in ways to encourage certain interpretations and discourage others. An effective leader recognizes that focusing on organizational interest (e.g., "We can increase productivity if we give people more time to rest and rejuvenate") will be a more effective frame than focusing on self-interest (e.g., "We've been working too hard and want time off").

> **Framing** means tailoring communication in ways to encourage certain interpretations and discourage others.

Effective leaders also know how to build relationships. They do what they can to be trustworthy, reliable, and respectful in not sharing or spreading information inappropriately. They understand that relationships are developed through **social exchange**, so they manage exchange processes and reciprocity to build partnerships and networks. They help others out when needed because they know that the **law of reciprocity** will invoke a sense of obligation by the other to return the favor ("if I do something for you, you will do something for me later if I need it"). This helps them build networks and relationships that serve as a key source of leadership influence.

> **Social exchange** means that people build human relationships and trust through exchanges of favors based on reciprocity.
>
> The **law of reciprocity** states that if someone does something for someone else it will invoke a sense of obligation to return the favor.

Leaders succeed when people follow them not because they have to, but because they *want* to. They are followed because others see the value of their ideas and

FINDING THE LEADER IN YOU

Michelle Greenfield Leads with a Sustainability Vision

When she was named as a recipient of the Ohio Department of Development's Keys to Success Award, Michelle Greenfield said, "It's exciting. It's kind of nice to be recognized as a good business owner. The goal is not to have the award, the goal is to have a good business and do well." She and her husband, Geoff, certainly do have a good business; it's called Third Sun Solar Wind and Power, Ltd.

The Greenfields began by building a rural home that used no electricity in rural Athens County, Ohio. Solar power was the replacement, and they have yet to pay an electric utility bill. As friends became interested, they helped others get into solar power, and the business kept growing from there. It has been ranked by *Inc.* magazine as thirty-second among the fastest-growing energy businesses in the United States. Third Sun is the largest provider of solar energy systems in the Midwest and has experienced a 390 percent growth in 3 years. Quite a story for an idea that began with a sustainable home!

Soon after its birth, Third Sun moved into a business incubator dedicated to helping local firms grow and prosper. Michelle says that they lived very frugally in their rural home, and this helped them start the business on a low budget. They have also benefited from tapping the local workforce in a university town and from having MBA students work with their firm in consulting capacities.

As their company grew, Geoff focused on technical issues while Michelle spent most of her time on the business and managerial ones. She's now the CEO and primarily concerned with strategic issues as the firm grows. "I do a lot of marketing," she says, "I do speaking engagements . . . I serve on the Board of Directors of Green Energy Ohio."

Christian Baird Photography

What's the Lesson Here?

Michelle Greenfield is proud of her accomplishments and says, "I think it's nice to be able to point out that there are women in the field that also have enough brains to be successful." She also points out that the name Third Sun was chosen to represent a "third son" for the couple, one requiring lots of nurturing in order to help it grow big and strong. Michelle's leadership combines entrepreneurship with vision to help save our planet. Could more people, even you, follow her path?

---

suggestions. This positive influence emerges from leaders' competence, persuasiveness, and human skills. Managers and team leaders, by virtue of their positions of authority, have the opportunity to act as leaders. But they don't always do so, or do so successfully. The "Finding the Leader in You" feature in each chapter is designed to provide role models and get you thinking about developing your leadership potential.

▎Effective Followers

Effective followers are those who work *with* leaders to produce positive outcomes. They support leaders by being willing to collaborate and defer when needed, rather than working against leaders or trying to undermine their power. At the same time, effective followers are not blindly obedient or subservient and passive. You are being an effective follower when you assume responsibility for telling leaders information they need to know, and not avoiding responsibility for passing along the "bad" news as well as the "good" news.

The best followers do not have to be micromanaged. They take responsibility for their own attitudes and behaviors and view themselves as partners with leaders in the leadership process. They help the manager by avoiding engaging in **upward delegation**, or passing their problems on to managers and burdening them with even more work. The best followers bring solutions along with problems. Overall, they try to identify things that could cause problems for leaders and then work to seek solutions before the problems escalate into big issues.

Organizations today are undergoing major transitions. They require successful leadership at all levels, and the need for more effective followership is on the rise. Followers today cannot get away with shrugging off responsibility or passing along blame as they might have

Upward delegation means passing problems or responsibilities upward in the hierarchy in ways that burden managers with more work.

in the past. They are expected to question and challenge leaders when needed, and to bring new ideas and creativity to their work. But to do so effectively they must act with respect, and keep the higher purpose in mind—the focus is on working with leaders in ways that advance the mission and purpose of the organization. And when leaders and followers partner effectively together, the result is a more meaningful, engaging and fulfilling work experience.

Study Guide

Key Questions and Answers

What is organizational behavior, and why is it important?
- Organizational behavior (OB) is the study of human behavior in organizations, focusing on individuals, teams, interpersonal processes, and organizational dynamics.
- OB is a body of knowledge with real applications to everyday living and careers, particularly in respect to a smart workforce where connections and collaboration are the keys to success.
- Trends and issues of interest in OB include ethical behavior, the importance of human capital, an emphasis on teams, the growing influence of information technology, new workforce expectations, changing notions of careers, and concerns for sustainability.
- OB is an applied discipline developed through scientific methods and taking a contingency perspective that there is no single best way to handle people and the situations that develop as they work together in organizations.

How do we learn about organizational behavior?
- Learning is an enduring change in behavior that results from experience.
- Lifelong learning about organizational behavior requires a commitment to continuous learning from one's work and everyday experiences.
- Most organizational behavior courses use a variety of instructional methods—self-assessments, experiential exercises, team projects, and case studies—to take advantage of the experiential learning cycle.

What is the context of organizational behavior?
- An organization is a collection of people working together in a division of labor for a common purpose.
- Organizations are open and adaptive systems that change over time while interacting with their environments to obtain resource and transform them into useful products and services.
- Key stakeholders in the external environments of organizations include customers, owners, suppliers, regulators, local communities, employees, and future generations.
- The organizational culture is the internal "personality" of the organization, including the beliefs and values that are shared by members.
- Positive organizational cultures place a high value on workforce diversity and multiculturalism, emphasizing respect and inclusiveness for all members.

What are the challenges of management in organizations?
- Effective managers directly support and help others reach high levels of both performance and job satisfaction; they are increasingly expected to act more like "coaches" and "facilitators" than like "bosses" and "controllers."

- The four functions of management are planning—to set directions; organizing—to assemble resources and systems; leading—to create workforce enthusiasm; and controlling—to ensure desired results.
- Managers use a combination of essential technical, human, and conceptual skills while working in networks of people to fulfill a variety of interpersonal, informational, and decisional roles.

What are the challenges of leadership in organizations?
- Effective leaders are individuals who successfully use influence to create change that benefits the mission and vision of the team or organization.
- Not all managers are good leaders that attract followers because their ideas or suggestions are valued and others choose to go along or align with them.
- Essential leadership skills include building competence and reputation, being an effective communicator, and developing relationships and influence.
- Essential followership skills involve being supportive of leaders, not delegating upward, and proactively anticipating problems or issues that could disrupt the team or the leader's ability to meet organizational goals.

Terms to Know

Amoral manager (p. 19)
Complex adaptive systems (p. 12)
Conceptual skill (p. 18)
Contingency thinking (p. 8)
Controlling (p. 15)
Dependent variables (p. 7)
Effective manager (p. 15)
Emotional intelligence (p. 16)
Ethics mindfulness (p. 19)
Evidence-based management (p. 8)
Framing (p. 20)
Human skills (p. 16)
Immoral manager (p. 18)
Inclusion (p. 14)

Independent variables (p. 7)
Job satisfaction (p. 15)
Law of Reciprocity (p. 20)
Leadership process (p. 20)
Leading (p. 15)
Learning (p. 9)
Lifelong learning (p. 9)
Management process (p. 15)
Manager (p. 14)
Models (p. 7)
Moral manager (p. 19)
Multiculturalism (p. 14)
Open systems (p. 12)
Organization (p. 11)

Organizational behavior (p. 4)
Organizational climate (p. 13)
Organizational culture (p. 13)
Organizing (p. 15)
Planning (p. 15)
Skill (p. 16)
Smart workforce (p. 4)
Social capital (p. 17)
Social exchange (p. 20)
Stakeholders (p. 12)
Task performance (p. 15)
Technical skill (p. 16)
Upward delegation (p. 21)
Workforce diversity (p. 13)

Self-Test 1

■ Multiple Choice

1. Which of the following issues would be most central to the field of organizational behavior (OB)?
   (a) How to improve advertising for a new product.
   (b) How to increase job satisfaction and performance among members of a team.
   (c) Making plans for a new strategy for organizational growth.
   (d) Designing a new management information system.

2. What is the best description of the context for organizational behavior today?
   (a) Command-and-control is in.
   (b) The new generation is similar to the old.
   (c) Empowerment is out.
   (d) Work–life balance concerns are in.
3. The term workforce diversity typically refers to differences in race, age, gender, ethnicity, and _____ among people at work.
   (a) social status
   (b) personal wealth
   (c) able-bodiedness
   (d) political preference
4. Which statement about OB is most correct?
   (a) OB seeks "one-best-way" solutions to management problems.
   (b) OB is a unique science that has little relationship to other scientific disciplines.
   (c) OB is focused on using social science knowledge for practical applications.
   (d) OB is so modern that it has no historical roots.
5. In the open-systems view of organizations, such things as technology, information, and money are considered _____.
   (a) transformation elements
   (b) feedback
   (c) inputs
   (d) outputs
6. If the organization culture represents the character of an organization in terms of shared values, the _____ represents the shared perceptions of members about day-to-day management practices.
   (a) value chain
   (b) organization climate
   (c) transformation process
   (d) organization strategy
7. Which of the following is *not* a good match of organizational stakeholder and the interests they often hold important?
   (a) customers—high-quality products
   (b) owners—returns on investments
   (c) future generations—value pricing
   (d) regulators—compliance with laws
8. Which word best describes an organizational culture that embraces multiculturalism and in which workforce diversity is highly valued?
   (a) inclusion
   (b) effectiveness
   (c) dynamism
   (d) predictability
9. The management function of _____ is concerned with creating enthusiasm for hard work among organizational members.
   (a) planning
   (b) motivating
   (c) controlling
   (d) leading
10. In the management process, _____ is concerned with measuring performance results and taking action to improve future performance.
    (a) transforming
    (b) organizing
    (c) leading
    (d) controlling
11. Among Mintzberg's ten managerial roles, acting as a figurehead and liaison are examples of _____ roles.
    (a) interpersonal
    (b) informational
    (c) decisional
    (d) conceptual

12. When a manager moves upward in responsibility, Katz suggests _____ skills decrease in importance and _____ skills increase in importance.
    (a) human, conceptual
    (b) conceptual, emotional
    (c) technical, conceptual
    (d) emotional, human

13. A person with high emotional intelligence would be strong in _____, the ability to think before acting and to control disruptive impulses.
    (a) motivation
    (b) perseverance
    (c) self-regulation
    (d) empathy

14. When a person's human skills are so good that he or she has relationships with other people who can be confidently asked for help and assistance at work, these skills have created _____ social capital for the individual.
    (a) analytical capacity
    (b) ethics mindfulness
    (c) social capital
    (d) multiculturalism

15. Class discussions, "debriefs," and individual papers based on case studies, team projects, and in-class activities are all ways an instructor tries to engage students in which part of the experiential learning cycle?
    (a) initial experience
    (b) reflection
    (c) theory building
    (d) experimentation

Short Response

16. What are the key characteristics of OB as a scientific discipline?
17. What does "valuing diversity" mean in the workplace?
18. What does "self-regulation" mean in the context of emotional intelligence?
19. When is a manager an effective leader?

Applications Essay

20. Carla, a college junior, is participating in a special "elementary education outreach" project in her local community. Along with other students from the business school, she is going to spend the day with fourth- and fifth-grade students and introduce them to the opportunities of going to college. One of her tasks is to lead a class discussion of the question "How is the world of work changing today?" Help Carla out by creating an outline of the major points she should discuss with the students.

Steps to Further Learning 1
Top Choices from *The OB Skills Workbook*

These learning activities from *The OB Skills Workbook* found at the back of the book are suggested for Chapter 1.

Case for Critical Thinking	Team and Experiential Exercises	Self-Assessment Portfolio
• Trader Joe's • Management Training Dilemma	• My Best Manager • My Best Job • Graffiti Needs Assessment • Sweet Tooth	• Learning Styles • Student Leadership Practices Inventory • Managerial Assumptions • 21st-Century Manager

2

Diversity, Personality, and Values

The Key Point

An understanding of organizational behavior begins with the individual. People vary in their personalities, traits, values, and individual characteristics. These individual differences influence how we behave and work together in organizations. ■

What's Inside?

- **Bringing OB to LIFE**
  TAKING STEPS TO CURB BIAS IN PERFORMANCE ASSESSMENT
- **Worth Considering . . . or Best Avoided?**
  WOULD YOU PLEASE MOVE OVER? WE'RE MAKING ROOM FOR GENERATION Y
- **Checking Ethics in OB**
  PERSONALITY TESTING
- **Finding the Leader in you**
  STEPHEN HAWKING INSPIRES AND SOARS DESPITE DISABILITY
- **OB in Popular Culture**
  AMBITION AND *THE SOCIAL NETWORK*
- **Research Insight**
  TWIN STUDIES: NATURE OR NURTURE?

Chapter at a Glance

- Why Are Individual Differences and Diversity Important?
- What Is Personality?
- How Are Personality and Stress Related?
- What Are Values, and How Do They Vary Across Cultures?

Individual Differences and Diversity

SELF CONCEPT, SELF-AWARENESS, AND AWARENESS OF OTHERS
VALUING-OR NOT VALUING-DIVERSITY • DIVERSITY ISSUES IN THE WORKPLACE
DIVERSITY AND SOCIAL IDENTITY

TEACHING NOTE: Have students write five adjectives they believe are consistent with their self concepts. Ask for examples and make a list. Have students describe how each adjective—if accurate—might be a source of career strengths or weaknesses for a person with this self concept.

People are complex. You approach a situation one way, and someone else may approach it quite differently. These differences among people can make it difficult to predict and understand individual behavior in relationships, teams, and organizations. They also contribute to what makes the study of organizational behavior so fascinating. The term **individual differences** refers to the ways in which people are similar and dissimilar in personal characteristics.

The mix of individual differences in organizations creates workforce diversity. Some of these differences are easily observable and often demographic. They represent **surface-level diversity** based on quite visible physical attributes such as ethnicity, race, sex, age, and abilities. Other individual differences—such as personalities, values, and attitudes—are more psychologically innate and less immediately visible. They represent **deep-level diversity** that may take time and effort to understand.[1]

Regardless of the level, diversity issues are of great interest in OB. Women, for example, now lead global companies such as PepsiCo, Xerox, IBM, and Kraft. But they still hold only 3 percent of top jobs in American firms.[2] Why have so few women so far made it to the top?[3] Society is becoming more diverse in its racial and ethnic makeup. But a research study found that résumés of people with white-sounding first names—such as Brett—received 50 percent more responses from potential employers than those with black-sounding first names—such as Kareem.[4] How can these results be explained given that the résumés were created equal?

Individual differences are the ways in which people are similar and dissimilar in personal characteristics.

Surface-level diversity involves individual differences in visible attributes such as race, sex, age, and physical abilities.

Deep-level diversity involves individual differences in attributes such as personality and values.

Self-Concept, Self-Awareness, and Awareness of Others

To best understand and deal well with individual differences and diversity, it only makes sense that it's important to have a strong sense of self. The **self-concept** is the view individuals have of themselves as physical, social, and spiritual or moral beings.[5] It is a way of recognizing oneself as a distinct human being. Two factors that increase awareness of individual differences—our own and others—are self-awareness and awareness of others. **Self-awareness** means being aware of our own behaviors, preferences, styles, biases, personalities, and so on. **Awareness of others** means being aware of these same things in others.

A person's self concept shows up in **self-esteem**, a belief about one's own worth based on an overall self-evaluation.[6] People high in self-esteem see themselves as capable, worthwhile, and acceptable; they tend to have few doubts about themselves. People who are low in self-esteem are full of self-doubt and are often afraid to act because of it. Someone's self-concept is also displayed in **self-efficacy**, sometimes called the *effectance motive*, which is a more specific version of self-esteem. It is an individual's belief about the likelihood of successfully completing a specific task. You could have high self-esteem and yet have a feeling of low self-efficacy about performing a certain task, such as public speaking.

What determines the development of the self? How, for example, can we explain **prejudice** in the form of negative, irrational, and superior opinions and attitudes toward persons who are different from ourselves? Perhaps you have heard someone say "She acts like her mother," or "Bobby is the way he is because of the way he was raised." These two comments illustrate the *nature/nurture controversy*: Are we the way we are because of *heredity*—genetic endowment, or because of *environment*—the cultural places and situations in which we have been raised and live? It is most likely that these two forces act in combination, with heredity setting the limits and environment determining how a person develops within them.[7]

Self-concept is the view individuals have of themselves as physical, social, spiritual, or moral beings.

Self-awareness means being aware of one's own behaviors, preferences, styles, biases, personalities, and so on.

Awareness of others is being aware of the behaviors, preferences, styles, biases, and personalities of others.

Self-esteem is a belief about one's own worth based on an overall self-evaluation.

Self-efficacy is an individual's belief about the likelihood of successfully completing a specific task.

Prejudice is the display of negative, irrational, and superior opinions and attitudes toward persons who are different from ourselves.

Research Insight

Twin Studies: Nature or Nurture?

There is a long-standing question in individual differences psychology: How much of who we are is determined by nature and how much by nurture? Research findings are beginning to provide fascinating insights into this question by investigating samples of twins. Before you read on, take a guess at the following: In thinking about leadership, how much of leadership capacity do you think is determined by nature and how much by nurture?

This question is being investigated in a research program by Rich Arvey and colleagues. In a recent study, he and his researchers used a sample of 178 fraternal and 214 identical female twins to see if they could generalize their findings that 30 percent of the variance in leadership role occupancy among the male twins could be accounted for by genetic factors. Their sample came from the Minnesota Twin Registry—a registry of twins born in the state between 1936 and 1951 who had been reared together during childhood. Surveys were sent to the female twins with measures assessing their history of holding leadership roles (i.e., leadership role occupancy) and an assessment of developmental life experiences, including family and work experiences.

The results supported the pattern shown in the male sample—32 percent of the variance in the women's leadership role occupancy was associated with hereditability. Family experience and work experience were also related to leadership role occupancy although, not surprisingly, experiences at work are more important than family experiences in shaping women's leadership development. The findings are important because they indicate that developmental experiences can help both men and women move into leadership roles.

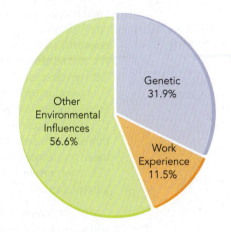

Do the Research How close was your guess? Do these findings correspond with what you see in your own families (e.g., with brothers and sisters or with parents and children)? How would you test the question of nature versus nurture?

Source: R. Arvey, Z. Zhang, B. Avolio, and R. Krueger, "Developmental and Genetic Determinants of Leadership Role Occupancy among Women," *Journal of Applied Psychology* 92.3 (2007), pp. 693–706.

◼ Valuing-or Not Valuing-Diversity

The U.S. population is not just getting bigger; it is more racially and ethnically diverse, and it is getting older. The U.S. Census Bureau predicts that the country will become a true plurality by 2060, with no one ethnic or racial group being in the majority. Hispanics are now the fastest growing community and by 2060 will constitute one-third of the population. America is also growing demographically older; by 2050 one in five people will be aged 65-plus.[8] What do these and other such demographic trends mean for everyday living, for our personal relationships, for the way we work?

More and more organizations are embracing policies and practices to value diversity in their workforces as a way to increase competitiveness, build talent, expand organizational capabilities, and enhance access to diverse customers.[9] Individual differences are fast becoming valued for the strengths that diversity can bring to a workforce.[10] If you need creativity, for example, do you turn to people who think like you or to people who can help you think differently? Moreover, when you need to understand something you have never encountered before, such as another culture or an emerging market, do you turn to people who are the same as you or would you want access to co-workers familiar with those cultures?

The flip side of valuing diversity is outright **discrimination** against women and minorities in the workplace. It occurs when minority members are unfairly treated and

Discrimination actively denies minority members the full benefits of organizational membership.

denied the full benefits of organizational membership. An example is when a manager fabricates reasons not to interview a minority job candidate, or refuses to promote a working mother on the belief that "she has too many parenting responsibilities to do a good job at this level." Such thinking underlies a form of discrimination called the **glass ceiling effect**, an invisible barrier or "ceiling" that prevents women and minorities from rising above a certain level of organizational responsibility.[11]

> The **glass ceiling effect** is an invisible barrier limiting career advancement of women and minorities.

Diversity Issues in the Workplace

Race and Ethnicity

The value of heterogeneous perspectives within teams and organizations can be gained from multicultural workforces with a rich mix of racial and ethnic diversity. And **Title VII of the Civil Rights Act of 1964** protects individuals against employment discrimination on the basis of race and ethnicity, as well as national origin, sex, and religion. It applies to employers with 15 or more employees, including state and local governments.

According to Title VII, equal employment opportunity cannot be denied any person because of his/her racial group or perceived racial group, his/her race-linked characteristics (e.g., hair texture, color, facial features), or because of his/her marriage to or association with someone of a particular race or color. It also prohibits employment decisions based on stereotypes and assumptions about abilities, traits, or the performance of individuals of certain racial groups. But, as noted earlier in the research showing prejudice in job searches against person's with black-sounding first names, it's still an imperfect world.[12]

> **Title VII of the Civil Rights Act of 1964** protects individuals against employment discrimination on the basis of race and color, as well as national origin, sex, and religion.

Gender

Women are bringing not just task expertise but valuable interpersonal skills and styles to the workplace, such as listening and collaborative skills, and abilities to multitask and synthesize alternative viewpoints effectively and quickly. Research shows that companies with a higher percentage of female board directors and corporate officers, on average, financially outperform companies with the lowest percentages by significant margins.[13] The presence of women leaders is also beneficial because they encourage more women in the pipeline and act as role models and mentors for younger women. Moreover, the presence of women leaders sends important signals that an organization has a broad and deep talent pool, and offers an inclusive workplace.

Despite these benefits to organizations and anti-discrimination protections afforded them under Title VII of the U.S. Civil Rights Act of 1964, women have not penetrated the highest level of organizational leadership to the extent we would expect. Even worse, many are still abandoning corporate careers just as they are positioned to attain higher-level responsibilities. The term **leaking pipeline** was coined by Professor Lynda Gratton and colleagues of the London Business School to describe this phenomenon.[14] In one study of 61 organizations operating in 12 European countries, they found that the number of women decreases the more senior the roles become.

> The **leaking pipeline** describes how women drop out of careers before reaching the top levels of organizations.

The nonprofit research organization Catalyst reports that women consistently identify gender stereotypes as a significant barrier to advancement and cause for the leaking pipeline.[15] They describe a "think-leader-think-male" mind-set in which men are largely seen as leaders by default because of stereotypically masculine "take charge" skills such as influencing superiors and problem solving. Women, by contrast are stereotyped for "caretaking skills" such as supporting and encouraging others. This creates what is called a **leadership double bind** for women. If they conform to the stereotype they are seen as weak, and if they go against the stereotype they are breaking norms of femininity. As some describe it, female leaders are "damned if they do, doomed if they don't."[16] Organizations can help address these stereotypes by creating workplaces that are more meaningful and satisfying to successful women, such as cultures that are less command-and-control and status-based. As *Catalyst* reports, "Ultimately, it is not women's leadership styles that need to change but the structures and perceptions that must keep up with today's changing times."[17]

> The **leadership double bind** describes how women are seen as weak in leadership if they conform to the feminine stereotype and also weak if they go against it.

BRINGING OB TO LIFE

> *"If you have several pair of shoes available, you're much more likely to be able to compare different attributes of the shoes."*

Taking Steps to Curb Bias in Performance Assessment

Try as we might, bias has a way of creeping into performance assessments and other human resource management decisions. But Harvard scholars Iris Bohnet, Alexandra van Geen, and Max H. Bazerman may have found a way to minimize or eliminate such implicit discrimination. The key, they say, is to make sure evaluators compare candidates directly rather than one by one.

This advice comes from research that asked 100 participants to act as candidates for a new job. They performed a variety of math and verbal tasks chosen by the researchers because of the common gender stereotype that "females are believed to be worse at math tasks and better at verbal tasks than males." Another 554 study participants then acted as evaluators to select candidates for a second round of testing. They were given test results and gender for each candidate. Some evaluators were asked to evaluate the candidates one at a time while others directly compared male and female candidates.

Gender stereotypes influenced the one-by-one evaluations, with female candidates more often chosen for further verbal testing and male candidates for further math testing. When male and female candidates were evaluated together, however, gender stereotypes largely disappeared.

Bohnet et al. summarize the research by noting that "if you look at one pair of shoes, it's hard to evaluate the quality of those shoes. You will be much more likely to go with stereotypes or heuristics or rules of thumb about shoes. But if you have several pair of shoes available, you're much more likely to be able to compare different attributes of the shoes."

Jon Feingersh Photography/SuperStock/Corbis

Has this OB research put its finger on a simple way to remove bias from human resource decisions? Is it time to stop assessing candidates one at a time and instead compare them to one another directly?

Sexual Orientation The first U.S. corporation to add sexual orientation to its non-discrimination policy did so 30 years ago. That company was AT&T and its chairman, John DeButts, said that his company would "respect the human rights of our employees."[18] Although employment discrimination based on sexual orientation or gender identity is not yet protected by federal legislation, such legislation has been proposed to Congress (the Employment Non-Discrimination Act), and individuals are protected from sexual harassment bullying at work and school.[19] Also, many states now have executive orders protecting the rights of lesbian, gay, bisexual, and transgender workers.[20]

Regardless of weak and incomplete legislative support, the workplace is beginning to improve for gay Americans. Harris polling shows that 78 percent of heterosexual adults in the United States agree that how an employee performs at his or her job should be the standard for judging an employee, not one's sexual orientation, while 62 percent agree that all employees are entitled to equal benefits on the job, such as health insurance for partners or spouses.[21]

Age Age or generational diversity is affecting the workplace like never before. Population demographics and economic trends have created a workforce where Millennials, Gen Xers, and Baby Boomers have to work and get along together. Nonetheless, there are

WORTH CONSIDERING ...OR BEST AVOIDED?

Would You Please Move Over? We're Making Room for Generation Y

Employers find a lot to like in the skills Generation Y members—the Millennials—bring to the workplace. No problem with technology—they're always on the cusp of things. No problem with collaboration—they've grown up with teamwork and social media. No problem either with motivation—they're task oriented and career focused.

But Gen Ys also need special handling. They can be spoiled and self-centered, quick to complain when their bosses don't communicate enough, when their skills aren't fully tapped, and when work rules and bureaucracy get too restrictive. They're also impatient for new assignments and promotions, and flexible work arrangements. And when they don't get them they're quick to move on. Loyalty to a single-employer career isn't part of their DNA.

Some employers go to great lengths to keep their Gen Ys happy, even to the point where "older" employers feel a bit put upon. The online book service Chegg cut middle management positions to make room for younger employees to advance. CEO Dan Rosensweig said, "If they don't feel like they're making a contribution to a company overall quickly, they don't stay." Software firm Aprimo guarantees Gen Ys promotion and a raise in a year if they perform up to expectations. When some of the older workers balked at this special treatment, President Bob Boehnlein said, "I had to strong-arm a little bit."

Barry Austin/Moodboard/Corbis

Do the Analysis

Do Gen Ys deserve special treatment? And when they get it, should it come at the expense of their more senior co-workers? Just how do you blend the needs and interests of a new generation of workers with others who have been around awhile—perhaps quite awhile? Who gains and who loses when the new generation pushes employers to rethink the nature of the employment contract?

---

points of conflict based on age stereotypes. Baby Boomers may view Millennials as feeling a sense of entitlement and not being hard working due to the way they dress and their interest in flexible hours. Millennials may view Baby Boomers and Gen Xers as more concerned about the hours they work than what they produce.[22]

The generational mix in organizations provides an excellent example of how diversity can deliver benefits. For example, Millennials seem to embrace gender equality and sexual, cultural, and racial diversity more than any previous generation, and they bring these values to work. Millennials also have an appreciation for community and collaboration. They can help create a more relaxed workplace that reduces some of the problems that come from too much focus on status and hierarchy. At the same time, Boomers and Gen Xers bring a wealth of experience, dedication, and commitment that contribute to productivity, and a sense of professionalism that is benefiting their younger counterparts.[23]

Ability In recent years the "disability rights movement" has been working to bring attention and support to the needs of disabled workers.[24] Estimates indicate that over 50 million Americans have one or more physical or mental disabilities, and studies show these workers do their jobs as well as, or better than, nondisabled workers. Despite this, nearly three-quarters of severely disabled persons are reported to be unemployed, and almost 80 percent of those with disabilities say they want to work.[25]

FINDING THE LEADER IN YOU

Stephen Hawking Inspires and Soars Despite Disability

Stephen Hawking cannot speak and does not have use of his motor skills, but he doesn't let that stop him. Renowned for his work in theoretical physics, Hawking has been an influential voice in redefining the way we see black holes and the origin of the universe. He is perhaps most recognized for his book *A Brief History of Time*, in which he works to translate Einstein's general theory of relatively and quantum theory for a general audience.

Hawking was diagnosed with ALS, or Lou Gehrig's disease, a few years after his twenty-first birthday. Over time, ALS has gradually crippled his body, first making him dependent on a wheelchair and private nurse, and then requiring 24/7 nursing care. He uses a voice synthesizer devised by a colleague that allows him to type rather than having to check letters off a card.

Despite his disability, Hawking has maintained an extensive program of travel, public lectures, and television appearances—even defying gravity by experiencing weightlessness on a zero-gravity flight for two hours over the Atlantic. His accomplishments and ability to live a full life, with three children and three grandchildren, have inspired people around the world. As Hawking says, "I'm sure my disability has a bearing on why I'm well known. People are fascinated by the contrast between my very limited physical powers, and the vast nature of the universe I deal with. I'm the archetype of a disabled genius, or should I say a physically challenged genius, to be politically correct. At least I'm obviously physically challenged. Whether I'm a genius is more open to doubt."

Menahem Kahana AFP/GettyImages/NewsCom

What's the Lesson Here?

How do you respond to individual differences in the workplace? Are you understanding of the strengths and limitations of others? What about your own limitations and challenges? Do you work to overcome them, or do you let them bring you down?

The passage of the **Americans with Disabilities Act** (ADA) in 1990 has been a significant catalyst in advancing their efforts. The focus of the ADA is to eliminate employers' practices that treat people with disabilities unnecessarily different. The ADA has helped to generate a more inclusive climate in which organizations are reaching out more to people with disabilities. The most visible changes from the ADA have been in issues of **universal design**—the practice of designing products, buildings, public spaces, and programs to be usable by the greatest number of people. You may see this in your own college or university's actions to make their campus and classrooms more accessible.[26]

The disability rights movement is working passionately to advance a redefinition of what it means to be disabled in U.S. society. The goal is to overcome the stigmas attached to disability. A **stigma** is a phenomenon whereby an individual with an attribute that is deeply discredited by his or her society is rejected as a result of the attribute. Because of stigmas, many are reluctant to seek coverage under the ADA because they do not want to experience discrimination in the form of stigmas.

The **Americans with Disabilities Act** is a federal civil rights statute that protects the rights of people with disabilities.

Universal design is the practice of designing products, buildings, public spaces, and programs to be usable by the greatest number of people.

A **stigma** is a phenomenon whereby an individual is rejected as a result of an attribute that is deeply discredited by his or her society.

▶ Diversity and Social Identity

Although in the past many organizations addressed the issue of diversity from the standpoint of compliance with legal mandates, the focus is now on policies and practices of inclusion.[27] This new focus represents a shift in thinking about how organizations can create inclusive cultures for everyone.[28]

The move from compliance to inclusion occurred primarily because employers began to learn that although they were able to recruit diverse individuals, they were not able to retain them. In work settings where upper ranks of organizations continued to be mostly composed of white males, difficult questions started to be asked and answered: Do employees in all groups and categories feel comfortable and welcomed in the organization? Do they feel included, and do they experience the environment as inclusive?[29]

Social identity theory is a theory developed to understand the psychological basis of discrimination.

Questions like those just posed are the focus of **social identity theory** as developed by social psychologists Henri Tajfel and John Turner in their quest to understand the psychological basis of discrimination.[30] According to the theory, individuals have not one but multiple "personal selves." Which self is activated depends on the group with which the person identifies. The mere act of identifying, or "categorizing," oneself as a member of a group will generate favoritism toward that group, and this favoritism is displayed in the form of "in-group" enhancement. This in-group favoritism occurs *at the expense of* the out-group. In terms of diversity, social identity theory suggests that simply having diversity in groups makes that identity salient in peoples' minds. Individuals engage these identities and experience feelings of **in-group membership** and **out-group membership**.

A feeling of **in-group membership** exists when individuals sense they are part of a group and experience favorable status and a sense of belonging.

A feeling of **out-group membership** exists when individuals sense they are not part of a group and experience discomfort and low belongingness.

The implications of social identity theory are straightforward. When organizations have strong identities formed around in-group and out-group categorizations based on diversity, this will work against a feeling of inclusion. Such in-group and out-group categorizations can be subtle but powerful, and they may be most noticeable to those in the "out-group" category. Organizations may not intend to create discriminatory environments, but when only a few members of a group are present, this may evoke a strong out-group identity. They may end up feeling uncomfortable and less a part of the organization. Managers and organizations try to deal with all this by creating work cultures and environments that welcome and embrace inclusion. The concept of valuing diversity emphasizes an appreciation of differences while creating a workplace where everyone feels valued and accepted.[31]

Personality

> TEACHING NOTE: Ask for examples of situations where a "bad" personality was dysfunctional for a work or study team. Engage a discussion of how such situations can best be handled. Include the question: Can someone's personality be changed?

LEARNING ROADMAP BIG FIVE PERSONALITY TRAITS • SOCIAL TRAITS • PERSONAL CONCEPTION TRAITS

The term **personality** encompasses the overall combination of characteristics that capture the unique nature of a person as that person reacts to and interacts with others. It combines a set of physical and mental characteristics that reflect how a person looks, thinks, acts, and feels. Think of yourself, and of your family and friends. A key part of how you interact with others depends on your own and their personalities, doesn't it? If you have a friend who has a sensitive personality, do you interact with that person differently than you do with a friend or family member who likes to joke around?

Personality is the overall combination of characteristics that capture the unique nature of a person as that person reacts to and interacts with others.

Sometimes attempts are made to measure personality with questionnaires or special tests. Frequently, personality can be inferred from behavior alone. Either way, personality is an important individual characteristic to understand. It helps us identify predictable interplays between people's individual differences and their tendencies to behave in certain ways.

▎Big Five Personality Traits

Personality traits are enduring characteristics describing an individual's behavior.

Numerous lists of **personality traits**—enduring characteristics describing an individual's behavior—have been developed, and used in OB research. A key starting point is to consider the personality dimensions known as the "Big Five Model":[32]

▶ Big Five Personality Dimensions

- *Extraversion*—the degree to which someone is outgoing, sociable, and assertive. An extravert is comfortable and confident in interpersonal relationships; an introvert is more withdrawn and reserved.
- *Agreeableness*—the degree to which someone is good-natured, cooperative, and trusting. An agreeable person gets along well with others; a disagreeable person is a source of conflict and discomfort for others.
- *Conscientiousness*—the degree to which someone is responsible, dependable, and careful. A conscientious person focuses on what can be accomplished and meets

Attractiveness Good for Men But Bad for Women When Job Hunting

Physical attractiveness is often considered a pathway to advancement and career success. The better looking among us, the reasoning goes, tend to fare better. But researchers from Ben Gurion University and Ariel University Centre in Israel faced unusual results when they tackled "attractiveness" in a study of employment practices. They sent similar résumés with and without photos of the job applicants to prospective employers. These photos of the male and female applicants were rated for attractiveness. Findings showed that attractive males were better off sending photos with their résumés, but attractive females were not. The hiring bias against attractive women in the study was explained as jealousy on the part of human resource staffers who are mostly female.

StockLite/Shutterstock

commitments; a person who lacks conscientiousness is careless, often trying to do too much and failing, or doing little.

- *Emotional stability*—the degree to which someone is relaxed, secure, and unworried. A person who is emotionally stable is calm and confident; a person lacking in emotional stability is anxious, nervous, and tense.
- *Openness to experience*—the degree to which someone is curious, open to new ideas, and imaginative. An open person is broad-minded, receptive to new things, and comfortable with change; a person who lacks openness is narrow-minded, has few interests, and is resistant to change.

A considerable body of literature links the personality dimensions of the Big Five model with behavior at work and in life overall. For example, conscientiousness is a good predictor of job performance for most occupations, and extraversion is often associated with success in management and sales. Indications are that extraverts tend to be happier than introverts in their lives overall, that conscientious people tend to be less risky, and that those more open to experience are more creative.[33]

You can easily spot the Big Five personality traits in people with whom you work, study, and socialize. But don't forget that they also apply to you. Others form impressions of your personality, and respond to it, just as you do in response to theirs. Managers often use these and other personality judgments when making job assignments, building teams, and otherwise engaging in the daily social give-and-take of work.

Social Traits

Social traits are surface-level traits that reflect the way a person appears to others when interacting in various social settings. A person's **problem-solving style**, based on the work of noted psychologist Carl Jung, is a good example. It reflects the way someone goes about gathering and evaluating information in solving problems and making decisions. Problem-solving styles are most frequently measured by the typically 100-item *Myers-Briggs Type Indicator (MBTI)*, which asks individuals how they usually act or feel in specific situations. The MBTI is often used by organizations to improve self-awareness of participants in management development programs.[34]

The first component in Jung's typology, information gathering, involves getting and organizing data for use. Styles of information gathering vary from sensation to intuitive. *Sensation-type individuals* prefer routine and order and emphasize well-defined details in gathering information; they would rather work with known facts than look for possibilities. By contrast, *intuitive-type individuals* prefer the "big picture." They like solving new problems, dislike routine, and would rather look for possibilities than work with facts.

Social traits reflect how a person appears to others in social settings.

Problem-solving style is how we gather and evaluate information when solving problems.

OB IN POPULAR CULTURE

Ambition and *The Social Network*

Columbia Pictures/Photofest

Sony's movie *The Social Network* is based on Facebook's story and especially the role of visionary and controversial founder Mark Zuckerberg (played by Jesse Eisenberg). Although Zuckerberg calls the film pure "fiction," it raises ethical questions about his actions while developing the initial Web site, refining it, and eventually turning it into a global company valued at over $50 billion. Two former Harvard classmates, Cameron and Tyler Winklevoss, sued him, claiming the original idea was theirs. Another early collaborator and co-founder, Eduardo Saverin, was initially left out of the new firm's financial gains.

In its reaction to the film, *Entertainment Weekly* asks, "Why did Zuckerberg betray these people? Or, in fact, did he really?"

One thing that cannot be denied is Zuckerberg's ambition, the desire to succeed and reach for high goals. He's the youngest self-made billionaire in business history. As the movie shows, ambition is one of those personality traits that can certainly have a big impact on individual behavior—both for the good and for the bad.

Get to Know Yourself Better
Watch *The Social Network* and discuss with your friends and classmates how different personalities and talents played out in creating the Facebook revolution. What can you learn that might help you deal with the ethics and intricacies of human behavior in work situations? Then take "Assessment 19: Your Personality Type" in the *OB Skills Workbook*. Personality is a good starting point for exploring your preferences and gaining a better understanding of who you are. How difficult would it be for someone else to understand you? Spend a few minutes looking at that. After you score the assessment, sit down with your roommate or a close friend and discuss the results. Is what you discovered consistent with how they see you?

The second component of problem solving, evaluation, involves making judgments about how to deal with information once it has been collected. Styles of information evaluation vary from an emphasis on feeling to an emphasis on thinking. *Feeling-type individuals* are oriented toward conformity and try to accommodate themselves to other people. They try to avoid problems that may result in disagreements. *Thinking-type individuals* use reason and intellect to deal with problems and downplay emotions.

When the two dimensions of information gathering and evaluation are combined, four basic problem-solving styles can be identified. As shown in Figure 2.1, people can be classified into combinations of sensation–feeling (SF), intuitive–feeling (IF), sensation–thinking (ST), and intuitive–thinking (IT).

Research indicates that there is a fit between the styles of individuals and the kinds of decisions they prefer. For example, STs (sensation–thinkers) prefer analytical strategies—those that emphasize detail and method. IFs (intuitive–feelers) prefer intuitive strategies—those that emphasize an overall pattern and fit. Not surprisingly, mixed styles (sensation–feelers or intuitive–thinkers) select both analytical and intuitive strategies. Other findings also indicate that thinkers tend to have higher motivation than do feelers, and that individuals who emphasize sensations tend to have higher job satisfaction than do intuitives. These and other findings suggest a number of basic differences among

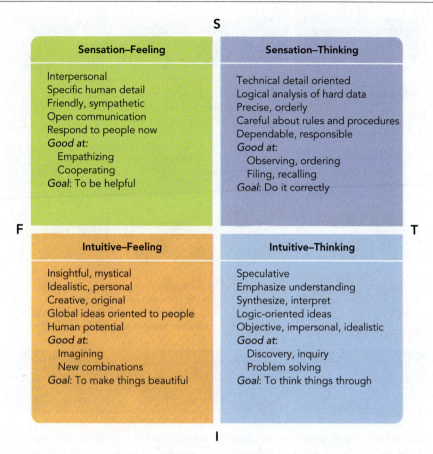

FIGURE 2.1 Four problem-solving styles of the Jungian typology.

different problem-solving styles, emphasizing the importance of fitting such styles with a task's information processing and evaluation requirements.[35]

Personal Conception Traits

What are known as **personal conception traits** represent various ways people think about their social and physical setting, their major beliefs, and personal orientations toward a range of issues. Personal conception traits often discussed in the work context include locus of control, proactive personality, authoritarianism/dogmatism, Machiavellianism, and self-monitoring.

Personal conception traits show up as personal beliefs and orientations toward settings and issues.

Locus of Control
The extent to which a person feels able to control his or her own life is known as **locus of control**.[36] People have personal conceptions about whether events are controlled primarily by themselves, which indicates an internal orientation, or by outside forces, such as their social and physical environment, which indicates an external orientation. *Internals*, or persons with an internal locus of control, believe that they control their own fate or destiny. In contrast, *externals*, or persons with an external locus of control, believe that much of what happens to them is beyond their control and is determined by environmental forces (such as fate).

In general, externals are more extraverted in their interpersonal relationships and are more oriented toward the world around them. Internals tend to be more introverted and are more oriented toward their own feelings and ideas. Figure 2.2 suggests that internals tend to do better on tasks requiring complex information processing and learning as well as initiative.

Locus of control is the extent a person feels able to control his or her own life and is concerned with a person's internal–external orientation.

Proactive Personality
Some people in organizations are passive recipients when faced with constraints, whereas others take direct and intentional action to change their

FIGURE 2.2 Ways in which internal locus of control differs from external locus of control.

A **proactive personality** is the disposition that identifies whether or not individuals act to influence their environments.

circumstances. The disposition that identifies whether or not individuals act to influence their environments is known as **proactive personality**. Individuals with high proactive personalities identify opportunities and act on them, show initiative, take action, and persevere until meaningful change occurs. Those low in proactivity are the opposite. They fail to identify—let alone seize—opportunities to change things. They tend to be passive and reactive, preferring to adapt to circumstances rather than change them.[37]

In the ever more demanding world of work, many employers are seeking individuals with more proactive qualities—individuals willing to take initiative and engage in proactive problem solving. Research supports this, showing that proactive personality is positively related to job performance, creativity, leadership, and career success. Other studies have shown that proactive personality is related to team effectiveness and entrepreneurship. Moreover, when organizations try to make positive and innovative change, these changes have more positive effects for proactive individuals—they are more involved and more receptive to change. This research is showing that proactive personality is an important and desirable element in today's work environment.

Authoritarianism/Dogmatism

Both authoritarianism and dogmatism as personal conception traits deal with the rigidity of someone's beliefs. A person high in **authoritarianism** tends to adhere rigidly to conventional values and to obey recognized authority. This person is concerned with toughness and power and opposes the use of subjective feelings. Highly authoritarian individuals present a special problem because they can be so eager to comply with directives from authority figures that they end up willing to behave unethically.[38]

Authoritarianism is a tendency to adhere rigidly to conventional values and to obey recognized authority.

Dogmatism leads a person to see the world as a threatening place and to regard authority as absolute.

An individual high in **dogmatism** sees the world as a threatening place. This person regards legitimate authority as absolute, and accepts or rejects others according to how much they agree with accepted authority. Superiors who possess these latter traits tend to be rigid and closed. At the same time, dogmatic subordinates tend to want certainty imposed on them.

CHECKING ETHICS IN OB

Personality Testing

Dear [your name goes here]:

I am very pleased to invite you to a second round of screening interviews with XYZ Corporation. Your on-campus session with our representative went very well, and we would like to consider you further for a full-time position. Please contact me to arrange a visit date. We will need a full day. The schedule will include several meetings with executives and your potential team members, as well as a round of personality tests.

Thank you again for your interest in XYZ Corp. I look forward to meeting you during the next step in our recruiting process.

Sincerely,

/signed/

Human Resource Director

Getting a letter like this is great news: a nice confirmation of your hard work and performance in college. You obviously made a good first impression. But have you thought about this "personality test" thing? What do you know about them and how they are used for employment screening?

Tek Image/Photo Researchers, Inc.

The U.S. Equal Employment Opportunity Commission says that personality tests can't have an adverse impact on members of protected groups. And, a report in the *Wall Street Journal* advises that lawsuits can result when employers use personality tests that weren't specifically designed for hiring decisions. Some people might even consider their use an invasion of privacy.

Make the Decision

What are the ethical issues of personality testing? When might the use of personality tests be considered an invasion of privacy? When might their use be considered unethical? Now go back to the situation just described: Will you take the tests at XYZ? Will you ask any questions about the tests when you contact the human resources director? Is the fact that XYZ uses personality tests a positive or a negative in terms of your likely fit with the firm?

Machiavellianism The very name of the sixteenth-century author Niccolo Machiavelli often evokes visions of someone who acts with guile, deceit, and opportunism. Machiavelli earned his place in history by writing *The Prince*, a nobleman's guide to the acquisition and use of power.[39] The subject of Machiavelli's book is manipulation as the basic means of gaining and keeping control of others. From its pages emerges the personality profile of **Machiavellianism**—the practice of viewing and manipulating others purely for personal gain.

Persons high in Machiavellianism approach situations logically and thoughtfully, and are even capable of lying to achieve personal goals.[40] They are rarely swayed by loyalty, friendships, past promises, or the opinions of others, and they are skilled at influencing others. They can also be expected to take control and try to exploit loosely structured environmental situations but will perform in a perfunctory, even detached, manner in highly structured situations. Where the situation permits, they might be expected to do or say whatever it takes to get their way. Those low in Machiavellianism, by contrast, tend to be more strongly guided by ethical considerations and are less likely to lie, cheat, or get away with lying or cheating.

Machiavellianism causes someone to view and manipulate others purely for personal gain.

Self-monitoring is a person's ability to adjust his or her behavior to external situational (environmental) factors.

Self-Monitoring

Self-monitoring reflects a person's ability to adjust his or her behavior to external, situational (environmental) factors.[41] High self-monitors are sensitive to external cues and tend to behave differently in different situations. High self-monitors can present a very different appearance from their true self. In contrast, low self-monitors, are less able to disguise their behaviors—"What you see is what you get." There is also evidence that high self-monitors are closely attuned to the behavior of others and conform more readily than do low self-monitors.[42] Thus, they appear flexible and may be especially good at adjusting their behavior to fit different kinds of situations and the people in them.

> TEACHING NOTE: Have students read the photo essay on page 41. Ask these or similar questions. Do we (really) work too much? When we do, is it mainly self-imposed or forced on us? Is taking more time off a true pathway to higher performance?

Personality and Stress

LEARNING ROADMAP TYPE A ORIENTATION AND STRESS • WORK AND LIFE STRESSORS
OUTCOMES OF STRESS • APPROACHES TO MANAGING STRESS

An individual's personality can also be described in terms of **emotional adjustment traits** that indicate how one handles emotional distress or displays unacceptable acts, such as impatience, irritability, or aggression.[43] Among these, a personality with **Type A orientation** is characterized by impatience, desire for achievement, and perfectionism. In contrast, those with a **Type B orientation** are characterized as more easygoing and less competitive in relation to daily events.[44] Type A people tend to work fast and to be abrupt, uncomfortable, irritable, and aggressive. Such tendencies may show up as "obsessive" behavior. When carried to the extreme, it may lead to greater concerns for details than for results, resistance to change, and overzealous attempts to exert control. In contrast, Type B people tend to be much more laid back and patient in their relationships with others.

Emotional adjustment traits are traits related to how much an individual experiences emotional distress or displays unacceptable acts.

Persons with **Type A orientations** tend to be impatient, achievement oriented, and competitive.

Persons with **Type B orientations** tend to be easygoing and less competitive.

Stress is a state of tension in response to extraordinary demands, constraints, or opportunities.

▮ Type A Orientation and Stress

In one survey of college graduates, 31 percent reported working over 50 hours per week, 60 percent rushed meals and 34 percent ate lunches "on the run," and 47 percent of those under 35 and 28 percent of those over 35 had feelings of job burnout. A study by the Society for Human Resources Management found that 70 percent of those surveyed worked over and above scheduled hours, including putting in extra time on the weekends; over 50 percent said that the pressure to do the extra work was "self-imposed."[45]

The situations just described all evidence the presence of **stress** as a state of internal tension experienced by individuals who perceive themselves as facing extraordinary demands, constraints, or opportunities.[46] If you look back to the discussion of Type A and Type B personalities, the fact is that Type As often bring stress upon themselves. They may even do this in situations others may find relatively stress free. You can spot Type A personality tendencies in yourself and others through the following patterns of behavior:

▸ Type A Behaviors

- Always moving, walking, and eating rapidly
- Acting impatient, hurrying others, put off by waiting
- Doing, or trying to do, several things at once
- Feeling guilty when relaxing
- Hurrying or interrupting the speech of others[47]

▮ Work and Life Stressors

Not all stress that we experience is personality driven. Any variety of things can cause stress for individuals. Some stressors can be traced directly to what people experience in the workplace, whereas others derive from life situations and nonwork factors.

Work Stressors There is no doubt that work can be stressful and job demands can sometimes disrupt one's work–life balance. Work stressors can arise from excessively high or low task demands, role conflicts or ambiguities, poor interpersonal relations, career progress that is either too slow or too fast, and more. The following is a list of common stressors:

- *Task demands*—being asked to do too much or being asked to do too little
- *Role ambiguities*—not knowing what one is expected to do or how work performance is evaluated
- *Role conflicts*—feeling unable to satisfy multiple, possibly conflicting, performance expectations
- *Ethical dilemmas*—being asked to do things that violate the law or personal values
- *Interpersonal problems*—experiencing bad relationships or working with others with whom one does not get along
- *Career developments*—moving too fast and feeling stretched; moving too slowly and feeling stuck on a plateau
- *Physical setting*—being bothered by noise, lack of privacy, pollution, or other unpleasant working conditions

◀ Common Work Stressors

Life Stressors Life stressors such as family events (e.g., the birth of a new child), economic difficulties (e.g., loss of income by a spouse), and personal affairs (e.g., a separation or divorce) can all be extremely stressful. That pretty much goes without saying. But it's also true that people can easily suffer from *spillover effects* that result when forces in their personal lives spill over to affect them at work or when forces at work spill over to affect their personal lives. Because it is often difficult to completely separate work and nonwork lives, especially in this age of smart devices that keep us continually in touch with work and personal affairs, life stressors and spillover effects are highly significant.

Outcomes of Stress

The stress we experience at work or in personal affairs isn't always negative. Scholars talk about two types of stress.[48] The first is **eustress**—constructive stress that results in positive outcomes. It occurs when moderate—not extreme—stress levels prompt things like increased work effort, greater creativity, and more diligence. You may know such stress as the tension that causes you to study hard before exams, pay attention in class, and complete assignments on time. The second type of stress is **distress**—destructive stress that turns out to be dysfunctional for both the individual. Key symptoms of individuals suffering distress are changes from regular attendance to absenteeism, from punctuality to tardiness, from diligent work to careless work, from a positive attitude to

Eustress is constructive stress that results in positive outcomes for the individual.

Distress is destructive stress that is dysfunctional for the individual.

Learning to Power Down: Vacation Habits Vary Around the World

"Most years I leave my vacation days on the table"—so says a bank marketing manager. Sound farfetched? Not necessarily; perhaps a bit extreme but still indicative of a pattern. A global survey of vacation habits finds that Americans on the average take fewer vacation days than they are allowed: an average of 12 out of 14. They leave anywhere from 2 to 11 days unused. This contrasts with French and Spanish workers who take all of their allocated 30 days, whereas the Japanese take only 4 of 10. One worker says, "It's almost not worth the stress of having double the work when you get back." Some employers are trying to curb tendencies to "work too much" as a way of helping people "do better work." The consulting firm KPMG uses a wellness scorecard to track and counsel workers who skip vacations and work excessive overtime.

Photomorphic/Robert Churchill

Job burnout is a loss of interest in or satisfaction with a job due to stressful working conditions.

a negative attitude, from openness to change to resistance to change, or from cooperation to hostility.

One possible outcome of extended distress, for example, is the **job burnout** that shows up as loss of interest in and satisfaction with a job due to stressful working conditions. Someone who is "burned out" feels emotionally and physically exhausted, and is less able to deal positively with work responsibilities and opportunities. More extreme reactions to distress include bullying of co-workers and even workplace violence. It is also clear that too much stress can overload and break down a person's physical and mental systems, resulting in absenteeism, turnover, errors, accidents, dissatisfaction, reduced performance, unethical behavior, and even illness.[49]

■ Approaches to Managing Stress

Coping Mechanisms

Coping is a response or reaction to distress that has occurred or is threatened.

Problem-focused coping mechanisms manage the problem that is causing the distress.

Emotion-focused coping are mechanisms that regulate emotions or distress.

Along with rising sensitivities to stress in the workplace, interest is also growing in how to manage, or *cope*, with distress. **Coping** is a response or reaction to distress that has occurred or is threatened. It involves cognitive and behavioral efforts to master, reduce, or tolerate the demands created by the stressful situation.

There are two major types of coping mechanisms. **Problem-focused coping** strategies try to manage the problem that is causing the distress. Indicators of this type of coping are comments like "I'll get the person responsible to change his or her mind," "I'll make a new plan of action and follow it," and "I'm going to stand my ground and fight for what I need." **Emotion-focused coping** strategies try to regulate the emotions drawn forth by stress. Indicators of this type of coping include comments like "I'll look for the silver lining, try to look on the bright side of things," "I'll accept the sympathy and understanding offered by others," and "I'll just try to forget the whole thing."[50]

People with different personalities tend to cope with stress in different ways. In respect to the Big Five, emotional stability has been found linked with increased use of hostile reaction, escapism/fantasy, self-blame, withdrawal, wishful thinking, passivity, and indecisiveness. People high in extraversion and optimism tend to show rational action, positive thinking, substitution, and restraint. And individuals high in openness to experience are likely to use humor in dealing with stress.

Stress Prevention

Stress prevention is the best first-line strategy in the battle against stress. It involves taking action to present stress from reaching destructive levels. Work and life stressors must be recognized before one can take action to prevent their occurrence or to minimize their adverse impacts. Persons with Type A personalities, for example, may exercise self-discipline, whereas supervisors of Type A employees may try to model a lower-key, more relaxed approach to work. Family

---

Achievement-Striving, and Learning to Say "No"

Persons high in achievement-striving can be overwhelmed by opportunities. They may end up over committed and less successful in the long run. A key element of managing stress is learning to say "No."[51]

When to Say No

- Focus on what matters most—focus on your priorities.
- Weigh the yes-to-stress ratio—how much added stress will this cause? Is it worth it?
- Take guilt out of the equation—guilt is inflated due to feeling of self-importance—it's okay to say no.
- Sleep on it—discipline yourself to not automatically say yes; what will it cost you?

How to Say No

- Just say no—or "I'm sorry but I can't...."
- Be brief—state your reason and avoid elaborations or justifications—"I'm swamped."
- Be honest—don't fabricate reasons; the truth is always best and people do understand.
- Be respectful—"I am honored to be asked but I can't do it."
- Be ready to repeat—stick to it if they ask again; just hit the replay button, don't give in.

problems may be partially relieved by a change of work schedule; simply knowing that your supervisor understands your situation may also help to reduce the anxiety caused by pressing family concerns.

Personal Wellness To keep stress from reaching a destructive point, special techniques of stress management can be implemented. This process begins with the recognition of stress symptoms and continues with actions to maintain a positive performance edge. The term *wellness* is increasingly used these days. **Personal wellness** involves the pursuit of one's job and career goals with the support of a personal health promotion program. The concept recognizes individual responsibility to enhance and maintain wellness through a disciplined approach to physical and mental health. It requires attention to such factors as smoking, weight management, diet, alcohol use, and physical fitness.

> **Personal wellness** involves the pursuit of one's job and career goals with the support of a personal health promotion program.

Values

LEARNING ROADMAP   SOURCES OF VALUES • PERSONAL VALUES • CULTURAL VALUES

> TEACHING NOTE: Option A: Do the class exercise—Alligator River Story. Launch a discussion of how values differences can influence teamwork. Option B: Have students use Hofstede's model to describe a cross-cultural experience that they found perplexing or especially interesting during international travels.

Values are broad preferences concerning appropriate courses of action or outcomes. They reflect a person's sense of right and wrong or what "ought" to be.[52] Statements like "Equal rights for all" and "People should be treated with respect and dignity" are indicators of values. And we recognize that values tend to influence attitudes and behavior.

■ Sources of Values

Parents, friends, teachers, siblings, education, experience, and external reference groups are all possible influences on individual values. Our values develop as a product of the learning and experience we encounter in the cultural setting in which we live, as learning and experiences differ from one person to another. Value differences result. Such differences are likely to be deep seated and difficult (though not impossible) to change. Many have their roots in early childhood and the way a person has been raised.[53]

> **Values** are broad preferences concerning appropriate courses of action or outcomes.

■ Personal Values

The noted psychologist Milton Rokeach classified values into two broad categories.[54] **Terminal values** reflect a person's preferences concerning the "ends" to be achieved; they are the goals an individual would like to achieve during his or her lifetime. **Instrumental values** reflect the "means" for achieving desired ends. They represent *how* you might go about achieving your important goals. Rokeach identifies the eighteen terminal values and eighteen instrumental values shown in Figure 2.3. Take a look at the list. Then ask this: What are my top five values, and what do they say about me and how I relate or work with others?

Bruce Meglino and colleagues discuss the importance of value congruence between leaders and followers.[55] It occurs when individuals express positive feelings upon encountering others who exhibit values similar to their own. When values differ, or are incongruent, conflicts over such things as goals and the means to achieve them may result. Research finds that satisfaction with a leader is greater when there is congruence among the four values of achievement, helping, honesty, and fairness.[56]

> **Terminal values** reflect a person's preferences concerning the "ends" to be achieved.
>
> **Instrumental values** reflect a person's beliefs about the means to achieve desired ends.

- *Achievement*—getting things done and working hard to accomplish difficult things in life
- *Helping and concern for others*—being concerned for other people and with helping others
- *Honesty*—telling the truth and doing what you feel is right
- *Fairness*—being impartial and doing what is fair for all concerned

◀ Megilino Values Schema

Terminal Values	Instrumental Values
• A comfortable life (and prosperous) • An exciting life (stimulating) • A sense of accomplishment (lasting contribution) • A world at peace (free of war and conflict) • A world of beauty (beauty of nature and the arts) • Equality (brotherhood, equal opportunity) • Family security (taking care of loved ones) • Freedom (independence, free choice) • Happiness (contentedness) • Inner harmony (freedom from inner conflict) • Mature love (sexual and spiritual intimacy) • National security (attack protection) • Pleasure (leisurely, enjoyable life) • Salvation (saved, eternal life) • Self-respect (self-esteem) • Social recognition (admiration, respect) • True friendship (close companionship) • Wisdom (mature understanding of life)	• Ambitious (hardworking) • Broad-minded (open-minded) • Capable (competent, effective) • Cheerful (lighthearted, joyful) • Clean (neat, tidy) • Courageous (standing up for beliefs) • Forgiving (willing to pardon) • Helpful (working for others' welfare) • Honest (sincere, truthful) • Imaginative (creative, daring) • Independent (self-sufficient, self-reliant) • Intellectual (intelligent, reflective) • Logical (rational, consistent) • Loving (affectionate, tender) • Obedient (dutiful, respectful) • Polite (courteous, well mannered) • Responsible (reliable, dependable) • Self-controlled (self-disciplined)

FIGURE 2.3 Terminal and Instrumental Values in the Rokeach value survey.

Cultural Values

Values can also be discussed for their presence at the level of national or societal culture. In this sense, **culture** can be defined as the learned, shared way of doing things in a particular society. It is the way, for example, in which its members eat, dress, greet and treat one another, teach their children, solve everyday problems, and so on.[57] Geert Hofstede, a Dutch scholar and consultant, refers to culture as the "software of the mind," making the analogy that the mind's "hardware" is universal among human beings.[58] But the software of culture takes many different forms. We are not born with a culture; we are born into a society that teaches us its culture. And because culture is shared among people, it helps to define the boundaries between different groups and affect how their members relate to one another.

Cultures are known to vary in their underlying patterns of values, and these differences are important in OB. The way people think about such matters as achievement, wealth and material gain, risk, and change, for example, may influence how they approach work and their relationships with organizations. Increasingly now you will hear the term **cultural quotient (CQ)** used to describe someone's ability to work effectively across cultures. And it's a point well worth considering in terms of personal growth and professional development.

One framework for understanding how value differences across national cultures was developed by the cross-cultural psychologist Hofstede. His framework is shown in Figure 2.4 and includes these five dimensions of national culture:

- **Power distance** is the willingness of a culture to accept status and power differences among its members. It reflects the degree to which people are likely to respect hierarchy and rank in organizations. Indonesia is considered a high-power-distance culture, whereas Sweden is considered a relatively low-power-distance culture.

- **Uncertainty avoidance** is a cultural tendency toward discomfort with risk and ambiguity. It reflects the degree to which people are likely to prefer structured versus unstructured organizational situations. France is considered a high-uncertainty-avoidance culture, whereas Hong Kong is considered a low-uncertainty-avoidance culture.

Culture is the learned and shared way of thinking and acting among a group of people or society.

Cultural quotient, or CQ, describes someone's ability to work effectively across cultures.

Power distance is a culture's acceptance of the status and power differences among its members.

Uncertainty avoidance is the cultural tendency to be uncomfortable with uncertainty and risk in everyday life.

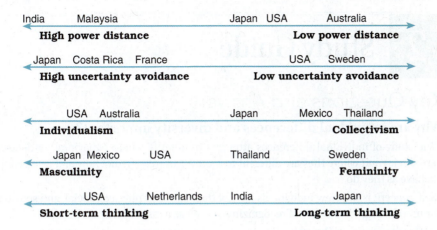

FIGURE 2.4 Sample country clusters on Hofstede's five dimensions of national values.

- **Individualism–collectivism** is the tendency of a culture to emphasize either individual or group interests. It reflects the degree to which people are likely to prefer working as individuals or working together in groups. The United States is a highly individualistic culture, whereas Mexico is a more collectivist one.
- **Masculinity–femininity** is the tendency of a culture to value stereotypical masculine or feminine traits. It reflects the degree to which organizations emphasize competition and assertiveness versus interpersonal sensitivity and concerns for relationships. Japan is considered a very masculine culture, whereas Thailand is considered a more feminine culture.
- **Long-term/short-term orientation** is the tendency of a culture to emphasize values associated with the future, such as thrift and persistence, or values that focus largely on the present. It reflects the degree to which people and organizations adopt long-term or short-term performance horizons. South Korea is high on long-term orientation, whereas the United States is a more short-term-oriented country.[59]

The first four dimensions in Hofstede's framework were identified in an extensive study of thousands of employees of a multinational corporation operating in more than forty countries.[60] The fifth dimension, long-term/short-term orientation, was added from research using the Chinese Values Survey conducted by cross-cultural psychologist Michael Bond and his colleagues.[61] Their research suggested the cultural importance of a value they called *Confucian dynamism*, with its emphasis on persistence, the ordering of relationships, thrift, sense of shame, personal steadiness, reciprocity, protection of "face," and respect for tradition.[62]

When using the Hofstede framework, it is important to remember that the five cultural value dimensions are interrelated, not independent.[63] National cultures may best be understood in terms of cluster maps or collages that combine multiple dimensions. For example, high power distance and collectivism are often found together, as are low power distance and individualism. Whereas high collectivism may lead us to expect a work team in Indonesia to operate by consensus, the high power distance may cause the consensus to be heavily influenced by the desires of a formal leader. A similar team operating in more individualist and low-power-distance Great Britain or America might make decisions with more open debate, including expressions of disagreement with a leader's stated preferences.

Hofstede also warns against falling prey to the **ecological fallacy**. This is acting with the mistaken assumption that a generalized cultural value, such as individualism in American culture or masculinity in Japanese culture, applies equally to all members of the culture.[64] And, finally, this model is just one starting point for developing cross-cultural awareness of values and value differences, and other frameworks of interest are available.[65]

Individualism–collectivism is the tendency of members of a culture to emphasize individual self-interests or group relationships.

Masculinity–femininity is the degree to which a society values assertiveness or relationships.

Long-term/short-term orientation is the degree to which a culture emphasizes long-term or short-term thinking.

Ecological fallacy is acting with the mistaken assumption that a generalized cultural value applies equally to all members of the culture.

2 Study Guide

Key Questions and Answers

Why are individual differences and diversity important?

- The study of individual differences attempts to identify where behavioral tendencies are similar and where they are different to more accurately predict how and why people behave as they do.
- Self-concept is the view individuals have of themselves as physical, social, and spiritual or moral beings. It is a way of recognizing oneself as a distinct human being.
- Both self-awareness (being aware of our own behaviors, preferences, styles, biases, and personalities) and awareness of others (being aware of these same things in others) are important capabilities if we are to best understand individual differences and diversity.
- The nature/nurture controversy addresses whether we are the way we are because of heredity or because of the environments in which we have been raised and live.
- There are many types of diversity, but the most commonly discussed in the workplace are racial/ethnic, gender, age, disability, and sexual orientation.
- In recent years there has been a shift from a focus on diversity to a focus on inclusion. This represents a need to emphasize not only recruitment but retention.
- Social identity theory suggests that many forms of discrimination are subtle but powerful, and may occur in subconscious psychological processes that individuals of out-groups perceive in the workplace.
- Organizations can value diversity by promoting cultures of inclusion that implement policies and practices to help create a more equitable and opportunity-based environment for all.

What is personality?

- Personality captures the overall profile, or combination of characteristics, that represents the unique nature of an individual as that individual interacts with others.
- Personality is determined by both heredity and environment; across all personality characteristics, the mix of heredity and environment is about 50–50. The Big Five personality traits are extraversion, agreeableness, conscientiousness, emotional stability, and openness to experience.
- A useful personality framework consists of social traits, personal conception traits, emotional adjustment traits, and personality dynamics, where each category represents one or more personality dimensions.

How are personality and stress related?

- Stress emerges when people experience tensions caused by extraordinary demands, constraints, or opportunities in their jobs.
- Personal stressors derive from personality type, needs, and values; they can influence how stressful different situations become for different people.
- Work stressors arise from such things as excessive task demands, interpersonal problems, unclear roles, ethical dilemmas, and career disappointments.
- Nonwork stress can spill over to affect people at work; nonwork stressors may be traced to family situations, economic difficulties, and personal problems.
- Stress can be managed by prevention—such as making adjustments in work and nonwork factors; it can also be dealt with through coping mechanisms and personal wellness—taking steps to maintain a healthy body and mind capable of better withstanding stressful situations.

What are values, and how do they vary across cultures?

- Values are broad preferences concerning courses of action or outcomes.
- Rokeach identifies terminal values (preferences concerning ends) and instrumental values (preferences concerning means); Meglino and his associates classify values into achievement, helping and concern for others, honesty, and fairness.
- Hofstede's five dimensions of national culture values are power distance, individualism–collectivism, uncertainty avoidance, masculinity–femininity, and long-term/short-term orientation.
- Culture is the learned and shared way of doing things in a society; it represents deeply ingrained influences on the way people from different societies think, behave, and solve problems.

Terms to Know

Americans with Disabilities Act (p. 33)
Authoritarianism (p. 38)
Awareness of others (p. 28)
Coping (p. 42)
Culture (p. 44)
Cultural quotient (p. 44)
Deep-level diversity (p. 28)
Discrimination (p. 29)
Distress (p. 41)
Dogmatism (p. 38)
Ecological fallacy (p. 45)
Emotion-focused coping (p. 42)
Emotional adjustment traits (p. 40)
Eustress (p. 41)
Glass ceiling effect (p. 30)
In-group membership (p. 34)
Individual differences (p. 28)
Individualism–collectivism (p. 45)
Instrumental values (p. 43)
Job burnout (p. 42)
Leaking pipeline (p. 30)
Leadership double bind (p. 30)
Locus of control (p. 37)
Long-term/short-term orientation (p. 45)
Machiavellianism (p. 39)
Masculinity–femininity (p. 45)
Out-group membership (p. 34)
Personal conception traits (p. 37)
Personal wellness (p. 43)
Personality (p. 34)
Personality traits (p. 34)
Power distance (p. 44)
Prejudice (p. 28)
Proactive personality (p. 38)
Problem-focused coping (p. 42)
Problem-solving style (p. 35)
Self-awareness (p. 28)
Self-concept (p. 28)
Self-efficacy (p. 28)
Self-esteem (p. 28)
Self-monitoring (p. 40)
Social identity theory (p. 34)
Social traits (p. 35)
Stigma (p. 33)
Stress (p. 40)
Surface-level diversity (p. 28)
Terminal values (p. 43)
Title VII of the Civil Rights Act of 1964 (p. 30)
Type A orientation (p. 40)
Type B orientation (p. 40)
Uncertainty avoidance (p. 44)
Universal design (p. 33)
Values (p. 43)

Self-Test 2

Multiple Choice

1. Individual differences are important because they _____.
   (a) mean we have to be different
   (b) reduce the importance of individuality
   (c) show that some cultural groups are superior to others
   (d) help us more accurately predict how and why people act as they do

2. Self-awareness is _____ awareness of others.
   (a) more important than
   (b) less important than
   (c) as important as
   (d) not at all related to

3. Self-efficacy is a form of _____.
   (a) self-awareness
   (b) self-esteem
   (c) nurture
   (d) agreeableness

4. Personality encompasses _____.
   (a) the overall combination of characteristics that capture the unique nature of a person
   (b) only the nurture components of self
   (c) only the nature components of self
   (d) how self-aware someone is

5. People who are high in internal locus of control _____.
   (a) believe what happens to them is determined by environmental forces such as fate
   (b) believe that they control their own fate or destiny
   (c) are highly extraverted
   (d) do worse on tasks requiring learning and initiative

6. Proactive personality is _____ in today's work environments.
   (a) punished
   (b) missing
   (c) becoming more important
   (d) losing importance

7. People who would follow unethical orders without question would likely be high in _____.
   (a) internal locus of control
   (b) Machiavellianism
   (c) proactive personality and extraversion
   (d) authoritarianism and dogmatism

8. Managers who are hard-driving, detail-oriented, have high performance standards, and thrive on routine could be characterized as _____.
   (a) Type B
   (b) Type A
   (c) high self-monitors
   (d) low Machs

9. Eustress is _____ stress, while distress is _____ stress.
   (a) constructive, destructive
   (b) destructive, constructive
   (c) negative, positive
   (d) the most common, the most relevant

10. Coping involves both _____ and _____ elements.
    (a) cognitive, intellectual
    (b) promotion, prevention
    (c) problem-focused, emotion-focused
    (d) cultural, psychological

11. When it comes to values, _____.
    (a) instrumental values are more important than terminal values
    (b) value congruence is what seems to be most important for satisfaction
    (c) it is rare that people hold similar values
    (d) most cultures share the same values

12. Culture is _____.
    (a) a person's major beliefs and personal orientation concerning a range of issues
    (b) the way a person gathers and evaluates information
    (c) the way someone appears to others when interacting in social settings
    (d) the learned, shared way of doing things in a particular society

13. The demographic makeup of the workforce _____.
    (a) has been relatively stable
    (b) is not related to managerial practices
    (c) has experienced dramatic changes in recent decades
    (d) is becoming less of an issue for management.

14. Companies that _____ experience the greatest benefits of workforce diversity.
    (a) have learned to employ people because of their differences
    (b) have learned to employ people in spite of their differences
    (c) have not worried about people's differences
    (d) have implemented diversity programs based only on affirmative action

15. The experience in which simply having various diversity groups makes that group category salient in people's minds is an example of _____.
    (a) stigma
    (b) leaking pipeline
    (c) inclusion
    (d) social identity theory

Short Response

16. What are individual differences, and why are they important to organizational behavior?
17. What is more influential in determining personality: nature or nurture?
18. What values were identified by Meglino and associates, and how do they relate to workplace behavior?
19. With respect to diversity and inclusion, what do we know about environments that are most conducive to valuing and supporting diversity?

Applications Essay

20. Your boss has noticed that stress levels have been increasing in your work unit and has asked you to assess the problem and propose a plan of action for addressing it. What steps would you take to meet this request? What would be the first thing you would do, what factors would you take into consideration in conducting your assessment, and what plan of action do you think would be most promising?

Steps for Further Learning 2
Top Choices from *The OB Skills Workbook*

These learning activities from *The OB Skills Workbook* found at the back of the book are suggested for Chapter 2.

Case for Critical Thinking	Team and Experiential Exercises	Self-Assessment Portfolio
• Diversity Commitment Worth Copying	• What Do You Value in Work? • Prejudice in Our Lives • How We View Differences • Alligator River Story	• Turbulence Tolerance Test • Personal Values • Time Management Profile • Personality Type

A discerning eye tells the story

Perception, Attribution, and Learning

3

The Key Point

It can be a shock when people view the same thing and come to different conclusions. But this is reality—people often perceive and respond to situations in different ways. The better we understand perception and attribution and their effects on how people behave and learn, the better we can be at dealing with events, people, and relationships. ■

What's Inside?

- **Bringing OB to LIFE**
  RAISING EXPECTATIONS AND GETTING BETTER FEEDBACK
- **Worth Considering . . . or Best Avoided?**
  NOT ENOUGH WOMEN ON BOARD? EUROPE TURNS TO QUOTAS
- **Checking Ethics in OB**
  WORKERS REPORT VIEWS ON ETHICAL WORKPLACE CONDUCT
- **Finding the Leader in You**
  RICHARD BRANSON LEADS WITH PERSONALITY AND POSITIVE REINFORCEMENT
- **OB in Popular Culture**
  POSITIVE REINFORCEMENT AND *BIG BANG THEORY*
- **Research Insight**
  INTERACTIONAL JUSTICE PERCEPTIONS AFFECT INTENT TO LEAVE

Chapter at a Glance

- What Is Perception, and Why Is It Important?
- What Are the Common Perceptual Distortions?
- What Is the Link Between Perception, Attribution, and Social Learning?
- What Is Involved in Learning by Reinforcement?

The Perception Process

> **LEARNING ROADMAP**
> FACTORS INFLUENCING PERCEPTION
> INFORMATION PROCESSING AND THE PERCEPTION PROCESS
> PERCEPTION, IMPRESSION MANAGEMENT, AND SOCIAL MEDIA

Perception is the process by which people select, organize, interpret, retrieve, and respond to information from the world around them.[1] It is a way of forming impressions about ourselves, other people, and daily life experiences. It also serves as a screen or filter through which information passes before it has an effect on people. Because perceptions are influenced by many factors, different people may perceive the same situation quite differently. Since people behave according to their perceptions, the consequences of these differences can be great in terms of what happens next.

Consider the example shown in Figure 3.1. It shows substantial differences in how performance-review discussions are perceived by managers and members of their work teams. The managers here may end up not giving much attention to things like career development, performance goals, and supervisory support since they perceive that these issues were adequately addressed at performance-review time. However, the team members may end up frustrated and unsatisfied because they perceive that less attention was given and they want more.

▌ Factors Influencing Perception

We can think of perception as a bubble that surrounds us and influences significantly the way we receive, interpret, and process information received from our environments. As the perception process varies, so too can things like decisions made and actions taken. When someone does things that we don't understand or in ways that we don't understand or that surprise us, the reason may well be due to the fact that their perceptions in the situation differed from ours or what we would normally

> TEACHING NOTE: Call for "Believe it or Not" time. Ask students for examples of the worst impression management mistakes they have seen or committed. Use this to launch a discussion of perception, how it influences behavior, and how it can be managed.

Perception is the process through which people receive and interpret information from the environment.

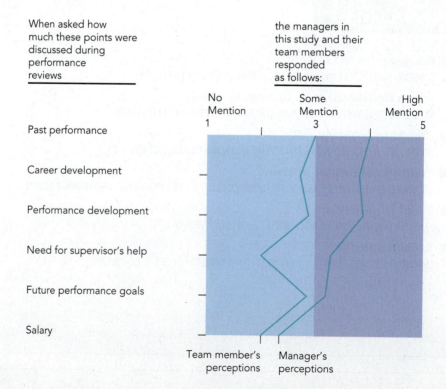

FIGURE 3.1 Contrasting perceptions between managers and subordinates regarding performance appraisal interviews.

expect. The many factors influencing perception include characteristics of the *perceiver*, the *setting*, and the *perceived*.

Characteristics of the Perceiver
A person's past experiences, needs or motives, personality, values, and attitudes may all influence the perceptual process. Someone with a strong need for achievement need tends to perceive a situation in terms of that need. If doing well in class is perceived as a way to help meet your achievement need, for example, you will tend to emphasize that aspect when choosing classes to take. In the same way, a person with a negative attitude toward younger workers may react poorly when asked to work for a young, newly hired but very competent team leader.

Characteristics of the Setting
The physical, social, and organizational context can influence the perception process. A teammate perceived by peers as temperamental may well be tolerated on the team. But take that person and make them the team leader and the same temperamental behavior may be perceived as bullying or intimidating.

Characteristics of the Perceived
Characteristics of the perceived person, object, or event are also important in the perception process. We talk about them in terms of contrast, intensity, figure–ground separation, size, motion, and repetition or novelty. In respect to contrast, for example, one iPad among six Android tablets or one man among six women will be perceived differently than one of six iPad computers or one of six men. In respect to intensity, a bright red sports car stands out from a group of gray sedans; whispering or shouting stands out from ordinary conversation. This links with a concept known as *figure–ground separation*. Look, for example, at the margin illustration. What do you see, faces or a vase? It depends on which image is perceived as the background and which as the figure or object of our attention.

In the matter of size, very small or very large objects or people tend to be perceived differently. In terms of motion, moving objects and people are perceived differently than stationary ones. In addition, repetition or frequency can also influence perceptions. Television advertisers well know that the more they put something in front of us the more likely we are to give it attention. Finally, the novelty of a situation affects its perception. A college student who enters class with streaks of hair dyed purple may be perceived quite differently by an instructor than others with a more common hair color.

◾ Information Processing and the Perception Process

The ways we process information during the perception process affect how we respond to experiences through feelings, thoughts, and actions taken. The four stages of this information processing are attention and selection, organization, interpretation, and retrieval. A good understanding of these stages can help us manage our own perceptions better, as well as both understand and influence the perceptions of others.

Attention and Selection
Our senses are constantly bombarded with so much information that if we don't screen it, we quickly become incapacitated with information overload. We tend to deal with this through **selective screening** that lets in only a tiny portion of all the information available.

Some of the selective screening that we do comes from controlled processing: consciously deciding what information to pay attention to and what to ignore. Think, for example, about the last time you were at a noisy restaurant and screened out all the sounds but those of the person with whom you were talking. Some screening also takes

Selective screening allows only a portion of available information to enter our perceptions.

Bringing OB to Life

> "If you want your friends to experience something as better than it truly is, go for it and exaggerate. But don't exaggerate by too much."

Raising Expectations and Getting Better Feedback

Wine tasting test: Does a glass of wine taste better if you have never heard of the vintage or if you have previously read a positive review of it? As you might expect, it will most often be the one that you taste after reading the positive review. The reason traces to a common OB understanding of perception and expectations. We basically end up perceiving things—the glass of wine, a test drive of a new BMW, or a new teammate—as we expect them to be.

Does this mean that before your next big presentation to the class or to an executive team you should prepare the audience by announcing ahead of time "You're going to like this one"? Well, perhaps—but some caution is in order. Raising expectations can be overplayed with the result that disappointment sets in. Think of a movie or restaurant recommendation you might have made to a friend. You raved about it and just couldn't wait for him to have the same experience. Instead, he reports, "It was okay but not great. I was hoping for better." What happened is that the high bar of excellence set in your expectations created a situation ripe for a letdown.

Dan Ariely, professor of psychology and behavioral economics, advises that we have to be careful in communicating expectations. If we overhype something because we're hoping for positive feedback, we may end up getting a negative review. His rule of thumb is to go ahead and send out the high expectations, but don't

MarkSwallow/iStockphoto

overexaggerate too much. You have to stay in a range where reality can deliver the results. He suggests shooting for about a 20 percent stretch of positive expectations. That's a comfortable target for pulling the perceiver's feedback in a positive direction.

This notion of raising expectations for positive feedback is an interesting one to test in everyday experience. Why not try it? See how well you can manage expectations of friends and teammates. Maybe this is a skill that could serve you well in many life and work situations.

---

place without conscious awareness. We often drive cars without thinking about the process; we're aware of things like traffic lights and other cars, but we don't pay conscious attention to them. This selectivity of attention and automatic information processing works well most of the time. But if a nonroutine event occurs, such as an animal darting in front of your vehicle, you may have an accident unless you quickly shift to controlled processing.

Organization

Even when selective screening takes place in the attention stage, it's still necessary for us to organize information efficiently. This is done to some extent through **schemas**. These are cognitive frameworks that represent organized knowledge developed through experience about a concept or stimulus.[2] The schemas most commonly used are script schemas, person schemas, and person-in-situation schemas.

A *script schema* is a knowledge framework that describes the appropriate sequence of events in a given situation.[3] For example, an experienced team leader might use a script

Schemas are cognitive frameworks that represent organized knowledge developed through experience about people, objects, or events.

Research Insight

Interactional Justice Perceptions Affect Intent to Leave

Research reported by Merideth Ferguson, Neta Moye, and Ray Friedman links perceptions of interactional justice during recruitment interviews with effects on long-term employment relationships. Focusing on issues of fairness in the workplace, a substantial literature on organizational justice shows that people respond to perceived fair and unfair treatments in positive and negative ways, with the links between perceived injustice and negative behaviors being particularly strong.

intentions to leave. The second study asked a sample of recent MBA graduates to report perceptions of interactional justice during their job negotiations; they were asked six months later to report on their intentions to leave the new employer. Results from both studies offered confirmation for the two hypotheses.

In conclusion, Ferguson et al. state that "the sense of injustice one feels during a negotiation affects an employee's turnover intentions with the hiring organization . . . negotiations in the recruitment process can set the tone for the future employment relationship." They recommend future research to examine how negotiating tactics like slow responses, dishonesty, disrespect, and lack of concessions influence justice perceptions and later intent to leave. They also suggest that perceived injustice in recruiting when jobs are plentiful may lead to applicants making alternative job choices, whereas such injustice when jobs are scarce may result in employees accepting the jobs but harboring intent to leave when the opportunity permits.

```
                    Hypothesis 1                Hypothesis 2
  [Perceived          ------>    [Less perceived    ------>    [More long-term
   high pressure                  interactional                  intent to leave by
   negotiating tactics            justice in job                 employees]
   by recruiters]                 negotiation]
```

This research examined fairness perceptions regarding negotiations taking place during the recruitment process and how these perceptions affected later intentions to leave. Two hypotheses were tested. First, it was hypothesized that perceived use of negotiation pressure by recruiters would have a negative impact on perceived interactional justice by job applicants. Second, it was hypothesized that perceived interactional injustice during recruiting negotiations would have a positive long-term impact on later intentions to leave by the newly hired employees.

Two studies were conducted. The first study asked a sample of sixty-eight university alumni of a business program about their retrospective perceptions of interactional justice during job negotiations and their current

Do the Research What is your experience with interactional justice in the recruiting process? Can you design a study to gather the experiences of your cohorts, friends, and others on campus? How can your study pinpoint the impact of tactics such as setting a tight time limit on a job offer?

Source: Merideth Ferguson, Neta Moye, and Ray Friedman, "The Lingering Effects of the Recruitment Experience on the Long-Term Employment Relationship," *Negotiation and Conflict Management Research* 1 (2008), pp. 246–262.

---

schema to think about the appropriate steps involved in running a meeting. A *self schema* contains information about a person's own appearance, behavior, and personality. For instance, people with decisiveness schemas tend to perceive themselves in terms of that aspect, especially in circumstances calling for leadership.

Person schemas sort people into categories—types or groups, in terms of similar perceived features. They include **prototypes** which are pre-set bundles of features expected to be characteristic of people in certain categories or roles. An example might be the prototype of a "good teammate" as someone who is intelligent, dependable, and

A **prototype** is a bundle of features expected to be characteristic of people in certain categories or roles.

hard-working. Once formed, person schemas are stored in long-term memory and retrieved only when needed for a comparison of how well a person matches the schema's features.[4]

Interpretation

Once your attention has been drawn to certain stimuli and you have grouped or organized this information, the next step is to uncover the reasons behind the actions. Even if your attention is called to the same information and you organize it in the same way your friend does, you may still interpret it differently or make different assumptions about what you have perceived. As a team leader, for example, you might interpret compliments from a team member as due to his being eager and enthusiastic about a task; your friend might interpret the team member's behavior as an attempt at insincere flattery.

Retrieval

Each stage of the perception process becomes part of memory. This information stored in our memory must be retrieved if it is to be used. But all of us at times have trouble retrieving stored information. Memory decays, so that only some of the information may be retrieved. Schemas can make it difficult for people to remember things not included in them. If you hold the prototype of a "good worker" as someone showing lots of effort, punctuality, intelligence, articulateness, and decisiveness, you may emphasize these traits and overlook others when evaluating the performance of a team member whom you generally consider good.

■ Perception, Impression Management, and Social Media

Impression management is the systematic attempt to influence how others perceive us.

Richard Branson, CEO of the Virgin Group, is one of the richest and most famous executives in the world. He may also be the ultimate master of **impression management**, the systematic attempt to behave in ways that will create and maintain desired impressions in the eyes of others.[5] One of Branson's early business accomplishments was the successful start-up of Virgin Airlines, now a global competitor to the legacy airlines. In a memoir, the former head of British Airways, Lord King, said, "If Richard Branson had worn a shirt and tie instead of a goatee and jumper, I would not have underestimated him."[6]

How to Build Your Personal Brand Through Impression Management in Social Networks

Don't let your social media presence get out of control. Impression management counts online as well as face to face, and here are some things to help you make it work for you.

- Ask: How do I want to be viewed? What are my goals in this forum?
- Ask: What am I communicating, or about to communicate, to my "public" audience?
- Ask: Before I post this item, is it something that I want my family, loved ones, or a potential employer to see?
- Do: Choose a respectable username.
- Do: Profile yourself only as you really would like to be known to others; keep everything consistent.
- Do: View your online persona as a "brand" that you are going to wear for a long time; make sure your persona and desired brand are a "fit" and not a "misfit."
- Do: Post and participate in an online forum only in ways that meet your goals for your personal brand; don't do anything that might damage it.

Don't you wonder if creating a casual impression was part of Branson's business strategy? Whether intended or not, the chances are he's used this persona to very good advantage in other business dealings as well. It's an example of how much our impressions can count, both positive and negative, in how others perceive us. And it's not a new lesson; we've all heard it before. Who hasn't been told when heading off to a job interview "Don't forget to make a good first impression"?

The fact is that we already practice a lot of impression management as a matter of routine in everyday life. Impression management is taking place when we dress, talk, act, and surround ourselves with what reinforces a desirable self-image and helps to convey that image to other persons. When well done, that can help us to advance in jobs and careers, form relationships with people we admire, and even create pathways to group memberships. We manage impressions by such activities as associating with the "right" people, "dressing up" and "dressing down" at the right times, making eye contact when introduced to someone, doing favors to gain approval, flattering others to impress them, taking credit for a favorable event and apologizing for a negative one, and agreeing with the opinions of others.[7]

One of the most powerful forces in impression management today might be the one least recognized—how we communicate our presence in the online world of social media. It might even be the case that this short message deserves to go viral: User beware! The brand you are building through social media may last a lifetime. For tips to remember, check the sidebar on "How to Build Your Personal Brand Through Impression Management in Social Networks."

It's no secret that more and more employers are intensely scouring the Web to learn what they can about job candidates. What they are gathering are impressions left in the trails of the candidates' past social media journeys. One bad photo, one bad nickname, or one bad comment sends the wrong impression and can kill a great job opportunity. We are creating impressions of ourselves whenever we are active in the online world. The problem is that those impressions may be fun in social space but harmful in professional space. There's a lot to learn about impression management and social media. At a minimum it pays to keep the two social media spaces—the social and the professional—separated with a good firewall between them.

Common Perceptual Distortions

LEARNING ROADMAP STEREOTYPES • HALO EFFECTS • SELECTIVE PERCEPTION PROJECTION • CONTRAST EFFECTS • SELF-FULFILLING PROPHECIES

> TEACHING NOTE: Have students form teams and then assign them the exercise—How We View Differences. Use your own version or the one from the OB Skills Workbook. Debrief according to the instructions.

Given the complexity of the information streaming toward us from various environments, we use various means of simplifying and organizing our perceptions. However, these simplifications can cause inaccuracies in our impressions and in the perception process more generally. Common perceptual distortions trace to the use of stereotypes, halo effects, selective perception, projection, contrast effects, and self-fulfilling prophecies.

Stereotypes

One of the most common simplifying devices in perception is the **stereotype**. It occurs when we identify someone with a group or category, and then use the attributes perceived to be associated with the group or category to describe the individual. Although this makes matters easier for us by reducing the need to deal with unique individual characteristics, it is an oversimplification. Because stereotypes obscure individual differences, we can easily end up missing the real individual. For managers this means not accurately understanding the needs, preferences, and abilities of others in the workplace.

Some of the most common stereotypes, at work and in life in general, relate to such factors as gender, age, race, and physical ability. Why are so few top executives in industry African Americans or Hispanics? Legitimate questions can be asked about *racial and ethnic stereotypes* and about the slow progress of minority managers into America's corporate mainstream.[8] Why is it that women constitute only a small

> A **stereotype** assigns attributes commonly associated with a group to an individual.

percentage of American managers sent abroad to work on international business assignments? A Catalyst study of opportunities for women in global business points to *gender stereotypes* that place women at a disadvantage compared to men for these types of opportunities. The tendency is to assume women lack the ability and/or willingness to work abroad.[9] Gender stereotypes may cause even everyday behavior to be misconstrued. For example, consider "He's talking with co-workers" (Interpretation: He's discussing a new deal) and "She's talking with co-workers" (Interpretation: She's gossiping).[10]

Ability stereotypes and *age stereotypes* also exist in the workplace. Physically or mentally challenged candidates may be overlooked by a recruiter even though they possess skills that are perfect for the job. A talented older worker may not be promoted because a manager assumes older workers are cautious and tend to avoid risk.[11] Yet a Conference Board survey of workers age 50 and older reports that 72 percent felt they could take on additional responsibilities, and two-thirds were interested in further training and development.[12] Then there's the flip side: Can a young person be a real leader, even a CEO? Facebook's founder and CEO Mark Zuckerberg is still in his twenties. When current CEO Sheryl Sandberg was being recruited from Google, she admits to having had this thought: "Wow, I'm going to work for a CEO who is quite young." "Mark is a great leader," she now says. After working for him, her perception has changed. "Mark has a real purity of vision. . . . He brings people along with him."[13]

Halo Effects

A **halo effect** occurs when one attribute of a person or situation is used to develop an overall impression of that individual or situation. Like stereotypes, these distortions are more likely to occur in the organization stage of perception. Halo effects are common in our everyday lives. When meeting a new person, for example, a pleasant smile can lead to a positive first impression of an overall "warm" and "honest" person. The result of a halo effect is the same as that associated with a stereotype, however, in that individual differences are obscured.

Halo effects are particularly important in the performance appraisal process because they can influence a manager's evaluations of subordinates' work performance. For example, people with good attendance records may be viewed as intelligent and responsible while those with poor attendance records are considered poor performers. Such conclusions may or may not be valid. It is the manager's job to try to get true impressions rather than allowing halo effects to result in biased and erroneous evaluations.

A **halo effect** uses one attribute to develop an overall impression of a person or situation.

Selective Perception

Selective perception is the tendency to single out those aspects of a situation, person, or object that are consistent with one's needs, values, or attitudes. Its strongest impact occurs in the attention stage of the perceptual process. This perceptual distortion was identified in a classic research study involving executives in a manufacturing company.[14] When asked to identify the key problem in a comprehensive business policy case, each executive selected a problem consistent with his or her functional area work assignments. Most marketing executives viewed the key problem area as sales, whereas production people tended to see the problem as one of production and organization. These differing viewpoints would likely affect how each executive would approach the problem; they might also create difficulties as the executives tried to work together to improve things.

Selective perception is the tendency to define problems from one's own point of view.

| WORTH CONSIDERING | ...OR BEST AVOIDED? |

Not Enough Women on Board? Europe Turns to Quotas

The consulting firm McKinsey & Company reports that women are hired to fill more than 50 percent of professional jobs in America's large corporations. Then they start leaking from the career pipeline. They hold 3 percent of CEO positions, 14 percent of C-suite jobs, and 28 percent of director positions on corporate boards. That's the good news. Data from the rest of the world are worse. Women hold just 13.7 percent of seats on corporate boards in Europe and 7.1 percent elsewhere in the world.

The low percentage of women serving at the top of corporate hierarchy doesn't match well with data showing their presence has a positive performance impact. A Millward Brown Optimor study found that top global companies with women on their boards showed 66 percent brand growth over a 5-year period and those with no female board members had 6 percent brand growth. An Ernst & Young study concludes, "The undisputed conclusion from all the research is that having more women at the top improves financial performance." The report went on to say that "Performance increased significantly once a certain critical mass was attained, namely at least three women on management committees for an average membership of 10 people."

Rather than leave the future of female representation on corporate boards to chance, Europe has started to consider quotas. Norway, Spain, Iceland, and France have already passed 40 percent quotas. When legislation requiring all EU-listed companies to appoint women to 40 percent of nonexecutive board seats by 2020 was proposed by the European Commission, it was later pulled for lack of support. Some member countries say they plan to file it again in the future.

© Trista Weibell/iStockphoto

A Heidrick & Struggles survey showed 51 percent of women directors supporting quotas like those appearing in Europe. Only 25 percent of men directors voiced similar support.

Do the Analysis

Is Europe on the right path with quotas to correct gender disparities in corporate boards? Should this conversation be limited to women in general? What about women of color? What about other minorities—male or female? When it comes to career advancement for women and minorities in the corporate world, is it time for quotas, or are we better off waiting for changes to take a natural course?

▌ Projection

Projection is the assignment of one's personal attributes to other individuals. It is especially likely to occur in the interpretation stage of perception. A classic error is projecting your needs, values, and views onto others. This causes their individual differences to get lost. Such projection errors can be controlled through a high degree of self-awareness and empathy—the ability to view a situation as others see it.

Suppose, for example, that you enjoy responsibility and achievement in your work. Suppose, too, that you are the newly appointed leader of a team whose jobs seem dull and routine. You may move quickly to expand these jobs so that members get increased satisfaction from more challenging tasks. Basically, you want them to experience what you value in work. However, this may not be a good decision. Instead of designing team members' jobs to best fit their needs, you have designed their jobs to best fit yours.

Projection assigns personal attributes to other individuals.

Contrast Effects

A **contrast effect** occurs when the meaning of something that takes place is based on a contrast with another recent event or situation.

We mentioned earlier how a bright red sports car would stand out from a group of gray sedans. This shows a **contrast effect** in which the meaning or interpretation of something is arrived at by contrasting it with a recently occurring event or situation. This form of perceptual distortion can occur, say, when a person gives a talk following a strong speaker or is interviewed for a job following a series of mediocre applicants. A contrast effect occurs when an individual's characteristics are contrasted with those of others recently encountered who rank higher or lower on the same characteristics.

Self-Fulfilling Prophecies

A **self-fulfilling prophecy** is creating or finding in a situation that which you expected to find in the first place.

A final perceptual distortion is the **self-fulfilling prophecy**: the tendency to create or find in another situation or individual that which you expected to find in the first place. A self-fulfilling prophecy is sometimes referred to as the "Pygmalion effect," named for a mythical Greek sculptor who created a statue of his ideal mate and then made her come to life.[15]

Self-fulfilling prophecies can have both positive and negative outcomes. In effect, they may create in work and personal situations that which we expect to find. Suppose you assume that team members prefer to satisfy most of their needs outside the work setting and want only minimal involvement with their jobs. Consequently, you assign simple,

---

CHECKING ETHICS IN OB

Workers Report Views on Ethical Workplace Conduct

Izvorinka Jankovic/iStockphoto

These data on ethical workplace conduct are from a survey conducted for Deloitte & Touche USA.

- 42 percent of workers say the behavior of their managers is a major influence on an ethical workplace.
- Most common unethical acts by managers and supervisors include verbal, sexual, and racial harassment, misuse of company property, and giving preferential treatment.
- Most workers consider it unacceptable to steal from an employer, cheat on expense reports, take credit for another's accomplishments, and lie on time sheets.
- Most workers consider it acceptable to ask a work colleague for a personal favor, take sick days when not ill, and use company technology for personal affairs.
- Top reasons for unethical behavior are lack of personal integrity (80 percent) and lack of job satisfaction (60 percent).
- Among workers, 91 percent are more likely to behave ethically when they have work–life balance; 30 percent say they suffer from poor work–life balance.

Whose Ethics Count? Shouldn't an individual be accountable for her or his own ethical reasoning and analysis? How and why is it that the ethics practices of others, including managers, influence our ethics behaviors? What can be done to strengthen people's confidence in their own ethical frameworks so that even bad management won't result in unethical practices?

highly structured tasks designed to require little involvement. Can you predict what response they will have to this situation? In fact, they may show the very same lack of commitment you assumed they would have in the first place. In this case your initial expectations get confirmed as a negative self-fulfilling prophecy.

Self-fulfilling prophecies can also have a positive side. In a study of army tank crews, one set of tank commanders was told that some members of their assigned crews had exceptional abilities whereas others were only average. However, the crew members had been assigned randomly so that the two test groups were equal in ability. The commanders later reported that the so-called "exceptional" crew members performed better than the "average" ones. The study also revealed that the commanders had given more attention and praise to the crew members for whom they had the higher expectations.[16] Don't you wonder what might happen with students and workers in general if teachers and managers adopted more uniformly positive and optimistic approaches toward them?

Perception, Attribution, and Social Learning

LEARNING ROADMAP   IMPORTANCE OF ATTRIBUTIONS • ATTRIBUTION ERRORS • ATTRIBUTION AND SOCIAL LEARNING

One of the ways in which perception exerts its influence on behavior is through **attribution**. This is the process of developing explanations or assigning perceived causes for events. It is natural for people to try to explain what they observe and what happens to them. What happens when you perceive that someone in a job or student group isn't performing up to expectations? How do you explain this? And, depending on the explanation, what do you do to try and correct things?

> TEACHING NOTE: Ask students to use the insights of attribution theory and tendencies toward attribution errors to describe how a class interaction might go wrong for the professor. Push them for specifics and then discuss the implications for work and personal situations in general.

Attribution is the process of creating explanations for events.

▶ Importance of Attributions

Attribution theory helps us understand how people perceive the causes of events, assess responsibility for outcomes, and evaluate the personal qualities of the people involved.[17] It is especially concerned with whether the assumption is that an individual's behavior, such as poor performance, has been internally or externally caused. Internal causes are believed to be under an individual's control—you believe Jake's performance is poor because he is lazy. External causes are seen as coming from outside a person—you believe Kellie's performance is poor because the software she's using is out of date.

According to attribution theory, three factors influence this internal or external determination of causality: distinctiveness, consensus, and consistency. *Distinctiveness* considers how consistent a person's behavior is across different situations. If Jake's performance is typically low, regardless of the technology with which he is working, we tend to assign the poor performance to an internal attribution—there's something wrong with Jake. If the poor performance is unusual, we tend to assign an external cause to explain it—there's something happening in the work context. *Consensus* takes into account how likely all those facing a similar situation are to respond in the same way. If all the people using the same technology as Jake perform poorly, we tend to assign his performance problem to an external attribution. If others do not perform poorly, we attribute Jake's poor performance to internal causation. *Consistency* concerns whether an individual responds the same way across time. If Jake performs poorly over a sustained period of time, we tend to give the poor performance an

Bias against Black Leaders Found on the Football Field

Are black leaders at a disadvantage when leadership success is evaluated? The answer is "yes" according to research reported in the *Academy of Management Journal*.

Scholars Andrew M. Carton and Ashleigh Shelby Rosette studied how the performance of football quarterbacks was reported in the news. They found that successful performances by black quarterbacks were attributed in news articles less often to the players' competence, such as "making decisions under pressure," and more often to factors that made up for incompetence, such as having "the speed to get away." The researchers expressed concern that black leaders may suffer from poor career advancement because of biased evaluations.

Sportschrome/NewsCom

internal attribution. If his low performance is an isolated incident, we may well attribute it to an external cause.

▶ Attribution Errors

People often fall prey to perception errors when making attributions about what caused certain events.[18] Look, for example, at the data reported in Figure 3.2. When executives were asked to attribute causes of poor performance among their subordinates, they most often blamed internal deficiencies of the individual—lack of ability and effort, rather than external deficiencies in the situation—lack of support. This demonstrates what is known as **fundamental attribution error**—the tendency to underestimate the influence of situational factors and to overestimate the influence of personal factors when evaluating someone else's behavior. When asked to identify causes of their own poor performance, however, the executives mostly cited lack of support—an external, or situational, deficiency. This demonstrates **self-serving bias**—the tendency to deny personal responsibility for performance problems but to accept personal responsibility for performance success.

The managerial implications of attribution errors trace back to the fact that perceptions influence behavior.[19] For example, a team leader who believes that members are not performing well and perceives the reason to be an internal lack of effort is likely to respond with attempts to "motivate" them to work harder. The possibility of changing external, situational factors that may remove job constraints and provide better organizational support may be largely ignored. This oversight could sacrifice major performance gains for the team.

▶ Attribution and Social Learning

Perception and attribution are important components in **social learning theory**, which describes how learning takes place through the reciprocal interactions among people,

Fundamental attribution error overestimates internal factors and underestimates external factors as influences on someone's behavior.

Self-serving bias underestimates internal factors and overestimates external factors as influences on someone's behavior.

Social learning theory describes how learning occurs through interactions among people, behavior, and environment.

FIGURE 3.2 Attribution errors by executives when explaining poor performance by others and themselves.

Cause of Poor Performance by Others	Most Frequent Attribution	Cause of Poor Performance by Themselves
Many	Lack of *ability*	Few
Many	Lack of *effort*	Few
Few	Lack of *support*	Many

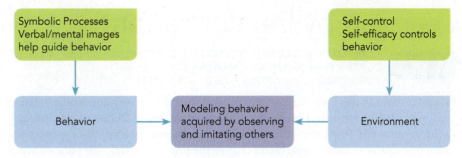

FIGURE 3.3 Simplified model of social learning.

behavior, and environment. According to the work of Albert Bandura, an individual uses modeling or vicarious learning to acquire behavior by observing and imitating others.[20] In a work situation, the model may be a higher manager or co-worker who demonstrates desired behaviors. Mentors or senior workers who befriend younger and more inexperienced protégés can also be important models. Indeed, some have argued that a shortage of mentors for women in senior management has been a major constraint to their progression up the career ladder.[21]

The symbolic processes shown in Figure 3.3 are important in social learning. Words and symbols used by managers and others in the workplace help communicate values, beliefs, and goals and thus serve as guides to an individual's behavior. For example, a "thumbs up" or other signal from the boss lets you know your behavior is appropriate. At the same time, the person's self-control is important in influencing his or her own behavior. And self-efficacy—the person's belief that he or she can perform adequately in a situation—is an important part of such self-control. Closely associated with the concept of self-efficacy are such terms as confidence, competence, and ability.[22]

People with high self-efficacy believe that they have the necessary abilities for a given job, that they are capable of the effort required, and that no outside events will hinder them from attaining their desired performance level.[23] In contrast, people with low self-efficacy believe that no matter how hard they try, they cannot manage their environment well enough to be successful. If you feel high self-efficacy as a student, a low grade on one test is likely to encourage you to study harder, talk to the instructor, or do other things to enable you to do well the next time. In contrast, a person low in self-efficacy would probably drop the course or give up studying. Of course, even people who are high in self-efficacy do not control their environment entirely.

Four Ways to Build or Enhance Self-Efficacy

Scholars generally recognize the following four ways of building or enhancing our self-efficacy:

1. *Enactive mastery*—gaining confidence through positive experience. The more you work at a task, so to speak, the more your experience builds and the more confident you become at doing it.

2. *Vicarious modeling*—gaining confidence by observing others. When someone else is good at a task and we are able to observe how they do it, we gain confidence in being able to do it ourselves.

3. *Verbal persuasion*—gaining confidence from someone telling us or encouraging us that we can perform the task. Hearing others praise our efforts and link those efforts with performance successes is often very motivational.

4. *Emotional arousal*—gaining confidence when we are highly stimulated or energized to perform well in a situation. A good analogy for arousal is how athletes get "psyched up" and highly motivated to perform in key competitions.

Learning by Reinforcement

LEARNING ROADMAP — CLASSICAL CONDITIONING • OPERANT CONDITIONING AND THE LAW OF EFFECT POSITIVE REINFORCEMENT • NEGATIVE REINFORCEMENT PUNISHMENT • EXTINCTION • REINFORCEMENT PROS AND CONS

> TEACHING NOTE: Find a YouTube version of the Big Bang Theory episode in the OB in Popular Culture feature. Show it in class and discuss reinforcement principles. Alternatively, have students suggest sitcom episodes or movie scenes that show something similar.

When it comes to learning, the concept of reinforcement is very important in OB. It has a very specific meaning that has its origin in some classic studies in psychology.[24] **Reinforcement** is the administration of a consequence as a result of a behavior. Managing reinforcement properly can change the direction, level, and persistence of an individual's behavior. This idea is best understood through the concepts of conditioning and reinforcement that you may have already learned in a basic psychology course.

Reinforcement is the delivery of a consequence as a result of behavior.

■ Classical Conditioning

Ivan Pavlov described **classical conditioning** as a form of learning through association that involves the manipulation of stimuli to influence behavior. The Russian psychologist "taught" dogs to salivate at the sound of a bell by ringing the bell when feeding the dogs. The sight of the food naturally caused the dogs to salivate. The dogs "learned" to associate the bell ringing with the presentation of food and to salivate at the ringing of the bell alone.

The key here is to understand stimulus and conditioned stimulus. A stimulus is something that incites action and draws forth a response, such as food for the dogs. The trick is to associate one neutral stimulus—the bell ringing—with another stimulus that already affects behavior—the food. The once-neutral stimulus is called a conditioned stimulus when it affects behavior in the same way as the initial stimulus. Such learning through association is so common in organizations that it is often ignored until it causes considerable confusion.

Take a look at the following figure for an example of how **classical conditioning** might occur in the workplace. Here, the boss's smiling has become a conditioned stimulus because of its association with his criticisms. The employee has learned to feel nervous and grit her teeth whenever the boss smiles.

Classical conditioning involves learning to display a behavior through its association with a stimulus.

Classical Conditioning	Stimulus	Behavior
Learning occurs through conditioned stimuli	A person sees the boss smile and hears boss's criticisms →	feels nervous grits teeth
	The person later sees the boss smile →	feels nervous grits teeth

■ Operant Conditioning and the Law of Effect

The well-known psychologist B. F. Skinner extended the applications of learning by reinforcement to include more than just conditioned stimulus and response behavior.[25] He focused on **operant conditioning** as the process of controlling behavior by manipulating its consequences. You may think of operant conditioning as learning by reinforcement. In a work setting the goal is to use reinforcement principles to systematically reinforce desirable behavior and discourage undesirable behavior.[26]

Operant conditioning is the control of behavior by manipulating its consequences.

Operant conditioning occurs by linking behavior and consequences. The following figure uses the example of an agreement with the boss to work overtime. When the employee actually does work overtime, this is the *behavior*. The *consequence* in the example is receiving the boss's praise. In operant conditioning, this consequence strengthens the behavior and makes it more likely to reoccur when the boss next requests overtime work.

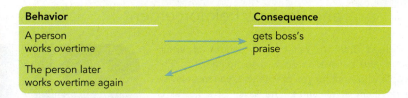

The basis for operant conditioning rests in E. L. Thorndike's **law of effect**.[27] It is simple but powerful: Behavior that results in a pleasant outcome is likely to be repeated, whereas behavior that results in an unpleasant outcome is not likely to be repeated. The implications of this law are rather straightforward. If you want more of a behavior—say the willingness of someone to stay and work overtime when things are rushed—you must make sure the consequences of performing the desired behavior are positive for the individual.

The consequences that reinforce behavior under the Law of Effect are **extrinsic rewards**—positively valued work outcomes given to the individual by another person.[28] Some of these are *contrived rewards* like pay increases and cash bonuses. These rewards have direct costs and budgetary implications. Other outcomes could be *natural rewards* such as verbal praise and recognition. These have no real cost other than the time and effort expended to deliver them.

The use of extrinsic rewards to systematically reinforce desirable work behavior and to discourage unwanted work behavior is known as **organizational behavior modification**, or OB Mod for short. It involves the use of four basic reinforcement strategies: positive reinforcement, negative reinforcement (or avoidance), punishment, and extinction.[29]

Positive Reinforcement

B. F. Skinner and his followers place great emphasis on the power of **positive reinforcement** in operant conditioning. This is the administration of positive consequences that tend to increase the likelihood that desirable behavior will be repeated. An example is when a team leader nods to a team member to express approval after she makes a useful comment during a sales meeting. For example, this increases the likelihood of future useful comments from the team member, something that might not happen if the useful comments went unrecognized when first offered in the meeting.

It's easy to waste rewards by giving them in ways that have little impact on future desired behaviors. In order to have maximum reinforcement value, a reward should be delivered only when a desired behavior—such as giving constructive comments in a meeting—is exhibited. That is, the reward must be contingent on the desired behavior. This principle is known as the **law of contingent reinforcement**. In addition, the reward should be given as soon as possible after the desired behavior. This is known as the **law of immediate reinforcement**.[30] If a team leader waits for the annual performance review to praise a team member for providing constructive comments during meetings, the law of immediate reinforcement would be violated.

Shaping
The power of positive reinforcement can be mobilized through a process known as **shaping**: the creation of a new behavior by the positive reinforcement of successive approximations to it. For example, new machine operators in the Ford Motor casting operation in Ohio must learn a complex series of tasks in pouring molten metal

---

The **law of effect** is that behavior followed by pleasant consequences is likely to be repeated; behavior followed by unpleasant consequences is not.

Extrinsic rewards are positively valued work outcomes that are given to the individual by some other person.

Organizational behavior modification is the use of extrinsic rewards to systematically reinforce desirable work behavior and discourage undesirable behavior.

Positive reinforcement strengthens a behavior by making a desirable consequence contingent on its occurrence.

The **law of contingent reinforcement** states that a reward should only be given when the desired behavior occurs.

The **law of immediate reinforcement** states that a reward should be given as soon as possible after the desired behavior occurs.

Shaping is positive reinforcement of successive approximations to the desired behavior.

FINDING THE LEADER IN YOU

Richard Branson Leads with Personality and Positive Reinforcement

Sir Richard Branson, well-known founder of Virgin Group, is a believer in positive reinforcement. "For the people who work for you or with you, you must lavish praise on them at all times," he says. "If a flower is watered, it flourishes. If not it shrivels up and dies." And besides, he goes on to add, "It's much more fun looking for the best in people."

Virgin Group is a business conglomerate employing many thousands of people around the globe. It even holds a space venture: Virgin Galactic. It's all very creative and ambitious—but that's Branson. "I love to learn things I know little about," he says.

Yet if you bump into Branson on the street you might be surprised. He's casual, he's smiling, and he's fun; he's also considered brilliant when it comes to business and leadership. His goal is to build Virgin into "the most respected brand in the world."

As the man behind the Virgin brand, Branson is described as "flamboyant," something that he doesn't deny and also considers a major business advantage that keeps him and his ventures in the public eye.

About leadership Branson says, "Having a personality of caring about people is important. . . . You can't be a good leader unless you generally like people. That is how you bring out the best in them." He claims his own style was shaped by his family and childhood. At age 10 his mother put him on a 300-mile bike ride to build character and endurance. At 16, he started a student magazine. By the age of 22, he was launching Virgin record stores. And by the time he was 30, Virgin Group was running at high speed.

As for himself, Branson says he'll probably never retire. Now known as Sir Richard after being knighted, he enjoys Virgin today "as a way of life." But he also says that "In the next stage of my life I want to use our business skills to tackle social issues around the world. . . . Malaria in Africa kills four million people a year. AIDS kills even more. . . . I don't want to waste this fabulous situation in which I've found myself."

Rosie Greenway/Getty Images, Inc.

What's the Lesson Here?

Sir Richard obviously has confidence in himself as both a person and a leader. How much of his business and leadership success comes from management of his public impression? Is this something we might all use to advantage? And when he says "you must lavish praise all the time" on the people who work for you, is he giving us an example of the law of effect in action? Finally, Branson seems to have moved beyond the quest for personal business success; he's now talking about real social impact. Is that a natural progression for successful entrepreneurs and business executives?

---

into castings in order to avoid gaps, overfills, or cracks.[31] The molds are filled in a three-step process, with each step progressively more difficult than its predecessor. Astute master craftspersons first show newcomers how to pour as the first step and give praise based on what they did right. As the apprentices gain experience, they are given praise only when all of the elements of the first step are completed successfully. Once the apprentices have mastered the first step, they move to the second. Reinforcement is given only when the entire first step and an aspect of the second step are completed successfully. Over time, apprentices learn all three steps and are given contingent positive

OB IN POPULAR CULTURE

Positive Reinforcement and *Big Bang Theory*

Cliff Lipson/CBS/Getty Images

Learning is an important part of an individual's development. In the workplace, reinforcement can be used to help employees learn proper behavior. Through the principle of operant conditioning, reinforcement uses consequences to help mold the behavior of others.

In one episode of "The Big Bang Theory," Leonard, Penny, and Sheldon are watching anime on television. Penny is bored with a show she does not understand and begins to tell a story about a high school classmate named Anna Mae. Sheldon uses chocolate to get her to stop talking. Later, when Penny's cell phone rings, Sheldon again uses chocolate to get Penny to take the call in the hallway. Leonard discovers the tactic and forbids Sheldon from experimenting with Penny. Sheldon then sprays Leonard with a water bottle (punishment).

The episode is hilarious yet serious. It demonstrates how easily behavior can be influenced through the proper application of operant conditioning techniques. However, it's important to remember that what works at one point in time may not work at another. If Sheldon continues to give Penny chocolates, for example, will she eventually lose her desire for them and the reinforcement will no longer be effective?

Get to Know Yourself Better
Take Assessment 12, The Downside of Punishment, in the *OB Skills Workbook*. Have you ever experienced punishment as a student or an employee? What was your reaction? Have you ever seen a boss punish an employee in front of co-workers or customers? Is this an effective way to change behavior? If you were a teacher, how would you handle a behavior problem with a student—such as unwanted text messaging in class?

---

rewards immediately upon completing a casting that has no cracks or gaps. In this way behavior is shaped gradually rather than changed all at once.

Scheduling Positive Reinforcement
Positive reinforcement can be given on either continuous or intermittent schedules. **Continuous reinforcement** administers a reward each time a desired behavior occurs, whereas **intermittent reinforcement** rewards behavior only periodically. In general, continuous reinforcement draws forth a desired behavior more quickly than does intermittent reinforcement. However, it is easily extinguished when reinforcement is no longer present. Behavior acquired under intermittent reinforcement is more resistant to extinction and lasts longer upon the discontinuance of reinforcement. This is why shaping typically begins with a continuous reinforcement schedule and then gradually shifts to an intermittent one.

Figure 3.4 shows that intermittent reinforcement can be given according to fixed or variable schedules. *Variable schedules* typically result in more consistent patterns of desired behavior than do fixed reinforcement schedules. *Fixed-interval schedules* provide

Continuous reinforcement administers a reward each time a desired behavior occurs.

Intermittent reinforcement rewards behavior only periodically.

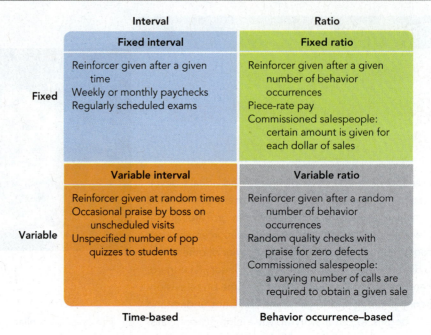

FIGURE 3.4 Alternative ways to schedule positive reinforcement.

rewards at the first appearance of a behavior after a given time has elapsed. *Fixed-ratio schedules* result in a reward each time a certain number of the behaviors have occurred. A *variable-interval schedule* rewards behavior at random times, whereas a *variable-ratio schedule* rewards behavior after a random number of occurrences.

▇ Negative Reinforcement

A second reinforcement strategy in operant conditioning is **negative reinforcement** or avoidance learning. It uses the withdrawal of negative consequences to increase the likelihood of desirable behavior being repeated. An example might be the manager regularly nags a worker about being late for work and then doesn't nag when the worker next shows up on time. The term *negative reinforcement* comes from this withdrawal of the negative consequences. The strategy is also called *avoidance learning* because its intent is for the person to avoid the negative consequence by performing the desired behavior. Think of it this way. Even when the streets are deserted, we still stop at red lights to avoid getting a traffic ticket.

Negative reinforcement strengthens a behavior by making the avoidance of an undesirable consequence contingent on its occurrence.

▇ Punishment

Unlike positive reinforcement and negative reinforcement which are intended to encourage desired behavior, **punishment** intends to discourage undesirable behavior. It is the administration of negative consequences or the withdrawal of positive consequences to reduce the likelihood of a behavior being repeated.

Evidence does show that punishment administered for poor performance can lead to better performance. Yet, when punishment is perceived as arbitrary and capricious, it leads to low satisfaction and low performance.[32] The lesson here and highlighted in the "How to Make Positive Reinforcement and Punishment Work for You" sidebar is that punishment can be handled poorly, or it can be handled well. If it is necessary to use punishment as a reinforcement strategy, be sure to do it well.

Punishment discourages a behavior by making an unpleasant consequence contingent on its occurrence.

It's also worth noting that punishment may be offset by positive reinforcement received from another source. Take the case of someone being positively reinforced by peers at the same time as he or she is receiving punishment from a boss, parent, or teacher. Sometimes the positive value of peer support is so great that the individual chooses to put up with punishment and continues the bad behavior. As many times as a child may be verbally reprimanded by a teacher for playing jokes, for example, the "grins" offered by classmates may keep the jokes flowing in the future.

Extinction

The final reinforcement strategy is **extinction**—the withdrawal of reinforcing consequences in order to weaken undesirable behavior. For example, Enya is often late for work and co-workers provide positive reinforcement by covering for her. The manager instructs Enya's co-workers to stop covering, thus withdrawing the positive consequences of her tardiness. This is a use of extinction to try and get rid of an undesirable behavior. Still, even though a successful extinction strategy decreases the frequency of or weakens behavior, the behavior is not "unlearned." It simply is not exhibited and will reappear if reinforced again.

> ### How to Make Positive Reinforcement and Punishment Work for You
>
> **Positive Reinforcement**
> - Clearly identify desired work behaviors.
> - Maintain a diverse inventory of rewards.
> - Inform everyone what must be done to get rewards.
> - Recognize individual differences when allocating rewards.
> - Follow the laws of immediate and contingent reinforcement.
>
> **Punishment**
> - Tell the person what is being done wrong.
> - Tell the person what is being done right.
> - Make sure the punishment matches the behavior.
> - Administer the punishment in private.
> - Follow the laws of immediate and contingent reinforcement.

Extinction discourages a behavior by making the removal of a desirable consequence contingent on its occurrence.

Reinforcement Pros and Cons

The effective use of the four reinforcement strategies presented in these pages can help in the management of human behavior at work, but their use is not without criticism.[33] A major criticism is that using reinforcement to influence human behavior is demeaning and dehumanizing.[34] Another criticism is that it becomes too easy for managers to abuse the power of their positions when they exert this type of external control over individual behavior.

Advocates of the reinforcement approach attack its critics head on. They agree that behavior modification involves the control of behavior, but they also argue that such control is an irrevocable part of every manager's job. The real question, they say, is how to ensure that the reinforcement strategies are done in positive and constructive ways.[35]

3 Study Guide

Key Questions and Answers

What is perception, and why is it important?
- Individuals use the perception process to select, organize, interpret, and retrieve information from the world around them.
- Perception acts as a filter through which all communication passes as it travels from one person to the next.

- Because people tend to perceive things differently, the same situation may be interpreted and responded to differently by different people.
- Factors influencing perceptions include characteristics of the perceiver, the setting, and the perceived.

What are the common perceptual distortions?
- Stereotypes occur when a person is identified with a category and is assumed to display characteristics otherwise associated with members of that category.
- Halo effects occur when one attribute of a person or situation is used to develop an overall impression of the person or situation.
- Selective perception is the tendency to single out for attention those aspects of a situation or person that reinforce or emerge and are consistent with existing beliefs, values, and needs.
- Projection involves the assignment of personal attributes to other individuals.
- Contrast effects occur when an individual's characteristics are contrasted with those of others recently encountered who rank higher or lower on the same characteristics.

What is the link between perception, attribution, and social learning?
- Attribution theory addresses tendencies to view events or behaviors as primarily the results of external causes or internal causes.
- Three factors that influence the attribution of external or internal causation are distinctiveness, consensus, and consistency.
- Fundamental attribution error occurs when we blame others for performance problems while excluding possible external causes.
- Self-serving bias occurs when, in judging our own performance, we take personal credit for successes and blame failures on external factors.
- Social learning theory links perception and attribution by recognizing how learning is achieved through the reciprocal interactions among people, behavior, and environment.

What is involved in learning by reinforcement?
- Reinforcement theory recognizes that behavior is influenced by environmental consequences.
- The law of effect states that behavior followed by a pleasant consequence is likely to be repeated; behavior followed by an unpleasant consequence is unlikely to be repeated.
- Positive reinforcement is the administration of positive consequences that tend to increase the likelihood of a person's repeating a behavior in similar settings.
- Positive reinforcement should be contingent and immediate, and it can be scheduled continuously or intermittently depending on resources and desired outcomes.
- Negative reinforcement, or avoidance learning, is used to encourage desirable behavior through the withdrawal of negative consequences for previously undesirable behavior.
- Punishment is the administration of negative consequences or the withdrawal of positive consequences to reduce the likelihood of an undesirable behavior being repeated.
- Extinction is the withdrawal of reinforcing consequences to weaken or eliminate an undesirable behavior.

Terms to Know

Attribution (p. 61)
Classical conditioning (p. 64)
Continuous reinforcement (p. 67)
Contrast effect (p. 60)
Extinction (p. 69)
Extrinsic rewards (p. 65)
Fundamental attribution error (p. 62)
Halo effect (p. 58)
Impression management (p. 56)
Intermittent reinforcement (p. 67)
Law of contingent reinforcement (p. 65)
Law of effect (p. 65)
Law of immediate reinforcement (p. 65)
Negative reinforcement (p. 68)
Operant conditioning (p. 64)
Organizational behavior modification (p. 65)
Perception (p. 52)
Positive reinforcement (p. 65)
Projection (p. 59)
Prototype (p. 55)
Punishment (p. 68)
Reinforcement (p. 64)
Schemas (p. 54)
Selective perception (p. 58)
Selective screening (p. 53)
Self-fulfilling prophecy (p. 60)
Self-serving bias (p. 62)
Shaping (p. 65)
Social learning theory (p. 62)
Stereotype (p. 57)

Self-Test 3

Multiple Choice

1. Perception is the process by which people _____ and interpret information.
   (a) generate
   (b) retrieve
   (c) transmit
   (d) verify

2. When an individual attends to only a small portion of the vast information available in the environment, this tendency in the perception process is called _____.
   (a) interpretation
   (b) self scripting
   (c) attribution
   (d) selective screening

3. Self-serving bias is a form of attribution error that involves _____.
   (a) blaming yourself for problems caused by others
   (b) blaming the environment for problems you caused
   (c) poor emotional intelligence
   (d) low self-efficacy

4. In fundamental attribution error, the influence of _____ as causes of a problem are _____.
   (a) situational factors, overestimated
   (b) personal factors, underestimated
   (c) personal factors, overestimated
   (d) situational factors, underestimated

5. If a new team leader changes tasks for persons on his or her work team mainly "because I would prefer to work the new way rather than the old," she may be committing a perceptual error known as _____.
   (a) halo effect
   (b) stereotype
   (c) selective perception
   (d) projection

6. Use of special dress, manners, gestures, and vocabulary words when meeting a prospective employer in a job interview are all examples of how people use _____.

   (a) projection
   (b) selective perception
   (c) impression management
   (d) self-serving bias

7. The perceptual tendency known as a/an _____ is associated with the "Pygmalion effect" and refers to finding or creating in a situation that which was originally expected.

   (a) self-efficacy   (b) projection
   (c) self-fulfilling prophecy   (d) halo effect

8. If a manager allows one characteristic of a person, say a pleasant personality, to bias performance ratings of that individual overall, the manager is falling prey to a perceptual distortion known as _____.

   (a) halo effect   (b) stereotype
   (c) selective perception   (d) projection

9. The underlying premise of reinforcement theory is that _____.

   (a) behavior is a function of environment
   (b) motivation comes from positive expectancy
   (c) higher-order needs stimulate hard work
   (d) rewards considered unfair are de-motivators

10. The law of _____ states that behavior followed by a positive consequence is likely to be repeated, whereas behavior followed by an undesirable consequence is not likely to be repeated.

    (a) reinforcement   (b) contingency
    (c) goal setting   (d) effect

11. _____ is a positive reinforcement strategy that rewards successive approximations to a desirable behavior.

    (a) Extinction   (b) Negative reinforcement
    (c) Shaping   (d) Merit pay

12. B. F. Skinner would argue that "getting a paycheck on Friday" reinforces a person for coming to work on Friday but would not reinforce the person for doing an extraordinary job on Tuesday. This is because the Friday paycheck fails the law of _____ reinforcement.

    (a) negative   (b) continuous
    (c) immediate   (d) intermittent

13. The purpose of negative reinforcement as an operant conditioning technique is to _____.

    (a) punish bad behavior
    (b) discourage bad behavior
    (c) encourage desirable behavior
    (d) offset the effects of shaping

14. Punishment _____.
    (a) may be offset by positive reinforcement from another source
    (b) generally is the most effective kind of reinforcement
    (c) is best given anonymously
    (d) should never be directly linked with its cause.

15. A defining characteristic of social learning theory is that it _____.
    (a) recognizes the existence of vicarious learning
    (b) is not concerned with extrinsic rewards
    (c) relies only on use of negative reinforcement
    (d) avoids any interest in self-efficacy

Short Response

16. Draw and briefly discuss a model showing the important stages of the perception process.
17. Select two perceptual distortions, briefly define them, and show how they can lead to poor decisions by managers.
18. Why is the law of effect useful in management?
19. Explain how the reinforcement learning and social learning approaches are similar and dissimilar to one another.

Applications Essay

20. One of your friends has just been appointed as leader of a work team. This is her first leadership assignment and she has recently heard a little about attribution theory. She has asked you to explain it to her in more detail, focusing on its possible usefulness and risks in managing the team. What will you tell her?

Steps to Further Learning 3
Top Choices from *The OB Skills Workbook*

These learning activities from *The OB Skills Workbook* found at the back of the book are suggested for Chapter 3.

Case for Critical Thinking	Team and Experiential Exercises	Self-Assessment Portfolio
• The Jim Donovan Case	• Decode	• Turbulence Tolerance Test
	• How We View Differences	• Global Readiness Index
	• Alligator River Story	• Intolerance for Ambiguity
	• Expatriate Assignments	
	• Cultural Cues	
	• Downside of Punishment	

Emotions, Attitudes, and Job Satisfaction

The Key Point

Emotions test us in everyday living. When we're feeling good, there's hardly anything better. When we're feeling down, it takes a toll on us and possibly others. OB scholars are very interested in how emotions and attitudes—such as job satisfaction—influence how people feel and behave.

What's Inside?

- **Bringing OB to LIFE**
  PAYING A HIGH PRICE FOR INCIVILITY AT WORK
- **Worth Considering . . . or Best Avoided?**
  GOT A YOGA MAT? MEDITATION CAN BE GOOD FOR YOU AND YOUR JOB
- **Checking Ethics in OB**
  THE DOWNSIDE OF FACEBOOK FOLLIES
- **Finding the Leader in You**
  DON THOMPSON LETS EMOTIONS AND LISTENING TAKE THE LEAD
- **OB in Popular Culture**
  MOODS AND *CRASH*
- **Research Insight**
  JOB SATISFACTION SPILLOVER HAS IMPACT ON FAMILY LIVES

Chapter at a Glance

- What Are Emotions and Moods?
- How Do Emotions and Moods Influence Behavior in Organizations?
- What Are Attitudes, and How Do They Influence Behavior in Organizations?
- What Is Job Satisfaction, and Why Is It Important?

Understanding Emotions and Moods

LEARNING ROADMAP — THE NATURE OF EMOTIONS • EMOTIONAL INTELLIGENCE • TYPES OF EMOTIONS • THE NATURE OF MOODS

> TEACHING NOTE: Put emotional intelligence into action. Ask students to describe situations in which they believe emotional intelligence worked for them. Discuss how the examples show (or not) the EI competencies in Figure 4.1.

How do you feel when . . . You are driving a car and are halted by a police officer? You are in class and receive a poor grade on an exam? A favorite pet passes away? You check e-mail and discover that you are being offered a job interview? A good friend walks right by without speaking? A parent or sibling or child loses his job? You get this SMS from a new acquaintance: "Ur gr8!"?

These are examples of things that draw out feelings of many forms, such as happy or sad, angry or pleased, anxious or elated. Such feelings constitute what scholars call **affect**, the range of emotions and moods that people experience in their life context.[1] Our affects have important implications not only for our lives in general but also our work experiences and careers.[2]

> **Affect** is the range of feelings in the forms of emotions and moods that people experience.

◼ The Nature of Emotions

Anger, excitement, apprehension, attraction, sadness, elation, grief are all **emotions** that appear as strong positive or negative feelings directed toward someone or something.[3] Emotions are usually intense and not long-lasting. They are always associated with a source. That is, someone or something makes us feel the way we do. You might feel the positive emotion of elation when an instructor congratulates you on a fine class presentation; you might feel the negative emotion of anger when an instructor criticizes you in front of the class. In both situations the object of your emotion is the instructor, but the impact of the instructor's behavior on your feelings is quite different in each case. And your response to the aroused emotions is likely to differ as well—perhaps breaking into a wide smile after the compliment, or making a nasty side comment or withdrawing from further participation after the criticism.

> **Emotions** are strong positive or negative feelings directed toward someone or something.

◼ Emotional Intelligence

All of us are familiar with the notions of cognitive ability and intelligence, or IQ, which have been measured for many years. A related concept is **emotional intelligence**, or EI as it is often called. It is defined by scholar Daniel Goleman as an ability to understand emotions in ourselves and others and to use that understanding to manage relationships effectively.[4] EI is demonstrated in the ways in which we deal with affect—for example, by knowing when a negative emotion is about to cause problems and being able to control that emotion so that it doesn't become disruptive.

> **Emotional intelligence** is an ability to understand emotions and manage relationships effectively.

Goleman's point about emotional intelligence is that we perform better when we are good at recognizing and dealing with emotions in ourselves and others. When high in EI, we are more likely to behave in ways that avoid having our emotions "get the better of us." Knowing that an instructor's criticism causes us to feel anger, for example, EI might help us control that anger, maintain a positive face, and perhaps earn the instructor's praise when we make future class contributions. If the unchecked anger caused us to act in a verbally aggressive way—creating a negative impression in the instructor's eyes—or to withdraw from all class participation—causing the instructor to believe we have no interest in the course, our course experience would likely suffer.

If you are good at knowing and managing your emotions and are good at reading others' emotions, you may perform better while interacting with other people. This applies to life in general, as well as to work leadership situations.[5] Figure 4.1 identifies

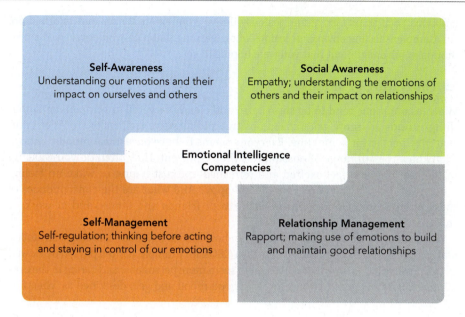

FIGURE 4.1 Four key emotional intelligence competencies for success in leadership and relationships.

four essential *emotional intelligence competencies* that can and should be developed for leadership success and success more generally in all types of interpersonal situations.[6] The competencies are self-awareness, social awareness, self-management, and relationship management.

Self-awareness in emotional intelligence is the ability to understand our emotions and their impact on our work and on others. You can think of this as a continuing appraisal of your emotions that results in a good understanding of them and the capacity to express them naturally. **Social awareness** is the ability to empathize, to understand the emotions of others, and to use this understanding to better relate to them. It involves continuous appraisal and recognition of others' emotions, resulting in better perception and understanding of them.

Self-management in emotional intelligence is the ability to think before acting and to be in control of otherwise disruptive impulses. It is a form of *self-regulation* in which we stay in control of our emotions and avoid letting them take over. **Relationship management** is an ability to establish rapport with others in ways that build good relationships and influence their emotions in positive ways. It shows up as the capacity to make good use of emotions by directing them toward constructive activities and improved relationships.

Self-awareness is the ability to understand our emotions and their impact on us and others.

Social awareness is the ability to empathize and understand the emotions of others.

Self-management is the ability to think before acting and to control disruptive impulses.

Relationship management is the ability to establish rapport with others to build good relationships.

Types of Emotions

Researchers have identified six major types of emotions: anger, fear, joy, love, sadness, and surprise. The key question from an emotional intelligence perspective is this: Do we recognize these emotions in ourselves and others, and can we manage them well? Anger, for example, may involve disgust and envy, both of which can have very negative consequences. Fear may contain alarm and anxiety; joy may contain cheerfulness and contentment; love may contain affection, longing, and lust; sadness may contain disappointment, neglect, and shame.

It is also common to differentiate between **self-conscious emotions** that arise from internal sources and **social emotions** that are stimulated by external sources.[7] Shame, guilt, embarrassment, and pride are examples of internal emotions. Understanding self-conscious emotions helps individuals regulate their relationships with others. Social

Self-conscious emotions arise from internal sources.

Social emotions derive from external sources.

emotions such as pity, envy, and jealousy derive from external cues and information. An example is feeling envious or jealous upon learning that a co-worker received a promotion or job assignment that you were hoping to get.

The Nature of Moods

Whereas emotions tend to be short term and clearly targeted at someone or something, **moods** are more generalized positive and negative feelings or states of mind that may persist for some time. Everyone seems to have occasional moods, and we each know the full range of possibilities they represent. How often do you wake up in the morning and feel excited and refreshed and just happy, or wake up feeling grouchy and depressed and generally unhappy? And what are the consequences of these different moods for your behavior with friends and family, and at work or school?

The field of OB is especially interested in how moods influence someone's likeability and relationships at work. When it comes to CEOs, for example, it often pays to be viewed as in a positive mood, one that makes them seem more personable and caring in the eyes of others. If a CEO goes to a meeting in a good mood and gets described as "cheerful,"

Moods are generalized positive and negative feelings or states of mind.

CHECKING ETHICS IN OB

The Downside of Facebook Follies

Facebook is fun, but if you're having a bad day or are in a bad or snarky mood and post the wrong things on it—inappropriate photo, snide comment, complaint about your boss, and such, you might get hurt. Some Facebook follies have caused users to change their online status to "Just got fired!"

Bed Surfing Banker—After a Swiss bank employee called in sick with the excuse that she "needed to lie in the dark," company officials observed her surfing Facebook. She was fired, and the bank's statement said it "had lost trust in the employee."

Angry Mascot—The Pittsburgh Pirates fired their mascot after he posted criticisms of team management on his Facebook page. A Twitter campaign by supporters helped him get hired back.

Loic Venance/AFP/Getty Images, Inc.

Shortchanged Server—A former server at a pizza parlor in North Carolina used Facebook to call her customers "cheap" for not giving good tips. After finding out about the posting, her bosses fired her for breaking company policy.

Who's Right and Wrong? You may know of similar cases where employees ended up being penalized for things they posted on their Facebook pages. But where do you draw the line? Isn't a person's Facebook page separate from one's work? Shouldn't people be able to speak freely about their jobs, co-workers, and even bosses when outside the workplace? Or is there an ethical boundary that travels from work into one's public communications that we must respect? What are the ethics here—on the employee and the employer sides?

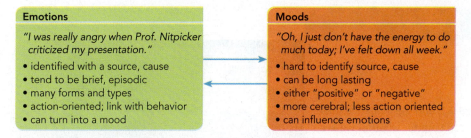

FIGURE 4.2 Emotions and moods are different, but they can also influence one another.

"charming," "humorous," "friendly," and "candid," she or he may be viewed as on the upswing. If the CEO goes into a meeting in a bad mood and is perceived as "prickly," "impatient," "remote," "tough," "acrimonious," or even "ruthless," the perception will more likely be of a CEO on the downslide.[8]

Figure 4.2 offers a brief comparison of emotions and moods. In general, emotions are intense feelings directed at someone or something; they always have rather specific triggers; and they come in many types: anger, fear, happiness, and the like. Moods tend to be more generalized positive or negative feelings. They are less intense than emotions and most often seem to lack a clear source; it's often hard to identify how or why we end up in a particular mood.[9] In addition, moods tend to be more long lasting than emotions. When someone says or does something that causes a quick and intense positive or negative reaction from you, that emotion will probably quickly pass. However, a bad or good mood is likely to linger for hours or even days and influence a wide range of behaviors.

How Emotions and Moods Influence Behavior

 EMOTION AND MOOD CONTAGION • EMOTIONAL LABOR
EMOTIONAL EMPATHY • CULTURAL ASPECTS OF EMOTIONS AND MOODS
EMOTIONS AND MOODS AS AFFECTIVE EVENTS

Although emotions and moods are influenced by different events and situations, each of us may display some relatively predictable tendencies.[10] Some people seem almost always positive and upbeat about things. For these *optimists* we might say the glass is nearly always half full. Others, by contrast, seem to be often negative or downbeat. They tend to be *pessimists* viewing the glass as half empty. Such tendencies toward optimism and pessimism influence the individual's behavior. They can also influence the people with whom he or she interacts.

> TEACHING NOTE: Make moods real. Ask for student examples of (a) where their moods had positive or negative spill-over effects on others, and (b) where the moods of others had positive or negative spill-over effects on them. Ask also: Could there be such a thing as "impression management for moods?"

▶ Emotion and Mood Contagion

Researchers are increasingly interested in **emotion and mood contagion**—the spillover effects of one's emotions and mood onto others.[11] You might think this as a bit like catching a cold from someone. Such contagion can have up and down effects on the emotions and moods of co-workers and teammates as well as family and friends.

Daniel Goleman and his colleagues studying emotional intelligence believe leaders should manage emotion and mood contagion with care. "Moods that start at the top tend to move the fastest," they say, "because everyone watches the boss."[12] When mood

Emotion and mood contagion is the spillover of one's emotions and mood onto others.

OB IN POPULAR CULTURE

Moods and *Crash*

None of us is immune to feelings and the influence they have on our lives, and it doesn't matter whether we are at work, at home, or at play. We are generally expected to be in charge of our feelings, particularly when we interact with others. This requires a good deal of self-control, and that can be difficult when moods take over our feelings. Moods are positive or negative states that persist, perhaps for quite a long time.

In the film *Crash*, Jean Cabot (Sandra Bullock) is talking on the telephone with her best friend, Carol. When she begins to complain about her housekeeper, Carol's response is skeptical and a bit critical. Jean starts to justify her reaction but then admits she is angry at practically everyone with whom she interacts. Her final admission is quite telling—Jean informs Carol that she wakes up angry every day. When Carol ends the conversation prematurely, Jean loses focus and ends up falling down the stairs in her home.

Bull's Eye Entertainment/Lions GateFilms//Photofest

This scene from the movie illustrates how moods can be all consuming—affecting not only our outlook but also our relationships and even behaviors. When emotions and moods get the best of us, we may say or do things that are not in our best interests and that we may regret later. Emotional intelligence involves understanding moods, recognizing how they affect behavior, and learning to control emotions.

Get to Know Yourself Better
Take Assessment 3, The Turbulence Tolerance Test, in the *OB Skills Workbook*. Remember to respond as if you were the manager. What is your tolerance level for turbulence? What role might moods and emotions play in how you react to these and other situations? How can better self-awareness and emotional intelligence help you prepare to handle such things more effectively?

---

contagion is positive, followers report being more attracted to their leaders and rate the leaders more highly.[13] In teams, one study found, team members shared good and bad moods within two hours of being together. Interestingly, the contagion of bad moods traveled person to person in teams faster than good moods did.[14]

■ Emotional Labor

The concept of **emotional labor** relates to the need to show certain emotions in order to perform a job well.[15] Good examples come from service settings such as airline check-in personnel or flight attendants. Persons in such jobs are supposed to appear approachable, receptive, and friendly while taking care of the things you require as a customer. Some airlines, such as Southwest, go even further in asking service employees to be "funny" and "caring" and "cheerful" while doing their jobs.

Emotional labor isn't always easy; it can be hard to be consistently "on" in displaying the desired emotions in one's work. If you're having a bad mood day or have just experienced an emotional run-in with a neighbor, for example, being "happy" and "helpful" with

Emotional labor is a situation in which a person displays organizationally desired emotions in a job.

a demanding customer might seem a little much to ask. Such situations can cause **emotional dissonance** in which the emotions we actually feel are inconsistent with the emotions we try to project.[16] That is, we are expected to act with one emotion while we actually feel quite another.

It often requires a lot of self-regulation to display organizationally desired emotions in one's job. Imagine, for example, how often service workers struggling with personal emotions and moods experience dissonance when having to act positive toward customers.[17] *Deep acting* occurs when someone tries to modify his or her feelings to better fit the situation—such as putting yourself in the position of the air travelers whose luggage went missing and feeling the same sense of loss. *Surface acting* occurs when someone hides true feelings while displaying very different ones—such as smiling at a customer even though the words they used to express a complaint just offended you.

Emotional dissonance is inconsistency between emotions we feel and those we try to project.

■ Emotional Empathy

It was noted previously that empathy is an important component of emotional intelligence. Although empathy itself can be thought of as a generalized sensitivity to other persons and their states of mind, it can be further considered at both the cognitive and emotional levels.[18] Daniel Goleman differentiates between **cognitive empathy**—an ability to know how others are viewing things—and **emotional empathy**—an ability to feel what the other person is experiencing in a particular situation.[19]

Emotional empathy is considered important in how relationships play out, be they relationships between spouses and family members, friends, or co-workers. Simply the perception that a partner is putting forth the effort to seek emotional empathy has been linked to relationship satisfaction among spouses.[20] In the work context, emotional empathy and management affect trust and collaboration in interpersonal relationships.[21] And when it comes to the distribution of empathic emotional skills, Goleman cites research showing that women score better than men.[22]

Cognitive empathy is the ability to know how others are viewing things.

Emotional empathy is the ability to feel what the other person is experiencing in a particular situation.

■ Cultural Aspects of Emotions and Moods

Issues of emotional intelligence, emotion and mood contagion, and emotional labor can be complicated in cross-cultural situations. General interpretations of emotions and moods appear similar across cultures, with the major emotions of happiness, joy, and love all valued positively.[23] However, the frequency and intensity of emotions are known to vary somewhat. In China, for example, research suggests that people report fewer positive and negative emotions as well as less intense emotions than in other cultures.[24] Norms for emotional expression also vary across cultures. In collectivist cultures that emphasize group relationships such as Japan, individual emotional displays are less likely to occur and less likely to be accepted than in individualistic cultures.[25]

Informal cultural standards called **display rules** govern the degree to which it is appropriate to show emotions. The display rules of British culture, for example, tend to encourage downplaying emotions. Those of Mexican culture tend to allow emotions to be more publicly demonstrative. Overall, the lesson is that the way emotions are displayed in one culture may not be the same in another culture. When Walmart first went to Germany, its executives found that an emphasis on friendliness embedded in its U.S. roots didn't work as well in the local culture. The more serious German shoppers did not respond well to Walmart's friendly greeters and helpful personnel.[26]

Display rules govern the degree to which it is appropriate to display emotions.

Believe It or Not, Video Games May Be Good for Our Brains

Believe it or not, researchers are starting to talk about gaming being good for our brains. Consider these data. Starcraft players show faster thought and movements; players of action video games were 25 percent faster than nonplayers in decision making; game players can track six things at once, and non-players track four; surgeons who play games at least three hours a week make fewer surgical errors. Of course there's a lot of downside risk, too. Players of violent video games seem to have more aggressive thoughts and are less caring toward others. Perhaps your gaming, well considered, can be a decision-making asset—boosting creativity and multitasking skills.

Jerzyworks/Masterfile

Emotions and Moods as Affective Events

The affective events theory (AET) shown in Figure 4.3 is one way of summarizing how emotions and moods end up influencing human behavior in organizations.[27] The basic notion of the theory is that day-to-day events involving other people and situations end up having an impact on our emotions and moods. They, in turn, influence our job performance and satisfaction.

The left-hand side of the figure shows how the work environment—including the job and its emotional labor requirements, daily work events, everyday hassles and uplifts—elicit positive and negative emotional reactions. These reactions affect one's job satisfaction and performance.[28] Notice that personal predispositions in the form of personality and moods also affect the connection between work events and emotional reactions. Someone's mood at the time can exaggerate the emotions experienced as a result of an event. If you have just been criticized by your boss, for example, you are likely to feel worse than you would otherwise when a colleague makes a joke about the length of your coffee breaks.

FIGURE 4.3 Figurative summary of affective events theory.

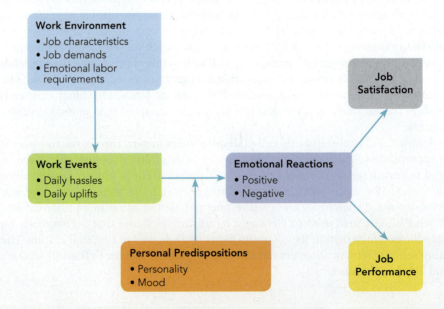

How Attitudes Influence Behavior

LEARNING ROADMAP WHAT IS AN ATTITUDE? • COMPONENTS OF ATTITUDES
ATTITUDES AND COGNITIVE CONSISTENCY
ATTITUDES AND THE WORKPLACE

> TEACHING NOTE: Do a quick exercise. Have students list the job and organizational characteristics that would cause them to show high levels of employee engagement. Jot examples on the board or screen and discuss how their points relate to issues of job satisfaction, job involvement, and organizational commitment.

At one time Challis M. Lowe was one of only two African-American women among the five highest-paid executives in U.S. companies.[29] Her 25-year career included several changes of employers and lots of stressors—working-mother guilt, a failed marriage, gender bias on the job, and an MBA degree earned part time. Looking back she said: "I've never let being scared stop me from doing something. Just because you haven't done it before doesn't mean you shouldn't try." That, simply put, is what we would call a "can-do" attitude.

What Is an Attitude?

An **attitude** is a predisposition to respond in a positive or negative way to someone or something in one's environment. When you say, for example, that you "like" or "dislike" someone or something, you are expressing an attitude. It's important to remember that an attitude, like a value, is a hypothetical construct; one never sees, touches, or actually isolates an attitude. Rather, attitudes are *inferred* from the things people say or through their behavior.

*An **attitude** is a predisposition to respond positively or negatively to someone or something.*

Attitudes are influenced by values and are acquired from the same sources—friends, teachers, parents, role models, and culture. Attitudes, however, focus on specific people or objects. The notion that shareholders should have a voice in setting CEO pay is a value. Your positive or negative feeling about a specific company due to the presence or absence of shareholder inputs on CEO pay is an attitude.

Components of Attitudes

The three components of an attitude are shown in Figure 4.4: cognitive, affective, and behavioral.[30] The *cognitive component* of an attitude reflects underlying beliefs, opinions, knowledge, or information a person possesses. It represents a person's ideas about someone or something and the conclusions drawn about them. The statement "My job lacks responsibility" is a belief as shown in the figure. The statement "and this is important to me" reflects an underlying value. Together they comprise the cognitive component of an attitude toward one's work or workplace.

FIGURE 4.4 A work-related example of the three components of attitudes.

The *affective component* of an attitude is a specific feeling regarding the personal impact of the antecedent conditions evidenced in the cognitive component. In essence this becomes the actual attitude, such as the feeling "I don't like my job." Notice that the affect in this statement displays a negative attitude; "I don't like my job" is a very different condition than "I do like my job."

The *behavioral component* is an intention to behave in a certain way based on the affect in one's attitude. It is a predisposition to act, but may or may not be implemented. The example in the figure shows behavioral intent expressed as "I'm going to quit my job." Yet even with such intent, it remains to be seen whether or not the person really quits.

As just pointed out, the link between attitudes and behavior is tentative. An attitude expresses an intended behavior that may or may not be carried out. In general, the more specific attitudes are, the stronger the relationship with eventual behavior. A person who feels "I don't like my job" may be less likely to actually quit than someone who feels "I can't stand another day with Alex harassing me at work." For an attitude to actually influence behavior, it's also necessary to have the opportunity or freedom to behave in the intended way. There are lots of people who stick with their jobs while still holding negative job attitudes, perhaps you know some. The fact is they may not have any other choice.[31]

Attitudes and Cognitive Consistency

Cognitive dissonance is experienced inconsistency between one's attitudes and/or between attitudes and behavior.

Social psychologist Leon Festinger used the term **cognitive dissonance** to describe a state of inconsistency between an individual's attitudes and/or between attitudes and behavior.[32] This is an important issue. Perhaps you have the attitude that recycling is good for the economy. You also realize you aren't always recycling everything you can. Festinger points out that such cognitive inconsistency between attitude and behavior is uncomfortable. We tend to deal with the discomfort by trying to do things to reduce or eliminate the dissonance: (1) changing the underlying attitude, (2) changing future behavior, or (3) developing new ways of explaining or rationalizing the inconsistency.

The way we respond to cognitive dissonance is influenced by the degree of control we seem to have over the situation and the rewards involved. In the case of recycling dissonance, for example, the lack of convenient recycling containers would make rationalizing easier and changing the positive attitude less likely. A reaffirmation of intention to recycle in the future might also reduce the dissonance.

Attitudes and the Workplace

Even though attitudes do not always predict behavior, the link between attitudes and potential or intended behavior is an important workplace issue. Think about your daily experiences or conversations with other people about their work. It isn't uncommon to hear concerns expressed about a co-worker's "bad attitude" or another's "good attitude." Such feelings get reflected in things like job satisfaction, job involvement, organizational commitment, organizational identification, and employee engagement.

Job satisfaction is the degree to which an individual feels positive or negative about a job.

Job Satisfaction
You often hear the term *morale* used to describe how people feel about their jobs and employers. It relates to the more specific notion of **job satisfaction**, an attitude reflecting a person's positive and negative feelings toward a job, co-workers, and the work environment. Indeed, you should remember that helping others realize job satisfaction is considered one hallmark of effective team leaders and managers—those who create work environments in which people achieve high performance and experience high job satisfaction.

| WORTH CONSIDERING | ...OR BEST AVOIDED? |

Got a Yoga Mat? Meditation Can Be Good for You and Your Job

Gone are the days when the only investment employers make in training is on "hard skills." It's a whole new world out there. Take a peek at the new normal at global giant General Mills.

> 4 pm—large room on premises—50 or more smiling faces topping off loose fitting clothes – lots of meditation cushions. Tibetan prayer bells are rung three times and the session leader says to everyone: "Take a posture that for you in this moment embodies dignity and strength. Allow the body to rest, to step out of busyness, bringing attention to the sensation of each breath." A collective sigh rises from the room and stress moves out as mindfulness settles in.

This is a glimpse into General Mills's Mindful Leadership Program, one supported by senior management to the point where meditation and yoga are becoming part of the corporate culture. And the evaluations back up the investment: over 80 percent of participants say it helps them be productive, improves their decision making, and makes them better listeners.

General Mills isn't alone in turning toward meditation and yoga as pathways to stress release and work engagement. Google, Aetna, and Target are among those committing to similar approaches. William George, former CEO of Medtronic, has written an article in the *Harvard Business Review* extolling the virtues of meditation. He claims that in his busy life meditation helps keep him focused and "if you're fully present on the job, you will be more effective as a leader, you will make better decisions, and you will work better with other people."

Hero Images/Corbis

Do the Analysis

Is corporate attention to meditation and yoga just a passing fad? Is General Mills onto something that other employers, large and small alike, should be copying? Or is this just a luxury item that few employers can afford and few employees really want to bother with? Just how far should organizations go in trying to encourage people to join in these types of activities?

Job Involvement In addition to job satisfaction, OB scholars and researchers are interested in **job involvement**. This is the extent to which an individual feels dedicated to a job. Someone with high job involvement psychologically identifies with her or his job and, for example, shows willingness to work beyond expectations to complete a special project. A high level of job involvement is generally linked with lower tendencies to withdraw from work, either physically by quitting or psychologically by reducing one's work efforts.

Job involvement is the extent to which an individual is dedicated to a job.

Organizational Commitment and Organizational Identification

Another work attitude is **organizational commitment**, or the degree of loyalty an individual feels toward the organization. Individuals with a high organizational commitment want to maintain their membership in the organization. Just as persons with a high sense of job involvement, their inclination is to stay and contribute rather than withdraw either physically or psychologically.

Organizational commitment is the sense of loyalty an individual has to the organization.

Two types of organizational commitment are often discussed. *Rational commitment* reflects feelings that the job serves one's financial, and career development, interests—in other words, "I am committed because I need what the organization offers in return for my labor." *Emotional commitment* reflects feelings that what one does is important, valuable, and of real benefit to others—in other words, "I am committed because of the self-satisfaction I experience from my membership in the organization." Research shows that strong emotional commitments to the organization are more powerful than rational commitments in positively influencing performance.[33]

The concept of emotional commitment is linked in OB research to something called **organizational identification**, or OID. It is the extent to which one feels personally identified with one's membership organization to the point that it becomes part of the self-concept. This notion derives from social identity theory and the premise that the memberships individuals maintain contribute to their feelings of self-esteem.[34]

Organizational identification is the extent to which a person identifies with his or her membership organization.

When organizational identification is positive for one's esteem, the expectation is that the individual will strive to be a good team player, a responsible organizational citizen, and generally a positive work contributor and performer.[35] It's also recognized that positive identification can work to the negative if it causes someone to commit unethical acts perceived as necessary to maintain organizational membership.[36] But, organizational identification can be negative as well as positive. Think of a person saying "I belong to this organization, and I don't feel good about myself because of it." In such cases individuals may struggle to psychologically balance their self-concept with the reality of the organizational membership.[37]

Employee Engagement

A survey of 55,000 American workers by the Gallup, Inc., suggests that profits for employers rise when workers' attitudes reflect high levels of job involvement, organizational commitment, and organizational identification. This combination creates a high sense of **employee engagement**—defined by Gallup as feeling "a profound connection" with the organization and "a passion" for one's job.[38] Scholar Jeffrey Pfeffer describes it as a "conceptual cousin" of job satisfaction.[39]

Employee engagement is a strong sense of connection with the organization and passion for one's job.

A highly engaged individual tends to have an enthusiastic attitude toward work as well as being willing to help others, to always try to do something extra to improve performance, and to speak positively about the organization. Individuals with high employee engagement also report more positive moods and better handling of workplace stress.[40]

When Students Share Assignments, Is It Collaborating . . . Or Cheating?

When a Harvard professor finished reading take-home final examinations from more than a hundred students in a government class, the conclusion was that too many answers said close to the same things. When the faculty member reported the incident to the university administration, Harvard had a "cheating" scandal on its hands. Or did it? From the perspective of some students, "collaborating" is a better choice of words. That's the view of a generation that grew up using the Internet and all sorts of collaborative media, and for whom online courses or class activities are a way of life. So, whose perspective is correct? Are the professors out of date? Do test-taking rules need better clarification? Are students taking advantage of new situations and technologies?

© Lighthaunter.iStockphoto

The drivers of high engagement in the Gallup research held the beliefs that one has the opportunity to do one's best every day, one's opinions count, fellow workers are committed to quality, and a direct connection exists between one's work and the organization's mission.[41]

Given all this, do you have a sense of how engaged most people are in their work? The fact is that recent Gallup research shows that 52 percent of American workers are "not engaged"—think "mentally checked out"—and another 18 percent are "actively disengaged"—think "undermining and disrupting." Even though high employee engagement is good for organizations and probably for the individual, only about 30 percent of American workers on the average report experiencing it.[42]

Job Satisfaction Trends and Issues

LEARNING ROADMAP — COMPONENTS OF JOB SATISFACTION • JOB SATISFACTION TRENDS • HOW JOB SATISFACTION INFLUENCES WORK BEHAVIOR • LINKING JOB SATISFACTION AND JOB PERFORMANCE

There is no doubt that job satisfaction—a person's feelings toward his or her job or job setting at a particular point in time—is one of the most talked about of all job attitudes.[43] And when it comes to job satisfaction, several good questions can be asked. What are the major components of job satisfaction? What are the main job satisfaction findings and trends? What is the relationship between job satisfaction and job performance?

> TEACHING NOTE: Have everyone read the Bringing OB to Life feature "Paying a High Price for Incivility at Work." Ask for real examples of incivilities from students' experiences and have a vote to identify the "worst of the worst." Discuss the potential complexities of trying to penalize incivility in teams and organizations.

■ Components of Job Satisfaction

It is possible to infer the job satisfaction of others by careful observation and interpretation of what they say and do while going about their jobs. Interviews and questionnaires can also be used to more formally assess levels of job satisfaction on a team or in an organization.[44] Two of the more popular job satisfaction questionnaires used over the years are the Minnesota Satisfaction Questionnaire (MSQ) and the Job Descriptive Index (JDI).[45] The MSQ measures satisfaction with working conditions, chances for advancement, freedom to use one's own judgment, praise for doing a good job, and feelings of accomplishment, among others. The JDI measures these five job satisfaction facets:

- ■ *The work itself*—responsibility, interest, and growth
- ■ *Quality of supervision*—technical help and social support
- ■ *Relationships with co-workers*—social harmony and respect
- ■ *Promotion opportunities*—chances for further advancement
- ■ *Pay*—adequacy of pay and perceived equity vis-á-vis others

◀ Common facets of job satisfaction

■ Job Satisfaction Trends

If you watch or read the news, you'll regularly find reports on the job satisfaction of workers. You'll also find lots of job satisfaction studies in the academic literature. The results don't always agree, but they usually fall within a common range. Until recently, we generally concluded that the majority of U.S. workers are at least somewhat satisfied with their jobs. Now, the trend has turned down.[46]

Surveys conducted by The Conference Board showed in 1987 that about 61 percent of American workers said they were satisfied; in 2009 only 45 percent were reporting job satisfaction.[47] The report states, "Fewer Americans are satisfied with all aspects of employment, and no age or income group is immune. In fact, the youngest cohort of employees (those currently under age 25) expresses the highest level of dissatisfaction ever recorded by the survey for that age group." In terms of other patterns, just 51 percent of workers surveyed in 2009 said their jobs were interesting versus 70 percent in 1987. And, only 51 percent said they were satisfied with their bosses versus 60 percent in 1987.

A global survey in 2011 by Accenture contacted 3,400 professionals from 29 countries around the world.[48] Results showed less than one-half were satisfied with their jobs, and that the percentage of job satisfaction was about equal between women (43 percent) and men (42 percent). But about three-quarters of the respondents said they had no plans to leave their current jobs. These data prompt an important question: What are the implications for both employees and employers when people stick with jobs that give them little satisfaction?

FINDING THE LEADER IN YOU: Don Thompson Lets Emotions and Listening Take the Lead

The open floor plan at McDonald's world headquarters in Oak Brook, Illinois, fits nicely with CEO Don Thompson's management style and personality. His former mentor Raymond Mines says, "He has the ability to listen, blend in, analyze and communicate. People feel at ease with him. A lot of corporate executives have little time for those below them. Don makes everyone a part of the process."

When Thompson was previously appointed president and chief operating officer, his boss, McDonald's vice chairman and chief executive officer, Jim Skinner said, "Don has done an outstanding job leading our U.S. business, and I am confident he will bring the same energy and innovative thinking to his new global role."

Although these rosy accolades are well deserved, there was a time when Thompson had to make a bold choice in his career. After grand success when first joining McDonald's, he ran into a period of routine accomplishment. He was getting stuck and thought it might be time to change employers. However, the firm's diversity officer recommended he speak with Raymond Mines, at the time the firm's highest-ranking African-American executive. When Thompson confided that he "wanted to have an impact on decisions," Mines told him to move out of engineering and into the operations side of the business.

Thompson listened to the advice and moved into unfamiliar territory. It got him the attention he needed to advance to ever-higher responsibilities that spanned restaurant operations, franchisee relations, and global strategic management.

Thompson now says, "I want to make sure others achieve their goals, just as I have."

Yves Logghe/AP

What's the Lesson Here?

How attuned are you to your own emotions and to those of others? What do you do when you feel frustrated? Do you ignore it, or do you try to address it by seeking out the advice of others? Are you willing to help others by sharing your own learning with them?

Both men and women in the Accenture survey generally agreed on the least satisfying things about their jobs: being underpaid, lacking career advancement opportunities, and feeling trapped in their jobs. Gender differences were also evident. Women are less likely than men to ask for pay raises (44 percent vs. 48 percent) and for promotions (28 percent vs. 39 percent). Women are more likely to believe their careers are not fast tracked (63 percent vs. 55 percent) and more likely to report that getting ahead in careers is due to hard work and long hours (68 percent vs. 55 percent). In respect to generational differences, Gen Y workers ranked pay higher as a source of motivation (73 percent) than either Gen Xers (67 percent) or Baby Boomers (58 percent).

How Job Satisfaction Influences Work Behavior

Would you agree that people deserve to have satisfying work experiences? You probably do. But, is job satisfaction important in other than a "feel good" sense? How does it impact work behaviors and job performance? In commenting on the Conference Board data just summarized, for example, Lynn Franco, the director of the organization's Consumer Research Center, said, "The downward trend in job satisfaction could spell trouble for the engagement of U.S. employees and ultimately employee productivity."[49]

Physical Withdrawal There is a strong relationship between job satisfaction and physical withdrawal behaviors of absenteeism and turnover. Workers who are more satisfied with their jobs are absent less often than those who are dissatisfied. Satisfied workers are also more likely to remain with their present employers, and dissatisfied workers are more likely to quit or at least be on the lookout for other jobs.[50] Withdrawal through absenteeism and turnover can be very costly in terms of lost experience and the expenses for recruiting and training of replacements.[51]

A survey by Salary.com showed that employers tend not only to overestimate the job satisfaction of their employees; they also underestimate the amount of job seeking they are doing.[52] Whereas employers estimated that 37 percent of employees were on the lookout for new jobs, 65 percent of the employees said they were job seeking by networking, Web surfing, posting résumés, or checking new job possibilities. Millennials in their twenties and early thirties were most likely to engage in these "just-in-case" job searches. The report concluded that "most employers have not placed enough emphasis on important retention strategies."

Psychological Withdrawal There is also a relationship between job satisfaction and psychological withdrawal behaviors. Think of the employee engagement concept introduced previously and discussed in the positive sense. Now we are talking about work disengagement as the negative side of things. It shows up in such forms as daydreaming, cyber-loafing via Internet surfing or personal electronic communications, excessive socializing, and even just giving the appearance of being busy when one is not. These disengagement behaviors are something that Gallup researchers say as many as 71 percent of workers report feeling at times.[53]

Organizational Citizenship Job satisfaction is also linked with **organizational citizenship behaviors**.[54] These are discretionary behaviors, sometimes called OCBs, that represent a willingness to "go beyond the call of duty" or "go the extra mile" in one's work.[55] A person who is a good organizational citizen does extra things that help others—*interpersonal OCBs*—or advance the performance of the organization as a whole—*organizational OCBs*.[56] You might observe interpersonal OCBs in a service worker who is extraordinarily courteous

Organizational citizenship behaviors are the extras people do to go the extra mile in their work.

BRINGING OB TO LIFE

> "Just one habitually offensive employee critically positioned in your organizations can cost you dearly in lost employees, lost customers, and lost productivity."

Paying a High Price for Incivility at Work

There's more downside to incivility at work than hurt feelings and bad relationships. When rudeness rules behavior, look for losses in the bottom line. The costs of incivility are the subject of research by Harvard scholars Christine Porath and Christine Pearson. They admit that most managers say they are against incivility and try to stop it whenever they can. It's also the case that managers don't have a good handle on the real costs incurred when employees are rude and disrespectful toward one another.

When the researchers asked 800 workers from different industries about how they responded to incivility at work, results showed:

- 48 percent decreased work effort
- 47 percent cut back time spent at work
- 80 percent lost work time due to worry
- 63 percent performed less well
- 78 percent were less committed to the organization
- 25 percent took frustration out on customers

There are lots of things managers, leaders, and employers can do to improve workplace civility—from modeling positive behaviors to teaching about civility to penalizing unacceptable behavior. An example is found at Cisco Systems. It has a global workforce civility program designed to decrease incivility and make civility part of

© Ariel Skelley/Corbis

the culture. The program was started after a study by the company concluded that incivility behaviors were costing the firm some $12 million a year.

Porath and Pearson conclude their article with this warning: "Just one habitually offensive employee critically positioned in your organizations can cost you dearly in lost employees, lost customers, and lost productivity." How about it? Is incivility taking a toll on the teams and organizations in your life? Is improved civility a hidden pathway to higher performance?

---

while taking care of an upset customer, or a team member who takes on extra tasks when a co-worker is ill or absent. Examples of organizational OCBs are co-workers who are always willing volunteers for special committee or task force assignments, and those whose voices are always positive when commenting publicly on their employer.

Counterproductive Behavior The flip side of organizational citizenship shows up as **counterproductive work behaviors**.[57] Often associated with a lack of job satisfaction, they purposely disrupt relationships, processes, satisfaction and/or performance in the workplace.[58] Counterproductive workplace behaviors cover a wide range of behaviors from work avoidance, to physical and verbal aggression, to bad-mouthing, to outright work sabotage and even theft. **Workplace bullying** is a special type of counterproductive behavior that manifests itself as one person acting in an abusive, demeaning, intimidating, and/or violent manner toward another on a continuing basis. It is continuing occurrence rather than one-off or occasional behavior that differentiates "bullying" from essentially "bad" behavior. Although bullying has roots in the personality of the perpetrator and power differentials between perpetrator and victim, it can also reflect the bully's personal lack of satisfaction with work.[59]

Counterproductive work behaviors intentionally disrupt relationships or performance at work.

Workplace bullying is one person acting in an abusive, demeaning, intimidating, and/or violent manner toward another on a continuing basis.

Work-Home Spillover OB scholars are very aware that what happens to us at home can affect our attitudes and behaviors at work. They also recognize that job satisfaction can spill over to influence **at-home affect**, basically how we feel at home as represented by emotions and moods. Research finds that people with higher daily job satisfaction show more positive affect after work.[60] In a study that measured spouse or significant-other evaluations, more positive at-home affect scores were reported on days when workers experienced higher job satisfaction.[61] This issue of the job satisfaction and at-home affect link is proving especially significant as workers in today's high-tech and always-connected world struggle with work–life balance.

> **Spotting Counterproductive or Deviant Workplace Behaviors**
>
> Whereas organizational citizenship behaviors help make the organization a better and more pleasant place, counterproductive or deviant behaviors do just the opposite. To varying degrees of severity, they harm the work, the people, and the organizational culture. Here are some things to look for:
>
> - *Personal aggression*—sexual harassment, verbal abuse, physical abuse, intimidation, humiliation
> - *Production deviance*—wasting resources, avoiding work, disrupting work flow, making deliberate work errors
> - *Political deviance*—spreading harmful rumors, gossiping, using bad language, lacking civility in relationships
> - *Property deviance*—destroying or sabotaging facilities and equipment, stealing money and other resources

At-home affect is how we feel at home as reflected by our emotions and moods.

Linking Job Satisfaction and Job Performance

We might say that people make two key decisions about their employment and organizational memberships—the *decision to belong* and the *decision to perform*. But, we also know that not everyone who belongs to an organization—whether it's a classroom or workplace or sports team or voluntary group—performs up to expectations. So, just how does the relationship between job satisfaction and performance enter into this puzzle?[62]

Three different positions have been advanced about causality in the satisfaction–performance relationship. The first is that job satisfaction causes performance; in other words, a happy worker is a productive worker. The second is that performance causes job satisfaction. The third is that job satisfaction and performance influence one another, and they are mutually affected by other factors such as the availability of rewards. Perhaps you can make a case for one or more of these positions based on your work experiences.

Satisfaction Causes Performance If job satisfaction causes high levels of performance, the message is clear. To increase someone's work performance, make them happy. But, research hasn't found a simple and direct link between individual job satisfaction at one point in time and later work performance. A sign once posted in a tavern near one of Ford's Michigan plants helps tell the story: "I spend 40 hours a week here. Am I supposed to work, too?" Even though some evidence exists for the satisfaction-causes-performance relationship among professional or higher-level employees, the best conclusion is that job satisfaction alone is not a consistent predictor of individual work performance.

Performance Causes Satisfaction If high levels of performance cause job satisfaction, the message is quite different. Instead of focusing on job satisfaction as the precursor to performance, try to create high performance as a pathway to job satisfaction. It generally makes sense that people should feel good about their jobs when they

Research Insight

Job Satisfaction Spillover Has Impact on Family Lives

The spillover of job satisfaction onto workers' family lives is the subject of a study published in the *Academy of Management Journal* by Remus Ilies, Kelly Schwind Wilson, and David T. Wagner. Noting that communication technologies and flexibility in work schedules have narrowed the gap between work and home, the researchers asked this question: How does daily job satisfaction spill over to affect a person's feelings and attitudes in the family role?

The research was conducted by survey and telephone interviews with 101 university employees and their spouses or significant others over a 2-week period. High work–family role integration was defined as making "little distinction between their work and family roles," and low work–family role integration meant that work and family were quite segmented from one another. A key hypothesis in the research was that job satisfaction spillover from work to home on any given day would be greater for the high work–family role integration employees.

Results showed that workers displayed higher positive affect at home on days when they also reported higher job satisfaction. As shown in the figure, the expected moderating effect of work–family integration also held. Workers with high work–family role integration showed a stronger relationship between daily job satisfaction and positive affect at home versus those with low work–family role integration. In fact, among workers with low work–family integration, those who tended to segment work and family roles, positive home affect actually declined as job satisfaction increased.

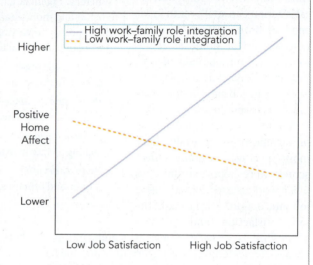

Do the Research How can the findings for the low work–family integration group be explained? What research questions does this study raise in your mind that might become the topics for further study in this area? Would you hypothesize that the job satisfaction–home spillover effects would vary by type of occupation, age of worker, family responsibilities such as number of at-home children, or other factors? Could you suggest a study that might empirically investigate these possibilities?

Source: Remus Ilies, Kelly Schwind Wilson, and David T. Wagner, "The Spillover of Daily Job Satisfaction onto Employees' Family Lives: The Facilitating Role of Work-Family Integration," *Academy of Management Journal*, Vol. 52, No. 1 (2009), pp. 87–102.

---

perform well. And, research does find a link between individual performance measured at one time and later job satisfaction. Figure 4.5 shows this relationship using a model from the work of Edward E. Lawler and Lyman Porter. It suggests that performance leads to rewards that, in turn, lead to satisfaction.[63]

Rewards are intervening variables in the Porter-Lawler model. When valued by the recipient, they link performance with later satisfaction. The model also includes perceived equity of rewards as a moderator variable. This indicates that performance leads to satisfaction only if rewards are perceived as fair and equitable. Although this model is insightful, we also know from experience that some people may perform well but still not like the jobs that they have to do.

Rewards Cause Both Satisfaction and Performance The third alternative in the job satisfaction–performance discussion suggests that the right rewards

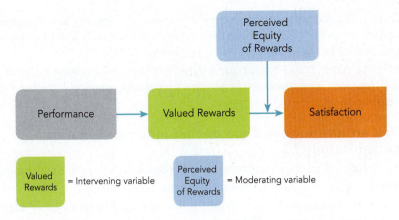

FIGURE 4.5 Simplified Porter-Lawler model of the performance → satisfaction relationship.

allocated in the right ways will positively influence both performance and satisfaction. A key issue here is *performance contingency* in the allocation of rewards. This means that the size of the reward varies in proportion to the level of performance.

Research generally finds that rewards in general influence satisfaction, while performance-contingent rewards influence performance.[64] The prevailing advice is to make good use of performance contingency when giving out rewards. A high performer receiving a large reward is likely to strive for more of the same in the future. And although giving a low performer a small reward may lead to dissatisfaction at first, the expectation is that he or she will make efforts to improve performance in order to obtain higher rewards in the future.[65]

4 Study Guide

Key Questions and Answers

What are emotions and moods?
- Affect is a generic term that covers a broad range of feelings that individuals experience as emotions and moods.
- Emotions are strong feelings directed at someone or something and that influence behavior, often with intensity and for short periods of time.
- Moods are generalized positive or negative states of mind that can be persistent influences on one's behavior.
- Emotional intelligence is the ability to detect and manage emotional cues and information. Four emotional intelligence skills or competencies are self-awareness, self-management, social awareness, and relationship management.

How do emotions and moods influence behavior in organizations?
- Emotional contagion involves the spillover effects onto others of one's emotions and moods; in other words, emotions and moods can spread from person to person.
- Emotional labor is a situation in which a person displays organizationally desired emotions while performing a job.

- Emotional dissonance is a discrepancy between true feelings and organizationally desired emotions; it is linked with deep acting to try to modify true inner feelings and with surface acting to hide one's true inner feelings.
- Affective events theory relates characteristics of the work environment, work events, and personal predispositions to positive or negative emotional reactions and job satisfaction.

What are attitudes, and how do they influence behavior in organizations?

- An attitude is a predisposition to respond in a certain way to people and things.
- Attitudes have affective, cognitive, and behavioral components.
- Although attitudes predispose individuals toward certain behaviors, they do not guarantee that such behaviors will take place.
- Individuals desire consistency between their attitudes and their behaviors, and cognitive dissonance occurs when a person's attitude and behavior are inconsistent.
- Job satisfaction is an attitude toward one's job, co-workers, and workplace.
- Job involvement is a positive attitude that shows up in the extent to which an individual is dedicated to a job.
- Organizational commitment is a positive attitude that shows up in the loyalty of an individual to the organization.

What is job satisfaction, and why is it important?

- Five components of job satisfaction are the work itself, quality of supervision, relationships with co-workers, promotion opportunities, and pay.
- Job satisfaction influences physical withdrawal behaviors of absenteeism; turnover; and psychological withdrawal behaviors such as daydreaming and cyber-loafing.
- Job satisfaction is linked with organizational citizenship behaviors that are both interpersonal—such as doing extra work for a sick teammate—and organizational—such as always speaking positively about the organization.
- A lack of job satisfaction may be reflected in counterproductive work behaviors such as purposely performing poorly, avoiding work, acting violently at work, or even engaging in workplace theft.
- Three possibilities in the job satisfaction and performance relationship are that satisfaction causes performance, performance causes satisfaction, and rewards cause both performance and satisfaction.

Terms to Know

Affect (p. 76)
At-home affect (p. 91)
Attitude (p. 83)
Cognitive dissonance (p. 84)
Cognitive empathy (p. 81)
Counterproductive work behaviors (p. 90)
Display rules (p. 81)
Emotion and mood contagion (p. 79)
Emotional dissonance (p. 81)

Emotional intelligence (p. 76)
Emotional empathy (p. 81)
Emotional labor (p. 80)
Emotions (p. 76)
Employee engagement (p. 86)
Job involvement (p. 85)
Job satisfaction (p. 84)
Moods (p. 78)
Organizational citizenship behaviors (p. 89)
Organizational commitment (p. 85)

Organizational identification (p. 86)
Relationship management (p. 77)
Self-awareness (p. 77)
Self-conscious emotions (p. 77)
Self-management (p. 77)
Social awareness (p. 77)
Social emotions (p. 77)
Workplace bullying (p. 90)

Self-Test 4

Multiple Choice

1. A/an _____ is a rather intense but short-lived feeling about a person or a situation, whereas a/an _____ is a more generalized positive or negative state of mind.
   (a) stressor, satisfier
   (b) affect, attitude
   (c) spillover, moderator
   (d) emotion, mood

2. When someone is feeling anger about something a co-worker did, she is experiencing a/an _____, but when just having a bad day overall she is experiencing a/an _____.
   (a) mood, emotion
   (b) emotion, mood
   (c) affect, effect
   (d) dissonance, consonance

3. Emotions and moods as personal affects are known to influence _____.
   (a) attitudes
   (b) ability
   (c) aptitude
   (d) intelligence

4. If a person shows empathy and understanding of the emotions of others and uses this to better relate to them, she is displaying the emotional intelligence competency of _____.
   (a) self-awareness
   (b) emotional contagion
   (c) relationship management
   (d) social awareness

5. The _____ component of an attitude indicates a person's belief about something, whereas the _____ component indicates positive or negative feeling about it.
   (a) cognitive, affective
   (b) emotional, affective
   (c) cognitive, mood
   (d) behavioral, mood

6. _____ describes the discomfort someone feels when his or her behavior is inconsistent with an expressed attitude.
   (a) Alienation
   (b) Cognitive dissonance
   (c) Job dissatisfaction
   (d) Person–job imbalance

7. Affective events theory shows how one's emotional reactions to work events, environment, and personal predispositions can influence _____.
   (a) job satisfaction and performance
   (b) emotional labor
   (c) emotional intelligence
   (d) emotional contagion

8. The tendency of people at work to display feelings consistent with the moods of their co-workers and bosses is known as _____.
   (a) emotional dissonance
   (b) emotional labor
   (c) mood contagion
   (d) mood stability

9. When an airline flight attendant displays organizationally desired emotions when interacting with passengers, this is an example of _____.
   (a) emotional labor
   (b) emotional contagion
   (c) job commitment
   (d) negative affect

10. A person who always volunteers for extra work or helps someone else with their work is said to be high in _____.
    (a) emotional labor
    (b) affect
    (c) emotional intelligence
    (d) organizational commitment

11. The main difference between job involvement and _____ is that the former shows a positive attitude toward the job and the latter shows a positive attitude toward the organization.
    (a) organizational commitment
    (b) employee engagement
    (c) job satisfaction
    (d) cognitive dissonance

12. Job satisfaction is known to be a good predictor of _____.
    (a) deep acting
    (b) emotional intelligence
    (c) cognitive dissonance
    (d) absenteeism

13. The best conclusion about job satisfaction in today's workforce is probably that _____.
    (a) it isn't an important issue
    (b) the only real concern is pay
    (c) most people are not satisfied with their jobs most of the time
    (d) trends show declining job satisfaction

14. Which statement about the job satisfaction–job performance relationship is most consistent with research?

    (a) A happy worker will be productive.
    (b) A productive worker will be happy.
    (c) A well-rewarded productive worker will be happy.
    (d) A poorly rewarded productive worker will be happy.

15. What does "performance contingent" mean when rewards are discussed as possible influences on satisfaction and performance?

    (a) Rewards are highly valued.
    (b) Rewards are frequent.
    (c) Rewards are in proportion to performance
    (d) Rewards are based only on seniority.

▶ Short Response

16. What are the major differences between emotions and moods as personal affects?

17. Describe and give examples of the three components of an attitude.

18. List five facets of job satisfaction and briefly discuss their importance.

19. Why is cognitive dissonance an important concept for managers to understand?

▶ Applications Essay

20. Your boss has a sign posted in her office: "A satisfied worker is a high-performing worker." In a half-joking and half-serious way she points to it and says, "You are fresh out of college as a business and management major. Am I right or wrong?" What is your response?

Steps to Further Learning 4
Top Choices from *The OB Skills Workbook*

These learning activities from *The OB Skills Workbook* found at the back of the book are suggested for Chapter 4.

Case for Critical Thinking	Team and Experiential Exercises	Self-Assessment Portfolio
• Tough Situation at Magrec, Inc.	• My Best Manager • My Best Job • Graffiti Needs Assessment • Sweet Tooth	• Learning Style Inventory • Student Leadership Practices Inventory • 21st-Century Manager • Global Readiness Index

5

Motivation

The Key Point

Even with great talents some people fail to achieve great things. In some cases it's because they just aren't willing to work hard enough to achieve high performance. When individuals underachieve, so do their organizations. An understanding of motivation theories can help turn such situations around. ■

What's Inside?

- **Bringing OB to LIFE**
  HITTING THE SNOOZE BUTTON TO IMPROVE PERFORMANCE

- **Worth Considering . . . or Best Avoided?**
  HIRING HOURLY WORKERS? PAYING MORE THAN THE MINIMUM MAY BE THE BEST CHOICE

- **Checking Ethics in OB**
  INFORMATION GOLDMINE CREATES A DILEMMA

- **Finding the Leader in You**
  LORRAINE MONROE TURNS LEADERSHIP VISION INTO INSPIRATION

- **OB in Popular Culture**
  EQUITY THEORY AND ALLY BANK

- **Research Insight**
  CONSCIOUS AND SUBCONSCIOUS GOALS HAVE MOTIVATIONAL IMPACT

Chapter at a Glance

- What Is Motivation?
- What Can We Learn from the Needs Theories of Motivation?
- Why Is the Equity Theory of Motivation Important?
- What Are the Insights of the Expectancy Theory of Motivation?
- How Does Goal Setting Influence Motivation?

What Is Motivation?

LEARNING ROADMAP: MOTIVATION DEFINED • MOTIVATION THEORIES

> TEACHING NOTE: Ask students to read the opening parable and then make up ones of their own to illustrate common errors in our approaches to motivation—both attempts to motivate others and at self motivation.

Motivation Defined

Parable: Once upon a time there was a horse standing knee deep in a field of carrots, contentedly munching away. A farmer wanted the horse to pull a wagon to another field, but she couldn't get the horse to come over to the fence and be harnessed. So, she stood by the wagon and held up a bunch of carrots for the horse to see. But, the horse continued to munch away on the carrots in the field.[1]

"What," you might be asking, "do horses and carrots have to do with human behavior in organizations?" The answer is **motivation**. Think of it as the forces within the individual that account for the direction, level, and persistence of effort expended at work. *Direction* refers to an individual's choice among alternative ends or goals. *Level* refers to the amount of effort put forth. *Persistence* refers to the length of time a person sticks with a path of action, even in face of difficulty.

With our co-workers and teammates, and with those we supervise and those who supervise us, we are often like the farmer in our opening parable: We'd really like someone to do something for us or for the team or organization, and we reach for some sort of incentive to try and "motivate" them to do so. All too often these attempts aren't any more successful than that of the farmer in the field.

Motivation refers to forces within an individual that account for the level, direction, and persistence of effort expended at work.

Motivation Theories

Many years of OB scholarship have created a rich foundation of research and thinking about motivation. Even as that research continues to evolve, a number of core "content" and "process" theories help us to think more rigorously and systematically about what turns people on and off in their work.[2] Although no single theory offers an absolutely best explanation, each is valuable in its own way. By combining insights from the available theories with wisdom gained through our experiences, we have a good chance of developing personal models of motivation that work well for us in most situations.

The **content theories** of motivation focus primarily on individual needs—physiological or psychological deficiencies that we feel a compulsion to reduce or eliminate. These theories try to explain the behaviors people display at work as a search for pathways to satisfy important needs or as reactions to blocked needs. Examples to be discussed in this chapter are Maslow's hierarchy of needs theory, Alderfer's ERG theory, McClelland's acquired needs theory, and Herzberg's two-factor theory.

Content or needs theories identify different needs that may motivate individual behavior.

Something to Read—*Drive: The Surprising Truth About What Motivates Us*

Author Daniel Pink believes that real drive—think of it as a willingness to work hard to accomplish a goal—comes from intrinsic motivation. In his book, *Drive*, Pink sets out the notion that we are more motivated to do things that we enjoy than to do things merely to get extrinsic rewards. Although most of us need to work for a living, once a minimum amount of pay and job security is achieved the motivational kick comes mainly from intrinsic motivation. This "motivation from the inside" happens when we are able to do things that are meaningful to us, things we pursue because we want to and not because we're told we have to do them. Employers can tap the potential of intrinsic motivation by giving workers discretion to make decisions about how their jobs get done and free time to pursue their own ideas on how things can be done better.

Larry Busacca/Getty Images

The **process theories** of motivation focus on how cognitive processes—individual thoughts and decision tendencies—influence work behavior. The focus is on understanding how and why certain factors influence people's decisions to work hard or not in certain situations. Three process theories discussed in this chapter are equity theory, expectancy theory, and goal-setting theory.

Process theories examine the thought processes that motivate individual behavior.

Motivation and Human Needs

LEARNING ROADMAP HIERARCHY OF NEEDS THEORY • ERG THEORY
ACQUIRED NEEDS THEORY • TWO FACTOR THEORY
EMOTIONAL DRIVES OR NEEDS MODEL

> TEACHING NOTE: Researchers like to criticize Herzberg's two-factor theory. But does it have face validity? Let the students decide. Lead a discussion on whether or not this theory has anything to offer in terms of work realities.

The premise of the content or needs theories is that motivation results from our attempts to satisfy important needs. They suggest that once an individual's needs are understood, it should be possible to create situations—work, family, sport, or otherwise—that respond positively to them.

◼ Hierarchy of Needs Theory

Perhaps the most well-known of the content approaches to motivation is Abraham Maslow's **hierarchy of needs theory**. As depicted in Figure 5.1, this theory identifies five levels of individual needs. They range from self-actualization and esteem needs at the top, to social, safety, and physiological needs at the bottom.[3] The concept of a needs "hierarchy" assumes that some needs are more important than others and must be satisfied before the other needs can serve as motivators. For example, physiological needs must be satisfied before safety needs are activated; safety needs must be satisfied before social needs are activated; and so on.

Maslow's model is easy to understand and has been quite popular for many years. However, it needs to be considered with caution. Research fails to support the existence of a

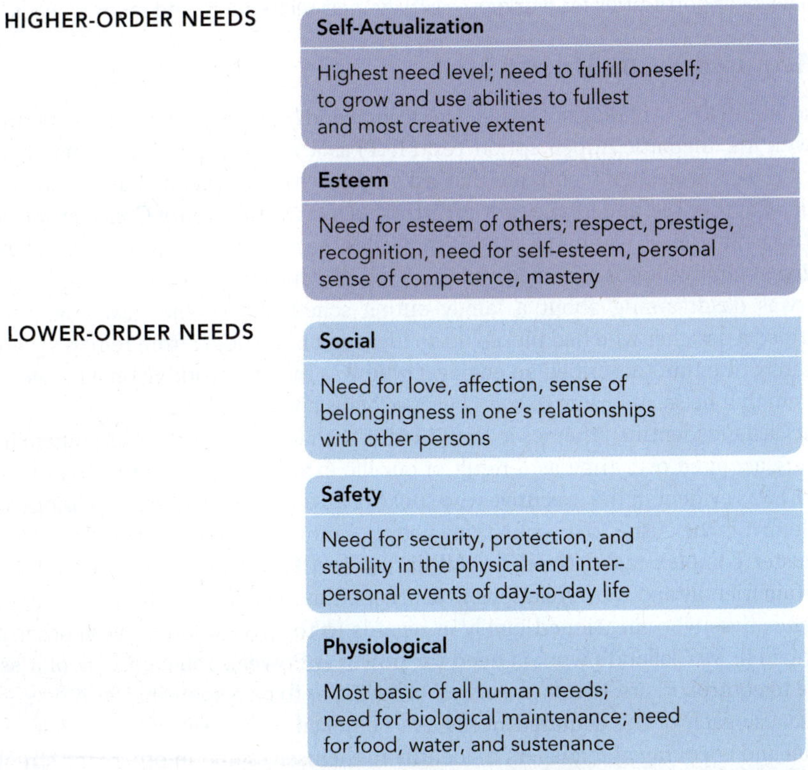

*Maslow's **hierarchy of needs theory** offers a pyramid of physiological, safety, social, esteem, and self-actualization needs.*

HIGHER-ORDER NEEDS

Self-Actualization
Highest need level; need to fulfill oneself; to grow and use abilities to fullest and most creative extent

Esteem
Need for esteem of others; respect, prestige, recognition, need for self-esteem, personal sense of competence, mastery

LOWER-ORDER NEEDS

Social
Need for love, affection, sense of belongingness in one's relationships with other persons

Safety
Need for security, protection, and stability in the physical and interpersonal events of day-to-day life

Physiological
Most basic of all human needs; need for biological maintenance; need for food, water, and sustenance

FIGURE 5.1 Pathways to satisfaction of Maslow's higher-order and lower-order needs.

> **Higher-order needs** in Maslow's hierarchy are esteem and self-actualization.
>
> **Lower-order needs** in Maslow's hierarchy are physiological, safety, and social.

precise five-step hierarchy of needs. If anything, the needs are more likely to operate in a flexible rather than in a strict, step-by-step sequence. The **higher-order needs** of self-actualization and esteem, for example, may grow more important than the **lower-order needs**—physiological, safety, and social, as one moves to higher levels of work responsibility.[4]

Studies report that needs may vary according to a person's career stage, the size of the organization, and even geographic location.[5] There is also no consistent evidence that the satisfaction of a need at one level decreases its importance and increases the importance of the next-higher need.[6] In addition, the presumed hierarchy of needs may vary across cultures. Findings suggest, for instance, that social needs tend to take on higher importance in more collectivist societies, such as Mexico, than in individualistic ones, such as the United States.[7]

ERG Theory

> Alderfer's **ERG theory** identifies existence, relatedness, and growth needs.
>
> **Existence needs** are desires for physiological and material well-being.
>
> **Relatedness needs** are desires for satisfying interpersonal relationships.
>
> **Growth needs** are desires for continued personal growth and development.

Clayton Alderfer's **ERG theory** is also based on needs, but it differs from Maslow's theory in important ways.[8] To begin, the theory collapses Maslow's five needs categories into three. **Existence needs** are desires for physiological and material well-being. **Relatedness needs** are desires for satisfying interpersonal relationships. **Growth needs** are desires for continued personal growth and development. ERG theory also abandons Maslow's strict hierarchy and contends that more than one of these needs need may be active at the same time.

One of the most unique aspects of ERG theory is its allowance for *frustration–regression* in how needs become activated. Alderfer believes an already satisfied lower-level need can become reactivated when a higher-level need cannot be satisfied. When someone is continually frustrated in attempts to satisfy growth needs, for example, relatedness and existence needs can again surface as key motivators.[9] This frustration-regression dynamic might explain why complaints about wages, benefits, and working conditions are often heard in many work settings. In addition to possible absolute deficiencies in these matters, concerns for them may also get exaggerated attention due to a lack of opportunities for workers to satisfy their relatedness and growth needs.

Acquired Needs Theory

In the late 1940s psychologist David I. McClelland and his co-workers began experimenting with the Thematic Apperception Test (TAT) as a way of measuring human needs.[10] The TAT is a projective technique that asks people to view pictures and write stories about what they see, and its use proved historic in motivation theory. Consider, for example, these differences when McClelland showed three executives a photograph of a man looking at family photos arranged on his work desk. One executive wrote of an engineer who was daydreaming about a family outing scheduled for the next day. Another described a designer who had picked up an idea for a new gadget from remarks made by his family. The third described an engineer who was intently working on a bridge stress problem that he seemed sure to solve because of his confident look.[11]

> **Need for achievement (nAch)** is the desire to do better, solve problems, or master complex tasks.
>
> **Need for affiliation (nAff)** is the desire for friendly and warm relations with others.
>
> **Need for power (nPower)** is the desire to control others and influence their behavior.

McClelland identified themes in the TAT stories that he believed correspond to needs that are acquired over time as a result of our life experiences. **Need for achievement (nAch)** was evident in the executive who spoke of an engineer working on a bridge stress problem. It is the desire to do something better or more efficiently, to solve problems, or to master complex tasks. **Need for affiliation (nAff)** is the desire to establish and maintain friendly and warm relations with others. This need may be more represented in the executives who mentioned family in regards to the TAT photos. Yet another need identified in McClelland's work is **need for power (nPower)**. You can think of it as the desire to control others, to influence their behavior, or to be responsible for others.

Because each of the acquired needs can be linked with a set of work preferences, McClelland encouraged managers to identify in themselves and in others the strengths

> **BRINGING OB TO LIFE**
>
> "'Chronic exhaustion'—meaning employees who don't get enough rest—is estimated to cost U.S. companies $60 billion a year in lost productivity."
>
> ## Hitting the Snooze Button to Improve Performance
>
> Not all of us can quietly close the office door and take a midday power nap. Yet, facts are suggesting that napping should become an accepted norm. Perhaps it's time for organizations to have dedicated "Quiet, I'm napping!" zones just as they have wellness and day care centers. After all, feeling sleepy at work can't be good for business.
>
> Did you know that medical researchers find that about one-third of American workers don't get enough sleep to perform at high levels on the job? And "chronic exhaustion"—meaning employees who don't get enough rest—comes at high cost to not just the individual but also the organization. It is estimated to cost U.S. companies $60 billion a year in lost productivity. That's a big number, and many employers are taking notice.
>
> What we are talking about here are people who come to work tired and end up cranky, listless, and underperforming. They don't intend to be that way, but lack of sleep caused by pressures of balancing work demands with complicated personal lives leaves them that way. The problem is especially common among shift workers whose work and personal schedules are out of balance.
>
> Is it time to put the snooze button on the desk and disassociate the office nap from perceived loafing? If we
>
>
> Photo-Dave/iStockphoto
>
> made the quick nap acceptable in the organizational culture, everyone might gain. That's part of the message in a book, *Sleep for Success*, by Psychologist James Maas. He writes, "If we treated machinery like we treat the human body, there would be breakdowns all the time."
>
> Organizational behavior researchers are always interested in studying things like motivation, effort, ability, and performance. It may be time for them to put "well rested" on their lists of research variables.

of nAch, nAff, and nPower. Armed with this understanding, it is possible to create work environments that will satisfy people with different need profiles. Someone with a high need for achievement, for example, will prefer individual responsibilities, challenging goals, and performance feedback. Someone with a high need for affiliation is drawn to interpersonal relationships and opportunities for communication. Someone with a high need for power seeks influence over others and likes attention and recognition.

Since these three needs are acquired, McClelland also believed it may be possible to teach people to develop need profiles required for success in various types of jobs. His research indicated, for example, that a moderate-to-high need for power that is stronger than a need for affiliation is linked with success as a senior executive. The high nPower creates the willingness to exercise influence and control over others; the lower nAff allows the executive to make difficult decisions without undue worry over being disliked.[12]

■ Two-Factor Theory

As scholarship on work motivation continued to develop, Frederick Herzberg took yet another approach that proved insightful to some and controversial to many. He began by asking workers to report the times they felt exceptionally good about their jobs and the times they felt exceptionally bad about them.[13] Results showed that people talked about

FIGURE 5.2 Sources of dissatisfaction and satisfaction in Herzberg's two-factor theory.

Herzberg's two-factor theory identifies job context as the source of job dissatisfaction and job content as the source of job satisfaction.

Hygiene factors in the job context are sources of job dissatisfaction.

very different things when they reported feeling good or bad about their jobs. Herzberg explained these results using what he called the **two-factor theory**, also known as the motivator–hygiene theory. This theory identifies motivator factors as primary causes of job satisfaction and hygiene factors as primary causes of job dissatisfaction.

Hygiene factors, shown to the left in Figure 5.2, are sources of job dissatisfaction, and they are found in the *job context* or work setting. They relate more to the setting in which people work than to the nature of the work itself. The two-factor theory suggests that job dissatisfaction occurs when hygiene is poor. It also suggests that improving the hygiene factors will not increase job satisfaction; it will only decrease job dissatisfaction. Among the hygiene factors, perhaps the most surprising is salary. Herzberg found that paying a low base salary or wage makes people dissatisfied, but paying more does not necessarily satisfy or motivate them.

Motivator factors in the job content are sources of job satisfaction.

Motivator factors, shown on the right in Figure 5.2, are sources of job satisfaction. These factors are found in *job content*—what people actually do in their work. They include such things as a sense of achievement, opportunities for personal growth, recognition, and responsibility. According to two-factor theory, the presence or absence of satisfiers or motivators in people's jobs is the key to satisfaction, motivation, and performance. When motivator factors are minimal, low job satisfaction decreases motivation and performance. When motivator factors are substantial, high job satisfaction raises motivation and performance.

A controversial point in the two-factor theory is Herzberg's belief that job satisfaction and job dissatisfaction are separate dimensions. Taking action to improve a hygiene factor, such as by giving pay raises or creating better physical working conditions, will not make people satisfied and more motivated in their work; it will only prevent them from being less dissatisfied on these matters. To improve job satisfaction, Herzberg believes job content must be enriched by adding more motivator factors. His technique of **job enrichment** is given special attention in the next chapter as a job design alternative. For now, the implication is well summarized in this statement by Herzberg: "If you want people to do a good job, give them a good job to do."[14]

Job enrichment tries to build more motivator factors into job content.

OB scholars have long debated the merits of the two-factor theory.[15] It is criticized as being method bound, or replicable only when Herzberg's original methods are used. This is a serious criticism, since the scientific approach valued in OB requires that theories be verifiable under different research methods.[16] Yet, the distinction between hygiene and motivator factors has been a useful contribution to OB. As will be apparent in the discussions of job designs and alternative work schedules in the next chapter, the notion of two factors—job content and job context—has a practical validity that adds useful discipline to management thinking.

■ Emotional Drives or Needs Model

An example of continuing attention to the link between human needs and motivation is found in the emotional drives or needs model described by Harvard scholars Paul Lawrence and Nitin Nohria. Their model of motivation identifies four emotional drives or needs that people seek to satisfy at work and in daily living. The *drive to acquire* is the need to obtain physical and psychological gratification. The *drive to bond* is the need to connect with other people individually and in groups. The *drive to comprehend* is the need to understand things and gain a sense of mastery. And, the *drive to defend* is the need to be protected from threats and obtain justice.[17]

The emotional drives or needs model ties each of the four drives with specific things that organizations and managers can do to satisfy them as ways to gain a positive impact on motivation. As shown in the figure, the drive to acquire is satisfied through reward systems that clearly distinguish between high and low performers and that distribute rewards contingently based on performance. The drive to bond is satisfied through a collaborative organizational and team culture that encourages friendship and positive social identity. The drive to comprehend is satisfied by job designs that provide a sense of meaning and importance in work being done, as well as the opportunity to learn and improve in one's competencies. The drive to defend is satisfied by information transparency and fair practices that build confidence and trust, especially in relation to rewards and resource allocations.

When the four emotional drives or needs were examined in empirical studies of 685 workers in major businesses, researchers found that their satisfaction explained 60 percent of the motivation workers experienced in their organizations.[18] Perhaps more important, they also reached this conclusion: "Employees in our study attributed as much importance to their boss's meeting their four drives as to the organization's policies."[19]

Motivation and Equity

 EQUITY AND SOCIAL COMPARISONS
EQUITY THEORY PREDICTIONS AND FINDINGS
EQUITY AND ORGANIZATIONAL JUSTICE

What happens when you get a grade back on a written assignment or test? How do you interpret your results, and what happens to your future motivation in the course? Such questions fall in the motivational domain of process theory, specifically **equity theory**. As known in OB through the writing of J. Stacy Adams, equity theory argues that any perceived inequity becomes a motivating state. In other words, people are motivated to behave in ways that restore or maintain a sense of balance—perceived equity—in their minds. These tendencies are found in work situations and the full variety of our personal affairs.[20]

■ Equity and Social Comparisons

The act of social comparison is a basic foundation of equity theory. Think back to the earlier questions. When you receive a grade, do you quickly try to find out what others received as well? When you do, does the interpretation of your grade depend on how well

> TEACHING NOTE: Ask students to make equity theory personal. When have they experienced felt negative inequity and how did they respond? How about positive inequity? What are the lessons for work and careers?

Adams's **equity theory** posits that people will act to eliminate any felt inequity in the rewards received for their work in comparison with others.

FINDING THE LEADER IN YOU

Lorraine Monroe Turns Leadership Vision into Inspiration

Dr. Lorraine Monroe began her career in the New York City schools as a teacher. She went on to serve as assistant principal, principal, and vice-chancellor for curriculum and instruction. Her career really took off when she founded the Frederick Douglass Academy, a public school in Harlem, where she had grown up. The academy's namesake was an escaped slave who later became a prominent abolitionist and civil rights leader. Under her leadership as principal, the school became highly respected for educational excellence.

Through her experiences, Monroe formed a set of beliefs centered on a leader being vision driven and follower centered. She believes leaders must always start at the "heart of the matter" and that "the job of a good leader is to articulate a vision that others are inspired to follow." She believes in making sure all workers know they are valued, that their advice is welcome, and that workers and managers should always try to help and support one another. "I have never undertaken any project," she says, "without first imagining on paper what it would ultimately look like. . . . All the doers who would be responsible for carrying out my imaginings have to be informed and let in on the dream."

About her commitment to public leadership, Monroe states, "We can reform society only if every place we live—every school, workplace, church, and family—becomes a site of reform." She now serves as a leadership consultant and runs the Lorraine Monroe Leadership Institute. Its goal is to train educational leaders in visionary leadership and help them go forth to build high-performing schools that transform children's lives.

Lorraine Monroe's many leadership ideas are summarized in what is called the "Monroe Doctrine." It begins with this advice: "The job of the leader is to uplift her people—not just as members of and contributors to the organization, but as individuals of infinite worth in their own right."

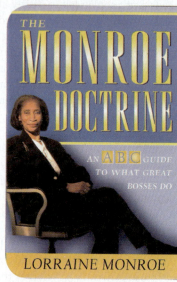

Copyright © 2003 by Lorraine Monroe. Reprinted by permission of PUBLICAFFAIRS, a member of Perseus Books Group. All rights reserved.

What's the Lesson Here?

How good are you at visioning? Are you able to generate visions that are persuasive and engaging to others? Do others feel inspired by your visions? If not, could it be that you need to think about how to make the vision more about them and less about you?

---

your grade compared to those of others? Equity theory predicts that your behavior upon receiving a grade—working less or harder in the course—will be based on whether or not you perceive it as fair and equitable. Furthermore, that determination is made only after you compare your results with those received by others.

Adams argues that the motivational consequences of rewards are a function of how one evaluates rewards received relative to efforts made, and as compared to the rewards received by others relative to their efforts made. A key issue in this comparison is "fairness." **Perceived inequity** occurs when someone believes that he or she has been under-rewarded or over-rewarded for work contributions in comparison to other people. As you might expect, any feelings of unfairness or perceived inequity are uncomfortable. They create a state of mind that equity theory says we are motivated to eliminate.

Perceived inequity is feeling under-rewarded or over-rewarded in comparison with others.

■ Equity Theory Predictions and Findings

The basic equity comparison can be summarized as follows:

$$\frac{\text{Individual Outcomes}}{\text{Individual Efforts}} =? \frac{\text{Others' Outcomes}}{\text{Others' Efforts}}$$

The preceding equity comparison shows that **felt negative inequity** exists when an individual believes that he or she has received relatively less than others in proportion to work efforts. Think of this as *under-reward inequity*. By contrast, **felt positive inequity** exists when an individual believes that he or she has received relatively more than others. Think of this as *over-reward inequity*. When either felt negative or positive inequity exists, the theory suggests that people will be motivated to act in ways that remove the cognitive discomfort and restore a sense of perceived equity to the situation. In both cases the motivational value of rewards is determined by social comparison. It isn't the reward giver's intentions that count in terms of motivational impact. What counts is how the recipient perceives the reward in his or her social context. In figurative terms:

Felt negative inequity occurs when an individual believes he or she has received relatively less than others in proportion to efforts.

Felt positive inequity occurs when an individual believes he or she has received relatively more than others in proportion to efforts.

Research on equity theory indicates that people who feel they are overpaid (perceived positive inequity) are likely to try to increase the quantity or quality of their work, whereas those who feel they are underpaid (perceived negative inequity) are likely to try to decrease the quantity or quality of their work.[21] The research is most conclusive with respect to felt negative inequity. It appears that people are less comfortable when they are under-rewarded than when they are over-rewarded.[22] And it is important to understand how people may react, particularly in felt negative inequity situations. In these cases, an individual might engage one of the following alternatives as a way of restoring a sense of perceived equity to the situation.

- Reduce work inputs (e.g., don't do anything extra in future: "If that is all I'm going to get, this is all I'm going to do.").
- Change the outcomes received (e.g., ask for a bigger raise: "Given my contributions and what I see others getting for their work, I believe I deserve more.").
- Leave the situation (e.g., quit: "That's it, I'm out of here.").
- Change the comparison points (e.g., compare to a different co-worker: "Perhaps I'm looking at this the wrong way. My situation is more similar to Henry's than Alicia's.").
- Psychologically distort things (e.g., rationalize the inequity as temporary: "The boss has been under a lot of pressure and misses a lot of things going on in the office. Things should improve in the future.").
- Try to change the efforts of the comparison person (e.g., get a teammate to accept more work: "Look, Miranda, I know you've had a hard time at home, but it's only fair that you do a bit more to justify the raises that were just given out.").

◀ Ways to reduce perceived negative inequity

▶ Equity and Organizational Justice

Fairness is a basic element of equity theory. It raises an issue in organizational behavior known as **organizational justice**—how fair and equitable people view the practices and outcomes of their workplace.[23]

Procedural justice is the degree to which the process, such as rules and procedures specified by policies, is properly followed in all cases to which it applies. In a sexual harassment case, for example, this may mean that required formal hearings are held for every case submitted for administrative review. **Distributive justice** is the degree to which all people are treated the same, regardless of race, ethnicity, gender, age, or any other demographic characteristic. In a sexual harassment case, this might mean that a complaint filed by a man against a woman would receive the same consideration as one filed by a woman against a man.

Organizational justice concerns how fair and equitable people view workplace practices and outcomes.

Procedural justice is the degree to which rules are always properly followed to implement policies.

Distributive justice is the degree to which all people are treated the same under a policy.

OB IN POPULAR CULTURE

Equity Theory and Ally Bank

Equity theory tells us that employees are motivated to eliminate perceived inequity: the feeling that stems from unfair distributions of rewards. These perceptions develop when employees receive outcomes as a result of their work effort and then make comparisons with similar others, known as referents.

Ally Bank has a number of child-themed commercials to depict unfair practices in the banking industry. The commercials resonate with viewers because we all have a fundamental understanding of what is fair and what is not. In one particular commercial, two little girls are sitting at a table with a grown man. The man turns to the first little girl and asks, "Would you like a pony?" The girl smiles and nods affirmatively, and he hands her a toy pony. Then the man turns and repeats his question to the second little girl. Only this time, when the girl indicates she would like a pony, the man makes a clicking noise and a real pony emerges from behind a playhouse.

The second little girl is overjoyed. But the first—initially quite happy with the toy pony, becomes upset. Her reaction illustrates equity theory and shows that we evaluate rewards within the context in which they are given. Rewards may look good on the surface. However, if someone else gets the same reward while doing less or gets a bigger reward for similar work, it makes your reward pale by comparison. That's not a good feeling.

Emmerich-Webb/Getty Images

Get to Know Yourself Better Take Assessment 17, Annual Pay Raises, in the *OB Skills Workbook*. It asks you to determine pay raises for a group of employees based on information provided about performance, co-worker assessments, and other nonperformance factors. Consider your inclinations when making these decisions. Take a close look at employee Z. Davis. He is a good worker, but others do not see it that way. How would you handle this situation? If Davis is truly deserving and does not get a pay raise, what will he do? If you give Davis a raise, on the other hand, how will co-workers react?

Interactional justice is the degree to which people are treated with dignity and respect in decisions affecting them.

Commutative justice is the degree to which exchanges and transactions are considered fair.

Interactional justice is the degree to which the people affected by a decision are treated with dignity and respect. Interactional justice in a sexual harassment case, for example, may mean that both the accused and accusing parties believe they have received a complete explanation of any decision made. **Commutative justice** is the degree to which exchanges and transactions among parties is considered free and fair. In the sexual harassment example again, commutative justice is present when everyone involved perceives themselves as having full access to all the available facts and information.[24]

CHECKING ETHICS IN OB

Information Goldmine Creates a Dilemma

DAJ/Getty Images

A worker opens the top of the office photocopier and finds a document someone has left behind. It's a list of performance evaluations, pay, and bonuses for eighty co-workers. She reads the document.

Lo and behold, someone considered a "nonstarter" is getting paid more than others regarded as "super workers." New hires are being brought in at substantially higher pay and bonuses than are paid to existing staff. To make matters worse, she's in the middle of the list and not near the top, where she would have expected to be. She makes a lot less money than some others are getting.

Looking at the data, she begins to wonder why she is spending extra hours working on her laptop in the evenings and on weekends at home, trying to do a really great job for the firm. She wonders to herself, "Should I pass this information around anonymously so that everyone knows what's going on? Or should I quit and find another employer who fully values me for my talents and hard work?"

In the end she decides to quit because she couldn't stand the inequity. She also decided not to distribute the information to others in the office because "It would make them depressed, like it made me depressed."

What Would You Do? Would you hit "Print," make about eighty copies, and put them in everyone's mailboxes—or even just leave them stacked in a couple of convenient locations? That would get the information out and right into the gossip chains pretty quickly. Is this ethical? On the other hand, if you don't send out the information, is it ethical to let other workers go about their days with inaccurate assumptions about pay practices at the firm? By quitting and not sharing the information, did this worker commit an ethics miscue?

Motivation and Expectancy

LEARNING ROADMAP EXPECTANCY TERMS AND CONCEPTS • EXPECTANCY THEORY PREDICTIONS
EXPECTANCY THEORY IMPLICATIONS AND RESEARCH

Another of the process theories of motivation achieving substantial scholarly impact is Victor Vroom's **expectancy theory**.[25] It's legacy value rests with the suggestion that motivation is a result of a rational calculation—people will do what they can do when they want to do it. In other words, work motivation is determined by individual beliefs regarding effort–performance relationships and work outcomes.

■ Expectancy Terms and Concepts

In expectancy theory, and as summarized in Figure 5.3, a person is motivated to the degree that he or she believes that (1) effort will yield acceptable performance (expectancy), (2) performance will be rewarded (instrumentality), and (3) the value of the rewards is highly positive (valence). Each of the key terms is defined as follows:

- **Expectancy** is the probability assigned by an individual that work effort will be followed by a given level of achieved task performance. Expectancy would equal zero if the person felt it were impossible to achieve the given performance level; it

> TEACHING NOTE: Have students use expectancy theory to explain their motivation to work hard—or not—in a course of their choosing. After discussing some examples, ask them how instructors might use this theory to boost students' motivation to work hard in their courses.

Vroom's **expectancy theory** argues that work motivation is determined by individual beliefs regarding effort–performance relationships and work outcomes.

Expectancy is the probability that work effort will be followed by performance accomplishment.

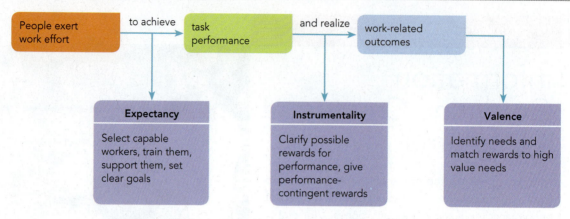

FIGURE 5.3 Key terms and managerial implications of Vroom's expectancy theory.

would equal one if a person were 100 percent certain that the performance could be achieved.

- **Instrumentality** is the probability assigned by the individual that a given level of achieved task performance will lead to various work outcomes. Instrumentality also varies from 0 to 1. Strictly speaking, Vroom's treatment of instrumentality would allow it to vary from −1 to +1. We use the probability definition here and the 0 to +1 range for pedagogical purposes; it is consistent with the instrumentality notion.
- **Valence** is the value attached by the individual to various work outcomes. Valences form a scale from −1 (very undesirable outcome) to +1 (very desirable outcome).

Instrumentality is the probability that performance will lead to various work outcomes.

Valence is the value to the individual of various work outcomes.

Expectancy Theory Predictions

Vroom posits that motivation, expectancy, instrumentality, and valence are related to one another in multiplicative fashion.

$$\text{Motivation} = \text{Expectancy} \times \text{Instrumentality} \times \text{Valence}$$

You can remember this expectancy equation simply as $M \times E \times I \times V$, and the multiplier effect described by the "x" signs is significant. It means that the motivational appeal of a work path is sharply reduced whenever any one or more of these factors—E, I, or V—diminishes and at the extreme approaches the value of zero. In order for a reward to have a high and positive motivational impact as a work outcome, the expectancy, instrumentality, and valence associated with it must each be high and positive.

Suppose, for example, that a team leader is wondering whether or not the prospect of earning a merit pay raise will be motivational to employee team member. Expectancy theory predicts that motivation to work hard to earn the merit pay will be low if *expectancy* is low: a person feels that he or she cannot achieve the necessary performance level. Motivation will also be low if *instrumentality* is low—the person is not confident that a high level of task performance will result in a high merit pay raise. Motivation will also be low if *valence* is low: the person places little value on a merit pay increase. Finally, motivation will be low if any combination of these exists.

Expectancy Theory Implications and Research

The logic of expectancy theory suggests that work situations should be adjusted or created to maximize expectancies, instrumentalities, and valences for people in their jobs.[26] To influence expectancies, the advice is to select people with proper abilities, train them well, support them with needed resources, and identify clear performance goals. To influence instrumentality, the advice is to clarify performance–reward relationships, and then live up to them when rewards are actually given for performance

WORTH CONSIDERING ...OR BEST AVOIDED?

Hiring Hourly Workers? Paying More than the Minimum May Be the Best Choice

More and more Americans are finding themselves in hourly paid jobs, and they don't pay real great on the average. The U.S. minimum wage is $7.25 per hour for non-tipped employees, and in some locations—like Ohio where the wage is $7.70 per hour—set higher minimums. That minimum wage may come with or without benefits such as health insurance and retirement programs.

For some employers, wages are viewed strictly as costs of production, and when it comes to costs, the tendency is to try and minimize or control them. The less you can pay for labor, the argument goes, the better off the "bottom line" is.

Whole Foods takes a different approach. It views business as a balancing act between owner–shareholders, customers, and employees as key stakeholders. Although the interest of each stakeholder is important, balance among all three is the goal. At Whole Foods this concept is described as "conscious capitalism," and one of its characteristics is paying employees more than either the law or market conditions require. At the moment this is about $15.00 per hour, often with benefits. Although this may not sound great, it's twice the minimum wage and about $3.00 plus benefits more than what an average worker earns at Walmart, for example.

David McNew/Getty Images

Do the Analysis

Whole Foods co-CEO Walter Robb believes that paying more than the minimum and competitors builds a stronger and more committed workforce. The payoff from paying more than you have to is having workers who are loyal, stable, and good for customers. How about it? Should more employers be adopting this philosophy on hourly pay? Or, is this just an interesting case that probably wouldn't apply in most other settings?

---

accomplishments. To influence valences, the advice is to identify the needs that are important to each individual and adjust available rewards to match these needs.

A great deal of research on expectancy theory has been conducted.[27] Even though the theory has received substantial support, specific details, such as the operation of the multiplier effect, remain subject to some question. In addition, expectancy theory has proven interesting in terms of helping to explain some apparently counterintuitive findings in cross-cultural management situations. For example, one study found that a pay raise motivated a group of Mexican workers to work fewer hours. Why? They wanted a certain amount of money in order to enjoy things other than work, rather than just getting more money in general. And, a Japanese sales representative's promotion to sales manager at a U.S. company adversely affected his performance. Why? His superiors did not realize that the promotion embarrassed him and distanced him from his colleagues.[28]

Motivation and Goals

LEARNING ROADMAP MOTIVATIONAL PROPERTIES OF GOALS • GOAL-SETTING GUIDELINES GOAL SETTING AND THE MANAGEMENT PROCESS

Every so often a defensive football player makes a dramatic error—scooping up an opponent's fumble and then with obvious effort and delight running the ball into the wrong end zone. These players don't lack motivation, but they fail by not focusing their energies toward the right goal. Less dramatic but similar goal and goal-setting problems occur regularly in work settings. People work hard, but end up disappointing themselves and

> TEACHING NOTE: Pose this situation: a team leader or course instructor sets the goals but allows for participation on how to best achieve them. Ask this discussion question: Is this sufficient to unlock the motivational power of goal-setting theory?

> ### How to Make Goal Setting Work for You
>
> - *Set challenging goals:* When viewed as realistic and attainable, more difficult goals lead to higher performance than do easy goals.
> - *Set specific goals:* They lead to higher performance than do more generally stated ones, such as "Do your best."
> - *Provide feedback on goal accomplishment:* Make sure that people know how well they are doing with respect to goal accomplishment.
> - *Build goal acceptance and commitment:* People work harder for goals they accept and believe in; they resist goals forced on them.
> - *Clarify goal priorities:* Make sure that expectations are clear as to which goals should be accomplished first, and why.
> - *Reward goal accomplishment:* Don't let positive accomplishments pass unnoticed; reward people for doing what they set out to do.

Goal setting is the process of setting performance targets.

their bosses because they pursued the wrong goals. When goals are clear and properly set, motivation is both activated and directed toward the right accomplishments.

Motivational Properties of Goals

Goal setting is the process of developing, negotiating, and formalizing the targets or objectives that a person is responsible for accomplishing.[29] Over a number of years Edwin Locke, Gary Latham, and their associates have developed a comprehensive framework linking goals to performance. They say: "Purposeful activity is the essence of living action. If the purpose is not clear, not challenging, very little gets accomplished."[30]

Goal-Setting Guidelines

Although the theory has its critics, the basic precepts of goal setting remain a respected source of advice for managing human behavior in the work setting.[31] The major implications of research are highlighted in the "How to Make Goal Setting Work for You" sidebar and can be summarized as follows:[32]

Key findings of goal-setting research

- *Difficult goals are more likely to lead to higher performance than are less difficult ones.* If the goals are seen as too difficult or impossible, however, the relationship with performance no longer holds. For example, you will likely perform better as a financial services agent if you have a goal of selling six annuities a week than if you have a goal of selling three. But if your goal is selling fifteen annuities a week, you may consider that impossible to achieve, and your performance may well be lower than what it would be with a more realistic goal.

- *Specific goals are more likely to lead to higher performance than are no goals or vague or very general ones.* All too often people work with very general goals such as the encouragement of "Do your best." Research indicates that more specific goals, such as selling six annuities a week, are much more motivational than a simple "Do your best" goal.

- *Task feedback, or knowledge of results, is likely to motivate people toward higher performance by encouraging the setting of higher performance goals.* Feedback lets people know where they stand and whether they are on course or off course in their efforts. Think, for example, about how eager you may be to find out how well you did on an examination. Think also about the instructor who often waits until the end of the course to find out how well students really liked his or her approach.

- *Goals are most likely to lead to higher performance when people have the abilities and the feelings of self-efficacy required to accomplish them.* The individual must be able to accomplish the goals and feel confident in those abilities. To take the financial services example again, you may be able to do what is required to sell six annuities a week and feel confident that you can. If your goal is to sell fifteen, however, you may believe that your abilities are insufficient to the task, and thus you may lack the confidence to work hard enough to accomplish it.

- *Goals are most likely to motivate people toward higher performance when they are accepted and there is commitment to them.* Participating in the goal-setting process helps build acceptance and commitment; it creates a sense of "ownership" of the goals that is motivating. However, even when goals are assigned, they can still be motivating if they come from a respected authority figure and are perceived as attainable. Assigned goals are most likely to lose motivational value when they are curtly or inadequately explained, and/or seem impossible to achieve.

Goal Setting and the Management Process

The entire management process is affected by goal setting. Goals set during planning provide the focus for organizing and leading, and they also facilitate controlling by identifying desired outcomes that can then be measured. One approach that tries to integrate goals across these management functions is known as **management by objectives (MBO)**. MBO is essentially a process of joint goal setting between managers or team leaders and those who report to them.[33] An example is the team leader who works with team members to set performance goals consistent with higher-level organizational objectives.

Management by objectives or MBO is a process of joint goal setting between a manager or team leader and those who report to them.

Research Insight

Conscious and Subconscious Goals Have Motivational Impact

Writing in the *Journal of Applied Psychology*, Alexander D. Stajkovic, Edwin A. Locke, and Eden S. Blair note that the literature on goal-setting theory and motivation is well established, but they point out that it deals only with conscious motivation. In two empirical studies they attempt to link this set of findings with a body of literature in social psychology concerned with subconscious goal motivation.

One of the key findings of research on goal-setting theory is that difficult goals lead to higher performance than do general "Do your best" or easy goals when performance feedback, goal commitment, and task knowledge are present. A research stream of social psychology literature deals with the subconscious activation of goals by primers found in environments in which goals are regularly pursued. Using this background, the researchers stated that their purpose "was to link subconscious and conscious goals by empirically examining the interaction between the two."

A pilot study and a main study were conducted with samples of undergraduate and graduate students at a university in the Midwest. Study participants were divided into two groups, with one group receiving a "priming" treatment where subjects did setup work involving identification or use of achievement-related words before they completed a performance task. In the second, or "no prime" group, only achievement-neutral words were identified or used in the setup work prior to the performance task.

In both studies the results confirmed predictions from goal-setting theory by showing that "difficult" conscious goals increased performance relative to "easy" and "Do your best" goal-setting conditions. In addition, the

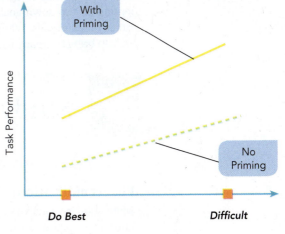

researchers found that subjects in primed subconscious conditions performed better than did those in unprimed subconscious conditions on both "difficult" and "Do your best" goals. In other words, primed subconscious goals had positive interactions with conscious goals for both "difficult" and "Do your best" goals.

The overall conclusions from these studies show that more research is needed on the links between conscious and subconscious goals with task performance, but the initial findings are favorable in suggesting that when both types of goals are used together, their motivational impact is increased.

Source: Alexander D. Stajkovic, Edwin A. Locke, and Eden S. Blair, "A First Examination of the Relationships between Primed Subconscious Goals, Assigned Conscious Goals, and Task Performance," *Journal of Applied Psychology* 91 (2006), pp. 1172–1180.

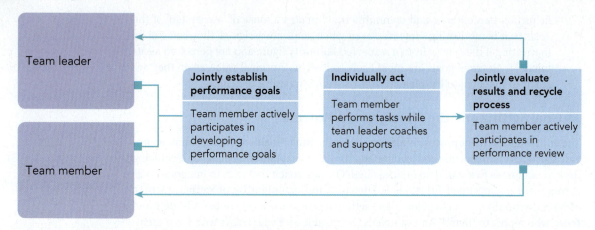

FIGURE 5.4 How a management by objectives process works.

Figure 5.4 shows how the MBO process can take advantage of goal-setting principles. The joint team leader and team member discussions are designed to extend participation from the point of setting initial goals all the way to evaluating results in terms of goal attainment. As team members work to achieve their goals, the team leader's role is to actively coach them.

Researchers identify a number of common difficulties with MBO in practice.[34] These include overemphasizing paperwork to document goals and accomplishments, and focusing on top-down goals, goals that are easily stated and achieved, and individual instead of team goals. When these issues are resolved, however, an MBO-type approach can help bring the many benefits and insights of goal-setting theory to life.

5 Study Guide

Key Questions and Answers

What is motivation?
- Motivation is an internal force that accounts for the level, direction, and persistence of effort expended at work.
- Content theories—including the work of Maslow, Alderfer, McClelland, and Herzberg—focus on identifying human needs that influence behavior in the workplace.
- Process theories, such as equity theory and expectancy theory, examine the thought processes that affect decisions people make about their work efforts.

What can we learn from the needs theories of motivation?
- Maslow's hierarchy of needs theory views human needs as activated in a five-step hierarchy ranging from physiological (lowest) to safety, to social, to esteem, to self-actualization (highest).
- Alderfer's ERG theory collapses the five needs into three: existence, relatedness, and growth; it maintains that more than one need can be activated at a time.
- McClelland's acquired needs theory focuses on the needs for achievement, affiliation, and power, and it views needs as developed over time through experience and training.
- Herzberg's two-factor theory links job satisfaction to motivator factors, such as responsibility and challenge, associated with job content; it links job dissatisfaction to hygiene factors, such as pay and working conditions, associated with job context.

Why is the equity theory of motivation important?
- Equity theory points out that social comparison takes place when people receive rewards.
- Any felt inequity in social comparison will motivate people to behave in ways that restore a sense of perceived equity to the situation.
- When felt inequity is negative—that is, when the individual feels unfairly treated—he or she may decide to work less hard in the future or to quit a job for other, more attractive opportunities.
- Organizational justice is an issue of how fair and equitable people view workplace practices; it is described in respect to distributive, procedural, interactive, and commutative justice.

What are the insights of the expectancy theory of motivation?
- Vroom's expectancy theory describes motivation as a function of an individual's beliefs concerning effort–performance relationships (expectancy), work–outcome relationships (instrumentality), and the desirability of various work outcomes (valence).
- Expectancy theory states that Motivation = Expectancy × Instrumentality × Valence, and argues that managers should make each factor strong and positive in order to ensure high levels of motivation.

How does goal setting influence motivation?
- Goal setting is the process of developing, negotiating, and formalizing performance targets or objectives.
- Goals are the most motivational when they are challenging and specific, allow for feedback on results, and create commitment and acceptance.
- Management by objectives, a process of joint goal setting between a team leader and team member, is a way of applying goal-setting theory in day-to-day management practice.

Terms to Know

Commutative justice (p. 108)
Content theories (p. 100)
Distributive justice (p. 107)
Equity theory (p. 105)
ERG theory (p. 102)
Existence needs (p. 102)
Expectancy (p. 109)
Expectancy theory (p. 109)
Felt negative inequity (p. 107)
Felt positive inequity (p. 107)
Goal setting (p. 112)
Growth needs (p. 102)
Hierarchy of needs theory (p. 101)
Higher-order needs (p. 102)
Hygiene factors (p. 104)
Instrumentality (p. 110)
Interactional justice (p. 108)
Job enrichment (p. 104)
Lower-order needs (p. 102)
Management by objectives (MBO) (p. 113)
Motivation (p. 100)
Motivator factors (p. 104)
Need for achievement (nAch) (p. 102)
Need for affiliation (nAff) (p. 102)
Need for power (nPower) (p. 102)
Organizational justice (p. 107)
Perceived inequity (p. 106)
Procedural justice (p. 107)
Process theories (p. 101)
Relatedness needs (p. 102)
Two-factor theory (p. 104)
Valence (p. 110)

Self-Test 5

■ Multiple Choice

1. Motivation is defined as the level and persistence of _____.
   - (a) effort
   - (b) performance
   - (c) need satisfaction
   - (d) instrumentalities

2. A content theory of motivation is most likely to focus on _____.
   (a) organizational justice
   (b) expectancy
   (c) equity
   (d) individual needs

3. A process theory of motivation is most likely to focus attention on _____.
   (a) frustration–regression
   (b) expectancies regarding work outcomes
   (c) lower-order needs
   (d) hygiene factors

4. When a team member shows strong ego needs in Maslow's hierarchy, the team leader should find ways to link this person's work on the team task with _____.
   (a) compensation tied to group performance
   (b) individual praise and recognition for work well done
   (c) lots of social interaction with other team members
   (d) challenging individual performance goals

5. According to McClelland, a person high in need achievement will be motivated by _____.
   (a) status of being an executive
   (b) control and influence over other people
   (c) teamwork and collective responsibility
   (d) challenging but achievable goals

6. In Alderfer's ERG theory, the _____ needs best correspond with Maslow's higher-order needs of esteem and self-actualization.
   (a) existence
   (b) relatedness
   (c) recognition
   (d) growth

7. Improvements in job satisfaction are most likely under Herzberg's two-factor theory when _____ are improved.
   (a) working conditions
   (b) base salaries
   (c) co-worker relationships
   (d) opportunities for responsibility

8. In Herzberg's two-factor theory _____ factors are found in job context.
   (a) motivator
   (b) satisfier
   (c) hygiene
   (d) enrichment

9. Both Barry and Marissa are highly motivated college students. Knowing this I can expect them to be _____ in my class.
   (a) hard working
   (b) high performing
   (c) highly satisfied
   (d) highly dissatisfied

10. In equity theory, the _____ is a key issue.
    (a) social comparison of rewards
    (b) equality of rewards
    (c) equality of efforts
    (d) absolute value of rewards

11. A manager's failure to enforce a late-to-work policy the same way for all employees is a violation of _____ justice.
    (a) interactional
    (b) moral
    (c) distributive
    (d) procedural

12. When someone has a high and positive expectancy in expectancy theory of motivation, this means that the person _____.
    (a) believes he or she can meet performance expectations
    (b) highly values the rewards being offered
    (c) sees a relationship between high performance and the available rewards
    (d) believes that rewards are equitable

13. In expectancy theory, _____ is the perceived value of a reward.
    (a) expectancy   (b) instrumentality
    (c) motivation   (d) valence

14. Which goals tend to be more motivating?
    (a) challenging goals   (b) easy goals
    (c) general goals   (d) no goals

15. The MBO process emphasizes _____ as a way of building worker commitment to goal accomplishment.
    (a) authority   (b) joint goal setting
    (c) infrequent feedback (d) rewards

Short Response

16. What is the frustration–regression component in Alderfer's ERG theory?
17. What does job enrichment mean in Herzberg's two-factor theory?
18. What is the difference between distributive and procedural justice?
19. What is the multiplier effect in expectancy theory?

Applications Essay

20. While attending a business luncheon, you overhear the following conversation at a nearby table. Person A: "I'll tell you this: If you satisfy your workers' needs, they'll be productive." Person B: "I'm not so sure. If I satisfy their needs, maybe they'll be real good about coming to work but not very good about working really hard while they are there." Which person do you agree with and why?

Steps to Further Learning 5
Top Choices from *The OB Skills Workbook*

These learning activities from *The OB Skills Workbook* found at the back of the book are suggested for Chapter 5.

Case for Critical Thinking	Team and Experiential Exercises	Self-Assessment Portfolio
• "It Isn't Fair . . ."	• What Do You Value in Work? • Teamwork and Motivation • Downsides of Punishment • Annual Pay Raises	• Managerial Assumptions • Two-Factor Profile

It's all about person–job fit

6

Motivation and Performance

The Key Point

Work, family, and leisure are highly intertwined in our busy multitasking world. There's a lot to balance in the quest for life and career satisfaction. Things go a lot better for people and organizations when work activities and outcomes fit well with individual needs and responsibilities. ■

What's Inside?

- **Bringing OB to LIFE**
  PAYING OR NOT PAYING FOR KIDS' GRADES
- **Worth Considering . . . or Best Avoided?**
  WANT VACATION? NO PROBLEM, TAKE AS MUCH AS YOU WANT
- **Checking Ethics in OB**
  SNIFFLING AT WORK TAKES ITS TOLL
- **Finding the Leader in You**
  SARA BLAKELY LEADS SPANX FROM IDEA TO BOTTOM LINE
- **OB in Popular Culture**
  SELF-MANAGEMENT AND *SLUMDOG MILLIONAIRE*
- **Research Insight**
  RACIAL BIAS MAY EXIST IN SUPERVISOR RATINGS OF WORKERS

Chapter at a Glance

- What Is the Link Between Motivation, Performance, and Rewards?
- What Are the Essentials of Performance Management?
- How Do Job Designs Influence Motivation and Performance?
- What Are the Motivational Opportunities of Alternative Work Arrangements?

Motivation, Rewards, and Performance

LEARNING ROADMAP
EMPLOYEE VALUE PROPOSITION AND FIT
INTEGRATED MODEL OF MOTIVATION
INTRINSIC AND EXTRINSIC REWARDS • PAY FOR PERFORMANCE

Motivation is defined as forces within the individual that account for the level and persistence of an effort expended at work. And because motivation is a property of the individual, we basically motivate ourselves. All managers and team leaders or parents and teachers can do is try to create environments that offer other individuals appealing sources of motivation. Whether they respond positively or not is up to them. But, one way to unlock this motivational potential is to provide opportunities to earn rewards that match well with individual needs and goals.

> TEACHING NOTE: Hold a quick debate. Ask one group of students to defend performance-contingent pay plans and ask another group to criticize them. After discussion, have students suggest ideas for innovative pay plans that they believe would be motivational to most people.

Motivation accounts for the level and persistence of a person's effort expended at work.

▎Employee Value Proposition and Fit

Perhaps the best place to start any discussion of the link between motivation, rewards, and performance is the concept of an **employee value proposition**, or EVP. Think of it as an exchange of value, what the organization offers the employee in return for his or her work contributions.[1] The value offered by the individual includes things like effort, loyalty, commitment, creativity, and skills. The value offered by the employer includes things like pay, benefits, meaningful work, flexible schedules, and personal development opportunities. It is common to call this exchange of values the *psychological contract*.

The **employee value proposition**, or EVP, is an exchange of value in what the organization offers the employee in return for his or her work contributions.

When everything comes together in an EVP and the psychological contract is in balance, the foundations for motivation are well set—not perfect yet, but well set. The key starting point is that each party perceives the exchange of values as fair and that it is getting what it needs from the other. Any perceived imbalance is likely to cause problems. From the individual's side, a perceived lack of inducements from the employer may reduce motivation and ultimately poor performance. From the employer's side, a perceived lack of contributions from the individual may cause a loss of confidence in and commitment to the employee, and reduced rewards for work delivered.

The foundation for a healthy and positive employee value proposition is "fit." **Person–job fit** is the extent to which an individual's skills, interests, and personal characteristics match well with the requirements of the job. **Person–organization fit** is the extent to which an individual's values, interests, and behaviors are consistent with the culture of the organization. A poor fit in either case increases the likelihood that imbalance will creep into the EVP. The importance of a good fit to the employee value proposition is highlighted to the extreme at Zappos.com. Believe it or not, if a new employee is unhappy with the firm after going through initial training, Zappos pays them to quit. At last check the "bye-bye bounty" was $4,000, and between 2 and 3 percent of new hires were taking it each year.[2]

Person–job fit is the extent to which an individual's skills, interests, and personal characteristics match well with the requirements of the job.

Person–organization fit is the extent to which an individual's values, interests, and behaviors are consistent with the culture of the organization.

▎Integrated Model of Motivation

Wouldn't it be nice if we all worked with a great employee value proposition and could connect with our jobs and organizations in positive and inspirational ways? In fact, there are lots of great workplaces out there. And, they become great because people and practices throughout the organization turn members on to their jobs rather than off of them. Making this happen requires a good understanding of motivation, a true appreciation for diversity and individual differences, and the ability to make rewards for good work truly meaningful.

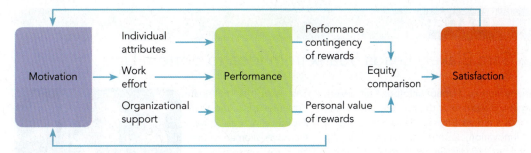

FIGURE 6.1 An integrated model of individual motivation to work.

Figure 6.1 outlines an integrated model of motivation that ties together the basic effort–performance–rewards relationship. The figure shows job performance and satisfaction as separate but interdependent work results. Performance is influenced by *individual attributes* such as ability and experience; *organizational support* comes from things such as goals, resources, and technology; and *effort* is the willingness of people to work hard at what they are doing. The individual experiences satisfaction when the rewards received for work accomplishments are perceived as both performance contingent and equitable.

Double-check Figure 6.1 and locate where various motivation theories come into play. Reinforcement theory highlights performance contingency and immediacy in determining how rewards affect future performance. Equity theory points to the influence on behavior of the perceived fairness of rewards. Content theories offer insight into individual needs that can give motivational value to the possible rewards. And, expectancy theory is central to the effort–performance–rewards linkage.

■ Intrinsic and Extrinsic Rewards

The typical reward systems of organizations offer a mix both intrinsic and extrinsic rewards. **Intrinsic rewards** are positively valued work outcomes that the individual receives directly as a result of task performance. Think of them as the reasons we do things just to enjoy them—play a sport, listen to certain music, and even do certain jobs. A feeling of achievement after completing a particularly challenging task is an example. Yves Chouinard, founder and CEO of Patagonia, Inc., puts it this way: "It's easy to go to work when you get paid to do what you love to do."[3] One of the most important things to remember about intrinsic rewards is that we give them to ourselves. Their positive impact doesn't require anyone else—boss or team leader included—to be involved.

Extrinsic rewards are positively valued work outcomes that are given to an individual or a group by another person. We don't get them by ourselves; someone else has to be the provider. Common extrinsic rewards include symbolic gestures, such as praise for a job well done, or material perks, such as pay raises or bonuses and so on. All such rewards have to be well managed if they are to have positive motivational impact. And the process can be tricky. How often have you heard someone say, "I'll do the minimum to keep the pay and benefits of this job, but that's it," or "For what I get paid with not even a thank-you, this job is hardly worth the effort I put into it."

■ Pay for Performance

Pay is a common and often talked about extrinsic reward. It's also an especially complex one that may not always deliver the hoped-for results. When pay functions well, it can help an organization attract and retain highly capable workers. It can also help satisfy and motivate these workers to work hard to achieve high performance. But when something goes wrong with pay, the results may decrease motivation performance. Pay

Intrinsic rewards are valued outcomes received as internal enjoyment of task performance.

Extrinsic rewards are valued outcomes received from an external source or person.

FINDING THE LEADER IN YOU

Sara Blakely Leads Spanx from Idea to Bottom Line

"Like so many women, I bought clothes that looked amazing in a magazine or the hanger, but in reality...." The words are Sara Blakely's, and her concerns led to product innovation, entrepreneurship, and ultimately a successful big business: Spanx. With $5,000 of her own money and a new idea for "body shaping" underwear, she cut the feet out of a pair of pantyhose and never looked back.

When her first attempts to convince manufacturers to make product samples met with resistance—with one calling it "a stupid idea"—she persisted until one agreed. She aspired to place Spanx in high-end department stores. But again, she didn't give up, finally persuading a Neiman-Marcus buyer to sell them. Blakely kept at it, traveling extensively and energetically, some might say exhaustively. "I'm the face of the brand," she says, "and we didn't have money to advertise. I had to be out. Sitting in the office wasn't helping." She sent Oprah Winfrey samples, and with Oprah's endorsement as "one of her favorite things," sales and the firm took off.

After about a year of fast-paced growth, Blakely turned operations over to a chief executive officer. This left her free to pursue creative efforts, new products, and brand development. She says that she recognized her limits and "was eager to delegate my weaknesses." It worked.

She won the national Entrepreneur of the Year Award and was voted Georgia's Woman of the Year. Her motivation to succeed extends beyond product and business goals alone. She has since started the Sara Blakely Foundation with the express purpose of "supporting and empowering women around the world."

Joe Kohen/Wireimage/GettyImages

What's the Lesson Here?

Blakely's success story obviously began with having a great product idea. It's also tied to who she is as a person. Where would she be today without her special personality? What about her persistence in the face of adversity? What role did goal setting play in her journey to success? Can you combine qualities like these with your ideas to build a motivational capacity for long-term career achievement?

The essence of **performance-contingent pay** is that you earn more when you produce more and earn less when you produce less.

Merit pay links an individual's salary or wage increase directly to measures of performance accomplishment.

dissatisfaction often shows up as bad attitudes, increased absenteeism, intentions to leave and actual turnover, poor organizational citizenship, and even adverse impacts on employees' physical and mental health.

The research of scholar and consultant Edward Lawler generally concludes that pay only serves as a motivator when high levels of job performance are viewed as the paths through which high pay can be achieved.⁴ This is the logic of **performance-contingent pay**, or pay for performance, where you earn more when you produce more and earn less when you produce less. Organizations pursue various options when implementing performance-contingent pay systems.

Merit Pay   It is most common to talk about pay for performance in respect to **merit pay**, a compensation system that directly ties an individual's salary or wage increase to measures of performance accomplishments during a specified time period.

Although the concept of merit pay is compelling, a survey by the Hudson Institute demonstrates that it is more easily said than done. When asked if employees who perform better really get paid more, only 48 percent of managers and 31 percent of nonmanagers responded with agreement. When asked if their last pay raise had been based on performance, 46 percent of managers and just 29 percent of nonmanagers said yes.⁵ In fact, surveys often show that people do not believe their pay is an adequate reward for a job well done.⁶

In order to work well a merit pay plan should create a belief among employees that the way to achieve high pay is to perform at high levels. This means that the merit system

BRINGING OB TO LIFE

> "It gets the kid's attention . . . and motivates them to study more."

Paying or Not Paying for Kids' Grades

Managing is a lot like parenting, and allocating rewards isn't easy in either situation. How often have you heard someone say "We pay kids for 'A's'?" Perhaps you've said this yourself, or plan to someday. But is paying for grades the correct thing to do? Can paying for grades improve control over children's study habits?

Those in favor of paying for grades are likely to say: "It gets the kid's attention . . . and motivates them to study more." "It prepares them for real work where pay and performance go together." Those against paying for grades are likely to say "Once kids get paid for As, they'll be studying for financial gain not real learning." Or "It hurts those who work hard but still can't get the high grades." Or "If there's more than one child in the family, it's unfair when they don't all get rewards."

OB scholars might be viewing this situation as a contrast between extrinsic and intrinsic rewards. They might worry that paying for grades (an extrinsic reward) removes the stimulus value of studying to gain a sense of personal accomplishment (an intrinsic reward). They might also point out that you better make sure the "pay" is really "contingent" on the grades if you expect the outcome to be as planned. With more kids in the family or in the neighborhood, they'd probably be saying "Watch out for equity dynamics."

Tetra Images/Getty Images

Take a position. As a parent will you pay for grades or not, and why? Take the situation a step further. What can parenting teach us about managing people at work?

---

should be based on realistic and accurate measures of work performance. It means that the merit system should clearly discriminate between high and low performers in the amount of pay increases awarded. It also means that any "merit" aspects of a pay increase are clearly and contingently linked with the desired performance.

Bonuses Some employers award cash **bonuses** as extra pay for performance that meets certain benchmarks or is over and above expectations. The bonus becomes "cash in hand" without raising the base salary or wage rate. This practice is especially common in senior executive ranks. However, a current trend is to extend bonus opportunities to workers at all levels. Employees at Applebee's, for example, may earn "Applebucks"—small cash bonuses that are given to reward performance and increase loyalty to the firm.[7]

> **Bonuses** are extra pay awards for special performance accomplishments.

Gain Sharing and Profit Sharing Another way to link pay with performance is **gain sharing**. This gives workers the opportunity to earn more by receiving shares of any productivity gains that they help to create at the team or work unit levels. An alternative is **profit sharing**, which rewards workers for contributions to increased organizational profits.[8] Both gain-sharing and profit-sharing plans are supposed to create a greater sense of personal responsibility for performance improvements and increase motivation to work hard. They are also supposed to encourage cooperation and teamwork to increase productivity.[9]

> **Gain sharing** rewards employees in some proportion to productivity gains.
>
> **Profit sharing** rewards employees in some proportion to changes in organizational profits.

Stock options give the right to purchase shares at a fixed price in the future.

Employee stock ownership plans (ESOPs) give stock to employees or allow them to purchase stock at special prices.

Stock Options and Employee Stock Ownership

Some companies offer employees **stock options** that give the owner the right to buy shares of stock at a future date at a fixed or "strike" price.[10] The expectation is that because employees gain financially as the stock price increases, those with stock options will be highly motivated to do their best so that the firm performs well. In **employee stock ownership plans (ESOPs)**, companies allow stock to be purchased by employees at a price below market value. The incentive value is like the stock options: Employee owners are expected to work hard so that the organization will perform well, the stock price will rise, and, as owners, they will benefit from the gains. Of course, there are risks to both options and stock ownership since a firm's stock prices can fall in the future as well as rise.[11]

Skill-based pay rewards people for acquiring and developing job-relevant skills.

Skill-Based Pay

Skill-based pay rewards people for acquiring and developing job-relevant skills. Pay systems of this sort pay people for the mix and depth of skills they have, not for the particular job assignment they hold. The expected motivational advantages include more willingness to engage in cross-training to learn other jobs in a team or work unit as well as to take on more self-management responsibilities, thus reducing the need to pay for more supervisors.[12]

WORTH CONSIDERING ...OR BEST AVOIDED?

Want Vacation? No Problem, Take as Much as You Want

Sound unreal? It isn't. Netflix operates with what CEO Reed Hastings calls a "freedom and responsibility culture." He describes this culture and the firm's vacation policy this way:

> We want responsible people who are self-motivating and self-disciplined, and we reward them with freedom. The best example is our vacation policy. It's simple and understandable: We don't have one. We focus on what people get done, not on how many days they worked.

Hasting says that the firm used to use a "standard vacation model" but rejected it as "an industrial era habit." His logic is that if people don't keep track of the number of hours they work, why should the employer keep track of how many days they spend on vacation? As for himself, Hastings says, "I make sure to take lots of vacation to set a good example, and I do some of my creative thinking on vacation."

A Society for Human Resource management survey says the practice of unlimited vacation time is found in only about 1 percent of employers, and then mostly in smaller ones. Among those that do ascribe to it, a high-trust culture seems to be a big success factor. Red Frog Events is a small entertainment organizer with 80 full-time employees, and it lets them take vacation when they want. According to the firm's HR director no abuses have been spotted. Another user, Dov Seidman, CEO of the 300-employee firm LRN, says, "People are a lot more honest and responsible when they are trusted."

Gareth Cattermole/Getty Images

Do the Analysis

Based on your experience alone, can this approach to vacation time work for all employers? Is this the next hot thing in employee perks? What are its limits, if any? Do the motivation theories in this chapter support the practice, or warn about its limits? And when it comes to trusting employees, why isn't this standard practice anyhow?

Motivation and Performance Management

LEARNING ROADMAP
PERFORMANCE MANAGEMENT PROCESS
PERFORMANCE MEASUREMENT APPROACHES AND ERRORS
PERFORMANCE ASSESSMENT METHODS

> TEACHING NOTE: Start with the Class Exercise—Upward Appraisal. It's easily modified to fit your course design. Use it to improve things right now for you and the students. Use it also to discuss 360° feedback, and what it requires from both the receiver and giver of performance feedback.

If you want to get hired by Procter & Gamble and get rewarded by advancements to upper management, you had better be good. Not only is the company highly selective in hiring; it also carefully tracks the performance of every manager in every job they are asked to do. The firm always has at least three performance-proven replacements ready to fill any vacancy that occurs. By linking performance to career advancement, motivation to work hard is built into the P&G management model.[13]

The approach followed by P&G can be highly motivating to those who want to work hard, advance in rank, and have successful top executive careers. However, we shouldn't underestimate the challenge of implementing this type of performance-based reward system. Such systems falter and fail to deliver desired results when the process and/or the performance measurement isn't respected by everyone involved.

Performance Management Process

The foundations for performance management are shown in Figure 6.2. And if the process is to work well, everyone involved must have good answers to both the "Why?" and the "What?" questions.

The "Why?" question in performance management is "What is the purpose?" Performance management serves an *evaluation purpose* when it lets people know where their actual performance stands relative to objectives and standards. Such an evaluation feeds into decisions that allocate rewards and otherwise administer the organization's human resource management systems. Performance management serves a *developmental purpose* when it provides insights into individual strengths and weaknesses. This can be used to plan helpful training and career development activities.

The "What?" question in performance management is "What is being measured?" It takes us back to the adage "What gets measured happens"—that is, people tend to do what they know is going to be measured. Given this, we have to make sure we are measuring the right things in the right ways in the performance management process. If a dean wants faculty members to be great teachers, for example, teaching has to be measured in valid ways and rewards tied to the results. Of course, the definition of "great" teaching and the measurement of it are both open to controversy. This is one reason we often talk about the importance of teaching while rewarding faculty members for easier-to-measure research output.

FIGURE 6.2 Four steps in the performance management process.

Performance Measurement Approaches and Errors

Performance measurements should be based on clear criteria, be accurate and defensible in differentiating between high and low performance, and be useful as feedback that can help improve performance in the future. Yet, talking about good measurement is easier than actually doing it. It's good to use **output measures** that assess what is accomplished in respect to concrete work results. But when measuring outputs is hard, **activity measures** that assess work inputs in respect to activities tried and efforts expended are

Output measures of performance assess achievements in terms of actual work results.

Activity measures of performance assess inputs in terms of work efforts.

Tough Talk from Bosses a Real Turnoff for Workers

Lots of times the answer to this question is "It's my boss." A survey by Development Dimensions International reports that difficult conversations with bosses are what employees often dread the most. Those conversations rank ahead of going back to work after vacation. They even rank higher than getting a speeding ticket or paying taxes. The influence of boss behavior—words and actions—on motivation was clear. Some 98 percent of those working for their "best boss ever" said they were highly motivated in their jobs; only 13 percent of those working for their "worst boss ever" said so.

Ice Tea Images/Age Fotostock America, Inc.

often used as replacements. An example might be to use the number of customer visits made per day—an activity measure—to assess a salesperson, instead of or in addition to counting the number of actual sales made—an output measure.

Regardless of the method being employed, any performance assessment system should satisfy two criteria. First, the measures should past the test of **reliability**. This means they provide consistent results each time they are used for the same person and situation. Second, the measures should pass the test of **validity**. This means that they actually measure something of direct relevance to job performance. The following are examples of measurement errors that can reduce the reliability or validity of any performance assessment.[14]

Reliability means a performance measure gives consistent results.

Validity means a performance measure addresses job-relevant dimensions.

▶ Common performance measurement errors

- *Halo error*—results when one person rates another person on several different dimensions and gives a similar rating for each dimension.
- *Leniency error*—just as some professors are known as "easy A's," some managers tend to give relatively high ratings to virtually everyone under their supervision; the opposite is *strictness error*—giving everyone a low rating.
- *Central tendency error*—occurs when managers lump everyone together around the average, or middle, category; this gives the impression that there are no very good or very poor performers on the dimensions being rated.
- *Recency error*—occurs when a rater allows recent events to influence a performance rating over earlier events; an example is being critical of an employee who is usually on time but shows up one hour late for work the day before his or her performance rating.
- *Personal bias error*—displays expectations and prejudices that fail to give the jobholder complete respect, such as showing racial bias in ratings.

▌Performance Assessment Methods

The formal procedure or event that evaluates a person's work performance is often called *performance review*, *performance appraisal*, or *performance assessment*. A variety of methods can be used. But, each has strengths and weaknesses that may make it a better choice in some situations than in others.[15]

Comparative Methods Comparative methods of performance assessment identify one worker's standing relative to others. **Ranking** is the simplest approach and is done by rank ordering each individual from best to worst on overall performance or on specific performance dimensions. Although relatively simple to use, this method can be difficult

Ranking in performance appraisal orders each person from best to worst.

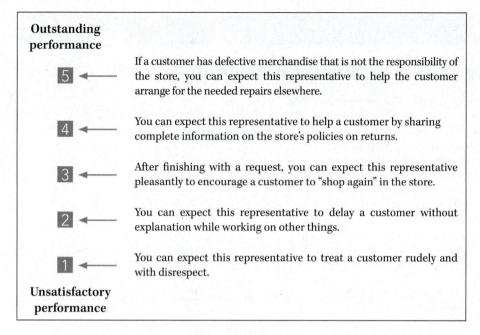

FIGURE 6.3 Sample behaviorally anchored rating scale (BARS) for a customer service representative.

when many people must be considered. An alternative is the **paired comparison** in which each person is directly compared with every other one. A person's final ranking is determined by the number of pairs for which she or he emerges as the "winner." Yet another alternative is **forced distribution**. It forces a set percentage of all persons being assessed into predetermined performance categories, such as outstanding, good, average, and poor. For example, it might be that a team leader must assign 10 percent of members to "outstanding," another 10 percent to "poor," and another 40 percent each to "good" and "average." One goal of this method is to eliminate tendencies to rate everyone about the same.

Paired comparison in performance appraisal compares each person with every other one.

Forced distribution in performance appraisal forces a set percentage of persons into predetermined rating categories.

Rating Scales
Graphic rating scales list a variety of performance dimensions, such as quality or quality of work, or personal traits, such as punctuality or diligence that an individual is expected to exhibit. The scales allow the manager to easily assign the individual scores on each dimension, but the descriptions are often very generalized and lack solid performance links to a given job. The **behaviorally anchored rating scale (BARS)** adds more sophistication by linking ratings to specific and observable job-relevant behaviors. These include descriptions of superior and inferior performance. The sample BARS for a customer service representative in Figure 6.3 shows a focus on discriminating among very specific work behaviors. This specificity makes the BARS more valuable for both evaluation and development purposes.[16]

Graphic rating scales in performance appraisal assign scores to specific performance dimensions.

The **behaviorally anchored rating scale (BARS)** links performance ratings to specific and observable job behaviors.

Critical Incident Diary
Critical incident diaries are written records that give examples of a person's work behavior that leads to either unusual performance success or failure. The incidents are typically recorded in a diary-type log that is kept daily or weekly according to predetermined dimensions. This approach is excellent for employee development and feedback. However, because it consists of qualitative statements rather than quantitative ratings, it is more debatable as an evaluation tool. This is why the critical incident technique is often used in combination with one of the other methods.

Critical incident diaries record actual examples of positive and negative work behaviors and results.

360° Review
Many organizations now make assessments based on a combination of feedback from a person's bosses, peers, and subordinates, internal and external customers,

Research Insight

Racial Bias May Exist in Supervisor Ratings of Workers

That racial bias may exist in supervisor ratings of workers is a conclusion of a research study by Joseph M. Stauffer and M. Ronald Buckley reported in a recent *Journal of Applied Psychology*. The authors point out that it is important to have performance criteria and supervisory ratings that are free of bias. They cite a meta-analysis by Kraiger and Ford (1985) that showed white raters tended to rate white employees more favorably than black employees, whereas black raters rated blacks more favorably than whites. They also cite a later study by Sackett and DuBois (1991) that disputed the finding that raters tended to favor members of their own racial groups.

In their study, Stauffer and Buckley reanalyzed the Sackett and DuBois data to pursue in more depth the possible interactions between rater and ratee race. The data included samples of military and civilian workers, each of whom was rated by black and white supervisors. Their findings are that, in both samples, white supervisors gave significantly higher ratings to white workers than they did to black workers, whereas black supervisors also tended to favor white workers in their ratings.

Stauffer and Buckley advise caution in interpreting these results as meaning that the rating differences are the result of racial prejudice; instead they maintain that the data aren't sufficient to address this issue. The researchers call for additional studies designed to further examine both the existence of bias in supervisory ratings and the causes of such bias. In terms of workplace implications, however, the authors are quite definitive: "If you are a White ratee then it doesn't matter if your supervisor is Black or White. If you are a Black ratee, then it is important whether your supervisor is Black or White."

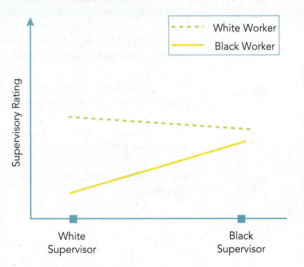

Do the Research These findings raise questions that certainly deserve answering. Can you design a research study that could discover whether or not racial bias affects instructor ratings of students? Also, when you bring this issue up with family and friends, do their experiences seem to support or deny the findings reported here?

Source: Joseph M. Stauffer and M. Ronald Buckley, "The Existence and Nature of Racial Bias in Supervisory Ratings," *Journal of Applied Psychology* 90 (2005), pp. 586–591. Also cited: K. Kraiger and J. K. Ford, "A Meta-analysis of Ratee Race Effects in Performance Ratings," *Journal of Applied Psychology* 70 (1985), pp. 56–65; and P. R. Sackett and C. L. Z. DuBois, "Rater-Ratee Race Effects on Performance Evaluations: Challenging Meta-Analytic Conclusions," *Journal of Applied Psychology* 76 (1991), pp. 873–877.

A **360° review** or assessment gathers feedback from a jobholder's bosses, peers, and subordinates, internal and external customers, and self-ratings. Known as the **360° review**, or *360° assessment*, it is quite common in today's team-oriented organizations. A typical approach asks the jobholder to complete a self rating and meet with a set of 360° participants to discuss it as well as their ratings. The jobholder learns from how well one's self-rating compares with the viewpoints of others, and the results are useful for both evaluation and development purposes.

New technologies allow 360° feedback to be continuous rather than periodic. Accenture uses a computer program called Performance Multiplier that allows users to post projects, goals, and status updates for review by others. And Microsoft-Rypple software allows users to post assessment questions in 140 characters or less. Examples might be—"What did you think of my presentation?" or "How could I have run that meeting better?" Anonymous responses are compiled by the program, and the 360° feedback is then sent to the person posting the query.[17]

Does Success Come from Hard Work, Luck, or a Bit of Both?

A survey of LinkedIn members in 15 countries reports that 84 percent believe that luck influences their careers—both good and bad. But they also say that luck is something we create for ourselves and that good luck tends to come to those who have a strong work ethic. In addition to work ethics, other things that are believed to drive good luck include communication skills, networking, being flexible, and acting on opportunities when they arise. Among survey respondents, Japanese considered themselves most lucky in their careers whereas Americans ranked in the middle.

John Turner/Stone/Getty Images

Motivation and Job Design

LEARNING ROADMAP — SCIENTIFIC MANAGEMENT • JOB ENLARGEMENT AND JOB ROTATION • JOB ENRICHMENT • JOB CHARACTERISTICS MODEL

> TEACHING NOTE: Pick a job, or have students suggest jobs. Engage students in a job redesign exercise using the Job Characteristics Model. Have them score the job and then suggest changes to increase its motivational appeal to workers like themselves.

When it comes to motivation, we might say that nothing beats a good person–job fit. A match of job requirements with individual abilities and needs is often a high satisfaction and high performance combination. By contrast, a bad person–job fit is likely to result in poor motivation and performance problems. You might think of the goal this way:

Person + Good Job Fit = High Motivation

Job design is the process of planning and specifying job tasks and work arrangements.[18] Figure 6.4 shows how three alternative job design approaches differ in the way tasks are defined and availability of intrinsic rewards. The "best" job design is one that meets organizational performance requirements, offers a good fit with individual skills and needs, and provides opportunities for job satisfaction.

> **Job design** is the process of specifying job tasks and work arrangements.

▶ Scientific Management

The history of scholarly interest in job design can be traced in part to Frederick Taylor's work with **scientific management** in the early 1900s.[19] Taylor and his contemporaries wanted to create management and organizational practices that would increase people's efficiency at work. Their approach was to study a job carefully, break it into its smallest components, establish exact time and motion requirements for each task to be done, and

> Taylor's **scientific management** used systematic study of job components to develop practices to increase people's efficiency at work.

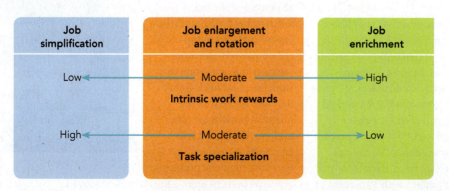

FIGURE 6.4 A continuum of job design strategies.

then train workers to do these tasks in the same way over and over again. Taylor's principles of scientific management can be summarized as follows:

1. Develop a "science" for each job that covers rules of motion, standard work tools, and supportive work conditions.
2. Hire workers with the right abilities for the job.
3. Train and motivate workers to do their jobs according to the science.
4. Support workers by planning and assisting their work using the job science.

Today, the term **job simplification** is used to describe a scientific management approach that standardizes work procedures and employs people in routine, clearly defined, and highly specialized tasks. The machine-paced automobile assembly line is a classic example. Why is it used? The answer is to increase operating efficiency. Job simplification reduces the number of skills required, allows for hiring low-cost labor, keeps the need for job training to a minimum, and focuses expertise on repetitive tasks. Why is it often criticized? Jobs designed this way come with potential disadvantages—lower work quality, high rates of absenteeism and turnover, and demands for ever-higher wages to compensate for unappealing work. One response is more automation to replace people with technology. In automobile manufacturing, for example, robots now do many different kinds of work previously accomplished with human labor.

Job simplification standardizes work to create clearly defined and highly specialized tasks.

Job Enlargement and Job Rotation

Although job simplification makes the limited number of tasks easier to master, the repetitiveness of the work can reduce motivation. This has prompted alternative job design approaches that try to make jobs more interesting by adding breadth to the variety of tasks performed.

Job enlargement increases task variety by combining into one job two or more tasks that were previously assigned to separate workers. Sometimes called *horizontal loading*, this approach increases job breadth by having the worker perform more and different tasks, but all at the same level of responsibility and challenge.

Job rotation increases task variety by periodically shifting workers among jobs involving different tasks. Also a form of horizontal loading, the responsibility level of the tasks stays the same. The rotation can be arranged according to almost any time schedule, such as hourly, daily, or weekly schedules. An important benefit of job rotation is training.

Job enlargement increases task variety by combining into one job two or more tasks that were previously assigned to separate workers.

Job rotation increases task variety by periodically shifting workers among jobs involving different tasks.

If You Want More Job Satisfaction, Consider Being Your Own Boss

Are you working for money alone, or will you be? If so, perhaps you might try self-employment. A survey from the Pew Research Center Social & Demographics Trends project found that the motivation to work differed somewhat between the self-employed and others. Whereas 50 percent of those not self-employed said they worked because they needed the money, this was the case for only 38 percent of the self-employed. Of them, 32 percent said they worked because they wanted to; for the not self-employed that figure was 19 percent. Results for job satisfaction followed a similar pattern with 39 percent of the self-employed reporting "complete satisfaction" versus 28 percent of the not self-employed. Although the Pew researchers found the self-employed to be more satisfied and less prone to work for a paycheck alone, they also noted that the financial benefits are less evident. Among the self-employed, 40 percent say they have financial problems versus 30 percent among the not self-employed.

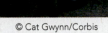
© Cat Gwynn/Corbis

It allows workers to become more familiar with different tasks and increases the flexibility with which they can be moved from one job to another.

Job Enrichment

When it comes to job rotation and enlargement, psychologist Frederick Herzberg asks: "Why should workers become motivated when one or more 'meaningless' tasks are added to previously existing ones or when work assignments are rotated among equally 'meaningless' tasks?"[20] He recommends **job enrichment**. It designs job that create opportunities to experiene responsibility, achievement, recognition, and personal growth. This is done by *vertical loading* that moves into a job many planning and evaluating tasks normally performed by supervisors. The increased job depth provides pathways to higher-order need satisfaction, and is supposed to increase both motivation and performance.

Job enrichment builds high-content jobs that involve planning and evaluating duties normally done by supervisors.

Job Characteristics Model

OB scholars have been reluctant to recommend job enrichment as a universal approach to job design. There are just too many individual differences among people at work for it to solve all performance and satisfaction problems. Their answer to the question "Is job enrichment for everyone?" is a clear "No." Present thinking focuses more on a diagnostic and contingency approach to job design. A good example is the job characteristics model developed by Richard Hackman and Greg Oldham.[21]

Core Characteristics

Figure 6.5 shows how the Hackman and Oldham model informs the process of job design. The higher a job scores on each of the following five core characteristics, the higher its motivational potential and the more it is considered to be enriched:[22]

- *Skill variety*—the degree to which a job includes a variety of different activities and involves the use of a number of different skills and talents
- *Task identity*—the degree to which the job requires completion of a "whole" and identifiable piece of work, one that involves doing a job from beginning to end with a visible outcome
- *Task significance*—the degree to which the job is important and involves a meaningful contribution to the organization or society in general
- *Autonomy*—the degree to which the job gives the employee substantial freedom, independence, and discretion in scheduling the work and determining the procedures used in carrying it out
- *Job feedback*—the degree to which carrying out the work activities provides direct and clear information to the employee regarding how well the job has been done

◀ Five core job characteristics

A job's motivating potential can be raised by combining tasks to create larger jobs, opening feedback channels to enable workers to know how well they are doing, establishing client relationships to experience such feedback directly from customers, and employing vertical loading to create more planning and controlling responsibilities. When the core characteristics are enriched in these ways, the job creates what is often called psychological empowerment—a sense of personal fulfillment and purpose that arouses one's feelings of competency and commitment to the work.[23] Figure 6.5 identifies three critical psychological states that have a positive impact on individual motivation, performance, and

FIGURE 6.5 Job design considerations according to the job characteristics model.

satisfaction: experienced meaningfulness of the work, experienced responsibility for the outcomes of the work, and knowledge of actual results of the work.

Moderator Variables The five core job characteristics do not affect all people in the same way. Rather than accept the notion that enriched jobs should be good for everyone, Hackman and Oldham take a contingency view that suggests enriched jobs will lead to positive outcomes only for those persons who are a good match for them—the person–job fit issue again.

"Fit" in the job characteristics model is based on the three moderators shown in Figure 6.5. The first is *growth-need strength*, or the degree to which a person desires the opportunity for self-direction, learning, and personal accomplishment at work. The expectation here is that people high in growth-need strengths will respond positively to enriched jobs, whereas people low in growth-need strengths will find enriched jobs to be sources of anxiety. The second moderator is *knowledge and skill*. People whose capabilities fit the demands of enriched jobs are predicted to feel good about them and perform

OB IN POPULAR CULTURE

Self-Management and *Slumdog Millionaire*

MCT/NewsCom

The *Times* of London called this movie an "exotic, edgy thriller," and the *New York Times* described it as a "gaudy, gorgeous rush of color, sound and motion." What's your take on this rags-to-riches story of an orphan growing up in Mumbai, India, and finding his way to a TV game show offering him the chance to be a "slumdog millionaire"?

When the disgruntled game-show host has the police chief rough up the main character, Jamal (Dev Patel), the night before the big show, he asks, "What the hell can a slum boy possibly know?" Facing the chief and the prospect of more mistreatment, Jamal looks him in the eye and says in return, "The answers."

This movie is a study in discipline, confidence, and self-management—the capacity to act with a strong sense of self-awareness. As a career skill, this ability helps us stay confident, build on strengths, overcome weaknesses, and avoid viewing ourselves both more favorably or more negatively than is justified.

You have to admire Jamal's motivation and the way he held up under the police chief's torture. He also didn't fall prey to the quiz master's repeated attempts to deceive and pressure him into not believing his own best answers. It's a classic case of self-management in action.

Even if you've already seen it, *Slumdog Millionaire* is worth another viewing. Watch for lessons on management and personal career development that you might explore with your friends and classmates.

Get to Know Yourself Better
Take Assessment 7, Two Factor Profile, in the *OB Skills Workbook*. Think about your capacity for self-management: what really motivates you in work situations. What are your primary sources of motivation, and what role do intrinsic and extrinsic rewards play in them? How confident are you that self-management will lead you through situations where extrinsic rewards may be high but the behaviors you might engage in to reach them may be questionable?

well. Those who are inadequate or who feel inadequate in this regard are likely to experience difficulties. The third moderator is *context satisfaction*, or the extent to which an employee is satisfied with aspects of the work setting such as salary, quality of supervision, relationships with co-workers, and working conditions. In general, people who are satisfied with job context are more likely to do well in enriched jobs.

Research Concerns and Questions Experts generally agree that the job characteristics model and its diagnostic approach are useful but not perfect, guides to job design.[24] One concern is whether or not jobs have stable and objective characteristics to which individuals will respond predictably and consistently over time.[25] It's quite possible that individual needs and task perceptions are a result of socially constructed realities. Suppose, for example, that several of your friends tell you that the instructor for a course is bad, the content is boring, and the requirements involve too much work. You may then think that the critical characteristics of the class are the instructor, the content, and the workload, and that they are all bad. All of this may substantially influence the way you perceive your instructor and the course, and the way you deal with the class—regardless of the core characteristics discussed in the Hackman and Oldham model.

Finally, research provides the following answers for three common questions about job enrichment and its applications. (1) *Should everyone's job be enriched*? The answer is clearly "No." The logic of individual differences suggests that not everyone will want an enriched job. Individuals most likely to have positive reactions to job enrichment are those who need achievement, who exhibit a strong work ethic, or who are seeking higher-order growth-need satisfaction at work. Job enrichment also appears to work best when the job context is positive and when workers have the abilities needed to do the enriched job. Costs, technological constraints, and workgroup or union opposition may also make it difficult to enrich some jobs. (2) *With so much attention on teams in organizations today, can job enrichment apply to groups*? The answer is "Yes." The result is called a self managing team. (3) *For those who don't want an enriched job, what can be done to make their work more motivating?* One answer rests in the following section and its focus on alternative work schedules. Even if the job content can't be changed, a redesign of the job context or setting may have a positive impact on motivation and performance.

Alternative Work Schedules

  COMPRESSED WORKWEEKS • FLEXIBLE WORKING HOURS
JOB SHARING • TELECOMMUTING • PART-TIME WORK

Another way that organizations are reshaping employee value propositions is through alternative work arrangements that do away with the traditional forty-hour weeks and nine-to-five schedules where work is done at the place of business. New alternatives are designed to improve satisfaction by helping employees balance the demands of work with their nonwork lives.[26] The value from the employee side is more support for work–life balance by a "family-friendly" employer.

If you have any doubts at all about the forces at play, consider these facts: 78 percent of American couples are dual wage earners; 63 percent believe they don't have enough time for spouses and partners; 74 percent believe they don't have enough time for their children; 35 percent are spending time caring for elderly relatives. Furthermore, both Baby Boomers and Gen Ys believe flexible work is important and want opportunities to work remotely at least part of the time.[27]

> TEACHING NOTE: Take up the Yahoo CEO Melissa Mayer decision to disallow telecommuting. Ask students to discuss its pros and cons, and the potential risks and rewards to her and the company. Push for good critical thinking on the realities of flexible work arrangements for employers and employees alike.

Compressed Workweeks

A **compressed workweek** allows a full-time job to be completed in fewer than the standard five days.

A **compressed workweek** is any schedule that allows a full-time job to be completed in fewer than the standard five days. The most common form is the "4/40"—40 hours of work accomplished in four 10-hour days, leaving a 3-day break. The additional time off gives workers longer weekends, free weekdays to pursue personal business, and lower commuting costs. In return, the organization hopes for less absenteeism, greater work motivation, and improved recruiting of new employees.[28] However, scheduling compressed workweeks can be more complicated, overtime pay for time over 8 hours in one day may be required by law, and union opposition to the longer workday is also a possibility.

Flexible Working Hours

Flexible working hours give individuals some amount of choice in scheduling their daily work hours.

Another alternative is some form of **flexible working hours** or *flextime* that gives individuals daily choice in work hours. A common flex schedule requires certain hours of "core" time but leaves employees free to choose their remaining hours from flexible time blocks. One person, for example, may start early and leave early, whereas another may start later and leave later.

All top 100 companies in *Working Mother* magazine's list of best employers for working moms offer flexible scheduling. Reports indicate that the flexibility gained to deal with nonwork obligations can lower turnover, absenteeism, and tardiness for the organization while reducing stress and raising commitment and performance by workers.[29] Flexible hours help employees manage children's schedules, fulfill elder care responsibilities, and attend to personal affairs such as medical and dental appointments, home emergencies, banking, and so on.

Job Sharing

In **job sharing**, one full-time job is split between two or more persons who divide the work according to agreed-upon hours.

Work sharing is when employees agree to work fewer hours to avoid layoffs.

In **job sharing**, two or more persons split one full-time job. This can be done, for example, on a half day, weekly, or monthly basis. Organizations benefit from job sharing when they can attract talented people who would otherwise be unable to work. Some job sharers report less burnout and claim that they feel recharged each time they report for work. The tricky part of this arrangement is finding two people who will stay coordinated and work well with each other.

Job sharing should not be confused with something called **work sharing**. This occurs when workers agree to cut back on the number of hours they work in order to protect against layoffs. In the recent economic crisis, for example, workers in some organizations agreed to voluntarily reduce their paid hours worked so that others would not lose their jobs.

How Employers Can Beat the Mommy Drain

It's no secret that more and more employers are turning to flexibility in work schedules to better accommodate today's workers. Among them, Accenture and Booz Allen Hamilton are taking special steps to make sure they can attract and retain talented working mothers. Here is a selection of ways top employers are counteracting the "Mommy drain" and responding to Daddy's needs as well:

- Offer increased pay and extended time for maternity leave.
- Offer increased pay and extended time for parental leave.
- Allow employee pay set-asides to buy more time for maternal and parental leave.
- Create alternative and challenging jobs that require less travel.
- Make sure pay for performance plans do not discriminate against those on maternal or parental leave.
- Set up mentoring and networking systems to support working parents.
- Make sure new mothers feel they are wanted back at work.
- Keep in contact with employees on maternity and parental leaves.

Mango Productions/Corbis

Telecommuting

Technology has enabled yet another alternative work arrangement that is now highly visible in employment sectors ranging from higher education to government, and from manufacturing to services.[30] **Telecommuting** is work done at home or in a remote location via the use of computers, tablets, and smart phone connections with bosses, co-workers, and customers. And it's popular. About four out of five employees say they would like the option and consider it a "significant job perk."[31]

When asked what they like, telecommuters report increased productivity, fewer distractions, the freedom to be their own boss, and the benefit of having more time for themselves. They also like the added flexibility, comforts of home, and being able to live and work in locations consistent with personal lifestyles. Potential negatives are reported as well. Some telecommuters say they end up working too much while having difficulty separating work and personal life. Other complaints include not being considered as important as on-site workers, feeling isolated from co-workers and less identified with the work team, and even having trouble managing interruptions from everyday family affairs. One telecommuter says, "You have to have self-discipline and pride in what you do, but you also have to have a boss that trusts you enough to get out of the way."[32]

Employers that allow telecommuting expect it to help improve work–life balance and job satisfaction for employees. But, some also worry that too much telecommuting disrupts schedules and reduces important face-to-face time among co-workers. Yahoo CEO Marissa Mayer, for example, was willing to face criticism when she decided to disallow it. Her reasoning was that working from home detracted from Yahoo!'s collaborative culture and ability to innovate.[33]

Telecommuting is work done at home or from a remote location using computers, tablets, and smart phone devices.

CHECKING ETHICS IN OB

Sniffling at Work Takes Its Toll

You wake up feeling even worse than the day before. Sniffling, sneezing, coughing, you make your way to work, hoping to get through the day as best as you can. Fine, but what about everyone whom you'll come into contact with that day, and what about the impact your *presenteeism*—basically meaning that you go to work sick—can have on office productivity and your co-workers' and customers' lives in general?

Brett Gorovsky of CCH, a business information resource, says that when people come to work sick it "can take a very real hit on the bottom line." His firm reports that 56 percent of executives in one poll considered this a problem; that figure is up some 17 percent in a two-year period. Estimates are that the cost of lost productivity is as much as $180 billion annually. Just think of the costs of swine flu season.

Rubberball/iStockphoto

WebMD reports a study claiming that the cost of lost productivity could be higher than what might be paid out in authorized sick days. Still, the fact remains: Many of us work sick because we have to if we want to be paid.

You Tell Us What are the ethics of coming to work sick and sharing our illnesses with others? From the management side of things, what are the ethics of not providing benefits sufficient to allow employees to stay home from work when they aren't feeling well?

Part-Time Work

Part-time work is an increasingly prominent and controversial work arrangement. One of the big downsides is that part-timers often fail to qualify for fringe benefits such as health care insurance and retirement plans. In addition, they may be paid less than their full-time counterparts. Because part-timers are easily released and hired as needs dictate, they are also likely to be laid off before full-timers during difficult business times.

The number of part-time workers is growing as today's employers try to stay flexible and manage costs in a demanding global economy. This is reflected in what you might hear called a "permanent temp economy," one where working as a permanent part timer—or—*permatemp* is a new reality for many job hunters.[34] Some choose this schedule voluntarily. Recent data, for example, show that many Millennials are opting for a shifting portfolio of freelance jobs that give them flexibility while still providing earning power.[35] But, there's no doubt that part-time work is an involuntary alternative for many who would prefer full-time work but are unable to get it.

6 Study Guide

Key Questions and Answers

What is the link between motivation, performance, and rewards?
- The integrated model of motivation brings together insights from content, process, and learning theories around the basic effort–performance–reward linkage.
- Reward systems emphasize a mix of intrinsic rewards, such as a sense of achievement from completing a challenging task, and extrinsic rewards, such as receiving a pay increase.
- Pay-for-performance systems takes a variety of forms, including merit pay, gain-sharing and profit-sharing plans, stock options, and employee stock ownership.

What are the essentials of performance management?
- Performance management is the process of managing performance measurement and the variety of human resource decisions associated with such measurement.
- Performance measurement serves both an evaluative purpose for reward allocation and a development purpose for future performance improvement.
- Performance measurement can be done using output measures of performance accomplishment or activity measures of performance efforts.
- The ranking, paired comparison, and forced-distribution approaches are examples of comparative performance appraisal methods.
- The graphic rating scale and the behaviorally anchored rating scale use individual ratings on personal and performance characteristics to appraise performance.
- 360° appraisals involve the full circle of contacts a person may have in job performance—from bosses to peers to subordinates to internal and external customers.
- Common performance measurement errors include halo errors, central tendency errors, recency errors, personal bias errors, and cultural bias errors.

How do job designs influence motivation and performance?
- Job design by scientific management or job simplification standardizes work and employs people in clearly defined and specialized tasks.

- Job enlargement increases task variety by combining two or more tasks previously assigned to separate workers; job rotation increases task variety by periodically rotating workers among jobs involving different tasks; job enrichment builds bigger and more responsible jobs by adding planning and evaluating duties.
- The job characteristics model offers a diagnostic approach to job enrichment based on analysis of five core job characteristics: skill variety, task identity, task significance, autonomy, and feedback.
- The job characteristics model does not assume that everyone wants an enriched job; it indicates that job enrichment will be more successful for persons with high-growth needs, requisite job skills, and context satisfaction.

What are the motivational opportunities of alternative work arrangements?

- The compressed workweek allows a full-time workweek to be completed in fewer than five days, typically offering four ten-hour days of work and three days free.
- Flexible working hours allow employees some daily choice in scheduling core and flex time.
- Job sharing occurs when two or more people divide one full-time job according to agreements among themselves and the employer.
- Telecommuting involves work at home or at a remote location while communicating with the home office as needed via computer and related technologies.
- Part-time work requires less than a forty-hour workweek and can be done on a temporary or permanent schedule.

Terms to Know

360° review (p. 128)
Activity measures (p. 125)
Behaviorally anchored rating scale (BARS) (p. 127)
Bonuses (p. 123)
Compressed workweek (p. 134)
Critical incident diaries (p. 127)
Employee stock ownership plans (ESOPs) (p. 124)
Employee value proposition (p. 120)
Extrinsic rewards (p. 121)
Flexible working hours (p. 134)
Forced distribution (p. 127)

Gain sharing (p. 123)
Graphic rating scales (p. 127)
Intrinsic rewards (p. 121)
Job design (p. 129)
Job enlargement (p. 130)
Job enrichment (p. 131)
Job rotation (p. 130)
Job sharing (p. 134)
Job simplification (p. 130)
Merit pay (p. 122)
Motivation (p. 120)
Output measures (p. 125)
Paired comparison (p. 127)
Performance-contingent pay (p. 122)

Person–job fit (p. 120)
Person–organization fit (p. 120)
Profit sharing (p. 123)
Ranking (p. 126)
Reliability (p. 126)
Scientific management (p. 129)
Skill-based pay (p. 124)
Stock options (p. 124)
Telecommuting (p. 135)
Validity (p. 126)
Work sharing (p. 134)

Self-Test 6

■ Multiple Choice

1. In the integrated model of motivation, what predicts effort?
   (a) rewards
   (b) organizational support
   (c) ability
   (d) motivation

2. Pay is generally considered a/an _____ reward, whereas a sense of personal growth experienced from working at a task is an example of a/an _____ reward.
   (a) extrinsic, skill-based
   (b) skill-based, intrinsic
   (c) extrinsic, intrinsic
   (d) absolute, comparative

3. If someone improves productivity by developing a new work process and receives a portion of the productivity savings as a monetary reward, this is an example of a/an _____ pay plan.
   (a) cost-sharing
   (b) gain-sharing
   (c) ESOP
   (d) stock option

4. Performance measurement serves both evaluation and _____ purposes.
   (a) reward allocation
   (b) counseling
   (c) discipline
   (d) benefits calculations

5. Which form of performance assessment is an example of the comparative approach?
   (a) forced distribution
   (b) graphic rating scale
   (c) BARS
   (d) critical incident diary

6. If a performance assessment method fails to accurately measure a person's performance on actual job content, it lacks _____.
   (a) performance contingency
   (b) leniency
   (c) validity
   (d) strictness

7. A written record that describes in detail various examples of a person's positive and negative work behaviors is most likely part of which performance appraisal method?
   (a) forced distribution
   (b) critical incident diary
   (c) paired comparison
   (d) graphic rating scale

8. When a team leader evaluates the performance of all team members as "average," the possibility for _____ error in the performance appraisal is quite high.
   (a) personal bias
   (b) recency
   (c) halo
   (d) central tendency

9. Job simplification is closely associated with _____ as originally developed by Frederick Taylor.
   (a) vertical loading
   (b) horizontal loading
   (c) scientific management
   (d) self-efficacy

10. Job _____ increases job _____ by combining into one job several tasks of similar difficulty.
    (a) rotation, depth
    (b) enlargement, depth
    (c) rotation, breadth
    (d) enlargement, breadth

11. If a manager redesigns a job through vertical loading, she would most likely _____.
    (a) bring tasks from earlier in the workflow into the job
    (b) bring tasks from later in the workflow into the job
    (c) bring higher-level or managerial responsibilities into the job
    (d) raise the standards for high performance

12. In the job characteristics model, a person will be most likely to find an enriched job motivating if he or she _____.
    (a) receives stock options
    (b) has ability and support
    (c) is unhappy with job context
    (d) has strong growth needs

13. In the job characteristics model, _____ indicates the degree to which an individual is able to make decisions affecting his or her work.
    (a) task variety
    (b) task identity
    (c) task significance
    (d) autonomy

14. When a job allows a person to do a complete unit of work—for example, process an insurance claim from point of receipt from the customer to the point of final resolution—it would be considered high on which core characteristic?
    (a) task identity
    (b) task significance
    (c) task autonomy
    (d) feedback

15. The 4/40 is a type of _____ work arrangement.
    (a) compressed workweek
    (b) "allow workers to change machine configurations to make different products"
    (c) job-sharing
    (d) permanent part-time

Short Response

16. Explain how a 360° review works as a performance appraisal approach.
17. Explain the difference between halo errors and recency errors in performance assessment.
18. What role does growth-need strength play in the job characteristics model?
19. What are the potential advantages and disadvantages of a compressed workweek?

Applications Essay

20. Choose a student organization on your campus. Discuss in detail how the concepts and ideas in this chapter could be applied in various ways to improve motivation and performance among its members.

Steps to Further Learning 6
Top Choices from *The OB Skills Workbook*

These learning activities from *The OB Skills Workbook* found at the back of the book are suggested for Chapter 6.

Case for Critical Thinking	Team and Experiential Exercises	Self-Assessment Portfolio
• Perfect Pizzeria, or Not? • OB Classic: Hovey and Beard Company	• My Fantasy Job • Upward Appraisal • Tinkertoys • Job Design Preferences	• Personal Values • Are You Cosmopolitan? • Managerial Assumptions • Twenty-First Century Manager

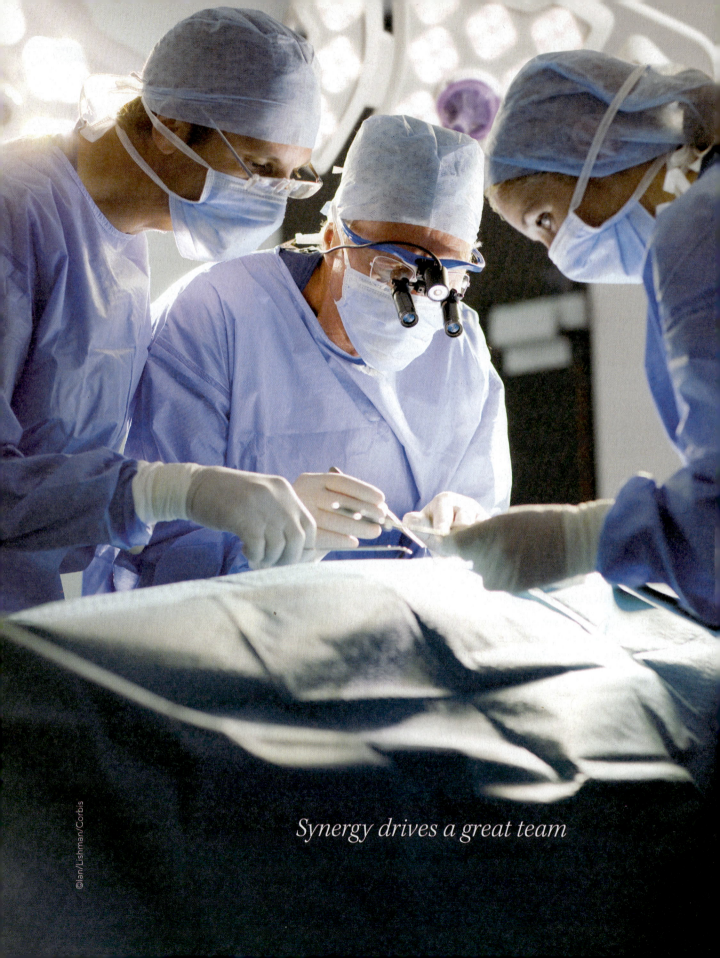

The Nature of Teams

7

The Key Point

When teams achieve synergy they unlock member talents and rally enthusiasm for creativity and high performance. But, we all know that teamwork isn't always easy and that teams sometimes underperform. It takes special skills and commitment—from leaders and team members alike—to bring out the best that teams have to offer. ■

What's Inside?

- **Bringing OB to LIFE**
  REMOVING THE HEADPHONES TO SHOW TEAM SPIRIT
- **Worth Considering . . . or Best Avoided?**
  SOFTWARE MAKES ONLINE MEETINGS EASY. IS IT TIME TO KILL FACE-TO-FACE SIT-DOWNS?
- **Checking Ethics in OB**
  CHEAT NOW . . . CHEAT LATER
- **Finding the Leader in You**
  TEAMWORK LEADS NASCAR'S RACE IN THE FAST LANE
- **OB in Popular Culture**
  SOCIAL LOAFING AND *SURVIVOR*
- **Research Insight**
  MEMBERSHIP, INTERACTIONS, AND EVALUATION INFLUENCE SOCIAL LOAFING IN GROUPS

Chapter at a Glance

- What Are Teams, and How Are They Used in Organizations?
- When Is a Team Effective?
- What Are the Stages of Team Development?
- How Can We Understand Teams at Work?

Teams in Organizations

LEARNING ROADMAP
TEAMS AND TEAMWORK • WHAT TEAMS DO
ORGANIZATIONS AS NETWORKS OF TEAMS
CROSS-FUNCTIONAL AND PROBLEM-SOLVING TEAMS
SELF-MANAGING TEAMS • VIRTUAL TEAMS

> TEACHING NOTE: Option A) Ask students for their team "horror stories." Discuss and deconstruct some to identify useful teamwork themes and issues. Option B) Ask students to describe the best-run team they have ever been on. Ask what made this team so different from others? Again, discuss and deconstruct some examples.

When we hear the word *team*, a variety of popular sports teams often comes to mind, perhaps a favorite from the college ranks or the professional leagues. For a moment, let's stick with basketball. *Scene—NBA Basketball:* Scholars find that both good and bad basketball teams win more games the longer the players have been together. Why? They claim it's a "teamwork effect" that creates wins because players know each other's moves and playing tendencies.[1]

Let's not forget that teams are important in work settings as well. And whether or not a team lives up to expectations can have a major impact on how well its customers and clients are served. *Scene—Hospital Operating Room:* Scholars notice that the same heart surgeons have lower death rates for similar procedures when performed in hospitals where they do more operations. They claim it's because the doctors spend more time working together with members of these surgery teams. The scholars argue it's not only the surgeon's skills that count: "The skills of the team, and of the organization, matter."[2]

Teams and Teamwork

What is going on in the prior examples? Whereas a group of people milling around a coffee shop counter is just that—a "group" of people, teams like those in the examples are supposed to be something more—"groups +" if you will. That "+" factor is what distinguishes the successful NBA basketball teams from the also-rans and the best surgery teams from all the others.

In OB we define a **team** as a group of people brought together to use their complementary skills to achieve a common purpose for which they are collectively accountable.[3] Real **teamwork** occurs when team members accept and live up to their collective accountability by actively working together so that all of their respective skills are best used to achieve team goals.[4] Of course, there is a lot more to teamwork than simply assigning members to the same group, calling it a team, appointing someone as team leader, and then expecting everybody to do a great job.[5] The responsibilities for building high-performance teams rest not only with the team leader, manager, or coach, but also with the team members. If you look now at the "Heads Up: Don't Forget" sidebar, you'll find a checklist of several team must-haves, the types of contributions that team members and leaders can make to help their teams achieve high performance.[6]

> A **team** is a group of people holding themselves collectively accountable for using complementary skills to achieve a common purpose.
>
> **Teamwork** occurs when team members live up to their collective accountability for goal accomplishment.

Heads Up: Don't Forget These Must-Have Contributions by Team Members

- Putting personal talents to work
- Encouraging and motivating others
- Accepting suggestions
- Listening to different points of view
- Communicating information and ideas
- Persuading others to cooperate
- Resolving and negotiating conflict
- Building consensus
- Fulfilling commitments
- Avoiding disruptive acts and words

© Monalyn Gracia Corbis

What Teams Do

One of the first things to understand about teams in organizations is that they do many things and make many types of performance contributions. In general, we can describe them as teams that recommend things, run things, and make or do things.[7]

Teams that recommend things are set up to study specific problems and recommend solutions for them. These teams typically work with a target completion date and often disband once the purpose has been fulfilled. The teams include task forces, ad hoc committees, special project teams, and the like. Members of these teams must be able to learn quickly how to pool talents, work well together, and accomplish the assigned task.

Teams that run things lead organizations and their component parts. A good example is a top-management team composed of a CEO and other senior executives. Key issues addressed by top-management teams include identifying overall organizational purposes, goals, and values as well as crafting strategies and persuading others to support them.[8]

Teams that make or do things are work units that perform ongoing tasks such as marketing, sales, systems analysis, manufacturing, or working on special projects with assigned due dates. Members of these action teams must have good working relationships with one another, the right technologies and operating systems, and the external support needed to achieve performance effectiveness over the long term or within an assigned deadline.

■ Organizations as Networks of Teams

The many **formal teams** found in organizations are created and officially designated to serve specific purposes. Some are permanent and appear on organization charts as departments (e.g., market research department), divisions (e.g., consumer products division), or teams (e.g., product-assembly team). Such teams can vary in size from very small departments or teams consisting of just a few people to large divisions employing 100 or more people. Other formal teams are temporary and short lived. They are created to solve specific problems or perform defined tasks and are then disbanded once the purpose has been accomplished. Examples include temporary committees and task forces.[9]

Formal teams are official and designated to serve a specific purpose.

Interlocking networks of formal teams create the basic structure of an organization. On the vertical dimension, the team leader at one level is a team member at the next higher level.[10] On the horizontal dimension, a team member may also serve on organization-wide task forces and committees.

Organizations also have vast networks of **informal groups**, which emerge and coexist as a shadow to the formal structure and without any assigned purpose or official endorsement. As shown in the nearby figure, these informal groups develop through personal relationships and create their own interlocking networks within the organization. *Friendship groups* consist of persons who like one another. Their members tend to work together, sit together, take breaks together, and even do things together outside of the workplace. *Interest groups* consist of persons who share job-related interests, such as an intense desire to learn more about computers, or non work interests, such as community service, sports, or religion.

Informal groups are unofficial and emerge to serve special interests.

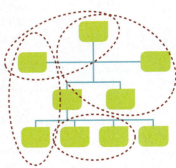

Although informal groups can be places where people meet to complain, spread rumors, and disagree with what is happening in the organization, they can also be quite helpful. The personal connections activated within informal networks can speed up workflows as people assist each other in ways that cut across the formal structures. They also create interpersonal relationships that can satisfy individual needs, such as by providing companionship (meeting a social need) or a sense of personal importance (meeting an ego need).

A tool known as **social network analysis** is used to identify the informal groups and networks of relationships that are active in an organization. The analysis typically asks people to identify co-workers who most often help them, who communicate with them regularly, and who motivate and demotivate them. When these social networks are mapped, you learn a lot about how work really gets done and who communicates most often with whom. The results often contrast markedly with the formal arrangements depicted on organization charts. And, this information can be used to redo the charts and reorganize teamwork for better performance.

Social network analysis identifies the informal structures and their embedded social relationships that are active in an organization.

FINDING THE LEADER IN YOU

Teamwork Leads NASCAR's Race in the Fast Lane

What distinguishes a group of people from a high-performance team? For one, it's the way members work with one another to achieve common goals.

A vivid example is a NASCAR pit crew. When a driver pulls in for a pit stop, the team must rapidly perform multiple tasks flawlessly and in perfect order and unison. A second gained or lost can be crucial to a NASCAR driver's performance. Team members must be well trained and rehearsed to efficiently perform on race day. "You can't win a race with a twelve-second stop, but you can lose it with an eighteen-second stop," says pit crew coach Trent Cherry.

Pit crew members are conditioned and trained to execute intricate maneuvers while taking care of tire changes, car adjustments, fueling, and related matters on a crowded pit lane. Each crew member is an expert at one task. Each is also fully aware of how that job fits into every other task that must be performed in a few-second pit-stop interval.

The duties are carefully scripted for each individual's performance and equally choreographed to fit together seamlessly at the team level. Every task is highly specialized and interdependent; if the jacker is late, for example, the wheel changer can't pull the wheel.

Pit crews plan and practice again and again, getting ready for the big test of race-day performance. The crew chief makes sure that everyone is in shape, well trained, and ready to contribute to the team. "I don't want seven all-stars," Trent Cherry says, "I want seven guys who work as a team."

© GeorgeTiedemann/GT Image/Corbis

The NASCAR pit crews don't just get together and wing it on race days. The members are carefully selected for their skills and attitudes, the teams practice–practice–practice, and the pit crew leader doesn't hesitate to make changes when things aren't going well.

What's the Lesson Here?

When in groups do you encourage teamwork, or do you do some things as a leader that might be harmful to team dynamics? Are you able to see ways to make positive changes even when things are going well? How open are you to suggestions for improvement from team members?

Cross-Functional and Problem-Solving Teams

A **cross-functional team** consists of people brought together from different functional departments or work units to achieve more horizontal integration and better lateral relations. Members of cross-functional teams are supposed to work together with a positive combination of functional expertise and integrative team thinking. The expected result is higher performance driven by the advantages of better information and faster decision making.

Cross-functional teams are a way of trying to beat the **functional silos problem**, also called the *functional chimneys problem*. It occurs when members of functional units stay focused on internal matters and minimize their interactions and cooperation with other functions. In this sense, the functional departments or work teams create artificial boundaries, or "silos," that discourage rather than encourage interaction with other units. The result is poor integration and poor coordination with other parts of the organization. The cross-functional team helps break down these barriers by creating a forum in which members from different functions work together as one team with a common purpose.[11]

Organizations also use any number of **problem-solving teams**, which are created temporarily to serve a specific purpose by dealing with a specific problem or opportunity. The president of a company, for example, might convene a task force to examine the possibility of implementing flexible work hours; a human resource director might bring together a committee to advise her on changes in employee benefit policies; a project team might be formed to plan and implement a new organization-wide information system.

The term **employee involvement team** applies to a wide variety of teams whose members meet regularly to collectively examine important workplace issues. They might discuss,

---

A **cross-functional team** consists of members from different functions or work units.

The **functional silos problem** occurs when members of one functional team fail to interact with others from other functional teams.

A **problem-solving team** is set up to deal with a specific problem or opportunity.

An **employee involvement team** meets regularly to address workplace issues.

for example, ways to enhance quality, better satisfy customers, raise productivity, and improve the quality of work life. Such employee involvement teams are supposed to mobilize the full extent of workers' know-how and experiences for continuous improvements. An example is what some organizations call a **quality circle**, a small team of persons who meet periodically to discuss and make proposals for ways to improve quality.[12]

> A **quality circle** team meets regularly to address quality issues.

Self-Managing Teams

The **self-managing team** is a high-involvement workgroup design that is becoming increasingly well established. Sometimes called *self-directed work teams*, these teams are empowered to make the decisions needed to manage themselves on a day-to-day basis.[13] They basically replace traditional work units with teams whose members assume duties otherwise performed by a manager or first-line supervisor. Figure 7.1 shows that members of true self-managing teams make their own decisions about scheduling work, allocating tasks, training for job skills, evaluating performance, selecting new team members, and controlling the quality of work.

> **Self-managing teams** are empowered to make decisions to manage themselves in day-to-day work.

Most self-managing teams include between five and fifteen members. They need to be large enough to provide a good mix of skills and resources but small enough to function efficiently. Because team members have a lot of discretion in determining work pace and in distributing tasks, **multiskilling** is important. This means that team members are expected to perform many different jobs—even all of the team's jobs—as needed. Pay is ideally skill based: The more skills someone masters, the higher the base pay.

> In **multiskilling**, team members are each capable of performing many different jobs.

The expected benefits of self-managing teams include better work quality, faster response to change, reduced absenteeism and turnover, and improved work attitudes and quality of work life. As with all organizational changes, however, the shift from traditional work units to self-managing teams may encounter difficulties. It may be hard for some team members to adjust to the "self-managing" responsibilities, and higher-level managers may have problems dealing with the absence of a first-line supervisor. Given all this, self-managing teams are probably not right for all organizations, situations, and people. They have great potential, but they also require the right setting and a great deal of

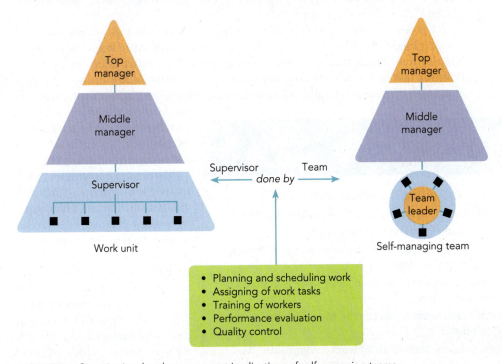

FIGURE 7.1 Organizational and management implications of self-managing teams.

Teamwork Makes "Worker-Owner" an Attractive Alternative to "Working-for-Others"

James Johnson says repairing computers at a local store in Richmond, California, "was just another job." Now he's a turned-on worker-owner in a bicycle shop. Called "hippie capitalism" by some, a worker cooperative tries to make teamwork a way of life. Everyone owns a financial share, and no one person is boss; work and leadership are evenly distributed. In Johnson's case, as he says, "you have to oversee people without actually being in charge." The city of Richmond is promoting cooperatives as a way of combating a bad economy. But the mayor's former assistant, Marilyn Langois, says the cooperative model "is really about creating democracy in the workplace and giving workers a sense that they own their own jobs."

© Raphye Alexius/Corbis

management support. At a minimum, the essence of any self-managing team—high involvement, participation, and empowerment—must be consistent with the values and culture of the organization.

Virtual Teams

Members of **virtual teams** work together through computer mediation.

It used to be that teamwork was confined in concept and practice to those circumstances in which members could meet face to face. Information technology has changed all that. The **virtual team**, one whose members work together through computer mediation rather than face to face, is now common.[14] Working in electronic space and free from the constraints of geographical distance, members of virtual teams do the same things members of face-to-face groups do. They share information, make decisions, and complete tasks together. And just like face-to-face teams, they have to be set up and managed well to achieve their full benefits. Some steps to successful teams are summarized in the "Don't Neglect These Steps to Successful Virtual Teams" sidebar.[15]

The potential advantages of virtual teams begin with the cost and time efficiencies of bringing together people located at some, perhaps great, distance from one another.[16] The electronic rather than face-to-face environment of the virtual team can help keep things on task by focusing attention and decision making on objective issues rather than emotional considerations and distracting interpersonal problems. Discussions and information shared among team members can also be stored electronically for continuous access and historical record keeping.

The potential downsides to virtual teams are also real. Members of virtual teams may find it hard to get up to speed and work well with one another. When the computer is the go-between, relationships and interactions can be different and require special attention. The lack of face-to-face interaction limits the role of emotions and nonverbal cues in the communication process, perhaps depersonalizing relations among team members.

Don't Neglect These Steps to Successful Virtual Teams

- Select team members high in initiative and capable of self-starting.
- Select members who will join and engage the team with positive attitudes.
- Select members known for working hard to meet team goals.
- Begin with social messaging that allows members to exchange information about each other to personalize the process.
- Assign clear goals and roles so that members can focus while working alone and also know what others are doing.
- Gather regular feedback from members about how they think the team is doing and how it might do better.
- Provide regular feedback to team members about team accomplishments.

| WORTH CONSIDERING | ...OR BEST AVOIDED? |

Software Makes Online Meetings Easy. Is It Time to Kill Face-to-Face Sit-downs?

"I just can't do another meeting," you say? Well, why not just connect virtually with those who would be involved and let things go at that? If you work for a tech firm the chances are that's the way things often get done. The question is this: Why aren't more people in more organizations abandoning the sit-down meeting and going online?

"When you're operating on the maker's schedule, meetings are a disaster," says software engineer Paul Graham. Meetings just don't fit the creativity and flexible timetables that bring most software to life. Some firms, such as Facebook, Dropbox, and Square, are trying to limit the time people spend in sit-downs. The experience of a former Microsoft engineer lends credibility to their moves. He claims that his 40-hour week was often consumed with 20 to 30 hours of meetings where "too little was accomplished." He left Microsoft to join GitHub, a small start-up that supports virtual teamwork.

One advantage of moving meetings online is that the tendency of manager-dominated discussions is lessened. In virtual space, people show less deference to job titles and status. Power tends to be distributed among all members and flows toward those with information and expertise and insight.

Even when the sit-down is unavoidable, some firms are trying to limit time spent and boost meeting productivity. At Grouper, another start-up, meetings are limited to 10 minutes maximum—and everyone has to stand, no sitting allowed.

Masterfile

Do the Analysis

This discussion is prompted by developments in the tech industry where highly talented people—often engineers—work on complex projects. How might the "no sit-down" approach work in other organizational settings? Make a list of two or three factors that you believe are most critical to the success of virtual teamwork. Check the scholarly literature to see if it supports your observations. And finally, what difference do the people in the meeting make. Is virtual teamwork or the standing face-to-face meeting approach good for everyone?

Team Effectiveness

LEARNING ROADMAP   CRITERIA OF AN EFFECTIVE TEAM • SYNERGY AND TEAM BENEFITS • SOCIAL FACILITATION • SOCIAL LOAFING AND TEAM PROBLEMS

> TEACHING NOTE: Have students share their social loafing experiences in course teams. Discuss their examples and use the discussion to develop guidelines for how leaders and members might handle social loafing teammates.

There is no doubt that teams are pervasive and important in organizations. They accomplish important tasks and help members achieve satisfaction in their work. We also know from personal experiences that teams and teamwork have their difficulties; not all teams perform well, and not all team members are always satisfied. Surely you've heard the sayings "A camel is a horse put together by a committee" and "Too many cooks spoil the broth." They raise an important question: Just what are the foundations of team effectiveness?[17]

■ Criteria of an Effective Team

Teams in all forms and types, just like individuals, should be held accountable for their performance. To do this we need to have some understanding of team effectiveness. In

> An **effective team** is one that achieves high levels of task performance, member satisfaction, and team viability.

OB we describe an **effective team** as one that achieves high levels of task performance, member satisfaction, and team viability.

With regard to *task performance*, an effective team achieves its performance goals in the standard sense of quantity, quality, and timeliness of work results. For a formal work unit such as a manufacturing team, this may mean meeting daily production targets. For a temporary team such as a new policy task force, this may involve meeting a deadline for submitting a new organizational policy to the company president.

With regard to *member satisfaction*, an effective team is one whose members believe that their participation and experiences are positive and meet important personal needs. They are satisfied with their team tasks, accomplishments, and interpersonal relationships. And, with regard to *team viability*, the members of an effective team are sufficiently satisfied to continue working well together on an ongoing basis. When one task is finished, they look forward to working on others in the future. Such a team has all-important long-term performance potential.

Synergy and Team Benefits

> **Synergy** is the creation of a whole greater than the sum of its parts.

Effective teams offer the benefits of **synergy**—the creation of a whole that is greater than the sum of its parts. Synergy works within a team, and it works across teams as their collective efforts are harnessed to serve the organization as a whole. It creates the great beauty of teams: people working together and accomplishing more through teamwork than they ever could by working alone.

The performance advantages of teams over individuals are most evident in three situations.[18] First, when there is no clear "expert" for a particular task or problem, teams tend to make better judgments than does the average individual alone. Second, teams are typically more successful than individuals when problems are complex and require a division of labor and the sharing of information. Third, because they tend to make riskier decisions, teams can be more creative and innovative than individuals.

Teams are interactive settings where people learn from one another and share job skills and knowledge. The learning environment and the pool of experience within a team can be used to solve difficult and unique problems. This is especially helpful to newcomers, who often need help in their jobs. When team members support and help each other in acquiring and improving job competencies, they may even make up for deficiencies in organizational training systems.

Teams are also important sources of need satisfaction for their members. Opportunities for social interaction within a team can provide individuals with a sense of security through work assistance and technical advice. Team members can also provide emotional support for one another in times of special crisis or pressure. The many contributions individuals make to teams can help members experience self-esteem and personal involvement.

Social Facilitation

> **Social facilitation** is the tendency for one's behavior to be influenced by the presence of others in a group.

Teams are also settings for something known as **social facilitation**—the tendency for one's behavior to be influenced by the presence of others in a group or social setting.[19] In a team context it can be a boost or a detriment to an individual member's performance contributions.

Social facilitation theory suggests that working in the presence of others creates an emotional arousal or excitement that stimulates behavior and affects performance. The effect is positive and stimulates extra effort when one is proficient with the task at hand. An example is the team member who enthusiastically responds when asked to do something she is really good at, such as making slides for a team presentation. But the effect of social facilitation can be negative when the task is unfamiliar or a person lacks the

Team Effectiveness

OB IN POPULAR CULTURE

Social Loafing and *Survivor*

Although teams offer tremendous performance potential, there are also unique problems in the team context. Social loafing is the tendency for an individual to do less in a group than he or she would individually. Two factors increase the likelihood of loafing. The first relates to the difficulty of identifying how individuals perform. When you do not know what others are doing, they can avoid working less hard. It is tempting to say the second factor is individual laziness. However, many times individuals simply recognize that others will pick up the slack and make sure tasks are accomplished. As a result, they simply opt out.

In the ever-popular reality show *Survivor*, individual players must balance cunning and competitiveness against the need for teamwork and collaboration. In Season 10, Willard Smith finds himself a member of the successful Koror tribe. Willard's contributions are limited, so his tribe assigns him to tend the fire at night. Instead

CBS/Landov LLC

of fulfilling his obligation, Willard sleeps in the only hammock available. When morning comes, eventual winner Tom Westman complains about losing sleep because he has to "cover" for Willard. He and Gregg Carey talk about how easy it is to make a contribution to the team even if physical ability is lacking.

Westman's assessment of Willard's motives (e.g., "Why should I do it if somebody else is going to do it for me") shows that social loafing can be a difficult problem to address even when others know it is happening.

Get to Know Yourself Better Take Assessment 9, Team Effectiveness, in the *OB Skills Workbook*. What does it say about you and your teamwork tendencies? If the score suggests previous groups were ineffective, explore the reasons. If social loafing was a problem, how would you deal with it in the future? If there were issues with other dynamics, think about ways that you could help future group members develop greater trust, communicate more effectively, and become more committed.

---

necessary skills. A team member might withdraw, for example, when asked to do something he or she isn't very good at.

■ Social Loafing and Team Problems

Although teams have enormous performance potential, one of their problems is **social loafing**. Also known as the *Ringlemann effect*, it is the tendency of people to work less hard in a group than they would individually.[20] Max Ringlemann, a German psychologist, pinpointed the phenomenon by asking people to pull on a rope as hard as they could, first alone and then as part of a team.[21] Average productivity dropped as more people joined the rope-pulling task. Ringlemann suggested that people may not work as hard in groups because their individual contributions are less noticeable in the group context and because they prefer to see others carry the workload.

You may have encountered social loafing in your work and study teams, and been perplexed in terms of how to best handle it. Perhaps you have even been surprised at your own social loafing in some performance situations. Rather than give in to the

Social loafing occurs when people work less hard in groups than they would individually.

phenomenon and its potential performance losses, you can often reverse or prevent social loafing. Steps that team leaders can take include keeping group size small and redefining roles so that free-riders are more visible and peer pressures to perform are more likely, increasing accountability by making individual performance expectations clear and specific, and making rewards directly contingent on an individual's performance contributions.[22]

Other common problems and difficulties can easily turn the great potential of teams into frustration and failure. Personality conflicts and differences in work styles can disrupt relationships and create antagonisms. Task uncertainties and competing goals or visions may cause some team members to withdraw and reduce their participation. Ambiguous agendas or ill-defined problems can also cause fatigue and loss of motivation when teams work too long on the wrong things with little to show for it. Finally, not everyone is always ready to do group work. This might be due to lack of motivation, but it may also stem from conflicts with other work deadlines and priorities. Low enthusiasm may also result from perceptions of poor team organization or progress, as well as from meetings that seem to lack purpose.

Research Insight

Membership, Interactions, and Evaluation Influence Social Loafing in Groups

"Why do individuals reduce their efforts or withhold inputs when in team contexts?" This question led researchers Kenneth H. Price, David A. Harrison, and Joanne H. Gavin into social loafing theory. The authors designed a study of natural teams consisting of students working together in course study groups for a semester. They posed hypotheses linking the presence of individual evaluation, perceived dispensability, and perceived fairness of group processes with the presence or absence of social loafing.

Price and colleagues studied 144 groups with a total of 515 students in 13 undergraduate and graduate university courses. Participants completed a questionnaire before group work started and again at the end. The final questionnaire included a section asking respondents to rate the extent to which each other group member "loafed by not doing his or her share of the tasks, by leaving work for others to do, by goofing off, and by having other things to do when asked to help out."

Findings showed that social loafing was negatively related to perceived fairness of group processes and positively related to perceived dispensability of one's contributions. The relationship between social loafing and perceived dispensability strengthened when individual

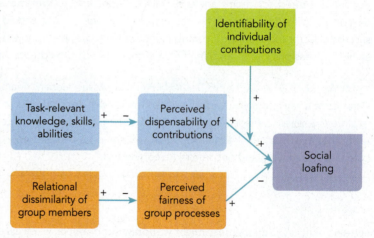

contributions were more identifiable. Task-relevant ability was negatively associated with perceived dispensability; the presence of relational differences among members was negatively associated with perceived fairness of group processes.

Do the Research
Build a model that explains social loafing in the teams you often work with. What are the major hypotheses? How might you test them in an actual research study?

Source: Kenneth H. Price, David A. Harrison, and Joanne H. Gavin, "Withholding Inputs in Team Contexts: Member Composition, Interaction Processes, Evaluation Structure, and Social Loafing," *Journal of Applied Psychology* 91.6 (2006), pp. 1375–1384.

Stages of Team Development

LEARNING ROADMAP — FORMING STAGE • STORMING STAGE • NORMING STAGE • PERFORMING STAGE • ADJOURNING STAGE

> TEACHING NOTE: Ask students to discuss if and how the five stages of team development apply to virtual rather than face-to-face teams. Is the model relevant in both team contexts? Ask for suggestions on modifying the model to best fit the world of virtual teamwork.

There is no doubt that the pathways to team effectiveness are often complicated and challenging. One of the first things to consider—whether we are talking about a formal work unit, a task force, a virtual team, or a self-managing team—is the fact that the team passes through a series of life cycle stages.[23] Depending on the stage the team has reached, the leader and members can face very different challenges and the team may be more or less effective. Figure 7.2 describes the five stages of team development as forming, storming, norming, performing, and adjourning.[24]

▌ Forming Stage

In the **forming stage** of team development, a primary concern is the initial entry of members to a group. During this stage, individuals ask a number of questions as they begin to identify with other group members and with the team itself. Their concerns may include "What can the group offer me?" "What will I be asked to contribute?" "Can my needs be met at the same time that I contribute to the group?" Members are interested in getting to know each other and discovering what is considered acceptable behavior, in determining the real task of the team, and in defining group rules.

*The **forming stage** focuses around the initial entry of members to a team.*

▌ Storming Stage

The **storming stage** of team development is a period of high emotionality and tension among the group members. During this stage, hostility and infighting may occur, and the team typically experiences many changes. Coalitions or cliques may form as individuals compete to impose their preferences on the group and to achieve a desired status position. Outside demands such as premature performance expectations may create uncomfortable pressures. In the process, membership expectations tend to be clarified, and attention shifts toward obstacles standing in the way of team goals. Individuals begin to understand one another's interpersonal styles, and efforts are made to find ways to accomplish team goals while also satisfying individual needs.

*The **storming stage** is one of high emotionality and tension among team members.*

▌ Norming Stage

The **norming stage** of team development, sometimes called initial integration, is the point at which the members really start to come together as a coordinated unit. The turmoil of the storming stage gives way to a precarious balancing of forces. While enjoying a new sense of harmony, team members will strive to maintain positive balance, but holding the team together may become more important to some than successfully working on the team tasks. Minority viewpoints, deviations from team directions, and criticisms

*The **norming stage** is reached when members start to work together as a coordinated team.*

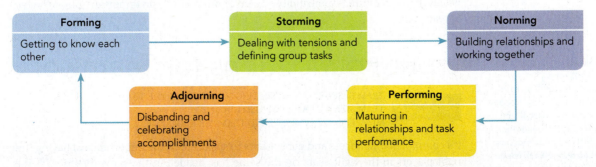

FIGURE 7.2 Five stages of team development.

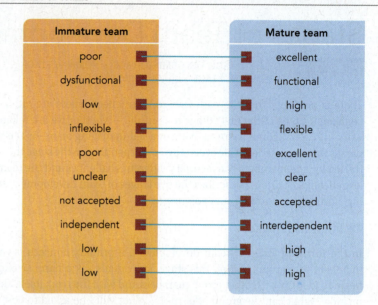

FIGURE 7.3 Ten criteria for measuring the maturity of a team.

may be discouraged as members experience a preliminary sense of closeness. Some members may mistakenly perceive this stage as one of ultimate maturity. In fact, a premature sense of accomplishment at this point needs to be carefully managed in order to reach the next level of team development: performing.

Performing Stage

The **performing stage** marks the emergence of a mature and well-functioning team.

The **performing stage** of team development, sometimes called total integration, marks the emergence of a mature, organized, and well-functioning team. Team members are now able to deal with complex tasks and handle internal disagreements in creative ways. The structure is stable, and members are motivated by team goals and are generally satisfied. The primary challenges are continued efforts to improve relationships and performance. Team members should be able to adapt successfully as opportunities and demands change over time. A team that has achieved the level of total integration typically scores high on the criteria of team maturity as shown in Figure 7.3.

Adjourning Stage

In the **adjourning stage,** teams disband when their work is finished.

A well-integrated team is able to disband, if required, when its work is accomplished. The **adjourning stage** of team development is especially important for the many temporary teams such as task forces, committees, project teams, and the like. Their members must be able to convene quickly, do their jobs on a tight schedule, and then adjourn—often to reconvene later if needed. Their willingness to disband when the job is done and to work well together in future responsibilities, team or otherwise, is an important long-term test of team success.

Input Foundations for Teamwork

TEACHING NOTE: Have students review Figure 7.4. Ask them to a) choose a team that they have recently been part of, and b) analyze the influence that each of these input factors had on team effectiveness.

TEAM RESOURCES AND SETTING • NATURE OF THE TEAM TASK
TEAM SIZE • TEAM COMPOSITION
MEMBERSHIP DIVERSITY AND TEAM PERFORMANCE

It's common for managers and consultants to speak about the importance of having "the right players in the right seats on the same bus, headed in the same direction."[25] This wisdom is quite consistent with the findings of OB scholars. One of the ways to put it into

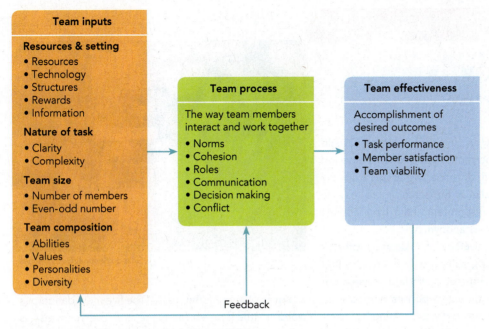

FIGURE 7.4 An open systems model of team effectiveness.

practice is to understand the open systems model presented in Figure 7.4. It shows team effectiveness being influenced by both team inputs—"right players in the right seats"—and team processes—"on the same bus, headed in the same direction."[26] You can remember the point with this equation:

Team effectiveness = Quality of inputs × (Process gains − Process losses)

As shown in the above equation, team inputs establish the initial foundations for team performance. They set the stage for how processes like communication, conflict, and decision making play out in action. And the fact is that the stronger the input foundations of a team, the more likely it is that processes will be smooth and performance will be effective. Key team inputs include resources and setting, the nature of the task, team size, and team composition.

Team Resources and Setting

Appropriate goals, well-designed reward systems, adequate resources, and appropriate technology are all essential to support the work of teams. Performance can suffer when team goals are unclear, insufficiently challenging, or arbitrarily imposed. It can also suffer if goals and rewards are focused too much on individual-level instead of group-level accomplishments. In addition, it can suffer when resources—information, budgets, work space, deadlines, rules and procedures, technologies, and the like—are insufficient to accomplish the task. By contrast, getting the right resources in place sets a strong launching pad for team success.

The importance of physical setting to teamwork is evident in the attention now being given to office architecture. Simply said, putting a team in the right workspace can go a long way toward nurturing teamwork. At SEI Investments, for example, employees work in a large, open space without cubicles or dividers. Each person has a private set of office furniture and fixtures, but everything is on wheels. Technology easily plugs and unplugs from suspended power beams that run overhead. This makes it easy for project teams to convene and disband as needed and for people to meet and converse intensely within the ebb and flow of daily work.[27]

CHECKING ETHICS IN OB

Cheat Now...
Cheat Later

A study reported by Rutgers University professor Donald McCabe found that 56 percent of MBA students reported cheating by plagiarizing, downloading essays from the Web, and more. He believes the actual figure may be higher and that some respondents held back confessions for fear of losing their anonymity.

Another study, by University of Arkansas professor Tim West and colleagues, surveyed students who had cheated on an accounting test by finding answers online. When asked why, student responses ranged from being unsure that what they did was cheating, to blaming West for giving a test that had answers available on the Web, to rationalizing that "everyone cheats" and "this is how business operates." Berkshire Hathaway

Orlando Sentinel/Getty Images

chairman Warren Buffett says, "The five most dangerous words in the English language are 'Everyone else is doing it.'" Professor Alma Acevedo of the University of Puerto Rico Rio Piedras calls this the fallacy of the "assumed authority of the majority."

What's Your Position? Is this the way business operates? Just because "everyone" may be doing something, does that make it okay for us to do it as well? How often does cheating creep into your thinking?

■ Team Task

The nature of the task is always an important team input because different tasks place different demands on teamwork. When tasks are clear and well defined, it's quite easy for members to both know what they are trying to accomplish and work together while doing it. But, team effectiveness is harder to achieve with complex tasks.[28] Such tasks require lots of information exchange and intense interaction, and everything takes place under conditions of some uncertainty. To deal well with complexity and achieve desired results, team members have to fully mobilize their talents and use the available resources well. When teams succeed with complex tasks, however, members tend to experience high satisfaction.

One way to analyze the nature of the team task is in terms of its technical and social demands. The *technical demands* of a task include the degree to which it is routine or not, the level of difficulty involved, and the information requirements. The *social demands* of a task involve the degree to which issues of interpersonal relationships, egos, controversies over ends and means, and the like come into play. Tasks that are complex in technical demands require unique solutions and more information processing. Those that are complex in social demands pose difficulties for reaching agreement on goals and methods to accomplish them.

■ Team Size

The size of a team can have an impact on team effectiveness. As a team becomes larger, more people are available to divide up the work and accomplish needed tasks. This can boost performance and member satisfaction, but only up to a point. Communication and coordination problems arise at some point because of the sheer number of linkages that must be maintained. Satisfaction may dip, and turnover, absenteeism, and social loafing

BRINGING OB TO LIFE

> "You should take off the headphones in the office, that's not the way we do things here."

Removing the Headphones to Show Team Spirit

When you put on headphones at work and tune in some nice sounds, are you tuning out team spirit? That's a question that is finding its way into more and more work settings. Maybe it's a Generation Y thing. Maybe it's just the influence of new technology on everyday living. Headphones are as common in some offices as they are on the streets. But, when someone puts on headphones, the signal being broadcast—intended or not—may be "Don't disturb!"

Willie B. Thomas/iStockphoto

Situation: Saul has just started a new job where everyone works in an open-plan office. He's just out of college and is happy and getting into his new responsibilities. A music lover, he has been wearing headphones during the day while working on the computer at his work station. Yesterday an older colleague came over and offered him some advice. "You should take off the headphones in the office," she said. "It's not the way we do things here. People are starting to say that you aren't a team player."

What Saul is bumping up against is a team culture that apparently doesn't fit well with his headphones. There's no company policy against them, but the "advice" he's getting suggests he's taking individuality a step too far in this setting.

Even though teams are built from individuals, OB recognizes that individual differences and preferences can fuel bad team dynamics. It's the type of thing that makes team leaders cringe and researchers take notice. But this situation should be manageable. The issues boil down to norms, cohesiveness, and team leadership in conditions of diversity. The new generation has pretty much grown up with headphones on. It shouldn't be too hard to find a way to fit them in at work.

---

may increase. Even logistical matters, such as finding time and locations for meetings, become more difficult for larger teams.[29]

The ideal size of creative and problem-solving teams is probably between five and seven members, or just slightly larger. Those with fewer than five may be too small to adequately share all the team responsibilities. With more than seven, individuals may find it harder to join in the discussions, contribute their talents, and offer ideas. Larger teams are also more prone to possible domination by aggressive members and have tendencies to split into coalitions or subgroups.[30] Amazon.com's founder and CEO, Jeff Bezos, is a great fan of teams. But he also has a simple rule when it comes to the size of Amazon's product development teams: No team should be larger than two pizzas can feed.[31]

When voting is required, odd-numbered teams are preferred to help rule out tie votes. When careful deliberations are required and the emphasis is more on consensus, such as in jury duty or very complex problem solving, even-numbered teams may be more effective. The even number forces members to confront disagreements and deadlocks rather than simply resolve them by majority voting.[32]

▶ Team Composition

"If you want a team to perform well, you've got to put the right members on the team to begin with." It's advice we hear a lot. There is no doubt that one of the most important

Team composition is the mix of abilities, skills, personalities, and experiences that the members bring to the team.

input factors is the **team composition**. You can think of this as the mix of abilities, personalities, backgrounds, and experiences that the members bring to the team. The basic rule of thumb for team composition is to choose members whose talents and interests fit well with the tasks to be accomplished, and whose personal characteristics increase the likelihood of being able to work well with others.

Ability counts in team composition, and it's a top priority when selecting members. The team is more likely to perform better when its members have skills and competencies that best fit task demands. Although talents alone cannot guarantee desired results, they do establish an important baseline of high performance potential. Let's not forget, however, that it takes more than raw talent to generate team success. Surely you've been on teams or observed teams where there was lots of talent but very little teamwork. A likely cause is that the blend of members caused relationship problems over everything from needs to personality to experience to age and other background characteristics.

FIRO-B theory examines differences in how people relate to one another based on their needs to express and receive feelings of inclusion, control, and affection.

Needs count too. The **FIRO-B theory** (FIRO = fundamental interpersonal relations orientation) identifies differences in how people relate to one another in groups based on their needs to express and receive feelings of inclusion, control, and affection.[33] Developed by William Schultz, the theory suggests that teams whose members have compatible needs are likely to be more effective than teams whose members are more incompatible. Symptoms of incompatibilities include withdrawn members, open hostilities, struggles over control, and domination by a few members. Schultz states the management implications of the FIRO–B theory this way: "If at the outset we can choose a group of people who can work together harmoniously, we shall go far toward avoiding situations where a group's efforts are wasted in interpersonal conflicts."[34]

Status congruence involves consistency between a person's status within and outside a group.

Another issue in team composition is status in terms relative rank, prestige, or social standing. **Status congruence** occurs when a person's position within the team is equivalent in status to positions the individual holds outside of it. Any status incongruence may create problems. Consider something that is increasingly common today—generationally blended teams. Things may not go smoothly, for example, when a young college graduate is asked to head a project team on social media and whose members largely include senior and more experienced workers.

▶ Membership Diversity and Team Performance

Diversity is always an important aspect of team composition. The presence of different values, personalities, experiences, demographics, and cultures among members can bring both opportunities and problems.[35]

In **homogeneous teams** members share many similar characteristics.

Teamwork usually isn't much of a problem in **homogeneous teams** where members are very similar to one another. The members typically find it quite easy to work together and enjoy the team experience. Yet, researchers warn about the risks of homogeneity.

Cross-Cultural Teamwork Finds a Home in Officeless Companies

Automattic Inc. has 123 employees. They work in 26 countries, 94 cities, and 28 U.S. states. So where is the headquarters? Well, it's really nowhere and everywhere. At this Web services company, everyone works from their home. The term "officeless" is used to describe a growing number of firms that operate this way. With Internet chat, Skype, and other technologies—including the telephone—people can easily work together across time and distance. Add in new advances in social media and cloud computing and it's almost a no-brainer. Being officeless can be a real boon for cross-cultural teams, making virtual meetings and teamwork commonplace. Instead of waiting for scheduled travel, the team is available at the touch of a screen or keyboard.

© Thomas Rodriguez/Corbis

Although it may seem logical that having members similar to one another is an asset, it doesn't necessarily work out that way. Research points out that teams composed of members who are highly similar in background, training, and experience often underperform even though the members may enjoy a sense of harmony and feel very comfortable with one another.[36]

Teamwork problems are likely in **heterogeneous teams** where members are very dissimilar to one another. The mix of diverse personalities, experiences, backgrounds, ages, and other personal characteristics may create difficulties as members try to define problems, share information, mobilize talents, and deal with obstacles or opportunities. Nevertheless, if—and this is a big "if"—members can work well together, the diversity can be a source of advantage and enhanced performance potential.[37]

Team process and performance difficulties due to diversity issues are especially likely to occur in the initial stages of team development. The so-called **diversity–consensus dilemma** is the tendency for diversity to make it harder for team members to work together, especially in the early stages of their team lives, even though the diversity itself expands the skills and perspectives available for problem solving.[38] These dilemmas may be most pronounced in the critical zone of the storming and norming stages of development as described in Figure 7.5. Problems may occur as interpersonal stresses and conflicts emerge from the heterogeneity. The challenge to team effectiveness is to take advantage of diversity without suffering process disadvantages.[39]

Working through the diversity–consensus dilemma can slow team development and impede relationship building, information sharing, and problem solving.[40] Some teams get stuck here and can't overcome their process problems. If and when such difficulties are resolved, diverse teams can emerge from the critical zone with effectiveness and often outperform less diverse ones. Research also shows that the most creative teams include a mix of old-timers and newcomers.[41] The old-timers have the experience and connections; the newcomers bring in new talents and fresh thinking.

The diversity and performance relationship is evident in research on **collective intelligence**—the ability of a group or team to perform well across a range of tasks.[42] Researchers have found only a slight correlation between average or maximum individual member intelligence and the collective intelligence of teams. But, they find strong correlations between collective intelligence and two process variables—social sensitivities within the teams and absence of conversational domination by a few members. Furthermore, collective intelligence is associated with gender diversity, specifically the proportion of females on the team. This finding also links to process, with researchers pointing out that females in their studies scored higher than males on social sensitivity.

In **heterogeneous teams** members differ in many characteristics.

Diversity–consensus dilemma is the tendency for diversity in groups to create process difficulties even as it offers improved potential for problem solving.

Collective intelligence is the ability of a team to perform well across a range of tasks.

FIGURE 7.5 Member diversity, stages of team development, and team performance.

7 Study Guide

Key Questions and Answers

What are teams, and how are they used in organizations?

- A team is a group of people working together to achieve a common purpose for which they hold themselves collectively accountable.
- Teams help organizations by improving task performance; teams help members experience satisfaction from their work.
- Teams in organizations serve different purposes—some teams run things, some teams recommend things, and some teams make or do things.
- Organizations consist of formal teams that are designated by the organization to serve an official purpose, as well as informal groups that emerge from special relationships but are not part of the formal structure.
- Organizations can be viewed as interlocking networks of permanent teams such as project teams and cross-functional teams, as well as temporary teams such as committees and task forces.
- Members of self-managing teams typically plan, complete, and evaluate their own work, train and evaluate one another in job tasks, and share tasks and responsibilities.
- Virtual teams, whose members meet and work together through computer mediation, are increasingly common and pose special management challenges.

When is a team effective?

- An effective team achieves high levels of task accomplishment, member satisfaction, and viability to perform successfully over the long term.
- Teams help organizations through synergy in task performance, the creation of a whole that is greater than the sum of its parts.
- Teams help satisfy important needs for their members by providing them with things like job support and social interactions.
- Team performance can suffer from social loafing when a member slacks off and lets others do the work.
- Social facilitation occurs when the behavior of individuals is influenced positively or negatively by the presence of others on a team.

What are the stages of team development?

- In the forming stage, team members come together and form initial impressions; it is a time of task orientation and interpersonal testing.
- In the storming stage, team members struggle to deal with expectations and status; it is a time when conflicts over tasks and how the team works are likely.
- In the norming or initial integration stage, team members start to come together around rules of behavior and what needs to be accomplished; it is a time of growing cooperation.
- In the performing or total integration stage, team members are well organized and well functioning; it is a time of team maturity when performance of even complex tasks becomes possible.
- In the adjourning stage, team members achieve closure on task performance and their personal relationships; it is a time of managing task completion and the process of disbanding.

How can we understand teams at work?

- Teams are open systems that interact with their environments to obtain resources that are transformed into outputs.
- The equation summarizing the open systems model for team performance is this:
  Team effectiveness = Quality of inputs × (Process gains − Process losses)
- Input factors such as resources and setting, nature of the task, team size, and team composition, establish the core performance foundations of a team.
- Team processes include basic group or team dynamics that show up as the ways members work together to use inputs and complete tasks.

Terms to Know

Adjourning stage (p. 152)
Collective intelligence (p. 157)
Cross-functional team (p. 144)
Diversity–consensus dilemma (p. 157)
Effective team (p. 148)
Employee involvement team (p. 144)
FIRO-B theory (p. 156)
Formal teams (p. 143)
Forming stage (p. 151)
Functional silos problem (p. 144)
Heterogeneous teams (p. 157)
Homogeneous teams (p. 156)
Informal groups (p. 143)
Multiskilling (p. 145)
Norming stage (p. 151)
Performing stage (p. 152)
Problem-solving team (p. 144)
Quality circle (p. 145)
Self-managing team (p. 145)
Social facilitation (p. 148)
Social loafing (p. 149)
Social network analysis (p. 143)
Status congruence (p. 156)
Storming stage (p. 151)
Synergy (p. 148)
Team (p. 142)
Team composition (p. 156)
Teamwork (p. 142)
Virtual team (p. 146)

Self-Test 7

Multiple Choice

1. The FIRO-B theory deals with _____ in teams.
   (a) membership compatibilities
   (b) social loafing
   (c) dominating members
   (d) conformity

2. It is during the _____ stage of team development that members begin to come together as a coordinated unit.
   (a) storming
   (b) norming
   (c) performing
   (d) total integration

3. An effective team is defined as one that achieves high levels of task performance, member satisfaction, and _____.
   (a) coordination
   (b) harmony
   (c) creativity
   (d) team viability

4. Task characteristics, reward systems, and team size are all _____ that can make a difference in team effectiveness.
   (a) processes
   (b) dynamics
   (c) inputs
   (d) rewards

5. The best size for a problem-solving team is usually _____ members.
   (a) no more than 3 or 4
   (b) 5 to 7
   (c) 8 to 10
   (d) around 12 to 13

6. When a new team member is anxious about questions such as "Will I be able to influence what takes place?" the underlying issue is one of _____.
   (a) relationships
   (b) goals
   (c) processes
   (d) control

7. Self-managing teams _____.
   (a) reduce the number of different job tasks members need to master
   (b) largely eliminate the need for a traditional supervisor
   (c) rely heavily on outside training to maintain job skills
   (d) add another management layer to overhead costs

8. Which statement about self-managing teams is most accurate?
   (a) They always improve performance but not satisfaction.
   (b) They should have limited decision-making authority.
   (c) They operate with elected team leaders.
   (d) They should let members plan and control their own work.

9. When a team of people is able to achieve more than what its members could by working individually, this is called _____.
   (a) distributed leadership
   (b) consensus
   (c) team viability
   (d) synergy

10. Members of a team tend to become more motivated and better able to deal with conflict during the _____ stage of team development.
    (a) forming
    (b) norming
    (c) performing
    (d) adjourning

11. The Ringlemann effect describes _____.
    (a) the tendency of groups to make risky decisions
    (b) social loafing
    (c) social facilitation
    (d) the satisfaction of members' social needs

12. Members of a multinational task force in a large international business should probably be aware that _____ might initially slow the progress of the team.
    (a) synergy
    (b) groupthink
    (c) the diversity–consensus dilemma
    (d) intergroup dynamics

13. When a team member engages in social loafing, one of the recommended strategies for dealing with this situation is to _____.
    (a) forget about it
    (b) ask another member to force this person to work harder
    (c) give the person extra rewards and hope he or she will feel guilty
    (d) better define member roles to improve individual accountability

14. When a person holds a prestigious position as a vice president in a top management team, but is considered just another member of an employee involvement team that a lower-level supervisor heads, the person might experience _____.
    (a) role underload   (b) role overload
    (c) status incongruence   (d) the diversity–consensus dilemma

15. The team effectiveness equation states: Team effectiveness = _____ × (Process gains − Process losses).
    (a) Nature of setting   (b) Nature of task
    (c) Quality of inputs   (d) Available rewards

Short Response

16. In what ways are teams good for organizations?
17. What types of formal teams are found in organizations today?
18. What are members of self-managing teams typically expected to do?
19. What is the diversity–consensus dilemma?

Applications Essay

20. One of your Facebook friends has posted this note: "Help! I have just been assigned to head a new product design team at my company. The division manager has high expectations for the team and me, but I have been a technical design engineer for four years since graduating from college. I have never 'managed' anyone, let alone led a team. The manager keeps talking about her confidence that I will be very good at creating lots of teamwork. Does anyone out there have any tips to help me master this challenge?" You smile while reading the message and start immediately to formulate your recommendations. Exactly what message will you send?

Steps to Further Learning 7
Top Choices from *The OB Skills Workbook*

These learning activities from *The OB Skills Workbook* found at the back of the book are suggested for Chapter 7.

Case for Critical Thinking	Team and Experiential Exercises	Self-Assessment Portfolio
• The Forgotten Team Member	• Sweet Tooth • Interrogatories • Teamwork and Motivation • Serving on the Boundary • *Eggs*periential Exercise	• Team Effectiveness • Decision-Making Biases

Teams are worth the hard work

8

Teamwork and Team Performance

The Key Point

In order for any virtual or face-to-face team to work well and do great things, its members must get things right. This means paying attention to accomplishments and building strong team processes. Team performance can't be left to chance. For sure teams can be hard work, but they're also worth the effort. ■

What's Inside?

- **Bringing OB to LIFE**
  WELCOMING THE ELEPHANT TO THE CONFERENCE ROOM
- **Worth Considering . . . or Best Avoided?**
  TEAMMATES MAY KNOW YOU BEST. SHOULD THEY PAY YOU AS WELL?
- **Checking Ethics in OB**
  SOCIAL LOAFING MAY BE CLOSER THAN YOU THINK
- **Finding the Leader in You**
  AMAZON'S JEFF BEZOS HARNESSES TEAMWORK TO DRIVE INNOVATION
- **OB in Popular Culture**
  GROUPTHINK AND *MADAGASCAR*
- **Research Insight**
  DEMOGRAPHIC FAULTLINES POSE IMPLICATIONS FOR LEADING TEAMS IN ORGANIZATIONS

Chapter at a Glance

- What Are High-Performance Teams?
- How Can Team Processes Be Improved?
- How Can Team Communications Be Improved?
- How Can Team Decisions Be Improved?

163

> **TEACHING NOTE:** Ask students to review the text discussion of team building. Next pose the following discussion question: How can team building be accomplished in virtual versus face-to-face teams. Push them for specifics and solid, usable suggestions.

High-Performance Teams

LEARNING ROADMAP — CHARACTERISTICS OF HIGH-PERFORMANCE TEAMS • THE TEAM-BUILDING PROCESS • TEAM-BUILDING ALTERNATIVES

Are you an iPad, Kindle Fire, Samsung Galaxy, or Google Nexus user? Have you ever wondered why the companies behind these products keep giving us a stream of innovative and trend-setting choices?

In many ways today's smartphone and tablet stories started years ago with Apple, Inc., its co-founder Steve Jobs, the first Macintosh computer, and a very special team. The "Mac" was Jobs's brainchild. To create it, he put together a team of high achievers who were excited and motivated by a highly challenging task. They worked all hours and at an unrelenting pace free from Apple's normal bureaucracy. Team members combined high talent with commitment to an exciting goal: change the world through computing. They ended up setting a benchmark for high-tech product innovation as well as new standards for what makes for a high-performance team.[1]

The smartphone, tablet, and notebook computer industry today is crowded and very competitive. But you can bet that all the players follow some version of the original Apple model, making their firms hotbeds of high-performing teams that harness great talents to achieve innovation. But even as we celebrate great teams and the teamwork that drives them, scholar J. Richard Hackman warns that many teams in organizations underperform and fail to live up to their potential. He says that they simply "don't work."[2] The question for us is: What differentiates high-performing teams from the also-rans?

Characteristics of High-Performance Teams

It's quite easy to agree on must-have team leadership skills like those described in the "Teams Gain from Great Leaders . . ." sidebar. It also makes sense that having a leader set a clear and challenging team direction is at the top of the list.[3] Again, Apple's original Macintosh story gives us an example. After getting a sneak look at what he had been told was the "machine that was supposed to change the world," *Wired* magazine's Steven Levy wrote: "I also met the people who created that machine. They were groggy and almost giddy from three years of creation. Their eyes blazed with Visine and fire. They told me that with Macintosh, they were going to 'put a dent in the Universe.' Their leader, Steven P. Jobs, told them so. They also told me how Jobs referred to this new computer: 'Insanely Great.'"[4]

High-performing teams have members who believe in team goals and are motivated to work hard to accomplish them. They feel "collectively accountable" for moving in what Hackman calls "a compelling direction." Getting to this point isn't always easy. All too often a team's members don't agree on the goal and don't share an understanding of what the team is supposed to accomplish.[5]

Whereas a shared sense of purpose gives general direction to a team, commitment to targeted—

Teams Gain from Great Leaders and Talented Members Who Do the Right Things

- Set a clear and challenging direction
- Keep goals and expectations clear
- Communicate high standards
- Create a sense of urgency
- Make sure members have the right skills
- Model positive team member behaviors
- Create early performance "successes"
- Introduce useful information
- Help members share useful information
- Give positive feedback

Helen King/©Corbis Images

not general or vague—performance results makes this purpose truly meaningful. High-performance teams turn a general sense of purpose into specific performance objectives. They set standards for taking action, measuring results, and gathering performance feedback. They also provide a clear focus when team members have to find common ground to solve problems and resolve conflicts.

Talent is essential. High-performance teams have members with the right mix of skills—technical, problem-solving, and interpersonal. Values count too. High-performance teams have strong core values that help guide team members' attitudes and behaviors in consistent directions. These values act as an internal control system that keeps team members on track without outside direction and supervisory attention.

The concept of **collective intelligence** applies in a high-performance team. Think of it as the ability of a team to do well on a wide variety of tasks. It fuels a team to excel not just once, but over and over again. Researchers point out that collective intelligence is higher in teams whose processes are not dominated by one or a few members. Collective intelligence is also higher on teams having more female members, a finding researchers link to higher social sensitivity in team dynamics.[6]

Collective intelligence is the ability of a team to perform well across a range of tasks.

▶ The Team-Building Process

Coaches and managers in the sports world spend a lot of time at the start of each season joining new members with old ones and forming a strong team. Yet, we all know that even the most experienced teams can run into problems as a season progresses. Members slack off or become disgruntled with one another; some have performance "slumps," and others criticize them for it; some are traded gladly or unhappily to other teams.

Even world-champion teams have losing streaks. At times even the most talented players can lose motivation, quibble among themselves, and end up contributing little to team success. When such things happen, concerned owners, managers, and players are apt to examine their problems, take corrective action to rebuild the team, and restore the teamwork needed to achieve high-performance results.[7]

Work teams face similar challenges. When newly formed, they must master many challenges as members learn how to work together while passing through the stages of team development. Even when mature, most work teams encounter problems of insufficient teamwork at different points in time. At the very least we can say that teams sometimes need help to perform well and that teamwork always needs to be nurtured.

Boot Camps Help Start Entrepreneurial Teams on the Fast Track

Picture this. A number of people sit around a table playing poker. Are they gambling for fun? No, according to James Barlow, director of entrepreneurial leadership at Tufts University, they are aspiring entrepreneurs learning about team risk taking. How about working together to assemble jigsaw puzzles? It's an exercise in team problem solving. What's happening here is a boot camp for entrepreneurs, one that helps them step back from start-up enterprises and reconsider their directions in a team environment. One participant at a camp led by Barlow says, "The luxury of being away from campus or the field and being able to immerse yourself in this thinking for five days nonstop with your team members is a rarity."

Fabrizio Costantini/Redux Pictures

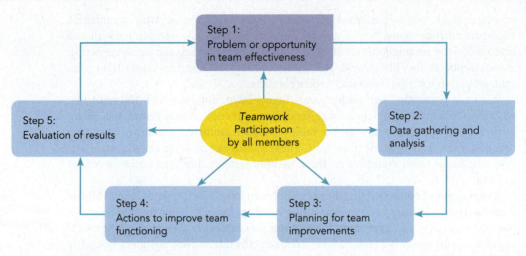

FIGURE 8.1 Steps in the team-building process.

Team building is a collaborative way to gather and analyze data to improve teamwork.

The occasional need for a performance "tune up" is why a process known as **team building** is so important. It is a sequence of planned activities designed to gather and analyze data on the functioning of a team and to initiate changes designed to improve teamwork and increase team effectiveness.[8] When done well and at the right times, team building can be a good way to deal with actual or potential teamwork problems.

The action steps for team building are highlighted in Figure 8.1. Although it is tempting to view the process as something that consultants or outside experts are hired to do, the fact is that it can and should be part of any team leader and manager's skill set.

Team building begins when someone notices an actual or a potential problem with team effectiveness. Data are gathered to examine the problem. This can be done by questionnaire, interview, nominal group meeting, or other creative methods. The goal is to get good answers to such questions as "How well are we doing in terms of task accomplishment?" "How satisfied are we as individuals with the group and the way it operates?" After the answers to such questions are analyzed by team members, they then work together to plan for and accomplish improvements. This team-building process is highly collaborative and participation by all members is essential.

Team-Building Alternatives

One fall day, a team of employees from American Electric Power (AEP) went to an outdoor camp. They worked on problems such as how to get six members through a spider-web maze of bungee cords strung 2 feet above the ground. When her colleagues lifted Judy Gallo into their hands to pass her over the obstacle, she was nervous. A trainer addressed her anxiety by telling the team this was just like solving a problem together at the office. The spider web was just another performance constraint, like the difficult policy issues or financial limits they might face at work. After high-fives for making it through the web, Judy's team jumped tree stumps together, passed hula hoops while holding hands, and more. Says one outdoor team trainer, "We throw clients into situations to try and bring out the traits of a good team."[9]

This was an example of the *outdoor experience approach* to team building. It is increasingly popular and can be done on its own or in combination with other approaches. The outdoor experience places teams in a variety of physically challenging situations. By having to work together to master difficult obstacles, team members are supposed to grow in self-confidence, gain more respect for each others' capabilities, and leave with a greater capacity for and commitment to teamwork.

In the *formal retreat approach*, team building takes place during an off-site retreat. The agenda, which may cover one or more days, is designed to engage team members in the variety of assessment and planning tasks. Formal retreats are often held with the assistance of a consultant, who is either hired from the outside or made available from in-house staff. Team-building retreats are opportunities to take time away from the job to assess team accomplishments, operations, and future potential.

In a *continuous improvement approach*, the manager, team leader, or group members themselves take responsibility for regularly engaging in the team-building process. This method can be as simple as periodic meetings that implement the team-building steps; it can also include self-managed formal retreats. In all cases, the goal is to engage team members in a process that leaves them more capable and committed to continuous performance assessment and improved teamwork.

Improving Team Processes

LEARNING ROADMAP ENTRY OF NEW MEMBERS • ROLES AND ROLE DYNAMICS • TASK AND MAINTENANCE LEADERSHIP • TEAM NORMS • TEAM COHESIVENESS • INTER-TEAM DYNAMICS

Team building should be an ongoing concern for leaders and members alike. It's a way of updating and strengthening the processes through which people work together in teams, something often called **team or group dynamics**. These are forces operating in teams that affect the way members relate to and work with one another.[10] They are especially important and at risk when teams are taking on new members, addressing disagreements on goals and responsibilities, resolving decision-making delays and disputes, reducing personality friction, and managing conflicts.

TEACHING NOTE: Have students read the Research Insight feature on group fault lines. Ask for examples of fault line experiences they have had in teams. Use the examples to engage a discussion of how fault line situations can best be handled by team leaders and team members alike.

Team or group dynamics are the forces operating in teams that affect the ways members work together.

▬ Entry of New Members

Special team process difficulties are likely to occur when members first get together in a new group or team, or when new members join an existing team. Problems arise as new members try to understand what is expected of them while dealing with the anxiety and discomfort of a new social setting. New members, for example, may worry about any of the following:

◂ New member concerns in teams

- *Participation*—"Will I be allowed to participate?"
- *Goals*—"Do I share the same goals as others?"
- *Control*—"Will I be able to influence what takes place?"
- *Relationships*—"How close do people get?"
- *Processes*—"Are conflicts likely to be upsetting?"

Scholar and consultant Edgar Schein points out that people may try to cope with individual entry problems in self-serving ways that may hinder team development and performance.[11] He identifies three behavior profiles that are common in such situations.

Tough Battler The *tough battler* is frustrated by a lack of identity in the new group and may act aggressively or reject authority. This person wants answers to this question: "Who am I in this group?" The best team response may be to allow the new member to share his or her skills and interests, and then have a discussion about how these qualities can best be used to help the team.

Friendly Helper The *friendly helper* is insecure, suffering uncertainties of intimacy and control. This person may show extraordinary support for others, behave in a dependent way, and seek alliances in subgroups or cliques. The friendly helper needs to know whether he or she will be liked. The best team response may be to offer support and encouragement while encouraging the new member to be more confident in joining team activities and discussions.

Objective Thinker The *objective thinker* is anxious about how personal needs will be met in the group. This person may act in a passive, reflective, and even single-minded manner while struggling with the fit between individual goals and group directions. The best team response may be to engage in a discussion to clarify team goals and expectations, and to clarify member roles in meeting them.

Roles and Role Dynamics

New and old team members alike need to know what others expect of them and what they can expect from others. A **role** is a set of expectations associated with a job or position on a team. We know that teams tend to perform better when their members have clear and realistic expectations about one another's tasks and responsibilities. When team members are unclear about their roles or face conflicting role demands, process problems are likely and team effectiveness can suffer. Although this is a common situation, it can be managed with proper attention to role dynamics and their causes.

Role ambiguity occurs when a person is uncertain about his or her role or job on a team. Role ambiguities may create problems as team members find that their work efforts are wasted or unappreciated. This can even happen in mature groups if team members fail to share expectations and listen to one another's concerns.

Being asked to do too much or too little as a team member can also create problems. **Role overload** occurs when too much is expected and someone feels overwhelmed. **Role underload** occurs when too little is expected and the individual feels underused. Both role overload and role underload can cause stress, dissatisfaction, and performance problems.

Role conflict occurs when a person is unable to meet the expectations of others. The individual understands what needs to be done but for some reason cannot comply. The resulting tension is stressful and can reduce satisfaction. It can affect an individual's performance and relationships with other group members. People at work and in teams can experience four common forms of role conflict:

- *Intrasender role conflict* occurs when the same person sends conflicting expectations. Example: Team leader—"You need to get the report written right away, but now I need you to help me get the PowerPoints ready."
- *Intersender role conflict* occurs when different people send conflicting and mutually exclusive expectations. Example: Team leader (to you)—"Your job is to criticize our decisions so that we don't make mistakes." Team member (to you)—"You always seem so negative. Can't you be more positive for a change?"
- *Person–role conflict* occurs when a person's values and needs come into conflict with role expectations. Example: Other team members (showing agreement with each other)—"We didn't get enough questionnaires back, so let's each fill out five more and add them to the data set." You (to yourself)—"Mmm, I don't think this is right."
- *Inter-role conflict* occurs when the expectations of two or more roles held by the same individual become incompatible, such as the conflict between work and family demands. Example: Team leader—"Don't forget the big meeting we have scheduled for Thursday evening." You (to yourself)—"But my daughter is playing in her first little-league soccer game at that same time."

A technique known as **role negotiation** is a helpful way of managing role dynamics. It's a process whereby team members meet to discuss, clarify, and agree on the role expectations each holds for the other. Such a negotiation might begin, for example, with one member writing down this request of another: "If you were to do the following, it would help me to improve my performance on the team." Her list of requests might include such specifics as "Respect it when I say that I can't meet some evenings because I have family obligations to fulfill"—indicating role conflict; "Stop asking for so much detail when we are working hard with tight deadlines"—indicating role overload; and "Try to make yourself available when I need to speak with you to clarify goals and expectations"—indicating role ambiguity.

> **Role negotiation** is a process for discussing and agreeing on what team members expect of one another.

Task and Maintenance Leadership

Research in social psychology suggests that teams have both task needs and maintenance needs, and that both must be met for teams to be successful.[12] Even though a team leader should be able to meet these needs at the appropriate times, each team member is responsible as well. This sharing of responsibilities for making task and maintenance contributions to move a team forward is called **distributed leadership**. And, it is well evidenced in high-performance teams.

Figure 8.2 describes **task activities** as what team members and leaders do that directly contribute to the performance of important group tasks. They include initiating discussion, sharing information, asking information of others, clarifying something that has been said, and summarizing the status of a deliberation.[13] A team will have difficulty accomplishing its objectives when task activities are not well performed. In an effective team, by contrast, all members pitch in to contribute important task leadership as needed.

> **Distributed leadership** shares responsibility among members for meeting team task and maintenance needs.
>
> **Task activities** directly contribute to the performance of important tasks.

Figure 8.2 also shows that **maintenance activities** support the social and interpersonal relationships among team members. They help a team stay intact and healthy as an ongoing and well-functioning social system. A team member or leader can contribute maintenance leadership by encouraging the participation of others, trying to harmonize differences of opinion, praising the contributions of others, and agreeing to go along with a popular course of action. When maintenance leadership is poor, members become dissatisfied with one another, the value of their group membership diminishes, and emotional conflicts may drain energies otherwise needed for task performance. In an effective team, by contrast, maintenance activities support the relationships needed for team members to work well together over time.

> **Maintenance activities** support the emotional life of the team as an ongoing social system.

In addition to helping meet a group's task and maintenance needs, team members share additional responsibility for avoiding and eliminating any **disruptive behaviors** that harm the group process. These dysfunctional activities include bullying and being overly aggressive toward other members, showing incivility and disrespect, withdrawing and refusing to cooperate, horsing around when there is work to be done, using meetings as forums for self-confession, talking too much about irrelevant matters, and trying to

> **Disruptive behaviors** in teams harm the group process and limit team effectiveness.

FIGURE 8.2 Task and maintenance leadership in team dynamics.

Research Insight

Demographic Faultlines Pose Implications for Leading Teams in Organizations

According to researchers Dora Lau and Keith Murnighan, strong "faultlines" occur in groups when demographic diversity results in the formation of two or more subgroups whose members are similar to and strongly identify with one another. Examples include teams with subgroups forming around age, gender, race, ethnic, occupational, or tenure differences. When strong faultlines are present, members are expected to identify more strongly with their subgroups than with the team as a whole. Lau and Murnighan predict that this will affect what happens with the team in terms of conflict, politics, and performance.

Using subjects from ten organizational behavior classes at a university, the researchers randomly assigned students to casework groups based on sex and ethnicity. After working on their cases, group members completed questionnaires about group processes and outcomes. Results showed, as predicted, that members in strong faultline groups evaluated those in their subgroups more favorably than did members of weak faultline groups. Members of weak faultline groups also experienced less conflict, more psychological safety, and more satisfaction than did those in strong faultline groups. More communication across faultlines had a positive effect on outcomes for weak faultline groups but not for strong faultline groups.

Strong faultline group
members identify more with subgroups than team
- more conflict
- less sense of safety
- less team satisfaction

Weak faultline group
members identify more with team than subgroups
- less conflict
- more sense of safety
- more team satisfaction

Do the Research See if you can verify these findings. Be a "participant observer" in your work teams. Focus on faultlines and their effects. Keep a diary, make notes, and compare your experiences with this study in mind.

Source: Dora C. Lau and J. Keith Murnighan, "Interactions within Groups and Subgroups: The Effects of Demographic Faultlines," *Academy of Management Journal* 48 (2005), pp. 645–659; and "Demographic Diversity and Faultlines: The Compositional Dynamics of Organizational Groups," *Academy of Management Review* 23 (1998), pp. 325–340.

---

compete for attention and recognition. *Incivility* or *antisocial behavior* by members can be especially disruptive of team dynamics and performance. Research shows that persons who are targets of harsh leadership, social exclusion, and harmful rumors often end up working less hard, performing less well, being late and absent more, and reducing their commitment.[14]

Team Norms

The entry issues, role dynamics, and task and maintenance needs we have just discussed all relate to what team members expect of one another and of themselves. This brings up the issue of team **norms**—beliefs about how members are expected to behave. They can be considered as rules or standards of team conduct.[15] Norms help members to guide their own behavior and predict what others will do. When someone violates a team

Norms are rules or standards for the behavior of group members.

| WORTH CONSIDERING | ...OR BEST AVOIDED? |

Teammates May Know You Best. Should They Pay You As Well?

Picture this. A group of fifteen co-workers is given a pool of 1,200 stock options to distribute among themselves as their annual bonuses. The only rule is you can't give any to yourself. The idea is that teammates know one another best and know who deserves to be recognized at raise time. In fact, they may notice what managers don't and thus reward people who would otherwise be missed. "Who knows better than employees themselves who the contributors are or [who is] the go-to person with a technical problem?" asks management professor Denise Rousseau.

This example is real. It's from Coffee & Power, a San Francisco start-up. It was initiated by entrepreneur and co-founder Philip Rosedale. His notion is that workers should be allowed to invest in their co-workers and financially reward them for performance and contributions. Becky Neil, a marketing employee at the firm, says the approach "lets me reward people that management may not always recognize."

No one knows who gives who the options, but they do get a report on the highest and lowest options grants with no names attached. Neil points out that it was "nerve wracking" as she waited to find out what others gave her and was "psyched" to learn if her self-evaluation matched theirs. "You don't always know what other people think of you,". she says.

Helder Almeida/Shutterstock

Do the Analysis

Does theory support the practice in this case? What is your gut reaction to this approach to pay: positive or negative or in between? In what types of situations might this practice work best? When should it be avoided altogether? Could the Coffee & Power version be modified in any way to make it a smoother fit elsewhere?

---

norm, other members typically respond in ways that are aimed at enforcing it and bring behavior back into alignment with the norm. These responses may include subtle hints, direct criticisms, and even reprimands. At the extreme, someone violating team norms may be ostracized or even expelled.

Types of Team Norms
A key norm in any team setting is the **performance norm**. It conveys expectations about how hard team members should work and what the team should accomplish. In some teams, the performance norm is high and strong. There is no doubt that all members are expected to work very hard and that high performance is the goal. If someone slacks off, they get reminded to work hard or end up removed from the team. In other teams, the performance norm is low and weak; members are left to work hard or not as they like, with little concern shown by the other members.

Many other norms also influence the day-to-day functioning of teams. Norms regarding attendance at meetings, punctuality, preparedness, criticism, and social behavior are important. So, too, are norms on how members deal with supervisors, colleagues, and customers, as well as norms about honesty and ethical behavior. Consider the following

The **performance norm** sets expectations for how hard members work and what the team should accomplish.

examples of norms that can have positive and negative implications for team processes and effectiveness:[16]

Common team norms ▶

- *Ethics norms*—"We try to make ethical decisions, and we expect others to do the same" (positive); "Don't worry about inflating your expense account; everyone does it here" (negative).
- *Organizational and personal pride norms*—"It's a tradition around here for people to stand up for the company when others criticize it unfairly" (positive); "In our company, they are always trying to take advantage of us" (negative).
- *High-achievement norms*—"On our team, people always want to win or be the best" (positive); "No one really cares on this team whether we win or lose" (negative).
- *Support and helpfulness norms*—"People on this committee are good listeners and actively seek out the ideas and opinions of others" (positive); "On this committee it's dog-eat-dog and save your own skin" (negative).
- *Improvement and change norms*—"In our department people are always looking for better ways of doing things" (positive); "Around here, people hang on to the old ways even after they have outlived their usefulness" (negative).

CHECKING ETHICS IN OB

Social Loafing May Be Closer Than You Think

Tetra Images/Getty Images, Inc.

- *Psychology study:* A German researcher asked people to pull on a rope as hard as they could. First, they pulled alone. Second, they pulled as part of a group. Results showed that people pull harder when working alone than when working as part of a team. Such social loafing is the tendency to reduce effort when working in groups.
- *Faculty office:* A student wants to speak with the instructor about his team's performance on the last group project. There were four members, but two did almost all of the work. The other two largely disappeared, showing up only at the last minute to be part of the formal presentation. His point is that the team was disadvantaged because the two free-riders caused reduced performance capacity for his team.
- *Telephone call from the boss:* "John, I really need you to serve on this committee. Will you do it? Let me know tomorrow." John thinks, "I'm overloaded, but I don't want to turn down the boss. I'll accept but let the committee members know about my limits. I'll be active in discussions and try to offer viewpoints and perspectives that are helpful. However, I'll tell them up front that I can't be a leader or volunteer for any extra work." Some might say this is an excuse to "slack off while still doing what the boss wants." John views it as being honest.

You Decide
Whether you call it social loafing, free-riding or just plain old slacking off, the issue is the same: What right do some people have to sit back in team situations and let other people do all the work? Is this ethical? Does everyone on a team have an ethical obligation to do his or her fair share of the work? Why isn't this always the norm? Regarding John, does the fact that he is going to be honest with the other committee members make any difference? Isn't he still going to be a loafer, and yet earn credit with the boss for serving on the committee? Would it be more ethical for John to decline becoming a part of this committee?

How to Influence Team Norms Team leaders and members can do several things to help their teams develop positive norms that foster high performance as well as membership satisfaction. The first thing is to always *act as a positive role model*. In other words, be the exemplar of the norm, always living up to the norm in everyday behavior. It is helpful to hold meetings where time is set aside to *discuss team goals* and also *discuss team norms* that can best contribute to their achievement. Norms are too important to be left to chance. The more directly they are discussed and confronted in the early stages of team development, the better.

It's always best to *select members who can and will live up to the desired norms*. They should be given the *right training and support*, and their *rewards should positively reinforce desired behaviors*. Finally, teams should remember the power of team building and *hold regular meetings to discuss team performance and plan how to improve* it in the future. This is a full-cycle approach to developing positive team norms: select the right people, provide them support, give positive reinforcement for doing things right, and continuously review progress and make constructive adjustments.

BRINGING OB TO LIFE

> "The 'elephant room' is where people go to work things out face to face. When you are in the room, nothing is to be held back and full transparency is expected."

Welcoming the Elephant to the Conference Room

It's called "passive aggression." An example is walking away from a disagreement with a friend or colleague only to turn around and attack them via e-mail. The impersonal e-mail seems to be a more comfortable medium for engaging conflict than face-to-face confrontation. However, the price may be bad problem solving, lost creativity, and poor interpersonal and team dynamics.

That price was too high for Paul English, chief technology officer at the travel website Kayak.com. Things were moving too fast at his growing firm, and he couldn't afford to have team members holding back with one another and failing to work through problems in real time. The open office design wasn't helping. So much public space seemed to make it harder to express and discuss disagreements. "So often at work," he says, "people have issues they can't resolve because they won't talk about it."

English realized people needed a space where uncomfortable disagreements could be addressed and resolved across the table. He responded by buying a stuffed elephant, naming her Annabelle, and putting her in a prominent place in a glass-walled conference room. Called "the elephant room," it's where people go to work things out face to face. English believes Annabelle "sends a positive signal to people that you are interested in sorting out problems." When you are in the room,

Gualtiero Boffi/Shutterstock

nothing is to be held back and full transparency is expected. After all, the elephant is in the room, not outside it.

Teamwork isn't easy and sometimes a simple structural solution like the elephant room can make it easier to engage in a bit of constructive conflict. The insights of OB don't only apply to training people to better deal with motives, emotions, and interpersonal relations. They also remind us that sometimes the best approach to difficult situations is to give people a better opportunity to do the right thing.

Team Cohesiveness

Cohesiveness is the degree to which members are attracted to a group and motivated to remain a part of it.

The **cohesiveness** of a group or team is the degree to which members are attracted to and motivated to remain part of it.[17] We might think of it as the feel-good factor that causes people to value their membership on a team, positively identify with it, and strive to maintain positive relationships with other members. Feelings of cohesion can be a source of need satisfaction, often providing a source of loyalty, security, and esteem for team members. Because cohesive teams are such a source of personal satisfaction, their members tend to be energetic when working on team activities, less likely to be absent, less likely to quit the team, and more likely to be happy about performance success and sad about failures.

Team Cohesiveness and Conformity to Norms

Even though cohesive teams are good for their members, they may or may not be good for the organization. The question is this: Will the cohesive team also be a high-performance team? The answer to this question depends on the match of cohesiveness with conformity to norms.

The **rule of conformity** is the greater the cohesiveness, the greater the conformity of members to team norms.

The **rule of conformity** in team dynamics states that the greater the cohesiveness of a team, the greater the conformity of members to team norms. So when the performance norms are positive in highly cohesive teams, the resulting conformity to the norm should have a positive effect on both team performance and member satisfaction. This is a best-case situation for team members, the team leader, and the organization.

When the performance norms are negative in a highly cohesive team, as shown in Figure 8.3, the rule of conformity creates a worst-case situation for the team leader and the organization. Although the high cohesiveness leaves the team members feeling loyal and satisfied, they are also highly motivated to conform to the negative performance norm. In between these two extremes are two mixed-case situations for teams low in cohesion. Because there is little conformity to either the positive or negative norms, team performance will most likely fall on the moderate or low side.

How to Influence Team Cohesiveness

What can be done to tackle the worst-case and mixed-case scenarios just described? The answer rests with the factors influencing team cohesiveness. Cohesiveness tends to be high in teams that are homogeneous in makeup—that is, when members are similar in age, attitudes, needs,

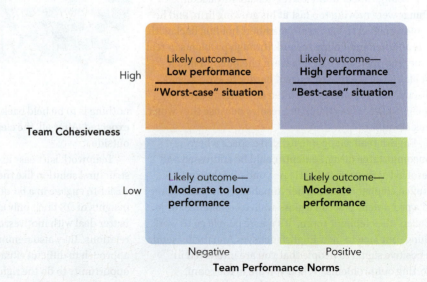

FIGURE 8.3 How cohesiveness and conformity to norms influence team performance.

How to Decrease Cohesion	Targets	How to Increase Cohesion
• Create disagreement • Increase heterogeneity • Restrict within team • Make team bigger • Focus within team • Reward individual results • Open up to other teams • Disband the team	• Goals • Membership • Interactions • Size • Competition • Rewards • Location • Duration	• Get agreement • Increase homogeneity • Enhance within team • Make team smaller • Focus on other teams • Reward team results • Isolate from other teams • Keep team together

FIGURE 8.4 Ways to increase and decrease team cohesiveness.

and backgrounds. Cohesiveness also tends to be high in teams of small size, where members respect one another's competencies, agree on common goals, and like to work together rather than alone on team tasks. Cohesiveness tends to rise when groups are physically isolated from others and when they experience performance success or crisis.

Figure 8.4 shows how team cohesiveness can be increased or decreased by making changes in goals, membership composition, interactions, size, rewards, competition, location, and duration. When the team norms are positive but cohesiveness is low, the goal is to take actions to increase cohesion and gain more conformity to the positive norms. When team norms are negative and cohesiveness is high, just the opposite may have to be done. If efforts to change the norms fail, it may be necessary to reduce cohesiveness and thus reduce conformity to the negative norms.

Inter-Team Dynamics

Organizations ideally operate as cooperative systems in which the various groups and teams support one another. In the real world, however, competition and inter-team problems often develop. Their consequences can be good or bad for the host organization and the teams themselves. This raises the issue of what happens between, not just within, teams. We call this **inter-team dynamics**.

On the positive side of inter-team dynamics, competition among teams can stimulate them to become more cohesive, work harder, become more focused on key tasks, develop more internal loyalty and satisfaction, or achieve a higher level of creativity in problem solving. This effect is demonstrated at virtually any intercollegiate athletic event, and it is common in work settings as well.[18] On the negative side, such as when manufacturing and sales units don't get along, inter-team dynamics may drain and divert work energies. Members may spend too much time focusing on their animosities or conflicts with another team and too little time focusing on their own team's performance.[19]

A variety of steps can be taken to avoid negative and achieve positive effects from inter-team dynamics. Teams engaged in destructive competition, for example, can be refocused on a common enemy or a common goal. Direct negotiations can be held among the teams. Members can be engaged in intergroup team building that encourages positive interactions and helps members of different teams learn how to work more cooperatively together. Reward systems can also be refocused to emphasize team contributions to overall organizational performance and on how much teams help out one another.

Inter-team dynamics occur as groups cooperate and compete with one another.

FINDING THE LEADER IN YOU

Amazon's Jeff Bezos Harnesses Teamwork to Drive Innovation

Amazon.com's founder and CEO Jeff Bezos is considered one of America's top businesspersons and a technology visionary. He's also a great fan of teams. Bezos coined a simple rule when it comes to sizing the firm's product development teams: If two pizzas aren't enough to feed a team, it's too big.

The business plan for Amazon originated while Bezos was driving cross-country. He started the firm in his garage, and even when his Amazon stock grew to $500 million, he was still driving a Honda and living in a small apartment in downtown Seattle. Clearly, he's a unique personality and also one with a great business mind. His goal with Amazon was to "create the world's most customer-centric company, the place where you can find and buy anything you want online."

If you go to Amazon.com and click on the "Gold Box" at the top, you'll be tuning in to his vision. It's a place for special deals, lasting only an hour and offering everything from a power tool to a new pair of shoes. Such online innovations don't just come out of the blue. They're part and parcel of the management philosophy Bezos has instilled at the firm. The Gold Box and many of Amazon's successful innovations are products of many "two-pizza teams." Described as "small," "fast-moving," and "innovation engines," these teams typically have five to eight members and thrive on turning new ideas into business potential.

Don't expect to spot a stereotyped corporate CEO in Jeff Bezos. His standard office attire is still blue jeans and blue-collared shirt. A family friend describes him and his wife as "very playful people." Bezos views Amazon's small teams as a way of fighting bureaucracy and decentralizing, even as a company grows large and very complex. He is also a fan of what he calls fact-based decisions. He says they help to "overrule the hierarchy. The most junior person in the company can win an argument with the most senior person with fact-based decisions."

David Strick/Redux Pictures

What's the Lesson Here?

Do you need to be in control as a team leader, or are you comfortable delegating? Do you consider yourself more informal or formal in your approach to leadership? How would you feel if a person junior to you had more say in a decision than you did?

TEACHING NOTE: Have students read the Bringing OB to Life feature on the elephant in the conference room. After discussing it for relevance, turn the conversation to virtual teamwork. Ask: How do you get the elephant into the virtual conference room?

Improving Team Communications

LEARNING ROADMAP INTERACTION PATTERNS AND COMMUNICATION NETWORKS • PROXEMICS AND USE OF SPACE • COMMUNICATION TECHNOLOGIES

It is important in teams to make sure that every member is strong and capable in basic communication and collaboration skills. In addition, however, teams must address questions like these: What communication networks are being used by the team and why? How does space affect communication among team members? Is the team making good use of the available communication technologies?

■ Interaction Patterns and Communication Networks

Three interaction patterns are common when team members work with one another on team tasks. We call these patterns the interacting team, the co-acting team, and the counteracting team as shown in Figure 8.5.

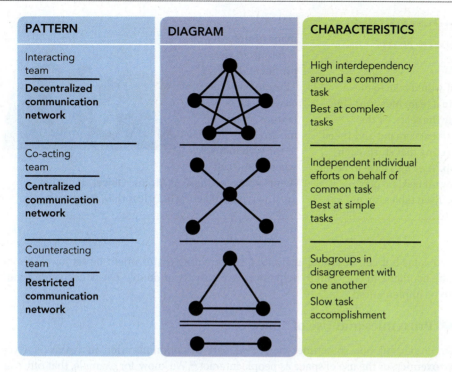

FIGURE 8.5 Interaction patterns and communication networks found in teams.

One of the most common teamwork mistakes is that members are not using the right interaction patterns. An example might be a student project team whose members believe every member must always be present when any work gets done on the project; in other words, no one works on his own and everything is done together. Team effectiveness requires that the interaction pattern should fit the task at hand. Because tasks vary, a team ideally shifts among the alternative interaction patterns as task demands emerge and change over time.

Figure 8.5 links interaction patterns with team communication networks.[20] Tasks that require intense interaction among team members are best done with a **decentralized communication network**. Also called the *star network* or *all-channel network*, it operates with everyone communicating and sharing information with everyone else. Information flows back and forth constantly, with no one person serving as the center point.[21] Decentralized communication networks work well when team tasks are complex and nonroutine, perhaps tasks that involve uncertainty and require creativity. Member satisfaction on such interacting teams is usually high.

Tasks that allow team members to work independently are best done using a **centralized communication network**. Also called the *wheel network* or *chain network*, it operates with a central hub through which one member—often a formal or informal team leader—collects and distributes information. Members of such coacting teams work on assigned tasks independently while the hub keeps everyone and everything coordinated. Work is divided among members, and results are pooled to create the finished product. The centralized network works well when team tasks are routine and easily subdivided. It is usually the hub member who experiences the most satisfaction on successful co-acting teams.

Counteracting teams form when subgroups emerge within a team due to issue-specific disagreements, such as a temporary debate over the best means to achieve a goal, or emotional disagreements, such as personality clashes. This creates a **restricted communication network** in which the subgroups contest each other's positions and restrict interactions with one another. The poor communication often creates

In **decentralized communication networks** members communicate directly with one another.

Centralized communication networks link group members through a central control point.

Restricted communication networks link subgroups that disagree with one another's positions.

When Team Members Stand Up, Team Decisions May Speed Up

Did you ever wonder what it would take to move decisions along a lot faster in a team meeting? One solution is simple: Take away the seats. At the software firm Atomic Object, seats are out and speed is in. At the regular team meeting that starts each workday, everyone stands up. They also have to be on time and are expected to stay on task; no playing Angry Birds or chit-chatting. Even tables are out at many Atomic Object meetings. A vice president declares, "They make it too easy to lean or rest laptops." Stand-up meetings are popular in the tech industry, where some call them "agile meetings." At Atomic Object, agile they are; the typical meeting lasts less than five minutes.

GlobalStock/iStockphoto

---

problems but can be useful at times. Counteracting teams might be set up to stimulate conflict and criticism to help improve creativity or double-check decisions about to be implemented.

Proxemics and Use of Space

Proxemics involves the use of space as people interact.

An important but sometimes neglected part of communication in teams involves **proxemics**, or the use of space as people interact.[22] We know, for example, that office or workspace architecture is an important influence on communication behavior. It only makes sense that communication in teams might be improved by arranging physical space to best support it. This might be done by moving chairs and tables closer together, or by choosing to meet in physical spaces that are most conducive to communication. Meeting in a small conference room at the library, for example, may be a better choice than meeting in a busy coffee shop.

Some architects and consultants specialize in office design for communication and teamwork. When Sun Microsystems built its facility in San Jose, California, public spaces were designed to encourage communication among persons from different departments. Many meeting areas had no walls, and most walls were glass.[23] At Google headquarters, often called Googleplex, specially designed office "tents" are made of acrylics to allow both the sense of private personal space and transparency.[24]

Communication Technologies

It hardly seems necessary in the age of Facebook, Twitter, and Skype to mention that teams now have access to many useful technologies that can facilitate communication and reduce the need to be face to face. We live and work in an age of instant messaging, tweets and texting, online discussions, video chats, videoconferencing, and more. We are networked socially 24/7 to the extent we want, and there's no reason the members of a team can't utilize the same technologies to good advantage.

Virtual communication networks link team members through electronic communication.

Think of technology as empowering teams to use **virtual communication networks** in which members communicate electronically all or most of the time. Technology in virtual teamwork acts as the "hub member" in the centralized communication network and as an ever-present "electronic router" that links members in decentralized networks on an as-needed and always-ready basis. New developments with social media keep pushing these capabilities forward. General Electric, for example, started a "Tweet Squad" to advise employees how social networking could be used to improve internal collaboration. The insurer MetLife has its own social network, Connect MetLife, which facilitates collaboration through a Facebook-like setting.[25] Of course, certain steps need to be taken to ensure that virtual teams and communication technologies are as successful as possible. This means doing things like online team building so that members get to know one another, learn about and identify team goals, and otherwise develop a sense of cohesiveness.[26]

Improving Team Decisions

LEARNING ROADMAP WAYS TEAMS MAKE DECISIONS • ASSETS AND LIABILITIES OF TEAM DECISIONS • GROUPTHINK SYMPTOMS AND REMEDIES • TEAM DECISION TECHNIQUES

One of the most important activities for any team is **decision making**, the process of choosing among alternative courses of action. The quality and timeliness of decisions and the processes through which they are made can have an important impact on how teams work and what they achieve.

▍Ways Teams Make Decisions

Consider the many teams of which you have been and are a part. Just how do major decisions get made? Most often there's a lot more going on than meets the eye. Edgar Schein has worked extensively with teams to identify, analyze, and improve their decision processes.[27] He observes that teams may make decisions through any of the six methods shown in Figure 8.6. Although Schein doesn't rule out any method, he does point out their advantages and disadvantages.

Lack of Response In *decision by lack of response*, one idea after another is suggested without any discussion taking place. When the team finally accepts an idea, all others have been bypassed and discarded by simple lack of response rather than by critical evaluation. This may happen early in a team's development when new members are struggling for identities and confidence. It's also common in teams with low-performance norms and when members just don't care enough to get involved in what is taking place. Whenever lack of response drives decisions, it's relatively easy for a team to move off in the wrong, or at least not the best, direction.

Authority Rule In *decision by authority rule*, the chairperson, manager, or leader makes a decision for the team. This is very time efficient and can be done with or without inputs by other members. Whether the decision is a good one or a bad one depends on whether or not the authority figure has the necessary information and if other group

> TEACHING NOTE: Have students to go back and read the Worth Considering… Or Best Avoided? feature on teammates paying one another for performance. Ask them to critique this approach to making pay decisions for its positives and negatives. Ask also if this situation is prone to groupthink, or not.

Decision making is the process of choosing among alternative courses of action.

FIGURE 8.6 Alternative ways that teams can make decisions.

members accept this approach. When an authority decision is made without expertise or member commitment, problems are likely.

Minority Rule
In *decision by minority rule*, two or three people are able to dominate, or railroad, the group into making a decision with which they agree. This is often done by providing a suggestion and then forcing quick agreement. The railroader may challenge the group with statements such as "Does anyone object?... No? Well, let's go ahead then." Although such forcing and bullying may get the team moving in a certain direction, member commitment to making the decision successful will probably be low. Kickback and resistance, especially when things get difficult, aren't unusual in these situations.

Majority Rule
One of the most common ways that groups make decisions is through *decision by majority rule*. This usually takes place as a formal vote to find the majority viewpoint. When team members get into disagreements that seem irreconcilable, for example, voting is seen to be an easy way out of the situation. Nonetheless, majority rule is often used without awareness of its potential problems. The very process creates coalitions, especially when votes are taken and results are close. Those in the minority—the "losers"—may feel left out or discarded without having had a fair say. They may not be enthusiastic about implementing the decision of the "winners." Lingering resentments may hurt team effectiveness in the future if they become more concerned about winning the next vote than doing what is best for the team.

Consensus
Another of the decision alternatives is **consensus**. It results when discussion leads to one alternative being favored by most team members and other members agree to support it. When a consensus is reached, even those who may have opposed the chosen course of action know that they have been listened to and have had a fair chance to influence the outcome. Consensus does not require unanimity. What it does require is the opportunity for any dissenting members to feel that they have been able to speak and that their voices have been heard.[28] Because of the extensive process involved in reaching a consensus decision, it may be inefficient from a time perspective. Still, consensus is very powerful in terms of generating commitments among members to making the final decision work best for the team.

Consensus is a group decision that has the expressed support of most members.

Unanimity
A *decision by unanimity* may be the ideal state of affairs. Here, all team members wholeheartedly agree on the course of action to be taken. This "logically perfect" decision situation is extremely difficult to attain in actual practice. One reason that teams sometimes turn to authority decisions, majority voting, or even minority decisions, in fact, is the difficulty of managing the team process to achieve decisions by consensus or unanimity.

When in Doubt, Follow the Seven Steps for Consensus

It's easy to say that consensus is good. It's a lot harder to achieve consensus, especially when tough decisions are needed. Here are some tips for how members should behave in consensus-seeking teams:

- Don't argue blindly; consider others' reactions to your points.
- Be open and flexible, but don't change your mind just to reach quick agreement.
- Avoid voting, coin tossing, and bargaining to avoid or reduce conflict.
- Act in ways that encourage everyone's involvement in the decision process.
- Allow disagreements to surface so that information and opinions can be deliberated.
- Don't focus on winning versus losing; seek alternatives acceptable to all.
- Discuss assumptions, listen carefully, and encourage participation by everyone.

▪ Assets and Liabilities of Team Decisions

The best teams don't limit themselves to any one of the decision methods just described. Instead, they move back and forth among them. Each method is used in circumstances for which it is a best fit. As professors, for example, we never complain when a department head makes an authority decision to have a welcome reception for new students at the start of the academic year or calls for a faculty vote on a proposed new travel policy. Yet we'd quickly disapprove if a department head made an authority decision to hire a new faculty member—something we believe should be made by faculty consensus.

It's important for any team leader to use the right decision method for the situation at hand. Without doubt, there are many times when the best choice is to go with the more team-oriented decisions. However, even they have potential disadvantages as well as advantages.[29] On the positive side, team decisions by consensus and unanimity offer the advantages of bringing more information, knowledge, and expertise to bear on a problem. Extensive discussion tends to create broader understanding of the final decision, and this increases acceptance. It also strengthens the commitments of members to follow through and support the decision.

On the negative side, we all know that team decisions can be imperfect. It usually takes a team longer to make a decision than it does an individual. Then too, social pressures to conform might make some members unwilling to go against or criticize what appears to be the will of the majority. Furthermore, in the guise of a so-called team decision, a team leader or a few members might railroad or force other members to accept their preferred decision.

Groupthink Symptoms and Remedies

One important problem that sometimes occurs when teams try to make decisions is **groupthink**—the tendency of members in highly cohesive groups to lose their critical evaluative capabilities.[30] As identified by social psychologist Irving Janis, groupthink is a property of highly cohesive teams, and it occurs because team members are so concerned with harmony that they become unwilling to criticize each other's ideas and suggestions. Desires to hold the team together, feel good, and avoid unpleasantries bring about an overemphasis on agreement and an underemphasis on critical discussion. This often results in a poor decision.

By way of historical examples, Janis suggests that groupthink played a role in the U.S. forces' lack of preparedness at Pearl Harbor before the United States entered World War II. It has also been linked to flawed U.S. decision making during the Vietnam War, to events leading up to the space shuttle disasters, and, most recently, to failures of American intelligence agencies regarding the status of weapons of mass destruction in Iraq. Perhaps you can think of other examples from your own experiences where otherwise well-intentioned teams end up doing the wrong things.

The following symptoms of teams displaying groupthink should be well within the sights of any team leader and member:[31]

- *Illusions of invulnerability*—Members assume that the team is too good for criticism or beyond attack.
- *Rationalizing unpleasant and disconfirming data*—Members refuse to accept contradictory data or to thoroughly consider alternatives.
- *Belief in inherent group morality*—Members act as though the group is inherently right and above reproach.
- *Stereotyping competitors as weak, evil, and stupid*—Members refuse to look realistically at other groups.
- *Applying direct pressure to deviants to conform to group wishes*—Members refuse to tolerate anyone who suggests the team may be wrong.
- *Self-censorship by members*—Members refuse to communicate personal concerns to the whole team.

Groupthink is the tendency of cohesive group members to lose their critical evaluative capabilities.

◀ Symptoms of groupthink

- *Illusions of unanimity*—Members are quick to accept consensus prematurely, without testing its completeness.
- *Mind guarding*—Members try to protect the team from hearing disturbing ideas or outside viewpoints.

Even though groupthink is a serious threat to teams at all levels and in all types of organizations, it can be managed. To do so, team leaders and members must stay alert to the preceding symptoms and be quick to take action when they are spotted.[32] The sidebar offers a number of steps that can be taken to prevent or minimize groupthink. During the Cuban missile crisis, for example, President John F. Kennedy chose to absent himself from certain strategy discussions conducted by his cabinet. This made it easier for them to engage in critical discussion and avoided tendencies for cabinet members to try to figure out what the president wanted and then give it to him. The result was an open and expansive decision process, and the crisis was successfully resolved.

Team Decision Techniques

What can be done to improve decision making in teams that are having problems? It's not just things like groupthink and premature rush to agreement that can harm decision making. Decision deficits often occur, for example, when meetings are poorly structured or poorly led as members try to work together. Decisions can easily get bogged down or go awry when tasks are complex, information is uncertain, creativity is needed, time is short, "strong" voices are dominant, and debates turn emotional and personal. These are times when special team decision techniques can be helpful.[33]

Brainstorming In the time-tested technique of **brainstorming**, team members actively generate as many ideas and alternatives as possible. They are supposed to do so relatively quickly and without inhibitions. But scholar Leigh Thompson points out that you have to be careful because brainstorming doesn't always work as intended. She recommends a period of "solo thinking" before brainstorming begins, keeping the brainstorming groups small, and making sure that rules are clear and followed.[34]

brainstorming involves generating ideas through freewheeling and without criticism.

You are surely familiar with the rules of brainstorming. First, all criticism is ruled out. No one is allowed to judge or evaluate any ideas until they are all on the table. Second, freewheeling is welcomed. The emphasis is on creativity and imagination; the wilder or more radical the ideas, the better. Third, quantity is a goal. The assumption is that the greater the number, the more likely a superior idea will appear. Fourth, piggybacking is good. Everyone is encouraged to suggest how others' ideas can be turned into new ideas or how two or more ideas can be joined into still another new idea.

Remedies to Help Teams Avoid Groupthink

- Assign the role of critical evaluator to each team member.
- Have the leader avoid seeming partial to one course of action.
- Create subgroups that each work on the same problem.
- Have team members discuss issues with outsiders and report back.
- Invite outside experts to observe and react to team processes.
- Assign someone to be a "devil's advocate" at each team meeting.
- Hold "second-chance" meetings after consensus is apparently achieved.

Nominal Group Technique At times teams get so large that open discussion and brainstorming are awkward to manage. It's also common for teams to get into situations where the opinions of members differ so much that discussions become antagonistic and argumentative. In such cases, using the structured **nominal group technique** for face-to-face or virtual decision making may be helpful.[35]

The **nominal group technique** involves structured rules for generating and prioritizing ideas.

OB IN POPULAR CULTURE

Groupthink and *Madagascar*

Dreamworks/Photofest

In the movie *Madagascar*, four animals try to escape from the New York Central Zoo. Local residents complain about the danger, so the animals are shipped to Africa when they are captured. The animals' crates are tossed overboard during a storm, and they end up in Madagascar.

Local King Julian, leader of the lemurs, hatches a plan to make friends with the mysterious animals that arrive on the island. He suggests that Alex, the lion, might be helpful in protecting them from other predators on the island. When Maurice, Julian's assistant, asks why predators are scared of Alex, he is quickly silenced. All the other lemurs are quick to agree with King Julian. Alex is later discovered to be a hungry carnivore and banished from the lemur colony.

This movie segment shows how easy it is for dissension to be squelched in highly cohesive groups. King Julian, for example, demeans individuals that question his ideas or offer contrasting views. The scene also shows mind guarding. Acknowledging that Alex is a dangerous predator might force the lemurs to deal with an unpleasant reality, so they pretend it does not exist.

Get to Know Yourself Better
Take Assessment 21, Work Team Dynamics, in the *OB Skills Workbook*. It can be a good gauge of whether one of your groups or teams is working effectively or might be susceptible to groupthink. It's also a chance to think about your role in such situations. Take a minute and assess a group to which you currently belong. If you are the leader, what can you do to guard against groupthink? If you are not the leader, what actions would you take if your team was heading toward groupthink?

The nominal group technique begins by asking team members to respond individually and in writing to a *nominal question*, such as "What should be done to improve the effectiveness of this work team?" Everyone is encouraged to list as many alternatives or ideas as they can. Next, participants in round-robin fashion are asked to read or post their responses to the nominal question. Each response is recorded on large newsprint or in a computer database as it is offered. No criticism is allowed. The recorder asks for any questions that may clarify specific items on the list, but no evaluation is allowed. The goal is simply to make sure that everyone fully understands each response. A structured voting procedure is then used to prioritize responses to the nominal question and identify the choice or choices having most support. This procedure allows ideas to be evaluated without risking the inhibitions, hostilities, and distortions that may occur in an open and less structured team meeting.

Delphi Technique
The **Delphi technique** has evolved as a useful decision-making technique when team members are unable to meet face to face. It's virtual version basically collects online responses to a set of questions posed to a panel of decision makers. A coordinator summarizes responses, then sends the summary plus follow-up questions back to the panel. This process is repeated until a consensus is reached and a clear decision emerges.

*The **Delphi technique** involves generating decision-making alternatives through a series of survey questionnaires.*

8 Study Guide

Key Questions and Answers

What are high-performance teams?
- Team building is a collaborative approach to improving group process and performance.
- High-performance teams have core values, clear performance objectives, the right mix of skills, and creativity.
- Team building is a data-based approach to analyzing group performance and taking steps to improve performance in the future.
- Team building is participative and engages all group members in collaborative problem solving and action.

How can team processes be improved?
- Individual entry problems are common when new teams are formed and when new members join existing teams.
- Task leadership involves initiating, summarizing, and making direct contributions to the group's task agenda; maintenance leadership involves gate-keeping, encouraging, and supporting the social fabric of the group over time.
- Distributed leadership occurs when team members step in to provide helpful task and maintenance activities and discourage disruptive activities.
- Role difficulties occur when expectations for group members are unclear, overwhelming, underwhelming, or conflicting.
- Norms are the standards or rules of conduct that influence the behavior of team members; cohesiveness is the attractiveness of the team to its members.
- Members of highly cohesive groups value their membership and are very loyal to the group; they also tend to conform to group norms.
- The best situation is a team with positive performance norms and high cohesiveness; the worst is a team with negative performance norms and high cohesiveness.
- Inter-team dynamics are forces that operate between two or more groups as they cooperate and compete with one another.

How can team communications be improved?
- Effective teams vary their use of alternative communication networks and decision-making methods to best meet task and situation demands.
- Interacting groups with decentralized networks tend to perform well on complex tasks; co-acting groups with centralized networks may do well at simple tasks.
- Restricted communication networks are common in counteracting groups where subgroups form around disagreements.
- Wise choices on proxemics, or the use of space, can help teams improve communication among members.
- Information technology ranging from instant messaging, video chats, video conferencing, and more, can improve communication in teams, but it must be well used.

How can team decisions be improved?
- Teams can make decisions by lack of response, authority rule, minority rule, majority rule, consensus, and unanimity.

- Although team decisions often make more information available for problem solving and generate more understanding and commitment, their potential liabilities include social pressures to conform and greater time requirements.
- Groupthink is a tendency of members of highly cohesive teams to lose their critical evaluative capabilities and make poor decisions.
- Special techniques for team decision making include brainstorming, the nominal group technique, and the Delphi technique.

Terms to Know

Brainstorming (p. 182)
Centralized communication network (p. 177)
Cohesiveness (p. 174)
Collective intelligence (p. 165)
Consensus (p. 180)
Decentralized communication network (p. 177)
Decision making (p. 179)
Delphi technique (p. 183)
Disruptive behaviors (p. 169)
Distributed leadership (p. 169)
Groupthink (p. 181)
Inter-team dynamics (p. 175)
Maintenance activities (p. 169)
Nominal group technique (p. 182)
Norms (p. 170)
Performance norm (p. 171)
Proxemics (p. 178)
Restricted communication network (p. 177)
Role (p. 168)
Role ambiguity (p. 168)
Role conflict (p. 168)
Role negotiation (p. 169)
Role overload (p. 168)
Role underload (p. 168)
Rule of conformity (p. 174)
Task activities (p. 169)
Team or group dynamics (p. 167)
Team building (p. 166)
Virtual communication networks (p. 178)

Self-Test 8

▶ Multiple Choice

1. One of the essential criteria of a true team is _____.
   (a) large size
   (b) homogeneous membership
   (c) isolation from outsiders
   (d) collective accountability

2. The team-building process can best be described as participative, data based, and _____.
   (a) action oriented
   (b) leader centered
   (c) ineffective
   (d) short term

3. A person facing an ethical dilemma involving differences between personal values and the expectations of the team is experiencing _____ conflict.
   (a) person–role
   (b) intrasender role
   (c) intersender role
   (d) interrole

4. The statement "On our team, people always try to do their best" is an example of a(n) _____ norm.
   (a) support and helpfulness
   (b) high-achievement
   (c) organizational pride
   (d) personal improvement

5. Highly cohesive teams tend to be _____.
   (a) bad for organizations
   (b) good for members
   (c) good for social loafing
   (d) bad for norm conformity

6. To increase team cohesiveness, one would _____.
   (a) make the group bigger
   (b) increase membership diversity
   (c) isolate the group from others
   (d) relax performance pressures

7. A team member who does a good job at summarizing discussion, offering new ideas, and clarifying points made by others is providing leadership by contributing _____ activities to the group process.
   (a) required
   (b) disruptive
   (c) task
   (d) maintenance

8. Examples of _____ that can harm team performance include when someone is being aggressive, makes inappropriate jokes, or talks about irrelevant matters in a group meeting.
   (a) disruptive behaviors
   (b) maintenance activities
   (c) task activities
   (d) role dynamics

9. If you heard from an employee of a local bank "It's a tradition here for us to stand up and defend the bank when someone criticizes it," you could assume that the bank employees had strong _____ norms.
   (a) support and helpfulness
   (b) organizational and personal pride
   (c) ethical and social responsibility
   (d) improvement and change

10. What can be predicted when you know that a work team is highly cohesive?
    (a) high-performance results
    (b) high member satisfaction
    (c) positive performance norms
    (d) status congruity

11. When two groups are in competition with one another, _____ may be expected within each group.
    (a) greater cohesiveness
    (b) less reliance on the leader
    (c) poor task focus
    (d) more conflict

12. A co-acting group is most likely to use a(n) _____ communication network.
    (a) interacting
    (b) decentralized
    (c) centralized
    (d) restricted

13. A complex problem is best dealt with by a team using a(n) _____ communication network.
    (a) all-channel
    (b) wheel
    (c) chain
    (d) linear

14. The tendency of teams to lose their critical evaluative capabilities during decision making is a phenomenon called _____.
    (a) groupthink
    (b) the slippage effect
    (c) decision congruence
    (d) group consensus

15. When a team decision requires a high degree of commitment for its implementation, a(n) _____ decision is generally preferred.
    (a) authority
    (b) majority rule
    (c) consensus
    (d) minority rule

■ Short Response

16. Describe the steps in a typical team-building process.
17. How can a team leader build positive group norms?
18. How do cohesiveness and conformity to norms influence team performance?
19. How can inter-team competition be bad and good for organizations?

■ Applications Essay

20. Alejandra Purón recently encountered a dilemma in working with his employer's diversity task force. One of the team members claimed that a task force must always be unanimous in its recommendations. "Otherwise," she said, "we will not have a true consensus." Alejandro, the current task force leader, disagrees. He believes that unanimity is desirable but not always necessary to achieve consensus. You are a management consultant specializing in teams and teamwork. Alejandro asks for advice. What would you tell him and why?

Steps to Further Learning 8
Top Choices from *The OB Skills Workbook*

These learning activities from *The OB Skills Workbook* found at the back of the book are suggested for Chapter 8.

Case for Critical Thinking	Team and Experiential Exercises	Self-Assessment Portfolio
• Teams Drive the Racing Cars	• Scavenger Hunt Team Building • Work Team Dynamics • Identifying Team Norms • Work Team Culture • The Hot Seat	• Team Effectiveness • Empowering Others

Decision Making and Creativity

9

The Key Point

When, how, and with whom we make choices is a key to success. But, we don't always make good decisions or use the right decision-making approaches. There are times when it's best to be quick, intuitive, and creative, and others when we should be slow, deliberative, and cautious. Sometimes it's best to make choices alone and many times it's best to involve others. ■

Chapter at a Glance

- What Is Involved in the Decision-Making Process?
- What Are the Alternative Decision-Making Models?
- What Are the Key Decision-Making Traps and Issues?
- What Can Be Done to Stimulate Creativity in Decision Making?

What's Inside?

- **Bringing OB to LIFE**
  GETTING REAL TO MAKE THE RIGHT JOB CHOICE
- **Worth Considering . . . or Best Avoided?**
  NEED A BREAK? SOME WORKERS ARE SWAPPING CASH FOR TIME
- **Checking Ethics in OB**
  LIFE AND DEATH AT AN OUTSOURCING FACTORY
- **Finding the Leader in You**
  ARIANNA RUSSELL LEADS WITH INTUITION AT THE BODACIOUS BANDIT
- **OB in Popular Culture**
  INTUITION AND US AIRWAYS FLIGHT 1549
- **Research Insight**
  ANALYTICAL AND INTUITIVE DECISIONS: WHEN TO TRUST YOUR GUT

The Decision-Making Process

LEARNING ROADMAP
STEPS IN THE DECISION-MAKING PROCESS • THE DECISION TO DECIDE
ETHICAL REASONING AND DECISION MAKING
ALTERNATIVE DECISION ENVIRONMENTS
DECISIONS WITH EXTREME CONSEQUENCES

> **TEACHING NOTE:** Ask students to review Figure 9.2 Combinations of decision environments and types of decisions, and discuss when they should abandon a once sound programmed decision.

The world of the manager is the world of choice. It is also no wonder that a Graduate Management Admissions Council survey reports that 25 percent of business school alumni would like more training in managing the decision-making process.[1] Even in your first job, making the appropriate decisions to solve problems will be a key to success.

Steps in the Decision-Making Process

Decision making is the process of choosing a course of action to deal with a problem or opportunity.

A common definition of **decision making** is the process of choosing a course of action for dealing with a problem or an opportunity.[2] The process is usually described in five steps that constitute the ideal or so-called *rational decision model*.

1. *Recognize and define the problem or opportunity*—gather information and deliberate in order to specify exactly why a decision is needed and what it should accomplish. Three mistakes are common in this critical first step in decision making. First, we may define the problem too broadly or too narrowly. Second, we may focus on problem symptoms instead of causes. Third, we may choose the wrong problem to deal with.

2. *Identify and analyze alternative courses of action*—evaluate possible alternative courses of action and their anticipated consequences for costs and benefits. Decision makers at this stage must be clear on exactly what they know and what they need to know. They should identify key stakeholders and consider the effects of each possible course of action on them.

3. *Choose a preferred course of action*—a choice is made to pursue one course of action rather than others. Criteria used in making the choice typically involve costs and benefits, timeliness of results, impact on stakeholders, and ethical soundness. Another issue is who makes the decision: team leader, team members, or some combination?

4. *Implement the preferred course of action*—actions are taken to put the preferred course of action into practice. This is a point where teams may suffer from **lack-of-participation error** because they haven't included certain people in the decision-making process whose support is necessary for its implementation. Teams that use participation and involvement successfully gather information and insights for better decision making, and commitments from team members to put choices into action. Some of the participation techniques are quite simple, such as a checklist for an emergency room surgery team.

Lack-of-participation error occurs when important people are excluded from the decision-making process.

Something to Read—*The Checklist Manifesto: How to Get Things Right* by Atul Gawande

In his book *The Checklist Manifesto* (Picador, 2011), physician and author Atul Gawande suggests that the old-fashioned checklist is a good way to make sure that what he calls "avoidable errors" aren't made.

Bad decisions he says, often sometimes come from missing small things. The best checklists are short and focused on the essentials. If they are too long, they may not get used or key things may be skipped. In teams, such as a surgery team in a hospital emergency room, checklists are empowering because they allow every team member to be part of the control process.

Erik Jacobs/The New York Times

5. *Evaluate results and follow up as necessary*—performance results are measured against initial goals and both anticipated and unanticipated outcomes are examined. This is where decision makers exercise control over their actions, being careful to ensure that the desired results are achieved and undesired side effects are avoided. It is a stage that many individuals and teams often neglect, with negative implications for their performance effectiveness.

The Decision to Decide

The reality is that making and implementing the right choices is complicated. And one of the most critical aspects of the decision-making process is setting priorities. Not every problem requires an immediate response and the best decision may be the one not made. Asking and answering the following questions can sometimes help with the decision to decide.

- *What really matters?* Small and less significant problems should not get the same time and attention as bigger ones.
- *Might the problem resolve itself?* Putting problems in rank order leaves the less significant for last. Surprisingly, many of these less important problems resolve themselves or are solved by others before you get to them.
- *Is this my, or our, problem?* Many problems can be handled by other people. These should be delegated to people who are best prepared to deal with them. Ideally, they should be delegated to people whose work they most affect.
- *Will time spent make a difference?* A really effective decision maker recognizes the difference between problems that realistically can be solved and those that are simply not solvable.

◀ Questions on decision immediacy

Ethical Reasoning and Decision Making

Choices at each step in the decision-making process often have moral issues that can easily be overlooked. Figure 9.1 links the steps in the decision-making process with corresponding issues of ethical reasoning.[3] As suggested in the figure, we are advocating that

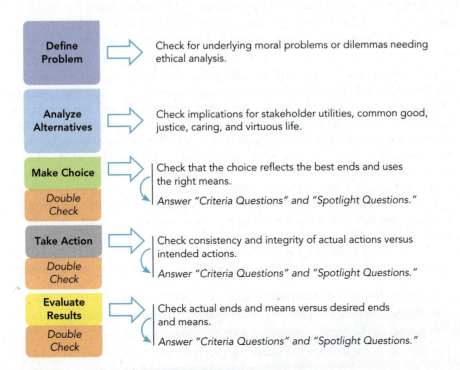

FIGURE 9.1 The decision-making process and ethical reasoning model.

an ethical reasoning approach be followed when decisions are made and that this approach be linked with steps in the decision-making process. In other words, decision making is incomplete without including ethical analysis.

Moral Problems and Dilemmas

Ethics is the philosophical study of morality or standards regarding good character and conduct.[4] When we apply ethical reasoning to decisions made by individuals and teams in organizations, the focus is on moral problems and dilemmas that are associated with the decision-making process.

A **moral problem** poses major ethical consequences for the decision maker or for others. It is possible to address a personal, management, or business problem and not properly consider any moral problems that might be associated with it, but the preferred approach is to carefully examine the ethics of each alternative for all stakeholders, and make choices that minimize negative impact and maximize respect for everyone's rights.

During the recession, for example, job layoffs were commonplace. For the manager or executive teams involved, layoffs may seem straightforward and necessary solutions to a business problem—there are insufficient sales to justify the payroll and some jobs must be cut. But this situation also involves a moral problem. The people who lose their jobs may have families, debts, and perhaps limited alternative job options. They will be hurt even if the business benefits from lowering its costs. Although addressing the moral problem might not change the business decision, it might change how the business decision is reached and implemented. This includes addressing whether or not better alternatives to job eliminations exist and what support is offered to those who do lose jobs.

Sometimes decision makers face **moral dilemmas** and need to decide between two or more ethically uncomfortable alternatives. An example might be having to make the decision to sign an outsourcing contract with a less expensive supplier in a country where employment discrimination exists but where the country is poor and new jobs are necessary for economic development, or contracting a local supplier whose high cost will affect the bottom line. A situation like this involves the uncomfortable position of choosing between alternatives that contain both potential benefits and harm.

Although such moral dilemmas are difficult to resolve, ethical reasoning helps ensure that the decisions will be made with rigor and thoughtful consideration. A willingness to pause to examine the ethics of a proposed decision may well result in a better decision, preservation of respect and reputation, and avoidance of costly litigation.

Ethics Double-Checks

In the preceding example of job layoffs, business executives who have been criticized for making job cuts might scramble to provide counseling and job search help to affected employees. This is after the fact, and moral conduct does not result from after-the-fact embarrassment. As ethicist Stephen Fineman suggests, "If people are unable to anticipate shame or guilt before they act in particular ways, then moral codes are invalid."[5] When you are the decision maker, decision making is not just a process followed for the good of the organization; it involves your values and your morality, and potential adverse impact on them should be anticipated.[6]

If you look at Figure 9.1, you will see that "ethics double-checks" are built into the ethical reasoning framework. This is a way of testing to make sure our decisions meet personal moral standards. The recommended ethics double-checks ask and answer two sets of questions: criteria questions and spotlight questions. Ethicist Gerald Cavanagh and his associates identify these four **criteria questions** for assessing ethics in decision making:[7]

- *Utility*—Does the decision satisfy all constituents or stakeholders?
- *Rights*—Does the decision respect the rights and duties of everyone?
- *Justice*—Is the decision consistent with the canons of justice?
- *Caring*—Is the decision consistent with my responsibilities to care?

Ethics is the philosophical study of morality.

A **moral problem** poses major ethical consequences for the decision maker or others.

A **moral dilemma** involves choosing among alternatives that contain both potential benefits and harm.

Criteria questions assess a decision in terms of utility, rights, justice, and caring.

CHECKING ETHICS IN OB

Life and Death at an Outsourcing Factory

Over 500,000 people work, and many employees live in dormitories, at the huge Foxconn complex in Shenzen, China that includes its own downtown, swimming pool, fire department and hospital. The company is not only known as a major outsourcing firm that makes products for Apple, Dell and Hewlett Packard, among others, but for labor unrest, industrial accidents and worker suicides.

Most workers are young and away from their homes for the first time. "Without their families," says a supervisor, "they're left without direction." The firm has been criticized for working conditions and labor practices that led to a rash of employee suicides. At one point the firm installed netting on the dormitories to prevent suicides by workers jumping from the roofs.

One Foxconn worker complains that the work is meaningless, no conversation is allowed on the production lines, and the bathroom breaks are limited. Another says, "I do the same things every day. I have no future."

In recent years, Foxconn has been working to improve conditions for workers and increase their pay. A supervisor

REUTERS/Jason Lee/Landov LLC

points out that the firm provides counseling services. "We try to provide them with direction and help."

One Foxconn worker complains that the work is meaningless, no conversation is allowed on the production lines, and bathroom breaks are limited. Another says: "I do the same thing every day. I have no future." A supervisor points out that the firm provides counseling services since most workers are young and this is the first time they are away from their homes. "Without their families," says the supervisor, "they're left without direction. We try to provide them with direction and help."

How Should We Act? People sometimes work in situations that are harmful to their health and well being. They face abuse in the form of sexual harassment, supervisor mistreatment, co-worker incivility, unsafe conditions, overly long hours, and more. What ethical responsibilities do the firms that contract for outsourcing in foreign plants have when it comes to the conditions under which the employees work? Whose responsibility is it to make sure workers are well treated? And when it comes to consumers, should we support bad practices by continuing to buy products from firms whose outsourcing partners have been revealed to treat workers poorly?

The **spotlight questions** expose a decision to public scrutiny and force us to consider a decision in the context of full transparency.[8] They include:

- "How would I feel if my family found out about this decision?"
- "How would I feel if this decision were published in the local newspaper or posted on the Internet?"
- "What would the person you know or know of who has the strongest character and best ethical judgment do in this situation?"

Spotlight questions expose a decision to public scrutiny and full transparency.

▪ Alternative Decision Environments

Decisions in organizations are typically made under the three conditions or environments—uncertainty, risk, and certainty—providing the decision maker with *nonprogrammed* or *programmed* types of decisions.[9] Combinations of these environments and types of decision

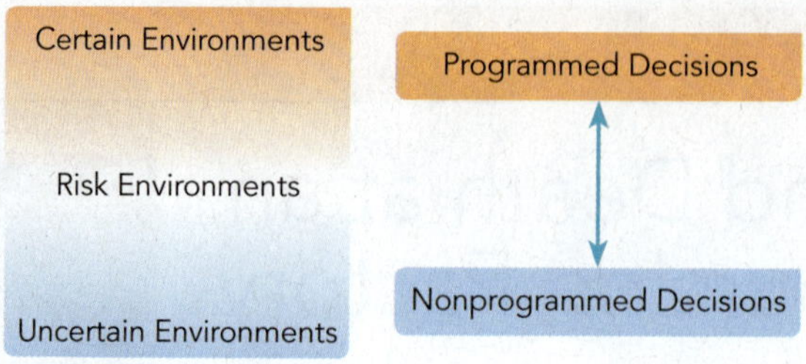

FIGURE 9.2 Combinations of decision environments and types of decisions.

are depicted in Figure 9.2. A quick examination of these combinations reveals interesting differences in the speed, accuracy, and efficiency of decision making.

Certain Environments and Programmed Decisions

Certain environments exist when information is sufficient to predict the results of each alternative in advance of implementation. When a person invests money in a savings account, for example, absolute certainty exists about the interest that will be earned on that money in a given period of time.

Programmed decisions are choices made as standardized responses to recurring situations and routine problems. They deal with things a decision maker or team already has experience with. Although it appears the choice has been made, there remains the question of implementation and tailoring the implementation to the exact problem at hand. For instance, even programmed decisions that deal with employee absences, compensation, or other standard human resource issues call for care in implementation.

The combination of a certain decision environment and programmed decisions appears trivial because it represents well established standard operating practice in a well-known setting. Choices should be activated when a choice is made for fast, accurate, and efficient choices. The astute manager also realizes there is an opportunity to delegate implementation, simplify decision rules, and/or investigate if new alternatives have arisen.

Uncertain Environments and Nonprogrammed Decisions

Uncertain environments exist when managers have so little information that they cannot even assign probabilities to various alternatives and their possible outcomes. This is the most difficult decision environment. As we will see in the rest of this chapter, uncertainty forces decision makers to rely heavily on unique, novel, and often totally innovative alternatives. This environment calls on managers to use their intuition, educated guesses, and even hunches to develop nonprogrammed decisions.

Nonprogrammed decisions are specifically crafted or tailored to fit a unique situation. They address novel or unexpected problems that demand a special response—one not available from a decision inventory. An example is a marketing team that has to respond to the introduction of a new product by a foreign competitor. Although past experience may help deal with this competitive threat, the immediate decision requires a creative solution based on the unique characteristics of the present market situation.

Risk Environments and Programmed Decisions

Risk environments exist when decision makers are aware of the probabilities associated with their likely occurrence. Decision makers often attempt to eliminate uncertainty by assigning probabilities to alternatives. The assignment can be made through objective statistical

---

Certain environments provide full information on the expected results for decision-making alternatives.

Programmed decisions implement solutions that have already been determined by past experience.

Uncertain environments provide no information to predict expected results for decision-making alternatives.

Nonprogrammed decisions are created to deal with a unique problem or opportunity at hand.

Risk environments provide probabilities regarding expected results for decision-making alternatives.

More Employers Use Computer Programs to Take the Guesswork Out of Hiring

It used to be that managers and human resource staffers followed job candidates from the point of application through the interview and into final job placement. Things are changing—fast. Computer software is replacing the human being in some aspects of hiring decisions. All call-center jobs at Xerox, for example, are filled by software that screens applications and responses to key job-related questions.

Software is often used to scan résumés for key words and phrases that are linked to the employer's hiring preferences. Personalities and decisions in simulated situations can easily be assessed by a variety of programs that organize the data and assign applicants to action categories such as *reject, hire,* and *consider further.* It's all part of what is called "talent management software." Users find that it takes the "hunch" factor out of hiring decisions and makes everything more data based.

Frances M. Roberts/NewsCom

procedures or through personal intuition. For instance, a senior production manager can make statistical estimates of quality rejects in production runs or make similar estimates based on personal past experience. Managers believe risk is a common decision environment.

In risk environments, decision makers often implement programmed decisions to gain speed and the appearance of efficiency. However, to the degree that the risk is manufactured from managerial estimates of conditions that are really uncertain, the accuracy of the choices could decline substantially.

Decision Environment and Decision Type Mismatches

The presence of unusual combinations of decision environments and types signals potentially serious decision-making deficiencies. When organizations rely on unprogrammed decisions in certain and risk environments, there is a potential loss of efficiency. Conversely, use of programmed decisions in an uncertain environment often fails because choices made don't solve the problem or match the opportunity. The use of programmed decisions in uncertain environments is perhaps more common than you might first think. This combination indicates that decision makers are unresponsive to changing, dynamic conditions.

■ Decisions with Extreme Consequences

Where the potential consequences of a decision are extreme, organizations often engage in planning to ensure their survival. One common type of planning involves systematic risk management and another focuses on responses to potential disasters.

Risk Management in Decision Making

Because so many decisions are made in risk and uncertain environments, there is heightened interest in **risk management**, often associated with insurance and finance. We use the term in general management as well, focusing on anticipating risk in situations and factoring risk alternatives into the decision-making process.[10] Risk management involves identifying critical risks and then developing strategies and assigning responsibilities for dealing with them.

KPMG, one of the world's largest consulting firms, has a large practice in enterprise risk management. It is designed to help executives identify risks to their firms and plan how to best deal with them.[11] KPMG consultants systematically ask managers to

Risk managemen involves anticipating risks and factoring them into decision making.

separately identify *strategic risks*—threats to overall business success; *operational risks*—threats inherent in the technologies used to reach business success; and *reputation risks*—threats to a brand or to the firm's reputation. Although they also note the importance of threats from regulatory sources, KPMG consultants pay special attention to financial threats, challenges to information systems, and new initiatives from competitors, in addition to change in the competitive setting such as economic recession or natural disasters.

Crisis Planning

> A **crisis decision** occurs when an unexpected problem can lead to disaster if not resolved quickly and appropriately.

The most extreme type of nonprogrammed decision is the **crisis decision** where an unexpected problem threatens major harm and disaster if it is not resolved quickly and appropriately.[12] Acts of terrorism, workplace violence, IT failures and security breaches, ethical scandals, and environmental catastrophes are all examples. The ability to handle crises could well be the ultimate decision-making test. Unfortunately, research indicates that we sometimes react to crises by doing exactly the wrong things.[13] Managers err in crisis situations when they isolate themselves and try to solve the problem alone or in a small, closed group. Teams do the same when they withdraw into the isolation of groupthink. In both instances, the decision makers cut themselves off from access to crucial information at the very time that they need it most.

Especially in our world of economic uncertainty, global crises, and IT security breaches, many organizations are developing formal crisis-management programs. They train managers in crisis, assign people to crisis-management teams, and develop crisis-management plans to deal with various contingencies. Just as fire and police departments, the Red Cross, and community groups plan ahead and train people how to best handle civil and natural disasters, and airline crews train for flight emergencies, so, too, can managers and work teams plan ahead and train to handle organizational crises. These preparedness programs often stress key points like the following on how to identify and respond to a crisis:[14]

> Crisis preparedness tips ▶

1. Take the time to understand what's happening and the conditions under which the crisis must be resolved.
2. Attack the crisis as quickly as possible, before it gets unmanageable.
3. Know when to back off and wait for a better opportunity to make progress with the crisis.
4. Understand the danger of all-new territory.
5. Value the skeptic—don't look for and get too comfortable with agreement. Appreciate skeptics and let them help you see things differently.
6. When things are going wrong and no one seems to care, you may have to start a crisis to get people's attention.

> TEACHING NOTE: Review with students a recent choice made in the heat of battle (could be a soccer game or political election debate) to note the difference between satisfying and optimal choice. Monday morning quarterbacks always criticize based on optimal choices.

Decision-Making Models

LEARNING ROADMAP CLASSICAL DECISION MODEL • BEHAVIORAL DECISION MODEL SYSTEMATIC AND INTUITIVE THINKING

Historically, field of organizational behavior has emphasized two alternative approaches to decision making as shown in Figure 9.3—classical and behavioral.[15] The classical decision model views rational people acting in a world of complete certainty, whereas the behavioral decision model accepts the notion of bounded rationality and suggests that people act only in terms of what they perceive about a given situation.

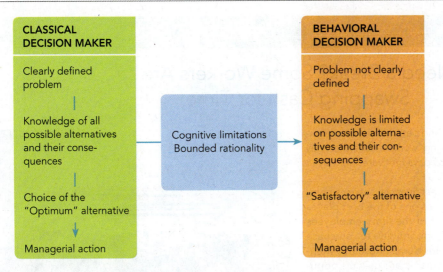

FIGURE 9.3 Decision making viewed from the classical and behavioral perspectives.

▶ Classical Decision Model

The **classical decision model** views the manager or team as acting rationally and in a fully informed manner. In a certain environment, the problem is clearly defined, all possible action alternatives are known, and their consequences are clear. This allows for an **optimizing decision** that gives the best solution to the problem. This model fits the five-step decision-making process described earlier. It is an ideal situation of complete information where the decision maker moves through the steps one by one in a logical fashion. And it nicely lends itself to various forms of quantitative decision analysis as well as to computer-based applications.[16]

Classical decision model views decision makers as acting in a world of complete certainty.

Optimizing decisions give the absolute best solution to a problem.

▶ Behavioral Decision Model

As Nobel laureate Herbert Simon noted, the reality is that many, perhaps most, decision situations faced by individuals and teams in organizations don't fit the assumptions of the model. Recognizing this, the premise of the alternative **behavioral decision model** is that people act only in terms of their perceptions, which are frequently imperfect.[17]

Behavioral scientists recognize that human beings have *cognitive limitations*—limits on what we are able to know at any point in time. These limitations restrict our information-processing capabilities. The result is that information deficiencies and overloads compromise the ability of decision makers to operate according to the classical model. Instead, they end up acting with *bounded rationality*, where things are interpreted and made sense of as perceptions and only within the context of the situation. They engage in decision making within the box of a simplified view of a more complex reality.

Armed with only partial knowledge about the available action alternatives and their consequences, decision makers in the behavioral model are likely to choose the first alternative that appears satisfactory to them. Herbert Simon calls this the tendency to make **satisficing decisions**. He states, "Most human decision making, whether individual or organizational, is concerned with the discovery and selection of satisfactory alternatives; only in exceptional cases is it concerned with the discovery and selection of optimal decisions."[18]

The **behavioral decision model** views decision makers as acting only in terms of what they perceive about a given situation.

Satisficing decisions choose the first alternative that appears to give an acceptable or satisfactory resolution of the problem.

WORTH CONSIDERING ...OR BEST AVOIDED?

Need a Break? Some Workers Are Swapping Cash for Time

If employers offer vacation, sick and personal days as incentives to employees, will allowing workers to either buy more time off or sell back unused days motivate them even more?

USAA is one of America's largest financial services companies and is consistently ranked as one of the best places to work. At last count 48 percent of the firm's employees had taken advantage of the opportunity to purchase additional time off. The Society for Human Resource Management reports that these programs are gaining popularity, with some 51 percent of organizations offering the option.

On the other hand, many employees don't use all their vacation or personal days. While the average U.S. employee gets 2.6 weeks of vacation each year, research firm Harris Interactive notes that 57 percent don't use all of their days. Selling unused days is a way for many to boost their paycheck.

Most plans that allow purchasing of time off use payroll deductions to make the financial impact less painful. At the building-materials maker USG, the program became so popular that management had to limit the purchases of vacation time to a maximum of one week a year.

Muharrem Oner/iStockphoto

Do the Analysis

Does it make sense that workers should be able to sell back and buy more time off? Does the practice hold up to real scrutiny? Are there disadvantages that must be considered? Can the practice be justified in terms of employee motivation and engagement? What is the cost of workers not taking enough vacation time?

Systematic and Intuitive Thinking

Individuals and teams may be described as using both comparatively slow "systematic" and quick "intuitive" thinking as they make decisions and try to solve problems. **Systematic thinking** is consistent with the rational model where a decision is approached in step-by-step and analytical fashion. You might recognize this style in a team member who tries to break a complex problem into smaller components that can be addressed one by one. Teams engaged in systematic thinking will try to make a plan before taking action, and to search for information and proceed with problem solving in a fact-based and logical fashion. Systematic thinking is also known as an analytical approach and is often recommended for superior decision making.[19]

We think of *intuition* as the ability to know or recognize quickly and readily the possibilities of a given situation.[20] Individuals and teams using **intuitive thinking** are more flexible and spontaneous in decision making.[21] You might observe this pattern in someone who always seems to come up with an imaginative response to a problem, often based on a quick and broad evaluation of the situation. Decision makers in this intuitive mode tend to deal with many aspects of a problem at once, search for the big picture, jump quickly from one issue to another, and act on hunches from experience or on spontaneous ideas. This approach is common under conditions of risk and uncertainty. Because intuitive thinkers take a flexible and spontaneous approach to

Systematic thinking approaches problems in a rational and analytical fashion.

Intuitive thinking approaches problems in a flexible and spontaneous fashion.

OB IN POPULAR CULTURE

Intuition and US Airways Flight 1549

During the afternoon of January 15, 2009, television news anchors began reporting about a plane in the Hudson River. The first reaction was "not another tragic plane crash." This incident, however, was different. Captain Chesley "Sully" Sullenberger successfully crash-land US Airways Flight 1549 in the river and save the lives of all passengers and crew.

In an interview with Greta van Susteren of Fox News, Sullenberger was asked to recount what happened. van Susteren commented, "It probably took about twenty seconds to explain; you had to make that decision like [snaps her fingers] that." Sullenberger responded, "It was sort of an instinctive move based upon my experience and my initial read of the situation."

What Captain Sullenberger describes is an intuitive decision. Think about it. If you had been a passenger on that plane, would you want him making a systematic decision under those circumstances? The plane would have been at the bottom of the Hudson River by the time he completed step 2. This is precisely why

Steven Day/© AP/Wide World Photos

pilots spend considerable time in flight simulators: to develop the experience necessary for dealing with problems that may only occur once, if ever, in a career.

Most descriptions of the decision-making process begin with the rational model. Systematic or rational thinking is often viewed as the most effective way to make decisions. By contrast, intuition involves being able to quickly size up a situation and make a decision. In some situations, like Sullenberger's, it may be a better way to approach a problem.

Get to Know Yourself Better
Take a look at Assessment 16, Intuitive Ability, in the *OB Skills Workbook* to determine the extent to which you use intuition in decision making. If your score suggests that you are uncomfortable with an intuitive decision style, you may need to work on it. Or perhaps you may simply need to rely on your experience and trust your judgment a little more.

---

decision making, their presence on a team adds potential for creative problem solving and innovation.

When US Airways Flight 1549 hit a flock of birds on takeoff from LaGuardia Airport, lost engine power, and was headed for a crash, Pilot Chesley "Sully" Sullenberger III made the decision to land in the Hudson River. The landing was successful, and no lives were lost. Called a hero for his efforts, Sullenberger described his thinking this way.[22]

> I needed to touch down with the wings exactly level. I needed to touch down with the nose slightly up. I needed to touch down at . . . a descent rate that was survivable. And I needed to touch down just above our minimum flying speed but not below it. And I needed to make all these things happen simultaneously.

Sullenberger did the right thing—he made the decision himself, betting on his training and experience and, stood behind it with his own life on the line.

Research Insight

Analytical and Intuitive Decisions: When to Trust Your Gut

Traditionally, managers have often been advised not to use intuitive decision making because it is often biased and may yield poor decisions. Managers have been advised by decisions experts to use analytical decision making. However, Dane and his colleagues noted recent work suggesting that this traditional recommendation might not hold for very experienced decision makers. For these individuals, intuitive heuristics might foster effective decision making.

The review of the literature suggested that intuition-based decision making might work well for experts facing tasks that could not be broken down into component parts. As they noted, "Experts are well equipped to capitalize on the potential benefits of intuition because they possess . . . domain knowledge that foster[s] rapid . . . accurate" choices.

To test this theory, the authors conducted a series of lab experiments. In the first experiment, the researchers asked student subjects to rate the difficulty of basketball shots. First, they took photos from a recent game of basketball players taking shots. They asked coaches to rate the difficulty of these shots on a scale of one to ten. Then they gathered the student participants. The student participants were first separated into two groups: one group had expensive experience with basketball (e.g., played three years of high school basketball) and the other did not. For each experience group, some students were asked to develop an analytic model with specific factors (e.g., the closeness of the defender) to make judgments about difficulty. The other students were asked to use their intuition. They then ran the experiment, giving all the students a limited amount of time to make the choices. So who do you think had the higher scores?

Results of the Basketball Experiment

	Intuition Used	Analysis Used
Low Expertise	21.34*	24.89
High Expertise	30.09	26.46

* Higher score is better.

It turns out that the individuals with the highest scores were the students who had played basketball and used intuition. The lowest scores came from the students without basketball expertise who used intuition.

The researchers also ran a similar test with fake versus real designer brand handbags. Here, the experts were students who owned several of the real bags versus those who did not. The results were virtually identical. They noted that their results might not hold for tasks, such as sequential statistical problems, that were decomposable.

Do the Research How much expertise do you think is necessary for intuition to be superior? Design a study with a non-decomposable task to examine this question.

Source: Erik Dane, Kevin W. Rockmann, and Michael G. Pratt, "When Should I Trust My Gut? Linking Domain Expertise to Intuitive Decision-Making Effectiveness," *Organizational Behavior and Human Decision Processes* 119 (2012), pp. 187–194.

Does this mean that we should always favor the more intuitive and less systematic approach? Most likely not—teams, like individuals, should use and combine the two approaches to solve complex problems. In other words, there's a place for both systematic and intuitive thinking in management decision making.

TEACHING NOTE: Preview an exam question by asking students to compare consultative decisions with team decisions and when each should be used.

Decision-Making Traps and Issues

LEARNING ROADMAP JUDGMENTAL HEURISTICS • DECISION BIASES • KNOWING WHEN TO QUIT • KNOWING WHO TO INVOLVE

The pathways to good decisions can seem like a minefield of challenging issues and troublesome traps. Whether working individually or as part of a team, it is important to understand the influence of judgmental heuristics and other potential decision biases, as well as be capable of making critical choices regarding if, when, and how decisions get made.

Judgmental Heuristics

Judgment, or the use of intellect, is important in all aspects of decision making. When we question the ethics of a decision, for example, we are questioning the judgment of the person making it. Work by Nobel laureate Daniel Kahneman, his colleagues, and many others shows that people are prone to mistakes and biases that often interfere with the quality of decision making.[23] Many of these mistakes and biases can be traced back to the use of **heuristics**. Heuristics serve a useful purpose by making it easier to deal with uncertainty and the limited information common to problem situations. However, they can also lead us toward systematic errors that affect the quality, and perhaps the ethical implications, of any decisions made.[24]

Heuristics are simplifying strategies or "rules of thumb" used to make decisions.

Availability Heuristic
The **availability heuristic** involves assessing a current event based on past occurrences that are easily available in one's memory. An example is the product development specialist who decides not to launch a new product because of a recent failure launching another one. In this case, the existence of a past product failure has negatively, and perhaps inappropriately, biased judgment regarding how best to handle the new product.

The **availability heuristic** bases a decision on recent events relating to the situation at hand.

Representativeness Heuristic
The **representativeness heuristic** involves assessing the likelihood that an event will occur based on its similarity to one's stereotypes of similar occurrences. An example is the team leader who selects a new member, not because of any special qualities of the person but because the individual comes from a department known to have produced high performers in the past. In this case, the individual's current place of employment—not job qualifications—is the basis for the selection decision.

The **representativeness heuristic** bases a decision on similarities between the situation at hand and stereotypes of similar occurrences.

Anchoring and Adjustment Heuristic
The **anchoring and adjustment heuristic** involves assessing an event by taking an initial value from historical precedent or an outside source and then incrementally adjusting this value to make a current assessment. An example is the executive who makes salary increase recommendations for key personnel by simply adjusting their current base salaries by a percentage. In this case, the existing base salary becomes an "anchor" that limits subsequent salary increases. This anchor may be inappropriate, such as in the case of an individual whose market value has become substantially higher than what is reflected by the base salary plus increment approach.

The **anchoring and adjustment heuristic** bases a decision on incremental adjustments to an initial value determined by historical precedent or some reference point.

Decision Biases

In addition to the common judgmental heuristics, decision makers are also prone to more general biases in decision making. One bias is **confirmation error**, whereby the decision maker seeks confirmation for what is already thought to be true and neglects opportunities to acknowledge or find disconfirming information. A form of selective perception, this bias involves seeking only information and cues in a situation that support a preexisting opinion.

The **confirmation error** is the tendency to seek confirmation for what is already thought to be true and not search for disconfirming information.

A second bias is the **hindsight trap** where the decision maker overestimates the degree to which he or she could have predicted an event that has already taken place. One risk of hindsight is that it may foster feelings of inadequacy or insecurity in dealing with future decision situations.

The **hindsight trap** is a tendency to overestimate the degree to which an event that has already taken place could have been predicted.

A third bias is the **framing error**. It occurs when managers and teams evaluate and resolve a problem in the context in which they perceive it—either positive or negative. Suppose research data show that a new product has a 40 percent market share. What does this really mean to the marketing team? A negative frame views the product as deficient because it is missing 60 percent of the market. Discussion and problem solving

Framing error is solving a problem in the context perceived.

BRINGING OB TO LIFE

> "Only 51 percent of new hires end up thinking they made the right decision. The main reason is that they had unrealistic expectations about the job."

Getting Real to Make the Right Job Choice

OB scholars have long talked about the importance of realistic recruitment or realistic job previews. Recruiters should provide job candidates with all relevant information about the prospective job and employer, including the possible downsides. This helps the candidates make better job choice decisions, avoiding job frustration and saving employers the cost of hiring again.

Injecting realism into job choice decisions makes good sense, but it's not the norm. A survey by Development Dimensions International, Inc. (DDI), reports that only 51 percent of new hires think they made the right decision. Unrealistic expectations and disengagement cause some employees to want out.

In the DDI survey of 2,300 new hires, many said they missed important information during the recruiting process. In retrospect, they would have liked answers to questions like these before accepting the job:

- What is the turnover rate? How often are you hiring for this position?
- How much travel is required, and what type of travel will it be?
- What are the actual hours of work, not just the official ones?
- How solid are the finances of this organization?
- Can I see the actual job description—the one my manager would be using?
- What is the structure of the team I will be joining, and how does it operate?
- Are there any team dynamics among existing members that I should know about?

Image Source/Corbis

From the OB point of view, everyone benefits from realistic recruiting. New hires who believe their decisions were fully informed are more likely to feel good about their new jobs. Employers providing full information are more likely to hire engaged workers who stick around. So, why do the gaps revealed in the DDI data persist? Why aren't more recruiters following OB and being fully open and transparent with job candidates?

within this frame would likely focus on "What are we doing wrong?" If the marketing team used a positive frame and considered a 40 percent share as a success, the conversation might have been quite different: "How can we do even better?" By the way, we are constantly exposed to framing in the world of politics; the word used to describe it is *spin*.

■ Knowing When to Quit

After the process of making a decision is completed and implementation begins, it can be hard for decision makers to change their minds and admit they made a mistake even when things are clearly not going well. Instead of backing off, the tendency is to press on to victory. This is called **escalating commitment**—continuing and renewing efforts on a previously chosen course of action, even though it is not working.[25] The tendency toward escalating commitment is reflected in the popular adage "If at first you don't succeed, try, try again."

Escalating commitments are a form of decision entrapment that leads people to do things that the facts of a situation do not justify. This is one of the most difficult aspects of decision making to convey to executives because so many of them rose to their positions by turning losing courses of action into winning ones.[26] Managers should be proactive in spotting "failures" and more open to reversing decisions or dropping plans that are not working. But this is easier said than done.

The tendency to escalate commitments often outweighs the willingness to disengage from them. Decision makers may rationalize negative feedback as a temporary condition, protect their egos by not admitting that the original decision was a mistake, or characterize any negative results as a "learning experience" that can be overcome with added future effort.

Perhaps you have experienced an inability to call it quits or been on teams with similar reluctance. It's hard to admit to a mistake, especially when a lot of thought and energy went into the decision in the first place; it can be even harder when one's ego and reputation are tied up with the decision. Fortunately, researchers suggest the following to avoid getting trapped in escalating commitments:

- Set advance limits on your involvement and commitment to a particular course of action; stick with these limits.
- Make your own decisions; don't follow the lead of others because they are also prone to escalation.
- Carefully determine just why you are continuing a course of action; if there are insufficient reasons to continue, don't.
- Remind yourself of the costs of a course of action; consider saving these costs as a reason to discontinue.

Escalating commitment is the tendency to continue a previously chosen course of action even when feedback suggests that it is failing.

◀ How to avoid escalating commitment

Knowing Who to Involve

In practice, good organizational decisions are made by individuals acting alone, by individuals consulting with others, and by people working together in teams.[27] In true contingency fashion, no one option is always superior to the others; who participates and how decisions are to be made should reflect the issues at hand.[28]

When **individual decisions**, also called *authority decisions*, are made, the manager or team leader uses information gathered and decides what to do without involving others. This decision method assumes that the decision maker is an expert on the problem at hand. In **consultative decisions**, by contrast, inputs are gathered from other persons and the decision maker uses this information to arrive at a final choice. In **team decisions**, group members work together to make the final choice, hopefully by consensus or unanimity.

Individual decisions, or authority decisions, are made by one person on behalf of the team.

Consultative decisions are made by one individual after seeking input from or consulting with members of a group.

Team decisions are made by all members of the team.

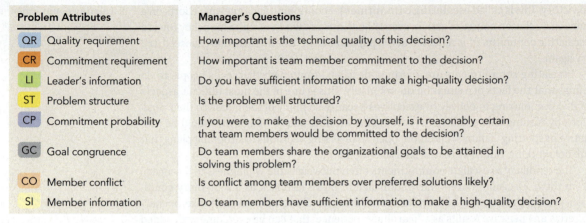

FIGURE 9.4 The Vroom-Jago model for a manager's use of alternative decision-making methods.

Victor Vroom, Phillip Yetton, and Arthur Jago developed the framework shown in Figure 9.4 for helping managers choose the right decision-making methods for various problem situations.[29] They identify these variants of the individual, consultative, and team decision options just described.

- *AI (first variant on the authority decision):* The manager solves the problem or makes the decision alone, using information available at that time.
- *AII (second variant on the authority decision):* The manager obtains the necessary information from team members and then decides on the problem's solution. The team members provide the necessary information but do not generate or evaluate alternatives.
- *CI (first variant on the consultative decision):* The manager shares the problem with team members individually, getting their ideas and suggestions without bringing them all together. The manager then makes a decision.

- *CII (second variant on the consultative decision):* The manager shares the problem with team members, collectively obtaining their ideas and suggestions. The manager then makes a decision.
- *G (the team or consensus decision):* The manager shares the problem with team members as a total group and engages them in consensus seeking to arrive at a final decision.

Figure 9.4 is a decision tree developed from the research of Vroom and his colleagues. Though complex, it helps to illustrate how decision makers can choose among the individual, consultative, and team decision options by considering these factors: (1) required quality of the decision, (2) commitment needed from team members to implement the decision, (3) amount of information available to the team leader, (4) problem structure, (5) chances team members will be committed if the leader makes the decision, (6) degree to which the team leader and members agree on goals, (7) conflict among team members, and (8) information available to team members.

Consultative and team decisions are recommended by this model when the leader lacks sufficient expertise and information to solve this problem alone; the problem is unclear and help is needed to clarify the situation; acceptance of the decision and commitment by others are necessary for implementation; and adequate time is available to allow for true participation. By contrast, authority decisions work best when team leaders have the expertise needed to solve the problem; they are confident and capable of acting alone; others are likely to accept and implement the decision they make; and little or no time is available for discussion. When problems must be resolved immediately, the authority decision made by the team leader may be the only option.[30]

Creativity in Decision Making

LEARNING ROADMAP PERSONAL CREATIVITY DRIVERS • TEAM CREATIVITY DRIVERS

Whether the choice is to make an individual decision, consult with others, or ask team members to work together, effective decision making often calls for creativity. **Creativity** is the generation of a novel idea or unique approach to solving performance problems or exploiting performance opportunities.[31] It often determines how well people, teams, and organizations do in response to complex challenges.[32]

Interestingly, researchers studying creativity rarely suggest that teams and organizations lack the potential for novel ideas or unique approaches. Yet, they also recognize that true creativity is rare. The critical question for a manager is how to turn the potential for creativity into real performance. The answer to this question rests with the individual team members, as well as the team and organizational context in which they are asked to perform.

■ Personal Creativity Drivers

One source of insight into personal creativity drivers is the three-component model of task expertise, task motivation, and creativity skills shown in Figure 9.5.[33]

Creative decisions are more likely to occur when a person has a lot of *task expertise*. Creativity typically extends a skill one is already good at in a new direction. Creative decisions are also more likely when the people making them are high in *task motivation*. Creativity happens in part because people work exceptionally hard to resolve a problem

> TEACHING NOTE: We like to stress that it is interactive combination of task experience, creativity skills, and task motivation that is important. If one is lacking, creativity is virtually nonexistent.

Creativity generates unique and novel responses to problems.

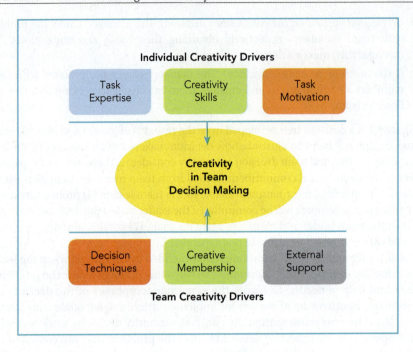

FIGURE 9.5 Individual and team creativity drivers.

or exploit an opportunity. Also, creative decisions are more likely when the people involved have strong creativity skills such as the following:[34]

Individual creativity skills ▸
- Work with high energy
- Hold ground in face of criticism
- Accept responsibility for what happens
- Are resourceful even in difficult situations
- Are both systematic and intuitive
- Are objective—step back and question assumptions
- Use divergent thinking—think outside of the box
- Use convergent thinking—synthesize and find correct answers
- Use lateral thinking—look at diverse ways to solve problems
- Transfer learning from one setting to others

■ Team Creativity Drivers

If you mix creative people together on a team, will you get creative results? Not necessarily.[35] Yes, the basic building block of team creativity is membership composition. If we want teams to be creative, they should be staffed with a *creative membership*. But beyond this, the use of special *decision techniques* such as brainstorming and the nominal group technique discussed in Chapter 8 can also be helpful. This is especially true when a team encounters process problems. Some useful decision making techniques teams can use to unleash their creativity include the following:[36]

Techniques for team creativity ▸
- *Associative play*—making up and telling stories, engaging in art projects, and building toy models that come to mind when dealing with a problem
- *Cross-pollination*—switching members among teams to gain insights from diverse interests, backgrounds, and experiences when working on problems
- *Analogies and metaphors*—using analogies and metaphors to describe a problem and open pathways to creative thinking

FINDING THE LEADER IN YOU

Arianna Russell Leads with Intuition at the Bodacious Bandit

Frustrated with the limited options of attractive and durable iPhone cases, Arianna Russell, a twenty-something entrepreneur, knew she could do better and decided to start her own business—Bodacious Cases—and created the 100% made in America, Band-It Case.

Russell wants to do more than save your iPhone from a devastating drop or a dunk in the water. She decided her iPhone cases should be attractive, practical and sturdy. As Yahoo! News reported, she "wanted . . . something truly bodacious. . . . with the Band-It Case, you have the best of several cases combined into one. It's sleek, thin, durable, and water-resistant."

The two piece, snap-together polycarbonate case was designed with an interchangeable colored band for protection and style. Standard features were not enough for Arianna, however. The iPhone case also holds a couple of credit cards and cash, and is super durable. And as a tribute to her father, a veteran, and all who have served in the military, it is made in the USA.

Bodacious Cases come in six brilliant colors with twelve different color changeable bands allowing users to match a combination of case and band to fit almost any outfit, mood, or even team or school colors. And the cases are super tough. On the company's web site you can pull up a video of Russell dumping a pitcher of water on the case, or pounding it with a croquet mallet. At the end of the video the iPhone is, of course, still working.

As for cost of manufacturing the cases, did Russell make a bad decision when she decided to produce her product in the USA? Most likely she would have saved money by outsourcing to another country, but Arianna did not even consider subcontracting or manufacturing abroad. During a holiday season interview with ABC's Diane Sawyer, the purchase of Bodacious Cases was touted as a patriotic purchase and the response was so great that Bodacious.com crashed due to overwhelming demand.

Arianna Russell

What's the Lesson Here?

Arianna's choices were intuitive and made without the traditional customer surveys, marketing analyses, or cost-benefit analyses. Did she make the right choice when deciding to manufacture her cases in the US?

Even with the right members and decision techniques available, the full creative potential of a team can only be unlocked when *external support* is added to the mix. At one level this involves making creativity a strategic priority in the broader organizational context. It also involves smaller, more everyday matters that are easily missed. Team creativity is enhanced by leaders who have the patience to allow creative processes time to work themselves through a decision situation. It is also enhanced by top management that is willing to provide the resources—technology, opportunity, and space, for example—that are helpful to the creative processes.

Think creativity nurtured the next time you see a young child playing with a unique toy. It may be from Fisher-Price toys, part of Mattel, Inc. In the firm's headquarters you'll find a special place called the "cave," and it's not your typical office space. Picture beanbag chairs, soft lighting, casual seats, and couches. It's a place for brainstorming where designers, marketers, engineers, and others can meet and join in freewheeling to come up with the next great toy for preschoolers. Consultants recommend that such innovation spaces be separated from the normal workplace and be large enough for no more than fifteen to twenty people.[37]

9 Study Guide

Key Questions and Answers

What is involved in the decision-making process?
- Decision making is a process of identifying problems and opportunities and choosing among alternative courses of action for dealing successfully with them.
- The steps in the decision-making process are (1) find and define the problem, (2) generate and evaluate alternatives, (3) decide on the preferred course of action, (4) implement the decision, and (5) evaluate the results.
- Ethical reasoning should be used in the decision-making process to ensure that all possible moral problems and dilemmas are dealt with properly.
- Decisions in organizations are made under conditions of certainty, risk, and uncertainty; the challenges to the decision maker are higher in risk and uncertain environments.
- Routine problems can be dealt with by programmed decisions; nonroutine or novel problems require specially crafted nonprogrammed decisions; crisis problems occur unexpectedly and can lead to disaster if not handled properly.

What are the alternative decision-making models?
- In the classical decision model, optimum decisions identifying the absolute best choice are made after analyzing with full information all possible alternatives and their consequences.
- In the behavioral decision model, satisficing decisions that choose the first acceptable alternative are made with limited information and bounded rationality.
- In the intuitive model, decision makers deal with many aspects of a problem at once, jump quickly from one issue to another, and act on hunches from experience or on spontaneous ideas.

What are the key decision-making traps and issues?
- The use of judgmental heuristics, or simplifying rules of thumb, can lead to biased results in decision making; such heuristics include availability decisions based on recent events, representativeness decisions based on similar events, and anchoring and adjustment decisions based on historical precedents.
- Other sources of decision-making bias are confirmation error, seeking information to justify a decision already made; hindsight trap, overestimating the extent to which current events could have been predicted; and framing error, viewing a problem in a limited context.
- Individuals and teams must know when to make decisions, realizing that not every problem requires an immediate decision.
- Individuals and teams must know who should be involved in making decisions, making use of individual, consultative, and team decisions as needed to best fit the problems and opportunities being faced.
- Individuals and teams must be able to counteract tendencies toward escalating commitment to previously chosen courses of action that are not working; they must know when to quit and abandon a course of action.

What can be done to stimulate creativity in decision making?
- Creativity is the generation of a novel idea or unique approach to solving performance problems or exploiting performance opportunities.

- Creativity in decision making can be enhanced by personal creativity drivers that include task expertise, motivation, and individual creativity skills.
- Creativity in decision making can be enhanced by team creativity drivers that include a creative membership, helpful decision techniques, and external support for creativity.

Terms to Know

Anchoring and adjustment heuristic (p. 201)
Availability heuristic (p. 201)
Behavioral decision model (p. 197)
Certain environments (p. 194)
Classical decision model (p. 197)
Confirmation error (p. 201)
Consultative decisions (p. 203)
Creativity (p. 205)
Crisis decision (p. 196)
Criteria questions (p. 192)
Decision making (p. 190)
Escalating commitment (p. 203)
Ethics (p. 192)
Framing error (p. 201)
Heuristics (p. 201)
Hindsight trap (p. 201)
Individual decisions (p. 203)
Intuitive thinking (p. 198)
Lack-of-participation error (p. 190)
Moral dilemmas (p. 192)
Moral problem (p. 192)
Nonprogrammed decisions (p. 194)
Optimizing decision (p. 197)
Programmed decisions (p. 194)
Representativeness heuristic (p. 201)
Risk environments (p. 209)
Risk management (p. 195)
Satisficing decisions (p. 197)
Spotlight questions (p. 197)
Systematic thinking (p. 198)
Team decisions (p. 203)
Uncertain environments (p. 194)

Self-Test 9

Multiple Choice

1. After a preferred course of action has been implemented, the next step in the decision-making process is to _____.
   (a) recycle the process
   (b) look for additional problems or opportunities
   (c) evaluate results
   (d) document the reasons for the decision

2. In which environment does the decision maker deal with probabilities regarding possible courses of action and their consequences?
   (a) certain
   (b) risk
   (c) organized anarchy
   (d) uncertain

3. If a team approaches problems in a rational and analytical way, with members trying to solve them in step-by-step fashion, it is well described as a team using _____.
   (a) systematic thinking
   (b) intuitive thinking
   (c) escalating thinking
   (d) associative thinking

4. An individual or team that must deal with limited information and substantial risk is most likely to make decisions based on _____.
   (a) optimizing
   (b) classical decision theory
   (c) behavioral decision theory
   (d) escalation

5. A team leader who makes a decision not to launch a new product because the last new product launch failed is falling prey to the _____ heuristic.
   (a) anchoring
   (b) availability
   (c) adjustment
   (d) representativeness

6. The criteria questions for assessing ethics in decision making include the issue of _____, making sure that the decision satisfies the interests of all stakeholders.
   (a) utility
   (b) justice
   (c) rights
   (d) caring

7. In Vroom's decision-making model, the choice among individual and team decision approaches is based on criteria that include quality requirements, availability of information, and _____.
   (a) need for implementation commitments
   (b) size of the organization
   (c) number of people involved
   (d) position power of the leader

8. The saying "If at first you don't succeed, try, try again" is most associated with a decision-making tendency called _____.
   (a) groupthink
   (b) the confirmation trap
   (c) escalating commitment
   (d) associative choice

9. The _____ decision model views individuals as making optimizing decisions, whereas the _____ decision model views them as making satisficing decisions.
   (a) behavioral/judgmental heuristics
   (b) classical/behavioral
   (c) judgmental heuristics/ethical
   (d) crisis/routine

10. A common mistake by managers facing crisis situations is _____.
    (a) trying to get too much information before responding
    (b) relying too much on team decision making
    (c) isolating themselves to make the decision alone
    (d) forgetting to use their crisis management plan.

11. What is a possible disadvantage of choosing to make a decision by the team rather than by the individual method?
    (a) People are better informed about the reason for the decision.
    (b) It takes too long to reach a decision.
    (c) More information is used to make the decision.
    (d) It won't ever result in a high-quality decision.

12. The _____ bases a decision on similarities between the situation at hand and stereotypes of similar occurrences.
    (a) representativeness heuristic
    (b) anchoring and adjustment heuristic
    (c) confirmation trap
    (d) hindsight trap

13. The _____ bases a decision on incremental adjustments to an initial value determined by historical precedent or some reference point.
    (a) representativeness heuristic
    (b) anchoring and adjustment heuristic
    (c) confirmation trap
    (d) hindsight trap

14. The _____ is the tendency to focus on what is already thought to be true and not to search for disconfirming information.
    (a) representativeness heuristic   (b) anchoring and adjustment heuristic
    (c) confirmation trap   (d) hindsight trap

15. Team creativity drivers include creative members, decision techniques, and _____.
    (a) task motivation   (b) task expertise
    (c) long-term goals   (d) external support

Short Response

16. What are heuristics, and how can they affect individual decision making?
17. What are the main differences among individual, consultative, and team decisions?
18. What is escalating commitment, and why is it important to recognize it in decision making?
19. What questions might a manager or team leader ask to help determine which problems to deal with and in which priority?

Applications Essay

20. As a participant in a new mentoring program between your university and a local high school, you have volunteered to give a presentation to a class of sophomores on the challenges of achieving creativity in teams. The goal is to motivate them to think creatively as individuals and to help ensure as well that their course teams achieve creativity when assignments call for it. What will you tell them?

Steps to Further Learning 9
Top Choices from *The OB Skills Workbook*

These learning activities from *The OB Skills Workbook* found at the back of the book are suggested for Chapter 9.

Case for Critical Thinking	Team and Experiential Exercises	Self-Assessment Portfolio
• Decisions, Decisions	• Decode • Lost at Sea • Entering the Unknown • Fostering the Creative Spirit	• Intuitive Ability • Decision-Making Biases

Don't neglect the power of "yes"

Conflict and Negotiation

10

The Key Point

Although cooperation and collaboration are ideal conditions, conflict and negotiation are ever present in team and organizational dynamics. Everyone has to be able to deal with them in positive ways. The word "yes" can often get things back on track when tensions build and communication falters in teamwork and interpersonal relationships. ■

What's Inside?

- **Bringing OB to LIFE**
  KEEPING IT ALL TOGETHER WHEN MOM'S THE BREADWINNER
- **Worth Considering . . . or Best Avoided?**
  LABOR AND MANAGEMENT SIDES DISAGREE. IS A STRIKE THE ANSWER?
- **Checking Ethics in OB**
  BLOGGING CAN BE FUN, BUT BLOGGERS BEWARE
- **Finding the Leader in You**
  ALAN MULALLY LEADS BY TRANSFORMING AN EXECUTIVE TEAM
- **OB in Popular Culture**
  CONFLICT AND *THE DEVIL WEARS PRADA*
- **Research Insight**
  WORDS AFFECT OUTCOMES IN ONLINE DISPUTE RESOLUTION

Chapter at a Glance

- What Is the Nature of Conflict in Organizations?
- How Can Conflict Be Managed?
- What Is the Nature of Negotiation in Organizations?
- What Are Alternative Strategies for Negotiation?

Conflict in Organizations

LEARNING ROADMAP — TYPES OF CONFLICT • LEVELS OF CONFLICT • FUNCTIONAL AND DYSFUNCTIONAL CONFLICT • CULTURE AND CONFLICT

> TEACHING NOTE: Ask students for examples of substantive and emotional conflicts they have experienced and that were particularly troublesome for them. Engage a class discussion of selected examples to identify underlying conflict dynamics.

We all need skills to work well with others who don't always agree with us, even in situations that are complicated and stressful.[1] **Conflict** occurs whenever disagreements exist in a social situation over issues of substance, or whenever emotional antagonisms create frictions between individuals or groups.[2] Team leaders and members can spend considerable time dealing with conflicts. Sometimes they are direct participants, and other times they act as mediators or neutral third parties to help resolve conflicts between other people.[3] The fact is that conflict dynamics are inevitable in the workplace, and it's best to know how to handle them.[4]

Conflict occurs when parties disagree over substantive issues or when emotional antagonisms create friction between them.

▌ Types of Conflict

Conflicts in teams, at work, and in our personal lives occur in at least two basic forms: substantive and emotional. Both types are common, ever present, and challenging. How well prepared are you to deal successfully with them?

Substantive conflict is a fundamental disagreement over ends or goals to be pursued and the means for their accomplishment.[5] A dispute with one's boss or other team members over a plan of action to be followed, such as the marketing strategy for a new product, is an example of substantive conflict. When people work together every day, it is only normal that different viewpoints on a variety of substantive workplace issues will arise. At times people will disagree over such things as team and organizational goals, the allocation of resources, the distribution of rewards, policies and procedures, and task assignments.

Substantive conflict involves fundamental disagreement over ends or goals to be pursued and the means for their accomplishment.

Emotional conflict involves interpersonal difficulties that arise over feelings of anger, mistrust, dislike, fear, resentment, and the like.[6] This conflict is commonly known as a "clash of personalities." How many times, for example, have you heard comments such as "I can't stand working with him" or "She always rubs me the wrong way" or "I wouldn't do what he asked if you begged me"? When emotional conflicts creep into work situations, they can drain energies and distract people from task priorities and goals. Yet, they emerge in a wide variety of settings and are common in teams, among co-workers, and in superior–subordinate relationships.

Emotional conflict involves interpersonal difficulties that arise over feelings of anger, mistrust, dislike, fear, resentment, and the like.

▌ Levels of Conflict

Our first tendency may be to think of conflict as something that happens between two people, something we call "interpersonal conflict." Conflicts in teams and organizations take other forms as well, and each needs to be understood. The full range of conflicts that we experience at work includes those emerging from the interpersonal, intrapersonal, intergroup, and interorganizational levels.

Interpersonal conflict occurs between two or more individuals who are in opposition to one another. It may be substantive, emotional, or both. Two teammates debating each other aggressively on the merits of hiring a specific job applicant for the team is an example of a substantive interpersonal conflict. Two persons continually in disagreement over each other's choice of words, work attire, personal appearance, or manners is an example of an emotional interpersonal conflict. Both types of interpersonal conflict often arise in the performance assessment process where the traditional focus has been on one person passing judgment on another. Sometimes the issue is one of substance—"Just exactly what does 'poor' performance mean?" asks the subordinate. Others times it is emotional—"I don't care if it is okay. Your long hair is a misfit with the rest of the team," says the boss. Even as performance reviews turn toward peer and 360° types, similar issues can make assessments difficult interpersonal moments.

Interpersonal conflict occurs between two or more individuals in opposition to each other.

Intrapersonal conflict is tension experienced within the individual due to actual or perceived pressures from incompatible goals or expectations. *Approach–approach conflict* occurs when a person must choose between two positive and equally attractive alternatives. An example is when someone has to choose between a valued promotion in the organization or a desirable new job with another firm. *Avoidance–avoidance conflict* occurs when a person must choose between two negative and equally unattractive alternatives. An example is being asked either to accept a job transfer to another town in an undesirable location or to have one's employment with an organization terminated. *Approach–avoidance conflict* occurs when a person must decide to do something that has both positive and negative consequences. An example is being offered a higher-paying job with responsibilities that make unwanted demands on one's personal time.

Intergroup conflict occurs between teams, perhaps ones competing for scarce resources or rewards or ones whose members have emotional problems with one another. The classic example is conflict among functional groups or departments, such as marketing and manufacturing. Sometimes these conflicts have substantive roots, such as marketing focusing on sales revenue goals and manufacturing focusing on cost-efficiency goals. Other times such conflicts have emotional roots, as when egotists in their respective departments want to look better than each other in a certain situation. Intergroup conflict is quite common in organizations, and it can make the coordination and integration of task activities very difficult.[7] The growing use of cross-functional teams and task forces is one way of trying to minimize such conflicts by improving horizontal communication.

Interorganizational conflict is most commonly thought of in terms of the rivalry that characterizes firms operating in the same markets. A good example is business competition between U.S. multinationals and their global rivals: Ford versus Hyundai, or AT&T versus Vodaphone, or Boeing versus Airbus, for example. But interorganizational conflict is a much broader issue than that represented by market competition alone. Other common examples include disagreements between unions and the organizations employing their members, between government regulatory agencies and the organizations subject to their surveillance, between organizations and their suppliers, and between organizations and outside activist groups.

Intrapersonal conflict occurs within the individual because of actual or perceived pressures from incompatible goals or expectations.

Intergroup conflict occurs among groups in an organization.

Interorganizational conflict occurs between organizations.

Functional and Dysfunctional Conflict

Any type of conflict in teams and organizations can be upsetting both to the individuals directly involved and to others affected by its occurrence. It can be quite uncomfortable, for example, to work on a team where two co-workers are continually hostile toward each other, or where your team is constantly battling another to get resources from top management attention. As Figure 10.1 points out, however, it's important to recognize that conflict can have a functional or constructive side as well as a dysfunctional or destructive side.

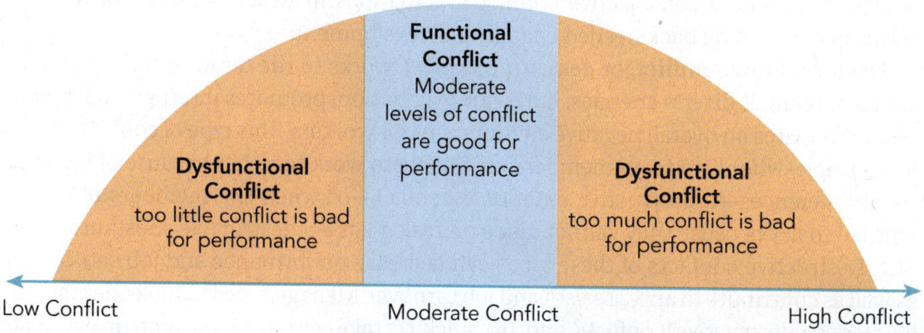

FIGURE 10.1 The two faces of conflict: functional conflict and dysfunctional conflict.

WORTH CONSIDERING …OR BEST AVOIDED?

Labor and Management Sides Disagree. Is a Strike the Answer?

It's hard to find a person who isn't in favor of good-quality schools. But when it comes time to change schools in search of a better future, teachers, administrators, and school boards sometimes have a hard time reaching agreement.

Take the case of Chicago. Mayor Rahm Emmanuel supported changes to lengthen school days, pay teachers on merit based in part on measures of student performance, and close some schools and open new ones. After months of negotiation teachers were given a 16 percent salary increase over 4 years. Nonetheless, the teacher's union went on strike over concerns about teacher evaluations, job security, and rules for hiring and firing teachers.

Even after a tentative agreement was reached by negotiators, the strike continued. Lewis said teachers were "not happy with the agreement. They'd like it to actually be a lot better." Robert Bruno, a labor law professor at the University of Illinois at Chicago, said, "I'm hard pressed to imagine how they could have done much better." A parent commented, "What's the point of going on strike if you don't get everything you need out of it?"

When the strike was over, more than 350,000 Chicago school kids had missed 9 days of school.

Scott Olson/Getty Images

Do the Analysis

In contrast to the Chicago school situation, Ford and the Canadian Auto Workers Union negotiated a new labor contract without a strike. The union's top negotiator said, "It's a damn good deal in these economic times," and Ford's negotiator said it "will improve competitiveness of the Canadian operations." So, is striking the answer when labor–management conflict hits the wall? Who wins and who loses when strikes occur? When conflicts occur, does having the threat of a strike on the table make management more willing to listen? What skills and conditions make reaching agreements more likely in high conflict situations?

Functional conflict results in positive benefits to the group.

Functional conflict, also called *constructive conflict*, results in benefits to individuals, the team, or the organization. This positive conflict can bring important problems to the surface so they can be addressed. It can cause decisions to be considered carefully and perhaps reconsidered to ensure that the right path of action is being followed. It can increase the amount of information used for decision making. It can offer opportunities for creativity that can improve performance. Indeed, an effective manager or team leader is able to stimulate constructive conflict in situations in which satisfaction with the status quo is holding back needed change and development.

Dysfunctional conflict works to the group's or organization's disadvantage.

Dysfunctional conflict, or *destructive conflict*, works to the disadvantage of an individual or team. It diverts energies, hurts group cohesion, promotes interpersonal hostilities, and creates an overall negative environment for workers. This type of conflict occurs, for example, when two team members are unable to work together because of interpersonal differences—a destructive emotional conflict—or when the members of a work unit fail to act because they cannot agree on task goals—a destructive substantive conflict. Destructive conflicts of these types can decrease performance and job satisfaction as well as contribute to absenteeism and job turnover. Managers and team leaders should be alert to destructive conflicts and be quick to take action to prevent or eliminate them—or at least minimize any harm done.

CHECKING ETHICS IN OB

Blogging Can Be Fun, But Bloggers Beware

Magali Delporte/eyevine/ReduxPictures

It is easy and tempting to set up your own blog, write about your experiences and impressions, and then share your thoughts with others online. So, why not do it?

Catherine Sanderson, a British citizen living and working in Paris, might have asked this question before launching her blog, *Le Petite Anglaise*. At one point it was so "successful" that she had 3,000 readers. But the Internet diary included reports on her experiences at work—and her employer, the accounting firm Dixon Wilson, wasn't at all happy when it became public knowledge.

Even though Sanderson was blogging anonymously, her photo was on the site, and the connection was eventually discovered. Noticed, too, was her running commentary about bosses, colleagues, and life at the office. One boss, she wrote, "calls secretaries 'typists.'" A Christmas party was described in detail, including an executive's "unforgivable faux pas." Under the heading "Titillation," she told how she displayed cleavage during a video conference at the office.

When it all came out, Sanderson says that she was "dooced"—a term used to describe being fired for what one writes in a blog. She sued for financial damages and confirmation of her rights, on principle, to have a private blog. The court awarded her a year's salary.

Who's in the Right? Would you agree with the observer who asks, "Say you worked for a large corporation, and in your spare time you wrote an anonymous 'insider's view' column for the Financial Times. Would you expect anything less than termination upon discovery?" Or would you agree with another, who asks, "Where does the influence your employer has on your day-to-day life stop?" Just what are the ethics issues here—from the blogger's and the employer's perspectives? Who has what rights when it comes to communicating in public about one's work experiences and impressions?

■ Culture and Conflict

Society today shows many signs of cultural wear and tear in social relationships. We experience difficulties born of racial tensions, homophobia, gender gaps, and more. They arise from tensions among people who are different from one another in some way. They are also a reminder that cultural differences must be considered for their conflict potential. Consider the cultural dimension of time orientation. When persons from short-term cultures such as the United States try to work with persons from long-term cultures such as Japan, the likelihood of conflict developing is high. The same holds true when individualists work with collectivists and when persons from high-power-distance cultures work with those from low-power-distance cultures.[8]

People who are not able or willing to recognize and respect cultural differences can cause dysfunctional conflicts in multicultural teams. On the other hand, members with cultural intelligence and sensitivity can help the team to unlock its performance advantages. Consider these comments from members of a joint European and American project team at Corning. *American engineer:* "Something magical happens. Europeans are very creative thinkers; they take time to really reflect on a problem to come up with the very best theoretical solution. Americans are more tactical and practical—we want to get down to developing a working solution as soon as possible." *French teammate:* "The French are more focused on ideas and concepts. If we get blocked in the execution of those ideas, we give up. Not the Americans. They pay more attention to details, processes, and time schedules. They make sure they are prepared and have involved everyone in the planning process so that they won't get blocked. But it's best if you mix the two approaches. In the end, you will achieve the best results."[9]

Conflict Management

LEARNING ROADMAP — STAGES OF CONFLICT • HIERARCHICAL CAUSES OF CONFLICT • CONTEXTUAL CAUSES OF CONFLICT • INDIRECT CONFLICT MANAGEMENT STRATEGIES • DIRECT CONFLICT MANAGEMENT STRATEGIES

> TEACHING NOTE: Have students study Figure 10.3 on conflict management strategies and identify which strategy is their most common or "default" option when in conflict situations. Ask what this tendency might imply about their performance and satisfaction in teams.

Conflict can be addressed in many ways, but true **conflict resolution**—a situation in which the underlying reasons for dysfunctional conflict are eliminated—can be elusive. When conflicts go unresolved, the stage is often set for future conflicts of the same or related sort. Rather than trying to deny the existence of conflict or settle on a temporary resolution, it is always best to deal with important conflicts in such ways that they are completely resolved.[10] This requires a good understanding of the stages of conflict, the potential causes of conflict, and indirect and direct approaches to conflict management.

Conflict resolution occurs when the reasons for a conflict are eliminated.

▣ Stages of Conflict

Most conflicts develop in the stages shown in the nearby figure. *Conflict antecedents* establish the conditions from which conflicts are likely to emerge. When the antecedent conditions become the basis for substantive or emotional differences between people or groups, the stage of *perceived conflict* exists. Of course, this perception may be held by only one of the conflicting parties.

There is quite a difference between perceived and *felt conflict*. When conflict is felt, it is experienced as tension that motivates the person to take action to reduce feelings of discomfort. For conflict to be resolved, all parties should perceive the conflict and feel the need to do something about it.

Manifest conflict is expressed openly in behavior. At this stage removing or correcting the antecedents results in *conflict resolution*, whereas failing to do so results in *conflict suppression*. With suppression, no change in antecedent conditions occurs even though the manifest conflict behaviors may be temporarily controlled. This occurs, for example, when one or both parties choose to ignore conflict in their dealings with one another. Conflict suppression is a superficial and often temporary state that leaves the situation open to future conflicts over similar issues. Only true conflict resolution establishes conditions that eliminate an existing conflict and reduce the potential for it to recur in the future.

▣ Hierarchical Causes of Conflict

The nature of organizations as hierarchical systems provides a convenient setting for conflicts as individuals and teams try to work with one another. *Vertical conflict* occurs between levels and commonly involves supervisor–subordinate and team leader–team member disagreements over resources, goals, deadlines, or performance results. *Horizontal conflict* occurs between persons or groups working at the same organizational level.

Research & Development Team	Manufacturing Team	Marketing Team
Emphasizes • Product quality • Long-time horizon	Emphasizes • Cost efficiency • Short-time horizon	Emphasizes • Customer needs • Short-time horizon

FIGURE 10.2 Structural differentiation as a potential source of conflict among functional teams.

Hierarchical conflicts commonly arise from goal incompatibilities, resource scarcities, or purely interpersonal factors. *Line–staff conflict* involves disagreements between line and staff personnel over who has authority and control over decisions on matters such as budgets, technology, and human resource practices. Also common are *role ambiguity conflicts* that occur when the communication of task expectations is unclear or upsetting in some way, such as a team member receiving different expectations from the leader and other members. Conflict is always likely when people are placed in ambiguous situations where it is hard to understand who is responsible for what, and why.

Contextual Causes of Conflict

The context of the organization as a complex network of interacting subsystems is a breeding ground for conflicts. *Task and workflow interdependencies* cause disputes and open disagreements among people and teams who are required to cooperate to meet challenging goals.[11] Conflict potential is especially great when interdependence is high—that is, when a person or group must rely on or ask for contributions from one or more others to achieve its goals. Conflict escalates with *structural differentiation*, when different teams and work units pursue different goals with different time horizons as shown in Figure 10.2. Conflict also develops out of *domain ambiguities*, when individuals or teams lack adequate task direction or goals and misunderstand such things as customer jurisdiction or scope of authority.

Actual or perceived *resource scarcity* can foster destructive conflict. Working relationships are likely to suffer as individuals or teams try to position themselves to gain or retain maximum shares of a limited resource pool. They are also likely to resist having their resources redistributed to others.

Power or value asymmetries in work relationships can also create conflict. They exist when interdependent people or teams differ substantially from one another in status and influence or in values. Conflict resulting from asymmetry is likely, for example, when a low-power person needs the help of a high-power person who does not respond, when people who hold dramatically different values are forced to work together on a task, or when a high-status person is required to interact with and perhaps be dependent on someone of lower status.

Stay Alert for These Common Causes of Conflicts in Organizations

- *Unresolved prior conflicts*—When conflicts go unresolved, they remain latent and often emerge again in the future as the basis for conflicts over the same or related matters.
- *Role ambiguities*—When people aren't sure what they are supposed to do, conflict with others is likely; task uncertainties increase the odds of working at cross-purposes at least some of the time.
- *Resource scarcities*—When people have to share resources with one another and/or when they have to compete with one another for resources, the conditions are ripe for conflict.
- *Task interdependencies*—When people must depend on others doing things first before they can do their own jobs, conflicts often occur; dependency on others creates anxieties and other pressures.
- *Domain ambiguities*—When people are unclear about how their objectives or those of their teams fit with those being pursued by others, or when their objectives directly compete in win–lose fashion, conflict is likely to occur.
- *Structural differentiation*—When people work in parts of the organization where structures, goals, time horizons, and even staff compositions are very different, conflict is likely with other units.

Indirect Conflict Management Strategies

Most people will tell you that not all conflict in teams and organizations can be resolved by getting everyone involved to adopt new attitudes, behaviors, and stances toward one another. Think about it. Aren't there likely to be times when personalities and emotions prove irreconcilable? In such cases an indirect or structural approach to conflict management can often help. It uses such strategies as reduced interdependence, appeals to common goals, hierarchical referral, and alterations in the use of mythology and scripts to deal with the conflict situation.

Managed Interdependence
When workflow conflicts exist, managers can adjust the level of interdependency among teams or individuals.[12] One simple option is *decoupling*, or taking action to eliminate or reduce the required contact between conflicting parties. In some cases, team tasks can be adjusted to reduce the number of required points of coordination. The conflicting parties are separated as much as possible from one another.

Buffering is another approach that can be used when the inputs of one team are the outputs of another. The classic buffering technique is to build an inventory, or buffer,

---

BRINGING OB TO LIFE

> "This puts me smack in the middle of a distinctively modern dilemma: how to handle the tensions of a marriage between an alpha woman and a beta man?"

Keeping It All Together When Mom's the Breadwinner

Members of today's new generation were largely raised with a sense of male–female equality. But is the man prepared for the woman to be the primary breadwinner? It wasn't too long ago that this question would have seemed out of the ordinary. After all, the female partner or spouse as breadwinner was pretty much an anomaly. Times have changed, and both men and women are facing adjustments.

The U.S. Bureau of Labor Statistics reports that some 40 percent of women earn more than their husbands, and wives out-earn husbands in 35 percent of families in top income brackets. Susan is one, and says, "This puts me smack in the middle of a distinctively modern dilemma: how to handle the tensions of a marriage between an alpha woman and a beta man?" Michelle is another and she says that gender role reversal—man takes care of the kids and chores while the woman goes to work—"puts immense pressure on our marriage."

Even though many, perhaps most, men don't have a problem with their partners or wives out-earning them, the stereotype still puts them in an awkward position. What does the label "house husband" mean to you— "slacker dude letting his wife do the heavy work" or "modern guy finding fulfillment in his role?" When Jon says, "I'm not the ambitious type like Alison, so I'm happy for her to make more money," does that make something less of him in their life partnership? When Greg says,

Sturti/iStockphoto

"I do feel angry and helpless because I can't support the family unit," what are the implications for his self-concept, work, and family relationships?

OB is heavy into issues of work–life balance, and the issues seem to be getting more complex than ever. More understanding of gender role reversals and female breadwinners would be useful. Indications are that relationships are better when couples are open with one another and in general agreement about what's taking place and why. Maybe OB can fill in the details and help couples increase the likelihood that both parties will be satisfied at home, at work, and in their relationship.

between the teams so that any output slowdown or excess is absorbed by the inventory and does not directly pressure the target group. Although it reduces conflict, this technique is increasingly out of favor because it increases inventory costs.

Conflict can sometimes be reduced by assigning people to serve as liaisons between groups that are prone to conflict.[13] Persons in these *linking-pin roles* are expected to understand the operations, members, needs, and norms of their host teams. They are supposed to use this knowledge to help the team work better with others in order to accomplish mutual tasks.

Appeals to Common Goals An *appeal to common goals* can focus the attention of conflicting individuals and teams on one mutually desirable conclusion. This elevates any dispute to the level of common ground where disagreements can be put in perspective. In a course team where members are arguing over content choices for a PowerPoint presentation, for example, it might help to remind everyone that the goal is to impress the instructor and get an "A" for the presentation and that this is only possible if everyone contributes their best.

OB IN POPULAR CULTURE

Conflict and *The Devil Wears Prada*

20th Century Fox/Photofest

Who wears Prada? In the hit movie *The Devil Wears Prada*, there is no doubt that it is Miranda Priestly (Meryl Streep). She's quite a contrast to her new assistant Andrea Sachs (Anne Hathaway). "Andy" is clearly out of her element when it comes to working in the fashion industry. As an assistant to the demanding Miranda, editor-in-chief of *Runway* magazine, she frequently finds herself assigned to impossible tasks.

In one scene, Andy is sent to retrieve sketches from designer James Holt (Daniel Sunjata) and gets buried in a party. She meets famed writer Christian Thompson (Simon Baker). Their conversation centers on career talk, but it's easy to see that Thompson has other motives. Although Andy recognizes this to a degree, she also realizes this relationship could have real value in terms of helping her meet Miranda's "impossible demands."

There are many work themes in this movie, from good boss–bad boss issues to everyday "How do you get along in a tough job" insights. The next time you watch it, however, check how the various players use or don't use conflict management and negotiation skills.

Management consultant William C. Byham says it is important to forge "deliberate connections" on the job. These connections become networks for learning, collaboration, and work accomplishment. They help us build all-important social capital: the capacity to enlist the help and support of others when it is needed.

Get to Know Yourself Better Take Assessment 18, Conflict Management Strategies, in the *OB Skills Workbook*. Think seriously about how you handle conflict and negotiation situations in your personal and work situations. What did you learn in this assessment about your preferred style for dealing with conflict? Sometimes the styles tend to be about equal. In other cases, we may learn that we have a dominant style. What about you? If you have a dominant style, how well does it serve you?

Upward Referral

Upward referral uses the chain of command for conflict resolution.[14] Problems are moved up from the level of conflicting individuals or teams for more senior managers to address. Although tempting, this has limitations. If conflict is severe and recurring, the continual use of upward referral may not result in true conflict resolution. Higher managers removed from day-to-day affairs may fail to see the real causes of a conflict, and attempts at resolution may be superficial. In addition, busy managers may tend to blame the people involved and perhaps act quickly to replace them.

Altering Scripts and Myths

In some situations, conflict is superficially managed by scripts, or behavioral routines, that are part of the organization's culture.[15] The scripts become rituals that allow the conflicting parties to vent their frustrations and to recognize that they are mutually dependent on one another. An example is a monthly meeting of department heads that is held presumably for purposes of coordination and problem solving but actually becomes just a polite forum for agreement.[16] Managers in such cases know their scripts and accept the difficulty of truly resolving any major conflicts. For instance, by sticking with the script, expressing only low-key disagreement, and then quickly acting as if everything has been taken care of, the managers can leave the meeting with everyone feeling a superficial sense of accomplishment.

■ Direct Conflict Management Strategies

In addition to the indirect conflict management strategies just discussed, it is also very important to understand how conflict management plays out in face-to-face fashion. Figure 10.3 shows five direct conflict management strategies that vary in their emphasis

FIGURE 10.3 Five direct conflict management strategies.

Accommodation or Smoothing
Letting the other's wishes rule. Smoothing over differences to maintain superficial harmony.

Collaboration and Problem Solving
Seeking true satisfaction of everyone's concerns by working through differences, finding and solving problems so everyone gains as a result.

Compromise
Working toward partial satisfaction of everyone's concerns; seeking "acceptable" rather than "optimal" solutions so that no one totally wins or loses.

Avoidance
Downplaying disagreement; failing to participate in the situation and/or staying neutral at all costs.

Competition and Authoritative Command
Working against the wishes of the other party, fighting to dominate in win–lose competition, and/or forcing things to a favorable conclusion through the exercise of authority.

Cooperativeness (attempting to satisfy the other party's concerns): Cooperative / Uncooperative

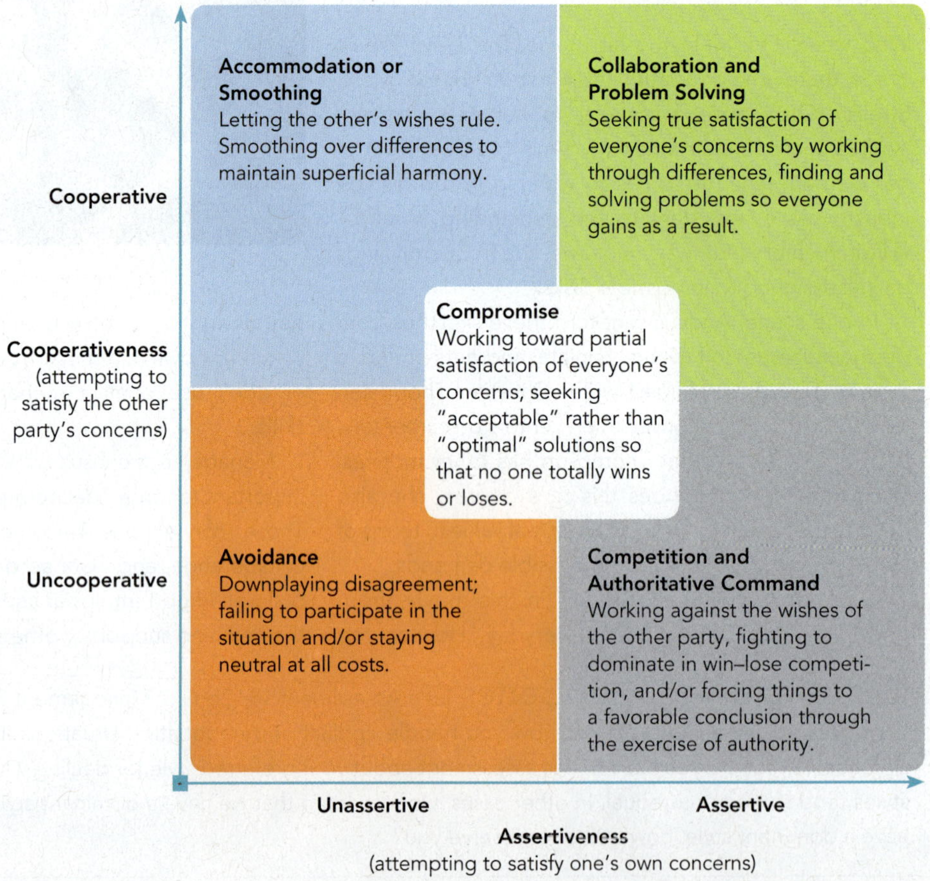

Assertiveness (attempting to satisfy one's own concerns): Unassertive / Assertive

on cooperativeness and assertiveness in the interpersonal dynamics of the situation. Although true conflict resolution can occur only when a conflict is dealt with through a solution that allows all conflicting parties to "win," the reality is that direct conflict management may also pursue lose–lose and win–lose outcomes.[17]

Lose–Lose Strategies

Lose–lose conflict occurs when nobody really gets what he or she wants in a conflict situation. The underlying reasons for the conflict remain unaffected, and a similar conflict is likely to occur in the future. Lose–lose outcomes are likely when the conflict management strategies involve little or no assertiveness. **Avoidance** is the extreme where no one acts assertively and everyone simply pretends the conflict doesn't exist and hopes it will go away. **Accommodation** (or **smoothing**) as it is sometimes called, involves playing down differences among the conflicting parties and highlighting similarities and areas of agreement. This peaceful coexistence ignores the real essence of a conflict and often creates frustration and resentment. **Compromise** occurs when each party shows moderate assertiveness and cooperation and is ultimately willing to give up something of value to the other. Because no one gets what they really wanted, the antecedent conditions for future conflicts are established.

> **Avoidance** involves pretending a conflict does not really exist.
>
> **Accommodation** (or **smoothing**) involves playing down differences and finding areas of agreement.
>
> **Compromise** occurs when each party gives up something of value to the other.

Win–Lose Strategies

In *win–lose conflict*, one party achieves its desires at the expense and to the exclusion of the other party's desires. This is a high-assertiveness and low-cooperativeness situation. It may result from outright **competition** in which one party achieves a victory through force, superior skill, or domination. It may also occur as a result of **authoritative command**, whereby a formal authority such as manager or team leader simply dictates a solution and specifies what is gained and what is lost by whom. Win–lose strategies fail to address the root causes of the conflict and tend to suppress the desires of at least one of the conflicting parties. As a result, future conflicts over the same issues are likely to occur.

> **Competition** seeks victory by force, superior skill, or domination.
>
> **Authoritative command** uses formal authority to end conflict.

Win–Win Strategies

Win–win conflict is achieved by a blend of both high cooperativeness and high assertiveness.[18] **Collaboration and problem solving** involve recognition by all conflicting parties that something is wrong and needs attention. It stresses gathering and evaluating information in solving disputes and making choices. All relevant issues are raised and openly discussed. Win–win outcomes eliminate the reasons for continuing or resurrecting the conflict because nothing has been avoided or suppressed.

> **Collaboration and problem solving** involve recognition that something is wrong and needs attention through problem solving.

The ultimate test for collaboration and problem solving is whether or not the conflicting parties see that the solution to the conflict: (1) achieves each party's goals, (2) is acceptable to both parties, and (3) establishes a process whereby all parties involved see a responsibility to be open and honest about facts and feelings. When success in each of these areas is achieved, the likelihood of true conflict resolution is greatly increased. However, this process often takes time and consumes lots of energy, to which the parties must be willing to commit. Collaboration and problem solving aren't always feasible, and the other strategies are sometimes useful if not preferred.[19] As the "You Should Know…" features points out, each of the conflict management strategies may have advantages under certain conditions.

Know When to Use Alternative Conflict Management Strategies

- *Avoidance* may be used when an issue is trivial, when more important issues are pressing, or when people need to cool down temporarily and regain perspective.
- *Accommodation* may be used when issues are more important to others than to yourself or when you want to build "credits" for use in later disagreements.
- *Compromise* may be used to arrive at temporary settlements of complex issues or to arrive at expedient solutions when time is limited.
- *Authoritative command* may be used when quick and decisive action is vital or when unpopular actions must be taken.
- *Collaboration and problem solving* are used to gain true conflict resolution when time and cost permit.

Negotiation

LEARNING ROADMAP — ORGANIZATIONAL SETTINGS FOR NEGOTIATION • NEGOTIATION GOALS AND OUTCOMES • ETHICAL ASPECTS OF NEGOTIATION

> TEACHING NOTE: Have students read both the Finding the Leader in You feature on Alan Mulally at Ford and the photo essay on two-tier wage systems. Ask them to use both to inform a discussion of how substance and process goals might or might not be achieved in labor-management negotiations in the auto industry.

Picture yourself trying to make a decision. *Situation:* You are about to order a new tablet device for a team member in your department. Then another team member submits a request for one of a different brand. Your boss says that only one brand can be ordered. *Situation:* You have been offered a new job in another city and want to take it, but you are disappointed with the salary. You've heard friends talk about how they "negotiated" better offers when taking jobs. You are concerned about the costs of relocating and would like a signing bonus as well as a guarantee of an early salary review.

The preceding examples are just two of the many situations that involve **negotiation**—the process of making joint decisions when the parties involved have different preferences.[20] Negotiation has special significance in teams and work settings, where disagreements are likely to arise over such diverse matters as wage rates, task objectives, performance evaluations, job assignments, work schedules, work locations, and more.

Negotiation is the process of making joint decisions when the parties involved have different preferences.

■ Organizational Settings for Negotiation

Managers and team leaders should be prepared to participate in at least four major action settings for negotiations. In a *two-party negotiation*, the manager negotiates directly with one other person. In a *group negotiation*, the manager is part of a team or group whose members are negotiating to arrive at a common decision. In an *intergroup negotiation*, the manager is part of a team that is negotiating with another group to arrive at a decision regarding a problem or situation affecting both. In a *constituency negotiation*, each party represents a broader constituency—for example, representatives of management and labor negotiating a collective bargaining agreement.

■ Negotiation Goals and Outcomes

Two important goals are at stake in any negotiation: substance goals and relationship goals. *Substance goals* deal with outcomes that relate to the content issues under negotiation. The dollar amount of a salary offer in a recruiting situation is one example. *Relationship goals* deal with outcomes that relate to how well people involved in the negotiation and any constituencies they may represent are able to work with one another once the process is concluded. An example is the ability of union members and management representatives to work together effectively after a labor contract dispute has been settled.

Effective negotiation occurs when substance issues are resolved and working relationships are maintained or even improved. In practice, think of this in terms of two criteria for effective negotiation:

Effective negotiation occurs when substance issues are resolved and working relationships are maintained or improved.

▶ Criteria of effective negotiation

- *Quality of outcomes*—The negotiation results in a "quality" agreement that is wise and satisfactory to all sides.
- *Harmony in relationships*—The negotiation is "harmonious" and fosters rather than inhibits good interpersonal relations.

■ Ethical Aspects of Negotiation

It would be ideal if everyone involved in a negotiation followed high ethical standards of conduct, but this goal can get sidetracked by an overemphasis on self-interests. The motivation to behave ethically in negotiations can be put to the test by each party's

FINDING THE LEADER IN YOU
Alan Mulally Leads by Transforming an Executive Team

Why did a CEO brought in from outside the industry fare the best as the Big Three automakers went into crisis mode during the economic downturn? That's a question that Ford Motor Company's chairman, William Clay Ford Jr., has been happy to answer. The person he's talking about is Alan Mulally, a former Boeing executive that Ford hired to retool the firm and put it back on a competitive track.

Many wondered at the time if an "airplane guy" could run an auto company. It isn't easy to come in from outside an industry and successfully lead a huge firm. Mulally's management experience and insights are proving well up to the task. One consultant remarked, "The speed with which Mulally has transformed Ford into a more nimble and healthy operation has been one of the more impressive jobs I've seen." He went on to say that without Mulally's impact, Ford might well have gone out of business.

In addition to making changes to modernize plants and streamline operations, Mulally tackled the bureaucratic problems common to many extremely large organizations—particularly those dealing with functional chimneys and a lack of open communication. William Ford says that the "old" Ford had a culture that "loved to meet" and in which managers got together to discuss the message they wanted to communicate to the top executives. Mulally changed all that.

He began with a focus on transparency and data-based decision making. He pushed for greater cooperation between Ford's divisions. He pursued a more centralized approach to global operations, one that focused on building vehicles to sell in many markets. When some of the senior executives balked and tried to go directly to Ford with their complaints, Mulally refused. "I didn't permit it," he says, thus reinforcing his authority to run the firm his way.

Ford's a dividend-paying stock once again, and Mulally has gained lots of respect for his executive prowess. One of his senior managers says, "I've never had such consistency

STAN HONDA/AFP/Getty Images, Inc.

of purpose before." The next big question is: "Who's going to replace Mulally?" He's due for retirement soon.

What's the Lesson Here?

How comfortable are you with conflict? Can you tolerate heated discussions around you, and can you recognize the difference between productive and nonproductive conflict? Would you be able to stand firm when others disagree with you (e.g., try to protect the status quo), or would you question your judgment?

desire to get more than the other from the negotiation and/or by a belief that there are insufficient resources to satisfy all parties.[21] After the heat of negotiations dies down, the parties may try to rationalize or explain away questionable ethics as unavoidable, harmless, or justified. Such after-the-fact rationalizations can have long-run negative consequences, such as not being able to achieve one's wishes again the next time. At the very least, the unethical party may be the target of revenge tactics by those who were disadvantaged. Once some people have behaved unethically in one situation, furthermore, they may become entrapped by such behavior and may be more likely to display it again in the future.[22]

Negotiation Strategies

APPROACHES TO DISTRIBUTIVE NEGOTIATION • HOW TO GAIN INTEGRATIVE AGREEMENTS • COMMON NEGOTIATION PITFALLS • THIRD-PARTY ROLES IN NEGOTIATION

> **TEACHING NOTE:** Do the recommended exercise—The Ugli Orange. Use it to launch a discussion of distributive versus integrative negotiation scenarios. Ask for comments on what the implications are for their future salary negotiations with employers.

When we think about negotiating for something, perhaps cars and salaries are the first things that pop into mind. But people in organizations are constantly negotiating over not only just pay and raises, but also such things as work rules or assignments, rewards, and access to any variety of scarce resources—money, time, people, facilities, equipment, and so on. The strategy used can have a major influence on how the negotiation transpires and its outcomes.

Two broad negotiation strategies differ markedly in approach and possible outcomes. **Distributive negotiation** focuses on positions staked out or declared by conflicting parties. Each party tries to claim certain portions of the available "pie" whose overall size is considered fixed. **Integrative negotiation**, sometimes called *principled negotiation*, focuses on the merits of the issues. Everyone involved tries to enlarge the available pie and find mutually agreed-on ways of distributing it, rather than stake claims to certain portions of it.[23] Think of the conversations you overhear and are part of in team situations. The notion of "my way or the highway" is analogous to distribution negotiation; "Let's find a way to make this work for both of us" is more akin to integrative negotiation.

Distributive negotiation focuses on positions staked out or declared by the parties involved, each of whom is trying to claim certain portions of the available pie.

Integrative negotiation focuses on the merits of the issues, and the parties involved try to enlarge the available pie rather than stake claims to certain portions of it.

Approaches to Distributive Negotiation

Participants in distributive negotiation usually approach it as a win–lose episode. Things tend to unfold in one of two directions—a hard battle for dominance or a soft and quick concession. Neither one nor the other delivers great results.

"Hard" distributive negotiation takes place when each party holds out to get its own way. This leads to competition, whereby each party seeks dominance over the other and tries to maximize self-interests. The hard approach may lead to a win–lose outcome in which one party dominates and gains, or it can lead to an impasse.

"Soft" distributive negotiation takes place when one party or both parties make concessions just to get things over with. This soft approach leads to accommodation—in which one party gives in to the other—or to compromise—in which each party gives up something of value in order to reach agreement. In either case at least some latent dissatisfaction is likely to remain.

Figure 10.4 illustrates classic two-party distributive negotiation by the example of the graduating senior negotiating a job offer with a recruiter.[24] Look at the situation first from the graduate's perspective. She has told the recruiter that she would like a salary of $60,000; this is her initial offer. However, she also has in mind a minimum reservation point of $50,000—the lowest salary that she will accept for this job. Thus she communicates a salary request of $60,000 but is willing to accept one as low as

FIGURE 10.4 The bargaining zone in classic two-party negotiation.

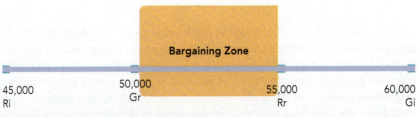

Ri   Recruiter's initial offer
Gr   Graduating senior's minimum reservation point
Rr   Recruiter's maximum reservation point
Gi   Graduating senior's initial offer

$50,000. The situation is somewhat the reverse from the recruiter's perspective. His initial offer to the graduate is $45,000, and his maximum reservation point is $55,000; this is the most he is prepared to pay.

The **bargaining zone** is the range between one party's minimum reservation point and the other party's maximum reservation point. In Figure 10.4, the bargaining zone is $50,000 to $55,000. This is a positive bargaining zone since the reservation points of the two parties overlap.

Whenever a positive bargaining zone exists, bargaining has room to unfold. Had the graduate's minimum reservation point been greater than the recruiter's maximum reservation point (for example, $57,000), no room would have existed for bargaining. Classic two-party bargaining always involves the delicate tasks of first discovering the respective reservation points—one's own and the other's. Progress can then be made toward an agreement that lies somewhere within the bargaining zone and is acceptable to each party.

Sooner or Later You'll Need to Know How to Negotiate a Better Raise

We've all done it—wish we'd asked for more when negotiating a starting salary or a pay raise. Why didn't we? And, even if we did, would it have made a difference? Chances are you'll go into a salary negotiation unprepared. And you may pay a price for that. There's quite a bit of advice around for how to negotiate pay raises. A compilation of thoughts and tips follows.

Josef Lindau/©Corbis

- *Prepare, prepare, prepare*—do the research and find out what others make for a similar position inside and outside the organization, including everything from salary to benefits, bonuses, incentives, and job perks.
- *Document and communicate*—identify and communicate your value; put forth a set of accomplishments that show how you have saved or made money and created value for an employer, or how your skills and attributes will do so for a prospective one.
- *Advocate and ask*—be your own best advocate; in salary negotiation, the rule is "Don't ask, don't get." But don't ask too soon; your boss or interviewer should be the first to bring up salary.
- *Stay focused on the goal*—the goal is to satisfy your interests to the maximum extent possible; this means everything from getting immediate satisfaction to being better positioned for future satisfaction.
- *View the details from the other side*—test your requests against the employer's point of view; ask if you are being reasonable, convincing, and fair; ask how the boss could explain to higher levels and to your peers a decision to grant your request.
- *Don't overreact to bad news*—never "quit on the spot" if you don't get what you want; be willing to search for and consider alternative job offers.

■ How to Gain Integrative Agreements

The integrative approach to negotiation is less confrontational than the distributive, and it permits a broader range of alternatives to be considered in the negotiation process. From the outset there is much more of a win–win orientation. Even though it may take longer, the time, energy, and effort needed to negotiate an integrated agreement can be well worth the investment. Always, the integrative or principled approach involves a willingness to negotiate based on the merits of the situation. The foundations for gaining truly integrative agreements can be described as supportive attitudes, constructive behaviors, and good information.[25]

The **bargaining zone** is the range between one party's minimum reservation point and the other party's maximum.

Attitudinal Foundations
There are three attitudinal foundations of integrative agreements. First, each party must approach the negotiation with a *willingness to trust* the other party. This is a reason why ethics and maintaining relationships are so important in negotiations. Second, each party must convey a *willingness to share* information with the other party. Without shared information, effective problem solving is unlikely to occur. Third, each party must show a *willingness to ask concrete questions* of the other party. This further facilitates information sharing.

Two-Tier Wages a Hot Button Issue in Labor–Management Negotiations

It was tough for automakers to sell cars and trucks when consumers were struggling. It was tough to earn a profit when costs, especially legacy pension costs, were high. And it was tough to compete with foreign carmakers who were building new cost-efficient plants. America's big firms—Chrysler, Ford, General Motors—responded with a two-tier wage system that pays new workers substantially less (up to one-half less) than existing workers doing the same job. So far the industry's labor unions have gone along with the two-tier system. It's appearing in other settings as well—many new teachers, for example, face similar two-tier systems. Some say two-tier wages are just a stopgap measure that will fade away with an improving economy? Others say they're here to stay.

Wolfgang Rattay/Reuters/Newscom

Behavioral Foundations
All behavior during a negotiation is important for both its actual impact and the impressions it leaves behind. This means the following behavioral foundations of integrative agreements must be carefully considered and included in any negotiator's repertoire of skills and capabilities:

▶ *How to gain integrative agreements*

- Separate people from the problem.
- Don't allow emotional considerations to affect the negotiation.
- Focus on interests rather than positions.
- Avoid premature judgments.
- Keep the identification of alternatives separate from their evaluation.
- Judge possible agreements by set criteria or standards.

Information Foundations
The information foundations of integrative agreements are substantial. They involve each party becoming familiar with the best alternative to a negotiated agreement (BATNA). That is, each party must know what he or she will do if an agreement cannot be reached. Both negotiating parties must identify and understand their personal interests in the situation. They must know what is really important to them in the case at hand and, they must come to understand what the other party values.

■ Common Negotiation Pitfalls

The negotiation process is admittedly complex on ethical and many other grounds. It is subject to all the possible confusions of complex, and sometimes even volatile, interpersonal and team dynamics. And as if this isn't enough, negotiators need to guard against some common negotiation pitfalls.[26]

One common pitfall is the tendency to stake out your negotiating position based on the assumption that in order to gain your way, something must be subtracted from the gains of the other party. This *myth of the fixed pie* is a purely distributive approach to negotiation. The whole concept of integrative negotiation is based on the premise that the pie can sometimes be expanded or used to the maximum advantage of all parties, not just one.

Second, the possibility of *escalating commitment* is high when negotiations begin with parties stating extreme demands. Once demands have been stated, people become committed to them and are reluctant to back down. Concerns for protecting one's ego and saving face may lead to the irrational escalation of a conflict. Self-discipline is needed to spot tendencies toward escalation in one's own behavior as well as in the behavior of others.

- Fixed pie myth
- Escalating commitment
- Over-confidence
- Too much telling
- Too little listening

Third, negotiators often develop *overconfidence* that their positions are the only correct ones. This can lead them to ignore the other party's needs. In some cases negotiators completely fail to see merits in the other party's position—merits that an outside observer would be sure to spot. Such overconfidence makes it harder to reach a positive common agreement.

Fourth, communication problems can cause difficulties during a negotiation. It has been said that "negotiation is the process of communicating back and forth for the purpose of reaching a joint decision."[27] This process can break down because of a *telling problem*—the parties don't really talk to each other, at least not in the sense of making themselves truly understood. It can also be damaged by a *hearing problem*—the parties are unable or unwilling to listen well enough to understand what the other is saying. Indeed, positive negotiation is most likely when each party engages in active listening and frequently asks questions to clarify what the other is saying. Each party occasionally needs to "stand in the other party's shoes" and to view the situation from the other's perspective.[28]

Research Insight

Words Affect Outcomes in Online Dispute Resolution

A study of dispute resolution among eBay buyers and sellers finds that using words that give "face" were more likely than words that attack "face" to result in the settlement of online disputes. Jeanne Brett, Marla Olekans, Ray Friedman, Nathan Goates, Cameron Anderson, and Cara Cherry Lisco studied real disputes being addressed through Square Trade, an online dispute resolution service to which eBay refers unhappy customers. For purposes of the study, a "dispute" was defined as a form of conflict in which one party to a transaction made a claim that the other party rejected.

The researchers point out that most past research on dispute resolution has focused on situational and participant characteristics. In this case, they adopted what they call a "language-based" approach based on the perspectives of face theory, essentially arguing that how participants use language to give and attack the face of the other party will have a major impact on results. In filing a claim, for example, an unhappy buyer might use polite words that preserve the positive self-image or face of the seller, or they might use negative words that attack this sense of face. Examples of negative words are *agitated*, *angry*, *apprehensive*, *despise*, *disgusted*, *frustrated*, *furious*, and *hate*.

This study examined 386 eBay-generated disputes processed through Square Trade. Words in the first social interchange between parties were analyzed. Results showed that expressing negative emotions and giving commands to the other party inhibited dispute resolution,

Dispute resolution less likely when
- Negative emotions are expressed
- Commands are issued

Dispute resolution more likely when
- Causal explanation given
- Suggestions are offered
- Communications are firm

whereas providing a causal explanation, offering suggestions, and communicating firmness all made dispute resolution more likely. A hypothesis that expressing positive emotions would increase the likelihood of dispute resolution was not supported. The study also showed that the longer a dispute played out, the less likely it was to be resolved.

In terms of practical implications, the researchers state, "Watch your language; avoid attacking the other's face either by showing your anger toward them, or expressing contempt; avoid signaling weakness; be firm in your claim. Provide causal accounts that take responsibility and give face." Finally, they note that these basic principles apply in other dispute resolution contexts, not just online.

Do the Research Consider the suggestions for successful online dispute resolution. Can you design a study to test how well they apply to disputes that may occur in virtual teamwork?

Source: Jeanne Brett, Marla Olekans, Ray Friedman, Nathan Goates, Cameron Anderson, and Cara Cherry Lisco, "Sticks and Stones: Language and On-Line Dispute Resolution," *Academy of Management Journal* 50 (February 2007).

Third-Party Roles in Negotiation

Negotiation may sometimes be accomplished through the intervention of third parties, such as when stalemates occur and matters appear to be irresolvable under current circumstances. In a process called *alternative dispute resolution*, a neutral third party works with persons involved in a negotiation to help them resolve impasses and settle disputes. There are two primary forms through which it is implemented.

In **arbitration**, such as the salary arbitration now common in professional sports, the neutral third party acts as a "judge" and has the power to issue a decision that is binding on all parties. This ruling takes place after the arbitrator listens to the positions advanced by the parties involved in a dispute. In **mediation**, the neutral third party tries to engage the parties in a negotiated solution through persuasion and rational argument. This is a common approach in labor–management negotiations, where trained mediators acceptable to both sides are called in to help resolve bargaining impasses. Unlike an arbitrator, the mediator is not able to dictate a solution.

In **arbitration** a neutral third party acts as judge with the power to issue a decision binding for all parties.

In **mediation** a neutral third party tries to engage the parties in a negotiated solution through persuasion and rational argument.

10 Study Guide

Key Questions and Answers

What is the nature of conflict in organizations?
- Conflict appears as a disagreement over issues of substance or emotional antagonisms that create friction between individuals or teams.
- Conflict situations in organizations occur at intrapersonal, interpersonal, intergroup, and interorganizational levels.
- Moderate levels of conflict can be functional for performance, stimulating effort and creativity.
- Too little conflict is dysfunctional when it leads to complacency; too much conflict is dysfunctional when it overwhelms us.

How can conflict be managed?
- Conflict typically develops through a series of stages, beginning with antecedent conditions and progressing into manifest conflict.
- Indirect conflict management strategies include appeals to common goals, upward referral, managed interdependence, and the use of mythology and scripts.
- Direct conflict management strategies of avoidance, accommodation, compromise, competition, and collaboration show different tendencies toward cooperativeness and assertiveness.
- Lose–lose conflict results from avoidance, smoothing or accommodation, and compromise; win–lose conflict is associated with competition and authoritative command; win–win conflict is achieved through collaboration and problem solving.

What is the nature of negotiation in organizations?
- Negotiation is the process of making decisions and reaching agreement in situations where participants have different preferences.
- Managers may find themselves involved in various types of negotiation situations, including two-party, group, intergroup, and constituency negotiation.

- Effective negotiation occurs when both substance goals (dealing with outcomes) and relationship goals (dealing with processes) are achieved.
- Ethical problems in negotiation can arise when people become manipulative and dishonest in trying to satisfy their self-interests at any cost.

What are alternative strategies for negotiation?
- The distributive approach to negotiation emphasizes win–lose outcomes; the integrative or principled approach to negotiation emphasizes win–win outcomes.
- In distributive negotiation, the focus of each party is on staking out positions in the attempt to claim desired portions of a fixed "pie."
- In integrative negotiation, sometimes called principled negotiation, the focus is on determining the merits of the issues and finding ways to satisfy one another's needs.
- The success of negotiations often depends on avoiding common pitfalls such as the myth of the fixed pie, escalating commitment, overconfidence, and both the telling and hearing problems.
- When negotiations are at an impasse, third-party approaches such as mediation and arbitration offer alternative and structured ways for dispute resolution.

Terms to Know

Accommodation (or smoothing) (p. 223)
Arbitration (p. 230)
Authoritative command (p. 223)
Avoidance (p. 223)
Bargaining zone (p. 227)
Collaboration and problem solving (p. 223)
Competition (p. 223)
Compromise (p. 223)
Conflict (p. 214)
Conflict resolution (p. 218)
Distributive negotiation (p. 226)
Dysfunctional conflict (p. 216)
Effective negotiation (p. 224)
Emotional conflict (p. 214)
Functional conflict (p. 216)
Integrative negotiation (p. 226)
Intergroup conflict (p. 215)
Interorganizational conflict (p. 215)
Interpersonal conflict (p. 214)
Intrapersonal conflict (p. 215)
Mediation (p. 230)
Negotiation (p. 224)
Substantive conflict (p. 214)

Self-Test 10

Multiple Choice

1. A/an _____ conflict occurs in the form of a fundamental disagreement over ends or goals and the means for accomplishment.
   - (a) relationship
   - (b) emotional
   - (c) substantive
   - (d) procedural

2. The indirect conflict management approach that uses the chain of command for conflict resolution is known as _____.
   - (a) upward referral
   - (b) avoidance
   - (c) smoothing
   - (d) appeal to common goals

3. Conflict that ends up being "functional" for the people and organization involved would most likely be _____.
   - (a) of high intensity
   - (b) of moderate intensity
   - (c) of low intensity
   - (d) nonexistent

4. One of the problems with the suppression of conflicts is that it _____.
   (a) creates winners and losers
   (b) is a temporary solution that sets the stage for future conflict
   (c) works only with emotional conflicts
   (d) works only with substantive conflicts

5. When a manager asks people in conflict to remember the mission and purpose of the organization and to try to reconcile their differences in that context, she is using a conflict management approach known as _____.
   (a) reduced interdependence   (b) buffering
   (c) resource expansion   (d) appeal to common goals

6. An _____ conflict occurs when a person must choose between two equally attractive alternative courses of action.
   (a) approach–avoidance   (b) avoidance–avoidance
   (c) approach–approach   (d) avoidance–approach

7. If two units or teams in an organization are engaged in almost continual conflict and the higher manager decides it is time to deal with matters through managed interdependence, which is a possible choice of conflict management approach?
   (a) compromise   (b) buffering
   (c) appeal to common goals   (d) upward referral

8. A lose–lose conflict is likely when the conflict management approach is one of _____.
   (a) collaborator   (b) altering scripts
   (c) accommodation   (d) problem solving

9. Which approach to conflict management can be best described as both highly cooperative and highly assertive?
   (a) competition   (b) compromise
   (c) accommodation   (d) collaboration

10. Both _____ goals should be considered in any negotiation.
    (a) performance and evaluation (b) task and substance
    (c) substance and relationship (d) task and performance

11. The three criteria for effective negotiation are _____.
    (a) harmony, efficiency, and quality
    (b) quality, efficiency, and effectiveness
    (c) ethical behavior, practicality, and cost-effectiveness
    (d) quality, practicality, and productivity

12. Of the following statements, only _____ is true.
    (a) Principled negotiation leads to accommodation.
    (b) Hard distributive negotiation leads to collaboration.
    (c) Soft distributive negotiation leads to accommodation or compromise.
    (d) Hard distributive negotiation leads to win–win conflicts.

13. Another name for integrative negotiation is _____.
    (a) arbitration
    (b) mediation
    (c) principled negotiation
    (d) smoothing

14. When a person approaches a negotiation with the assumption that in order for him to gain his way, the other party must lose or give up something, the _____ negotiation pitfall is being exhibited.
    (a) myth of the fixed pie
    (b) escalating commitment
    (c) overconfidence
    (d) hearing problem

15. In the process of alternative dispute resolution known as _____, a neutral third party acts as a judge to determine how a conflict will be resolved.
    (a) mediation
    (b) arbitration
    (c) conciliation
    (d) collaboration

▶ Short Response

16. List and discuss three conflict situations faced by managers.

17. List and discuss the major indirect conflict management approaches.

18. Under what conditions might a manager use avoidance or accommodation?

19. Compare and contrast distributive and integrative negotiation. Which is more desirable? Why?

▶ Applications Essay

20. Discuss the common pitfalls you would expect to encounter in negotiating your salary for your first job, and explain how you would best try to deal with them.

Steps to Further Learning 10
Top Choices from *The OB Skills Workbook*

These learning activities from *The OB Skills Workbook* found at the back of the book are suggested for Chapter 10.

Case for Critical Thinking	Team and Experiential Exercises	Self-Assessment Portfolio
• The Case of the Missing Raise	• Choices • The Ugli Orange • Vacation Puzzle • Conflict Dialogues	• Conflict Management Strategies

Communication builds relationships and results

Communication

11

The Key Point

How well do you communicate? Many people think they are effective communicators, but evidence suggests otherwise. In this chapter we identify the challenges of communication in organizational contexts, and describe what we can do to become more skilled communicators. ■

What's Inside?

- **Bringing OB to LIFE**
  REMOVING DOUBTS BY EMBRACING OPEN INFORMATION
- **Worth Considering . . . or Best Avoided?**
  EVERYONE ON THE TEAM SEEMS REALLY HAPPY. IS IT TIME TO CREATE SOME DISHARMONY?
- **Checking Ethics in OB**
  PRIVACY IN THE AGE OF SOCIAL NETWORKING
- **Finding the Leader in You**
  IDEO SELECTS FOR COLLABORATIVE LEADERS
- **OB in Popular Culture**
  CROSS-CULTURAL COMMUNICATION AND *THE AMAZING RACE*
- **Research Insight**
  LEADERSHIP BEHAVIOR AND EMPLOYEE VOICE: IS THE DOOR REALLY OPEN?

Chapter at a Glance

- What Is Communication?
- What Are Barriers to Effective Communication?
- What Is the Nature of Communication in Organizational Contexts?
- What Is the Nature of Communication in Relational Contexts?
- Why Is Feedback So Important?

The Nature of Communication

LEARNING ROADMAP THE IMPORTANCE OF COMMUNICATION • THE COMMUNICATION PROCESS • NONVERBAL COMMUNICATION

> TEACHING NOTE: Ask students to describe a situation in which nonverbal communication by themselves or someone else complicated a situation or relationship. Discuss implications for communication skills development.

Communication is the lifeblood of the organization. All organizational behavior—good and bad—stems from communication. Yet, despite the fact that we spend most of our lives communicating, we are not always very good at it.

In this chapter we examine communication in organizational and relational contexts to identify factors associated with effective and ineffective communication. A basic premise of this chapter is that to communicate effectively we need to have good relationships, and to have good relationships we need to communicate effectively.

Importance of Communication

Communication has always been important, but the nature of communication is changing in organizations and in the world. Widely available information is empowering people and societies in unprecedented ways. For example, the Egyptian Revolution of 2012 was called the "Facebook Revolution" because Egyptian citizens used Facebook to organize a revolution behind the scenes. In organizations, managers are not able to control information like they once could, and this is changing the nature of power in organizations. When Yahoo! announced that it would no longer allow employees to work at home, employees rebelled by anonymously posting company memos online. What managers had intended to be private company policy quickly snowballed into a major international news story and critique.

Communication is the glue that holds organizations together. It is the way we share information, ideas, and expectations as well as display emotions to coordinate action. Therefore we need to make effective communication a top priority in organizations.

The Communication Process

Although we all know what communication is, it is useful to review the basic communication model to set up a discussion of how and why communication breakdowns occur. As illustrated in Figure 11.1, **communication** is a process of sending and receiving

> **Communication** is the process of sending and receiving symbols with attached meanings.

FIGURE 11.1 The communication process.

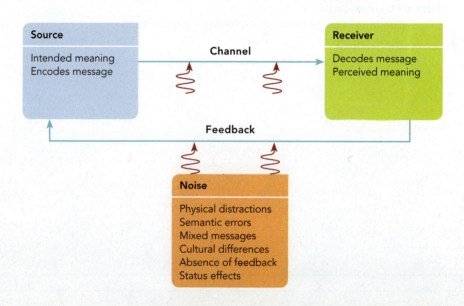

messages with attached meanings. The key elements in the communication process include a source, which encodes an intended meaning into a message, and a receiver, which decodes the message into a perceived meaning. The receiver may or may not give feedback to the source.

The information source, or **sender**, is a person or group trying to communicate with someone else. The source seeks to communicate, in part, to change the attitudes, knowledge, or behavior of the receiver. A team leader, for example, may want to communicate with a division manager in order to explain why the team needs more time or resources to finish an assigned project. This involves **encoding**—the process of translating an idea or thought into a message consisting of verbal, written, or nonverbal symbols (such as gestures), or some combination of these. Messages are transmitted through various **communication channels**, such as face-to-face meetings, e-mail, texts, videoconferencing, Skype, blogs, and newsletters. The choice of channel can have an important impact on the communication process. Some people are better at particular channels, and certain channels are better able to handle some types of messages. In the case of the team leader communicating with the division manager, for example, it can make quite a difference whether the message is delivered in person or electronically.

The communication process is not complete even though a message is sent. The **receiver** is the individual or group of individuals to whom a message is directed. In order for meaning to be assigned to any received message, its contents must be interpreted through decoding. This process of translation is complicated by many factors, including the knowledge and experience of the receiver and his or her relationship with the sender. A message may also be interpreted with the added influence of other points of view, such as those offered by co-workers, colleagues, or family members. Problems can occur in receiving when the decoding results in the message being interpreted differently from what was originally intended.

Feedback is the process through which the receiver communicates with the sender by returning another message. Feedback represents two-way communication, going from sender to receiver and back again. Compared to one-way communication, which flows from sender to receiver only, two-way communication is more accurate and effective, although it may also be more costly and time consuming. Because of their efficiency, one-way forms of communication—mass e-mails, reports, newsletters, division-wide meetings, and the like—are frequently used in work settings. Although one-way messages are

> The **sender** is a person or group trying to communicate with someone else.
>
> **Encoding** is the process of translating an idea or thought into a message consisting of verbal, written, or nonverbal symbols (such as gestures), or some combination of them.
>
> **Communication channels** are the pathways through which messages are communicated.
>
> The **receiver** is the individual or group of individuals to whom a message is directed.
>
> **Feedback** communicates how one feels about something that another person has done or said.

Perception Alert! Is Wealth Due to Good Connections or Hard Work?

If asked to choose which of the following statements is closest to the truth, how would you respond?

a. Most rich people today are wealthy mainly because of their own hard work, ambition, or education.
b. Most rich people today are wealthy mainly because they know the right people or were born into wealthy families.

This question was in a Pew Research survey with the following results. Overall, 46 percent of respondents chose B—the "good connections" alternative—while 42 percent chose A—the "hard work" alternative.

Interestingly, when respondents were categorized as upper or lower class, 56 percent of the uppers attributed their success to hard work while 53 percent of the lowers attributed the uppers' success to connections. In another Pew Research survey, 76 percent of respondents believed that "the rich get richer while the poor get poorer."

© Studio DL/Corbis

easy for the sender, they might be more time consuming in the long run when receivers are unsure what the sender means or wants done.

Although this process appears to be elementary, it is not as simple as it looks. Many factors can inhibit effective transmission of a message. One of these is noise. **Noise** is the term used to describe any disturbance that disrupts communication and interferes with the transference of messages within the communication process. If your stomach is growling because your class is right before lunch, or if you are worried about an exam later in the day, it can interfere with your ability to pay attention to what your professor and classmates are saying. In addition, if you don't like a person, your emotions may trigger a "voice" in your head that you can't turn off, disrupting your ability to hear and listen effectively. These are all *noise* in the communication process.

Noise is anything that interferes with the effectiveness of communication.

▶ Nonverbal Communication

Nonverbal communication is communication through means other than words. The most common forms are facial expressions, body position, eye contact, and other physical gestures. Studies show that when verbal and nonverbal communication do not match, receivers pay more attention to the nonverbal. This is because the nonverbal side of communication often holds the key to what someone is really thinking or meaning. Do you know how to tell if someone is lying? Watch for avoidance of eye contact and signs of stress, such as fidgeting, sweating, and, in more serious cases, dilated pupils.

Nonverbal communication occurs through facial expressions, body motions, eye contact, and other physical gestures.

Nonverbal communication affects the impressions we make on others. Because of this, we should pay careful attention to both verbal and nonverbal aspects of our communication, including dress, timeliness, and demeanor. It is well known that interviewers tend to respond more favorably to job candidates whose nonverbal cues are positive, such as eye contact and erect posture, than to those displaying negative nonverbal cues, such as looking down or slouching. The way we choose to design or arrange physical space also has powerful effects on how we interpret one another.[1] This can be seen in choice of workspace designs, such as that found in various office layouts or buildings. Figure 11.2 shows three different office arrangements and the messages they may communicate to visitors. Check the diagrams against the furniture arrangement in your office or that of your instructor or a person with whom you are familiar. What are you or they saying to visitors by the choice of furniture placement?[2]

"I am the boss!"

"I am the boss, but let's talk."

"Forget I'm the boss, let's talk."

FIGURE 11.2 Furniture placement and nonverbal communication in the office.

FINDING THE LEADER IN YOU: IDEO Selects for Collaborative Leaders

IDEO has built a business based on *design thinking*—an approach that engages diverse people in raucous dialogue to generate breakthrough ideas and creative solutions. Design thinking requires a certain kind of leader, so IDEO seeks out individuals who are smart and willing to engage in collaborative work: "We ask ourselves what will this person be like at dinner, or during a brainstorm, or during a conflict? We are eclectic, diverse, and there is always room for another angle."

Brainstorming is a fundamental element of design thinking, and failure is an accepted part of the culture. To succeed at IDEO, you have to be able to function with "confusion, incomplete information, paradox, irony, and fun for its own sake." Once ideas are developed, the key is storytelling through videos, skits, narratives, animations, and even comic strips. Free flow of ideas is enabled by discouraging formal titles, dress codes, and encouraging employees to move around—especially during mental blocks. According to general manager Tom Kelley, "It's suspicious when employees are at their desk all day because it makes you wonder how they pretend to work."

The creativity is reflected in the physical space that often looks like "cacophonous kindergarten classrooms." As described by Tom Peters, "Walk into the offices of IDEO design in Palo Alto, California, immediately you'll be caught up in the energy, buzz, creative disarray, and sheer lunacy of it all." Lunacy or not, for IDEO, design thinking is the key to success.

Courtesy of IDEO

What's the Lesson Here?

How would you fare at IDEO? Does the communication environment fit with your leadership style? Would you find the confusion and ambiguity exhilarating or frustrating?

Because nonverbal communication is so powerful, those who are more effective at communication are careful to use it to their advantage. For some, this means recognizing the importance of **presence**, or the act of speaking without using words. Analysis of Adolf Hitler's speeches shows he was a master at managing presence. Hitler knew how to use silence to great effect. He would stand in front of large audiences in complete silence for several minutes, all the while in total command of the room. Steve Jobs of Apple used the same technique during product demonstrations. In fact, Jobs was so good at managing presence that it made it more difficult for his successor, Tim Cook, who pales in comparison.

Presence is the act of speaking without using words.

Communication Barriers

LEARNING ROADMAP   INTERPERSONAL BARRIERS • PHYSICAL BARRIERS
SEMANTIC BARRIERS • CULTURAL BARRIERS

In interpersonal communication, it is important to understand the barriers that can easily create communication problems. The most common barriers in the workplace include interpersonal issues, physical distractions, meaning (or "semantic") barriers, and cultural barriers.

> TEACHING NOTE: Put students in discussion teams. Ask them to describe how each of the points about communication barriers—interpersonal, physical, semantic, cultural, applies to electronic as well as face-to-face communication.

▶ Interpersonal Barriers

Interpersonal barriers occur when individuals are not able to objectively listen to the sender due to things such as lack of trust, personality clashes, a bad reputation, or stereotypes/prejudices. Interpersonal barriers are reflected in a quote paraphrased from Ralph Waldo Emerson: "I can't hear what you say because who you are rings so loudly in my ears." When strong, interpersonal barriers are present, receivers and senders often distort communication by evaluating and judging a message or failing to communicate it effectively. Think of how you communicate with someone you don't like, or a co-worker or a classmate who

Interpersonal barriers occur when individuals are not able to objectively listen due to personality issues.

CHAPTER 11 ■ Communication

rubs you the wrong way. Do you listen effectively, or do you ignore them? Do you share information, or do you keep your interactions short, and perhaps even evasive?

Such problems are indicative of selective listening and filtering. In **selective listening**, individuals block out information or only hear things that match preconceived notions. Someone who does not trust will assume that the other is not telling the truth, or may "hear" things in the communication that are not accurate. An employee who believes a co-worker is incompetent may disregard important information if it comes from that person. Individuals may also **filter** information by conveying only some of the information. If we don't like a co-worker, we may decide to leave out critical details or pointers that would help him or her to be more successful in getting things done.

Another major problem in interpersonal communication is avoidance. **Avoidance** occurs when individuals choose to ignore or deny a problem or issue, rather than confront it. It is a major barrier to openness and honesty in communication. Avoidance occurs because individuals fear the conversation will be uncomfortable, or worry that trying to talk about the problem will only make it worse. This fear often comes with a lack of understanding about how to approach difficult conversations. Avoidance can be overcome by learning to use supportive communication principles, as described in a later section.

> **Selective listening** involves blocking out information and only hearing things that the listener wants to hear.

> **Filtering** leaves out critical details.

> **Avoidance** occurs when individuals ignore or deny a problem rather than confront it.

▶ Physical Barriers

Physical distractions are another barrier that can interfere with the effectiveness of a communication attempt. Some of these distractions are evident in the following conversation between an employee, George, and his manager.[3]

> Okay, George, let's hear your problem (phone rings, boss picks it up, promises to deliver the report "just as soon as I can get it done"). Uh, now, where were we—oh, you're having a problem with marketing. So (the manager's secretary brings in some papers that need immediate signatures; he scribbles his name and the secretary leaves) . . . you say they're not cooperative? I tell you what, George, why don't you (phone rings again, lunch partner drops by) . . . uh, take a stab at handling it yourself. I've got to go now.

Besides what may have been poor intentions in the first place, George's manager allowed physical distractions to create information overload. As a result, the communication with George suffered. Setting priorities and planning can eliminate this mistake. If George has something to say, his manager should set aside adequate time for the meeting. In addition, interruptions such as telephone calls, drop-in visitors, and the like should be prevented. At a minimum, George's manager could start by closing the door to the office and instructing his secretary not to disturb them.

> **Physical distractions** include interruptions from noises, visitors, and the like, that interfere with communication.

▶ Semantic Barriers

Semantic barriers involve a poor choice or use of words and mixed messages. When in doubt regarding the clarity of your written or spoken messages, the popular KISS principle of communication is always worth remembering: "*Keep it short and simple.*" Of course, that is often easier said than done. The following illustrations of the "bafflegab" that once tried to pass as actual "executive communication" are a case in point.[4]

> A. "We solicit any recommendations that you wish to make, and you may be assured that any such recommendations will be given our careful consideration."
> B. "Consumer elements are continuing to stress the fundamental necessity of a stabilization of the price structure at a lower level than exists at the present time."

> **Semantic barriers** involve a poor choice or use of words and mixed messages.

One has to wonder why these messages weren't stated more understandably: (A) "Send us your recommendations; they will be carefully considered." (B) "Consumers want lower prices."

▶ Cultural Barriers

We all know that globalization is here to stay. What we might not realize is that the success of international business often rests with the quality of cross-cultural communication. A common problem in cross-cultural communication is **ethnocentrism**, the tendency to believe one's culture and its values are superior to those of others. It is often accompanied by an unwillingness to try to understand alternative points of view and to take the values they represent seriously. Another problem in cross-cultural communication arises from **parochialism**—assuming that the ways of your culture are the only ways of doing things. It is parochial for traveling American businesspeople to insist that all of their business contacts speak English, whereas it is ethnocentric for them to think that anyone who dines with a spoon rather than a knife and fork lacks proper table manners.

Ethnocentrism is the tendency to believe one's culture and its values are superior to those of others.

Parochialism assumes that the ways of your culture are the only ways of doing things.

OB IN POPULAR CULTURE

Cross-Cultural Communication and *The Amazing Race*

CBS/Nancy Daniels/Landov LLC

You hear it often enough: To be successful in today's business world you must be culturally aware. This is particularly true when it comes to communication. Being proficient in other languages is an important skill. The ability to recognize the nuances of communication in other cultures, such as body language and the use of space, is even more important. Ethnocentrism, the belief that the ways of our own culture are superior, must be avoided in order to communicate effectively.

In Season 6 of *The Amazing Race*, contestants travel to Dakar, Senegal, to find the final resting place of a nationally famous poet. The stress of competition combined with the difficulties of a new culture cause problems for some of the teams. Gus and Hera are clearly uncomfortable with the conditions they face. Adam and Rebecca, limited in terms of language skills, nevertheless make fun of their taxi driver's inability to communicate with them. Freddy and Kendra get into an argument with a driver over the cab fare. Kris and Jon are excited by the prospects of experiencing a new culture. At the same time, Kris is appalled by how other competitors in the race are handling the situation.

When Jonathan screams for someone to speak to him in English, he is clearly exhibiting the "ugly American behavior" that Kris abhors. It is one thing to be uncomfortable with new surroundings, but to be abusive when individuals from other cultures do not respond the way you want shows disrespect for the host country.

Get to Know Yourself Better Assessment 4, Global Readiness Index, in the *OB Skills Workbook* measures your global readiness. The increasingly global nature of business demands workers who understand other cultures and are comfortable interacting with individuals whose values and practices may be quite different. If you were suddenly dropped into an unfamiliar country, how would you respond?

The difficulties with cross-cultural communication are perhaps most obvious in respect to language differences. Advertising messages, for example, may work well in one country but not when translated into the language of another. Problems accompanied the introduction of Ford's European small car model, the "Ka," into Japan (in Japanese, *ka* means "mosquito"). Gestures may also be used quite differently in the various cultures of the world. For example, crossed legs are quite acceptable in the United Kingdom but are rude in Saudi Arabia if the sole of the foot is directed toward someone. Pointing at someone to get his or her attention may be acceptable in Canada, but in Asia it is considered inappropriate and even offensive.[5]

The role of language in cross-cultural communication has additional and sometimes even more subtle sides. The anthropologist Edward T. Hall notes important differences in the ways different cultures use language, and he suggests that these differences often cause misunderstanding.[6] Members of **low-context cultures** are very explicit in using the spoken and written word. In these cultures, such as those of Australia, Canada, and the United States, the message is largely conveyed by the words someone uses, and not particularly by the context in which they are spoken. In contrast, members of **high-context cultures** use words to convey only a limited part of the message. The rest must be inferred or interpreted from the context, which includes body language, the physical setting, and past relationships—all of which add meaning to what is being said. Many Asian and Middle Eastern cultures are considered high context, according to Hall, whereas most Western cultures are low context.

International business experts advise that one of the best ways to gain understanding of cultural differences is to learn at least some of the language of the country with which one is dealing. Says one global manager: "Speaking and understanding the local language gives you more insight; you can avoid misunderstandings." A former American member of the board of a German multinational says: "Language proficiency gives a [non-German] board member a better grasp of what is going on . . . not just the facts and figures but also texture and nuance."[7] Although the prospect of learning another language may sound daunting, there is little doubt that it can be well worth the effort.

> In **low-context cultures**, messages are expressed mainly by the spoken and written word.
>
> In **high-context cultures**, words convey only part of a message, while the rest of the message must be inferred from body language and additional contextual cues.

Communication in Organizational Contexts

LEARNING ROADMAP COMMUNICATION CHANNELS • COMMUNICATION FLOWS • VOICE AND SILENCE

Communication Channels

Organizations are designed based on bureaucratic organizing principles; that is, jobs are arranged in hierarchical fashion with specified job descriptions and formal reporting relationships. However, much information in organizations is also passed along more spontaneously through informal communication networks. These illustrate two types of information flows in organizations: formal and informal communication channels.

Formal channels follow the chain of command established by an organization's hierarchy of authority. For example, an organization chart indicates the proper routing for official messages passing from one level or part of the hierarchy to another. Because formal channels are recognized as authoritative, it is typical for communication of policies, procedures, and other official announcements to adhere to them. On the other hand, much "networking" takes place through the use of **informal channels** that do not adhere to the organization's hierarchy of authority. They coexist with the formal channels but frequently diverge from them by skipping levels in the hierarchy or cutting across

> TEACHING NOTE: Do the recommended exercise—Upward Appraisal, or your own version of it. Use results to make constructive changes to your course and also discuss communication barriers in organizational contexts.
>
> **Formal channels** follow the official chain of command.
>
> **Informal channels** do not follow the chain of command.

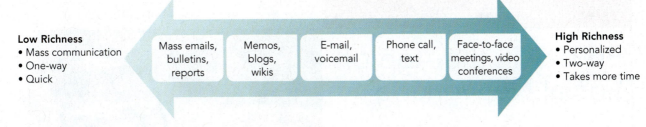

FIGURE 11.3 Richness of communication channels.

divisional lines. Informal channels help to create open communications in organizations and ensure that the right people are in contact with one another.

A common informal communication channel is the **grapevine**, or network of friendships and acquaintances through which rumors and other unofficial information are passed from person to person. Grapevines have the advantage of being able to transmit information quickly and efficiently. They also help fulfill the needs of people involved in them. Being part of a grapevine can provide a sense of security that comes from "being in the know" when important things are going on. It also provides social satisfaction as information is exchanged interpersonally. The primary disadvantage of grapevines arises when they transmit incorrect or untimely information. Rumors can be very dysfunctional, both to people and to organizations. One of the best ways to avoid rumors is to make sure that key persons in a grapevine get the right information from the start.

Channel richness indicates the capacity of a channel to convey information. And as indicated in Figure 11.3, the richest channels are face to face. Next are telephone, videoconferences and text, followed by e-mail, reports, and letters. The leanest channels are posted notices and bulletins. When messages get more complex and open ended, richer channels are necessary to achieve effective communication. Leaner channels work well for more routine and straightforward messages, such as announcing the location of a previously scheduled meeting.

A **grapevine** transfers information through networks of friendships and acquaintances.

Channel richness indicates the capacity of a channel to convey information.

Communication Flows

Information in organizations flows in many directions: downward, laterally, and upward. **Downward communication** follows the chain of command from top to bottom. Lower-level personnel need to know what higher levels are doing and be reminded of key policies, strategies, objectives, and technical developments. Of special importance are feedback and information on performance results. Sharing such information helps minimize the spread of rumors and inaccuracies regarding higher-level intentions, as well as create a sense of security and involvement among receivers who believe they know the whole story.

Lateral communication is the flow of information across the organization. The biggest barrier to lateral communication is **organizational silos**, units that are isolated from one another by strong departmental or divisional lines. In siloed organizations, units tend to communicate more inside than outside, and they often focus on protecting turf and information rather than sharing it. This is in direct contrast to what we need in today's organizations, which is timely and accurate information in the hands of workers.

Inside organizations, people must communicate across departmental or functional boundaries and listen to one another's needs as "internal customers." More effective organizations design lateral communication into the organizational structure, in the form of cross-departmental committees, teams, or task forces as well as matrix structures. There

Downward communication follows the chain of command from top to bottom.

Lateral communication is the flow of messages at the same levels across organizations.

Organizational silos are units that are isolated from one another by strong departmental or divisional lines.

CHECKING ETHICS IN OB

Privacy in the Age of Social Networking

CJG-Technology/Alamy

Is there a clear line between your personal and professional life? In the age of social networking, the answer to this question is becoming less clear. Today many companies are using the Internet to evaluate current and prospective employees, and if you fail to maintain a "professional" demeanor you could suffer consequences. There are stories of college athletes disciplined because of something they posted on their Web site, employees who are fired for what they say online about the company or their co-workers, or individuals who aren't hired because of a photo on their Facebook page.

To complicate matters, employment law in many states is still quite unclear and often provides little protection to workers who are punished for their online postings. Take the case of Stacy Snyder, age twenty-five, a senior at Millersville University in Millersville, Pennsylvania, who was dismissed from the student teaching program at a high school after the school staff came across a photograph on her MySpace profile showing her wearing a pirate's hat while sipping from a large plastic cup with the caption "drunken pirate."

Ms. Snyder filed a lawsuit in federal court in Philadelphia contending her rights to free expression had been violated. Millersville University, in a motion asking the court to dismiss the case, countered that Ms. Snyder's student teaching had been unsatisfactory—although school officials acknowledged that she was dismissed based on her MySpace photograph. They said her posting was unprofessional and might promote underage drinking, citing a passage in the teacher's handbook that staff members are "to be well-groomed and appropriately dressed."

Do the Research
The cases of Stacy Snyder and others raise interesting questions. As long as no laws are broken, should what an employee does after hours be the organization's business? Or should there be a line between an employee's professional and private life?

---

is also growing attention to organizational ecology—the study of how building design may influence communication and productivity by improving lateral communications.

The flow of messages from lower to higher organizational levels is **upward communication**. Upward communication keeps higher levels informed about what lower-level workers are doing and experiencing in their jobs. A key issue in upward communication is status differences. **Status differences** create potential communication barriers between persons of higher and lower ranks.

Communication is frequently biased when flowing upward in organizational hierarchies. Subordinates may filter information and tell their superiors only what they think the bosses want to hear. They do this out of fear of retribution for bringing bad news, an unwillingness to identify personal mistakes, or just a general desire to please. Regardless of the reason, the result is the same: The higher-level decision maker may end up taking the wrong actions because of biased and inaccurate information supplied from below.

Upward communication is the flow of messages from lower to higher organizational levels.

Status differences are differences between persons of higher and lower ranks.

Research Insight

Leadership Behavior and Employee Voice: Is the Door Really Open?

In today's environment, the willingness of all members to provide thoughts and ideas about critical work processes characterizes successful learning in various types of teams. Yet, despite this "learning imperative," many individuals do not work in environments where they feel it is safe to speak up. To address these issues, James Detert and Ethan Burris engaged in a study of employee *voice*—providing information intended to improve organizational functioning to those with authority to act, even if the information challenges and upsets the status quo.

Detert and Burris found that leaders being positive isn't enough. For employees to speak up they need leaders who are open to change and willing to act. Leaders being open is important because it provides a "safe" environment. The authors concluded that the signals leaders send are key inputs to employees in assessing the potential costs and benefits of speaking up.

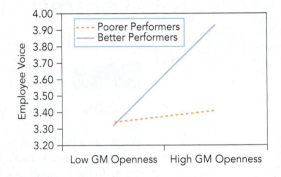

Do the Research Do you think the findings are applicable to your work situation? How would you conduct a study in your workplace to find out? What other variables would you include?

Source: J. Detert and E. Burris, "Leadership Behavior and Employee Voice: Is the Door Really Open?" *Academy of Management Journal* 50 (2007), pp. 869–884.

This is sometimes called the mum effect, in reference to tendencies to sometimes keep "mum" from a desire to be polite and a reluctance to transmit bad news.[8] One of the best ways to counteract the mum effect is to develop strong trusting relationships. Therefore, organizations that want to enhance upward communication and reduce the mum effect work hard to develop high-quality relationships and trusting work climates throughout the organization.

▶ Voice and Silence

The choice to speak up (i.e., to confront situations) rather than remain silent is known as **voice**.[9] Employees engage in voice when they share ideas, information, suggestions, or concerns upward in organizations. Voice is important because it helps improve decision making and promote responsiveness in dynamic business conditions. It also facilitates team performance by encouraging team members to share concerns if they think the team is missing information or headed in the wrong direction—correcting problems before they escalate.[10]

Despite this, many employees choose to remain silent rather than voice.[11] **Silence** occurs when employees have input that could be valuable but choose not to share it. Research shows that two key factors play into the choice to voice or remain silent. The first is the *perceived efficacy* of voice, or whether the employee believes their voice will make a difference. If perceived efficacy is low, employees will think "Why bother? No one will listen and nothing will change."

The second is *perceived risk*. Employees will be less likely to voice if they believe speaking up to authority will damage their credibility and/or relationships. Consistent with the mum effect, many employees deliberately withhold information from those in positions of power because they fear negative consequences, such as bad performance evaluations, undesirable job assignments, or even being fired.

Voice involves speaking up to share ideas, information, suggestions or concerns upward in organizations.

Silence occurs when employees choose not to share input that could be valuable.

Employees are more likely to remain silent in hierarchical or bureaucratic structures, and when they work in a fear climate. Therefore, organizations should create environments that are open and supportive. Formal structural channels for employees to provide information, such as hotlines, grievance procedures, and suggestion systems, are also helpful.

Communication in Relational Contexts

LEARNING ROADMAP RELATIONSHIP DEVELOPMENT • RELATIONSHIP MAINTENANCE
SUPPORTIVE COMMUNICATION PRINCIPLES • ACTIVE LISTENING

Much of the work that gets done in organizations occurs through relationships. Surprisingly, although we live our lives in relationships, most of us are not aware of, or ever taught, how to develop good-quality relationships. Many times people think relationships just happen. When relationships develop poorly, we have a tendency to blame the other: "There is something wrong with the other person," or "They are just impossible to deal with." But relationships are much more manageable than we might think ... it comes down to how we communicate in relational contexts.

▶ Relationship Development

Relationships develop through a **relational testing** process. This begins when one person makes a **disclosure**—an opening up or revelation about oneself—to another. For example, a simple disclosure is sharing one's likes or dislikes with another.

Once a disclosure is made, the other automatically begins to form a judgment. If the other shares the like or dislike, the individuals experience a sense of bonding, or attachment, with one another. If the other does not share the likes or dislikes, a positive connection is not felt and the relationship may remain at arm's length.

A deeper disclosure is a more intensely personal revelation, such as an intimate detail about one's personal history. Deeper disclosures are typically appropriate only in very high-quality relationships in which individuals know and trust one another. Inappropriate disclosures made too early in exchanges can derail the process and result in ineffective relationship development.

This sequential process represents the active "scorekeeping" stage of the testing process. If a test is passed, the relationship progresses, and disclosures may become more revealing. If a test is failed, individuals begin to hold back, and interactions may even take on a negative tone. This process is much like the classic game of Chutes and Ladders (see Figure 11.4). When relational tests go well they can act like "ladders," escalating the relationship to higher levels. When relational violations occur they can act like "chutes," dropping the relationship back down to lower levels.

Relational testing is really easy to see in the context of going out with someone. When you first hang out you share information with the other and watch for a reaction; you also listen for what the other shares with you. When things go well, you "hit it off" and things flow smoothly—you enjoy the interaction, and you like what the other person has to say. This leads you to share more information. When things go poorly, tests are not being passed for at least one individual and the interactions can become awkward and uncomfortable.

Because we are taught to be polite, sometimes it can be hard to tell how things are really going if individuals are covering up their true feelings or reactions. In professional settings, we engage in testing without even thinking about it. We don't do it on purpose—it's a natural part of how humans interact. Oftentimes, opinions get formed on a very trivial or limited information.

> TEACHING NOTE: Ask for examples of relationship violations students have experienced in work or academic situations. Choose one or more to deconstruct. Ask for suggestions on how good communication skills might have helped repair these relationships.

Relational testing is a process through which individuals make disclosures and form opinions or attributions about the other based on the disclosures.

A **disclosure** is an opening up or revelation to another of something about oneself.

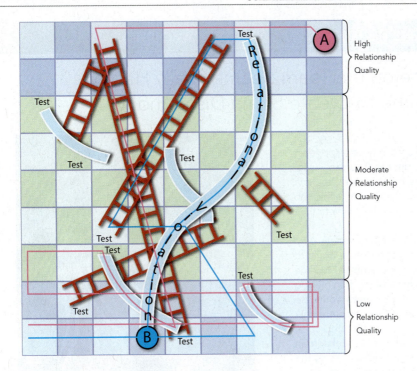

FIGURE 11.4 Relational Testing Process.

The key point is to understand that testing processes are going on around us all of the time, and if you want to more carefully manage your relationships, you need to be more consciously aware of when and how testing is occurring. When it is happening, you have to pay attention so you can manage the process more effectively. This does not mean being dishonest or fake; in fact, being fake is a quick way to fail a test! It does mean being careful how you engage with others with whom you have not yet established a relationship (e.g., a new boss).

■ Relationship Maintenance

Once relationships are established, testing processes take on a different form. They go from active testing to watching for relational violations.[12] A **relational violation** is a violation of the "boundary" of acceptable behavior in a relationship. These boundaries will vary depending on the nature of the relationship. In marriage, infidelity is a boundary violation. In a high-quality manager–subordinate relationship, breaking trust is a boundary violation. In a poor-quality manager–subordinate relationship, it may take more serious offense, such as sabotage or a work screwup, to constitute a boundary violation. The point is that the testing process is now not active "scorekeeping," or evaluating nearly every interaction, but rather one of noticing testing only when the relationship has been violated.[13]

As long as violations don't occur, individuals interact in the context of the relational boundaries, and the relationship proceeds just fine. When violations do occur, however, testing kicks back. If the relationship survives the violation—and some don't—it is now at a lower quality, or even in a negative state. For it to recover, it must go through relational repair.

Relational repair involves actions to return the relationship to a positive state. Relational repair is again a testing process, but this time the intention is to rebuild or reestablish the relationship quality. For example, a violation of trust can be repaired with a sincere apology, followed by actions demonstrating trustworthiness. A violation of professional respect can be repaired with strong displays of professional competence.

In most cases, relational repair requires effective communication. As you can imagine, not everyone has these skills, and those who have them often use them intuitively—not

A **relational violation** is a violation of the "boundary" of acceptable behavior in a relationship.

Relational repair involves actions to return the relationship to a positive state.

WORTH CONSIDERING ...OR BEST AVOIDED?

Everyone on the Team Seems Really Happy. Is It Time to Create Some Disharmony?

"There is no 'I' in team" goes the common cry. But basketball superstar Michael Jordan once responded, "There is an 'I' in win." What's the point here? Jordan is suggesting that someone as expert as he at a task shouldn't always be subordinated to the team. Rather, the team's job may be to support his or her talents so that they shine to their brightest.

In his book, *There Is an I in Team: What Elite Athletes and Coaches Really Know About High Performance* (Harvard Business Review Press, 2012), Cambridge scholar Mark de Rond turns to the world of sports to find insights into making the best of teams and teamwork in the business world. He notes that sports metaphors abound in the workplace. We talk about "heavy hitters" and ask teammates to "step up to the plate." But instead of the "I" in win that Michael Jordan talked about, the real world of teamwork is dominated by the quest for cooperation, perhaps at the cost of needed friction. And that's a performance problem.

Both du Rond and Harvard's Richard Hackman worry that harmony among teammates rather than high performance often becomes the team goal. Hackman says the problem is especially acute when the quest for harmony causes highly talented members to "self censor their contributions."

"When teams work well," du Rond says, "it is because, not in spite, of individual differences." Rather than trying to avoid or smooth over them, we need to find ways to accommodate these differences in teams. If superstars bring a bit of conflict to the situation, the result may well be added creativity and a performance boost that would otherwise not exist. Instead of trying to make everyone happy, perhaps it's time for managers and team leaders to accept that disharmony can be functional. A bit of team tension may be a price worth paying to bring someone with exceptional talents into the team equation.

© Duomo/Corbis

Do the Analysis

Okay, so maybe there is a superstar on your team. Does that mean that poor team contributions and even bad personality should be forgiven? Is there a point where talent simply overrides any negatives that the star brings to the team? Or is du Rond leading us, and our teams, astray? What is the line between real performance contribution and negative impact caused by personality and temperament clashes? Given what we know about teams and your personal experiences with them, should we be finding ways to accommodate the superstar or avoid them?

---

quite aware of what they are doing. One set of principles that can help individuals engage in relational repair, as well as in relationships, is *supportive communication principles*.

▶ Supportive Communication Principles

Supportive communication principles are a set of tools focused on joint problem solving.

Defensiveness occurs when individuals feel they are being attacked and need to protect themselves.

Supportive communication principles focus on joint problem solving. They are especially effective in dealing with relational breakdowns or in addressing problematic behaviors before they escalate into relational violations.[14]

Supportive communication principles help us avoid problems of *defensiveness* and *disconfirmation* in interpersonal communication. We all know these problems. You feel defensive when you think you are being attacked and need to protect yourself. Signs of **defensiveness** are people beginning to get angry or aggressive in a communication, or lashing out. You have a feeling of **disconfirmation** when you sense that you are being put down and your self-worth is being questioned. When people are disconfirmed they withdraw from a conversation or engage in show-off behaviors to try to build themselves back up.

Relationships under stress are particularly susceptible to problems of defensiveness and disconfirmation. Therefore, in situations of relational repair it is doubly important to watch for and diffuse defensiveness and disconfirmation by stopping and refocusing the conversation as soon as these problems begin to appear.

Supportive Communication Principles

1. Focus on the problem and not the person.
   Not "You are bad!" but rather "You are behaving badly."
2. Be specific, not global, and objective, not judgmental.
   Avoid using *never* or *always*, as in "You never listen to me."
3. Own, rather than disown, the communication.
   "I believe we need to change" rather than "Management tells us we have to change."
4. Be congruent—match the words with the body language.
   Don't say "No I'm not angry!" if your body language says you are.

Getty Images, Inc.

The first, and most important, technique to consider in supportive communication is to *focus on the problem and not the person*. If you focus on the person, the most likely reaction is for the other to become defensive or disconfirmed. A trick many people use to remember this is "I" statements rather than "you" statements. "You" statements are like finger pointing: "You screwed up the order I sent you" or "You undermined me in the meeting." An "I" statement, and a focus on the problem, would be "I had a problem with my order the other day and would like to talk with you about what went wrong with it" or "I felt undermined in the meeting the other day when I was interrupted in the middle of my presentation and not able to continue."

The second technique is to focus on a problem that the two of you can do something about. Remember that the focus should be on *joint problem solving*. This means the framing of the message should be on a shared problem, and the tone should be on how you can work together to fix it and both benefit in the process. It helps in this part of the conversation if you can make it clear to the other person how you care about him or her or the relationship and that the other person trusts your motives. If another perceives that you are out for yourself or out to attack, the conversation will break down. For example, "I'd like to talk with you about how we can manage the budget more effectively so we can avoid problems in the future" rather than "You overspent on the budget and now I have to fix your mess."

Beyond this, the other techniques help you think about the kinds of words you should choose to make the conversation more effective. For example, you should be *specific/not global*, and *objective/not judgmental*. Specific/not global means not using words like *never* or *always*. These words are easy to argue, and you will quickly find the other person saying "It's not true." Try to be more factual and objective. Instead of saying "You never listen to me," say "The other day in the meeting you interrupted me three times and that made it hard for me to get my point across."

The principles also tell you to *own the communication* and make sure to *be congruent*. Owning the communication means you take responsibility for what you say rather than place it on a third party. A manager who says, "Corporate tells us we need to better document our work hours," sends a weaker message than one who says, "I believe that better documenting our work hours will help us be more effective in running our business." Being congruent means matching the words (verbal) and the body language (nonverbal). If your words say, "No, I'm not mad," but your body language conveys anger, then you are not being honest or forthright. The other person will know it, and this may cause him or her to be less open and committed to the conversation in return.

Disconfirmation occurs when an individual feels his or her self-worth is being questioned.

Tough Talk from Bosses a Real Turnoff for Workers

Lots of times the answer to this question is "It's my boss." A survey by Development Dimensions International reports that difficult conversations with bosses are what employees often dread the most. Those conversations rank ahead of going back to work after vacation. They even rank higher than getting a speeding ticket or paying taxes. The influence of boss behavior—words and actions—on motivation was clear. Some 98 percent of those working for their "best boss ever" said they were highly motivated in their jobs; only 13 percent of those working for their "worst boss ever" said so.

Ice Tea Images/Age Fotostock America, Inc.

Active Listening

Active listening involves listening to another person with the purpose of helping a person think through his or her problem.

Reflecting involves paraphrasing back what the speaker said, summarizing what was said, or taking a step further by asking a question for clarification or elaboration.

Probing is asking for additional information that helps elaborate, clarify, or repeat if necessary.

Supportive communication principles emphasize the importance of **active listening**. Active listening again focuses on problem solving, but this time from the standpoint of trying to help another person. For example, active listening is often used in counseling situations. In these situations, your intent is to help the other person sort through problems involving emotions, attitudes, motivation, personality issues, and so on. To do this effectively, you need to keep the focus on the counselee and his or her issue(s) and not you and your issue(s).

The biggest mistake people make in this kind of listening is jumping to advice too early or changing the focus of the conversation onto themselves. A good principle to keep in mind during active listening is "We have two ears and one mouth, so we should listen twice as much as we speak."[15] When you are engaged in active listening, your goal is to keep the focus on the other person, and to help that other person engage in effective self-reflection and problem solving.

Active listening involves understanding the various types of listening responses and matching your response to the situation. What is most important to remember is that to counsel someone, you want to use *reflecting* and *probing* more often than *advising* or *deflecting*. Reflecting and probing are "opening" types of responses that encourage others to elaborate and process. Advising and deflecting are "closed" types of responses and should only be used sparingly, and at the end of the conversation rather than the beginning.[16]

Reflecting means paraphrasing back what the other said. Reflecting can also mean summarizing what was said or taking a step further by asking a question for clarification or elaboration. Reflecting allows us to show we are really listening and to give the speaker a chance to correct any misunderstanding we may have. **Probing** means asking for additional information. In probing you

Tips for Active Listening

- **Reflecting:** paraphrasing back what the speaker said, summarizing what was said, or taking a step further by asking a question for clarification or elaboration.

  "So you were upset by the way your manager treated you."

  "So do I hear you saying that you were upset by the way your manager treated you?"

- **Probing:** asking for additional information that helps elaborate, clarify, or repeat if necessary.

  "Why do you think you were so upset about the way your manager treated you?"

  "What else happened that made you upset?"

- **Deflecting:** shifting to another topic.

  "I know. That happens to me all the time."

  "Did you hear what happened to Raj the other day?"

- **Advising:** telling someone what to do.

  "You need to take care of that right away."

  "Talk to the manager and tell him you won't put up with it anymore."

want to be careful about the kinds of questions you ask so you do not come across as judgmental (e.g., "How could you have done that?"). You also don't want to change the subject before the current subject is resolved. Effective probing flows from what was previously said, and asks for elaboration, clarification, and repetition if needed.

Deflecting means shifting to another topic. When we deflect to another topic we risk coming across as uninterested in what is being said or being too preoccupied to listen. Many of us unwittingly deflect by sharing our own personal experiences. While we think this is being helpful in letting the speaker know he or she is not alone, it can be ineffective if it diverts the conversation to us and not them. The best listeners keep deflecting to a minimum.[17]

Advising means telling someone what to do. This is a closed response, because once you tell someone what to do that typically can end a conversation. While we think we are helping others by advising them, we actually may be hurting because doing so can communicate a position of superiority rather than mutuality. Again, the best listeners work to control their desire to advise unless specifically asked to do so and to deliver the advice in the context of supportiveness rather than presumptuousness.

> **Deflecting** is shifting the conversation to another topic.
>
> **Advising** is telling someone what to do.

Developmental Feedback

LEARNING ROADMAP FEEDBACK GIVING • FEEDBACK SEEKING • FEEDBACK ORIENTATION

In most workplaces, there is too little feedback rather than too much. This is particularly the case for negative feedback. People avoid giving unpleasant feedback because they fear heightening emotions in the other that they will not know how to handle. For example, words intended to be polite and helpful can easily be interpreted as unpleasant and hostile. This risk is especially evident in the performance appraisal process. To serve a person's developmental needs, feedback—both the praise and the criticism—must be well communicated.

> TEACHING NOTE: Ask students to use the Johari Window in Figure 11.5 to find reasons why a 360° performance feedback session might turn out to be less beneficial for the focal person than anticipated.

■ Feedback Giving

Feedback is vital for human development. Therefore, giving another person honest and **developmental feedback** in a sensitive and caring way is critically important. It lets us know what we are doing well and not so well, and what we can do to improve.

One tool that helps us understand this is the **Johari Window** (see Figure 11.5). The Johari Window shows us that we know some things about ourselves that others know ("open") and some things about ourselves that others don't know ("hidden"). But there are also some things about ourselves that we don't know but others do—this is our blind spot. The blind spot is blind to us but not to others. As you can imagine, this is a problem because it means others are aware of something about us, but we are in the dark! The only way to reduce blind spots is through feedback from others—which is why feedback is so important. It helps us reduce our blind spots.

Despite this, giving feedback is perhaps one of the most avoided activities in organizations. It doesn't have to be, however. When delivered properly, giving feedback can be a rewarding experience. It helps build relationships and strengthens trust. As with supportive communication principles, you should keep in mind certain important techniques when giving feedback:[18]

> **Developmental feedback** is giving feedback in an honest and constructive way that helps another to improve.
>
> The **Johari Window** is a tool that helps people understand their relationship with self and others.

1. *Make sure it is developmental:* Be positive and focus on improvement.
2. *Be timely:* Provide feedback soon after the issue occurs so it is fresh in mind.
3. *Prepare ahead of time:* Be clear about what you want to say so you stick to the issue.
4. *Be specific:* Don't use generalities, as that will just leave them wondering.

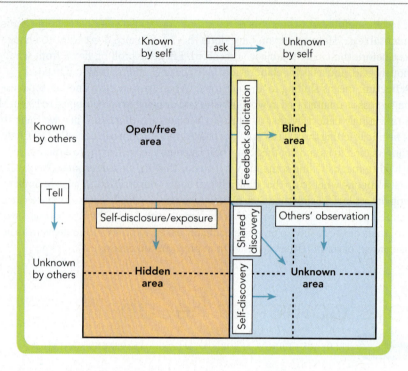

FIGURE 11.5 The Johari Window.

5. *Do it in private:* Have the discussion in a safe and comfortable place for the other.
6. *Limit the focus:* Stick to a behavior the person can do something about.
7. *Reinforce:* Don't bring the person down—make sure he or she knows there are good things about them too.
8. *Show caring:* Convey a sense of caring and that you are trying to help.

Feedback Seeking

The Johari Window implies we should not only give feedback—*we should also seek it*. Pursuing feedback allows us to learn more about ourselves and how others perceive us. In organizations, people engage in **feedback seeking** for multiple reasons: (1) to gather information for increasing performance, (2) to learn what others think about them, and (3) to regulate one's behavior.[19]

Because feedback can be emotionally charged, people typically like to see feedback involving favorable information. But this is not always the case. If individuals are more self-confident, they are more willing to seek feedback regarding performance issues, even if that feedback may be bad. The premise is that people prefer to know what they are doing wrong than perform poorly on a task. This seems to be less the case the longer that employees are in a job. Research shows that feedback seeking is lower for those who have been in a job longer, even though these employees find feedback just as valuable as newer employees do. This may be due to employees feeling they should be able to assess their own performance without needing to ask.[20]

When individuals fear that performance feedback will hurt their image, they are more likely to forego feedback seeking and therefore won't gain the benefits it can provide. Safe environments, where employees can trust others and there is little risk to their image or ego, can help overcome avoidance.[21]

Feedback Orientation

A concept that can help us understand individual differences in how people receive feedback is **feedback orientation**. Feedback orientation describes one's overall receptivity to

Feedback seeking is seeking feedback about yourself from others.

Feedback orientation is a person's overall receptivity to feedback.

BRINGING OB TO LIFE

> "I know where we are. I know the bottom line and how it's going to affect the bonus I get at the end of the year."

Removing Doubts by Embracing Open Information

Transparency is in and secrecy is falling by the wayside in more organizations. But is there a limit to how much co-workers should know about each other? It's hard to find an argument against transparency in any current discussion of leadership. So-called "open book management" is finding its way into more and more workplaces. In many ways it's a cornerstone of collaborative organizations.

© GlobalStock/iStockphoto

Scene: At a small software company, all seventy employees join monthly strategic management meetings and have free access to up-to-date financial information. New hires take a financial literacy workshop so that they can understand the numbers. One employee says, "I know where we are. I know the bottom line and how it's going to affect the bonus I get at the end of the year."

Sounds good, doesn't it? The firm is Tenmast Software of Lexington, Kentucky, and it's an example of transparency at work. But one thing you can't do at Tenmast is access salary information. That's still kept private.

Not so at SumAll, a small data-analytics firm in Manhattan. Salaries are part of CEO Dane Atkinson's commitment to running an open enterprise. Each employee is assigned to one of nine fixed-salary grades, and everyone knows where everyone else stands. Atkinson wants to take salary concerns off the table and refocus energies on the work to be done. "When it's secret, you want to know it more," says office manager Kimi Mongello.

From the OB side of things, such openness about financials, pay, and other matters is supposed to be a good thing—motivating employees and removing concerns about equity. But what about the possible downsides?

When RethinkDB, of Mountain View, California, tried pay transparency, it didn't work as expected. CEO Slava Akhmechet says too many employees used the information to try and negotiate for higher pay. It was also hard to pay well enough to get exceptional new hires. He had to either raise everyone's salaries or ask for exceptions. So, the open pay approach was dropped.

---

feedback. Those with a higher feedback orientation are better able to control and overcome their emotional reactions to feedback. They also process feedback more meaningfully by avoiding common attribution errors such as externalizing blame. This helps them to successfully apply feedback in establishing goals that will help them improve performance.[22]

Feedback orientation is composed of four dimensions. *Utility* represents the belief that feedback is useful in achieving goals or obtaining desired outcomes. *Accountability* is the feeling that one is accountable to act on feedback he or she receives (e.g., "It is my responsibility to utilize feedback to improve my performance"). *Social awareness* is consideration of others' views of oneself and being sensitive to these views. *Feedback self-efficacy* is an individual's perceived competence in interpreting and responding to feedback appropriately (e.g., "I feel self-assured when dealing with feedback").[23]

Those with feedback orientation tend to be higher in feedback-seeking behavior and have better relationships. They also tend to receive higher performance ratings from their managers. An important role for managers, however, is enhancing climates for developmental feedback. They can do this by being accessible, encouraging feedback seeking, and consistently providing credible, high-quality feedback in a tactful manner.[24]

11 Study Guide

Key Questions and Answers

What is communication?
- Communication is the process of sending and receiving messages with attached meanings.
- The communication process involves encoding an intended meaning into a message, sending the message through a channel, and receiving and decoding the message into perceived meaning.
- Noise is anything that interferes with the communication process.
- Feedback is a return message from the original recipient back to the sender.
- To be constructive, feedback must be direct, specific, and given at an appropriate time.
- Nonverbal communication occurs through means other than the spoken word (e.g., facial expressions, body position, eye contact, and other physical gestures).

What are barriers to effective communication?
- Interpersonal barriers detract from communication because individuals are not able to listen objectively to the sender due to personal biases; they include selective listening, filtering, and avoidance.
- Physical distractions are barriers due to interruptions from noises, visitors, and so on.
- Semantic barriers involve a poor choice or use of words and mixed messages.
- Cultural barriers include parochialism and ethnocentrism, as well as differences in low-context versus high-context cultures.

What is the nature of communication in organizational contexts?
- Organizational communication is the specific process through which information moves and is exchanged within an organization.
- Communication in organizations uses a variety of formal and informal channels; the richness of the channel, or its capacity to convey information, must be adequate for the message.
- Information flows upward, downward, and laterally in organizations.
- Organizational silos inhibit lateral communication, while upward communication is inhibited by status differences.
- The choice to speak up or remain silent is known as employee voice; voice is enhanced when employees perceive high efficacy that speaking up will make a difference and low risk that they will be harmed in the process.

What is the nature of communication in relational contexts?
- The most common types of relationships in organizations are manager–subordinate relationships, co-worker relationships, peer relationships, and customer–client relationships.
- Relationships develop through a process of relational testing; individuals make disclosures and, if the disclosure is positively received, the test is passed and the relationship will advance.
- Once relationships are established, they go from relational testing to watching for relational violations; relational violations occur when behavior goes outside the boundary of acceptable behavior in the relationship.

- Relational repair involves actions to return the relationship to a positive state.
- Supportive communication tools help in developing and repairing relationships; they focus on joint problem solving while reducing defensiveness and disconfirmation.
- Active listening is designed to help another person think through a problem; it focuses on reflecting and probing more than advising and deflecting.

Why is feedback so important?
- Most workplaces have too little feedback, not too much.
- Developmental feedback is important because it lets us know what we are doing well and not so well, and what we can do to improve.
- The Johari Window reveals the nature of blind spots—things others know about us that we don't know; feedback helps individuals reduce their blind spots.
- When done properly, giving feedback can be a rewarding experience because it helps build relationships and strengthen trust.
- Feedback seeking is seeking feedback about yourself from others.
- Feedback orientation describes one's overall receptivity to feedback.

Terms to Know

Active listening (p. 250)
Advising (p. 251)
Avoidance (p. 240)
Channel richness (p. 243)
Communication (p. 236)
Communication channels (p. 237)
Defensiveness (p. 248)
Deflecting (p. 251)
Developmental feedback (p. 251)
Disclosure (p. 246)
Disconfirmation (p. 249)
Downward communication (p. 243)
Encoding (p. 237)
Ethnocentrism (p. 241)
Feedback (p. 237)
Feedback orientation (p. 253)

Feedback seeking (p. 252)
Filter (p. 240)
Formal channels (p. 242)
Grapevine (p. 243)
High-context cultures (p. 242)
Informal channels (p. 242)
Interpersonal barriers (p. 239)
Johari window (p. 251)
Lateral communication (p. 243)
Low-context cultures (p. 242)
Noise (p. 238)
Nonverbal communication (p. 238)
Organizational silos (p. 243)
Parochialism (p. 241)

Physical distractions (p. 240)
Presence (p. 239)
Probing (p. 250)
Receiver (p. 237)
Reflecting (p. 250)
Relational repair (p. 247)
Relational testing (p. 246)
Relational violation (p. 247)
Selective listening (p. 240)
Semantic barriers (p. 240)
Sender (p. 237)
Silence (p. 245)
Status differences (p. 244)
Supportive communication principles (p. 248)
Upward communication (p. 244)
Voice (p. 245)

Self-Test 11

Multiple Choice

1. In communication, _____ is anything that interferes with the transference of the message.
   (a) channel
   (b) sender
   (c) receiver
   (d) noise

2. When you give constructive criticism to someone, the communication will be most effective when the criticism is _____.
   (a) general and nonspecific
   (b) given when the sender feels the need
   (c) tied to things the recipient can do something about
   (d) given all at once to get everything over with

3. Which communication is the best choice for sending a complex message?
   (a) face-to-face
   (b) written memorandum
   (c) e-mail
   (d) telephone call

4. _____ occurs when words convey one meaning but body posture conveys something else.
   (a) Ethnocentric message
   (b) Incongruence
   (c) Semantic problem
   (d) Status effect

5. Personal bias is an example of _____ in the communication process.
   (a) an interpersonal barrier
   (b) a semantic barrier
   (c) physical distractions
   (d) proxemics

6. Organizational silos _____ communication.
   (a) inhibit
   (b) enhance
   (c) do not affect
   (d) promote

7. _____ is an example of an informal channel through which information flows in an organization.
   (a) Top-down communication
   (b) The mum effect
   (c) The grapevine
   (d) Transparency

8. Relationships develop through a process of _____.
   (a) feedback seeking
   (b) feedback giving
   (c) active listening
   (d) relational testing

9. _____ cause a relationship to kick back into active testing processes.
   (a) Relational violations
   (b) Interpersonal barriers
   (c) Semantic barriers
   (d) Supportive communication principles

10. In _____ communication the sender is likely to be most comfortable, whereas in _____ communication the receiver is likely to feel most informed.
    (a) two-way; one-way
    (b) top-down; bottom-up
    (c) bottom-up; top-down
    (d) one-way; two-way

11. A manager who wants to increase voice in his department should increase _____.
    (a) bureaucracy
    (b) trust
    (c) hierarchy
    (d) the grapevine

12. _____ shows us why developmental feedback is so important.
    (a) The Johari Window
    (b) Relational testing
    (c) Active listening
    (d) Nonverbal communication

13. If someone is confused because they don't understand the word that the other is using the communication is suffering from a _____ barrier.
    (a) listening
    (b) interpersonal
    (c) semantic
    (d) cultural

14. Among the rules for active listening is _____.
    (a) remain silent and communicate only nonverbally
    (b) use primarily advising and deflecting
    (c) don't let feelings become part of the process
    (d) reflect back what you think you are hearing

15. The primary focus of supportive communication principles is _____.
    (a) reducing defensiveness and disconfirmation
    (b) increasing voice
    (c) reducing silence
    (d) increasing feedback orientation

▶ Short Response

16. Why is channel richness a useful concept for managers?
17. What is the role of informal communication channels in organizations today?
18. Why is communication between lower and higher levels sometimes filtered?
19. What is the key to using active listening effectively?

▶ Applications Essay

20. "People in this organization don't talk to one another any more. Everything is e-mail, e-mail, e-mail. If you are mad at someone, you can just say it and then hide behind your computer." With these words, Wesley expressed his frustrations with Delta General's operations. Xiaomei echoed his concerns, responding, "I agree, but surely the managing director should be able to improve organizational communication without losing the advantages of e-mail." As a consultant overhearing this conversation, how do you suggest the managing director respond to Xiaomei's challenge?

Steps to Further Learning 11
Top Choices from *The OB Skills Workbook*

These learning activities from *The OB Skills Workbook* found at the back of the book are suggested for Chapter 11.

Case for Critical Thinking	Team and Experiential Exercises	Self-Assessment Portfolio
• The Poorly Informed Walrus	• Active Listening • Upward Appraisal • 360 Feedback	• "TT" Leadership Style • Empowering Others

Make connections, gain power and influence

12

Power and Politics

The Key Point

Power and politics are a fact of life in organizations: To be successful, we must know how to gain power and use influence. But we also know that *power* and *politics* are often seen as dirty words. Why do these concepts have such a bad name and how can we overcome their negative connotations?

What's Inside?

- **Bringing OB to LIFE**
  FLIRTING AND CHATTING UP FOR SUCCESS
- **Worth Considering . . . or Best Avoided?**
  STRUGGLING TO GAIN INFLUENCE? TAP INTO THE SCIENCE OF PERSUADING
- **Checking Ethics in OB**
  FURLOUGH OR FIRE? WEIGHING ALTERNATIVE INTERESTS
- **Finding the Leader in You**
  CORRUPTIVE POWER OF CELEBRITY TURNS BLIND EYE TO PEDOPHILIA
- **OB in Popular Culture**
  TOOTING ONE'S HORN IN *SPANGLISH*
- **Research Insight**
  SOCIAL NETWORKS AND POWER IN ORGANIZATIONS

Chapter at a Glance

- What Is Power, and How Does It Operate in Organizations?
- What Are the Sources of Power and Influence?
- How Do People Respond to Power and Influence?
- What Are Organizational Politics?
- How Do Individuals Navigate Politics in Organizations?

Understanding Power

LEARNING ROADMAP WHAT IS POWER AND WHY IS IT IMPORTANT? • POWER AND DEPENDENCE • THE PROBLEM OF POWERLESSNESS • POWER AS AN EXPANDING PIE

> TEACHING NOTE: Have students pull up an image in their mind of a time when they were powerless. Once they have it, ask them to call out how it feels—what emotions are associated with it? What does it make them want to do (in terms of behavioral responses)?

Power and politics are among the most important, yet least understood, concepts in organizational behavior. When you hear the words *power* and *politics*, how do you feel? Do you want power?

If you say you don't want power you are likely missing out on important opportunities. Without power and influence you will be less effective in organizations. Did you know that the modern computer was first invented by Xerox in 1975? But name Xerox is not associated with computers because the engineers who designed it were not able to influence Xerox executives who saw themselves as a "paper company" to adopt their innovation. Instead, as we now know, Xerox showed it to Steve Jobs of Apple, who went on to commercialize it to great success.

The point is this: If you want to get things done, you have to be able to influence others. And influence comes from power and political skill. But engaging in power and politics is not what many people think. As you will see in this chapter, the key lies in building power for yourself while expanding the power of those around you.

■ What Is Power and Why Is It Important?

> *"The fundamental concept in social science is Power, in the same sense in which Energy is the fundamental concept in physics."*
>
> — Bertrand Russell

> **Power** is the ability of a person or group to influence or control some aspect of another person or group.

Power is the ability of a person or group to influence or control some aspect of another person or group.[1] In organizations, it is often associated with control over resources others need, such as money, information, decisions, work assignments, and so on.

Most people assume that power comes from hierarchical positions—that because managers have positions with authority embedded in them they have all the power. But this isn't always true. Can you think of a manager who was not very effective because no one listened to her, or a teacher who had no control over his classroom? When others do not comply with a person's authority that person doesn't really have power. In other words, power is not an absolute. It has to be *given* by others who are willing to be influenced.

> **Social power** is power that comes from the ability to influence another in a social relation.
>
> **Force** is power made operative against another's will.

For this reason, most of the power we study in organizations is social power. **Social power** is used to recognize that power comes from the ability to influence another in a social relation. It differs from **force**, which describes power that occurs against another's will. Social power is *earned* through relationships, and if it isn't used properly, it can be taken away. We see teenagers take their parents' power away when they don't listen or do as they are told. Employees remove managers' power when they do not act respectfully or badmouth managers to others in the organization.

■ Power and Dependence

> **Dependence** means that one person or group relies on another person or group to get what they want or need.
>
> **Control** is the authority or ability to exercise restraining or dominating influence over someone or something.

Power is based on dependence. This means that to understand power, we need to understand the nature of dependence. **Dependence** means that one person or group relies on another person or group to get what they want or need.[2] If dependence can be easily removed then an individual has power only as long as the other is willing to give it to him or her. If dependence cannot be easily removed individuals have little choice and must comply.

Dependence in organizations is most often associated with **control** over access to things other people need, such as information, resources, and decision-making.[3] For this reason, major organizational powerholders are usually those who have important competencies (e.g., influential executives, top salespeople, skilled technicians). Power is also associated with key decision-making functions, such as budgets, schedules, performance appraisals, organizational strategy, and the like.

Because power is based on dependence, we need to manage dependencies in order to manage power. We do this by increasing others' dependence on us and reducing our dependence on others. We increase others' dependence on us by establishing competence and being indispensable. Individuals who are highly competent are in great demand. They are seen as irreplaceable and organizations will work hard to keep them.

We reduce our dependence on others by increasing employability. This means that if we lose our job today we can soon get another. Individuals reduce dependence by keeping their options open, such as being willing to relocate if necessary to take another job. We reduce dependence on employers by not getting overextended financially, which can make us overly dependent on a particular organization for our livelihood. And, we reduce dependency and increase power and self-control by removing another's power over us. The decision to give someone or something power over us is a choice. Sometimes the choice to remove a dependency is difficult. It may mean changing jobs, leaving an organization, or blowing the whistle. But when we allow others to abuse power, we are complicit in their unethical and inappropriate behavior.

The Problem of Powerlessness

One of the biggest problems associated with power and dependence is the perception of powerlessness. **Powerlessness** is a lack of autonomy and participation.[4] It occurs when power imbalances make people feel that they have no option but to do what others say. When we experience powerlessness we feel little control over ourselves and our work processes. Research shows that when we feel powerless we display it in our body language—for example, by shrinking in, caving in our chests, physically withdrawing, or using less forceful hand gestures.[5]

Powerlessness is defined as a lack of autonomy and participation.

In organizations, powerlessness has debilitating effects. Perceptions of powerlessness create spirals of helplessness and alienation. Think for a minute about a situation in which you feel power*less*. How does it make you feel? Frustrated? Anxious? Angry? Afraid? Resentful? Isolated? These are destructive emotions in relationships and in organizations. When we feel power*ful*, on the other hand, we view power in a positive way. We feel energized, engaged, excited, and fulfilled by work.

Powerless people often try to regain some sense of control over themselves and their work environment. But the result can be extremely damaging to organizations (e.g., absenteeism, tardiness, theft, vandalism, grievances, shoddy workmanship, and

Removing Another's Power: The Case of Whistleblowing

You may find yourself in a situation where your boss, or someone in a position of power over you, asks you to do something unethical. Will you do it? This is the question faced by whistleblowers. For those who decide to act, research shows they will experience less retaliation if they have more power. They get that power through *perceived legitimacy* and *personal leverage*.

To know if you have these sources of power, ask yourself these questions: Will others see you as acting out of legitimate duty rather than self-interest? Will others trust and support you? Does your word carry weight? Is your evidence conclusive, showing that the perpetrator is also aware of the wrongdoing? If your answers are yes, then you have done a good job of building your power bases—and empowered yourself to be able to make a decision to act if needed.

© Ocean/Corbis

| WORTH CONSIDERING | ...OR BEST AVOIDED? |

Struggling to Gain Influence? Tap into the Science of Persuading

Scene 1. Hoteliers want to wash fewer towels. So how do they get their customers to reuse more of them? The science of persuading says it's best to identify the request with a social norm. Researchers found that guests reused 33 percent more towels when left a message card that said "75 percent of customers who stay in this room reuse their towels." *Influence Approach:* Identify with the social norm.

Scene 2. Restaurant servers want to maximize tips. How can they get more customers to leave tips? The science of persuading says it's best to create a sense of reciprocity in the server-customer relationship. Researchers found that tip giving increased when servers gave customers a piece of candy when presenting the bill. *Influence Approach:* Create sense of reciprocity.

Scene 3. A young executive is presenting a proposal to top management. What can she do to increase the chances of approval? The science of persuading says its best to emphasize what will be lost if the proposal is denied. Researchers found that executives presenting IT proposals were more successful when they identified project denial with a potential loss of $500,000 than when they identified project approval with a potential gain of $500,000. *Influence Approach:* Focus on how you frame your message.

Do the Analysis

Influencing is complicated in any setting. It requires thinking about how others will respond. The preceding scenes are examples of successful persuasion from the book *Yes! 50*

© Rana Faure/Fancy/Corbis

Scientifically Proven Ways to be Persuasive (Free Press, 2009) by Noah J. Goldstein, Steve J. Martin, and Robert B. Cialdini. Do a self-check of your success in influence situations: To what extent is persuasion part of your skill portfolio? How about others you work with? Do they pass or fail as masters of the science of persuasion? And if persuasion is so important, why don't we spend more time practicing how to do it really well?

---

counterproductive behavior).[6] Contrary to what we think, therefore, the problem in organizations *is not power, but powerlessness*. And this means that to gain and use power responsibly, we need to work to *expand* the power of others rather than restrict it to a few.

▶ Power as an Expanding Pie

The idea that social power can be an expanding pie is the basis for the trend in organizations over the past decades toward empowerment. **Empowerment** involves sharing power, information, and rewards with employees to make decisions and solve problems in their work. More than ever, managers in progressive organizations are expected to be good at and comfortable with empowering others. Rather than considering power to be something held only at higher levels in the traditional pyramid of organizations, this view considers power to be something that can be shared by everyone working in flatter and more collegial structures. When managers empower others, they also empower themselves by gaining a more dedicated and engaged workforce.

Although many firms want empowerment, it is extremely difficult to accomplish. It requires individuals to change their understanding of power away from it being a zero

Empowerment involves sharing power, information, and rewards with employees to make decisions and solve problems in their work.

sum game. A **zero sum game** means one person's gain is equal to another person's loss ("I win, you lose"). It represents a belief that "for me to gain power, you must lose power." Viewing power as a zero sum game causes you to lose power in the long run.

This is because increasing your own power while others lose power leads to power imbalances. When power imbalances get bad, they trigger forces that rise up to take power away to restore the balance. This is known as the **Iron Law of Responsibility**. An example is when lobbying groups work to take an organizations' power away by passing regulations.

The idea that force is met with countervailing force is also described by **psychological reactance theory**, which says that people rebel against constraints and efforts to control their behavior. The extent to which we do this varies, but for some of us, when we feel overpowered it will trigger us to push back very hard in an effort to maintain our autonomy—perhaps without even realizing we are doing it![7]

Empowerment views, therefore, change our understanding of power away from a focus on "power over" others to a focus on "power with" others.[8] It recognizes that the more power we allow others, the more power we will be given in return (e.g., treat people with respect and they will respect you back). The most sustainable way to gain and use power, therefore, is by increasing positive power all around.

Zero sum game describes a situation in which one person's gain is equal to another person's loss.

The **Iron Law of Responsibility** states that when power imbalances get bad enough, forces are triggered that will rise up and take the power away (to restore power balances).

Psychological reactance theory says that people rebel against constraints and efforts to control their behavior.

Sources of Power and Influence

LEARNING ROADMAP POSITION POWER • PERSONAL POWER
INFORMATION POWER • CONNECTION POWER

Over fifty years ago, John French and Bertram Raven identified a typology of five bases of power that is still used today.[9] These bases are classified into two main categories: position power and personal power. **Position power** stems from the formal hierarchy or authority vested in a particular role or position. **Personal power** resides in the individual and is independent of position; it is generated in relationships with others.

We can tell if the power a person holds is positional or personal because when a person leaves a position, their personal power goes with them. Have you ever had a really good boss or teacher who left a position and, when they did, it felt like a vacuum? This is because they had a lot of personal power. In the case of position power, however, the power stays with the position. For example, when the president of the United States leaves office, the daily security briefings that are a key source of information power are transferred to the new president.

TEACHING NOTE: Ask students which type of power is most important for managers to have? Which type of power is most important for employees to have?

Position power stems from the formal hierarchy or authority vested in a particular role.

Personal power resides in the individual, and is generated in relationships with others.

▶ Position Power

There are three main types of position power in organizations: *legitimate power*, *reward power*, and *coercive power*.

Legitimate Power
Legitimate power represents the formal hierarchical authority that comes from a position. It is called legitimate because it represents a belief that those holding certain positions have a legitimate right to prescribe behavior, and those reporting to the position have a legitimate obligation to follow (e.g., "After all, I am your supervisor, and you should feel some obligation to do what I ask").[10] In organizations, legitimate power is hierarchically structured. Managers have authority, and subordinates are expected to comply with that authority. This power is associated with offices (i.e., positions) rather than between persons, and remains in the office regardless of who the occupant is.[11]

• Managers who rely only on legitimate power are not likely to be powerful for very long. This is the mistake made by many first-time managers when they assume they are "the

Legitimate power is the formal hierarchical authority that comes with a position.

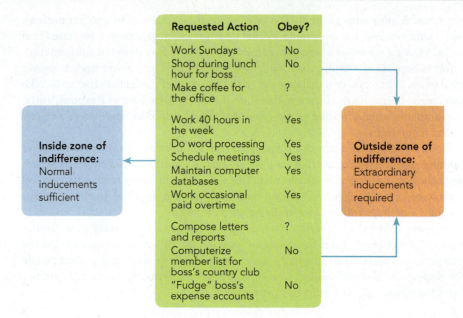

FIGURE 12.1 Hypothetical psychological contract for a secretary.

boss" but then find out that others are not willing to go along. Chester Barnard described an unwillingness to automatically comply with legitimate power as the **zone of indifference**. It represents the range of requests to which a person is willing to respond without subjecting the directives to critical evaluation or judgment.[12] When directives fall within the zone they are obeyed routinely, but when they fall outside the zone of indifference or are not considered legitimate, they are not necessarily obeyed, as is shown in Figure 12.1.

Because the mere possession of formal authority can generate power distance that isolates managers from employees, overuse of legitimate power is often accompanied by hierarchical thinking in organizations. **Hierarchical thinking** occurs when hierarchical systems create environments of superiority among managers (i.e., "superiors") and inferiority among employees (i.e., "subordinates"). Hierarchical thinking is a problem because it can lead employees to defer responsibility and initiative-taking, and cripple an organization that needs to be flexible and adaptive to survive.[13]

Zone of indifference is the range of authoritative requests to which a subordinate is willing to respond without subjecting the directives to critical evaluation or judgment.

Hierarchical thinking occurs when hierarchical systems create positions of superiority and inferiority in organizations.

Reward power comes from one's ability to administer positive rewards and remove or decrease negative rewards.

Reward Power
Reward power comes from the ability to administer outcomes that have positive valence (i.e., provide positive rewards) and remove or decrease outcomes that have negative valence (i.e., remove negative rewards). Examples of rewards include money, promotions, kudos, enriched jobs, or not assigning unpleasant task duties or undesirable work schedules. For rewards to be effective, they must be perceived as equitable. Problems arise in the use of reward power when rewards do not match expectations.

Coercive power is the use of punishment when others do not comply with influence attempts.

Coercive Power
Coercive power involves the use of threat or punishment. It stems from the expectation that one will be punished if he or she fails to conform to the influence attempt. For example, coercive power can involve the threat that one will be transferred, demoted, or fired if they do not act as desired. Pay can become a form of coercive power when a manager threatens to withhold a pay raise. Although coercive power is sometimes needed to correct performance or behavioral problems, when not used carefully and sparingly, it can reduce the strength and quality of relationships. For this reason, organizations often have policies on employee treatment to protect employees from abuses of coercive power.

Personal Power

Personal power resides in the individual and comes from personal qualities distinct from position power, such as a person's reputation, charm, charisma, perceived worth, and right to respect from others.[14] Because it resides in the person and not the position, it is available to anyone in the organization, not just those in formal or managerial roles. Sources of personal power include *expert power* and *referent power*.

Expert Power **Expert power** comes from special skills and abilities that others need but do not possess themselves. It can include knowledge, experience, and judgment. Expert power is often determined by the individual's performance record over time and the alternative sources of knowledge available. It also is highly influenced by the importance of the area of expertise. People who have expertise in steam engines have little expert power today compared to those with expertise in biotechnology. Expert power is also relative, not absolute. If you are the best cook in the kitchen, you have expert power until a real chef enters, and then the chef has the expert power.

Referent Power **Referent power** is the ability to alter another's behavior because the person wants to identify with you as the power source. Identification comes from a

> **Expert power** is the power a person has because of special skills and abilities that others need but do not possess themselves.

> **Referent power** is the ability to alter another's behavior because of the individual's desire to identify with the power source.

BRINGING OB TO LIFE

"When women use their sexuality at work, they are viewed as more feminine, and thus less than equal. Research shows sexuality is really a short-term power source."

Flirting and Chatting Up for Success

Surely you've seen a bit of flirting or friendly chatting up in the workplace. How did you react? And, can you deny that some of it was purposeful? We're not talking sex here. We're talking someone getting something job related from another person who controls what they want. The quick little flirt or positive chat-up is an attempt to make a work relationship a bit more personal and deliver favorable treatment.

It takes a lot of personal influence to get things done in collaborative workplaces. Formal top-down influence is losing prominence to that which unfolds peer to peer, side to side, upward, and informally. And in this context, flirting and chatting-up may be considered an influence strategy. But is it a good one? What are the boundaries? Should we hold it against someone who's really good at it?

Findings by OB researchers Arthur Brief and colleagues might slow down the urge to flirt. Although 50.6 percent of female business school graduates in their study said they did flirt to get ahead, the non-flirters got higher pay and were promoted more often than the flirters. Co-author Suzanne Chan-Serafin says, "When women use their sexuality at work, they are viewed as more feminine, and thus less than equal. Research shows sexuality is really a short-term power source."

But the world of OB is complicated and nuanced. A study of flirtation in negotiations concluded on the

© Andreas Baum/Corbis

positive side. Professor Laura Kay and colleagues found that "feminine charm" worked well in negotiations if kept within limits. The key, they suggest, is to avoid sexual flirtation and "flirt with your own natural personality in mind. Be authentic. Have fun."

Is it time to ratchet up OB scholarship in this area? Why all the focus on women? What about men flirting for career success? What are the limits? When does flirting cross the boundary and become sexual harassment? Stay alert for the office flirt: There may be more to it than you think.

feeling of oneness with another, and it is based on the sense of wanting to be associated with another person or to feel part of a group.[15] Identification acts as a source of referent power because it causes individuals to want to behave, believe, and perceive in ways similar to the leader. Individuals holding referent power are respected and looked up to by others. Although referent power is an invaluable source of power for individuals, it can be variable. To retain referent power, its holders are under constant pressure to maintain their exemplary images and live up to other's expectations.

Information Power

Another form of power that plays an important role in organizations—and can be either positional or personal—is information power. **Information power** is possession of or access to information that is valuable to others.[16] It can come from one's position in the organization, such as the information a manager has because he or she is in the chain of command. Or it can come from one's informal networks and being "in the know," such as personal relationships with others who have access to information. Individuals who have information power have wide discretion in how to use it. Some will guard it, and others will share it to build more personal relationships and more substantive networks in organization.

Information power comes with a cautionary note. Individuals who use information power must be very careful not to share or spread proprietary information. Violating confidentiality and trust can lead to loss of relationships, which is damaging to all forms of power an individual may hold in organizations.

Information power is possession of or access to information that is valuable to others.

Connection Power

In today's interconnected society and knowledge-based organizations, connection power from networks and relationships is becoming increasingly important. **Connection power** is the ability to call on connections and networks both inside and outside the organization for support in getting things done and in meeting one's goals.[17] It is another form of power that crosses both positional and personal power. Two forms of connection power are *association power* and *reciprocal alliances*.

Connection power is the ability to call on connections and networks both inside and outside the organization for support in getting things done and in meeting one's goals.

Association Power

Association power arises from influence with a powerful person on whom others depend. Individuals have association power when they know people in key positions or have networks of relationships with higher-ups who connect them to influential others. Association power is reflected in the expression "It's not what you know but who you know." It is valuable because so many things in organizations happen through personal connections and relationships. Association power can help

Association power arises from influence with a powerful person on whom others depend.

It's *What* You Know, Not *Who* You Know

A funny thing happened on the way to the Network Age. Things turned upside down.

Do you remember the old adage "It's not what you know but who you know?" Well, it turns out that in our hyper-networked world—where access to information is abundant and connecting people takes just a click on an e-mail—it's increasingly difficult to make yourself stand out in the crowd. As a result, knowledge has now become one of our most valuable commodities. And, knowledge comes from what you know.

In today's workplaces, others will seek you out if you have compelling knowledge. This isn't to say that networks aren't still important . . . they certainly are. But in a new world of easy access to information and abundant capital, it may be that *what* you know is becoming more vital than *who* you know.

Poba/iStockphoto

you cut through bureaucracy, provide greater access to sponsorship and promotions, and allow you to gain access to positions and resources needed to get things done.

Reciprocal Alliances

Reciprocal alliances describe a form of power arising from connections with others developed through reciprocity. Reciprocity is based on the concept that if one person does something for another, it will invoke an obligation to return the favor. For example, if your friend goes out of his way to give you a ride and you respond with "I owe you one," you are recognizing that you are now indebted to that friend until you can pay him back in some way. These bonds of indebtedness link individuals together in networks of relationships.

> **When It Comes to Networking . . .**
>
> High performers have networks that provide them access to people who:
>
> - Can offer them new information or expertise
> - Have formal power
> - Are powerful informal leaders
> - Give them developmental feedback
> - Challenge their decision and push them to be better

Effective networkers recognize that reciprocity and reciprocal alliances are a powerful way to form strong networks in organizations. Research shows that executives who consistently rank in the top 20 percent of their companies in both performance and well-being have developed strong networks made up of high-quality relationships from diverse areas and up and down the corporate hierarchy. Such networks are characterized by an exchange of resources and support, including access to information, expertise, best practices, mentoring, developmental feedback, and political support.[18]

Reciprocal alliances represent power arising from alliances with others developed through reciprocity (the trading of power or favors for mutual gain in organizational transactions).

Responses to Power and Influence

LEARNING ROADMAP CONFORMITY • RESISTANCE • HOW POWER CORRUPTS

Power is relational. Whether you have power depends on how others respond to your influence attempts. If individuals do not defer to your influence attempt, then you have no power. This means that to understand power you need to keep in mind how individuals respond to you and your influence.

> TEACHING NOTE: Divide students into discussion groups with some groups managers and some groups employees. Have them discuss Furlough or Fire? See if there are any differences in what managers decide versus what employees decide.

▪ Conformity

In the earliest formal research into power and influence, Herbert Kelman identified three levels of conformity one can make to another's influence attempt: *compliance*, *identification*, and *internalization*.

Compliance

Compliance occurs when individuals accept another's influence because of the positive or negative outcomes tied to it. When individuals comply, they go along not because they want to but because they have to. When you take a required class for a subject you are not interested in or study only because you have to, you are complying. The motivation here is purely instrumental—it is done to obtain the specific reward or avoid the punishment associated with not complying.

Compliance occurs when individuals accept another's influence not because they believe in the content but because of the rewards or punishment associated with the requested action.

Because compliance is an extrinsic form of motivation, it results in minimal effort (proportional to the reward or punishment). Because of this, it is not a very effective influence strategy in the long run. Moreover, it requires surveillance by management. For example, employees who are not committed to excellent customer service will typically slack off when the supervisor is not monitoring their behavior.

Responses to Power	
Conformity	**Resistance**
• *Compliance*—have to do it to avoid negative consequences	• *Constructive*—trying to help make things better
• *Commitment*—want to do it because you agree with it	• *Destructive*—trying to undermine, thwart, or harm

Commitment **Commitment** occurs when individuals accept an influence attempt out of duty or obligation. Committed individuals agree with the desired action and show initiative and persistence in completing it. Kelman identified two forms of commitment in response to influence attempts: *identification* and *internalization*.

Identification is displayed when individuals accept an influence attempt because they want to maintain a positive relationship with the person or group making the influence request.[19] Students who join a fraternity or sorority accept the influence of their peers because they identify with the organization and want to be part of the group. **Internalization** occurs when an individual accepts influence because the induced behavior is congruent with their value system. Internalization means you believe in the ideas and actions you are being asked to undertake. For example, members of religious organizations follow the dictates of the church because they truly believe in the principles and philosophies being advocated.

Commitment occurs when individuals accept an influence attempt out of duty or obligation.

Identification occurs when individuals accept an influence attempt because they want to maintain a positive relationship with the person or group making the influence request.

Internalization occurs when an individual accepts influence because the induced behavior is congruent with their value system.

▶ Resistance

Responses to power include not only conformity but also resistance. Resistance involves individuals saying no, making excuses, stalling or even arguing against the initiative. There are two main types of resistance strategies used by individuals when they perceive an impractical request from their supervisor: constructive resistance and dysfunctional resistance.[20]

Constructive Resistance **Constructive resistance** is characterized by thoughtful dissent aimed at constructively challenging the manager to rethink the issue. Individuals who use constructive resistance make suggestions for alternative actions accompanied by reasons for noncompliance. They do so in the hope of opening a dialogue to try to find a more appropriate solution to a problem.[21]

Constructive resistance is characterized by thoughtful dissent aimed at constructively challenging the influencing agent to rethink the issue.

Dysfunctional Resistance **Dysfunctional resistance** involves ignoring or dismissing the request of the influencing agent.[22] Employees who engage in dysfunctional resistance attempt to thwart and undermine the manager by disrupting workflows (e.g., ignoring requests, making only a half-hearted effort, or simply refusing to comply by just saying "no").

Dysfunctional resistance involves a more passive form of noncompliance in which individuals ignore or dismiss the request of the influencing agent.

Studies of dysfunctional resistance show that employees are more likely to refuse when their supervisors are abusive, but that these effects depend on the employee's personality. Conscientious employees are more likely to use constructive resistance, whereas less conscientious employees are more likely to use dysfunctional resistance.[23] Moreover, employees who use constructive resistance are more likely to receive positive performance ratings from managers, whereas employees who use dysfunctional resistance are more likely to receive negative ratings from managers.[24]

▶ How Power Corrupts

We have all heard the expression "Power corrupts, and absolute power corrupts absolutely." The question is why? What is it about power that causes people to lose perspective and do terrible things that cause great harm to themselves and others?

Dean Ludwig and Clinton Longenecker describe the problem as the **Bathsheba syndrome**.[25] The Bathsheba syndrome is based on the story of King David, a once great and revered leader who got caught up in a downward spiral of unethical decisions when

The **Bathsheba syndrome** is epitomized when men and women in the pinnacle of power with strong personal integrity and intelligence engage in unethical and selfish behavior because they mistakenly believe they are above the law.

his success led him to feel so privileged and self-indulgent that he took another man's wife (Bathsheba), and then covered it up through murder and deception. It describes what happens to men and women of otherwise strong personal integrity and intelligence, who just at the moment of seemingly "having it all"—and despite the fact that they know it is wrong—engage in unethical and selfish behavior with the mistaken belief that they have the power to conceal it.

The lesson from the Bathsheba syndrome is that power can have corruptive effects that, if not prepared for, may lead to devastating outcomes. To avoid the Bathsheba syndrome, individuals should prepare themselves for success. Success often leads to complacency—it can make those who have it too comfortable and inflate their ego, causing one to lose perspective. Power can have an intoxicating allure that makes people crave more and more of it.

A key to being powerful, therefore, is to manage yourself in the face of power. Maintaining humility and being around others who will push back on you can help keep you grounded and maintain perspective. Being powerful also means taking responsibility in the face of others' power. Responsibly managing power means acting to keep power in check.

FINDING THE LEADER IN YOU

Corruptive Power of Celebrity Turns Blind Eye to Pedophilia

It's a horrific picture. More than 200 cases of sexual abuse spanning half a century, with some victims as young as 8 years old. The abuse took place in broadcast studios, hospitals, homes for the mentally disabled, and other places of care for the vulnerable. At Stoke Mandeville Hospital, the site of 24 attacks alone, the offender was allowed to maintain living quarters and an office, free to roam as an honorary porter after raising millions of pounds for its spinal injuries unit.

What kind of monster could do this? And what kind of society could allow it to happen?

It was Jimmy Savile, one of Britain's most celebrated television hosts and someone revered for zany showmanship and working-class chumminess. His cult of celebrity was sealed by his "near-saintly" commitment to charity work. Knighted by Pope John Paul II and Queen Elizabeth II, he was considered untouchable. As one officer said, "Really, it came down to this: do we really want to take on this man, Saint Jimmy, who does all of this fund-raising and knows all of these people?" Despite his activities being an "open secret" to many who worked with him and acknowledgement in his book of his predilection for young girls, Saville escaped legal scrutiny. He died at the age of 84 without ever facing a single charge in court.

This story is of a man who "groomed a nation" while hiding in plain sight, and a society that let bad things happen. Saville's victims felt they could not speak and those in the press, the police, and TV who knew what was happening, chose not to speak.

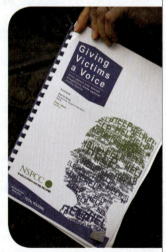

Carl Court/Getty Images

What's the Lesson Here?

As described by one investigator, "This whole sordid affair has demonstrated the true consequences of what happens when vulnerability collides with power." What can we do to make ourselves less vulnerable to the corruptive effects of power? How can we empower ourselves to speak up in the face of wrongdoing? We now know the cover-up was enabled by a highly dysfunctional, top-heavy culture in the BBC, characterized by rival factions, poor communication, and buck-passing. What can we do to prevent these kinds of political climates in organizations? What would you do if you worked in such an organization?

Understanding Organizational Politics

> **LEARNING ROADMAP** WHY DO WE HAVE ORGANIZATIONAL POLITICS? THE ROLE OF SELF-INTEREST • POLITICAL CLIMATES

> TEACHING NOTE: Ask students to use Figure 12.2 to analyze their power bases in either jobs they have had or in an organization of which they are part (or a family or friend group). How strong are their power bases? How can they improve areas that need further development?

For many, the word *politics* conjures up thoughts of illicit deals, favors, and advantageous personal relationships. It is important, however, to understand the importance of organizational politics and how they can help the workplace function in a much broader capacity.[26]

Why Do We Have Organizational Politics?

Politics occur because we have both formal and informal systems in organizations.[27] **Formal systems** tell us what is to be done in organizations and how work processes are to be coordinated and structured. They represent the "rational" side of organizations that controls behavior and reduces uncertainty. Not all behaviors in organizations can be prescribed, however, so informal systems arise to fill in the blanks. **Informal systems** are patterns of activity and relationships that arise in everyday activities when individuals and groups work to get things done. They are highly changeable and occur through personal connections. For example, when a salesperson uses a personal connection with someone in operations to help speed up an order for a customer, this is an example of the informal system.

Organizational politics involve efforts by organizational members to seek resources and achieve desired goals through informal systems and structures. Politics represent how people get ahead, how they gain and use power, and how they get things done (for good and bad) in organizations.

> **Formal systems** dictate what is to be done in organizations and how work processes are to be coordinated and structured.
>
> **Informal systems** are patterns of activity and relationships that arise in everyday activities as individuals and groups work to get things done.
>
> **Organizational politics** are efforts by organizational members to seek resources and achieve desired goals through informal systems and structures.

The Role of Self-Interest

Like power, organizational politics are neutral. Whether they are good or bad depends on how they are used. They are positive when they advance the interests of the organization and do not intentionally harm individuals. They are negative when they involve self-interested behaviors of individuals and groups who work to benefit themselves in ways that disadvantage others and the organization.

Self-interested politics occur when people work to shift otherwise ambiguous outcomes to their personal advantage. What makes this tricky is that individuals often disagree as to whose self-interests are most valuable. Self-interested politics are those that benefit, protect, or enhance self-interests without consideration of the welfare of co-workers or the organization.[28] They include illegitimate political activities such as coalition building, favoritism-based pay and promotions, scapegoating, backstabbing, and using information as a political tool to enhance one's self or harm others.

> **Self-interested politics** occur when individuals or groups work to shift otherwise ambiguous outcomes to their personal advantage without consideration of the organization or coworkers.

Political Climates

Political climate refers to whether people in organizations work "within" or "around" formal policies and procedures in getting their work done.[29] When people work around formal policies and procedures, the climate is perceived as more political. Less political climates involve more direct and straightforward activities, where there is less need to interpret and watch out for the behaviors happening behind the scenes.

> **Political climate** is the shared perceptions about the political nature of the organization.

Informal Systems and Workarounds
Consistent with the idea that politics manifest in and through informal systems, organizational political climates are seen in

CHECKING ETHICS IN OB

Furlough or Fire? Weighing Alternative Interests

Belterz/iStockphoto

You knew the news was bad, but it just got worse. The most severe economic crisis in decades is spreading, and your organization just announced another round of budget cuts. Unfortunately, all the low-hanging fruits are gone, and the cuts are now digging into core operating budgets. The decision has to be made: Do we furlough or do we fire?

This is the situation faced by organizations around the world in the aftermath of the global economic crisis. The option is to fire a few, or ask all employees in the organization to take pay cuts in the form of furloughs—mandatory leave without pay. A 2009 survey of 100 companies show that more than one-third of the companies use furloughs. But this isn't without costs. Furloughs can lead to perceptions that the psychological contract is broken, and it can increase stress and work overload for employees.

The question is whether it is better to furlough or fire. According to organizational psychologist Ann Huffman, "Employees see furloughs as the lesser of two evils and are more agreeable to them rather than being laid off or seeing colleagues lose their jobs." But if you knew you were not at risk for being cut what would you do? Would you vote for the furlough or for the cut?

You Tell Us Do you think it is better to make the many suffer or the few? Whose interest matters more? Is this a "political" decision? Why or why not?

---

the extent to which people engage in **workarounds**. Workarounds occur when people go around rules to accomplish a task or goal because the normal process or method isn't producing the desired result.[30] Workarounds can involve seeking assistance from influential people in one's network, exploiting loopholes in a system, or using one's connections to access potentially useful information or influence decisions.

How the political climate is seen depends on the nature and motivation of workarounds. Workarounds that benefit oneself or one's work unit at the expense of others will likely trigger copycat behaviors, fueling dysfunctional political climates. When workarounds are used to benefit the organization, however, such as when a policy loophole is used to make a process more efficient or to contribute to an innovative new service, they contribute to advancing organizational interests. In this case they serve a functional purpose.[31]

Connections and Perceptions Two people in the same work group may experience a political climate very differently. The difference depends on one's status and power in the political system. For someone in the know and highly connected, the political climate will likely be perceived as quite positive. For an individual who is disadvantaged or not well connected, the political climate can be seen as very negative.

> **Workarounds** occur when people work around the system to accomplish a task or goal when the normal process or method isn't producing the desired result.

OB IN POPULAR CULTURE

Tooting One's Horn in *Spanglish*

Everyone has a right to "toot their own horn." But when it means the job is not getting done, or others are suffering, then it can be a sign of negative political behavior.

This is the case in *Spanglish*, a movie in which John Clasky (Adam Sandler) is an exceptional chef with an exclusive restaurant in California. His assistants, Pietro (Phil Rosenthal) and Gwen (Angela Goethals), are always trying to impress him. Gwen is very political, constantly ingratiating the boss by telling him how great he is and trying to do favors for him. Pietro is equally political, just in a more cunning fashion. He controls the actions of others and uses his own cooking skills to make himself invaluable to the boss.

Columbia Pictures/Marshak, Bob/NewsCom

What we see in both cases are employees who want to be viewed favorably by the boss. There is nothing wrong with that. However, if the actions keep one from completing legitimate job responsibilities or are designed to mask performance deficiencies, then they represent bad political behaviors.

Get to Know Yourself Better Take a look at Assessment 14, Machiavellianism, in the *OB Skills Workbook*. Machiavellian tendencies are often associated with political behavior. Take this quick test and see how you score. What does it suggest about your own preferences? Do you have a desire to control and manipulate others? Could this lead to actions that might be viewed unfavorably by co-workers? How can you make sure that you use your power appropriately and effectively?

People who are connected with powerful others see the political climate as a vital and important part of their career and professional advancement. Those who are in the "out group" and without access to organizational power and status, have much more negative perceptions of organizational politics. They see political climates as rewarding employees who engage in manipulative influence tactics, which can include things like taking credit for others' work, coalition building, and using connections to create unfair advantage. Those who report stronger perceptions of organizational politics often experience greater job stress and strain, reduced job satisfaction and organizational commitment, and, ultimately, increased turnover.[32]

Navigating the Political Landscape

LEARNING ROADMAP BUILDING POWER BASES • DEVELOPING POLITICAL SKILLS • NETWORKING

Power and politics are facts of life in organizations. They are necessary for getting things done in social systems. So to be effective we need to manage our power successfully in political environments. Those who don't navigate politics in organizations are at a disadvantage not only in terms of winning raises and promotions, but maybe even in keeping their jobs.

A key to navigating power and politics is managing one's own attitude and behavior. People who are nonpolitical or cynical about power may find themselves not getting promoted and being left out of key decisions and activities in the organization. Those who are overly political and abuse their power may be perceived as Machiavellian, or self-serving. Ultimately these people may lose credibility and influence. A moderate amount of prudent political behavior, therefore, is a survival tool. It involves understanding how to establish power bases, develop political skills, and build strong and effective networks.

Building Power Bases

You have to establish your power bases—position, personal, information, connection—to do well at managing power and politics. **Power bases** are the sources of power (position, personal, information, connection) that individuals and subunits develop in organizations. As can be seen in Figure 12.2 shows these sources of power can help in navigating political climates in organizations. Individuals without established power bases are more susceptible to powerlessness. A lack of power limits ability to have real influence. Persons with power are able to advance important initiatives and gain access to key resources. They are also better able to protect themselves from powerful others. Power bases must be established before you need them, however. If you wait to develop them when needed, it is probably too late.

There are two main ways to build power bases in organizations. The first involves establishing competence and value added to the organization. This builds personal and position power by proving your ability to perform at higher levels and having competencies that are hard to replace. High competency and value added make an individual or work unit non-substitutable. They increase others' dependency on you. The goal for individuals and teams is to increase **non-substitutability** by making their work more critical, relevant, visible, and central to organizational performance.

The second way to build power bases is through developing information and connection power. You do this by building relationships and networks. Information comes from formal access to information (e.g., meetings, task forces, e-mails, policy documents), informal access to information (e.g., grapevine, hall talk) and the opportunity to distribute or share information with others (e.g., being the first to tell others about an organizational change).[33] Individuals who want to build information power often spend a lot of time making connections that let them be "in the know." They can use this information

Power bases are the sources of power individuals and subunits develop in organizations.

Non-substitutable means that the individual or the work performed by the subunit cannot be easily replaced.

FIGURE 12.2 Building power bases.

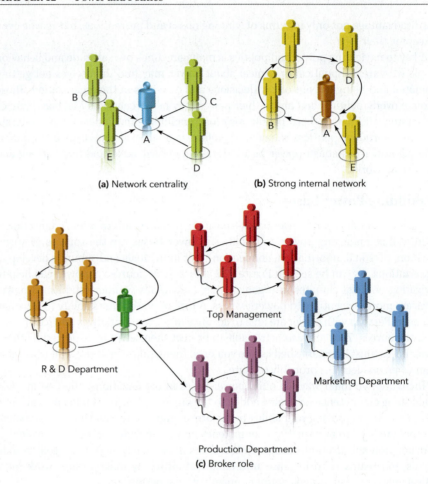

FIGURE 12.3 Sample scenarios for connections and networks in organizations.

in various (positive or negative) ways, such as telling others the "real" story, withholding information, filtering communication, and even selectively leaking key information to suit their purposes.

Connection power comes from internal networks, external networks, and being central in a network. The sample connection and network scenarios in Figure 12.3 show how you can build your connection power by aligning with others to gain advice, friendship, alliances, collaborations, information flows, and access to job opportunities.

Developing Political Skills

Rarely in organizational politics are things as they appear. Instead they are more like those 3D hidden stereogram images in which, on the surface, you see a bunch of dots, but when you peer deeply into the image a hidden picture emerges. Individuals who are successful at politics are like this. They know how to read political situations and uncover the real motivations and connections going on behind the scenes. They have what can be described as **political savvy**—skill and adroitness at reading political environments and understanding how to influence effectively in these environments.

Another term for political savvy is **political skill,** defined as the ability to understand and influence others to act in ways that enhance personal and/or organizational objectives.[35] Individuals who are high in political skill have the ability to read and understand people and get them to act in desired ways. They use connections to skillfully align themselves with others to attain goals. They adapt their behavior to the situ-

Political savvy is skill and adroitness at reading political environments and understanding how to influence effectively in these environments.

Political skill is an ability to use knowledge of others to influence them to act in desired ways.

Research Insight

Social Networks and Power in Organizations

Secretaries have more power than you might think! That is the finding of a recent study of secretaries in a university setting by H. Cenk Sozen published in *Personnel Review*. Secretaries have unique power bases due to their central positions in organizational networks. This allows them to control information flows and use power to their advantage. Findings show that secretaries are high in both network centrality and "betweenness" centrality, and that they serve as critical links between departments and people (a "broker" role).

Even more interesting, in many cases the secretaries in the university had higher network centrality than their bosses. The key, then, is how they use their power. And the picture is not always pretty. Secretaries serve as gatekeepers and can choose the type of information they share and whether to speed up or slow down the spread of information.

The implication is that you'd better not get on your secretary's bad side. As one faculty member said, "Nobody wants to have a bad relation with her in our department. She may decide not to transfer critical information . . . [or] give wrong information about my activities to our chair so as to create a negative impression about me."

Do the Research If you wanted to find out more about how secretaries use their power, how would you go about doing it? What research questions would you want to explore?

Source: H. C. Sozen, "Social Networks and Power in Organizations: A Research on the Roles and Positions of Junior Level Secretaries in an Organizational Network," *Personnel Review* 41 (2012), pp. 487–512.

---

ation, but with authenticity and genuineness to build trust and credibility rather than suspicion or disdain.

Developing political savvy involves learning to read the situation, increasing awareness of self and others, negotiating with rather than negating others and framing messages so that others will listen (e.g., a focus on organizational interest rather than self-interest). One of the best ways you can build these skills is to learn from and watch others who have them. It is also helpful to find mentors or sponsors who can provide developmental feedback and coaching in how to interpret and respond to political environments.

Networking

What you know is not enough. You also need connections, or social capital, to get ahead. **Social capital** is resources that come from networks of relationships.[36] It differs from **human capital**, which is knowledge, skills, and intellectual assets employees bring to the workplace. Whereas human capital represents *what* you know, social capital represents *who* you know. The importance of social capital is understanding that being smart, or having great ideas and information, is not sufficient—it is only beneficial if you are able to get the ideas communicated and implemented.

Networking helps individuals find better jobs and enjoy greater occupational success. If you have more network ties, you have greater opportunity to gain access to resources and influence others. Research has found that for many things—such as finding jobs or getting ahead—weak "acquaintance" ties work better than strong "friendship" ties. Individuals have greater access to more and different job opportunities when relying on weak ties.[37] This is good news because strong ties are costly to maintain—they require more time than weak associations.

Social capital is the current or potential resources gained through one's network.

Human capital is the knowledge, skills, and intellectual assets employees bring to the workplace.

Brokers serve as links between structural holes in a network, providing greater access to resources, information, and opportunities.

Structural holes are the gaps between individuals and groups in a social network.

Another way individuals can provide an advantage to themselves and to organizations is by acting as a **broker,** someone who bridges **structural holes** which exist as gaps between individuals and groups without connections in networks.[38] Brokers develop relationships that link formerly unconnected actors by building bridges that provide greater access to information, resources, and opportunities. Bridging ties provide access to a diverse set of opinions, which is important for creativity. Networking is vital to the performance of both individuals and organizations.

The most beneficial networks come from acquaintances one makes through everyday work activities and professional events, as well as from reciprocity in the exchange of resources. Skilled networkers know that a request for a favor is a great opportunity. If you do a favor for someone else, he or she will now feel obligated to pay you back when needed. People who get ahead keep themselves open to opportunities, continually develop their competencies and skills sets, and build connections and relationships that benefit both individual and organizational success.

12 Study Guide

Key Questions and Answers

What is power, and how does it operate in organizations?

- Power is the ability to get things done in organizations; it comes from being able to influence or control things that are important to another person or group.
- A key to managing power is managing dependencies, or the reliance we have on another person or group to get what we want or need.
- When people have strong dependencies on others, they often experience powerlessness; it is not power but powerlessness that has debilitating effects in relationships and organizations.
- Empowerment approaches move away from powerlessness by focusing on "power with" rather than "power over."

What are the sources of power and influence?

- Position power comes from the formal hierarchy or authority vested in a particular role; sources include *legitimate power*, *reward power*, and *coercive power*.
- Personal power is generated in relationships with others; sources include *expert power* and *referent power*.
- Information power can be either positional or personal, and comes from access to information that is valuable to others.
- Connection power is the ability to call on connections and networks both inside and outside the organization for support in getting things done and meeting one's goals; sources include *association power* and *reciprocal alliances*.

How do people respond to power and influence?

- When individuals go along with power and authority, they are conforming. Three levels of conformity include *compliance*, *identification*, and *internalization*.
- Individuals can also resist power. Research has distinguished two types of resistance strategies used by individuals when they perceive an impractical request from their supervisor: *constructive resistance* and *dysfunctional resistance*.
- Individuals who hold power can be corrupted by it; the Bathsheba syndrome describes a situation in which individuals who become successful abuse power.

- A key to responding to power is managing oneself in the face of it, both in terms of being a responsible power holder and in reacting responsibly to others' power.

What are organizational politics?
- Organizational politics represent efforts by organizational members to seek resources and achieve desired goals through informal systems and structures.
- Politics represent how people get ahead, how they gain and use power, and how they get things done (for good and bad) in organizations.
- Political behaviors are positive when they advance the interests of the organization and do not intentionally harm individuals; they are negative when they involve self-interested behaviors of individuals and groups who work to benefit themselves in ways that disadvantage others and the organization.
- An organization's political climate represents the shared perceptions about the political nature of the organization; when individuals hold negative perceptions of the political climate they experience greater job stress, lower job satisfaction, and increased turnover.

How do individuals navigate politics in organizations?
- A moderate amount of prudent political behavior is a survival tool; it involves understanding how to establish power bases, develop political skills, and build strong and effective networks.
- Power bases are the sources of power individuals and subunits develop in organizations; they help individuals advance important initiatives and gain access to key resources as well as protect themselves when threatened by powerful others.
- Two main ways to build power bases in organizations include establishing competence and building networks.
- Individuals who are high in political skill have the ability to read and understand people, and then act on that knowledge in influential ways.

Terms to Know

Association power (p. 266)
Bathsheba syndrome (p. 268)
Brokers (p. 276)
Coercive power (p. 264)
Commitment (p. 268)
Compliance (p. 267)
Connection power (p. 266)
Constructive resistance (p. 268)
Control (p. 260)
Dependence (p. 260)
Dysfunctional resistance (p. 268)
Empowerment (p. 262)
Expert power (p. 265)
Force (p. 260)
Formal systems (p. 270)
Hierarchical thinking (p. 264)
Human capital (p. 275)
Identification (p. 268)
Informal systems (p. 270)
Information power (p. 266)
Internalization (p. 268)
Iron Law of Responsibility (p. 263)
Legitimate power (p. 263)
Non-substitutable (p. 273)
Organizational politics (p. 270)
Political climate (p. 270)
Personal power (p. 263)
Political savvy (p. 274)
Political skill (p. 274)
Position power (p. 263)
Power (p. 260)
Power bases (p. 273)
Powerlessness (p. 261)
Psychological reactance theory (p. 263)
Reciprocal alliances (p. 267)
Referent power (p. 265)
Reward power (p. 264)
Self-interested politics (p. 270)
Social capital (p. 275)
Social power (p. 260)
Structural holes (p. 276)
Workarounds (p. 271)
Zero sum game (p. 261)
Zone of indifference (p. 264)

Self-Test 12

Multiple Choice

1. Social power differs from _____, which is power made operative against another's will.
   (a) powerlessness (b) force
   (c) dependence (d) zero sum game

2. The idea that social power can be an expanding pie is the basis for the trend toward _____.
   (a) hierarchical thinking (b) political climate
   (c) personal power (d) empowerment

3. _____ says that if you do not use power appropriately others will rise up to take it away.
   (a) Empowerment (b) Instrumental theory
   (c) The Iron Law of Responsibility (d) Coercive power

4. Legitimate power is a form of _____ power.
   (a) position (b) personal
   (c) connection (d) information

5. Failure to comply because a directive does not fall in the acceptable range of requests is called _____.
   (a) a zero sum game (b) powerlessness
   (c) political savvy (d) the zone of indifference

6. What form of power stems from the expectation that a person will be punished if he or she fails to conform to influence attempts?
   (a) reward power (b) legitimate power
   (c) coercive power (d) referent power

7. In today's interdependent society and knowledge-based organizations, _____ is becoming increasingly important.
   (a) connection power (b) coercive power
   (c) referent power (d) control

8. Power that comes from who you know is called _____.
   (a) human capital (b) association power
   (c) referent power (d) interpersonal power

9. When individuals respond to power because they want to obtain a reward or avoid punishment, they are being _____.
   (a) politically savvy (b) empowered
   (c) instrumental (d) resistant

10. _____ is a passive form of resistance that involves noncompliance.
    (a) Constructive resistance (b) Dysfunctional resistance
    (c) Controlled resistance (d) Conscientious resistance

11. Organizational politics occur in the _____ of an organization.
    (a) hierarchical structures (b) boundaries
    (c) formal systems (d) informal systems

12. A _____ is when individuals go outside the formal system to accomplish a task or goal.
    (a) workaround
    (b) power base
    (c) network
    (d) political climate

13. Individuals who have _____ know how to read political situations and respond effectively.
    (a) perceptions of organizational politics
    (b) networks
    (c) political savvy
    (d) power bases

14. Networking builds _____ in organizations.
    (a) human capital
    (b) social capital
    (c) informal systems
    (d) political savvy

15. _____ help individuals have influence in organizations and provide protection against powerful others.
    (a) Social skills
    (b) Political climates
    (c) Formal systems
    (d) Power bases

Short Response

16. What do we mean when we say power is based on dependencies?
17. Why is powerlessness a problem in organizations?
18. How can you tell if someone's power is positional or personal?
19. Why do we have politics in organizations?

Applications Essay

20. Cristos is starting his first job after graduating from college. He is very excited but also very nervous. He has heard from others that the organization he will be working in has a highly political environment and that he needs to be careful. What advice would you give him about how to best manage himself in terms of power and politics in his organization?

Steps to Further Learning 12
Top Choices from *The OB Skills Workbook*

These learning activities from *The OB Skills Workbook* found at the back of the book are suggested for Chapter 12.

Cases for Critical Thinking	Team and Experiential Exercises	Self-Assessment Portfolio
• Trader Joe's • Management Training Dilemma	• My Best Manager • My Best Job • Graffiti Needs Assessment • Sweet Tooth	• Learning Styles • Student Leadership Practices Inventory • Managerial Assumptions • 21st Century Manager

13

The Leadership Process

The Key Point

Although many people think of leadership as the behavior of leaders, it is actually generated in interactions and relationships between people. Understanding leadership as a process opens our eyes to the fact that leadership is co-produced by leaders and followers working together in organizational contexts. ■

What's Inside?

- **Bringing OB to LIFE**
  BUILDING CHARISMA THROUGH POLISHED RHETORIC
- **Worth Considering . . . or Best Avoided?**
  BOSSES ARE TO BE OBEYED AND MY JOB IS TO COMPLY. OR IS IT?
- **Checking Ethics in OB**
  WORKERS SHARE THEIR SALARY SECRETS
- **Finding the Leader in You**
  GOOGLE'S TRIUMVIRATE GIVES WAY TO NEW LEADERSHIP STRUCTURE
- **OB in Popular Culture**
  LEADER IDENTITY AND *FORREST GUMP*
- **Research Insight**
  PARTICIPATORY LEADERSHIP AND PEACE

Chapter at a Glance

- What Is Leadership?
- What Is Followership?
- What Do We Know about Leader–Follower Relationships?
- What Do We Mean by Leadership as a Collective Process?

Leadership

LEARNING ROADMAP — FORMAL AND INFORMAL LEADERSHIP • LEADERSHIP AS SOCIAL CONSTRUCTION • IMPLICIT LEADERSHIP THEORIES

> **TEACHING NOTE:** Have students analyze one of their group experiences from the standpoint of leader and follower claiming and granting. Do they see claiming and granting processes happening? How does it work?

When we think of leadership, we often think of leaders. But leaders are only one element of leadership. Other key elements are followers, leader–follower relationships, and context. It is only when all these elements come together effectively that leadership is produced. For this reason, leadership should be thought of as a process.

The leadership process shown in the nearby figure is co-created by leaders and followers acting in context. **Leadership** is generated when acts of leading (e.g., influencing) are combined with acts of following (e.g., deferring). It represents an influence relationship between two or more people who depend on one another for attainment of mutual goals.[1] The implication of this is that leadership is not only about the actions of leaders. It also involves the actions of followers who contribute to, or detract from, leaders' attempts to influence.

Because following is so important to leading, we could almost say that it is in following that leadership is created. If others do not follow then, even if a person has a leadership position, he or she is not really a leader. The person may be a manager—but not a leader. For example, when students in a class act up and do not respect the teacher, they are not following and the teacher is not leading. The teacher may try to use position power to manage the situation, but in this case the teacher is acting as a manager rather than a leader.

Leadership is an influence process generated when acts of leading (e.g., influencing) are combined with acts of following (e.g., deferring) as individuals work together to attain mutual goals.

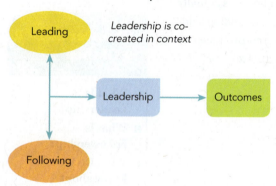

The Leadership Process
Leadership is co-created in context

Leadership influence can be located in one person (i.e., a "leader") or be distributed throughout the group (i.e., collective leadership). For example, some teams have one project leader who everyone follows. Other groups may be more self-managing, where team members share the leadership function and responsibilities. While in the past leadership was largely the domain of formal managerial leaders, in today's environments leadership is broadly distributed more throughout organizations, with everyone expected to play their part.

■ Formal and Informal Leadership

Formal leadership is exerted by persons appointed or elected to positions of formal authority in organizations.

Informal leaders is exerted by persons who become influential due to special skills or their ability to meet the needs of others.

Upward leadership occurs when leaders at lower levels influence those at higher levels to create change.

Leadership processes occur both inside and outside of formal positions and roles. When leadership is exerted by individuals appointed or elected to positions of formal authority, it is called **formal leadership**. Managers, teachers, ministers, politicians, and student organization presidents are all formal leaders. Leadership can also be exerted by individuals who do not hold formal roles but become influential due to special skills or their ability to meet the needs of others. These individuals are **informal leaders**.[2] Informal leaders can include opinion leaders, change agents, and idea champions.

Whereas formal leadership involves top-down influence flows, informal leadership can flow in any direction: up, down, across, and even outside the organization. Informal leadership allows us to recognize the importance of upward leadership (or "leading-up"). **Upward leadership** occurs when individuals at lower levels act as leaders by influencing those at higher levels. This concept of leadership flowing upward is often missed in discussions of leadership in organizations, but it is absolutely critical for organizational change and effectiveness.

Regardless of whether it is formal or informal, a key to effective leadership is "willing followership," as shown in Figure 13.1. Willing followership means that others follow because they *want* to, not because they have to. This is closely related to the concept of power. When leaders operate from a willing followership model, others follow out of

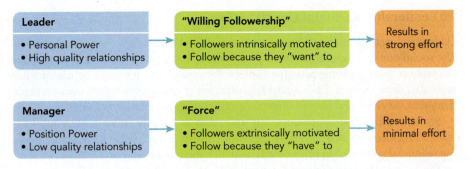

FIGURE 13.1 The role of "willing followership" in leadership.

intrinsic motivation and power comes from personal sources. This differs from more compliance-based approaches-common to managers who aren't leaders, where others follow out of extrinsic motivation and power is more position based. Managers who are also effective leaders have *both* position and personal power. On the other hand, informal leaders who do not have formal positions can only operate through personal power.

Research Insight

Participatory Leadership and Peace

In an unusual cross-cultural organizational behavior study, Gretchen Spreitzer examined the link between business leadership practices and indicators of peace in nations. She found that earlier research suggested that peaceful societies had (1) open and egalitarian decision making and (2) social control processes that limit the use of coercive power. These two characteristics are the hallmarks of participatory systems that empower people in the collective. Spreitzer reasoned that business firms can provide open egalitarian decisions by stressing participative leadership and empowerment.

Spreitzer recognized that broad cultural factors could also be important. The degree to which the culture is future oriented and low in power distance appeared relevant. And she reasoned that she needed specific measures of peace. She selected two major indicators: (1) the level of corruption and (2) the level of unrest. The measure of unrest was a combined measure of political instability, armed conflict, social unrest, and international disputes. While she found a large leadership database that directly measured participative leadership, she developed the measures of empowerment from another apparently unrelated survey. Two items appeared relevant: the decision freedom individuals reported (decision freedom), and the degree to which they felt they had to comply with their boss regardless of whether they agreed with an order (compliance).

You can schematically think of this research in terms of the following model.

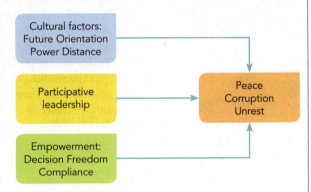

As one might expect with exploratory research, the findings support most of her hypotheses but not all. Participative leadership was related to less corruption and less unrest, as was the future-oriented aspect of culture. Regarding empowerment, there were mixed results; decision freedom was linked to less corruption and unrest, but the compliance measure was only linked to more unrest.

Do the Research Do you agree that when business used participatory leadership, it legitimated the democratically based style and increased the opportunity for individuals to express their voice? What other research could be done to determine the link between leadership and peace?[11]

Source: Gretchen Spreitzer, "Giving Peace a Chance: Organizational Leadership, Empowerment, and Peace," *Journal of Organizational Behavior* 28 (2007), pp. 1077–1095.

Leadership as Social Construction

Understanding leadership as a process helps us see that leadership is socially constructed. The **social construction of leadership** means that leadership is co-created in relational interactions among people acting in context. Because of this, it cannot be meaningfully separated from context. Each leadership situation is unique, having its own particular dynamics, variables, and players. There is no one-size-fits-all solution in leadership.

Social construction approaches see leadership as socially defined. They recognize leaders and followers as relational beings who "constitute" each other in dynamic, unfolding relational contexts.[3] In other words, whether you are a leader or a follower depends on the nature of the interactions you have with other people. Because of this, communication and the everyday interactions of people are a key element of constructionist approaches to leadership.

Leadership as Identity Construction

An example of social construction can be seen in DeRue and Ashford's model of the **leadership identity construction process**. This model shows how individuals negotiate identities as leaders and followers.[4] As seen in Figure 13.2, the identity construction process involves individuals "claiming" an identity (as a leader or follower) and others affirming or "granting" that identity by going along with the claim. **Claiming** refers to actions people take to assert their identity as a leader or follower. **Granting** refers to actions people take to bestow an identity of a leader or follower onto another person.[5]

We can see the identity construction process occurring every time a new group is formed. When there is no designated leader, group members negotiate who will be leaders and who will be followers. For example, some might say, "I am willing to take the leader role," or "Leadership is not really my thing, so I prefer to follow." It may also be more implicit, with some people doing more influencing and organizing and others doing more deferring and performing.

This process occurs even when there is a designated leader. In these cases it may be more subtle, however, such as when individuals choose not to follow the designated leader (i.e., when they do not grant the leader claim). In groups we often see informal

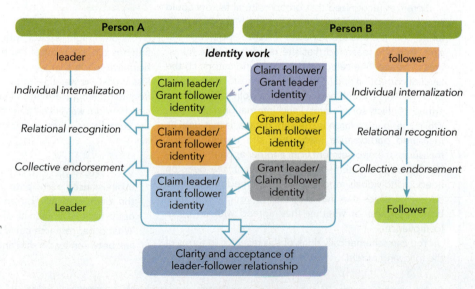

FIGURE 13.2 DeRue and Ashford Leadership Identity Construction Process.

OB IN POPULAR CULTURE

Leader Identity and *Forrest Gump*

In *Forrest Gump*, Tom Hanks plays a character who has a mental impairment but, despite this, always seems to find himself in extraordinary events and situations. One of the most memorable is when he decides to go out for a run, and ends up running for three and a half years. Forrest's passion for running began as a young boy when his best friend, Jenny, tells him, "Run, Forrest, run!" to get away from bullies. Forrest learns that running is a way to get *out* of his problems as well as to get *over* them.

As an adult, Forrest is distraught over Jenny leaving him and goes for a run. Once he starts, he just keeps going. He reaches one coast and decides he isn't done running, so he runs to the other coast. This coast-to-coast run goes on for years, with Forrest only stopping to sleep.

Forrest's run attracts media attention, and soon he has a large following of people who make attributions about meaning behind Forrest's running. Several of these followers are failing entrepreneurs who end up achieving success as a result of inspiration they take from Forrest. At the end of one scene we see Forrest on a highway with his followers trailing behind him. We hear Forrest say, "I had run for three years, two months, fourteen days, and sixteen hours," and then he stops running and turns around. The followers behind him also stop and look to Forrest to see what is going on. One says, "Quiet, quiet! He's gonna say something!" and after a pause Forrest says, "I'm pretty tired—I think I'll go home now."

Paramount Pictures/Photofest

Forrest's run raises fascinating questions for leadership. Was Forrest a leader? He had followers, so does this make him a leader? Others granted him leader identity and claimed their own identity as a follower of Forrest. But Forrest never claimed a leader identity himself. So was this leadership? How do we know when something is leadership and when it isn't?

Get to Know Yourself Better
Take a look at Experiential Exercise 25: Interview a Leader and Experiential Exercise 25: Leadership Skills Inventory in the *OB Skills Workbook*. These are designed to help you learn more about what makes a person a leader and what constitutes leadership processes. Do these help you understand whether Forrest was a leader in this case or do you need to know more? What would you add to these exercises to help you better assess leadership and followership in the case of Forrest Gump?

---

norms emerging around leader and follower grants and claims in the form of people supporting or resisting each other's claims.

Leader identity construction has important implications, particularly for those who are high in **motivation to lead**.[6] Although these individuals may want to lead, if others do not grant them a leadership identity their efforts will not succeed. It also helps us

Motivation to lead is the extent to which individuals choose to assume leadership training, roles and responsibilities.

understand why some individuals seem to find themselves in a leader role even if they don't want to be. For these "natural leaders," leadership is thrust upon them by others who grant them leadership identities regardless of their desire to claim leadership (see the "OB in Popular Culture" feature on *Forrest Gump*).

The leadership identity construction process brings a new understanding to the importance of followership. Contrary to views that depict followers as passive bystanders to leaders, identity construction shows that followers play an important role in leadership by (a) granting claims to leaders and (b) claiming roles as followers. When these grants and claims do not align—for example, when followers do not grant leaders' claims or when followers do not accept their own role as followers—the result is conflict and lack of legitimacy. Unless the problems are worked through, individuals will not be able to negotiate compatible identities. In these cases conflict will prevail, and the leadership process will break down.

Implicit Leadership Theories

A key element affecting whether leadership claims will be granted lies in the "implicit theories" we hold about leadership. **Implicit leadership theories** are beliefs or understanding about the attributes associated with leaders and leadership.[7] They can vary widely depending on our experiences and understandings of leadership. For example, some people believe leaders are charismatic, so they look for charismatic traits and behaviors in those vying for leadership status. Others believe leaders are directive and assertive, so they grant leadership status to those who take charge. Still others believe leaders are confident and considerate, so they identify leaders as those who have innovative and interesting ideas and involve others in bringing the idea to fruition.

Implicit theories cause us to naturally classify people as leaders or nonleaders. We are often not aware this process is occurring. It is based in the cognitive categorization processes associated with perception and attribution. These processes help us quickly and easily handle the overwhelming amounts of information we receive from our environments every day. The categorization process is often particularly salient when we are faced with new information. For example, on the first day of class did you look around the room and find yourself making assessments of the teacher, and even your classmates? If so, you did this using your cognitive categories and implicit theories.

To understand your own implicit leadership theories, think about the factors you associate with leadership. What traits and characteristics come to mind? Take a minute and make a list of those attributes. Now look at the sidebar on spotting implicit leadership prototypes.[8] How does your list compare? Did you identify the same prototypical leader behaviors as found in research? What is the nature of your implicit theory? Is it more positive, such as sensitivity, dedication, intelligence, and strength, or is it more negative, involving leaders' tendencies to dominate, control, or manipulate others? Why do you think you have the implicit theory you do? What experiences you've had make you see leadership in this way?

Implicit leadership theories are our beliefs or understanding about the attributes associated with leaders and leadership.

How to Spot Common Implicit Leadership Prototypes

People hold various prototypes of attributes they associate with leadership. Researchers find the following prototypes are most commonly used.

- *Sensitivity*—Sympathetic, compassionate, understanding
- *Dedication*—Disciplined, prepared, hard working
- *Tyranny*—Domineering, power hungry, manipulative
- *Charisma*—Inspiring, involved, dynamic
- *Attractiveness*—Classy, well dressed, tall
- *Intelligence*—Clever, knowledgeable, wise
- *Strength*—Forceful, bold, powerful

BRINGING OB TO LIFE

> *"Instead of putting charismatic leadership on an unreachable pedestal, perhaps learning specific charismatic communication techniques is a pathway to success."*

Building Charisma through Polished Rhetoric

The next time you give a presentation, check to see who's really listening. Better yet, check to see who's showing signs that they are ready to accept and act on what you are saying or proposing. That's one of the ways leadership claims get granted—framing and requesting things in ways that cause others to respond positively. We're talking about people who turn listeners into followers.

Some would argue this is a special skill associated with a magnetic or charismatic quality that you either have or don't have at birth. Recent OB thinking suggests there is a lot more to the story. Think of charisma as an ability to inspirationally persuade and motivate others. How is this positive impact achieved? In simple terms it's done by dropping bland business speech, such as "We need to operationalize this process," and practicing more emotive language, such as "once we put this into practice it'll feel like we all threw fifty-yard touchdown passes."

Professor John Antonakis at the University of Lausanne, Switzerland, believes that all of us should and can learn charismatic communication skills. "Some people are naturally more talented, but everyone can improve with practice," he says. And he has a training program designed to do just that. After one batch of corporate executives was trained, their leadership ratings went up 60 percent.

Some charismatic leadership techniques taught by Antonakis are verbal, breaking things down into basic

© Monalyn Gracia/Corbis

components: using metaphors and telling stories, asking rhetorical questions, taking a moral stand, and setting high goals. Others are nonverbal: using voice modulations, gestures, and facial expressions to accent what you are saying.

OB recognizes that not all managers are good leaders even though they should be. Instead of putting charismatic leadership on an unreachable pedestal, perhaps learning specific charismatic communication techniques is a pathway to success. Learning the techniques and putting them to work in everyday conversations is a way for more of us to be perceived as "leaderlike" by others.

Followership

LEARNING ROADMAP WHAT IS FOLLOWERSHIP? • HOW DO FOLLOWERS SEE THEIR ROLES? HOW DO LEADERS SEE FOLLOWER ROLES?

> TEACHING NOTE: Ask for a list of quotes regarding followership (e.g., "If you aren't the lead dog the view never changes"). What do these quotes convey about how followership is seen? Are they right?

Until very recently, followership has not been given serious consideration in leadership research. We are infatuated with leaders, but often disparage followers. Think about how often you are told the importance of being an effective leader. Now think about the times when you have been told it is important to be an effective follower—has it ever happened? If you are like most people, you have received recognition and accolades for leadership but rarely have you been encouraged or rewarded for being a follower.

What Is Followership?

Followership represents the capacity or willingness to follow a leader. It is a process through which individuals choose how they will engage with leaders to co-produce leadership and its outcomes. These co-productions can take many forms. For example, it may be heavily leader dominated, with passive followers who comply or go along. Or it may be a partnership, in which leaders and followers work collaboratively to produce leadership outcomes.

Our infatuation with leaders at the expense of followers is called the **romance of leadership**: the tendency to attribute all organizational outcomes—good or bad—to the acts and doings of leaders.[9] The romance of leadership reflects our needs and biases for strong leaders who we glorify or demonize in myths and stories of great and heroic leaders. We see it in our religious teachings, our children's fairy tales, and in news stories about political and business leaders.

The problem with the romance of leadership is that its corollary is the "subordination of followership."[10] The subordination of followership means that while we heroize (or demonize) leaders, we almost completely disregard followers. Leo Tolstoy's description of the French Revolution provides an excellent example. According to Tolstoy, the French Revolution was the product of the "spectacle of an extraordinary movement of millions of men" all over Europe and crossing decades, but "historians . . . lay before us the sayings and doings of some dozens of men in one of the buildings in the city of Paris," and the detailed biography and actions of *one* man, to whom it is all attributable: Napoleon. To overcome the problem of the romance of leadership, we need to better understand the role of followership in the leadership process.

How Do Followers See Their Roles?

Followers have long been considered in leadership research, but mainly from the standpoint of how they see leaders. The question we need to consider is this: How do followers see their own role? And how do leaders see the follower role? Research is now beginning to offer new insight into these issues.

The Social Construction of Followership

One of the first studies to examine follower views was a qualitative investigation in which individuals were asked to describe the characteristics and behaviors they associate with a follower (subordinate) role.[11] The findings support the socially constructed nature of followership and leadership in that, according to followers, they hold certain beliefs about how they should act in relation to leaders but whether they can act on these beliefs depends on context.

Some followers hold *passive beliefs*, viewing their roles in the classic sense of following—that is, passive, deferential, and obedient to authority. Others hold *proactive beliefs*, viewing their role as expressing opinions, taking initiative, and constructively questioning and challenging leaders. Proactive beliefs are particularly strong among "high potentials"—those identified by their organizations as demonstrating strong potential to be promoted to higher-level leadership positions in their organization.

Because social construction is dependent on context, individuals are not always able to act according to their beliefs. For example, individuals holding proactive beliefs reported not being able to be proactive in authoritarian or bureaucratic work climates. These environments suppress their ability to take initiative and speak up, often leaving them feeling frustrated and stifled—not able to work to their potential. In empowering climates, however, they work with leaders to co-produce positive outcomes. Individuals with passive beliefs are often uncomfortable in empowering climates because their

---

Followership is a process through which individuals choose how they will engage with leaders to co-produce leadership and its outcomes.

The **romance of leadership** refers to the tendency to attribute organizational outcomes (both good and bad) to the acts and doings of leaders.

CHECKING ETHICS IN OB

Workers Share Their Salary Secrets

Pay secrecy is a long-held tradition in the workplace. Workers are told they cannot discuss their pay or they will be fired. Managers say pay secrecy is necessary because it helps avoid potential conflicts and dissatisfaction among workers. But like many other things, Millennials are questioning this practice—and shaking up the workplace in the process.

Brian Bader took a tech-support job with Apple and during his orientation was told that he was not allowed to discuss his pay with co-workers. But this made the 25-year old Bader, curious, and he immediately set out to survey his new colleagues about their wages. What he learned was that he was twice as productive as the lowest performer in the group, but paid only 20 percent more. Bader decided to quit his job: "It irked me. If I'm doing double the work, why am I not seeing double the pay?" asked Mr. Bader.

Keeping salary information private is much harder for companies in today's environment of social media, with Web sites like Glassdoor, Facebook, and Twitter. Information is power, and despite company policies against it many people—especially young workers—are using their power to speak up against such policies. In addition to pay secrecy, the seniority system and annual performance reviews are two workplace institutions that

Maskot/Getty Images

Millennials are questioning. And answers like "because I said so" and "because we've always done it that way" are not enough for this generation. When they are dissatisfied, they take matters into their own hands, either by acting on information power, or quitting, as demonstrated by Brian Bader.

What Do You Think?
Should companies be able to reasonably expect workers to keep their pay secret? And if there is a company policy against sharing pay information, what is the obligation of the employee to follow this policy? How far does our obligation go? In 2013 we saw Edward Snowden break his company policy because he didn't agree with the NSA policy regarding the government's Internet and phone-tracking program. How does his action compare to that of Mr. Bader, who shared his pay information against company policy?

---

natural inclination is to follow rather than be empowered. In these environments they report feeling stressed by leaders' demands, and uncomfortable with requests to be more proactive. Passive followers are more comfortable in authoritarian climates where they receive more direction from leaders.

Follower Role Orientation
Follower beliefs are also being studied in research on follower role orientation. **Follower role orientation** represents the beliefs followers hold about the way they should engage and interact with leaders to meet the needs of the

> **Follower role orientation** is defined as the beliefs followers hold about the way they should engage and interact with leaders to meet the needs of the work unit.

FIGURE 13.3 Followership in Context.

work unit.[12] It reflects how followers define their role, how broadly they perceive the tasks associated with it, and how to approach a follower role to be effective.

Findings show that followers with hierarchical, **power distance orientation** believe leaders are in a better position than followers to make decisions and determine direction.[13] These individuals have lower self-efficacy, meaning they have less confidence in their ability to execute on their own, and they demonstrate higher obedience to leaders. They depend on leaders for structure and direction, which they follow without question. These followers report working in contexts of greater hierarchy of authority and lower job autonomy. This may be because these contexts are attractive to them, or it may be because those with more proactive follower orientations are less likely to remain in these environments.

Individuals with a **proactive follower orientation** approach their role from the standpoint of partnering with leaders to achieve goals.[14] These individuals are higher in proactive personality and self-efficacy. They believe followers are important contributors to the leadership process and that a strong follower role (e.g., voice) is necessary for accomplishing the organizational mission. Proactive followers tend to work in environments that support and reinforce their followership beliefs—that is, lower hierarchy of authority, greater autonomy, and higher supervisor support. These environments are important because proactive followers need support for their challenging styles. They need to trust leaders and to know that they will not be seen as overstepping their bounds.

The issue that is less clear is what managers want from followers. It seems that managers want voice, as long as that voice is provided in constructive ways. However, findings with obedience are not significant, indicating that managers may be mixed on whether obedience is positive or negative. This is true regardless of whether it comes from those with a power distance or proactive follower orientation. Therefore, we are not quite sure how obedience plays into followership. Do managers want obedience? Do only some managers want it, or do managers want only certain types of obedience? It turns out that although we have spent decades learning about what followers want from leaders, we still know very little about what leaders prefer in terms of follower behaviors and styles. Research is now underway to better investigate the manager side of the leadership story.

■ How Do Leaders See Follower Roles?

One area that helps us understand the manager's view is the study of **implicit followership theories**.[15] Research on implicit followership theories takes the approach described in implicit leadership theory research but reverses it—asking *leaders* (i.e., managers) to describe characteristics associated with *followers* (e.g., effective followers, ineffective followers). It then analyzes the data to identify prototypical and anti-prototypical follower characteristics.

Power distance orientation is the extent to which one accepts that power in institutions and organizations is distributed unequally.

Proactive follower orientation reflects the belief that followers should act in ways that are helpful, useful, and productive to leadership outcomes.

Implicit followership theories are preconceived notions about prototypical and antiprototypical followership behaviors and characteristics.

WORTH CONSIDERING ...OR BEST AVOIDED?

Bosses Are to Be Obeyed and My Job Is to Comply. Or Is It?

Before you answer the question in the headline, read further:

Yale University laboratory, 1963—Psychologist Stanley Milgram runs an experiment with collaborators posing as "learners" being taught word association tasks by their "teachers" – the real subjects. When the learners behind a wall missed a word association each of the 40 teachers was instructed to give them an electric shock. The learners faked their expressions of pain and cries to stop the process. When the teachers resisted going to higher levels of electric voltage, they were told by the experimenter: "You must go on. The experiment requires that you go on." Twenty-six of the teachers kept administering shocks until the final level was reached, a level they were told would be of danger to human life.

McDonald's Restaurant, 2004— A telephone caller tells an assistant store manager that he is a police officer investigating employee theft. Claiming to have "corporate" on the line he tells the assistant manager to take a female employee into the back room and interrogate her while he is on the line. The assistant manager does so for over three hours and follows "Officer Scott's" instructions to the point where the 18-year old employee is naked and doing jumping jacks. The hoax was discovered only when the assistant manager called her boss to check out the story. The caller was later arrested and was found to have tried similar tricks at over 70 McDonald's restaurants.

Managers are supposed to make decisions, and the rest of us are supposed to follow. Isn't that the conventional wisdom? But these incidents suggest that even though we may have a tendency to obey apparent authority figures, it isn't always the right thing to do.

There are times when it's best to disobey the boss or any other authority figure who is asking us to do something that seems odd or incorrect or just plain suspicious. And if what you are being asked to do is wrong but you still comply, you'll

Arcady/Shutterstock

share the blame. It can't be excused with the claim "I was just following orders."

Do the Analysis

If obedience isn't always the right choice, how do we know when it's time to disobey? Can you give some examples from personal experience when it was best not to comply with what you were asked to do? How would your behavior in the situation stack up under scrutiny? What does the literature have to say about reasons for obedience and how to double-check to make sure our obedience is justified in certain situations? How about the price of disobedience? Is it possible to educate and train people to be better followers—people who don't always follow orders and sometimes question them?

Findings shown in the sidebar on the next page indicate that characteristics associated with good followers include being industrious, having enthusiasm, and being a good organizational citizen.[16] Characteristics associated with ineffective followers (i.e., anti-prototypical characteristics) include conformity, insubordination, and incompetence. Of these anti-prototypical traits, it appears that incompetence is the most impactful. In other words, leaders see incompetence as the greatest factor associated with ineffective followership.

How to Spot Common Followership Prototypes and Antiprototypes

People hold various prototypes and antiprototypes of attributes they associate with followership. Researchers find the following are most common.

Prototypical
- *Industry*—Hardworking, productive, goes above and beyond
- *Enthusiasm*—Excited, outgoing, happy
- *Good citizen*—Loyal, reliable, team player

Antiprototypical
- *Conformity*—Easily influenced, follows trends, soft spoken
- *Insubordination*—Arrogant, rude, bad tempered
- *Incompetence*—Uneducated, slow, inexperienced

What is interesting about the findings on prototypes and antiprototypes (see the sidebar) is that they may show why we are uncertain of what managers desire from followers. What managers see as insubordination and incompetence, followers may see as proactive follower behaviors. There can be a fine line between these behaviors as provided by followers, and whether leaders are ready and able to effectively receive them. Although it hasn't been studied yet in research, we can be pretty sure that a key factor in influencing how managers view and receive proactive follower behaviors is the quality of the relationship between the manager and the subordinate.

TEACHING NOTE: Divide students into groups of those who currently have or have had high quality relationships with their managers and those with low quality relationships. Have them describe their relationships to one another and then report out to class.

The Leader–Follower Relationship

LEARNING ROADMAP LEADER–MEMBER EXCHANGE THEORY • SOCIAL EXCHANGE THEORY
HOLLANDER'S IDIOSYNCRASY CREDIT

Among the strongest findings in leadership research are studies showing that the nature of leader–follower relationships matter. When relationships are good, outcomes are positive. When relationships are bad, outcomes are negative, and potentially even destructive.

▌Leader–Member Exchange (LMX) Theory

Leader-member exchange (LMX) is the study of manager–subordinate relationship quality.

The underlying premise of **leader–member exchange (LMX)** theory is that leaders (i.e., managers) have differentiated relationships with followers (i.e., subordinates).[17] With some subordinates, managers have high-quality LMX relationships, characterized by trust, respect, liking, and loyalty. With other subordinates, managers have low-quality LMX relationships, characterized by lack of trust, respect, liking, and loyalty. Whereas the former (high LMX relationships) are more like partnerships between managers and subordinates in co-producing leadership, the latter (low LMX relationships) are more like traditional supervision, with managers supervising and monitoring and subordinates complying (or maybe resisting).

Leader–follower relationships are important because they are differentially related to leadership and work outcomes. As you would expect, when relationship quality is high it has all kinds of benefits: Performance is better, subordinates are more satisfied and feel more supported, commitment and citizenship are higher, and turnover is reduced. When relationship quality is low, outcomes are not only negative, they can also be destructive. At the very least, workers in low LMX relationships are less productive and have more negative job attitudes. At their worst, relationships are hostile, leading to abuse or even sabotage.[18]

The implications of leader–member exchange theory are very clear. Bad relationships are counterproductive for individuals and organizations, whereas good relationships bring tremendous benefits. If you have a bad relationship with your boss, you can expect it to negatively impact your work and possibly your career. In organizations, bad relationships create negative environments and poor morale. They drain organizations of the energy needed to perform, adapt, and thrive.

Social Exchange Theory

To avoid these problems, we need to work to develop better-quality relationships throughout the organization. The question is, how?

Social exchange theory helps explain the social dynamics behind relationship building. According to social exchange theory, relationships develop through exchanges—actions contingent upon rewarding reactions. We engage in exchanges every day when we say something or do something for another and those actions are rewarded or not rewarded. Relationships develop when exchanges are mutually rewarding and reinforcing. When exchanges are one sided or not satisfactory, relationships will not develop effectively, and will likely deteriorate or extinguish.

At the core of social exchange is the **norm of reciprocity**, the idea that when one party does something for another an obligation is generated, and that party is indebted to the other until the obligation is repaid.[19] We see this all the time when someone does us a favor and then, depending on how close we are to them, we feel indebted to pay them back. If the relationship is close (e.g., family) we don't worry about paying back right away because we know it will be repaid in some way in the future. If the exchange is with someone we don't know as well (e.g., a classmate we just met), we are more anxious to repay so that the other knows we are "good" for it.

The norm of reciprocity can be seen as involving three components.[20] **Equivalence** represents the extent to which the amount of what is given back is roughly the same as what was received (e.g., the exact same or something different). **Immediacy** refers to the *time span of reciprocity*—how quickly the repayment is made (e.g., immediately or an indeterminate length of time). **Interest** represents the motive the person has in making the exchange. Interest can range from pure self-interest, to mutual interest, to other interest (pure concern for the other person).

The way in which these components work together varies by the quality of leader-follower relationships. When relationships are first forming, or if they are low quality, reciprocity involves greater equivalence (we want back what we give), immediacy is low (we expect payback relatively quickly), and exchanges are based on self-interest (we are watching out for ourselves). As relationships develop and trust is built, equivalence reduces (we don't expect exact repayment), the time span of reciprocity extends (we aren't concerned about payback—we may bank it for when we need it at some time in the future), and exchanges become more mutually or other (rather than self) interested.

What makes this process social and not economic is that it is based on trust. **Trust** is based on the belief regarding the intention and ability of the other to repay. Economic exchanges are necessarily devoid of trust. The reason we make economic contracts is to create a legal obligation in case one party breaks the contract. In social exchange, trust is the foundational element upon which exchanges occur. If one party demonstrates that they are not trustworthy, the other party will see this and stop exchanging—and the relationship will degenerate.

If we want to build effective relationships, therefore, we need to pay attention to reciprocity

---

Social exchange theory describes how relationships initiate and develop through processes of exchange and reciprocity.

The **norm of reciprocity** says that when one party does something for another, that party is indebted to the other until the obligation is repaid.

Equivalence is the extent to which the amount given back is roughly the same as what was received.

Immediacy is how quickly the repayment is made.

Interest is the motive behind the exchange.

Trust in social exchange is based on the belief in the intention and ability of the other to repay.

Reciprocity and Social Exchange in Leader-Follower Relationships

Low quality or newly forming relationships	High quality relationships
• High immediacy	• Low immediacy
• High equivalence	• Low equivalence
• Self-interest	• Mutual interest

and social exchange processes. We need to make sure that we are engaging in exchanges, that we are doing so based on reciprocity, and that the exchanges are mutually satisfying and rewarding for all involved.

▌Hollander's Idiosyncrasy Credits

Another way to view the nature of exchange in relationships is idiosyncrasy credit theory, developed by social psychologist Edwin Hollander in the 1950s.[21] **Idiosyncrasy credits** represent our ability to violate norms with others based on whether we have enough "credits" to cover the violation. If we have enough credits, we can get away with idiosyncrasies (i.e., deviations from expected norms) as long as the violation does not exceed the amount of credits. If we do not have enough credits, the violation will create a deficit. When deficits become large enough, or go on for too long, our account becomes "bankrupt," and the deviations will no longer be tolerated, resulting in deterioration of relationships.

Idiosyncrasy credits offer a fun and simple way to think about some key concepts we need to keep in mind in relationship building. The main point is to manage your balances. If you are expending credits by behaving in idiosyncratic ways (deviating from expected norms), then you have to stop spending and start building. If you have a rich account and the relationship is flying high, you can afford to expend some credits by acting in a quirky way or doing things that might not be seen as positively in the other's eyes. Others will be willing to stick with you—as long as you don't go into a deficit.

Idiosyncrasy credits refer to our ability to violate norms with others based on whether we have enough "credits" to cover the violation.

Collective Leadership

TEACHING NOTE: Using the descriptions of collective leadership, ask student if they have worked in any groups or organizations that have used any of these forms of leadership. If not, why not?

LEARNING ROADMAP   DISTRIBUTED LEADERSHIP • CO-LEADERSHIP • SHARED LEADERSHIP

Relational interactions are the foundation of leadership, and relational approaches have allowed us to understand that leadership is more aptly described as a collective rather than an individual process. **Collective leadership** considers leadership not as a property of individuals and their behaviors but as a social phenomenon constructed in interaction. It advocates a shift in focus from traits and characteristics of leaders to a focus on the shared activities and interactive processes of leadership.

Collective leadership represents views of leadership not as a property of individuals and their behaviors but as a social phenomenon constructed in interaction.

▌Distributed Leadership

One of the first areas to recognize leadership as a collective process was **distributed leadership** research, distinguishing between "focused" and "distributed" forms of leadership. This research draws heavily on systems and process theory, and locates leadership in the relationships and interactions of multiple actors and the situations in which they are operating.[22]

Distributed leadership sees leadership as a group phenomenon that is distributed among individuals.

Distributed leadership is based on three main premises. First, leadership is an emergent property of a group or network of interacting individuals, i.e., it is co-constructed in interactions among people. Second, distributed leadership is not clearly bounded. It occurs in context, and therefore it is affected by local and historical influences. Third, distributed leadership draws from the variety of expertise across the many, rather than relying on the limited expertise of one or a few leaders. In this way it is a more democratic and inclusive form of leadership than hierarchical models.[23]

Leadership from this view is seen in the day-to-day activities and interactions of people working in organizations. Rather than simply being a hierarchical construct, it occurs in small, incremental, and emergent everyday acts that go on in organizations.

These emergent acts, interacting with large-scale change efforts from the top, can be mutually reinforcing to produce emergence and adaptability in organizations. Hence, leadership is about learning together and constructing meaning and knowledge collaboratively and collectively. For this to happen, though, formal leaders must let go of some of their authority and control and foster consultation and consensus over command and control.[24]

■ Co-Leadership

Another form of collective leadership is co-leadership. **Co-leadership** occurs when top leadership roles are structured in ways that no single individual is vested with the power to unilaterally lead.[25] Co-leadership can be found in professional organizations (e.g., law firms that have partnerships), the arts (the artistic side and administrative side), and healthcare (where power is divided between the community, administration, and medical sectors). Co-leadership has been used in some very famous and large businesses (e.g., Google, Goldman-Sachs).

> **Co-leadership** occurs when leadership is divided so that no one person has unilateral power to lead.

Co-leadership helps overcome problems related to the limitations of a single individual and of abuses of power and authority. It is more common today because challenges facing organizations are often too complex for one individual to handle. Co-leadership allows organizations to capitalize on the complementary and diverse strengths of multiple individuals. These forms are sometimes referred to as constellations, or collective leadership in which members play roles that are *specialized* (i.e., each operates in a particular area of expertise), *differentiated* (i.e., avoiding overlap that would create confusion), and *complementary* (i.e., jointly cover all required areas of leadership).[26]

FINDING THE LEADER IN YOU

Google's Triumvirate Gives Way to New Leadership Structure

The news came as a surprise: Eric Schmidt was out and Larry Page was in as head of Google. Schmidt had been brought in by the board of directors in 2001 to provide "adult supervision" to then twenty-seven-year-old founders Larry Page and Sergey Brin. For ten years Google's management structure represented triumvirate leadership, with Page, Brin, and Schmidt sharing the leadership role. To some, it was a three-ring circus, with co-founders Larry Page and Sergey Brin running the business behind the scenes and Schmidt as the public face. Now, the three decided, it was time for Page to take the stage.

"For the last ten years, we have all been equally involved in making decisions. This triumvirate approach has real benefits in terms of shared wisdom, and we will continue to discuss the big decisions among the three of us. But we have also agreed to clarify our individual roles so there's clear responsibility and accountability at the top of the company," said Eric Schmidt.

The objective is to simplify the management structure and speed up decision making. "Larry will now lead product development and technology strategy, his greatest strengths . . . and he will take charge of our day-to-day operations as Google's Chief Executive Officer," according to Schmidt.

That leaves Sergey Brin, with title of co-founder, to focus on strategic projects and new products, and Schmidt to serve as executive chairman, working externally on deals, partnerships, customers, and government outreach. As described on the official Google blog, "We are confident that this focus will serve Google and our users well in the future."

The question now is, with the leadership triumvirate dead, will the new leadership structure work?

David Strick/Redux

What's the Lesson Here?

Do you think co-leadership models work? And would they work for you—would you be able to operate effectively as part of a co-leadership structure? Why or why not?

Shared Leadership

Shared leadership is a dynamic, interactive influence process among team members working to achieve goals.

According to **shared leadership** approaches, leadership is a dynamic, interactive influence process among individuals in groups for which the objective is to lead one another to the achievement of group or organizational goals, or both.[27] This influence process occurs both laterally—among team members—and vertically, with the team leader. Vertical leadership is formal leadership; shared leadership is distributed leadership that emerges from within team dynamics. The main objective of shared leadership approaches is to understand and find alternate sources of leadership that will impact positively on organizational performance.

In shared leadership, leadership can come from outside or inside the team. Within a team, leadership can be assigned to one person, rotate across team members, or be shared simultaneously as different needs arise across time. Outside the team, leaders can be formally designated. Often these nontraditional leaders are called coordinators or facilitators. A key part of their job is to provide resources to their unit and serve as a liaison with other units.

According to the theory, the key to successful shared leadership and team performance is to create and maintain conditions for that performance. This occurs when vertical and shared leadership efforts are complementary. Although a wide variety of characteristics may be important for the success of a specific effort, five important characteristics have been identified across projects: (1) efficient, goal-directed effort; (2) adequate resources; (3) competent, motivated performance; (4) a productive, supportive climate; and (5) a commitment to continuous improvement.[28] The distinctive contribution of shared leadership approaches is in widening the notion of leadership to consider participation of all team members while maintaining focus on conditions for team effectiveness.

13 Study Guide

Key Questions and Answers

What is leadership?

- Leadership occurs in acts of leading and following as individuals work together to attain mutual goals.
- Formal leadership is found in positions of authority in organizations, whereas informal leadership is found in individuals who become influential due to special skills or abilities.
- Leadership involves an identity construction process in which individuals negotiate identities as leaders and followers through claiming and granting.
- Implicit leadership theories are beliefs or understanding about the attributes associated with leaders and leadership.

What is followership?

- Followership represents a process through which individuals choose how they will engage with leaders to co-produce leadership and its outcomes.
- Romance of leadership is the tendency to attribute organizational outcomes (both good and bad) to the acts and doings of leaders; its corollary is the "subordination of followership."
- The social construction of followership shows that followers hold beliefs about how they should act in relation to leaders, but whether they can act on these beliefs depends on context.

- Those with power distance orientation accept that power in institutions and organizations is distributed unequally, whereas those with proactive follower orientations believe followers should act in ways that are helpful and productive to leadership outcomes.
- Implicit followership theories show managers' views of characteristics associated with effective and ineffective followership.

What do we know about leader–follower relationships?
- Leader–member exchange theory shows that managers have differentiated relationships with subordinates depending on the amount of trust, respect, and loyalty in the relationship.
- These relationships are important because they are differentially related to leadership and work outcomes. When relationship quality is high, performance is better, subordinates are more satisfied and supported, commitment and citizenship are higher, and turnover is reduced.
- Relationships develop through processes of social exchange based on the norm of reciprocity (i.e., when one party does something for another, an obligation is generated until it is repaid).
- Reciprocity is determined based on three components: equivalence (whether the amount given back is same as what was received), immediacy (how quickly the repayment is made), and interest (the motive behind the exchange).
- Idiosyncrasy credits mean that when we have enough credits built up in relationships with others, we can get away with idiosyncrasies (i.e., deviations from expected norms) as long as the violation does not exceed the amount of credits.

What do we mean by leadership as a collective process?
- Collective leadership advocates a shift in focus from traits and characteristics of leaders to a focus on the shared activities and interactive processes of leadership.
- Distributed leadership sees leadership as drawing from the variety of expertise across the many, rather than relying on the limited expertise of one or a few leaders.
- Co-leadership is when top leadership roles are structured in ways that no single individual is vested with the power to unilaterally lead.
- Shared leadership defines leadership as a dynamic, interactive influence process among individuals in groups for which the objective is to lead one another to the achievement of group or organizational goals, or both.
- Shared leadership occurs both laterally, among team members, and vertically, with the team leader. The main objective is to understand and find alternate sources of leadership that will impact positively on organizational performance.

Terms to Know

Claiming (p. 284)
Co-leadership (p. 295)
Collective leadership (p. 294)
Distributed leadership (p. 294)
Equivalence (p. 293)
Followership (p. 288)
Follower role orientation (p. 289)
Formal leadership (p. 282)
Granting (p. 284)
Idiosyncrasy credits (p. 294)
Immediacy (p. 293)
Implicit followership theories (p. 290)
Implicit leadership theories (p. 286)
Informal leaders (p. 282)
Interest (p. 293)
Leader–member exchange (LMX) (p. 292)
Leadership (p. 282)
Leadership identity construction process (p. 284)
Motivation to lead (p. 285)
Norm of reciprocity (p. 293)
Power distance orientation (p. 290)
Proactive follower orientation (p. 290)
Romance of leadership (p. 288)
Shared leadership (p. 296)
social construction of leadership (p. 284)
Social exchange theory (p. 293)
Trust (p. 293)
Upward leadership (p. 282)

Self-Test 13

■ Multiple Choice

1. Leadership is a process of _____.
   (a) leading and following
   (b) deferring and obeying
   (c) managing and supervising
   (d) influencing and resisting

2. We could almost say that it is in _____ that leadership is created.
   (a) positions
   (b) authority
   (c) following
   (d) hierarchy

3. A type of leadership that is often missed in discussions of leadership is _____ leadership.
   (a) face-to-face
   (b) downward
   (c) hierarchical
   (d) upward

4. _____ occurs through processes of claiming and granting.
   (a) Followership
   (b) Leadership identity construction
   (c) Implicit theory
   (d) Status

5. People use _____ in deciding whether to grant a leadership claim.
   (a) implicit theories
   (b) social constructions
   (c) collective leadership
   (d) social exchange

6. _____ involves the choice of how to engage with leaders in producing leadership.
   (a) Implicit theories
   (b) Followership
   (c) Informal leadership
   (d) Reciprocity

7. Power distance is an example of _____.
   (a) an implicit followership theory
   (b) upward leadership
   (c) the leadership process
   (d) a follower role orientation

8. Individuals who engage in voice likely have a _____.
   (a) weak feedback orientation
   (b) prototypical leadership theory
   (c) constructive follower orientation
   (d) power distance orientation

9. _____ involves the process of revealing and reacting to disclosures.
   (a) Relational violations
   (b) Leadership identity construction
   (c) Shared leadership
   (d) Relational testing

10. The obligation created when someone does you a favor is _____.
    (a) feedback orientation
    (b) the norm of reciprocity
    (c) implicit followership theories
    (d) distributed leadership

11. A rule of thumb for whether you can violate norms in a relationship is to not overexpend your _____.
    (a) idiosyncrasy credits
    (b) relational disclosures
    (c) low LMX
    (d) reciprocity

12. _____ says that leadership is an emergent property of a group or network of interacting individuals.
    (a) Leadership identity construction (b) Distributed leadership
    (c) Leader–member exchange theory (d) Social exchange theory

13. If a manager and subordinate have a lot of trust and support for one another, we can say they have a _____.
    (a) weak norm of reciprocity (b) idiosyncratic relationship
    (c) low LMX relationship (d) high LMX relationship

14. When the leadership role at the top is divided among multiple people, it is called _____.
    (a) collective leadership (b) distributed leadership
    (c) co-leadership (d) shared leadership

15. Conformity is an example of _____.
    (a) power distance orientation (b) prototypical followership
    (c) anti-prototypical followership (d) constructive orientation

Short Response

16. What does it mean when we say leadership is socially constructed?
17. How do followers see their role in leadership?
18. How does the norm of reciprocity work in relationship development?
19. Why are scholars talking about collective leadership?

Applications Essay

20. Your roommate is student government president and has been having trouble getting others to listen to him. Each night it is a different complaint about how terrible the other people in student government are, and how they are lazy and not willing to do anything. You really want to help him figure out this problem. How do you go about it?

Steps to Further Learning 13
Top Choices from *The OB Skills Workbook*

These learning activities from *The OB Skills Workbook* found at the back of the book are suggested for Chapter 13.

Case for Critical Thinking	Team and Experiential Exercises	Self-Assessment Portfolio
• The New Vice President	• Interview a Leader • Leadership Skills Inventories • Leadership and Participation in Decision Making	• Student Leadership Practices Inventory • Least-Preferred Co-worker Scale • Leadership Style • "TT" Leadership Style • Empowering Others

Great leaders know the way

14

Leader Traits and Behavioral Styles

The Key Point

When leaders are effective, the people who are influenced by them tend to feel good and are most often productive. But when leaders are ineffective, people and performance suffer. This chapter explores why some leaders can be more successful than others, and identifies challenges facing leaders in today's changing organizational contexts. ■

What's Inside?

- **Bringing OB to LIFE**
  STAYING THIN TO GAIN A LEADERSHIP EDGE
- **Worth Considering . . . or Best Avoided?**
  NEWLY PROMOTED TO MANAGER? "DO NOTHING" MAY BE YOUR KEY TO SUCCESS
- **Checking Ethics in OB**
  TACKLING UNETHICAL LEADERSHIP IN THE WORKPLACE
- **Finding the Leader in You**
  PATRICIA KARTER USES CORE VALUES AS HER GUIDE
- **OB in Popular Culture**
  LINCOLN AND LEADERSHIP
- **Research Insight**
  WHEN INDIVIDUAL DIFFERENCES MATTER MORE THAN CULTURAL DIFFERENCES

Chapter at a Glance

- What Do We Know About Leader Traits and Behaviors?
- What Do Contingency Approaches Tell Us About leadership?
- What Are Charismatic and Transformational Theories of Leadership?
- What Are Complexity Leadership Views?
- How Do We Address Leadership Ethics?

Leader Traits and Behaviors

LEARNING ROADMAP — EARLY TRAIT APPROACHES • LATER TRAIT APPROACHES • BEHAVIORAL LEADERSHIP APPROACHES • ARE LEADERS BORN OR MADE?

> TEACHING NOTE: Have students develop a list of competencies they think leaders need to be effective in today's environment. What about the competencies of effective followers?

We all have experience with many different kinds of leaders. Some are task oriented and authoritarian. Others are inspirational and motivating. Still others are hands off, with laissez-faire or ineffectual styles that can make it frustrating when situations require strong leadership.

These characteristics represent traits and behavioral styles of leaders. Trait and behavioral approaches help us understand how characteristics of leaders are associated with their effectiveness. The basic premise is that we can identify more and less effective leadership styles by studying how followers perceive and react to different kinds of leaders.

As any of us who have worked in organizations know, managers play a crucial role in creating the climates in which we work. When a manager fosters a supportive and motivating climate, our work is meaningful and going to work is fun. But when we have a bad manager, morale plummets and we are drained of the energy we need to be productive in work—and in life. Research has shown us what makes some managers more effective than others. In this chapter we build from this knowledge to understand how we can become more effective managers and leaders in the workplace.

▶ Early Trait Approaches

For over a century, scholars have been on a quest to identify the elusive qualities that separate leaders from non-leaders. Based on the assumption that leaders are endowed with certain traits or characteristics, much of the early work focused on identifying qualities that predict who is a leader and who is not. These studies, collectively called **trait approaches**, assumed that if we could identify leadership qualities, we could select individuals for leadership positions based on their leadership traits.

The focus in this early work was on personality, needs, motives, values, and even physical characteristics such as height and sex. For this reason, these theories were often called "great man theories" because one of the key traits they associated with leadership was being male.

Trait approaches assume that leaders are endowed with certain traits or qualities associated with leader status and success.

Early review were discouraging. Scholars concluded that traits were not significantly associated with leadership. A primary reason was the failure to look for situational and mediating variables, such as communication or interpersonal behaviors, that would help explain how leader traits are causally linked to outcomes.[1] Instead, researchers looked for significant correlations between traits and leadership outcomes, such as group performance or leader advancement. When they failed to find strong relationships, they concluded that traits were not a significant predictor of leadership or its effectiveness.

▶ Later Trait Approaches

These early reviews saying there was not a pattern of significant correlations caused trait approaches to fall out of favor. In recent years, however, trait approaches have experienced a comeback as management scholars are developing new measures and new ways to analyze the relationship between a manager's traits and his or her leadership effectiveness.

Some scholars are using the Big Five dimensions of personality in an attempt to predict leader emergence (i.e., who is recognized as leader of a group) and leader effectiveness (i.e., how well a leader performs in the role). Findings show significant but small relationships for four of the Big Five traits: extraversion, conscientiousness, emotional

BRINGING OB TO LIFE

> "When we see a senior executive who's overweight, our initial reaction isn't positive.... If he can't keep his hand out of the cookie jar, how can he do his job?"

Staying Thin to Gain a Leadership Edge

A good workout may return more than good health and the body image you want. It might boost your leadership potential as well. Although OB scholarship has historically turned away from considering personal traits such as height, weight, and physical attractiveness in leadership, the real world may be moving in a different direction. OB researchers are starting to look at the workout as not only a personal wellness issue but also a leadership one.

After seeing a video replay of a presentation he made at the Center for Creative Leadership (CCL), Tim McNair was shocked at the prominence of his "gut." He guessed co-workers back home were looking at the same thing every time he spoke with them. Even worse, he wondered if they were saying to each other "If he can't keep his hand out of the cookie jar, how can he do his job?"

That question doesn't surprise OB professor and leadership consultant Barry Posner of Santa Clara University. "When we see a senior executive who's overweight," he says, "our initial reaction isn't positive." Recent research by CCL backs him up. A study of 757 executives showed that a leader's weight had a strong correlation with how good she or he was perceived as a leader by peers, bosses, and subordinates. A BMI of 25 seemed to be the dividing line. Below it and you score well as a leader; above it you score more poorly.

BelleMedia/Shutterstock

OB places a lot of importance on how perceptions influence attitudes and behavior. So if perceptions of our leadership abilities are affected in any part by our physical appearance, maybe it's time to get both weight and perceptions under control. Whether you call it our "leadership image" or something else, we own it. Even the CEO of Weight Watchers International has had to own up. He started the job at 245 pounds on a six-foot-two frame and says, "I sucked my gut in a lot." After losing 40 pounds he now says, "I probably carry myself with more confidence and authority."

stability, and openness to experience.[2] This means that effective leaders seem to have a bit more of these traits than ineffective and non-leaders.

Other scholars are pulling from evolutionary psychology to identify genetic factors associated with leadership that have evolved through natural selection. These scholars argue that our predilections toward leadership and followership are likely due to natural selection that caused certain traits and behaviors to be retained because they solved adaptive problems faced by our ancestors.[3] According to evolutionary psychology approaches, it may be engrained in some of us to voluntarily subordinate to others because our ancestors learned that, in certain situations, it is better to defer to a central command.

■ Behavioral Leadership Approaches

If you want to know whether a leader has a certain trait—that is, intelligence, extraversion, or persuasiveness—how would you find out? The answer is that you would look at his or her *behaviors*. Not surprisingly, then, when the early trait approaches failed to produce meaningful results, researchers began considering other types of leader characteristics, such as what leaders did, or how they behaved.

The **behavioral approach** focuses on identifying categories of relevant leadership behavior and examining their effects on performance and other outcomes.

This led to what is known as the **behavioral approach** in management research. The behavioral approach focuses on identifying categories of relevant leadership behavior and examining their relationships with outcomes. It does this primarily through the use of interviews and questionnaires that gather subordinates' perceptions of the supervisors' behaviors.

Much of the early work on behavioral approaches was centered at two universities, so they became known as the Ohio State and Michigan studies.[4] These studies discovered that the majority of a manager's leadership behaviors could be divided into two

Research Insight

When Individual Differences Matter More than Cultural Differences

When it comes to transformational leadership, whether subordinates like it or not may depend more on individual differences than cultural differences. At least this is what researchers found in a study of managers and subordinates in the United States and China. The findings, published in the *Academy of Management Journal*, show that when individuals have a low power distance orientation they see transformational leaders as more fair (i.e., procedural justice) than when they have a high power distance orientation. And this finding seems to hold across both Chinese and American respondents.

The authors suggest that the difference lies in one's power distance orientation. When individuals have a high power distance orientation, they expect their leaders to communicate strong directives. And they don't want leaders to provide explanation or clarification—their expectation is that solutions should come from leaders, not from followers. Transformational leaders, however, are focused on stimulating followers to think for themselves and take on more leadership responsibility. They use intellectual stimulation to encourage followers to think more like leaders. For those with high power distance orientation, this use of intellectual stimulation is viewed with suspicion. They believe it is unfair for leaders to pass on to followers what they should be taking care of themselves.

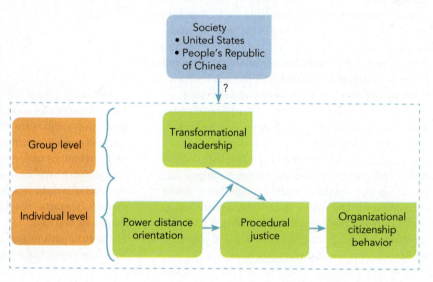

These findings indicate that cultural differences may matter less than we think. Individuals both in the United States and China appear to respond negatively to transformational leadership when they have high power distance orientation. When power distance orientation is low, transformational leadership is seen as fair. But when power distance is high, transformational leaders better beware: Subordinates might not like their style!

Do the Research Do you think these findings would hold for other leadership styles? The study looked at power distance orientation, but what other variables do you think might matter when it comes to considering individual differences across cultures?

Source: See Bradley Kirkman, Gilad Chen, Jiing-Lih Harh, Zhen Xiong Chen, and Kevin Lowe, "Individual Power Distance Orientation and Follower Reactions to Transformational Leaders: A Cross-Cultural Examination," *Academy of Management Journal* 52 (2009), pp. 744–764.

meta-categories: relations-oriented and task-oriented behavior. **Relations-oriented behavior**, or *consideration*, involves concern for relationships and interpersonal support. It focuses on employee-centered, or socioemotional, concerns. **Task-oriented behavior**, or *initiating structure*, involves directive behavior focused on providing clarity and task focus. It addresses production-centered, or task-related, concerns of management.

These two behavioral categories form the foundation for much of the management research that was to follow. Relations-oriented behavior focuses on the human relations aspects of management. It shows that highly considerate managers are sensitive to people's feelings and try to make things pleasant for followers. They do this by listening to subordinates and treating them as respected colleagues, defending subordinates when needed, being willing to accept suggestions, and consulting with subordinates on important matters.[5]

Task-oriented behavior focuses on production. Its key concern is to provide structure for subordinates by defining task requirements and specifying the work agenda. Task-oriented behaviors include maintaining performance standards, assigning tasks, identifying standard procedures, enforcing deadlines, correcting performance problems, and coordinating activities.[6]

> **Relations-oriented behavior**, also known as *consideration*, involves concern for relationships and socioemotional support.
>
> **Task-oriented behavior**, also known as *initiating structure*, involves providing direction and enforcing performance standards needed to drive production.

▶ Are Leaders Born or Made?

The focus on traits and behaviors raises another issue at the center of leadership. Is leadership restricted to those who are *born* with leadership ability, or can anyone be *made* into a leader? This is known as the "born/made" argument in leadership. The "born" argument aligns with trait theory, which says that leaders have certain traits—that they are natural-born leaders. The "made" argument aligns with the behavior approaches, which say that leadership is associated with behaviors (i.e., if you behave like a leader you are a leader). The made argument implies that anyone can be made into a leader through training and development.

Where do you fall on this issue? Do you think anyone can be made into a leader? Or do you think people have to have certain skills to be a leader? If the born argument is right, then we should focus on *selection* by screening new hires for leadership traits and skills. If the made argument is correct then we should focus on *development* by training individuals to better demonstrate leadership behaviors.

Potential insight into the answer can be found in a series of research studies by Rich Arvey and colleagues based on samples of fraternal and identical twins from the Minnesota Twin Registry. Examining how much leadership is determined by nature (i.e., genetics) and how much by nurture (i.e., environment), they found that 30 percent to 32 percent of the variance in role occupancy among twins could be accounted for by genetic factors. This means that roughly 70 percent can be developed.[7] The implication of these findings is that not everyone can be a leader. Instead, individuals must possess at least some set of basic leadership skills and abilities. In other words, just like being a musician or a star athlete, leadership is a talent—and some people have it more than others.

Contingency Theories

LEARNING ROADMAP THE CONTINGENCY MODEL • FINDINGS FROM CONTINGENCY THEORIES
FIEDLER'S LEADER MATCH • PROBLEMS WITH CONTINGENCY APPROACHES

> TEACHING NOTE: Run a mini debate, with one side arguing that contingency theories help us know more about leadership and the other side arguing that contingency theories are not very useful for learning how to be more effective leaders.

Common sense would tell us that not all traits or behaviors of leaders are positively related to effectiveness all of the time. Instead, whether a leader behavior is effective will depend on the situation. On the first day of class, what do you want from your professor: Do you want more considerate behavior, or do you want more structuring behavior? Most students want more structuring behavior. If your professor comes in and is nice and friendly (i.e., consideration) but does not hand out a syllabus (i.e., initiating structure), the

Contingency approaches state that the relationship between leader behavior and leadership effectiveness depends on the situation.

Directive leadership provides clarity and direction for subordinates.

Supportive leadership promotes a friendly work climate by focusing on subordinate needs and well-being.

Achievement-oriented leadership is motivation focused and builds subordinates' confidence to achieve high standards through its focus on excellence and goal setting.

Participative leadership is a democratic form of leadership that consults with subordinates and takes their suggestions into account before making decisions.

response will likely not be very positive. In other words, some situations call for certain types of behaviors more than others.

This is the premise behind the **contingency approaches** in leadership theory. Contingency approaches state that whether a leader style or behavior is positively associated with leadership effectiveness depends on (i.e., is *contingent* upon) the situation. In situations requiring more direction and structure, task-oriented behavior will be more effective and desired. In situations requiring more support and consideration, relations-oriented behavior will be more effective.

The Contingency Model

A general contingency model is shown in Figure 14.1. It indicates that a manager's leadership behavior or style (e.g., the independent variable) is related to leadership effectiveness (e.g., the outcome variable) depending on the situation (e.g., the moderator variable).

Contingency theories start with a manager's behavioral style. The most common leadership behaviors used by managers are task oriented and relations oriented. In contingency approaches, these are often referred to as **directive leadership** and **supportive leadership** styles. Two additional behavioral styles were added later: achievement-oriented and participative leadership.[8] **Achievement-oriented leadership** focuses on building subordinates' confidence in their ability to achieve high standards of performance through a focus on excellence and goal setting. **Participative leadership** focuses on consulting with subordinates and taking their suggestions into account before making decisions.

Contingency theories try to predict leadership effectiveness. The most common effectiveness variables are subordinate job satisfaction and performance. As described in previous chapters, job satisfaction is the positive feelings one has about the work and work setting. Performance is the quality and quantity of work produced. Performance can be measured at the individual level (i.e., the performance of a particular subordinate) or at the group level (i.e., the performance of a work unit).

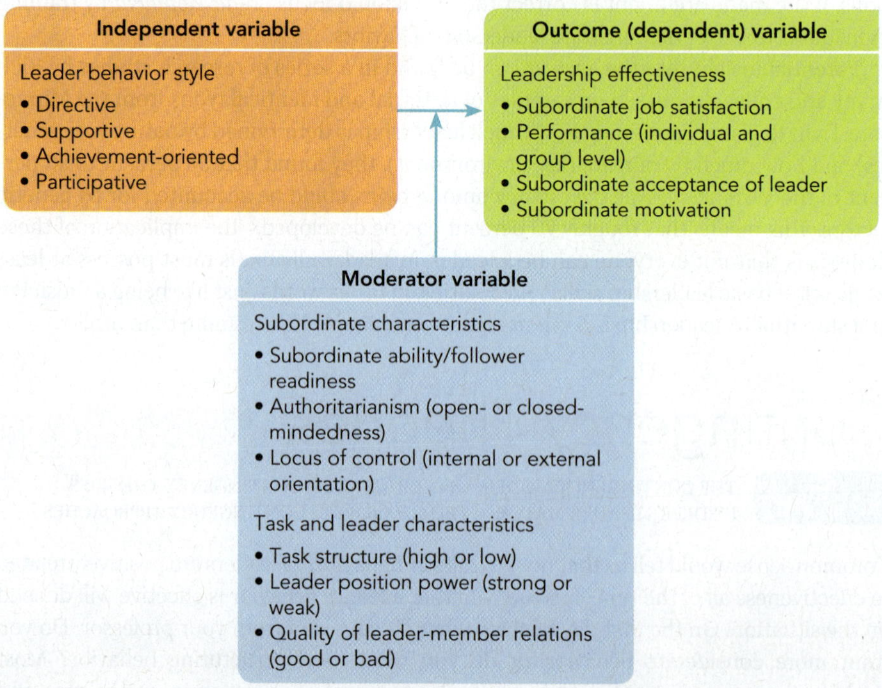

Independent variable	Outcome (dependent) variable
Leader behavior style • Directive • Supportive • Achievement-oriented • Participative	Leadership effectiveness • Subordinate job satisfaction • Performance (individual and group level) • Subordinate acceptance of leader • Subordinate motivation

Moderator variable

Subordinate characteristics
- Subordinate ability/follower readiness
- Authoritarianism (open- or closed-mindedness)
- Locus of control (internal or external orientation)

Task and leader characteristics
- Task structure (high or low)
- Leader position power (strong or weak)
- Quality of leader-member relations (good or bad)

FIGURE 14.1 A comprehensive contingency model.

The central argument of contingency theories is that situational factors moderate the association between a manager's leadership style and his or her effectiveness. Situational variables are assessed in a variety of ways. They include characteristics of the follower, such as **follower readiness**, or ability to do the task. They can be characteristics of the task, such as **task structure** (e.g., high or low task structure). Or they can be characteristics of the organizational structure, such as **leader position power** (e.g., formal or informal authority system).

▎Findings from Contingency Theories

Findings from contingency approaches show, in general, that certain situations favor certain leadership styles. Managers, therefore, need to understand, what the situation is and how to adjust their style to fit it.

Directive Leadership Directive leadership is needed when subordinates want guidance and direction in their jobs. It helps increases role clarity, self-efficacy, effort, and performance. When the task is clear, directive leadership will have a negative impact, as it will be seen as overly domineering—a "micromanaging" style—by subordinates.

Supportive Leadership Supportive leadership is needed when subordinates want emotional, not task, support. Supportive leadership is beneficial for highly repetitive or unpleasant tasks. It helps reduce stress by letting employees know the organization cares and will provide help.

Achievement-Oriented Leadership Achievement-oriented leadership is needed for challenging tasks or when subordinates need to take initiative. It helps employees gain confidence and strive for higher standards. It increases expectations that effort will lead to desired performance.

Participative Leadership Participative leadership is best when subordinates need limited direction and support. It allows employees to provide input. When tasks are repetitive, nonauthoritarian subordinates appreciate being involved to help break up the monotony.

▎Fiedler's Leader-Match

One contingency theory that differs from the others in how it handles the issue of fit between leader style and the situation is Fiedler's LPC (least-preferred co-worker) model. Fiedler's LPC model suggests that a manager's leadership style does not change. A manager has a certain style and that is the style he or she has to work with. Therefore, instead of modifying their style, managers need to match (i.e., **leader-match**) the situation to their style.

A match can be achieved in two ways: by selecting managers with the appropriate style to fit the situation, or by training managers to change the situation to make it fit their leadership style. In the latter case, Fiedler developed leader-match training, which Sears, Roebuck and Co. and other organizations used for training managers to diagnose the situation and match their style to it. A number of studies have been designed to test this leader match training. Although they are not uniformly supportive, more than a dozen such tests found increases in work unit effectiveness following the training.[9]

▎Problems with Contingency Approaches

Although contingency approaches focus managers on the importance of matching their styles to the situation, they do not describe exactly how to do this. The problem is that the guidelines coming out of contingency approaches are broad, and therefore not very

---

Follower readiness is the amount of experience or ability the follower has to do the job.

Task structure describes whether the task is highly defined (high structure) or ambiguous (low structure).

Leader position power describes the amount of formal authority associated with the position of the leader.

Leader-match means the leader cannot change his or her style and therefore needs to change the situation to match the style.

WORTH CONSIDERING ...OR BEST AVOIDED?

Newly Promoted to Manager? "Do Nothing" May Be Your Key to Success

Do nothing! Really? This sounds like the complete opposite of what leaders are supposed to be doing. After all they worked really hard to get the promotion. Shouldn't they be showing everyone else that they're still the best workers on the team?

Northwestern's Keith Murnighan has spent a lot of time studying leaders and people at work. He's the one pushing the "do nothing" approach to leadership. But he doesn't mean not showing up for work and being out of touch with what's going on. He does mean, however, not trying to do other people's jobs for them and continuing to do the tasks you excelled at before getting the promotion. Leaders need to understand that their jobs are to help others do great work, not do that work for them. They also need to understand that leadership today is more like coaching a team full of talented players: they need strategy, they need support, and they need encouragement and reminders to stay focused. When given all that, the likelihood is that teams can deliver great results.

In his book *Do Nothing: How to Stop Overmanaging and Become a Great Leader*, Murnighan identifies micromanaging—or overmanaging—as one of a leader's most common and costly mistakes. This basically means not trusting others to use their talents and instead trying to direct them in every last detail of their work. Murnighan describes this as a natural human tendency, one linked in part to the desire to be in control of things. He also says a good leader recognizes this tendency and guards against it. "As you move up," Murnighan points out, "you can't help but remember what made you successful and think that you should 'do' more of that. But as you get more responsibility you should actually do less."

The point is that leaders need time to work on the big picture and putting resources and support systems in place. They also need time to listen and learn from those reporting to them so that they can do these things best. Everyone, says

© Hero Images/Corbis

Murnighan, wants leaders who are willing to say "You're on the front lines and I'm not, so I want to hear your voice as I formulate strategy." If they try to do everything, they won't have time for these really important things. But if they "do nothing"—meaning nothing that someone else can do—they'll have time and energy left to do the right things, the things leaders are paid for and expected to do in support of their teams.

Do the Analysis

Can you buy into this notion of "doing nothing"? Is Murnighan on the right track, or is his advice potentially misleading in causing leaders to think that they don't have to be in charge of things at all? What's the proper dividing line between managing just enough and overmanaging? Does this line depend on the nature of the work being done, the skills of the work team, and even the industry? In other words, is "Do nothing" a universal prescription for leadership action or more of a useful reminder that leaders need to tread carefully and make sure they're doing the right things?

---

informative. In the workplace, managers face leadership situations that are complex and dynamic, and each situation is unique in its own way. There is no "magic toolbox" we can give managers for how to deal with these situations. Leaders need to understand the basic concepts but then be able to adapt their style to fit the needs of the particular situation.

Frustration with these limitations led to what some refer to as the "doom and gloom" period in leadership research. This period (the 1970s to 1980s) was characterized by disillusionment and criticism from scholars that leadership research had told us very little.[10] To address these criticisms, scholars turned to a new way to think about leadership. Instead of focusing on leadership contexts, they focused on leaders. This led to visionary, charismatic, and transformational approaches in leadership.

Charismatic/Transformational Views

CHARISMATIC LEADERSHIP • BURNS'S TRANSFORMING LEADERSHIP THEORY
BASS'S TRANSACTIONAL/TRANSFORMATIONAL LEADERSHIP THEORY
PROBLEMS OF "HEROIC" LEADERSHIP VIEWS

> **TEACHING NOTE:** Develop a list of people who can be considered charismatic leaders (you can have students generate the list). Then for each one ask students to raise their hands as to whether they see that leader as charismatic. Note and discuss the differences in views.

■ Charismatic Leadership

We are all familiar with charismatic leadership. We have been witness to the powerful effects, both good and bad, charismatic leaders can have on those around them. But what exactly is charisma, and how does it operate in leadership?

Charisma **Charisma** is a special personal quality or attractiveness that enables an individual to influence others. It is often characterized as personal magnetism or charm. Charisma evokes enthusiasm and commitment among followers. For example, John F. Kennedy, Oprah Winfrey, and Nelson Mandela are often described as charismatic leaders.

Charisma has its roots in Christianity. The earliest usage depicts leaders set apart from ordinary people by their divine calling, personal sacrifice, and devotion to a spiritual mission and duty.[11] People follow out of a sense of obedience and trust in the leader and his or her revelation. Mother Theresa and Gandhi were able to amass large followings because of their self-sacrifice and dedication to their mission. Their calling had broad appeal to the needs and hopes of the people around them.

Although charisma is often considered an individual trait, it is more aptly described as a relational process involving a leader, followers, and a situation. Katherine Klein and Robert House describe charisma as "a fire" produced by three elements: (1) a "spark"—a leader with charismatic qualities, (2) "flammable material"—followers who are open or susceptible to charisma, and (3) "oxygen"—an environment, such as a crisis or a situation of unrest among followers, that is conducive to charisma.[12] For example, Martin Luther King was a leader with charismatic qualities (a skilled communicator), who tapped into the needs of followers hungry for change (protestors for equality), in a time of great unrest (the Civil Rights Movement).

> **Charisma** is a special personal quality or attractiveness that enables an individual to influence others.

Charismatic Traits and Behaviors What most distinguishes charismatic leaders is their skill as communicators. Charismatic leaders connect with followers on a deep, emotional level. They use metaphors and symbols to articulate their vision in ways that captivate followers and build identification. Their vision may offer promises that otherwise appear impossible. For many, this was the appeal of Barack Obama's 2008 election platform of "Change We Can Believe In" and "Yes We Can." Charismatic leaders often use unconventional behavior to demonstrate their exceptional qualities. Virgin Group founder Richard Branson is often described as a charismatic leader, and his record-breaking crossing of the Pacific Ocean in a hot air balloon certainly qualifies as unconventional and exceptional behavior.

> **Socialized charismatics** focus on power for collective (e.g., societal) rather than personal benefit.

Characteristics of Charismatic Leaders

- Novel and inspiring vision
- Emotional appeals to values
- Expressive communication in articulating the vision
- Unconventional behavior
- Personal risk and self-sacrifice to attain the vision
- High expectations
- Confidence and optimism

Consequences of Charisma For charisma to achieve positive outcomes, it needs to be used from a **socialized charismatic** power orientation, where power is used for collective rather than personal benefit. When used for personal interests,

Personalized charismatics focus on power for personal rather than collective benefit.

or a **personalized charismatic** power orientation it can have destructive consequences. Personalized charismatics dominate followers and keep them weak and dependent on the leader. For example, many dictators oppress their people by not allowing access to schooling or meaningful employment. In organizations, personalized charismatics reduce followers' power by centralizing decision making, restricting information, and doing what they can to make themselves look more important than others.[13]

Research findings suggest that charisma is not a beneficial attribute for most chief executives.[14] Studies of CEO charisma have shown that financial performance was predicted by past performance but not by CEO charisma. Although charismatics are often able to persuade boards of directors to give them higher compensation, there is no evidence that these CEOs improve financial performance for their companies. One exception is in times of crisis or change management. For example, Steve Jobs's charisma was critical to the turnaround of Apple Computer in the late 1990s.

Dangers of Charismatic Leadership

Charisma is a powerful force, and can be a dangerous one. Because charismatic leaders arouse strong emotions among followers, they can produce radical behaviors, even when that is not their intention. This occurs because followers often have psychological needs causing them to want hero figures who make them feel motivated, special, or secure.[15] This can lead followers to interpret leaders as wanting them to do things even when leaders do not. For example, in the movie *Dead Poet's Society*, Robin Williams plays a charismatic teacher, John Keating, who inspires students in a conservative and aristocratic boarding school in Vermont to "seize the day" and live their lives to the fullest. His charisma goes out of control, however, when one of the students, Neil Perry, interprets Keating's message to mean he should rebel against his parents. When that doesn't work, Neil is so distraught that he commits suicide.

Followers' heroizing of charismatic leaders can also lead to disbelief and frustration when leaders don't live up to their expectations. Followers of charismatic leaders often put the leader on a pedestal and expect superhuman behavior. But the problem is all leaders are human, and rarely will they live up to these expectations.

Power distance is the extent to which followers see leaders as having much higher status than them.

Charismatic leaders can try to address these problems by reducing **power distance**. Power distance is the extent to which followers see the leader as having much higher status than them.[16] When power distance is high, followers are reluctant to speak up or question because they believe the leader knows best. Leaders can address these problems by empowering followers to think critically and encouraging them to push back when they have concerns. They can also share in the credit for success, letting followers know that it is the combined actions that allowed the success—not the leader acting alone.

▶ Burns's Transforming Leadership Theory

Transformational leadership theory is another approach that helped lift leadership out of the doom and gloom period in leadership studies. It began with publication of a book by political scientist James MacGregor Burns in 1978 analyzing the leadership styles of prominent political leaders.[17] Burns's approach focused on leadership from the standpoint of power, purpose, and relationships.[18] Key to his analysis was the distinction between leaders and power wielders.

Power wielders use power to advance their own interests without considering followers' needs.

According to Burns, leaders take followers' goals, motivations, needs, and feelings into consideration and use power for good. **Power wielders**, on the other hand, are egocentric and Machiavellian. They use power to advance their own interests without considering followers' needs. Whereas leaders elevate followers (and themselves)

FINDING THE LEADER IN YOU: Patricia Karter Uses Core Values as Her Guide

Sweet is what one gets when digging into one of Dancing Deer Baking's Cherry Almond Ginger Chew cookies. Co-founded by Trish Karter, Dancing Deer sells over $10 million of cookies, cakes, and brownies each year. Each product is made with all-natural ingredients, packaged in recycled materials, and comes from inner-city Boston.

This story began for Karter in 1994 when she and her husband made a $20,000 angel investment in a talented baker and set her up in a former pizza shop. Karter hadn't planned on working in the company, but growth came quickly and their baker partner, Suzanne Lombardi, needed more support for the company to prosper and Karter jumped in. Customer demand led to product development and expansion; many positive press callouts and industry awards, such as being recognized on national TV as having the "best cake in the nation" and winning (the first of eleven) Sophie awards, the food industry's equivalent of the Oscars, fueled growth further.

It isn't always easy for a leader to stay on course and in control while changing structures, adding people, and dealing with competition. For Karter, though, the anchor point has always been clear: let core values be the guide. Dancing Deer's employees get stock options and a package of benefits well above the industry standard; 35 percent of the sales price from the firm's Sweet Home line of cake and cookie gifts are donated to fund scholarships for homeless and at-risk mothers. When offered a chance to make a large cookie sale to Williams-Sonoma, Karter declined. Why? Because to fulfill the order would have required the use of preservatives, and that violated the company's values.

Williams-Sonoma was so impressed that it contracted to develop bakery mixes and, eventually, many more

Courtesy Dancing Deer Baking Company, Inc.

products and a substantial relationship. Instead of losing an opportunity, by sticking with her values Karter's firm gained more sales.

"There's more to life than selling cookies," says the Dancing Deer's Web site, "but it's not a bad way to make a living." Karter hopes growth will soon make Dancing Deer "big enough to make an impact, to be a social economic force." As she says on www.dancingdeer.com: "It has been an interesting journey. Our successes are due to luck, a tremendous amount of dedication and hard work, and a commitment to having fun while being true to our principles. We have had failures as well—and survived them with a sense of humor."

What's the Lesson Here?

Do you know your core values? Do those core values guide your leadership decisions? Have you ever had your core values tested, and how did you respond?

---

to new heights, power wielders gain power *over* followers in ways that cause followers to engage in behaviors they otherwise would not. In Burns's view, power wielders are not leaders.

Through his analysis, Burns noticed different styles and approaches used by leaders. Some used **transactional leadership** styles, in which they focused on exchanging valued goods in return for something they want (e.g., economic, political, or social exchanges, such as exchange of money for goods or support for votes). The focus here is purely instrumental. There is no expectation beyond the exchange. Other leaders—the ones Burns was most interested in learning about—used what he called **transformational leadership** styles. Transformational leaders developed inspirational relationships with followers in which both leaders and followers were positively transformed in the process. This transformation raised human conduct and enhanced the moral aspirations of both

Transformational leadership involves inspirational relationships in which both leaders and followers are positively transformed in the process.

Transactional leadership involves a focus on exchanging valued goods in return for something leaders want.

leaders and followers. In Burns's transforming leadership theory, the transformation is based on both leaders and followers attaining higher levels of moral purpose as they accomplished common goals.

The key element of Burns's theory is the moral foundation upon which transforming leadership rests.[19] A transforming leader is one who, though initially impelled by the quest for individual recognition, ultimately advances collective purpose by being attuned to the aspirations and needs of his or her followers. In Burns's theory, the transformation is a moral accomplishment because its outcome raises human conduct. According to Burns, Mao and Gandhi were quintessential transforming leaders. Instead of exploiting power they remained sensitive to higher purposes and aspirations.[20] Hitler, on the other hand, was not a leader in Burns's analysis, but a power wielder who used his power for selfish and destructive purpose.

Bass's Transactional/Transformational Leadership Theory

Bernard Bass drew from Burns's theory of political leadership to develop a theory of leadership for organizations. He called his approach "performance beyond expectations." Contrary to Burns's focus on transformation as a higher moral purpose and values, Bass's focus on transformation was on organizational performance. In his theory, the transformation occurs when followers are inspired to set aside their self-interest for organizational interest. In other words, they accept the purpose is attainment of pragmatic task objectives for the good of the organization.[21]

Bass's Transformational Leadership

Bass's transformational leadership styles move the follower beyond immediate self-interests by using four types of leader behaviors shown in Figure 14.2. *Idealized influence* and *inspirational leadership* are similar to charismatic leadership, described earlier in this chapter. They are displayed when the leader envisions a desirable future, articulates how it can be reached, sets an example to be followed, sets high standards of performance, and shows determination and

Bass's transformational leadership involves leaders motivating followers to transcend self-interest for the sake of the organization or team.

Transformational Leadership	Transactional Leadership
Idealized influence: Increases degree of followers' identification with the leader.	**Contingent reward:** Leader clarifies what the follower needs to do to be rewarded for the effort.
Inspirational leadership: Communicates high expectations, uses symbols and expresses important purposes in simple ways.	**Active management-by-exception:** Leader monitors the follower's performance and takes corrective action when needed.
Intellectual stimulation: Influencing followers to look for more creative solutions.	**Passive leadership:** Leader waits for problems to arise before taking corrective action.
Individualized consideration: Provides everyone personal attention, and coaches and advises.	**Laissez-faire:** Leader avoids taking any action.

FIGURE 14.2 Key Differences in Transformational and Transactional Leadership Styles.

confidence. *Intellectual stimulation* is displayed when the leader helps followers to become more innovative and creative. *Individualized consideration* is displayed when leaders pay attention to the developmental needs of followers by providing support, encouragement, and coaching.[22]

Transformational leaders articulate a shared vision of the future, intellectually stimulate subordinates, provide a great deal of support to individuals, recognize individual differences, and set high expectations for the work unit.[23] They increase followers' social identity by enhancing pride in contributing to a higher purpose, and make followers feel more secure in their membership and status in the group.

Bass's Transactional Leadership

Bass's transactional leadership is based in self-interest, and use exchanges between leaders and followers to attain desired behavior and outcomes. The transactional leadership styles shown in Figure 14.2 are associated with several kinds of behavior. *Contingent rewards* involve exchanging rewards for mutually agreed-upon goal accomplishment. *Active management by exception* involves watching for deviations from rules and standards and taking corrective action. *Passive management by exception* involves intervening only if standards are not met. And *laissez-faire* leadership involves abdicating responsibilities and avoiding decisions.[25]

> **Bass's transactional leadership** refers to the exchange relationship between leaders and followers to meet their own self-interests.

Findings from Bass's Approach

Bass's transactional and transformational leadership theory is one of the most prominent theories in organizational leadership research. To advance his work, Bass began by developing a measure known as the Multifactor Leadership Questionnaire (MLQ). This measure assesses transformational and transactional leadership styles.[24] Hundreds of studies have used the MLQ to investigate transformational and transactional styles of managerial leaders as perceived by their subordinates. Findings largely support Bass's premise that transformational leadership is associated with increased follower motivation and performance (more so than transactional leadership) and that effective leaders use a combination of both types of leadership.

Meta-analyses show that composite measures of transformational and transactional leadership are related to leadership effectiveness, particularly when ratings are provided by subordinates (e.g., subordinate satisfaction). One likely reason for this is that transformational leadership is highly correlated with trust. In other words, much of the relationship between transformational leaders and outcomes is likely due to the trust subordinates have in transformational leaders.[26]

One criticism of Bass's approach is that in focusing on organizational performance as the ultimate goal, Bass lost the moral underpinnings upon which Burns's theory is based. Burns's theory is based on the leader's allegiance to followers and to uplifting society. Bass's theory is based on allegiance to the organization and performance. Some argue that this makes the approach susceptible to problems of narcissism and exploitation when leaders interpret the transformation from self-interest to organizational interest to mean their wishes take precedence over others.[27] It is also morally questionable to ask subordinates to put aside their self-interest for organizational good.

Problems of "Heroic" Leadership Views

Charismatic and transformational approaches were key to revitalizing leadership studies after the doom and gloom period, so they hold a prominent place in leadership

OB IN POPULAR CULTURE

Lincoln and Leadership

Dreamworks/20th Century Fox/Photofest

From the time we are young, we are told stories of great leaders. In American culture one of these heroes is Abraham Lincoln. Known as Honest Abe, Lincoln's story conveys a man of great integrity and conviction.

But the movie *Lincoln* directed by Stephen Spielberg shows a more nuanced view of the realities and complexities facing Lincoln as a leader, and the sacrifices to personal integrity he made to accomplish his goal of abolishing slavery. Contrary to views of leaders as inspiring others to follow through vision and transformation, the story of Lincoln shows how very transactional Lincoln had to be to procure the votes needed to pass the Thirteenth Amendment. Much like our politicians today, Lincoln engaged in deal making and buying votes. In the process he resorted to relying on sleazy political operatives, and at times even misrepresented the truth.

Lincoln's key strengths, as portrayed in the movie, were his understanding of the complexities he faced and the need for a keen sense of timing. Speaking to Thaddeus Stevens, Lincoln says, "When the people disagree, bringing them together requires going slow until they're ready to make up the distance. . . . [I]f I'd listened to you I'd have declared every slave freed the minute the first shell struck Fort Sumter. And the border states would have gone over to the Confederacy, the war would have been lost, and the Union along with it, and instead of abolishing slavery . . . we'd be watching helpless as infants as it spread from the American South into South America."

Lincoln clearly motivated his followers through inspirational storytelling that diffused tension and helped maintain their support, but he also had to rely on his position power. In one scene with his cabinet secretaries, he tells them, "Two votes stand in its way. These votes must be procured . . . now get the hell out of here and get 'em!" When one member asks, "Yes, but how?" Lincoln responds in frustration, "Buzzard's guts, man. I am the president of the United States of America clothed in immense power. You will procure me these votes."

Get to Know Yourself Better Assessment 12, "TT" Leadership Style, in the *OB Skills Workbook* measures your transformational and transactional leadership styles. What does it show? Would you, like Lincoln, be able to draw from both transformational and transactional leadership as needed to accomplish goals? Do you understand the importance of timing? What do you think about the ethics of Lincoln's approach? Some question the methods Lincoln used—going to war in which 600,000 people lost their lives. Do the ends justify the means, or was there another way to accomplish his goals?

Heroic leadership views see leadership as the result of acts of great leaders who inspire and motivate others to accomplish extraordinary things.

theory and practice. One side effect of these approaches, however, is the rise of **heroic leadership views**. Heroic views see leadership as the acts of great leaders who inspire and motivate others to accomplish extraordinary things. Heroic views create pictures of leaders as white knights swooping in to save the day, and followers as weak and passive subordinates who are fully reliant on leaders for direction, trust and hope.[28]

In so doing, heroic views overlook the significance of everyday leaders influencing throughout the organization. They also miss the importance of process, and the key role of followers in the leadership process. They overestimate the influence of the leader and underestimate the importance of context and timing. To address these issues and others, new approaches such as complexity leadership theory are being introduced to leadership research.

Complexity Leadership Views

LEARNING ROADMAP TODAY'S COMPLEX ENVIRONMENTS • COMPLEXITY LEADERSHIP THEORY • CHALLENGES OF COMPLEXITY LEADERSHIP APPROACHES

Complexity leadership approaches draw from complexity science to bring a more dynamic and contextual view to leadership.[29] Complexity science originates in fields such as biology, physics, mathematics, economics, and meteorology. It is the study of **complex adaptive systems**—systems that adapt and evolve in the process of interacting with dynamic environments.[30]

Complex adaptive systems offer a valuable lens for organizational behavior because, contrary to bureaucratic organizing approaches, complex systems have no centralized coordination and control. Coordination comes from within the system, occurring through interactive dynamics and emergence among system components.[31] Many are beginning to see complex adaptive systems as powerful mechanisms for explaining phenomena in the physical and economic world, including weather (e.g., hurricanes, tornadoes), anthills, swarming fish, bee colonies, economies, and markets.

Complex adaptive systems help us think about how organizations can make themselves more adaptive rather than bureaucratic. They emphasize that a key goal of organizations and criteria for leadership effectiveness should be the extent to which they are able to adapt to survive.

> **TEACHING NOTE:** Ask students to generate examples of emergence (e.g., Arab Spring, Global Economic Crisis, Hurricane Katrina). What does leadership look like in these situations and how must we view leaders differently in these situations?

Complex adaptive systems are systems that adapt and evolve in the process of interacting with dynamic environments.

■ Today's Complex Environments

Interest in complexity approaches is increasing because our environments today are radically different from those of the industrial era when management theories first developed.[32] In the Industrial Age managers were trying to figure out how to organize semiskilled laborers in assembly lines and factories. To do this they turned to **bureaucracy**, which allowed managers to use hierarchy and control to achieve efficiency and results.[33]

In today's environments these approaches are no longer working. Managers no longer have control over information, and employees are less willing to just go along or do what they are told. They expect to be engaged at work and to be treated as active partners in the leadership process. Moreover, problems are too complex to be solved by one person. They require teams of people and distributed intelligence, rather than the limited intelligence of the leader at the top.

As seen in Figure 14.2, these changes are requiring radical differences in assumptions about what leaders need to do to be effective in today's workplace. We are gradually moving away from a hierarchical world into a more connectionist one. In this highly connected world leaders need to rely more on personal power than position power, and we need both "bottom up" and "top down" influence and information flows in organizations. This requires more proactive than passive followership, and leadership responsibility needs to be distributed throughout the organization. It is no longer just the responsibility of leaders (i.e., accountability up) but instead the responsibility of all (i.e., accountability all).

Bureaucracy is an organizing form in which division of labor, specification of titles and duties, and hierarchical reporting relationships provide efficiency and control.

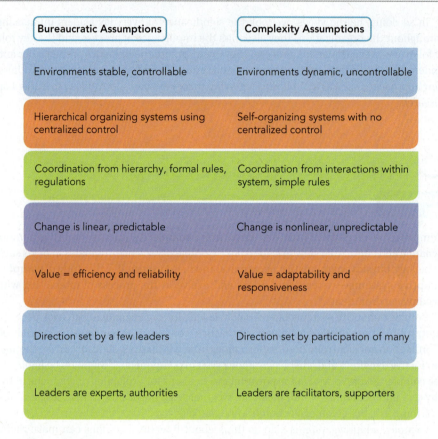

FIGURE 14.3 Major Differences Between Bureaucratic and Complexity Assumptions.

The major differences in complexity and bureaucratic assumptions are shown in Figure 14.3.[34] Perhaps the biggest difference lies in the nature of control. Unlike the Industrial Age when managers could control events, today's interconnected world means that things happen unexpectedly and without our ability to stop them. Managers today operate in workplaces where they are expected to think on their feet and respond quickly and creatively. And they can't respond to complex problems by themselves. All of this requires that leaders enable their organizations to cope with complexity by being more adaptive.

Complexity Leadership Theory

Today's leaders enable adaptability by fostering innovation, flexibility, and learning. These characteristics are the key to survival in complex (ever-changing) environments. That said, organizations are still bureaucracies: They still have hierarchical organizing systems, and they still need efficiency and control. Therefore, the key lies in effectively combining bureaucratic organizing structures with complex adaptive systems.[35]

Complexity leadership theory says we can do this by understanding three types of leadership systems in organizations.[36] The first, **administrative leadership**, focuses on how we can gain efficiency and meet the financial and performance needs of the organization. The goal of administrative leadership is to drive business results through tools such as policy, efficiency, strategic planning, resource allocation, budgeting, and scheduling. It occurs in formal roles (i.e., the administrative system) and is mainly performed by managers.

Entrepreneurial leadership represents the bottom-up, emergent forces that drive innovation, learning, and change in organizations. This form of leadership can be subtle,

Administrative leadership occurs in formal, managerial roles and focuses on alignment and control aimed at driving business results.

Entrepreneurial leadership fuels innovation, adaptability, and change.

New Venture Start-ups Led by Women More Likely to Succeed

© Mark Bowden/iStockphoto

Could it be that having women in executive roles could be a performance asset for start-up firms receiving venture capital? Research reported by Dow Jones VentureSource that the median presence of females on boards and in executive roles of successful start-ups was 73 percent versus only 31 percent in unsuccessful ones. Even though a small minority of firms in the survey—13 percent—had female founders, the presence of females as board members, vice presidents, and senior executives was a differentiating success factor. Still, women founders aren't getting their fair share of new venture start-up capital. Especially in the tech industry, venture capitalist Cameron Lester says, money tends to flow toward men who better fit the entrepreneurial stereotype. But the research on start-up success is refocusing attention on the advantages women bring to the situation—for example, they are more in tune with different customer and market groups, and more financially conservative in managing a firm's money.

---

such as when people develop new ways of working as part of their day-to-day functioning and these changes dissipate into the system. Or it can be more intentional, as in the case of entrepreneurial leaders acting as intrapreneurs: individuals who work to create and actively champion new ideas and innovations. These types of entrepreneurial leaders are often highly proactive, self-motivated, and action oriented in the pursuit of innovative products or services.

Top-down and bottom-up forces alone are not sufficient, however. They need to function together effectively to make the overall system adaptive. Therefore, complexity leadership adds a third function called adaptive leadership. **Adaptive leadership** operates in the interface between administrative and entrepreneurial systems.[37] Its job is to foster the conditions for productive emergence by helping generate new ideas and then enabling them within the formal administrative system to produce results (i.e., innovation). It does this by sponsoring ideas from the entrepreneurial system, providing critical resources, and helping innovations to flow into the formal administrative system to increase fitness for the firm.

Research findings provide support for complexity leadership models. They offer evidence for emergence and the importance of adaptive leadership in organizations. One of the most significant findings, however, is the overwhelming predominance of stifling bureaucratic leadership in organizations. This is because traditional leadership theories have socialized managers and organizational members into control-oriented approaches that respond to complexity with order and stability. Findings are beginning to show that traditional top-down approaches are not only insufficient in complex environments—they may even be harmful to organizational health when they stifle the adaptive dynamics needed to respond in complex environments.

Adaptive leadership operates in the interface between the administrative and entrepreneurial systems and fosters conditions for emergence.

■ Challenges of Complexity Leadership Approaches

Because complexity leadership is a new approach, more study is needed. Early findings are supportive, but we need greater understanding of how these processes work in organizations, particularly with respect to the adaptive system. Complexity is a broad and technical field so it needs to be translated appropriately for business leaders. It also represents a paradigm shift that will be uncomfortable to many. Although research findings show that leaders who use complexity approaches are successful in driving business results and adaptability, these approaches are so different that some individuals may

CHECKING ETHICS IN OB

Tackling Unethical Leadership in the Workplace

© LuminaStock/iStockphoto

A 2013 report released by the Institute of Leadership and Management reveals that unethical practices are common in U.K. workplaces. Over three-fifths (63 percent) of managers in the United Kingdom indicate that they have been expected to engage in unethical behavior at work. Among managers, 9 percent say they have been asked to break the law at some point in their career, and 1 in 10 say they left a job because they were asked to do something that made them feel uncomfortable.

It seems that efforts by organizations to curtail unethical leadership may not be working. Over 90 percent of the respondents said their organizations have a values statement, but 43 percent of respondents said they were pressured to act in direct violation of it. Worse, 12 percent of the managers said the association between employee behavior and company-stated values was "not close at all" in their workplace. Over a quarter of the respondents were concerned that their career would suffer if they reported an ethical violation, with whistle-blowing fears higher among more junior managers than directors.

The researchers recommend that businesses have a clear policy to encourage staff to report concerns over breaches and ethical violations. They also call for the need for ethical leadership from the top. Given the seeming severity of the problem, do you think this will work? It seems value statements are not enough to stem the problems of unethical leadership in the workplace.

What Do You Think?

We know that ethical problems exist in organizations and that much of this comes from managers asking employees to engage in unethical behavior. What can be done to stem this problem? Ethical statements and reporting programs do not seem to be working. What would you do to design a more ethical workplace, and what structural factors would you identify to help promote more ethical leadership? How would you deal with cases of ethical violations in your workplace?

---

not be recognized as leaders because they are not as directive and controlling as described in predominant thinking about leadership. As we continue to transition from a hierarchical to a complex world, however, these styles will not only be more recognized, they will be more expected.

> TEACHING NOTE: Have students debate the purpose of business. Should it be profit maximization? Shared value? How does this relate to ethics?

Leadership Ethics

LEARNING ROADMAP • SHARED VALUE VIEW • SERVANT LEADERSHIP • EMPOWERING LEADERSHIP • ETHICAL LEADERSHIP THEORY

At the core of leadership is the issue of the moral and ethical dilemmas that arise in leadership contexts. And leadership contexts are ripe for moral challenges. Leaders can be seduced by power, and pressure for results can tempt achievement-oriented leaders to cheat to avoid failure. The hierarchical nature of manager–subordinate relationships can make followers afraid to speak up, and the lack of checks and balances on leaders can lead to devastating outcomes.[38]

To address these challenges, scholars are focusing more seriously on leadership ethics. **Leadership ethics** is the study of ethical problems and challenges distinctive to and inherent in the processes, practices, and outcomes of leading and following.[39] It is concerned with the ethical use of power and the morality of leadership outcomes (e.g., fairness, equality, liberty). Paralleling the study of ethics more generally, leadership ethics examines right, wrong, good, evil, virtue, duty, obligation, rights, justice, and fairness as they apply to leadership relationships and leader and follower behaviors.

> **Leadership ethics** is the study of ethical problems and challenges distinctive to and inherent in the processes, practices, and outcomes of leading and following.

▮ Shared Value View

In organizational contexts, a challenge to leadership ethics comes from the way we socialize individuals into the purpose of business. Nearly all businesspeople have been indoctrinated in to Milton Friedman's dictum that the "social responsibility of business is to increase its profits."[40] This is known as the **profit motive**, and it drives the belief that the sole purpose of business is to make money.

> The **profit motive** is based on Milton Friedman's view that the sole purpose of business is to make money.

The profit motive is being seriously questioned in today's environment. Leaders such as John Mackey, the CEO of Whole Foods, and Michael Porter of Harvard University are offering alternative views based on conscious capitalism and creating shared value. These views, developed from purpose-driven mind-sets, argue that the problem is not profit but profit at what cost? To address this issue, recent discussions of the role of profit in business are arguing for a **shared value view**, stating that organizations should create economic value in a way that also creates value for society by addressing societal needs and challenges.[41] In a shared value view, the focus is on both profit and societal gain.

> The **shared value view** states that organizations should create economic value in a way that also creates value for society.

This more modern take advocates the need for business to reconnect company success with social progress. In the process, it addresses the issue at the very core of the debate in leadership ethics: Whose interests matter more . . . those of the individual (or company) or the collective (i.e., the "greater good")? Shared value argues that the answer is both.

> **Servant leadership** is a view in which servant leaders selflessly serve others first.

▮ Servant Leadership

Servant leadership, developed by Robert K. Greenleaf, is based on the notion that the primary purpose of business should be to create a positive impact on the organization's employees as well as the community. In an essay that Greenleaf wrote about servant leadership in 1970, he stated, "The servant-leader *is* servant first. . . . It begins with the natural feeling that one wants to serve, to serve *first*. Then conscious choice brings one to aspire to lead."[42]

The core characteristic of servant leadership as described by Greenleaf is "going beyond one's self-interest." Compared to other leadership styles, such as

Characteristics of Servant Leadership

1. *Empowerment:* fostering a proactive, self-confident attitude among followers
2. *Accountability:* showing confidence in followers by giving them responsibility and then holding them accountable for performance; allows them control and ensures they know what is expected of them
3. *Standing back:* giving priority to the interest of others first and giving them necessary support and credit
4. *Humility:* the ability to put one's own accomplishments and talents in a proper perspective and remain modest
5. *Authenticity:* being true to oneself, adherence to a generally perceived moral code, keeping professional role secondary to whom the individual is as a person
6. *Courage:* daring to take risks and try new approaches; challenging conventional modes of working and using values and convictions to govern one's actions
7. *Forgiveness:* having the ability to understand and experience the feelings of others, let go of perceived wrongdoings, and not carry a grudge into other situations
8. *Stewardship:* demonstrating the willingness to take responsibility for the larger institution sense of obligation to a common good that includes the self but that stretches beyond one's own self-interest

transformational leadership where the primary allegiance is to the organization, the servant leader emphasizes how the organization can create opportunities for followers to grow. It is a person-oriented approach focused on building safe and strong relationships in organizations. Leaders use power not for self-interest but for the growth of employees, survival of the organization, and responsibility to the community.[43]

The servant leader is attuned to basic spiritual values and in serving these assists others, including colleagues, the organization, and society. Servant leaders see their responsibility as increasing the autonomy of followers and encouraging them to think for themselves. They complement their focus on followers with a leadership style that places primary emphasis on humility and remaining true to themselves and their moral convictions in the face of power. Servant leaders accomplish this by empowering and developing people, having high integrity, accepting people for who they are, and being stewards who work for the good of the whole.[44]

▮ Empowering Leadership

Empowering leadership is similar to servant leadership in its focus on valuing and developing people. Although it was not developed as an ethical leadership theory, it is consistent with leadership ethics in its core premise that employees should be treated with dignity and respect.

Authoritarian (or autocratic) leadership involves making decisions independently with little or no input from others.

Empowering leadership enables power sharing with employees by clarifying the significance of the work, providing autonomy, expressing confidence in the employee's capabilities, and removing hindrances to performance.

Empowering leadership is in direct contrast to **authoritarian (or autocratic) leadership** styles that involve leaders dictating policies and procedures, making all decisions about what goals are to be achieved, and directing and controlling all activities without any meaningful participation by subordinates. **Empowering leadership** focuses instead on conveying the significance of the work, allowing participation in decision making, removing bureaucratic constraints, and instilling confidence that performance will be high.[45] Empowering leadership emphasizes the importance of leaders delegating authority and employees assuming responsibility. It argues that by sharing knowledge and information, and allowing employees responsibility and self-control, organizations will be rewarded with a more dedicated and intrinsically motivated workforce.

Research findings show that empowering leadership is related to increased employee creativity and, to some extent, performance.[46] Most views assume that empowering leadership is most appropriate for those with high follower readiness (e.g., high ability and experience). Interestingly, however, research findings have shown the opposite. A study of

Corruption Raises Leadership Questions in International Business

Avon and Walmart share a common problem. They are spending lots of money for attorney fees and internal audits relating to the 1977 U.S. Foreign Corrupt Practices Act (FCPA). The act makes it illegal for a U.S. firm to pay bribes to get international business opportunities. And it's become increasingly important as corruption in international business comes under great scrutiny around the world. If a corporate leader loses control or makes the wrong ethics decisions and runs afoul of this law, the financial costs and damage to his or her reputation can be huge. When claims emerged that Walmart was paying bribes in Mexico, a situation

Ronaldo Schemidt/AFP/Getty Images

subject to the FCPA, internal investigations cost the firm $51 million. When Avon faced the same problem in China, the cost of its compliance review was $280 million. And those figures don't include any FCPA prosecution or fines.

sales representatives showed that, contrary to expectations, empowering leadership was most beneficial for those with *low* levels of product and industry knowledge and *low* experience rather than those with high readiness. For those with high knowledge and experience, empowering leadership appeared to reap no benefits. Perhaps experienced individuals have little to gain from leader efforts toward empowerment.

Ethical Leadership Theory

Ethical leadership theory is a normative theory focused on understanding how ethical leaders behave. A **normative theory** implies or prescribes a norm or standard. Ethical leadership theory prescribes that leaders should be role models of appropriate behavior—such as openness, honesty, and trustworthiness—who are motivated by altruism, meaning they are unselfish and concerned for others (e.g., treating employees fairly and considerately). Ethical leaders should (1) communicate to followers what is ethical and allow followers to ask questions and provide feedback regarding ethical issues; (2) set clear ethical standards, and ensure followers comply with those standards by rewarding ethical conduct and disciplining those who don't follow standards; and (3) take into account ethical principles in making decisions and ensure that followers observe and follow this process.[47]

A **normative theory** implies or prescribes a norm or standard.

Ethical leaders create ethical climates by allowing followers voice and ensuring that processes are fair. **Ethical climates** are the ethical values, norms, attitudes, feelings, and behaviors of employees in an organization.[48] Ethical leaders foster such climates by creating moral awareness and concern, enhancing moral reasoning, clarifying moral values, and encouraging moral responsibility. They consider the consequences of their decisions and make principled and fair choices that can be observed and emulated by others.[49]

Ethical climates are the ethical values, norms, attitudes, feelings, and behaviors of employees in an organization.

Research shows that ethical leadership is linked to higher levels of follower performance and innovative behavior. Evidence also suggests a mitigating effect of ethical leadership on followers' misconduct, unethical behaviors, and workplace bullying.[50] Despite this, ethical leadership theory is limited in that it focuses primarily on leaders' responsibilities for ethics. For ethical leadership to truly take hold in organizations, it needs to be the responsibility of both leaders and followers.

14 Study Guide

Key Questions and Answers

What do we know about leader traits and behaviors?

- Trait approaches investigate the personal qualities and characteristics associated with leader emergence and effectiveness.
- Trait approaches find significant but small relationships between leadership and four of the Big Five traits, including extraversion, conscientiousness, emotional stability, and openness to experience.
- Behavioral approaches identify categories of managerial leadership behavior to examine their relationships with outcomes.
- The majority of leader behaviors represent two meta-categories: relations-oriented and task-oriented behavior.

What do contingency approaches tell us about leadership?

- Contingency approaches say that whether a leader style or behavior is positively associated with leadership effectiveness depends on (i.e., is *contingent* upon) the situation.
- In situations that require more direction and structure, task-oriented behavior will be more effective and desired; in situations requiring more support and consideration, relations-oriented behavior will be more effective.
- Fiedler's LPC model differs from other contingency approaches in that it argues that leaders cannot change their style, and therefore must match the situation to their style.

What are charismatic and transformational theories of leadership?

- Charismatic leaders are seen as exceptional people endowed with extraordinary characteristic and abilities that set them apart from ordinary people.
- Research on charismatic leadership in organizations suggests that charisma is not a beneficial attribute for most chief executives, and it is particularly dangerous in cases of personalized charismatics who use their skills primarily for personal benefit.
- Burns's transforming leadership theory says that leadership is a transforming process that ultimately becomes a moral achievement when it raises human conduct and the aspirations of both leaders and followers, having a "transforming" effect on both.
- Bass adapted Burns's theory to focus on organizational performance; in his theory, the transformation is getting people to set aside self-interest for organizational interest.

What are complexity leadership views?

- Complexity leadership views are grounded in complexity science and describe leadership in the context of complex adaptive systems.
- Complexity leadership views offer an alternative to traditional leadership approaches, grounded in bureaucratic organizing principles; instead of hierarchy and control, they focus on emergence and adaptability.
- A key contribution of complexity is emergence; emergence describes processes in which higher-level order emanates out of interactions of agents operating within the system.
- Complexity leadership theory describes three types of leadership in organizations: administrative leadership, entrepreneurial leadership, and adaptive leadership. These forms of leadership need to function together effectively to create productive emergence and adaptability in organizations.

How do we address leadership ethics?

- Leadership ethics is the study of ethical problems and challenges that are distinctive to and inherent in the processes, practices, and outcomes of leading and following.
- In organizations, the greatest challenge to ethics comes from pressures for results (e.g., profits) at all cost (e.g., individual or societal harm) and the tension between self-interest and the "greater good."
- Servant leaders use power not for self-interest but for the growth of employees, survival of the organization, and responsibility to the community.
- Empowering leadership focuses on valuing and developing people by allowing autonomy and removing bureaucratic constraints.
- Ethical leadership theory is a normative theory that says leaders should be role models for ethics and create ethical climates that enforce high ethical standards.

Terms to Know

Achievement-oriented leadership (p. 306)
Adaptive leadership (p. 317)
Administrative leadership (p. 316)
Authoritarian (or autocratic) leadership (p. 320)
Behavioral approach (p. 304)
Bass's transactional leadership (p. 313)
Bass's transformational leadership (p. 312)
Bureaucracy (p. 315)
Charisma (p. 309)
Complex adaptive systems (p. 315)
Contingency approaches (p. 306)
Directive leadership (p. 306)
Empowering leadership (p. 320)
Entrepreneurial leadership (p. 317)
Ethical climates (p. 321)
Follower readiness (p. 307)
Heroic leadership views (p. 314)
Leader-match (p. 307)
Leader position power (p. 307)
Leadership ethics (p. 319)
Normative theory (p. 321)
Participative leadership (p. 306)
Personalized charismatic (p. 310)
Power distance (p. 310)
Power wielders (p. 310)
Profit motive (p. 319)
Relations-oriented behavior (p. 305)
Servant leadership (p. 319)
Shared value view (p. 319)
Socialized charismatic (p. 309)
Supportive leadership (p. 306)
Task structure (p. 307)
Task-oriented behavior (p. 305)
Trait approaches (p. 302)
Transactional leadership (p. 311)
Transformational leadership (p. 311)

Self-Test 14

▶ Multiple Choice

1. _____ study the personal qualities and characteristics of leaders to identify their association with leader emergence and effectiveness.
   (a) Implicit leadership approaches
   (b) Managerial approaches
   (c) Behavior approaches
   (d) Trait approaches

2. The two meta-categories of leader behaviors found in the behavioral approaches are _____.
   (a) transformational and transactional leader behaviors
   (b) achievement-oriented and participative leadership
   (c) relations-oriented and task-oriented behaviors
   (d) directive and authoritarian behavioral styles

3. The "born" argument in leadership implies that leaders should be _____.
   (a) developed
   (b) selected
   (c) trained
   (d) transformed

4. According to _____, whether leader behaviors will be effective depends on the situation.
   (a) trait approaches
   (b) behavior approaches
   (c) contingency theories
   (d) transactional theories

5. The best leadership style to use when tasks are highly repetitive is _____.
   (a) supportive
   (b) directive
   (c) charismatic
   (d) entrepreneurial

6. Charisma is most aptly described as a _____ process.
   (a) leader
   (b) relational
   (c) follower
   (d) situational

7. Research has shown that charisma is _____ for most chief executives.
   (a) a neutralizer
   (b) a substitute
   (c) beneficial
   (d) not beneficial

8. To help avoid the dangers of charisma, leaders should reduce _____.
   (a) transactions
   (b) task-oriented behaviors
   (c) power distance
   (d) networks

9. According to Burns's theory, _____ are not leaders.
   (a) bureaucrats
   (b) power wielders
   (c) managers
   (d) socialized charismatics

10. Bass modified Burns's theory to focus on _____ rather than moral interests.
    (a) organizational
    (b) societal
    (c) follower
    (d) collective

11. Complexity leadership approaches offer an alternative to _____ organizing principles.
    (a) systems
    (b) political
    (c) transformational
    (d) bureaucratic

12. The key contribution complexity offers to leadership is the understanding of _____.
    (a) emergence
    (b) administrative leadership
    (c) entrepreneurial leadership
    (d) empowerment

13. Ethical leadership theory is a _____ theory of leadership.
    (a) transformational
    (b) transactional
    (c) normative
    (d) complexity

14. When leaders create moral awareness and concern, enhance moral reasoning, and encourage moral responsibility, they are creating more _____.
    (a) transformational leadership
    (b) ethical climates
    (c) empowering climates
    (d) authenticity

15. _____ are attuned to spiritual values and see their responsibility as being stewards for the good of the whole.
    (a) Servant leaders
    (b) Transformational leaders
    (c) Authoritarian leaders
    (d) Empowering leaders

Short Response

16. Why did the early trait approaches fall out of favor?
17. What are the problems with contingency approaches?
18. Why are complexity approaches being developed?
19. What are the challenges associated with leadership ethics?

Applications Essay

20. Jonathan knows he has a charismatic style of leadership. When he speaks, others listen, and when he leads, others are passionate in their desire to follow him. Although he has benefited from this style and enjoys the effects it has on others, he also knows there are risks associated with charismatic leadership. What are these risks, and how can he avoid them?

Steps to Further Learning 14
Top Choices from *The OB Skills Workbook*

These learning activities from *The OB Skills Workbook* found at the back of the book are suggested for Chapter 14.

Cases for Critical Thinking	Team and Experiential Exercises	Self-Assessment Portfolio
• Trader Joe's • Management Training Dilemma	• My Best Manager • My Best Job • Graffiti Needs Assessment • Sweet Tooth	• Learning Styles • Student Leadership Practices Inventory • Managerial Assumptions • 21st-Century Manager • Political Skills Inventory

15

Organizational Culture and Innovation

The Key Point

An organization's culture provides meaning, guidance, and a sense of stability to members, but most organizations also contain a number of subcultures and countercultures. We need to understand the types and layers of culture, the important roles of stories, rites, and rituals, and the links between cultures, performance, and innovation. ■

What's Inside?

- **Bringing OB to LIFE**
  RAISING THE OWNERSHIP STAKES TO BOOST INNOVATION
- **Worth Considering . . . or Best Avoided?**
  IS IT TIME TO MAKE THE WORKPLACE A FUN PLACE?
- **Checking Ethics in OB**
  AGE BECOMES AN ISSUE IN JOB LAYOFFS
- **Finding the Leader in You**
  CHRISTINE SPECHT PUTS A SMILE ON COUSINS SUBS
- **OB in Popular Culture**
  CORPORATE CULTURE AND *THE FIRM*
- **Research Insight**
  CEO VALUES, CULTURE, AND ASPECTS OF PERFORMANCE

Chapter at a Glance

- What Is Organizational Culture?
- How Do You Understand an Organizational Culture?
- How Can We Manage Organizational Culture and Innovation?
- What Is Innovation, and Why Is It Important?

Organizational Culture

FUNCTIONS OF ORGANIZATIONAL CULTURE
SUBCULTURES AND COUNTERCULTURES
NATIONAL CULTURE AND CORPORATE CULTURE

Organizational culture is the system of shared actions, values, and beliefs that develops within an organization and guides the behavior of its members.[1] In the business setting, this system is often referred to as the **corporate culture**. Each organization has its own unique culture. Just as no two individual personalities are the same, no two organizational cultures are identical. Yet, there are some common cultural elements that yield stability and meaning for organizations.[2]

> **TEACHING NOTE:** Ask students to describe acceptable and unacceptable behaviors for your school. Note differences between what the students say, the way the school publicizes itself, and the student honor code.

Organizational culture or **corporate culture** is the system of shared actions, values, and beliefs that develops within an organization and guides the behavior of its members.

■ Functions of Organizational Culture

It is important to recognize that the organizational culture of a firm emerges from (1) the dialogue and discourse among its members and their collective experience over time, (2) the attempts by managers to influence subordinates, and (3) pressures from the larger environment in which the members, the managers, and the organization operate. In this chapter we will examine the functions of organizational culture and various levels of cultural analysis to understand the powerful force of organizational culture. We will then turn to innovation and link innovation to managing organizational culture.

External Adaptation
An important function of organizational culture is to provide historically successful answers to external adaptation.[3] Issues of **external adaptation** deal with ways of reaching goals, tasks to be accomplished, methods used to achieve the goals, and cope with success and failure. Through their shared experiences, members can develop common views that help guide their day-to-day activities toward commonly shared goals.

External adaptation deals with reaching goals, the tasks to be accomplished, the methods used to achieve the goals, and the methods of coping with success and failure.

Although managers attempt to influence members and the organization in many ways, they have an important influence by emphasizing a limited number of goals that shape the shared actions, values, and beliefs of all organizational members and key external contributors.

For managers, this goal-setting aspect of external adaptation involves answering important instrumental or goal-related questions concerning reality: How do we (the organization) contribute? What is the real mission? What are our goals? How do we reach our goals? Organizational members need to know the real mission of the organization, not just the pronouncements to key constituencies, such as stockholders. If they know and accept organizational goals, members will develop an understanding of how they contribute to the mission.

Each group of individuals in an organization tends to (1) separate more important from less important external forces, (2) develop ways to measure accomplishments, and (3) create explanations for why goals are not always met. At Dell, for example, managers have moved away from judging their progress against specific targets to estimating the degree to which they are moving a development process forward. They work on improving participation and commitment.[4]

The final issues in external adaptation deal with two important, but often neglected, aspects of coping with external reality. First, individuals need to develop ways of promoting the firm and themselves. At 3M, for example, employees talk about the quality of their products and the many new, useful products the organization has brought to the market. Second, individuals must collectively know when and how to admit defeat. At the beginning of 3M's development process, team members establish "drop" points where they will quit the development effort and redirect it if necessary. When the decision is made to

WORTH CONSIDERING ...OR BEST AVOIDED?

Is It Time to Make the Workplace a Fun Place?

Do employees that have fun at work actually perform better? Should employers build fun into daily work routines?

"Goofing off" time is considered valuable time at the online retailer Zappos.com. Employees are encouraged to take breaks and have fun at work. The company even has a "cultural evangelist," John Walkses, whose job it is to make sure the organizational culture continues to be happy and productive. He says, "By allowing team members to participate in non-work activities and have fun, the office keeps a positive vibe and people are much happier. Also, they don't burn out as they are free to take time away from their duties."

Zappos isn't alone in its commitment to turning the workplace into a fun and interesting place for employees. At? What If?, an innovation consulting firm, PechaKucha, a presentation style in which twenty slides are shown for twenty seconds each, is used to engage employees in sharing interesting things about themselves and their activities outside of work. Presenters narrate their slide show as a way of helping co-workers get to know them better.

© Jared McMillen/Aurora Photos /Corbis

Are organizations like Zappos and? What If! ahead of the curve with others likely to follow? Or is this trend a fad that applies to just a few employers and work settings?

Do the Analysis

What do the scholars say about creating a happy and productive workplace? Should managers spend time and money to remake organizational cultures so that the workplace also becomes a fun place?

---

quit, project managers are careful not to suggest that the group has failed but stress that what they have learned increases the chances that the next project will succeed to market.[5]

In sum, external adaptation involves answering important instrumental or goal-related questions concerning coping with reality: What is the real mission? How do we contribute? What are our goals? How do we reach our goals? What external forces are important? How do we measure results? What do we do if we do not meet specific targets? When do we quit?

Internal Integration A second important function of the organizational culture, **internal integration**, centers on the collective identity of members and how they live and work together.[6] The process of internal integration often begins with the establishment of a unique identity. Through dialogue and interaction, members begin to characterize their world. They may see it as malleable or fixed, filled with opportunities or threats. As with external adaptation, there are important issues. These include a series of membership issues: Who is a group member, what behavior is acceptable, who is a friend?

For all organizational members, the three most important aspects of working together are (1) deciding who is a member of the group and who is not, (2) developing an informal understanding of acceptable and unacceptable behavior, and (3) separating friends from enemies. Aetna, one of the nation's leading health care benefits companies, describes its corporate culture as one in which employees "work together openly, share information freely and build on each other's ideas to continually create the next better way. Nothing is impossible to our Aetna team. We are eager, ambitious learners and continuous innovators. And we are succeeding. Every day."[7]

To work together effectively, individuals need to decide collectively how to allocate power, status, and authority. They need to establish a shared understanding of who will get rewards

Internal integration deals with the creation of a collective identity and with ways of working and living together.

Organizations with More Engaged Employees Perform Better

The Gallup organization uses an "engagement ratio" as an indicator of organizational health. And research finds that engagement can have a big performance impact. Data show that in the best organizations, actively engaged employees out number the disengaged ones by a ratio of 9.57 to 1. By contrast, the ratio falls to 1.83 to 1 in average organizations.

© moodboard/Corbis

The benefits derived from an actively engaged workforce extend to profitability, safety records, employee retention, and customer orientation. Gallup points out that in high-performing organizations "engagement is more than a human resources initiative—it is a strategic foundation for the way they do business."

and sanctions for specific types of actions. Too often, managers fail to recognize these important aspects of internal integration. A manager may fail, for example, to explain the basis for a promotion and to show why this reward, the status associated with it, and the power given to the newly promoted individual are consistent with commonly shared beliefs.

Individuals also need to work out acceptable ways to communicate and develop guidelines for relationships at work. Although these aspects of internal integration may appear esoteric, they are vital. For example, to function effectively as a team, all must recognize that some members will be closer than others; friendships are inevitable.[8]

Resolving the issues of internal integration helps individuals develop a shared identity and a collective commitment. It may well lead to longer-term stability and provide a lens for members to make sense of their part of the world. In sum, internal integration involves answers to important questions associated with living together. What is our unique identity? How do we allocate power, status, and authority? How do we communicate? Answering these questions is important to organizational members because the organization is more than just a place to work.

▶ Subcultures and Countercultures

Whereas smaller firms often have a single dominant culture with a universal set of shared actions, values, and beliefs, most larger organizations contain several subcultures as well as one or more countercultures.[9]

Subcultures are groups of individuals who exhibit unique patterns of values and philosophies consistent with the dominant culture of the larger organization or system.

Subcultures
Subcultures are groups of individuals who exhibit a unique pattern of values and a philosophy that is consistent with the organization's dominant values and philosophy.[10] Although subcultures are unique, their members' values do not clash with those of the larger organization. Strong subcultures are often found in task forces, teams, and special-project groups in organizations. The subculture emerges, binding individuals to work together intensely to accomplish a specific task. For example, there are strong subcultures of stress engineers and liaison engineers in the Boeing plant in Renton, Washington. These highly specialized groups must solve technical issues to ensure that Boeing planes are safe. Although they are distinct, these groups of engineers share in the core values at Boeing.

Countercultures are groups in which the patterns of values and philosophies outwardly reject those of the organization or social system.

Countercultures
In contrast, **countercultures** are groups whose patterns of values and philosophies reject those of the larger organization or social system.[11] The infamous story of Steve Jobs's return to Apple illustrates a counterculture. When Jobs returned to Apple as its CEO, he formed a counterculture within the company that did not follow the values and philosophies of the former CEO, Gil Amelio. Numerous clashes occurred as the followers of the former CEO fought to maintain their place in Apple and maintain the

old culture. Job's counterculture took off and so did Apple. His counterculture became dominant, and the company has continued to thrive, even after his death.[12]

Every large organization imports subcultural groupings when it hires employees from the larger society. In North America, for instance, subcultures and countercultures may naturally form based on ethnic, racial, gender, generational, or locational similarities. In Japanese organizations, subcultures often form based on the date of graduation from a university, gender, or geographic location. In European firms, ethnicity and language play an important part in developing subcultures, as does gender.

Within an organization, mergers and acquisitions may produce adjustment problems for established subcultures and countercultures.[13] Employers and managers of an acquired firm may hold values and assumptions that are inconsistent with those of the acquiring firm. This is known as the "clash of corporate cultures." One example of culture clash occurred at Bank of America when it acquired Merrill Lynch, the Wall Street trading firm. Old-line bank employees objected to the huge bonuses given to traders in its new Merrill Lynch unit.[14]

OB IN POPULAR CULTURE

Corporate Culture and *The Firm*

Paramount Pictures/Photofest

Corporate culture is reflected in the shared values, beliefs, and actions of an organization's employees. Culture is not only important, it can be a competitive advantage. Consider the cultures of the United States Marine Corps, for example, or most college fraternities and sororities. Membership in any of these organizations may create an identity that can define a person for life.

In *The Firm*, hotshot lawyer Mitch McDeere (Tom Cruise) accepts a position at the Memphis law firm of Bendini, Lambert & Locke. After graduating first in his Harvard Law School class, he knows what it means to work hard. He shows up early on the first day and finds himself alone in the firm's law library. Sometime later, Lamar Quin (Terry Kinney) arrives to show him around. When Mitch says he "thought he would jump start the bar exam," Lamar quickly responds, "Good, because no associate of the firm ever failed the bar exam." Throughout the day, McDeere is greeted by a series of lawyers bringing binders and offering help. Each leaves the office with the same admonishment: "No associate of the firm has ever failed the bar exam."

Corporate culture is reinforced through stories, rites, rituals, and symbols. Rites are special activities that hold important meaning throughout the organization. Like rites of passage, these activities may represent tests that employees are expected to pass. At Bendini, Lambert & Locke, passing the bar exam on the first try was the measure of success.

Get to Know Yourself Better Do you think much about organizational culture? Take a look at "Assessment 22, Which Culture Fits You?" in the *OB Skills Workbook*. What does it reveal about your preference? Although person–organization fit is important, you may not have the luxury of choosing the "right" organization upon graduating. Could you work in an organization that had any one of the other three cultures? What challenges might this present for you?

National Culture and Corporate Culture

Most organizations originate in one national culture and incorporate many features from this host culture even when they expand internationally. The difference between Toyota's corporate emphasis on group achievements and Ford's emphasis on individual engineering excellence, for example, can be traced to the Japanese emphasis on collective action versus the U.S. emphasis on individualism. National cultural values may also become embedded in the expectations of organizational constituencies and in generally accepted solutions to problems.

When moving across cultures, managers need to be sensitive to cultural differences so that their actions do not violate common assumptions in the underlying national culture. To improve morale at General Electric's French subsidiary, Chi. Générale de Radiologie, American managers invited the European managers to a get-acquainted meeting near Paris. The Americans gave out colorful T-shirts for everyone to wear, embellished with the GE slogan "Go for One." One outspoken employee said, "It was like Hitler was back, forcing us to wear uniforms. It was humiliating."[15] Firms often face problems like this in developing strong ethical standards, particularly when they import societal subgroups.

Importing Societal Subgroups
Beyond culturally sensitivity, difficulties often arise with importing groupings from the larger society. Some of these groupings are relevant to the organization, whereas others may be quite destructive. At the one extreme, senior managers can merely accept societal divisions and work within the confines of the larger culture. This approach presents three primary difficulties. First, subordinated groups, such as members of a specific religion or ethnic group, may form into a counterculture and to work more diligently to change their status than to better the firm. Second, the firm may find it difficult to cope with broader cultural changes. For instance, in the United States the treatment of women, ethnic minorities, and the disabled has changed dramatically over the last 20 years. Firms that don't change with the times and accept old customs and prejudices have experienced a greater loss of key personnel and increased communication difficulties, as well as greater interpersonal conflict, than have their more progressive counterparts. Third, firms that accept and build on natural divisions from a single larger culture may find it challenging to develop sound international operations. For example, some Japanese firms continue to experience difficulties adjusting to the equal treatment of women in their U.S. operations.[16]

Building on National Cultural Diversity
At the other extreme, managers can work to eradicate all naturally occurring national subcultures and countercultures. Firms are struggling to develop what Taylor Cox calls the **multicultural organization**, a firm that values diversity but systematically works to block the transfer of societally based subcultures into the fabric of the organization.[17] Because Cox focuses on some problems unique to the United States, his prescription for change may not apply to organizations located in other countries with more homogeneous populations.

Cox suggests a five-step program for developing the multicultural organization. First, the organization should develop pluralism with the objective of multibased socialization. To accomplish this objective, members of different occurring groups need to educate one another to increase knowledge and information and to help eliminate stereotyping. Second, the firm should fully integrate its structure so that there is no direct relationship between a naturally occurring group and any particular job—for instance, there are no distinct male or female jobs. Third, the firm must integrate the informal networks by eliminating barriers and increasing participation—that is, it must break down existing societally based informal groups. Fourth, the organization should break the linkage

> **Multicultural organization** is a firm that values diversity but systematically works to block the transfer of societally based subcultures into the fabric of the organization.

CHECKING ETHICS IN OB

Age Becomes an Issue in Job Layoffs

Sarah is young, single, and graduated from college just a few years ago; she is hard working, topped the performance ratings this year, and always steps forward when volunteers are needed for evening work or travel. Mary is in her mid-forties, has two children, and a husband who is a pediatrician; her performance is good, always at or above average during performance reviews, but she has limited time available for evening work and out-of-town travel.

Image Source/Getty Images, Inc.

Who gets picked for the layoff, Sarah or Mary? Chances are it's going to be Sarah. The *Wall Street Journal* reports that younger workers are at greater risk of layoffs because many employers use a "last in/first out" rule when cutting back on staff. This is true even though the younger workers tend to earn less than their older counterparts and may even be outperforming them. One reason is conflict avoidance; who wants to face an age discrimination lawsuit? Another is the emotional toll that making layoff decisions places on managers; it just seems easier to let go the younger person who probably has fewer complicating personal and family situations.

David Schauer, a school superintendent in Phoenix, says he sent layoff notices to sixty-eight teachers all in their first year of employment. He says, "My worst fear is that really good people will leave teaching." Nicole Ryan, a teacher in New York, received just such a notice. She says, "I knew it was coming because, based on seniority, I was lower on the totem pole." But, she adds, "It didn't make it any easier."

What's Right? Are managers doing the right thing when they lay off younger workers first, even when they are high performers? Is it right to take personal and family factors into account when making decisions about who gets to keep their jobs and who doesn't? Is it fair that younger workers have more to fear about keeping their jobs because some managers are unwilling to face possible age discrimination claims from older workers?

---

between naturally occurring group identity and the identity of the firm. Finally, the organization must actively work to eliminate interpersonal conflict based on either the group identity or the backlash of the largest societally based grouping.

Understanding Organizational Cultures

LEARNING ROADMAP LAYERS OF CULTURAL ANALYSIS • STORIES, RITES, RITUALS, AND SYMBOLS • CULTURAL RULES AND ROLES • SHARED VALUES, MEANINGS, AND ORGANIZATIONAL MYTHS

> TEACHING NOTE: Have students describe some of the organizational cultures they have worked in and how those cultures influenced their attitudes and performance.

Some aspects of organizational culture are easy to see. But not all aspects of organizational culture are readily apparent because they are buried deep in the shared experience of organizational members. It may take years to understand some deeper aspects of the

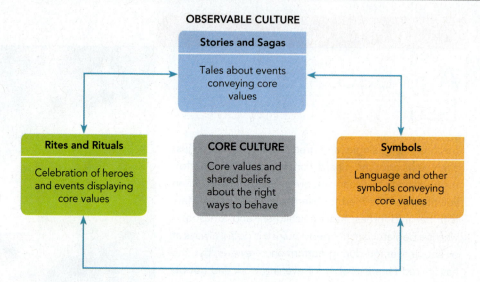

FIGURE 15.1 Three levels of analysis in studying organizational culture.

Observable culture is the way things are done in an organization.

culture. This complexity has led researchers to examine different layers of analysis ranging from easily observable to deeply hidden aspects of corporate culture.

Layers of Cultural Analysis

Figure 15.1 illustrates the observable aspects of culture, shared values, and underlying assumptions as three layers.[18] The deeper one digs, the more difficult it is to discover the culture but the more important an aspect becomes.

The first layer concerns **observable culture**, or "the way we do things around here." Important parts of an organization's culture emerge from the collective experience of its members. These emergent aspects of the culture help make it unique and may well provide a competitive advantage for the organization. Some of these aspects may be observed directly in day-to-day practices. Others may have to be discovered—for example, by asking members to tell stories of important incidents in the history of the organization. We often learn about the unique aspects of the organizational culture through descriptions of specific events.[19] By observing employee actions, listening to stories, and asking members to interpret what is going on, one can begin to understand the organization's culture. The observable culture includes the unique stories, ceremonies, and corporate rituals that make up the history of the firm or a group within the firm.

The second layer recognizes that shared values can play a critical part in linking together people and can provide a powerful motivational mechanism for members of the culture. Many consultants suggest that organizations should develop a "dominant and coherent set of shared values."[20] The term *shared* in cultural analysis implies that the group is a whole. Not every member of an organization may agree with the shared values, however, but they will continue to be exposed to them. At Microsoft, for example, a shared culture value is a passion for technology.

At the deepest layer of cultural analysis are common cultural assumptions. These are the taken-for-granted truths that collections of corporate members share as a result of their joint experience. It is often difficult to isolate these patterns, but doing so can help explain why culture invades every aspect of organizational life.

Stories, Rites, Rituals, and Symbols

To understand a corporate culture, it is often easiest to start with stories. Organizations are rich with tales of winners and losers, successes and failures. Perhaps one of the most important stories concerns the founding of the organization. The founding story often contains the lessons learned from the heroic efforts of an embattled entrepreneur, whose vision may still guide the firm. The story of the founding may be so embellished that it becomes a **saga**—a heroic account of accomplishments.[21] Sagas are important because they are used to tell new members the mission of the organization, how the organization operates, and how individuals can fit into the company. Rarely is the founding story totally accurate, and it often glosses over some of the more negative aspects of the founders.

Such is the case with Monterey Pasta[22] before it was purchased by a Korea-based holding company and its name was changed to Monterey Gourmet Foods. "The Monterey Pasta Company was launched from a 400-square-foot storefront on Lighthouse Avenue in Monterey, California in 1989. . . . The founders started their small fresh pasta company in response to the public's growing interest in healthy gourmet foods. Customers were increasingly excited about fresh pasta given its superior quality and nutritional value, as well as ease of preparation. . . . The company soon accepted its first major grocery account. . . . In 1993, the company completed its first public offering." An unsuccessful venture into the restaurant business in the mid-1990s provided a significant distraction, and substantial losses were incurred before the company refocused on its successful retail business. But why ruin a good founding story?

If you have job experience, you may have heard stories that address the following questions: How will the boss react to a mistake? Can someone move from the bottom to the top of the company? What will get me fired?[23] Often, the stories provide valuable but hidden information about who has the most power, whether or not jobs are secure, and how things are controlled within the organization. In essence, the stories begin to suggest how organizational members view the world and work together.

Some of the most obvious aspects of organizational culture are rites and rituals.[24] **Rites** are standardized and recurring activities that are used at special times to influence the behaviors and understanding of organizational members; **rituals** are systems of rites. It is common for Japanese workers and managers to start their workdays with group exercises and singing of the "company song." Separately, the exercises and song are rites. Together, they form part of a ritual. Another example is, Mary Kay Cosmetics, where scheduled ceremonies are reminiscent of the Miss America pageant (a ritual) and are used to spotlight positive work achievements and reinforce high-performance expectations with awards, including gold and diamond pins, and top performers are rewarded with a pink Cadillac.

Rituals and rites may be unique to particular groups within the organization. Subcultures often arise from the type of technology deployed by the unit, the function being performed, and the collection of specialists in the unit. A unique language may well maintain the boundaries of the subculture. Often, the language of a subculture, and its rituals and rites, emerge from the group as a form of jargon. In some cases, the special language starts to move outside the firm and begins to enter the larger society. For instance, look at Microsoft Word's specialized language, with such words as hyperlink, frames, and quick parts, that has become commonplace outside of the organization.

Another observable aspect of corporate culture centers on the symbols found in organizations. A **cultural symbol** is any object, act, or event that serves to transmit cultural meaning. Examples are the uniforms worn by UPS and Federal Express delivery personnel.

■ Cultural Rules and Roles

Organizational culture often specifies when various types of actions are appropriate and where individual members stand in the social system. These cultural rules and roles are part of the normative controls of the organization and emerge from its daily routines.[25] For instance, the timing, presentation, and methods of communicating authoritative directives are often quite specific to each organization. In one firm, meetings may follow a set rigid agenda. The manager could go into meetings to tell subordinates what to do and how to accomplish tasks. Private conversations prior to the meeting might be the

---

Saga is an embellished heroic account of accomplishments.

Rites are standardized and recurring activities used at special times to influence the behaviors and understanding of organizational members.

Rituals are systems of rites.

A **cultural symbol** is any object, act, or event that serves to transmit cultural meaning.

Healthy Living Sets the Values Tone At Clif Bar

Have you had your Clif Bar today? Lots of people have, thanks to a long bike ride during which Gary Erickson decided he just couldn't eat another of the available energy bars. He went back to experiment in his mother's kitchen and produced the first Clif Bar two years later. Despite its growth from a one-man operation to one employing 270+ people, Clif remains committed to what it calls the "5 aspirations"—"sustaining our planet... community... people... business... brands." Clif's core values are also evident in the quality of working life offered employees. Picture "Clifies" working this way:

- Every employee an owner
- Paid sabbatical leaves of 6 to 8 weeks after seven years
- Flexible schedule to get every other Friday free
- Pay for 2.5 hours of workout time each week
- Bring your pet to work and wear casual clothes
- Get $6,500 toward a hybrid or biodiesel automobile

MCT/Getty Images

place for any new ideas or critical examination. In other firms, meetings might be forums for dialogue and discussion, for which managers set agendas and then let others offer new ideas, critically examine alternatives, and fully participate.

▶ Shared Values, Meanings, and Organizational Myths

To describe an organization's culture more fully, it is necessary to go deeper than the observable aspects. To many researchers and managers, shared common values lie at the very heart of organizational culture.

Shared Values Shared values help turn routine activities into valuable and important actions, tie the corporation to the important values of society, and possibly provide a distinctive source of competitive advantage. Important values are then attributed to these solutions to everyday problems. By linking values and actions, the organization taps into some of the strongest and deepest realms of the individual. The tasks a person performs are given not only meaning but also value.

Successful organizations often share common cultural characteristics.[26] Those with "strong cultures" possess a broad and deeply shared value system. Unique, shared values can provide a strong corporate identity, enhance collective commitment, provide a stable social system, and reduce the need for formal and bureaucratic controls. When consultants suggest that organizations develop strong cultures, they basically mean the following:[27]

▶ **Characteristics of strong culture organizations**

- A widely shared understanding of what the organization stands for, often embodied in slogans
- A concern for individuals over rules, policies, procedures, and adherence to job duties
- A recognition of heroes whose actions illustrate the company's shared philosophy and concerns
- A belief in ritual and ceremony as important to members and to building a common identity
- A well-understood sense of the informal rules and expectations so that employees and managers understand what is expected of them
- A belief that what employees and managers do is important and that it is important to share information and ideas

A strong culture and value system can reinforce a singular and sometimes outdated view of the organization and its environment. If dramatic changes are needed, it may be very difficult to change the organization. For years General Motors had a strong culture. But as the global auto industry changed, GM did not. It took bankruptcy to shake it to its foundations and provide the impetus for radical change.

Shared Meanings
When you are observing the actions within an organization, it is important to keep in mind the three levels of analysis discussed earlier. What you see as an outside observer may not be what organizational members experience because members may link actions to values and unstated assumptions. For instance, in the aftermath of the 9/11 terrorist attacks, a new building and its meaning are contested. Is it just another gleaming office tower or the Freedom Tower symbolizing the resilience of the American people and New York City's ability to recover from the attacks?[28]

In this sense, organizational culture is a "shared" set of meanings and perceptions. The members of most organizations create and learn a deeper aspect of their shared culture.[29] Often one finds a series of common assumptions known to most everyone: "We are different." "We are better at. . . ." "We have unrecognized talents." Cisco Systems provides an excellent example. Senior managers often share common assumptions, such as "We are good stewards" and "We are competent managers" and "We are practical innovators." Like values, such assumptions become reflected in the organizational culture. Of course, shared meanings and perceptions can create a double-edged sword. In his book *How Do the Mighty Fall*, consultant Jim Collins notes that organizations may begin to decline if managers share an unrealistic positive perception of them.[30]

Organizational Myths
In many firms, a key aspect of the shared common assumptions involves organizational myths. **Organizational myths** are unproven and frequently unstated beliefs that are accepted without criticism. Often corporate mythology focuses on cause–effect relationships and assertions by senior management that cannot be empirically supported.[31] Although some may scoff at organizational myths and want to see rational analysis replace mythology, each firm needs a series of managerial myths.[32] Myths allow executives to redefine impossible problems into more manageable components. Myths can facilitate experimentation and creativity, and they allow managers to govern.

Organizational myth is a commonly held cause–effect relationship or assertion that cannot be supported empirically.

Managing Organizational Culture

LEARNING ROADMAP • DIRECT ATTEMPTS TO CHANGE VALUES • DEVELOPING SHARED GOALS • MODIFYING VISIBLE ASPECTS OF THE CULTURE

> TEACHING NOTE: Have students discuss ways a leader might modify the existing culture of an organization to rally members around a common high performance commitment.

The process of managing organizational culture is a complex challenge of the first order. A leader or manager must first understand the subculture at the top of the system be it the whole organization or just a department. A series of cascading goals from the societal contribution of the organization to the expectations for each unit and individual must be put into place. Once these goals are shared by all, reward systems consistent with the goals must be developed and consistently used to reward groups and individuals for the appropriate actions. This top-down view must also be accompanied by an understanding of the emergent aspects of organizational culture and a focus on helping individuals cope with the challenges of external adaptation and internal integration.

▌Direct Attempts to Change Values

Early research on culture and cultural change often emphasized direct attempts by senior management to alter the values and shared meanings of individuals by resocializing them—that is, trying to change their hearts so that their minds and actions would follow the desires of senior management.[33] Many top-level managers wanted all employees to adopt the organization's subculture in order to establish one clear, consistent organization-wide consensus. Key aspects of the top-down management subculture are often referred to in the OB literature by the term *management philosophy*. A **management philosophy** links important goals with key collaboration issues and comes up with a series of general ways by which the firm will manage its affairs.[34] Specifically, it (1) establishes generally understood boundaries for all members of the firm, (2) provides a consistent way of approaching new and novel situations, and (3) helps bond employees by ensuring them of a path toward success. In other words, it is the way in which top management addresses the questions of external adaptation.

More recent work suggests that this unified approach of working through the values of the top management subculture may not possible.[35] Although there are many reasons, two stand out. The first is that shared values and meanings evolve from the shared experiences, dialogue, and discussion of members, and that the "world" of top executives is often fundamentally different from the "world" of other employees. The second reason is that trying to change people's values from the top down without changing how the organization operates and rewards individuals and groups usually doesn't work.

In addition a narrowly diverse culture may not be desirable.[36] As the diversity of opinions values, and meaning in an organization narrows, it becomes more vulnerable to external change and less able to capitalize on external opportunities. The management philosophy at the top is often too narrow. For instance, recent research on the link between corporate culture and financial performance reaffirms the importance of helping employees adjust to the environment. And it suggests that a narrow emphasis is not sufficient. Neither is an emphasis solely on stockholders or customers associated with long-term economic performance. Instead, managers must emphasize responsiveness to competitive pressures, stockholder demands, and customer desires simultaneously.

A **management philosophy** links key goal-related issues with key collaboration issues to come up with general ways by which the firm will manage its affairs.

How to Become a Better Culture Manager

To develop a strong management culture, managers need to:

- Emphasize a shared understanding of what the unit stands for.
- Stress a concern for members over rules and procedures.
- Talk about heroes of the past and their contributions.
- Develop rituals and ceremonies for the members.
- Reinforce informal rules and expectations consistent with shared values.
- Promote the sharing of ideas and information.
- Provide employees with emotional support.
- Make a commitment to understand all members.
- Support progressive thinking by all members.

Southern Stock/Blend/Getty Images, Inc.

Developing Shared Goals

One of the most powerful ways managers influence organizational culture is through commonly shared goals that are specific to the organization. The choice of specific goals often begins with the type of contribution the firm makes to society and the types of outputs it seeks.[37] Astute managers recognize that they should specify a desired set of internal conditions that can be used to evaluate progress.

Societal Goals, Output Goals, and Mission Statements

Organizations normally serve a specific function or an enduring need of society. By emphasizing their contributions to the larger society, organizations gain legitimacy, a social right to operate, discretion to adopt non-societal goals, and freedom for operating practices.

Societal goals represent an organization's intended contributions to the broader society.[38] By claiming to provide specific societal contributions, an organization can also make legitimate claims over resources, individuals, markets, and products. And a clear articulation of the organization's societal contribution can become a foundation for positively shared meanings and values.

For most organizations, the societal goals are just the beginning and lead to more detailed statements concerning their products and services. These product and service goals provide not only an important basis for judging the firm but also a common basis for members to evaluate the organization's progress. **Output goals** define the type of business an organization is in and provide some substance to the more general social contribution.

Often, the social contribution of the firm and its stated output goals are part of its mission statement. **Mission statements** are written statements of organizational purpose. Weaving a mission statement together with an emphasis on implementation to provide direction and motivation is an executive order of the first magnitude. A good mission statement, in addition to specifying outcomes, also includes whom the firm will serve and how it will go about accomplishing its societal purpose.[39]

We would expect to see the mission statement of a political party linked to generating and allocating power for the betterment of citizens. Mission statements for universities often profess to both develop and disseminate knowledge. Courts are expected to integrate the interests and activities of citizens. Finally, business firms are expected to provide

> **Societal goals** represent an organization's intended contributions to the broader society.
>
> **Output goals** define the type of business an organization is in.
>
> **Mission statements** are written statements of organizational purpose.

Research Insight

CEO Values, Culture, and Aspects of Performance

Although there has been a lot of discussion about the link between the values of the CEO, corporate culture, and performance, few comprehensive studies have been done. Recently, Berson, Oreg, and Dvir started to remedy this gap with a study of CEO values, organizational culture, and performance. They suggested that individuals are drawn to and stay with organizations that have value priorities similar to their own. That includes the CEO. Furthermore, the CEO reinforces some values over others, and this has a measurable impact on the organizational culture. The organizational culture, then, emphasizes some aspects of performance over others. This emphasis on selected aspects of the culture naturally favors some aspects of performance over others.

The researchers hypothesized and found the following in a study of some twenty-two CEOs and their firms in Israel: CEOs tend to place a high priority on self-direction or security or benevolence. This priority tends to emphasize a particular aspect of organizational culture. Specifically, when a CEO values self-direction, there is more cultural emphasis on innovation; when a CEO values security, there is more cultural emphasis on bureaucracy; and when a CEO values benevolence, the culture is more supportive of its members.

The researchers then linked aspects of organizational culture with specific elements of performance. More innovation was associated with higher sales growth. A bureaucratic culture was linked to efficiency, whereas a supportive culture was associated with greater employee satisfaction. Schematically, it looks like this:

CEO Values	Organizational Culture	Organizational Effectiveness
Self-direction, Security, Benevolence	Innovation, Bureaucratic, Supportive	Sales growth, Efficiency, Satisfaction

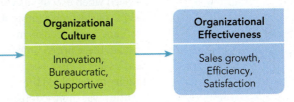

Do the Research Do you think this study would transfer to firms located in North America? Is it possible that firms with an established innovative culture select a CEO that values self-direction?

Source: Yair Berson, Shaul Oreg, and Taly Dvir, "CEO Values, Organizational Culture and Firm Outcomes," *Journal of Organizational Behavior* 29 (2008), pp. 615–633.

economic sustenance and material well-being.[40] As managers consider how they will accomplish their firm's mission, many begin by clarifying with refined output goals which business they are in.[41] This refinement spells out how managers hope to deal with external adaptation. The refined mission often targets efforts toward a very specific group and recognizes secondary contributions to powerful outsiders[42]—that is, organizations have a primary beneficiary, but the refined mission also recognizes the interests of many other parties. For example, business mission statements often stress profitability to shareholders but recognize the organization's obligations to customers as well as its intention to support the community.

Systems Goals

Managers also recognize that regardless of the mission or output goals, the organization needs to survive. **Systems goals** are concerned with the conditions within the organization that are expected to increase the organization's survival potential.[43] The list of systems goals is almost endless. For many organizations, however, the list includes growth, productivity, stability, harmony, flexibility, prestige, innovation, quality, and human-resource maintenance. Although technically market share and current profitability are not internal conditions, many businesses analysts consider them as important systems goals because of the link from profitability and market share to survival.

Systems goals must be balanced against one another and collectively present members with a natural tension among competing desires. For instance, a productivity and efficiency drive, if taken too far, may reduce the flexibility of an organization. To effectively manage the culture, systems goals must be well-defined, practical, and easy to understand. They must help focus attention on what should be done and provide a basis for employees to understand their contributions.

> **Systems goals** are concerned with the conditions within the organization that are expected to increase the organization's survival potential.

▶ Modifying Visible Aspects of Culture

Beyond focusing on goals and reward systems, managers can modify the visible aspects of culture, such as the language, stories, rites, rituals, and sagas. Because of their positions, senior managers can interpret situations in new ways and can adjust the meanings attached to important corporate events. They can create new rites and rituals. Executives can support these initiatives with both words and actions. All of this takes time and an enormous amount of energy, but the long-run benefits can be great. For example, examine the actions of Christine Specht of Cousins Subs in the "Finding the Leader in You" feature.

Reinforcing Ethical Standards

Although it seems obvious that managers at all levels need to establish and reinforce ethical cultural standards, in far too many cases this has not happened. The need to provide an ethics emphasis in managing culture can be seen when executives violate ethical and legal standards, as in the case of firms publishing misleading earning statements. One key study found that whereas the fines levied for "cooking the books" may appear small, other costs were far more substantial. The real costs to these firms came from a loss of their reputation in the business community. Customers lost confidence, suppliers demanded greater assurances, and the financial community undervalued the firm so that loan costs were higher, stock prices were lower, and scrutiny was more extensive. How big is big? The fines averaged about $23 million a firm. But the financial cost from the loss of reputation was estimated at 7.5 times the average fine. That yielded a loss of an average of $196 million.[44]

Modifying Reward Systems

To change the culture, managers need to develop a new, powerful, and meaningful reward system. In many larger U.S.-based firms, the reward system matches the overall way the firm competes and reinforces the culture emerging from day-to-day activities. Two patterns are common. The first is a steady-state way of competing matched with hierarchical rewards and consistent with what can be labeled a clan culture. Specifically, rewards emphasize and reinforce a culture

FINDING THE LEADER IN YOU

Christine Specht Puts a Smile on Cousins Subs

As the second generation to head Cousins Subs, Christine Specht stresses the importance of culture. She makes it perfectly clear that her focus is on the key attributes of the organization founded by her father and his cousin.

Specht notes, "Our food is better; our sandwiches are bigger. More importantly, they are made by people who really care about serving the guests . . . we have a great organizational culture of people who really care about the company and the guest."

For Christine Specht, it is imperative to continue the cultural traditions of Cousins while at the same time making sure the firm is new, vital, and viable. When Specht unveiled a new logo and restaurant design for Cousins Subs, she explained that it was a great time to evolve the company's look with a logo that, while fresh and modern, incorporated the "pride of our family heritage" and shared the story of Cousins Subs with their loyal patrons.

Although Specht emphasizes tradition at Cousins, she also looks to the future. When she first became president of the organization, she visited all of the franchise operations. Based on this experience, she reorganized the central office operations. The visits helped build trust, and as the economy entered the recession the new central office operations were instrumental in reducing costs for all the franchise holders. These changes also led to a revamped training program for those who own, or want to own, a Cousins franchise.

Since becoming president, Specht continues to focus on the cornerstone of the brand: "*Better Bread. Better Subs.*" And it is as true today as it was 30 years ago when cousins Bill Specht and Jim Sheppard started the company. The cousins worked with a local baker to create a unique recipe for their bread that is still baked fresh several times a day in every Cousins' store.

COURTESY OF COUSINS SUBMARINES, INC.

What's the Lesson Here?

How comfortable are you with managing change? How can you use stories, rituals, and symbols to reinforce aspects of the culture you want to keep? How much innovation would you introduce and how quickly?

---

characterized by long-term commitment, fraternal relationships, mutual interests, and collegiality with heavy pressures to conform from peers, and with superiors acting as mentors. Firms with this pattern are in power generation, chemicals, mining, and pharmaceuticals industries.

In contrast is a second pattern in which the firm competes by stressing evolution and change. Here the rewards emphasize and reinforce a more market culture. That is, rewards emphasize a contractual link between employee and employer, focus on short-term performance, and stress individual initiative with little pressure from peers to conform, and with supervisors acting as resource allocators. Firms with this pattern are often in restaurants, consumer products, and industrial services industries.[45]

Innovation in Organizations

LEARNING ROADMAP THE PROCESS OF INNOVATION • PRODUCT AND PROCESS INNOVATIONS
BALANCING EXPLORATION AND EXPLOITATION
MANAGING TENSIONS BETWEEN CULTURAL STABILITY AND INNOVATION

> TEACHING NOTE: Check the risk propensity of students by asking who has purchased lottery tickets? Ask at what dollar pay-off they would buy a one dollar lottery ticket with 5,000,000 to 1 odds of winning.

When analysis stresses commonly shared actions, values, and assumptions across the entire organization, firms can appear to be static, unchanging entities. It is clear that much of an organization's culture and its structure emphasize stability and control. Yet, the world is changing and firms must change with it. The best organizations don't

CHAPTER 15 ■ Organizational Culture and Innovation

stagnate; they consistently innovate to the extent that innovation becomes a part of everyday operations.

Innovation is the process of creating new ideas and putting them into practice.[46] It is the means by which creative ideas find their way into everyday practices—ideally ones that contribute to improved customer service or organizational productivity. There are a variety of ways to look at innovation. Here we will examine it as a process and a separate product from process innovation, and we will note the tensions between the early development of ideas and the task of implementation.

> **Innovation** is the process of creating new ideas and putting them into practice.

■ The Process of Innovation

One easy way to look at the complex process of innovation is to break it down into four steps as shown in Figure 15.2.

1. *Idea creation*—to create an idea through spontaneous creativity, ingenuity, and information processing
2. *Initial experimentation*—to establish the idea's potential value and application
3. *Feasibility determination*—to identify anticipated costs and benefits
4. *Final application*—to produce and market a new product or service, or to implement a new approach to operations

It takes many creative ideas to establish a base for initial experimentation. Moreover, many successful initial experiments are just not feasible. Even among the few feasible ideas, only the rare idea actually makes it into application. Finally, innovative entities benefit from and require top-management support. Senior managers can and must provide good examples for others, eliminate obstacles to innovation, and try to get things done that make innovation easier.

By emphasizing the innovation process, innovative entities often adapt a different culture from the ones typically found where more routine operations are paramount. Innovative entities look to the future, are willing to cannibalize existing products in their development of new ones, have a high tolerance for risk and mistakes, respect well-intentioned ideas that do not work, prize creativity, and reward and give special attention to idea generators, information keepers, product champions, and project leaders. They also prize empowerment and emphasize communication up, down, and across all individuals in the unit.[47]

Although it is convenient to depict the process as a sequential four-step affair, in practice the process of innovation is often messy. Take a look at Figure 15.2. With initial

FIGURE 15.2 The innovation process: a case of new product development.

experimentation, for example, the act of sharing ideas with others can, and often does, yield a completely new set of ideas. Even in final application, the process does not stop, as astute innovators listen to customers and clients to make further improvements. Also note that organizational support for innovation is needed in each step in this ongoing process.

Although the desire to improve financial performance is important in stimulating innovation, it is also essential to note that innovation can arise from the firm's desire to be more legitimate in the eyes of key stakeholders, such as government regulators. For example, one recent study suggested that pressures from regulators and a prior record of poor environmental performance yielded more innovative environmental responses from firms. There was an exception, however, in that firms with greater slack resources did not respond as positively to regulatory pressures even if they had a record of poorer prior environmental performance.[48]

Research also shows the results of the team factors associated with greater innovation.[49] It is clear from this work that a number of significant team processes are consistently linked to greater innovation. First, goal interdependence among the team members is important. Goal interdependence is the degree to which individuals can reach their goals only if other team members reach theirs. The higher the goal interdependence, the greater the innovation. Second, for a number of teams, a higher-quality process was linked to more innovation. Six team processes were particularly important for innovative success:

- *Vision*—the degree of clarity and commitment to goals
- *Support for innovation*—support both within and from outside
- *Task orientation*—a climate for excellence
- *Cohesion*—a commitment to the team and maintenance of group membership
- *Internal communications*—quality interactions within the group
- *External communications*—quality interactions with outsiders

◀ Team processes for successful innovation

Product and Process Innovations

Product innovations result in the introduction of new or improved goods or services to better meet customer needs. A number of studies suggest that the key difficulty associated with product development is the integration across all of the units needed to move from the idea stage to final implementation.[50] Culturally, new product development often challenges existing practice and existing value structures, and common understandings. For instance, product innovation means that the definition of the business will change. Many firms find it difficult to cannibalize their existing product lineup in the hope that new products will be even more successful. Yet, this is what often needs to be done.[51]

Product innovation is so crucial that a number of government-based initiatives have been launched to help spur the development of new products. Individuals proposing initiatives point to the revolution that has resulted from development of the Internet, green technologies, and medical breakthroughs with the potential to change the human condition. One recent study suggests that corporate culture, rather than national policy, makes the biggest difference with radical product innovation.[52]

A number of interrelated firms may share the product innovation process.[53] Generally speaking, complex products are often the result of a combinations of individual components from a variety of corporations. Control is exercised by a common design, often under the direction of a single integrator who maintains the dominant design. This is often the model in computer software, for example. It is important to note that

Product innovations introduce new goods or services to better meet customer needs.

the development and control of the dominant design can be linked to profitability.[54] Furthermore, the dominant design is often not the best technical solution—it is the solution most often adopted by a large number of users.

Where the product innovation process is less open, firms often find that coordination with lead users can help provide design insights.[55] Although no solution is perfect, several studies suggest that the development of multidisciplinary teams can help maintain broader commitment. Of course, just the inclusion of individuals with diverse skills, interests, and perspectives calls for astute management.

Process innovations result in the introduction of new and better work methods and operations. Perhaps one of the most interesting and difficult types of process improvement is that of management innovation.[56] Much management innovation comes from the vast industry known as management consulting. Unfortunately, many of the new management practices emanating from these outside units are more fashions and fads than workable solutions to the problems faced by individual firms. The key to successful managerial innovation often involves extensive interaction with peers, subordinates, and superiors. As astute managers try new practices, they compare initial implementation with the reactions of peers and subordinates to refine and modify the practice. Often this process of trial and error takes several iterations before the practice becomes accepted enough to provide the intended benefits.

Process innovations introduce into operations new and better ways of doing things.

BRINGING OB TO LIFE

> "Every Friday you'll find Fusenet engineers working on their own ideas. They do so knowing that if the ideas are good, they'll own any business that comes from them."

Raising the Ownership Stakes to Boost Innovation

Google borrowed 3M's time-tested willingness to let engineers take a portion of their work time—up to 20 percent—and devote it to free time to think about things outside their everyday jobs. At Fusenet, a Toronto based software developer, every Friday is a free day for employees to work on their own ideas. They end their week on a creative note, knowing that if their innovations are good, they will own any business that comes from them.

The goal is to break people free from tight job descriptions and organization structures, and encourage innovation. It's a move that OB researchers say is necessary to avoid the downsides of too much bureaucracy in dynamic environments.

Armed with a freedom to "tinker," the expectation is that employees will generate new ideas that have the potential to fuel useful and profitable innovation. Some call this "scheduled playtime at work." At 3M, such play brought us the Post-it note. At Google, it drove Gmail.

But what happens when free time doesn't result in innovation? Can you order someone to play? Can you take away what employees create and expect them to innovate willingly and successfully again?

David Paul Morris/Bloomberg/Getty

When employees feel a sense of ownership, they tend to work harder. Think participation in goal setting and profit-sharing compensation, for example. If ownership motivates, why not give innovative employees ownership rights and let them gain financially and emotionally from their creativity?

Balancing Exploration and Exploitation

In the early stages of innovation, time, energy, and exploration are necessary. These early phases are the result of the research and development units found in many companies. Yet, too much emphasis on exploration will yield a whole list of potential ideas for products and processes to new clients and customers in new markets, but will result in little payoff. It is important to stress exploitation to capture the economic value stemming from exploration.[57] **Exploitation** often focuses on refinement and reuse of existing products and processes. Refining an existing product to make it more saleable in a new market is an example of exploitation. Of course, too much emphasis on exploitation and the firm loses its competitive edge because its products become obsolete and its processes less effective and efficient than their competitors.

The admonition to balance exploration and exploitation sounds simple, but it comes with a major problem. **Exploration** calls for the organization and its managers to stress freedom and radical thinking and opens the firm to big changes—or what some call radical innovations.[58] Although some radical departures are built on existing competencies, often the adoption of a radically new product or process means that the existing knowledge within a firm is invalidated.[59] Conversely, an emphasis on exploitation stresses control and evolutionary development. Such exploitation can be planned with tight budgets, careful forecasts, and steady implementation. It is often easier to stress exploitation because most organizations have a structure and culture that emphasizes stability and control.[60]

Managers may attempt to solve this tension between exploration and exploitation in a variety of ways. One partial solution is to have separate units for the two types of activities. For example, some firms rely heavily on cooperative research and development (R&D) arrangements with other firms for exploration and keep a tight rein on exploitation within the firm.[61] Others rely on middle managers to reconcile the tensions stemming from attempts to link explorative and exploitative groups. However, the desired mix of explorative and exploitative may well depend on the industry setting.

Recent research suggests a more culturally oriented solution based on the notion of an ambidextrous organization. There appear to be four critical factors in building an ambidextrous organization:

- Managers must recognize the tension between exploration and exploitation.
- Managers should realize that one form of thinking based on a single perspective is inappropriate.
- Managers must discuss with their subordinates the paradoxes arising from simultaneously thinking about big ideas and sound incremental improvements.
- Managers must encourage subordinates to embrace these paradoxes and use them as motivations to provide creative solutions.[62]

Managing Tensions between Cultural Stability and Innovation

Although organizational cultures help individuals cope with external adaptation and internal integration, the enduring pattern of observable actions, shared values, and common assumptions often does not evolve as quickly as required by innovations.

Organizational Cultural Lag
Organizational cultural lag is a condition in which dominant cultural patterns are inconsistent with new emerging innovations.[63] As we suggested earlier, observable aspects of organizational culture such as rites, rituals, and cultural symbols often have powerful underlying meaning for organizational members. In a way they are symbols of successful ways of coping with external adaptation and internal integration. Individuals are often wary of abandoning successful strategies for an unproven new approach. One scholar notes that there can be

---

Exploitation focuses on refinement and reuse of existing products and processes.

Exploration calls for the organization and its managers to stress freedom and radical thinking and opens the firm to big changes–or what some call radical innovations.

◀ How to build an ambidextrous organization

Organizational cultural lag is a condition in which dominant cultural patterns are inconsistent with new emerging innovations.

a major "cultural drag on innovation from cultural legacies."[64] These legacy effects come from an overreliance on rule following and reinforcement of existing patterns of action.

One of the key challenges to management in promoting innovation where there are widely held and strong attachments to shared values and common assumptions, is to show how they apply to the new innovations. When managers see an opportunity to develop new visions, create new strategies, and move the organization in new directions, they need to balance rule changing and rule following.[65] If left uncontrolled, rule changing can yield runaway industry change that can quickly lead to chaos. Rule following can lead to a more stable industry structure and/or controlled industry change, yet there is also a danger of reinforcing cultural lag.

Purposeful Unintended Consequences With substantial innovation, three common myths may combine to present major risk problems.[66] The first common myth is the presumption that at least senior management has *no risk bias*. This myth is often expressed as "Although others may be biased, I am able to define problems and develop solutions objectively." We are all subject to bias in varying degrees and in varying ways. As an issue becomes more complex, it is also much more likely there are several biased viable interpretations.

A second common myth is *the presumption of administrative competence*. Managers at all levels are subject to believing that their part of the firm is okay and just needs minor improvements. This is rarely the case. In almost all firms, there is considerable room for improvement. One particularly damaging manifestation of this myth is that new process and product innovations can be managed in the same way as older ones.

A third common myth is *the denial of trade-offs*; where the group, unit, or firm can avoid making undesirable trade-offs and simultaneously please nearly every constituency. Whereas the denial of trade-offs is common, it can be a dangerous myth in some firms. An emphasis on a single goal often means that other goals are neglected. For example, ethics does not stem from the search for higher efficiency. It is a worthy goal among several.

As illustrated in Figure 15.3, these myths may combine to yield purposeful, yet unintended consequences. Purposeful, unintended consequences arise from the collective application of these three myths. Purposeful, unintended consequences are dramatic, unanticipated benefits or costs arising from the implementation of a way of doing business. Often these unintended consequences are dire. They are purposeful because they stem from unexamined myths—myths managers think apply to others and not themselves.

FIGURE 15.3 Purposeful unintended consequences arising from organizational myths.

The financial meltdown that took place between 2007–2009 is an example of purposeful unintended consequences.[67] Banks and financial institutions had bought and sold mortgage-backed derivatives (complex financial instruments) under the myths that they could (1) accurately judge the risk themselves and value them accurately (they were not risk biased); (2) administer these complex instruments in a manner similar to traditional mortgages (the presumption of administrative competence); and (3) gain great short-term returns without risking long-term profitability (denial of trade-offs). Combining these myths allowed the managers to dismiss the potential of a systematic meltdown of the entire financial system (the dire unintended consequence). Yet, by the end of 2008 and the beginning of 2009, the global financial system almost collapsed from these and related problems. Was the unintended consequence pursued on purpose? No one manager sought a meltdown. Yet millions of mortgages were granted to individuals with questionable credit and were then used to develop new types of financial instruments. It took unprecedented actions by many central banks and governments to avert a total collapse.

That said, mortgage-backed securities and derivatives were one of the financial system's major innovations toward the turn of the century. They were an important way to broaden the financial support for housing. And initially, they appeared successful and provided financial institutions with a way to grow and prosper. However, managers forgot that they needed to manage their corporate culture in the face of innovation.

15 Study Guide

Key Questions and Answers

What is organizational culture?
- Organizational culture or corporate culture is the system of shared actions, values, and beliefs that develops within an organization and guides the behavior of its members.
- The functions of the corporate culture include responding to both external adaptation and internal integration issues.
- Most organizations contain a variety of subcultures, and a few have countercultures that can sometimes become the source of potentially harmful conflicts.
- The corporate culture also reflects the values and implicit assumptions of the larger national culture.

How do you understand an organizational culture?
- Organizational cultures may be analyzed in terms of observable actions, shared values, and common assumptions (the taken-for-granted truths).
- Observable aspects of culture include the stories, rites, rituals, and symbols that are shared by organization members.
- Cultural rules and roles specify when various types of actions are appropriate and where individual members stand in the social system.

- Shared meanings and understandings help everyone know how to act and expect others to act in various circumstances.
- Common assumptions are the taken-for-granted truths that are shared by collections of corporate members.

How can we manage organizational culture and innovation?
- Executives may manage many aspects of the observable culture directly.
- Nurturing shared values among the membership is a major challenge for executives.
- Adjusting actions to common understandings limits the decision scope of even the CEO.

What is innovation, and why is it important?
- Innovation is the process of creating new ideas and then implementing them in practical applications.
- Steps in the innovation process normally include idea generation, initial experimentation, feasibility determination, and final application.
- Common features of highly innovative organizations include supportive strategies, cultures, structures, staffing, and senior leadership.
- Product innovations result in improved goods or services; process innovations result in improved work methods and operations.
- Process innovations introduce into operations new and better ways of doing things.
- Although it is necessary to balance exploration and exploitation, it is difficult to accomplish.
- There are tensions between the tendency for cultural stability in most firms and the need to innovate.

Terms to Know

Corporate culture (p. 328)
Countercultures (p. 330)
Cultural symbol (p. 335)
Exploitation (p. 345)
Exploration (p. 345)
External adaptation (p. 328)
Innovation (p. 342)
Internal integration (p. 329)
Management philosophy (p. 338)

Mission statements (p. 339)
Multicultural organization (p. 332)
Observable culture (p. 334)
Organizational cultural lag (p. 345)
Organizational culture (p. 328)
Organizational myths (p. 337)

Output goals (p. 339)
Process innovations (p. 344)
Product innovations (p. 343)
Rites (p. 335)
Rituals (p. 335)
Saga (p. 335)
Societal goals (p. 339)
Subcultures (p. 330)
Systems goals (p. 340)

Self-Test 15

■ Multiple Choice

1. Culture concerns all of the following except _____.
    (a) the collective concepts shared by members of a firm
    (b) acquired capabilities
    (c) the personality of the leader
    (d) the beliefs of members

2. The three levels of cultural analysis highlighted in the text concern _____.
   (a) observable culture, shared values, and common assumptions
   (b) stories, rites, and rituals
   (c) symbols, myths, and stories
   (d) manifest culture, latent culture, and observable artifacts

3. External adaptation concerns _____.
   (a) the unproven beliefs of senior executives
   (b) the process of coping with outside forces
   (c) the vision of the founder
   (d) the processes working together

4. Internal integration concerns _____.
   (a) the process of deciding the collective identity and how members will live together
   (b) the totality of the daily life of members as they see and describe it
   (c) expressed unproven beliefs that are accepted uncritically and used to justify current actions
   (d) groups of individuals with a pattern of values that rejects those of the larger society

5. When Japanese workers start each day with the company song, this is an example of a(n) _____.
   (a) symbol
   (b) myth
   (c) underlying assumption
   (d) ritual

6. _____ is a sense of broader purpose that workers infuse into their tasks as a result of interaction with one another.
   (a) A rite
   (b) A cultural symbol
   (c) A foundation myth
   (d) A shared meaning

7. The story of a corporate turnaround attributed to the efforts of a visionary manager is an example of _____.
   (a) a saga
   (b) a foundation myth
   (c) internal integration
   (d) a latent cultural artifact

8. The process of creating new ideas and putting them into practice is _____.
   (a) innovation
   (b) creative destruction
   (c) product innovation
   (d) process innovation

9. Any object, act, or event that serves to transmit cultural meaning is called _____.
   (a) a saga
   (b) a cultural symbol
   (c) a cultural lag
   (d) a cultural myth

10. Groups where the patterns of values outwardly reject those of the larger organization are _____.
    (a) external adaptation rejectionist
    (b) cultural lag
    (c) countercultures
    (d) organizational myths

11. Groups with unique patterns of values and philosophies that are consistent with the dominant organizational culture are called _____.
    (a) countercultures
    (b) subcultures
    (c) sagas
    (d) rituals

12. A _____ links key goal-related issues with key collaboration issues to come up with general ways by which the firm will manage its affairs.
    (a) managerial philosophy
    (b) cultural symbol
    (c) ritual
    (d) saga

13. Commonly held cause–effect relationships that cannot be empirically supported are referred to as _____.
    (a) cultural lags
    (b) rituals
    (c) management philosophy
    (d) organizational myths

14. The patterns of values and philosophies that outwardly reject those of the larger organization or social system are called _____.
    (a) sagas
    (b) organizational development
    (c) rituals
    (d) countercultures

15. _____ is a condition in which dominant cultural patterns are inconsistent with new emerging innovations.
    (a) Organizational cultural lag
    (b) Management philosophy
    (c) Internal integration
    (d) External adaptation

Short Response

16. Describe the five steps Taylor Cox suggests need to be developed to help generate a multicultural organization or pluralistic company culture.

17. List the three aspects that help individuals and groups work together effectively, and illustrate them through practical examples.

18. Give an example of how cultural rules and roles affect the atmosphere in a college classroom. Provide specific examples from your own perspective.

19. What are the major elements of a strong corporate culture?

Applications Essay

20. Discuss why managers should balance exploration and exploitation when seeking greater innovation.

Steps to Further Learning 15
Top Choices from *The OB Skills Workbook*

These learning activities from *The OB Skills Workbook* found at the back of the book are suggested for Chapter 15.

Case for Critical Thinking	Team and Experiential Exercises	Self-Assessment Portfolio
• Never on a Sunday	• How We View Differences • Workgroup Culture • Fast-Food Technology • Alien Invasion	• Are You Cosmopolitan? • Team Effectiveness • Which Culture Fits You?

16

Organizational Structure and Design

The Key Point

Organizations are collections of people working together to achieve common goals. In this chapter, we discuss how organizations design and structure themselves to reach their goals. Effective managers need to know how to establish a hierarchy and control it, and how to organize the work to be done and effectively coordinate with others. ∎

Chapter at a Glance

- What Is the Formal Structure of the Organization?
- How Is Work Organized and Coordinated?
- What Is Organizational Design?
- What Are Bureaucracies and Their Alternatives?

What's Inside?

- **Bringing OB to LIFE**
  FLATTENING STRUCTURES BY CROWDSOURCING PEER EVALUATIONS

- **Worth Considering . . . or Best Avoided?**
  DO FLEXIBLE FACTORIES HAVE STAYING POWER?

- **Checking Ethics in OB**
  FLATTENED INTO EXHAUSTION

- **Finding the Leader in You**
  DENISE WILSON KEEPS STRUCTURE SIMPLE AT DESERT JET

- **OB in Popular Culture**
  HIERARCHY AND *RATATOUILLE*

- **Research Insight**
  COORDINATION IN TEMPORARY ORGANIZATIONS

CHAPTER 16 ■ Organizational Structure and Design

Formal Organizational Structure

LEARNING ROADMAP ORGANIZATIONS AS HIERARCHIES • CONTROLS AS A BASIC FEATURE

> TEACHING NOTE: Have students describe the way their department or college is organized. Draw the chart as they talk. Ask them to discuss how it might be changed for the better.

Once the goals of an organization are clear, managers must decide how to organize work to accomplish these goals.[1] The static aspect of the process is known as organizational structure. Specifically, the formal structure of an organization outlines the jobs to be done, the people who are to perform specific activities, and the ways the tasks of the organization are to be accomplished. In other words, the formal structure is the skeleton of the firm.[2]

The formal structure shows the planned pattern of positions, job duties, and the lines of authority among different parts of the company. Traditionally, the formal structure of the firm also has been called the division of labor. This terminology is still used to isolate decisions concerning formal structure from choices regarding the division of markets and/or technology. We will deal with environmental and technology issues after we discuss the structure as a foundation for managerial action.

■ Organizations as Hierarchies

In most organizations, there is a clear separation of authority and duties by rank. How authority is specialized is known as vertical specialization. **Vertical specialization** is an organization's hierarchical division of labor that distributes formal authority and establishes where and how critical decisions will be made. This division creates a hierarchy of authority—an arrangement of work positions in order of increasing authority.[3]

Vertical specialization is an organization's hierarchical division of labor.

The Organization Chart
Organization charts are diagrams that depict the formal structures of organizations. A typical chart shows the various positions, the position holders, and the lines of authority that link them to one another. Figure 16.1 presents a partial organization chart for a large university. The chart allows university employees to locate their positions in the structure and to identify the lines of authority linking them with others in the organization. For instance, in this figure, the treasurer reports to the vice president of administration, who, in turn, reports to the president of the university.

Organization charts are diagrams that depict the formal structures of organizations.

Although an organization chart may indicate who each employee reports to, it is also important to recognize that it does not show how work is completed, who exercises the most power over specific issues, or how the firm will respond to its environment.

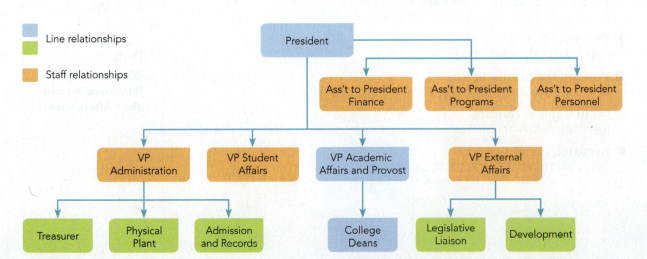

FIGURE 16.1 A partial organization chart for a state university.

However, organization charts can be important to the extent that they accurately represent the chain of command, a listing of who reports to whom up and down the firm's hierarchy and shows how executives, managers, and supervisors are connected. Traditional management theory suggests that each individual should have one boss, and each unit should have one leader. Under these circumstances, there is a unity of command which is necessary to avoid confusion, assign accountability to specific individuals, and provide clear channels of communication throughout the organization.

Span of Control The number of individuals reporting to a supervisor is called the **span of control**. Narrower spans of control are expected when tasks are complex, when subordinates are inexperienced or poorly trained, or when tasks call for team effort. Unfortunately, narrow spans of control yield many organizational levels. The excessive number of levels is not only expensive, but it also makes the organization unresponsive to necessary change. Communications often becomes less effective because information is successively screened and modified and subtle but important changes can be ignored.

> The **span of control** is the number of individuals reporting to a supervisor.

CHECKING ETHICS IN OB

Flattened into Exhaustion

© Jesper Elgaard/iStockphoto

Dear Stress Doctor:

My boss has come up with this great idea of cutting some supervisor positions, assigning more workers to those of us who remain, and calling us "coaches" instead of supervisors. She says this is all part of a new management approach to operate with a flatter structure and more empowerment.

For me this means a lot more work coordinating the activities of seventeen operators instead of the six that I previously supervised. I can't get everything cleaned up on my desk most days, and I end up taking a lot of paperwork home.

As my organization "restructures" and cuts back staff, it puts a greater burden on those of us who remain. We get exhausted, and our families get shortchanged and even angry. I even feel guilty now taking time to watch my daughter play soccer on Saturday mornings. Sure, there's some decent pay involved, but that doesn't make up for the heavy price I'm paying in terms of lost family times.

But you know what? My boss doesn't get it. I never hear her ask "Henry, are you working too much? Don't you think it's time to get back on a reasonable schedule?" No! What I often hear instead is "Look at Andy. He handles our new management model really well, and he's a real go-getter. I don't think he's been out of here one night this week before eight P.M."

What am I to do, just keep it up until everything falls apart one day? Is a flatter structure with fewer managers always best? Am I missing something in regard to this "new management?"

Sincerely,
Overworked in Cincinnati

Get the Ethics Straight
Is it ethical to restructure, cut management levels, and expect the remaining managers to do more work? Or is it simply the case that managers used to the "old" ways of doing things need extra training and care while learning "new" management approaches? And what about this person's boss—is she on track with her management skills? Aren't managers supposed to help people understand their jobs, set priorities, and fulfill them, while still maintaining a reasonable work–life balance?

When organizations have many levels, managers can get too far removed from the action and become isolated. Conversely with too few levels, organizations may experience coordination and control problems and managers are subject to burnout.

Line and Staff Units A useful way to examine the vertical division of labor is to separate line and staff units. **Line units** and personnel conduct the major business of the organization. The production and marketing functions are two examples. In contrast, **staff units** and personnel assist the line units by providing specialized expertise and services, such as accounting and public relations. For example, the vice president of administration in a university (see Figure 16.1) heads a staff unit, as does the vice president of student affairs.

Staff units can be assigned predominantly to senior-, middle-, or lower-level managers. When staff is assigned predominantly to senior management, the capability of senior management to develop alternatives and make decisions and monitor progress is expanded.

> **Line units** and personnel conduct the major business of the organization.

> **Staff units** assist the line units by providing specialized expertise and services.

Controls as a Basic Feature

Distributing formal authority calls for control. **Control** is the set of mechanisms used to keep action or outputs within predetermined limits.[4] Control deals with setting standards, measuring results versus standards, and instituting corrective action. We should stress that effective control occurs before action actually begins. For instance, in setting standards, managers must decide what will be measured and how accomplishment will be determined. Although there are a wide variety of organizational controls, they are roughly divided into output, process, and social controls.

> **Control** is the set of mechanisms used to keep action or outputs within predetermined limits.

Output Controls We have defined output goals and suggested that systems goals should be a road map to desirable conditions that tie together units to achieve the organization's output and societal goals. **Output controls** focus on desired targets for each unit in the organization. Developing targets or standards, measuring results against these targets, and taking corrective action are all steps involved in developing effective output controls.[5] When executives stress output controls, managers can use their own methods to reach defined targets. Most organizations use output controls as part of an overall method of managing by exception.

> **Output controls** focus on desired targets for each unit.

Output controls are popular because they promote flexibility and creativity and facilitate dialogue concerning corrective actions. Reliance on outcome controls separates what is to be accomplished from how it is to be accomplished, and the discussion of goals is separated from the dialogue concerning methods. This separation can facilitate the movement of power down the organization, as managers are reassured that individuals at all levels will be working toward the goals management believes are important, even as lower-level managers innovate and introduce new ways to accomplish these goals.

Process Controls Few organizations run on outcome controls alone. Once a solution to a problem is found and successfully implemented, managers do not want the problem to recur, so they institute process controls. **Process controls** attempt to specify the manner in which tasks are accomplished.[6] There are many types of process controls, but three groups have received considerable attention: (1) policies, procedures, and rules; (2) formalization and standardization; and (3) total quality management controls.

> **Process controls** attempt to specify the manner in which tasks are accomplished.

Most organizations implement a variety of policies, procedures, and rules to help specify how goals are to be accomplished. Usually, we think of a **policy** as a guideline for action that outlines important objectives and broadly indicates how an activity is to be performed. It sets boundaries but typically allows for some individual discretion. **Procedures** indicate the best method for performing a task, show which aspects of a task are the most important, or outline how an individual is to be rewarded.

> A **policy** sets forth a broad guideline for action.

> A **procedure** sets forth the best method for performing a task.

Rules are more specific, rigid, and impersonal than policies. They typically describe in detail how a task or a series of tasks is to be performed, or they indicate what cannot be done. They are designed to apply to all individuals, under specified conditions. For example, most car dealers have detailed instruction manuals for repairing a new car under warranty, and they must follow strict procedures to obtain reimbursement from the manufacturer for warranty work.

Rules, procedures, and policies are often employed as substitutes for direct managerial supervision. In OB, **formalization** refers to the written documentation of rules, procedures, and policies to guide behavior and decision making. Under the guidance of written rules and procedures, the organization can specifically direct the activities of many individuals. Written instructions allow individuals with less training to perform sophisticated tasks, as more complicated activities can be broken down into simplified steps. Written procedures may also ensure that a proper sequence of tasks is executed.

Formalization is the written documentation of rules, procedures and policies to guide behavior and decision making.

Most organizations have developed additional methods for dealing with recurring problems or situations. **Standardization** is the allowable actions in a job or series of jobs. It involves the creation of guidelines so that similar work activities are repeatedly performed in a consistent fashion. Such standardized methods may come from years of experience in dealing with typical situations, or they may come from outside training. For instance, if you are late in paying your credit card, the bank will automatically send you a notification and start an internal process of monitoring your account.

Standardization is the allowable actions in a job or series of jobs.

Total Quality Management

The process controls discussed so far—policies, procedures, rules, formalization, and standardization—represent the lessons of experience within an organization. Often there is no overall philosophy for using controls to improve the operations of the company. One way of instituting process controls is to establish a total quality management process within the firm.

The late W. Edwards Deming was the founder of the total quality management movement.[7] When Deming's ideas were not initially accepted in the United States, he found an audience in Japan. At the heart of Deming's approach is instituting a process approach to continual improvement based on statistical analyses of the firm's operations. Around this core idea, Deming developed a series of fourteen points for managers to implement. In Figure 16.2, note the emphasis on everyone working together using statistical controls in order to achieve continual improvement.

Deming's 14 Points of Quality Management

1. Create a consistency of purpose in the company to (a) innovate, (b) put resources into research and education, and (c) put resources into maintaining equipment and new production aids.
2. Learn a new philosophy of quality to improve every system.
3. Require statistical evidence of process control and eliminate financial controls on production.
4. Require statistical evidence of control in purchasing parts; this will mean dealing with fewer suppliers.
5. Use statistical methods to isolate the sources of trouble.
6. Institute modern on-the-job training.
7. Improve supervision to develop inspired leaders.
8. Drive out fear and instill learning.
9. Break down barriers between departments.
10. Eliminate numerical goals and slogans.
11. Constantly revamp work methods.
12. Institute massive training programs for employees in statistical methods.
13. Retrain people in new skills.
14. Create a structure that will push, every day, on the preceding thirteen points.

FIGURE 16.2 Deming's 14 Points of Quality Management.

When an organization's goals and outcomes are well defined, Deming's system and emphasis on quality work well. The approach is particularly effective when implemented in conjunction with empowerment and participative management. Success with a quality program requires high involvement by everyone as well as strong management support for skills training and keeping quality themes visible.

Centralization and Decentralization

Organizations use different mixes of vertical specialization, output controls, process controls, and managerial techniques to allocate the authority or discretion to act.[8] The farther up the hierarchy of authority the discretion to spend money, to hire people, and to make similar decisions is moved, the greater the degree of **centralization**. The more such decisions are delegated, or moved down the hierarchy of authority, the greater the degree of **decentralization**. Greater centralization is often adopted when the firm faces a single major threat to its survival. It is little wonder that armies tend to be centralized and that firms facing bankruptcy increase centralization. Recent research even suggests that governmental agencies may improve their performance via centralization when in a defensive mode.[9]

Centralization is the degree to which the authority to make decisions is restricted to higher levels of management.

Decentralization is the degree to which the authority to make decisions is given to lower levels in an organizations hierarchy.

BRINGING OB TO LIFE

> "We are decentralizing as much decision making as we can, so we also need to decentralize reviews."

Flattening Structures by Crowdsourcing Peer Evaluations

As executives look for ways to flatten organization structures and reduce administrative costs, going online with performance reviews and crowdsourcing feedback are becoming increasingly popular.

OB scholars have long suggested that it's good to get away from the traditional manager-driven, top-down performance evaluations. An example of how practice has responded to theory is the popularity of 360-degree reviews. They include feedback from peers and others working with or for the person under review.

Online reviews are in at the San Francisco-based social media outfit Hearsay Social, Inc. The firm runs on teamwork and involves constantly shifting projects. All ninety employees are part of a crowdsourced feedback system that allows them to comment on one another's work and the feedback is anonymous. Chief technology officer Steve Garrity says, "We are decentralizing as much decision making as we can, so we also need to decentralize reviews."

The daily deal company LivingSocial takes crowdsourcing of reviews a step further. Its employees can go online anytime and comment—in public or in private, on someone else's work. These peer reviews are factored into formal performance reviews done every three months, and are also used in making pay bonus decisions.

With more employees on the giving and receiving ends of crowdsourced performance feedback, San Francisco State management professor John Sullivan worries that people may end up evaluating others whose jobs they don't know enough about. As online peer reviews become more common, managers should make sure they understand how they affect those involved, and how they can best be implemented.

Bill O'Leary/The Washington Post/Getty

Greater decentralization generally provides higher subordinate satisfaction and a quicker response to a diverse series of unrelated problems. Decentralization also assists in the on-the-job training of subordinates for higher-level positions. Decentralization is now a popular approach in many industries.[10] For instance, Union Carbide is pushing responsibility down the chain of command, as are SYSCO and Hewlett-Packard. In each case, the senior managers hope to improve both performance quality and organizational responsiveness.

Decentralization and Participation Closely related to decentralization is the notion of participation. Many people want to be involved in making decisions that affect their work. Participation results when a manager delegates some authority for such decision making to subordinates. For example, Macy's has successfully experimented with moving decisions down the chain of command and increasing employee participation. In many cases, employees want a say both in what the unit objectives should be and in how they can be achieved.

The Illusion of Control One of the myths in management is the illusion of control. There are many variations of this, but one centers on the formal controls themselves. Many managers want to believe they can specify all of the relevant goals for subordinates as well as how they are to be accomplished. With too many output and process goals, subordinates appear to have very little flexibility. However, as the number of output and process controls escalates, so do the conflicts between the two. The result is that subordinates begin to pick and choose which controls they follow and managers only have the illusion that subordinates are reaching toward the specified goals.[11]

Organizing and Coordinating Work

LEARNING ROADMAP TRADITIONAL TYPES OF DEPARTMENTS • COORDINATION

Managers must divide the total task into separate duties and group similar people and resources together.[12] Organizing work is formally known as **horizontal specialization**, which is a division of labor that establishes specific work units or groups within an organization. This aspect of the organization is also called departmentation. Whatever is divided horizontally into two or more departments must also be integrated.[13] **Coordination** is the set of mechanisms that an organization uses to link the actions of its units into a consistent pattern. This includes mechanisms to connect managers and staff units, operating units, and divisions with each other. Managers use a mix of personal and impersonal methods of coordination to tie together the efforts of departments.

TEACHING NOTE: Ask students to redesign into a network structure an organization of their choice (use the university as a default option), and identify the possible advantages and disadvantages to stakeholders.

Horizontal specialization is a division of labor that establishes specific work units or groups within an organization.

Coordination is the set of mechanisms that an organization uses to link the actions of their units into a consistent pattern.

▰ Traditional Types of Departments

Since the pattern of departmentation is so visible and important in a firm, managers often refer to their pattern of departmentation as the departmental structure. Although most firms use a mix of various types of departments, it is important to look at the traditional types and what they do and do not provide the firm.[14]

Functional Departments Grouping individuals by skill, knowledge, and action yields a pattern of **functional departmentation**. Recall that Figure 16.1 shows the partial organization chart for a large university in which each department has a technical specialty. Marketing, finance, production, and personnel are important functions in business. In many small companies, this functional pattern dominates. Even large

Functional departmentation groups individuals by skill, knowledge, and action.

Major Advantages and Disadvantages of Functional Specialization	
Advantages	**Disadvantages**
1. Yields clear task assignments, consistent with an individual's training. 2. Individuals within a department can build on one another's knowledge, training, and experience. 3. Provides an excellent training ground for new managers. 4. It is easy to explain. 5. Takes advantage of employee technical quality.	1. May reinforce the narrow training of individuals. 2. May yield narrow, boring, and routine jobs. 3. Communication across technical area is complex and difficult. 4. "Top-management overload" with too much attention to cross-functional problems. 5. Individuals may look up the organizational hierarchy for direction and reinforcement rather than focus attention on products, services, or clients.

FIGURE 16.3 Major advantages and disadvantages of functional specialization.

organizations use this pattern in technically demanding areas. Figure 16.3 summarizes the advantages and disadvantages of the functional pattern.

With all of these advantages, it is not surprising that the functional form is popular. It is used in most organizations, particularly toward the bottom of the hierarchy. The extensive use of functional departments does have some disadvantages. Organizations that rely heavily on functional specialization may expect the following tendencies to emerge over time: an emphasis on quality from a technical standpoint, rigidity to change, and difficulty in coordinating the actions of different functional areas.

Divisional Departments With **divisional departments**, individuals and resources are grouped by products, territories, services, clients, or legal entities. A divisional pattern is often used to meet diverse external threats and opportunities. As shown in Figure 16.4, the major advantages of the divisional pattern are its flexibility in meeting external demands, spotting external changes, integrating specialized individuals deep within the organization, and focusing on the delivery of specific products to specific customers. Among its disadvantages are duplication of effort by function, the tendency for divisional goals to be placed above corporate interests, and conflict among divisions. It is also not the structure most desired for training individuals in technical areas. Firms relying on this pattern may fall behind technically to competitors with a functional pattern.

> **Divisional departmentation** groups individuals together by products, territories, services, clients, or legal entities.

Many larger, geographically dispersed organizations that sell to national and international markets may rely on departmentation by geography. The savings in time, effort, and travel can be substantial, and each territory can adjust to regional differences. Organizations that rely on a few major customers may organize their people and resources by client. Here, the idea is to focus attention on the needs of the individual customer. To the extent that customer needs are unique, departmentation by customer can also reduce confusion and increase synergy. Organizations expanding internationally may also form divisions to meet the demands of complex host-country ownership requirements. For example, NEC, Sony, Nissan, and many other Japanese corporations have developed U.S. divisional subsidiaries to service their customers in the U.S. market. Some European-based corporations such as Philips and Nestlé have also adopted a divisional structure in their expansion to the United States.

Matrix Structures Originally from the aerospace industry, a third unique form of departmentation is called the matrix structure.[15] In aerospace efforts, projects are technically complex, involving hundreds of subcontractors located throughout the world. Precise integration and control are needed across many functional specialties and

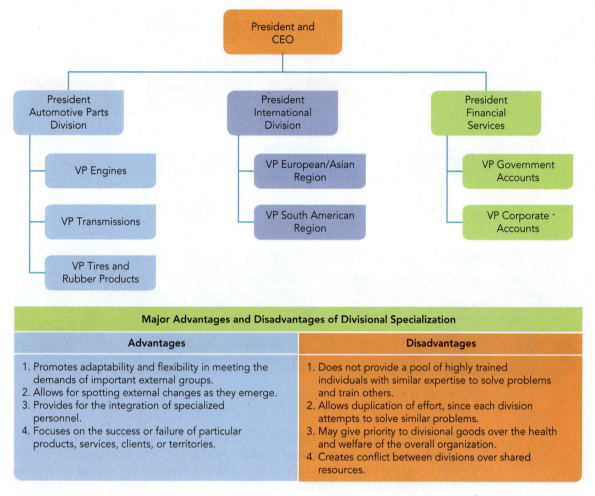

FIGURE 16.4 A divisional pattern of departmentation and the advantages and disadvantages of divisional specialization.

corporations. This is often more than a functional or divisional structure can provide, for many firms do not want to trade the responsiveness of the divisional form for the technical emphasis provided by the functional form. Therefore, **matrix departmentation** uses both the functional and divisional forms simultaneously. Figure 16.5 shows the basic matrix arrangement for an aerospace program. Note the functional departments on one side and the project efforts on the other. Workers and supervisors in the middle of the matrix have two bosses—one functional and one project manager.

Figure 16.5 summarizes the major advantages and disadvantages of the matrix form of departmentation. The key disadvantage of the matrix method is the loss of unity of command. Individuals can be unsure as to what their jobs are, who they report to for specific activities, and how various managers are to administer the effort. It can also be an expensive method because it relies on individual managers to coordinate efforts deep within the firm. Despite these limitations, the matrix structure provides a balance between functional and divisional concerns. Many problems can be resolved at the working level, where the balance among technical, cost, customer, and organizational concerns can be dealt with effectively.

Which form of departmentation should be used? As the matrix concept suggests, it is possible to departmentalize by two different methods at the same time. Actually, companies often use a mixture of departmentation forms. It is often desirable to divide the

Matrix departmentation uses both the functional and divisional forms simultaneously.

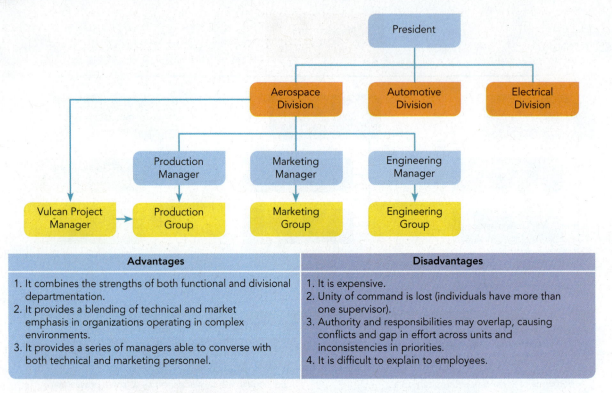

FIGURE 16.5 A matrix pattern of departmentation in an aerospace division.

effort (group people and resources) by two methods at the same time in order to balance the advantages and disadvantages of each. These mixed forms help organizations use their division of labor to capitalize on environmental opportunities, capture the benefits of larger size, and realize the potential of new technologies in pursuit of its strategy.

Coordination

Whatever is divided up horizontally in two departments should also be integrated.[16] Coordination, as noted previously, is the set of mechanisms that an organization uses to link the actions of its units into a consistent pattern. Coordination is needed at all levels of management, not just across a few scattered units. Much of the coordination within a unit is handled by its manager. Smaller organizations may rely on their management hierarchy to provide the necessary consistency and integration.

Personal Methods of Coordination

Personal methods of coordination produce synergy by promoting dialogue and discussion, innovation, creativity, and learning, both within and across organizational units. Personal methods allow the organization to address the needs of distinct units and individuals simultaneously. There is a wide variety of personal methods of coordination.[17] Perhaps the most popular is direct contact between and among organizational members. As new information technologies have moved into practice, the potential for developing and maintaining effective contact networks has expanded. For example, many executives use electronic communication to supplement direct personal communication. Direct personal contact is also associated with the ever-present "grapevine." Although the grapevine is notoriously inaccurate in its role as a rumor mill, it is often accurate and quick enough that managers cannot ignore it. Instead, managers need to work with and supplement the rumor mill with accurate information.

Managers are often assigned to committees in order to improve coordination across departments. Committees can be effective in communicating complex qualitative information and in helping managers whose units must work together to adjust schedules, workloads, and work assignments to increase productivity.

The appropriate mix of personal coordination methods, and tailoring them to the individual skills, abilities, and experience of subordinates, also varies with the type of task. As the "Research Insight" feature suggests, a variety of personal methods can be tailored to match different individuals and the settings in which they operate. Personal

Research Insight

Coordination in Temporary Organizations

In today's world, many individuals have jobs that take them to a number of different temporary settings such as a corporate task force, an alliance, or a special project. Coordinating the actions of the members in these temporary arrangements is often a challenge. However, recent research by Beth Bechky offers some insight. She studied the workers on a movie set—not the actors or producer—but the crew who set up and run the equipment, shoot the movie, and make sure the sound is perfect. These individuals are generally independent contractors whose work must mesh quickly even though they have only been together a few hours.

How do they do it in the short-lived organization of a movie set? According to Bechky, they negotiate their roles with each other. Each has his or her own specialization and assignment, and these must be coordinated with all others. Although each recognizes the others' career progression (some have more experience and are looked to for help), all recognize that the current assignment is one among many they may want in the future. All are on their best behavior with the hopes that they will be hired for the next movie.

Bechky found that the more experienced crew may provide enthusiastic appreciation and polite admonishing to the less-experienced crew members. To enforce an emerging order and maintain coordination, many use humor, Sarcasm, and teasing. Public displays of anger are rare and frowned upon. With these mechanisms in place it only takes a few hours for the crew to emerge as an integrated unit.

To transfer the findings to a student group, try and build a simplified model of the factors mentioned in the description. It might look somewhat like this:

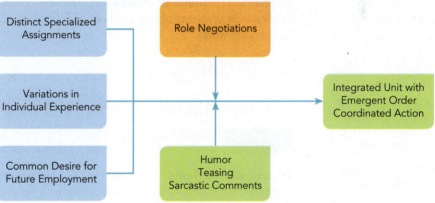

Pick a student group to perform a team case study with majors in different areas (such as accounting, finance, and management). See if the members self-assign to specialized areas based on their major. Look for variations in experience, and check if there is a common desire for high performance. As the group starts work on the project, observe if the members negotiate distinct roles. Do they use humor, teasing, or sarcastic comments to coalesce? Do they form an integrated group with an identified order and coordinated action, or do just a few actually run the show?

Do the Research Would you expect a student group to form much the way that professionals do? If the student group does not use humor or teasing, what do members use to gain coordinated action?

Source: Beth A. Bechky, "Gaffers, Gofers, and Grips: Role-Based Coordination in Temporary Organizations" *Organization Science* 17.1 (2006), pp. 3–23.

methods are only one important part of coordination. The manager may also establish a series of impersonal mechanisms.

Impersonal Methods of Coordination

Impersonal methods of coordination produce synergy by stressing consistency and standardization so that individual pieces fit together. Impersonal coordination methods are often refinements and extensions of process controls with an emphasis on formalization and standardization. Organizations often have written policies and procedures, such as schedules, budgets, and plans that are designed to mesh the operations of several units into a whole by providing predictability and consistency.

Managers often institute controls under the title of coordination. Since some of the techniques are used for both, many managers suggest that all efforts at control are for coordination. It is extremely important to separate these two functions because the reactions to controls and coordination are different. The underlying logic of control involves setting targets, measuring performance, and taking corrective action to meet goals normally assigned by higher management. Many employees see an increase in controls as a threat based on a presumption that they have been doing something wrong. The logic of coordination is to get unit actions and interactions meshed together into a unified whole. Although control involves the vertical exercise of formal authority, coordination stresses cooperative problem solving. Experienced employees recognize the difference between controls and coordination regardless of what their manager calls it.[18] Increasing controls rarely solves problems of coordination, and emphasizing coordination to solve control issues rarely works.

Organizational Design

LEARNING ROADMAP SIZE AND THE SIMPLE DESIGN • TECHNOLOGY AND ORGANIZATIONAL DESIGN • ENVIRONMENT AND ORGANIZATIONAL DESIGN

> TEACHING NOTE: Ask students which of the contingency factors of size, technology and environment should be the most heavily emphasized in designing a community hospital, a police department, and a department store.

Organizational design is the process of choosing and implementing a structural configuration.[19] It goes beyond indicating who reports to whom and what types of jobs are contained in each department. The design process takes the basic structural elements and molds them to the company's desires, demands, constraints, and choices. When managers chose their overall approach to reaching their mission, the choice of an appropriate organizational design is contingent on several factors, including the size of the organization, its operations and information technology, and its environment.

Organizational design is the process of choosing and implementing a structural configuration.

▶ Size and the Simple Design

The **simple design** is a configuration involving one or two ways of specializing individuals and units. Vertical specialization and control typically emphasize levels of supervision without elaborate formal mechanisms (e.g., rulebooks and policy manuals), and the majority of the control resides in the manager. The simple design tends to minimize bureaucracy and rest more heavily on the leadership of the manager.

The simple design pattern is appropriate for many small companies such as family businesses, retail stores, and small manufacturing firms.[20] The strengths of the simple design are simplicity, flexibility, and responsiveness to the desires of a central manager—in many cases, the owner. Because a simple design relies heavily on the manager's personal leadership, however, this configuration is only as effective as is the senior manager.

The **simple design** is a configuration involving one or two ways of specializing individuals and units.

Technology and Organizational Design

Although the design for an organization should reflect its size, it must also be adjusted to fit technological opportunities and requirements. Successful organizations arrange their internal structures to meet the dictates of their dominant "operations technologies" or workflows and, more recently, information technology opportunities.[21]

Operations Technology and Organizational Design

Operations technology is the combination of resources, knowledge, and techniques that creates a product or service output for an organization.[22] As researchers in OB have charted the links between operations technology and organizational design, two common classifications for operations technology have received considerable attention: Thompson's and Woodward's classifications.

> **Operations technology** is the combination of resources, knowledge, and techniques that creates a product or service output for an organization.

Thompson's View of Technology A classic description of alternative technologies was developed by James D. Thompson. As shown in Figure 16.6, it classified technologies based on degrees of specification and interdependence among work activities.[23] Under *intensive technology*, there is uncertainty as to how to produce desired outcomes. A group of specialists must be brought together and use a variety of techniques to solve problems. Examples are found in a hospital emergency room or a research and development laboratory. Coordination and knowledge exchange are of critical importance with this kind of technology.

Mediating technology links parties that want to become interdependent. For example, banks link creditors and depositors and store money and information to facilitate such exchanges. Whereas all depositors and creditors are indirectly interdependent, the reliance is pooled through the bank. The degree of coordination among the individual tasks with pooled technology is reduced, and information management becomes more important than coordinated knowledge application.

Under *long-linked technology*, also called mass production or industrial technology, the way to produce the desired outcomes is known. The task is broken down into a number of sequential steps. A classic example is the automobile assembly line. Control is critical, and coordination is restricted to making the sequential linkages work in harmony.

Joan Woodward's View of Technology Joan Woodward also divides technology into three categories: small-batch, mass production, and continuous-process manufacturing.[24] In units of *small-batch production*, a variety of custom products are tailored to fit customer specifications, such as tailor-made suits. The machinery and equipment used are generally not very elaborate, but considerable craftsmanship is often needed. In *mass production*, the organization produces one or a few products through an assembly-line system. The work of one group is dependent on that of another, the equipment is typically sophisticated, and the workers are given detailed instructions. Automobiles and refrigerators are produced in this way.

Stefano Lunardi/Age Fotostock America, Inc.

Keith Brofsky/Getty Images, Inc.

© vario images GmbH & Co. KG/Alamy Limited

FIGURE 16.6 Three Types of Operations Technologies: Intensive, Mediating, and Long linked.

FINDING THE LEADER IN YOU

Denise Wilson Keeps Structure Simple at Desert Jet

Founded in 2007, by Denise Wilson, Desert Jet provides private jet travel services to corporations throughout the United States. What makes this company, located in Thermal, California, really unique is that it also offers aircraft owners with professional aircraft management and the opportunity to generate revenue. When an aircraft would otherwise be sitting idle, Desert Jets enlists them in a certified leasing program.

Under this program, Desert Jet can lease an aircraft to a member of the general public for about $1,500 to $3,500 per hour. "Our clients will call us and tell us where they want to go and what time they want to go. We provide them not only with the aircraft, but also with ground transportation, catering on the flight, and any other special requests," says Wilson.

A quick look at the Desert Jet website shows that Wilson uses a simple organizational design. She has line positions (pilots) and staff slots (accountants). She has functional specialists (a certified head of maintenance, an accountant, a chief pilot, and a director of safety) reporting to her. And recently, Desert Jet advertised for a specialist to clean aircrafts to join the team. Desert Jet is among the fastest-growing new firms according to Inc., and it will probably take more than a decade of growth for the current simple design to be outmoded.

Courtesy Denise Wilson

What's the Lesson Here?

From the information provided in this chapter, speculate about the types of mechanisms you would likely see in use. What does the attention to the certifications and qualifications of the employees tell you about the use of controls in this firm?

Organizations using *continuous-process technology* produce a few products using considerable automation. Classic examples are automated chemical plants and oil refineries.

From her studies, Woodward concluded that the combination of structure and technology was critical to the success of organizations. When technology and organizational design were matched properly, a firm was more successful. Specifically, successful small-batch and continuous-process plants had flexible structures with small workgroups at the bottom; more rigidly structured plants were less successful. In contrast, successful mass-production operations were rigidly structured and had large workgroups at the bottom. Since Woodward's studies, other investigations supported this technological imperative. Today we recognize that operations technology is just one factor involved in the success of an organization.[25]

Operating Technology and Adhocracy

The influence of operations technology is seen in small organizations and in specific departments within large organizations. In some instances, managers and employees do not know the appropriate way to service a client or to produce a particular product. This is an extreme example of Thompson's intensive type of technology, and it may be found in some small-batch processes where a team of individuals must develop a unique product for a client.

Mintzberg suggests that at these technological extremes, the "adhocracy" may be an appropriate design.[26] An **adhocracy** is characterized by shared decentralized decision making, extreme horizontal specialization, few management levels and minimal formal controls with very few rules, policies, and procedures. This design emphasizes innovation. It is particularly useful when an operations technology presents two problems:

1. the tasks vary considerably and provide many exceptions, and
2. the problems are difficult to define and resolve.[27]

The adhocracy places a premium on professionalism and coordination in problem solving.[28] Large organizations may use temporary task forces, form special committees,

---

An **adhocracy** is characterized by shared decentralized decision making, extreme horizontal specialization, few management levels and minimal formal controls with very few rules, policies, and procedures.

and even contract with consulting firms to help solve problems the adhocracy promotes. For instance, Microsoft creates autonomous departments to encourage talented employees to develop new software programs. Allied Chemical and 3M set up groups to work through new ideas.

We should note that the adhocracy is notoriously inefficient. Further, many managers are reluctant to adopt this form because they appear to lose control of day-to-day operations. The strategy consistent with the adhocracy is a stress on quality and individual service as opposed to efficiency. With more advanced information technology, firms are beginning to combine an adhocracy with bureaucratic elements based on advanced information systems.

Information Technology and Organizational Design

Information technology is the combination of machines, artifacts, procedures, and systems used to gather, store, analyze, and disseminate information for translating it into knowledge.[29] Information technology (IT), the Web, and the computer (be it in tablet or phone form) are virtually inseparable and have fundamentally changed the organization design of firms to capture new competencies.[30]

From an organizational standpoint, IT can be used, among other things, as a substitute for some operations as well as some process controls and impersonal methods of coordination. IT has the capability to transform information to knowledge. For instance, most financial firms could not exist without IT, because it is now the base for the industry. Financial institutions created completely new aspects of their industry based on IT, such as exotic derivatives; it is now painfully obvious that these new aspects of the industry outpaced the ability of management to control them. Information technology, just as operations technology, can yield great good or great harm.

The Virtual Organization As IT has become widespread and it's importance for attaining valued goals has increased, some executives have started to develop "virtual organizations."[31]

A virtual organization is an ever-shifting constellation of firms, with a lead corporation (such as Amazon) that pools skills, resources, and experiences to thrive jointly. This ever-changing collection most likely has a relatively stable group of participants (usually independent firms) and includes key customers, research centers, suppliers, and distributors all connected to each other. The lead firm possesses a critical competence that all need and therefore directs the constellation. Although this critical competence may be a key operations technology or access to customers, it always includes IT as a base for connecting the firms.

The virtual organization works if it operates by some unique rules and is led in a most untypical way. First, the production system that yields the products and services needs to

> **Information technology (IT)** is the combination of machines, artifacts, procedures, and systems used to gather, store, analyze, and disseminate information for translating it into knowledge.

Too Much Technology May Cause Airline Flight Crews to Lose Critical Skills

As flight technology continues to evolve, pilots are spending more time monitoring computer readings. And that worries some observers. "They're becoming dependent on using the autopilot, the auto-throttles, the auto flight system, the computers, to actually operate the entire flight," says former pilot Kevin Hiatt.

Does the emphasis on computers in the cockpit reduce manual flying skills and a pilot's capacity to make judgments under unusual or crisis conditions?

Long ago the German sociologist Max Weber warned against trained incapacity in organizations when structure replaced human judgment. Are we at the point where it's time to put more manual flight time back into pilot training?

© carlosphotos/jStockphoto.com

be a partner network among independent firms where they are bound together by mutual trust and collective survival. As customers desire change, the proportion of work done by any member firm might also change and the membership itself may change. Second, this partner network needs to develop and maintain (1) an advanced information technology (rather than just face-to-face interaction), (2) trust and cross-owning of problems and solutions, and (3) a common shared culture.

The virtual organization can be highly resilient, extremely competent, innovative, and reasonably efficient—characteristics that are usually trade-offs. Executives in the lead firm need to have the vision to see how the network of participants will both effectively compete with patterns consistent enough to be recognizable and still rapidly adjust to technological and environmental changes.[32]

Many managers are involved with a "virtual" network of task forces and temporary teams in order to both define and solve problems. Here the members will only connect electronically. Recent work on participants of the virtual teams suggests managers will need to rethink what it means to "manage." Instead of telling others what to do, managers will need to treat colleagues as unpaid volunteers who expect to participate in governing the meetings and who are tied to the effort only by a commitment to identify and solve problems.[33]

Environment and Organizational Design

An effective organizational design reflects powerful external forces as well as size and technological factors. Organizations, as open systems, need to receive input from the environment and in turn to sell output to their environment. Therefore, understanding the environment is important.[34]

Segments of the Organization's Environment

The **general environment** is the set of cultural, economic, legal–political, and educational conditions found in the areas in which the organization operates. Firms expanding globally encounter multiple general environments.

The owners, suppliers, distributors, government agencies, and competitors with which an organization must interact in order to grow and survive constitute its **specific environment**. A firm typically has much more choice in the composition of its specific environment than its general environment. Although it is often convenient to separate the general and specific environmental influences on the firm, managers need to recognize the combined impact of both.

> The **general environment** is the set of cultural, economic, legal–political, and educational conditions found in the areas in which the organization operates.
>
> The **specific environment** is the set of owners, suppliers, distributors, government agencies, and competitors with which an organization must interact to grow and survive.
>
> **Environmental complexity** refers to the magnitude of the problems and opportunities in the organization's environment.

Environmental Complexity

A basic concern to address when analyzing the environment of the organization is its complexity. A more complex environment provides an organization with more opportunities and more problems. **Environmental complexity** refers to the magnitude of the problems and opportunities in the organization's environment, as evidenced by three main factors: the degree of richness, the degree of interdependence, and the degree of uncertainty stemming from both the general and the specific environment.

Environmental Richness Overall, the environment is richer when the economy is growing, when individuals are improving their education, and when everyone that the organization relies on is prospering. For businesses, a richer environment means that economic conditions are improving, customers are spending more money, and suppliers (especially banks) are willing to invest in the organization's future. In a rich environment, more organizations survive, even if they have poorly functioning organizational designs. A richer environment is also filled with more opportunities and dynamism—the potential for change. The organizational design must allow the company to recognize these opportunities and capitalize on them. The opposite of richness is decline. For most business firms, recession is a good example of a leaner environment.

Millennials Are Warming Up to Part-time Employment for Full-time Pay

As organizations streamline and adopt new forms, work preferences are also changing. Now it seems that free agency is in among millennials.

Look around your classroom and talk to friends. More and more of are opting to work freelance by personal choice, not just because there aren't alternatives. The term *permalancers* is even being used to describe recent college graduates who opt to string together multiple and shifting freelance and part-time contracts to create full-time income.

The key is employment independence and the personal flexibility that goes along with it. Judith Watson, an associate dean at the City University of New York, refers to this trend as employment entrepreneurship. "You have to craft your own career," she says.

Kzenon/Shutterstock

Environmental Interdependence The link between external interdependence and organizational design is often subtle and indirect. The organization may co-opt powerful outsiders by including them. For instance, many large companies have financial representatives from banks and insurance companies on their boards of directors.

The organization may also adjust its overall design strategy to absorb or buffer the demands of a more powerful external element. Perhaps the most common adjustment is the development of a centralized staff department to handle an important external group. Few large U.S. corporations lack some type of centralized governmental relations group.[35]

Uncertainty and Volatility Environmental uncertainty and volatility can be particularly damaging to large organizations. In times of change, investments quickly become outmoded, and internal operations no longer work as expected. The organizational design response to uncertainty and volatility is to opt for a more flexible organic form. At the extremes, movement toward an adhocracy may be important. However, these pressures may run counter to those that come from large size and operations technology. In these cases, it may be too hard or too time consuming for some organizations to make the design adjustments. The organization may continue to struggle while adjusting its design just a little bit at a time. Some firms can deal with the conflicting demands from environmental change and need for internal stability by developing alliances.

Networks and Alliances for Highly Complex Environments

In today's complex global economy, organizational design must go beyond the traditional boundaries of the firm.[36] Firms must learn to alter their environment as well as merely adjust to it. Two ways are becoming more popular: (1) the management of networks and (2) the development of alliances. Many North American firms are learning from their European and Japanese counterparts to develop networks of linkages to the key firms they rely upon. In Europe, for example, one finds *informal combines* or *cartels*. Here, competitors work cooperatively to share the market in order to decrease uncertainty and improve favorability for all. Except in rare cases, these arrangements are often illegal in the United States.

In Japan, the network of relationships among well-established firms in many industries is called a *keiretsu*. There are two common forms. The first is a bank-centered *keiretsu*, in which firms link to one another directly through cross-ownership and historical ties to one bank. The Mitsubishi group is a good example of a company that grew through cross-ownership. In the second type, a *vertical keiretsu*, a key manufacturer, is at the hub of a network of supplier firms or distributor firms. The manufacturer typically has both long-term supply contracts with members and cross-ownership ties. These arrangements help isolate Japanese firms from stockholders and provide a mechanism for sharing and developing technology. Toyota is an example of a firm at the center of a *vertical keiretsu*.

Interfirm alliances are cooperative agreements or joint ventures between two independent firms.

Another option is to develop **interfirm alliances**, which are cooperative agreements or joint ventures between two independent firms.[37] Often, these agreements involve corporations that are headquartered in different nations. In high-tech areas, such as robotics, semiconductors, advanced materials (ceramics and carbon fibers), and advanced information systems, a single company often does not have all of the knowledge necessary to bring new products to the market. Alliances are common in such high-technology industries. Via their international alliances, high-tech firms seek to develop technology and to ensure that their solutions standardize across regions of the world.

Developing and effectively managing an alliance is a managerial challenge of the first order. Firms are asked to cooperate rather than compete. The alliance's sponsors normally have different and unique strategies, cultures, and desires for the alliance itself. Both the alliance managers and sponsoring executives must be patient, flexible, and creative in pursuing the goals of the alliance and each sponsor.

Bureaucracy and Beyond

TEACHING NOTE: Let the students be creative. Put them in teams and give them a few minutes to sketch a visual design for an organization that would most appeal to them as employees. Have the designs presented and discussed.

LEARNING ROADMAP
MECHANISTIC STRUCTURES AND THE MACHINE BUREAUCRACY
ORGANIC STRUCTURES AND THE PROFESSIONAL BUREAUCRACY
HYBRID STRUCTURES

Bureaucracies rely on a division of labor, hierarchical control, promotion by merit with career opportunities for employees, and administration by rule.

Modern complex societies are not just dominated by organizations but contain a number of large powerful organizations know as *bureaucracies*. In OB this term has a special meaning, beyond its negative connotation. The German sociologist Max Weber suggested that organizations would thrive if they became bureaucracies by emphasizing legal authority, logic, and order.[38] Ideally, **bureaucracies** rely on a division of labor, hierarchical control, promotion by merit with career opportunities for employees, and administration by rule.

Weber argued that the rational and logical idea of bureaucracy was superior to building the firm based on charisma or cultural tradition. The "charismatic" ideal-type organization was overly reliant on the talents of one individual and could fail when the leader leaves. Too much reliance on cultural traditions blocked innovation, stifled efficiency, and was often unfair. Since the bureaucracy prizes efficiency, order, and logic, Weber hoped that it could also be fair to employees and provide more freedom for individual expression than is allowed when tradition dominates or dictators rule. Many interpreted Weber as suggesting that bureaucracy or some variation of this ideal form, although far from perfect, would dominate modern society.[39] For large organizations, the bureaucratic form is predominant. Yet, the bureaucracy poses a series of challenges for managers, including the following:

Challenges posed by bureaucracies ▶

- Overspecialization with conflicts between highly specialized units
- Overreliance on the chain of command rather than bottom-up problem solving
- Objectification of senior executives as rulers rather than problem solvers for others
- Overemphasis on conformity
- Rules as ends in and of themselves

Just as interpretations of Weber have evolved over time, so has the notion of a bureaucracy.[40] We will discuss some popular basic types of bureaucracies: the mechanistic structure and machine bureaucracy, the organic structure and professional bureaucracy,

OB IN POPULAR CULTURE

Hierarchy and *Ratatouille*

Buena Vista/Photofest

Bureaucracy tends to a get a bad rap most of the time. Yet organizations must have rules and structure to operate effectively. Large companies organize into departments and distribute responsibilities and authority in hierarchical fashion. This is known as vertical specialization, the division of labor that shows authority relationships, decision making, and the chain of command. This is usually spelled out in an organization chart.

Pixar's film *Ratatouille* is the story of a rat named Remy that aspires to be a great cook like his hero, Chef Auguste Gusteau. Following an accident, Remy is separated from the rest of his family and finds himself in Paris. He is soon peering down through a skylight into the restaurant made famous by the now departed Gusteau. He observes the cooking activity taking place in the kitchen and can name all the roles and relationships that exist between the staff. Guided by an apparition of Gusteau himself, he learns that all positions in the kitchen are critical—even that of the garbage boy.

What we learn from *Ratatouille* is that hierarchy and authority are necessary to keep the work flowing smoothly. Although some positions have more power and responsibility than others, each individual has a contribution to make and must be willing to do so if the organization is to be successful.

Get to Know Yourself Better By now, you are probably quite used to participating in organizations with a lot of structure. Take a look at Assessment 21, Organizational Design Preference, in the *OB Skills Workbook* to determine your comfort level with this environment. If you score high, you will probably function effectively in an organization with a high degree of vertical specialization. On the other hand, if your score is low, you may like working for a smaller, newer company in which the structure is a more flexible.

---

and some hybrid approaches. Each type is a different mix of the basic elements discussed in this chapter, and each mix yields firms with a slightly different blend of capabilities and natural tendencies.

■ Mechanistic Structures and the Machine Bureaucracy

The **mechanistic (or machine) type of bureaucracy** emphasizes vertical specialization and control.[41] Organizations of this type stress rules, policies, and procedures; specify techniques for decision making; and emphasize developing well-documented control systems backed by a strong middle management and supported by a centralized staff. There is often extensive use of the functional pattern of departmentation throughout the company. Henry Mintzberg uses the term *machine bureaucracy* to describe an organization structured in this manner.[42]

The mechanistic design results in a management emphasis on routine for efficiency. Firms often used this design in pursuing a strategy of becoming a low-cost leader. Until the implementation of new information systems, most large-scale firms in basic industries were machine bureaucracies. Included in this long list were all of the auto firms, banks, insurance companies, steel mills, large retail establishments, and government offices. Efficiency was achieved through extensive vertical and

The **mechanistic (or machine) type of bureaucracy** emphasizes vertical specialization and control.

horizontal specialization tied together with elaborate controls and impersonal coordination mechanisms.

There are, however, limits to the benefits of specialization backed by rigid controls. Employees generally do not like rigid designs, so motivation becomes a problem. Unions further solidify narrow job descriptions by demanding fixed work rules and regulations to protect employees from the extensive vertical controls. In short, using a machine bureaucracy can hinder an organization's capacity to adjust to subtle external changes or new technologies.

■ Organic Structures and the Professional Bureaucracy

The **organic (or professional) type of bureaucracy** is less vertically oriented than its mechanistic counterpart is; it emphasizes horizontal specialization. Procedures are minimal, and those that do exist are not as formalized. The organization relies on the judgments of experts and personal means of coordination. When controls are used, they are often based on professional standards, training, and individual reinforcement. Staff units are placed toward the middle of the organization. Because this is a popular design in professional firms, Mintzberg calls it a professional bureaucracy.[43]

Your university is probably a professional bureaucracy that looks like a broad, flat pyramid with a large bulge in the center for the professional staff. Power in this ideal type rests with knowledge. Other examples of organic types include most hospitals and social service agencies.

Compared to the machine bureaucracy, the professional bureaucracy is better for problem solving and for serving individual customer needs. Since lateral relations and coordination are emphasized, centralized direction by senior management is less intense. This type is good at detecting external changes and adjusting to new technologies, but at the sacrifice of responding to central management direction. Firms using this pattern have found it easier to pursue product quality, quick response to customers, and innovation as strategies.

■ Hybrid Structures

Many large firms have found that neither the mechanistic nor the organic approach is suitable for all of their operations. Adopting a machine bureaucracy overloads senior management and yields too many levels of management. Yet, adopting an organic type would mean losing control and becoming too inefficient. Senior managers may opt for one of a number of hybrid types.

We have briefly introduced two of the more common hybrid types. One is an extension of the divisional pattern of departmentation and is sometimes called a divisional firm. Here, the firm is composed of quasi-independent divisions so that different divisions can be more or less organic or mechanistic. Although the divisions may be treated as separate businesses, they often share a similar mission and systems goals.[44] When adopting this hybrid type, each division can pursue a different strategy.

A second hybrid is the true conglomerate. A **conglomerate** is a single corporation that contains a number of unrelated businesses. On the surface, these firms look like divisionalized firms, but when the various businesses of the divisions are unrelated, the term *conglomerate* is applied.[45] For instance, General Electric is a conglomerate that has divisions in unrelated businesses and industries, ranging from producing light bulbs, to designing and servicing nuclear reactors, to building jet engines. Most state and federal entities are also, by necessity, conglomerates. For instance, a state governor is the chief executive officer of those units concerned with higher education, welfare, prisons, highway construction and maintenance, police, and the like.

The **organic (or professional) type of bureaucracy** emphasizes horizontal specialization, use of personal coordination devices, and professional-based controls.

A **conglomerate** is a single corporation that contains a number of unrelated businesses.

| WORTH CONSIDERING | ...OR BEST AVOIDED? |

Do Flexible Factories Have Staying Power?

Flexibility at Harley Davidson's plant in York, Pennsylvania, means building "hogs" with less than half the workers previously employed. The factory has been consolidated from several buildings into one efficient facility. The thousand workers now fall into just five job classifications, versus sixty-two previously, and they perform many different tasks with a variety of skills. At least 10 percent are considered "casual workers" who are employed only as needed to meet production schedules. In addition, lots of robots are doing jobs once handled by human hands and computers are everywhere.

The company-wide cost savings due to Harley's new manufacturing strategy are estimated at $275+ million. It's enough to keep U.S.-made bikes on the road and at least some manufacturing jobs still in American hands. But flexibility means that workers take on more responsibilities, must learn more skills, and have to be "flexible" in working with management to solve problems and keep the production line moving.

Flexible manufacturing seems to be a way of saving some manufacturing jobs that might otherwise be lost overseas. However, companies need to invest in facilities and technology, and workers need to learn new skills and ways of working.

© Greg Dale/National GeographicSociety/Corbis

Do the Analysis

Just as organization structures and cultures are changing, work processes and human resource management practices are, too. Is this a win-win for everyone involved, or are there downsides to this move toward flexibility that may come back to haunt us in the future? Can you identify products or situations where manufacturing flexibility can't work? Overall, can we say that the recession prompted a shift into a new world of manufacturing strength for U.S. firms?

The conglomerate type illustrates three important points about organization structures. First, all structures are combinations of the basic elements. Second, no one structure is always best. What is best is situational and depends on a number of factors such as the size of the organization, its environment, its technology, and, of course, the goals it pursues. Third, no organization stands alone. It is always part of a larger complex network of other organizations and stakeholders.

16 Study Guide

Key Questions and Answers

What is the formal structure of the organization?
- The formal structure is also known as the firm's division of labor.
- The formal structure defines the intended configuration of positions, job duties, and lines of authority among different parts of the enterprise often as depicted in an organizational chart.

- Typically, a chain of command exists to link lower-level workers with senior managers.
- The distinction between line and staff units also indicates how authority is distributed, with line units conducting the major business of the firm and staff providing support.
- Control is the set of mechanisms the organization uses to keep action or outputs within predetermined levels.
- Output controls focus on desired targets and allow managers to use their own methods for reaching these targets.
- Process controls specify the manner in which tasks are to be accomplished through policies, rules, and procedures; formalization and standardization; and total quality management processes.

How is work organized and coordinated?
- Horizontal specialization results in various work units and departments in the organization.
- Three main types or patterns of departmentation are observed: functional, divisional, and matrix. Each pattern has a mix of advantages and disadvantages.
- Organizations may successfully use any type, or a mixture, as long as the strengths of the structure match the needs of the organization.
- Coordination is the set of mechanisms an organization uses to link the actions of separate units into a consistent pattern.
- Personal methods of coordination produce synergy by promoting dialogue, discussion, innovation, creativity, and learning.
- Impersonal methods of control produce synergy by stressing consistency and standardization so that individual pieces fit together.

What is organizational design?
- Organizational design is the process of choosing and implementing a structural configuration for an organization.
- The design of a large organization is far more complex than that of a small firm. Smaller firms often adopt a simple structure because it works, is cheap, and emphasizes the influence of the leader.
- Operations technology and organizational design should be interrelated to ensure that the firm produces the desired goods and/or services. Adhocracy is an organizational design used in technology-intense settings.
- Information technology is the combination of machines, artifacts, procedures, and systems used to gather, store, analyze, and disseminate information for translating it into knowledge and forms the basis for the virtual organization.
- The environment is more complex when it is richer and more interdependent with higher volatility and greater uncertainty. Firms need not stand alone but can develop network relationships and alliances to cope with greater environmental complexity.

What are bureaucracies and their alternatives?
- The bureaucracy is an ideal form based on legal authority, logic, and order that provides superior efficiency and effectiveness.
- Mechanistic, organic, and hybrid are common types of bureaucracies.
- Hybrid types include the divisionalized firm and the conglomerate. No one type is always superior to the others.

Terms to Know

Adhocracy (p. 366)
Bureaucracies (p. 370)
Centralization (p. 358)
Conglomerates (p. 372)
Control (p. 356)
Coordination (p. 359)
Decentralization (p. 358)
Divisional departmentation (p. 360)
Environmental complexity (p. 368)
Formalization (p. 357)
Functional departmentation (p. 359)
General environment (p. 368)
Horizontal specialization (p. 359)
Information technology (IT) (p. 367)
Interfirm alliances (p. 370)
Line Units (p. 356)
Matrix departmentation (p. 361)
Mechanistic (or machine) type of bureaucracy (p. 371)
Organic (or professional) type of bureaucracy (p. 372)
Operations technology (p. 365)
Organization charts (p. 354)
Output controls (p. 356)
Organizational design (p. 364)
Policy (p. 356)
Procedure (p. 356)
Process controls (p. 356)
Simple design (p. 364)
Span of control (p. 355)
Specific environment (p. 368)
Staff units (p. 356)
Standardization (p. 357)
Vertical specialization (p. 354)

Self-Test 16

Multiple Choice

1. The formal structures of organizations may be shown in a(n) _____.
   (a) environmental diagram
   (b) organization chart
   (c) horizontal diagram
   (d) matrix depiction
   (e) labor assignment chart

2. A major distinction between line and staff units concerns _____.
   (a) the amount of resources each is allowed to utilize
   (b) linkage of their jobs to the goals of the firm
   (c) the amount of education or training they possess
   (d) their use of computer information systems
   (e) their linkage to the outside world

3. Control involves all but _____.
   (a) measuring results
   (b) establishing goals
   (c) taking corrective action
   (d) comparing results with goals
   (e) selecting manpower

4. Grouping individuals and resources in the organization around products, services, clients, territories, or legal entities is an example of _____ specialization.
   (a) divisional
   (b) functional
   (c) matrix
   (d) mixed form
   (e) outsourced specialization

5. Grouping resources into departments by skill, knowledge, and action is the _____ pattern.
   (a) functional
   (b) divisional
   (c) vertical
   (d) means-endchains
   (e) matrix

6. A matrix structure _____.
   (a) reinforces unity of command
   (b) is inexpensive
   (c) is easy to explain to employees
   (d) gives some employees two bosses
   (e) yields a minimum of organizational politics

7. Compared to the machine bureaucracy (mechanistic type), the professional bureaucracy (organic type) _____.
   (a) is more efficient for routine operations
   (b) has more vertical specialization and control
   (c) is larger
   (d) has more horizontal specialization and coordination mechanism
   (e) is smaller

8. Environmental complexity _____.
   (a) refers to the set of alliances formed by senior management
   (b) refers to the overall level of problems and opportunities stemming from munificence, interdependence, and volatility
   (c) is restricted to the general environment of organizations
   (d) is restricted to other organizations with which an organization must interact in order to obtain inputs and dispose of outputs

9. _____ is grouping individuals by skill, knowledge, and action yields.
   (a) Divisional departmentation
   (b) Functional departmentation
   (c) Hybrid structuration
   (d) Matrix departmentation

10. The division of labor through the formation of work units or groups within an organization is called _____.
    (a) control
    (b) vertical specialization
    (c) horizontal specialization
    (d) coordination

11. _____ is the set of mechanisms used in an organization to link the actions of its subunits into a consistent pattern.
    (a) Departmentation
    (b) Coordination
    (c) Control
    (d) Formal authority

12. The design of the organization needs to be adjusted to all but _____.
    (a) the environment of the firm
    (b) the strategy of the firm
    (c) the size of the firm
    (d) the operations and information technology of the firm
    (e) the personnel to be hired by the firm

13. Regarding the organizational design for a small firm compared to a large firm, _____.
    (a) they are almost the same
    (b) they are fundamentally different
    (c) a large firm is just a larger version of a small one
    (d) the small firm has more opportunity to use information technology

14. Adhocracies tend to favor _____.
    (a) vertical specialization and control
    (b) horizontal specialization and coordination
    (c) extensive centralization
    (d) a rigid strategy

15. Which of the following is an accurate statement about an adhocracy?
    (a) The design facilitates information exchange and learning.
    (b) There are many rules and policies.
    (c) Use of IT is always minimal.
    (d) IT handles routine problems efficiently.
    (e) IT is quite common in older industries

▶ Short Response

16. Compare and contrast output goals with systems goals.
17. Describe the types of controls that are used in organizations.
18. Explain why a large firm could not use a simple structure.
19. Describe the effect of operations technology on an organization from both—Thompson's and Woodward's points of view.

▶ Applications Essay

20. Describe some of the side effects of organizational controls in a large mechanistically structured organization such as the United States Postal Service.

Steps to Further Learning 16
Top Choices from *The OB Skills Workbook*

These learning activities from *The OB Skills Workbook* found at the back of the book are suggested for Chapter 16.

Case for Critical Thinking	Team and Experiential Exercises	Self-Assessment Portfolio
• First Community Financial	• Tinkertoys • Organizations Alive • Fast-Food Technology • Alien Invasion • Force-Field Analysis	• A Twenty-First-Century Manager • Group Effectiveness • Organizational Design Preferences

Great jobs aren't easy to get. Career success today requires lots of initiative, self-awareness, and continuous personal improvement. The question is: "Are you ready?"

THE OB SKILLS WORKBOOK

FEATURING
The Jossey-Bass/Pfeiffer Classroom Collection

SUGGESTED USES AND APPLICATIONS OF WORKBOOK MATERIALS

1. Student Leadership Practices Inventory by Kouzes and Posner

Activity	Overview
1. Student Leadership Practices Inventory (LIP)— Student Workbook	This workbook includes a worksheet to help interpret feedback and plan improvement in each leadership practice assessed, sections on how to compare scores with the normative sample and how to share feedback with constituents, and more than 140 actual steps students can take to get results.
2. Student Leadership Practices Inventory— Self	This 30-item inventory will help students evaluate their performance and effectiveness as a leader. Results from the simple scoring process help students prepare plans for personal leadership development.
3. Student Leadership Practices Inventory— Observer	This version of the LPI is used by others to assess the individual's leadership tendencies, thus allowing for comparison with self-perceptions.

2. Learning Styles

Activity	Overview
1. Learning Styles Inventory— Online at: www.wiley.com/college/schermerhorn	This online inventory provides insight into a person's relative strengths on seven alternative approaches to learning, described as Visual Learner, Print Learner, Auditory Learner, Interactive Learner, Haptic Learner, Kinesthetic Learner, and Olfactory Learner.
2. Study Tips for Different Learning Styles	This reading included in the workbook provides study tips for learners with different tendencies and strengths.

3. Self-Assessment Portfolio

See companion Web site for online versions of many assessments: www.wiley.com/college/schermerhorn

Assessment	Suggested Chapter	Cross-References and Integration
1. Managerial Assumptions	1 Introducing Organizational Behavior	leadership
2. A Twenty-First-Century Manager	1 Introducing Organizational Behavior 14 Leader Traits and Behavioral Styles 16 Organizational Structure and Design	leadership; decision making; globalization
3. Turbulence Tolerance Test	1 Introducing Organizational Behavior 2 Diversity, Personality, and Values	perception; individual differences; organizational change and stress
4. Global Readiness Index	4 Emotions, Attitudes, and Job Satisfaction 13 The Leadership Process	diversity; culture; leading; perception; management skills; career readiness

Assessment	Suggested Chapter	Cross-References and Integration
5. Personal Values	4 Emotions, Attitudes, and Job Satisfaction 6 Motivation and Performance	perception; diversity and individual differences; leadership
6. Intolerance for Ambiguity	3 Perception, Attribution, and Learning	perception; leadership
7. Two-Factor Profile	5 Motivation 6 Motivation and Performance	job design; perception; culture; human resource management
8. Are You Cosmopolitan?	6 Motivation and Performance 15 Organizational Culture and Innovation	diversity and individual differences; organizational culture
9. Group Effectiveness	7 The Nature of Teams 8 Teamwork and Team Performance 15 Organizational Culture and Innovation	organizational designs and cultures; leadership
10. Least Preferred Co-worker Scale	14 Leader Traits and Behavior Styles	diversity and individual differences; perception; group dynamics and teamwork
11. Leadership Style	13 The Leadership Process	diversity and individual differences; perception; group dynamics and teamwork
12. "TT" Leadership Style	11 Communication 13 The Leadership Process	diversity and individual differences; perception; group dynamics and teamwork
13. Empowering Others	8 Teamwork and Team Performance 11 Communication 12 Power and Politics	leadership; perception and attribution
14. Machiavellianism	12 Power and Politics	leadership; diversity and individual differences
15. Personal Power Profile	12 Power and Politics	leadership; diversity and individual differences
16. Your Intuitive Ability	9 Decision Making and Creativity	diversity and individual differences
17. Decision-Making Biases	7 The Nature of Teams 9 Decision Making and Creativity	teams and teamwork; communication; perception
18. Conflict Management Strategies	10 Conflict and Negotiation	diversity and individual differences; communication
19. Your Personality Type	2 Diversity, Personality, and Values	diversity and individual differences; job design
20. Time Management Profile	2 Diversity, Personality, and Values	diversity and individual differences
21. Organizational Design Preference	16 Organizational Structure and Design	job design; diversity and individual differences
22. Which Culture Fits You?	15 Organizational Culture and Innovation	perception; diversity and individual differences

4. Team and Experiential Exercises

Exercise	Suggested Chapter(s)	Cross-References and Integration
1. My Best Manager	1 Introducing Organizational Behavior 4 Emotions, Attitudes, and Job Satisfaction	leadership
2. Graffiti Needs Assessment	1 Introducing Organizational Behavior	human resource management; communication
3. My Best Job	1 Introducing Organizational Behavior 6 Motivation and Performance	motivation; job design; organizational cultures
4. What Do You Value in Work?	5 Motivation	diversity and individual differences; performance management and rewards; motivation; job design; decision making
5. My Asset Base	3 Perception, Attribution, and Learning 4 Emotions, Attitudes, and Job Satisfaction	perception and attribution; diversity and individual differences; groups and teamwork; decision making
6. Expatriate Assignments	3 Perception, Attribution, and Learning 15 Organizational Culture and Innovation	perception and attribution; diversity and individual differences; decision making
7. Cultural Cues	13 Leadership Process	perception and attribution; diversity and individual differences; decision making; communication; conflict; groups and teamwork
8. Prejudice in Our Lives	4 Emotions, Attitudes, and Job Satisfaction	perception and attribution; decision making; conflict; groups and teamwork
9. How We View Differences	3 Perception, Attribution, and Learning 4 Emotions, Attitudes, and Job Satisfaction 15 Organizational Culture and Innovation	culture; international; diversity and individual differences; decision making; communication; conflict; groups and teamwork
10. Alligator River Story	3 Perception, Attribution, and Learning	diversity and individual differences; decision making; communication; conflict; groups and teamwork
11. Teamwork and Motivation	5 Motivation	performance management and rewards; groups and teamwork
12. The Downside of Punishment	5 Motivation	motivation; perception and attribution; performance management and rewards
13. Tinkertoys	6 Motivation and Performance 16 Organizational Structure and Design	organizational structure; design and culture; groups and teamwork
14. Job Design Preferences	6 Motivation and Performance	motivation; job design; organizational design; change
15. My Fantasy Job	6 Motivation and Performance	motivation; individual differences; organizational design; change
16. Motivation by Job Enrichment	6 Motivation and Performance	motivation; job design; perception; diversity and individual differences; change

Exercise	Suggested Chapter(s)	Cross-References and Integration
17. Annual Pay Raises	5 Motivation 6 Motivation and Performance	motivation; learning and reinforcement; perception and attribution; decision making; groups and teamwork
18. Serving on the Boundary	7 The Nature of Teams	intergroup dynamics; group dynamics; roles; communication; conflict; stress
19. Eggsperiential Exercise	7 The Nature of Teams	group dynamics and teamwork; diversity and individual differences; communication
20. Scavenger Hunt—Team Building	8 Teamwork and Team Performance	groups; leadership; diversity and individual differences; communication; leadership
21. Work Team Dynamics	8 Teamwork and Team Performance	groups; motivation; decision making; conflict; communication
22. Identifying Team Norms	8 Teamwork and Team Performance	groups; communication; perception and attribution
23. Workgroup Culture	8 Teamwork and Team Performance 15 Organizational Culture and Innovation	groups; communication; perception and attribution; job design; organizational culture
24. The Hot Seat	8 Teamwork and Team Performance	groups; communication; conflict and negotiation; power and politics
25. Interview a Leader	12 Power and Politics 13 The Leadership Process	performance management and rewards; groups and teamwork; new workplace; organizational change and stress
26. Leadership Skills Inventories	14 Leader Traits and Behavioral Styles	individual differences; perception and attribution; decision making
27. Leadership and Participation in Decision Making	13 The Leadership Process	decision making; communication; motivation; groups; teamwork
28. My Best Manager: Revisited	12 Power and Politics	diversity and individual differences; perception and attribution
29. Active Listening	11 Communication	group dynamics and teamwork; perception and attribution
30. Upward Appraisal	6 Motivation and Performance 11 Communication	perception and attribution; performance management and rewards
31. 360° Feedback	6 Motivation and Performance 11 Communication	communication; perception and attribution; performance management and rewards
32. Role Analysis Negotiation	9 Decision Making and Creativity	communication; group dynamics and teamwork; making perception and attribution; communication; decision making
33. Lost at Sea	9 Decision Making and Creativity	communication; group dynamics and teamwork; making conflict and negotiation
34. Entering the Unknown	9 Decision Making and Creativity 10 Conflict and Negotiation	communication; group dynamics and teamwork; perception and attribution
35. Vacation Puzzle	10 Conflict and Negotiation	conflict and negotiation; communication; power; leadership

Exercise	Suggested Chapter(s)	Cross-References and Integration
36. The Ugli Orange	9 Decision Making and Creativity 10 Conflict and Negotiation	communication; decision making
37. Conflict Dialogues	10 Conflict and Negotiation	conflict; communication; feedback; perception; stress
38. Force-Field Analysis	9 Decision Making and Creativity	decision making; organization structures, designs, cultures
39. Organizations Alive!	16 Organizational Structure and Design	organizational design and culture; performance management and rewards
40. Fast-Food Technology	15 Organizational Culture and Innovation 16 Organizational Structure and Design	organizational design; organizational culture; job design
41. Alien Invasion	15 Organizational Culture and Innovation 16 Organizational Structure and Design	organizational structure and design; international; diversity and individual differences; perception and attribution
42. Power Circles Exercise	12 Power and Politics	influence; power; leadership; change management

5. Class Activities from the *Pfeiffer Training Annuals*

Activity	Suggested Part(s)	Overview
A. Sweet Tooth: Bonding Strangers into a Team	Parts 1, 3, 4	perception, teamwork, decision making, communication
B. Interrogatories: Identifying Issues and Needs	Parts 1, 3, 4	current issues, group dynamics, communication
C. Decode: Working with Different Instructions	Parts 3, 4	decision making, leadership, conflict, teamwork
D. Choices: Learning Effective Conflict Management Strategies	Parts 1, 2, 3, 4, 5	conflict, negotiation, communication, decision making
E. Internal/External Motivators: Encouraging Creativity	Parts 2, 4, 5	creativity, motivation, job design, decision making
F. Quick Hitter: Fostering the Creative Spirit	Parts 4, 5	creativity, decision making, communication

STUDENT LEADERSHIP PRACTICES INVENTORY

Student Workbook

James M. Kouzes
Barry Z. Posner, Ph.D.

Jossey-Bass Publishers • San Francisco

Jossey-Bass/Pfeiffer Classroom Collection

 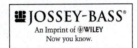

Copyright © 1998 by James M. Kouzes and Barry Z. Posner. All rights reserved.

ISBN: 0-7879-4425-4

Jossey-Bass is a registered trademark of Jossey-Bass Inc., a Wiley Company.

No part of this publication may be reproduced, stored in a retrieval system, or transmitted in any form or by any means, electronic, mechanical, photocopying, recording, scanning, or otherwise, except as permitted under Sections 107 or 108 of the 1976 United States Copyright Act, without either the prior written permission of the Publisher or authorization through payment of the appropriate per-copy fee to the Copyright Clearance Center, 222 Rosewood Drive, Danvers, MA 01923, (978) 750-8400, fax (978) 750-4744. Requests to the Publisher for permission should be addressed to the Permissions Department, John Wiley & Sons, Inc., 111 River Street, Hoboken, NJ. 07030-5774, (201) 748-6011, fax (201) 748-6008. permreq@wiley.com.

Printed in the United States of America.

Jossey-Bass books and products are available through most bookstores. To contact Jossey-Bass directly, call (888) 378-2537, fax to (800) 605-2665, or visit our Web site at www.josseybass.com.

Substantial discounts on bulk quantities of Jossey-Bass books are available to corporations, professional associations, and other organizations. For details and discount information, contact the special sales department at Jossey-Bass.

Printing 10 9 8 7 6 5 4 3 2

This book is printed on acid-free, recycled stock that meets or exceeds the minimum GPO and EPA requirements for recycled paper.

CONTENTS

CHAPTER 1
Leadership: What People Do When They're Leading
W-14

CHAPTER 2
Questions Frequently Asked About the Student LPI
W-15

CHAPTER 3
Recording Your Scores
W-17

CHAPTER 4
Interpreting Your Scores
W-20

CHAPTER 5
Summary and Action-Planning Worksheets
W-24

About the Authors
W-26

People WHO BECOME
leaders
DON'T *always* **seek**
THE **challenges**
THEY **face.**
CHALLENGES
also SEEK **leaders.**

1
Leadership: What People Do When They're Leading

"*Leadership is everyone's business.*" That's the conclusion we have come to after nearly two decades of research into the behaviors and actions of people who are making a difference in their organizations, clubs, teams, classes, schools, campuses, communities, and even their families. We found that leadership is an observable, learnable set of practices. Contrary to some myths, it is not a mystical and ethereal process that cannot be understood by ordinary people. Given the opportunity for feedback and practice, those with the desire and persistence to lead—to make a difference—can substantially improve their ability to do so.

The *Leadership Practices Inventory* (LPI) is part of an extensive research project into the everyday actions and behaviors of people, at all levels and across a variety of settings, as they are leading. Through our research we identified five practices that are common to all leadership experiences. In collaboration with others, we extended our findings to student leaders and to school and college environments and created the student version of the LPI.[1] The LPI is a tool, not a test, designed to assess your current leadership skills. It will identify your areas of strength as well as areas of leadership that need to be further developed.

The *Student LPI* helps you discover the extent to which you (in your role as a leader of a student group or organization) engage in the following five leadership practices:

Challenging the Process. Leaders are pioneers—people who seek out new opportunities and are willing to change the status quo. They innovate, experiment, and explore ways to improve the organization. They treat mistakes as learning experiences. Leaders also stay prepared to meet whatever challenges may confront them. *Challenging the Process* involves

- Searching for opportunities
- Experimenting and taking risks

As an example of Challenging the Process, one student related how innovative thinking helped him win a student class election: "I challenged the process in more than one way. First, I wanted people to understand that elections are not necessarily popularity contests, so I campaigned on the issues and did not promise things that could not possibly be done. Second, I challenged the incumbent positions. They thought they would win easily because they were incumbents, but I showed them that no one has an inherent right to a position."

Challenging the Process for a student serving as treasurer of her sorority meant examining and abandoning some of her leadership beliefs: "I used to believe, 'If you want to do something right, do it yourself.' I found out the hard way that this is impossible to do. . . . One day I was ready to just give up the position because I could no longer handle all of the work. My adviser noticed that I was overwhelmed, and she turned to me and said three magic words: 'Use your committee.' The best piece of advice I would pass along about being an effective leader is that it is okay to experiment with letting others do the work."

---

[1]For more information on our original work, see Barry Z. Posner and James M. Kouznes, *The Leadership Challenge: How to Keep Getting Extraordinary Things Done in Organizations* (San Francisco: Jossey-Bass Publishers, 1995).

Inspiring a Shared Vision. Leaders look toward and beyond the horizon. They envision the future with a positive and hopeful outlook. Leaders are expressive and attract other people to their organization and teams through their genuineness. They communicate and show others how their interests can be met through commitment to a common purpose. *Inspiring a Shared Vision* involves

- Envisioning an uplifting future
- Enlisting others in a common vision

Describing his experience as president of his high school class, one student wrote: "It was our vision to get the class united and to be able to win the spirit trophy.... I told my officers that we could do anything we set our minds on. Believe in yourself and believe in your ability to accomplish things."

Enabling Others to Act. Leaders infuse people with energy and confidence, developing relationships based on mutual trust. They stress collaborative goals. They actively involve others in planning, giving them discretion to make their own decisions. Leaders ensure that people feel strong and capable. *Enabling Others to Act* involves

- Fostering collaboration
- Strengthening people

It is not necessary to be in a traditional leadership position to put these principles into practice. Here is an example from a student who led his team as a team member, not from a traditional position of power: "I helped my team members feel strong and capable by encouraging everyone to practice with the same amount of intensity that they played games with. Our practices improved throughout the year, and by the end of the year had reached the point I was striving for: complete involvement among all players, helping each other to perform at our very best during practice times."

Modeling the Way. Leaders are clear about their personal values and beliefs. They keep people and projects on course by behaving consistently with these values and modeling how they expect others to act. Leaders also plan projects and break them down into achievable steps, creating opportunities for small wins. By focusing on key priorities, they make it easier for others to achieve goals. *Modeling the Way* involves

- Setting the example
- Achieving small wins

Working in a business environment taught one student the importance of Modeling the Way. She writes: "I proved I was serious because I was the first one on the job and the last one to leave. I came prepared to work and make the tools available to my crew. I worked alongside them and in no way portrayed an attitude of superiority. Instead, we were in this together."

Encouraging the Heart. Leaders encourage people to persist in their efforts by linking recognition with accomplishments and visibly recognizing contributions to the common vision. They express pride in the achievements of the group or organization, letting others know that their efforts are appreciated. Leaders also find ways to celebrate milestones. They nurture a team spirit, which enables people to sustain continued efforts. *Encouraging the Heart* involves

- Recognizing individual contributions
- Celebrating team accomplishments

While organizing and running a day camp, one student recognized volunteers and celebrated accomplishments through her actions. She explains: "We had a pizza party with the children on the last day of the day camp. Later, the volunteers were sent thank you notes and 'valuable volunteer awards' personally signed by the day campers. The pizza party, thank you notes, and awards served to encourage the hearts of the volunteers in the hopes that they might return for next year's day camp."

> **Somewhere,**
> sometime,
> THE *leader within*
> EACH OF US
> MAY get
> THE CALL
> *to* STEP **forward.**

2
Questions Frequently Asked About the *Student LPI*

Question 1: What are the right answers?

Answer: There are no universal right answers when it comes to leadership. Research indicates that the more frequently you are perceived as engaging in the behavior and actions identified in the *Student LPI,* the more likely it is that you will be perceived as an effective leader. The higher your scores on the Student LPI-Observer, the more others perceive you as (1) having personal credibility, (2) being effective in running meetings, (3) successfully representing your organization or group to non-members (4) generating a sense of enthusiasm and cooperation, and (5) having a high-performing team. In addition, findings show a strong and positive relationship between the extent to which people report their leaders engaging in this set of five leadership practices and how motivated, committed, and productive they feel.

Question 2: How reliable and valid is the Student LPI?

Answer: The question of reliability can be answered in two ways. First, the *Student LPI* has shown sound psychometric properties. The scale for each leadership practice is internally reliable, meaning that the statements within each practice are highly correlated with one another. Second, results of multivariate analyses indicate that the statements within each leadership practice are more highly correlated (or associated) with one another than they are between the five leadership practices.

In terms of validity (or "So what difference do the scores make?"), the *Student LPI* has good face validity and predictive validity. This means, first, that the results make sense to people. Second, scores on the *Student LPI* significantly differentiate high-performing leaders from their less successful counterparts. Whether measured by the leader, his or her peers, or student personnel administrators, those student leaders who engage more frequently, rather than less frequently, in the five leadership practices are more effective.

Question 3: Should my perceptions of my leadership practices be consistent with the ratings other people give me?

Answer: Research indicates that trust in the leader is essential if other people (for example, fellow members of a group, team, or organization) are going to follow that person over time. People must experience the leader as believable, credible, and trustworthy. Trust—whether in a leader or any other person—is developed through consistency in behavior. Trust is further established when words and deeds are congruent.

This does not mean, however, that you will always be perceived in exactly the same way by every person in every situation. Some people may not see you as often as others do, and therefore they may rate you differently on the same behavior. Some people simply may not know you as well as others do. Also you may appropriately behave differently in different situations, such as in a crisis versus during more stable times. Others may have different expectations of you, and still others may perceive the rating descriptions (such as "once in a while" or "fairly often") differently.

Therefore, the key issue is not whether your self-ratings and the ratings from others are exactly the same, but whether people perceive consistency between what you say you do and what you actually do. The only way you can know the answer to this question is to solicit feedback. The Student LPI-Observer has been designed for this purpose.

Research indicates that people tend to see themselves more positively than others do. The Student LPI-Self norms are consistent with this general trend; scores on the Student LPI-Self tend to be somewhat higher than scores on the Student LPI-Observer. *Student LPI* scores also tend to be higher than LPI scores of experienced managers and executives in the private and public sector.

Question 4: Can I change my leadership practices?

Answer: It is certainly possible—even for experienced people—to learn new skills. You will increase your chances of changing your behavior if you receive feedback on what level you have achieved with a particular skill, observe a positive model of that skill, set some improvement goals for yourself, practice the skill, ask for updated feedback on your performance, and then set new goals. The practices that are assessed with the *Student LPI* fall into the category of learnable skills.

But some things can be changed only if there is a strong and genuine inner desire to make a difference. For example, enthusiasm for a cause is unlikely to be developed through education or job assignments; it must come from within.

Use the information from the *Student LPI* to better understand how you currently behave as a leader, both from your own perspective and from the perspective of others. Note where there are consistencies and inconsistencies. Understand which leadership behaviors and practices you feel comfortable engaging in and which you feel uncomfortable with. Determine which leadership behaviors and practices you can improve on, and take steps to improve your leadership skills and gain confidence in leading other people and groups. The following sections will help you to become more effective in leadership.

> **Perhaps** NONE OF
> us knows
> OUR **true strength**
> UNTIL **challenged**
> TO **bring**
> **it** forth.

3
Recording Your Scores

On pages W-17 through W-20 are grids for recording your *Student LPI* scores. The first grid (Challenging the Process) is for recording scores for items 1, 6, 11, 16, 21, and 26 from the Student LPI-Self and Student LPI-Observer. These are the items that relate to behaviors involved in Challenging the Process, such as searching for opportunities, experimenting, and taking risks. An abbreviated form of each item is printed beside the grid as a handy reference.

In the first column, which is headed "Self-Rating," write the scores that you gave yourself. If others were asked to complete the Student LPI-Observer and if the forms were returned to you, enter their scores in the columns (A, B, C, D, E, and so on) under the heading "Observers' Ratings." Simply transfer the numbers from page W-18 of each Student LPI-Observer to your scoring grids, using one column for each observer. For example, enter the first observer's scores in column A, the second observer's scores in column B, and so on. The grids provide space for the scores of as many as ten observers.

After all scores have been entered for Challenging the Process, total each column in the row marked "Totals." Then add all of the totals for observers; do not include the "self" total. Write this grand total in the space marked "Total of All Observers' Scores." To obtain the average, divide the grand total by the number of people who completed the Student LPI-Observer. Write this average in the blank provided. The sample grid shows how the grid would look with scores for self and five observers entered.

Sample Grid with Scores from Self and Five Observers

	SELF-RATING	OBSERVERS' RATINGS									
		A	B	C	D	E	F	G	H	I	J
1. Seeks challenge	5	4	2	4	4	2					
6. Keeps current	4	4	3	4	4	3					
11. Initiates experiment	3	3	2	2	2	1					
16. Looks for ways to improve	4	3	2	3	5	3					
21. Asks "What can we learn?"	2	3	2	3	3	2					
26. Lets others take risks	5	3	3	2	3	2					
TOTALS	23	20	14	18	21	13					

TOTAL OF ALL OBSERVERS' SCORES: 86

TOTAL SELF-RATING: __23__

AVERAGE OF ALL OBSERVERS: __17.2__

The other four grids should be completed in the same manner.

The second grid (Inspiring a Shared Vision) is for recording scores to the items that pertain to envisioning the future and enlisting the support of others. These include items 2, 7, 12, 17, 22, and 27.

The third grid (Enabling Others to Act) pertains to items 3, 8, 13, 18, 23, and 28, which involve fostering collaboration and strengthening others.

The fourth grid (Modeling the Way) pertains to items about setting an example and planning small wins. These include items 4, 9, 14, 19, 24, and 29.

The fifth grid (Encouraging the Heart) pertains to items about recognizing contributions and celebrating accomplishments. These are items 5, 10, 15, 20, 25, and 30.

Grids for Recording *Student LPI* Scores

Scores should be recorded on the following grids in accordance with the instructions on page W-17. As you look at individual scores, remember the rating system that was used:

- "1" means that you *rarely or seldom* engage in the behavior.
- "2" means that you engage in the behavior *once in a while*.
- "3" means that you *sometimes* engage in the behavior.
- "4" means that you engage in the behavior *fairly often*.
- "5" means that you engage in the behavior *very frequently*.

After you have recorded all of your scores and calculated the totals and averages, turn to page W-20 and read the section on interpreting scores.

Challenging the Process

	SELF-RATING	OBSERVERS' RATINGS									
		A	B	C	D	E	F	G	H	I	J
1. Seeks challenge											
6. Keeps current											
11. Initiates experiment											
16. Looks for ways to improve											
21. Asks "What can we learn?"											
26. Lets others take risks											
TOTALS											

TOTAL OF ALL OBSERVERS' SCORES: _____

TOTAL SELF-RATING: _____   AVERAGE OF ALL OBSERVERS: _____

Inspiring a Shared Vision

	SELF-RATING	OBSERVERS' RATINGS									
		A	B	C	D	E	F	G	H	I	J
2. Describes ideal capabilities											
7. Looks ahead and communicates future											
12. Upbeat and positive communicator											
17. Finds common ground											
22. Communicates purpose and meaning											
27. Enthusiastic about possibilities											
TOTALS											

TOTAL OF ALL OBSERVERS' SCORES: _____

TOTAL SELF-RATING: _____   AVERAGE OF ALL OBSERVERS: _____

Enabling Others to Act

	SELF-RATING	OBSERVERS' RATINGS									
		A	B	C	D	E	F	G	H	I	J
3. Includes others in planning											
8. Treats others with respect											
13. Supports decisions of others											
18. Fosters cooperative relationships											
23. Provides freedom and choice											
28. Lets others lead											
TOTALS											

TOTAL OF ALL OBSERVERS' SCORES: _____

TOTAL SELF-RATING: _____   AVERAGE OF ALL OBSERVERS: _____

Modeling the Way

	SELF-RATING	OBSERVERS' RATINGS									
		A	B	C	D	E	F	G	H	I	J
4. Shares beliefs about leading											
9. Breaks projects into steps											
14. Sets personal example											
19. Talks about guiding values											
24. Follows through on promises											
29. Sets clear goals and plans											
TOTALS											

TOTAL OF ALL OBSERVERS' SCORES: _____

TOTAL SELF-RATING: _____   AVERAGE OF ALL OBSERVERS: _____

Encouraging the Heart

	SELF-RATING	OBSERVERS' RATINGS									
		A	B	C	D	E	F	G	H	I	J
5. Encourages other people											
10. Recognizes people's contributions											
15. Praises people for job well done											
20. Gives support and appreciation											
25. Finds ways to publicly celebrate											
30. Tells others about group's good work											
TOTALS											

TOTAL OF ALL OBSERVERS' SCORES

TOTAL SELF-RATING: _____

AVERAGE OF ALL OBSERVERS: _____

> THE unique ROLE
> OF leaders
> IS TO *take us*
> TO places
> WE'VE never
> *been* before.

4
Interpreting Your Scores

This section will help you to interpret your scores by looking at them in several ways and by making notes to yourself about what you can do to become a more effective leader.

Ranking Your Ratings

Refer to the previous chapter, "Recording Your Scores." On each grid, look at your scores in the blanks marked "Total Self-Rating." Each of these totals represents your responses to six statements about one of the five leadership practices. Each of your totals can range from a low of 6 to a high of 30.

In the blanks that follow, write "1" to the left of the leadership practice with the highest total self-rating, "2" by the next-highest total self-rating, and so on. This ranking represents the leadership practices with which you feel most comfortable, second-most comfortable, and so on. The practice you identify with a "5" is the practice with which you feel least comfortable.

Again refer to the previous chapter, but this time look at your scores in the blanks marked "Average of All Observers." The number in each blank is the average score given to you by the people you asked to complete the Student LPI-Observer. Like each of your total self-ratings, this number can range from 6 to 30.

In the blanks that follow, write "1" to the right of the leadership practice with the highest score, "2" by the next-highest score, and so on. This ranking represents the leadership practices that others feel you use most often, second-most often, and so on.

Self		Observers
_____	Challenging the Process	_____
_____	Inspiring a Shared Vision	_____
_____	Enabling Others to Act	_____
_____	Modeling the Way	_____
_____	Encouraging the Heart	_____

Comparing Your Self-Ratings to Observers' Ratings

To compare your Student LPI-Self and Student LPI-Observer assessments, refer to the "Chart for Graphing Your Scores." On the chart, designate your scores on the five leadership practices (Challenging, Inspiring, Enabling, Modeling, and Encouraging) by marking each of these points with a capital "S" (for "Self"). Connect the five resulting "S" scores with a *solid line* and label the end of this line "Self" (see the following sample chart).

If other people provided input through the Student LPI-Observer, designate the average observer scores (see the blanks labeled "Average of All Observers" on the scoring grids) by marking each of the points with a capital "O" (for "Observer"). Then connect the five resulting "O" scores with a *dashed line* and label the end of this line "Observer" (see sample chart). Completing this process will provide you with a graphic representation (one solid and one dashed line) illustrating the relationship between your self-perception and the observations of other people.

Chart for Graphing Your Scores

Chart for Graphing Your Scores

Percentile	Challenging the Process	Inspiring a Shared Vision	Enabling Others to Act	Modeling the Way	Encouraging the Heart
100%	30 29 28 27	30 29 28	30 29	30 29 28 27	30 29
90%	26	27			28
80%	25	26	28	26	27
70%	24	25	27	25	26
60%	23	24	26	24	25
50%	22	23 22	25	23	24
40%	21	21	24	22	23
30%	20	20	23	21	22
20%	19	19 18	22	20 19	21 20
10%	18 17 16 15	17 16 15 14	21 20 19 18	18 17 16	19 18 17 16

Percentile Scores

Look again at the "Chart for Graphing Your Scores." The column to the far left represents the Student LPI-Self percentile rankings for more than 1,200 student leaders. A percentile ranking is determined by the percentage of people who score at or below a given number. For example, if your total self-rating for "Challenging" is at the 60th percentile line on the "Chart for Graphing Your Scores," this means that you assessed yourself higher than 60 percent of all people who have completed the *Student LPI;* you would be in the top 40 percent in this leadership practice.

Studies indicate that a "high" score is one at or above the 70th percentile, a "low" score is one at or below the 30th percentile, and a score that falls between those ranges is considered "moderate."

Using these criteria, circle the "H" (for "High"), the "M" (for "Moderate"), or the "L" (for "Low") for each leadership practice on the following "Range of Scores" table. Compared to other student leaders around the country, where do your leadership practices tend to fall? (Given a "normal distribution," it is expected that most people's scores will fall within the moderate range.)

Range of Scores

In my perception				In others' perception			
Practice	**Rating**			**Practice**	**Rating**		
Challenging the Process	H	M	L	Challenging the Process	H	M	L
Inspiring a Shared Vision	H	M	L	Inspiring a Shared Vision	H	M	L
Enabling Others to Act	H	M	L	Enabling Others to Act	H	M	L
Modeling the Way	H	M	L	Modeling the Way	H	M	L
Encouraging the Heart	H	M	L	Encouraging the Heart	H	M	L

Exploring Specific Leadership Behaviors

Looking at your scoring grids, review each of the thirty items on the *Student LPI* by practice. One or two of the six behaviors within each leadership practice may be higher or lower than the rest. If so, on which specific items is there variation? What do these differences suggest? On which specific items is there agreement? Please write your thoughts in the following space.

Challenging the Process

_____
_____
_____
_____
_____
_____

Inspiring a Shared Vision

_____
_____
_____
_____
_____
_____
_____

Enabling Others to Act

_____
_____
_____
_____
_____

Modeling the Way

_____
_____
_____
_____
_____
_____

Encouraging the Heart

_____
_____
_____
_____
_____
_____

Comparing Observers' Responses to One Another

Study the Student LPI-Observer scores for each of the five leadership practices. Do some respondents' scores differ significantly from others? If so, are the differences localized in the scores of one or two people? On which leadership practices do the respondents agree? On which practices do they disagree? If you try to behave basically the same with all the people who assessed you, how do you explain the difference in ratings? Please write your thoughts in the following space.

_____
_____
_____
_____
_____
_____
_____
_____
_____
_____

Wanting TO LEAD AND
believing THAT
YOU *can lead* ARE THE
departure POINTS
ON THE PATH TO **leadership.**
LEADERSHIP IS AN ART—
A *performing* art—
AND THE **instrument**
IS THE **self.**

5
Summary and Action-Planning Worksheets

Take a few moments to summarize your *Student LPI* feedback by completing the following Strengths and Opportunities Summary Worksheet. Refer to the "Chart for Graphing Your Scores," the "Range of Scores" table, and any notes you have made.

After the summary worksheet you will find some suggestions for getting started on meeting the leadership challenge. With these suggestions in mind, review your *Student LPI* feedback and decide on the actions you will take to become an even more effective leader. Then complete the Action-Planning Worksheet to spell out the steps you will take. (One Action-Planning Worksheet is included in this workbook, but you may want to develop action plans for several practices or behaviors. You can make copies of the blank form before you fill it in or just use a separate sheet of paper for each leadership practice you plan to improve.)

Strengths and Opportunities Summary Worksheet

Strengths

Which of the leadership practices and behaviors are you most comfortable with? Why? Can you do more?

_____
_____
_____
_____
_____
_____
_____

Areas for Improvement

What can you do to use a practice more frequently? What will it take to feel more comfortable?

_____
_____
_____
_____
_____
_____
_____
_____

The following are ten suggestions for getting started on meeting the leadership challenge.

Prescriptions for Meeting the Leadership Challenge

Challenge the Process
- Fix something
- Adopt the "great ideas" of others

Inspire a Shared Vision
- Let others know how you feel
- Recount your "personal best"

Enable Others to Act
- Always say "we"
- Make heroes of other people

Model the Way
- Lead by example
- Create opportunities for small wins

Encourage the Heart
- Write "thank you" notes
- Celebrate, and link your celebrations to your organization's values

Action-Planning Worksheet

1. What would you like to be better able to do?

_____
_____
_____
_____

_____
_____
_____
_____

2. What specific actions will you take?

_____
_____
_____
_____
_____
_____
_____
_____

3. What is the first action you will take? Who will be involved? When will you begin?

Action _____
_____
_____

People Involved _____
_____
_____

Target Date _____

4. Complete this sentence: "I will know I have improved in this leadership skill when. . . ."

_____
_____
_____

5. When will you review your progress? _____

About the Authors

James M. Kouzes is chairman of TPG/Learning Systems, which makes leadership work through practical, performance-oriented learning programs. In 1993 *The Wall Street Journal* cited Jim as one of the twelve most requested "nonuniversity executive-education providers" to U.S. companies. His list of past and present clients includes AT&T, Boeing, Boy Scouts of America, Charles Schwab, Ciba-Geigy, Dell Computer, First Bank System, Honeywell, Johnson & Johnson, Levi Strauss & Co., Motorola, Pacific Bell, Stanford University, Xerox Corporation, and the YMCA.

Barry Z. Posner, Ph.D., is dean of the Leavey School of Business, Santa Clara University, and professor of organizational behavior. He has received several outstanding teaching and leadership awards, has published more than eighty research and practitioner-oriented articles, and currently is on the editorial review boards for *The Journal of Management Education, The Journal of Management Inquiry,* and *The Journal of Business Ethics*. Barry also serves on the board of directors for Public Allies and for The Center for Excellence in Non-Profits. His clients have ranged from retailers to firms in health care, high technology, financial services, manufacturing, and community service agencies.

Kouzes and Posner are co-authors of several bestselling and award-winning leadership books. *The Leadership Challenge: How to Keep Getting Extraordinary Things Done in Organizations* (2nd ed., 1995), with over 800,000 copies in print, has been reprinted in fifteen languages, has been featured in three video programs, and received a Critic's Choice award from the nation's newspaper book review editors. *Credibility: How Leaders Gain and Lose It, Why People Demand It* (1993) was chosen by *Industry Week* as one of the five best management books of the year.

Jossey-Bass is a registered trademark of Jossey-Bass Inc., a Wiley Company.

No part of this publication may be reproduced, stored in a retrieval system, or transmitted in any form or by any means, electronic, mechanical, photocopying, recording, scanning, or otherwise, except as permitted under Sections 107 or 108 of the 1976 United States Copyright Act, without either the prior written permission of the Publisher or authorization through payment of the appropriate percopy fee to the Copyright Clearance Center, 222 Rosewood Drive, Danvers, MA 01923, (978) 750-8400, fax (978) 750-4744. Requests to the Publisher for permission should be addressed to the Permissions Department, John Wiley & Sons, Inc. 111 River Street, Hoboken, NJ, 07030-5774, (201) 748-6011, fax (201) 748-6008.

Jossey-Bass Publishers
350 Sansome Street
San Francisco, California 94104
(888) 378-2537
Fax (800) 605-2665

www.josseybass.com   ISBN: 0-7879-4426-2

STUDENT LEADERSHIP PRACTICES INVENTORY—SELF

Your Name: _____

Instructions

What follows are thirty statements describing various leadership behaviors. Please read each statement carefully. Then rate *yourself* in terms of *how frequently* you engage in the behavior described. *This is not a test* (there are no right or wrong answers).

Consider each statement in the context of the student organization (e.g., club, team, chapter, group, unit, hall, program, project) with which you are most involved. The rating scale provides five choices:

(1) If you RARELY or SELDOM do what is described in the statement, circle 1.
(2) If you do what is described ONCE IN A WHILE, circle 2.
(3) If you SOMETIMES do what is described, circle 3.
(4) If you do what is described FAIRLY OFTEN, circle 4.
(5) If you do what is described VERY FREQUENTLY or ALMOST ALWAYS, circle 5.

Please respond to every statement.

In selecting the response, be realistic about the extent to which you *actually* engage in the behavior. Do *not* answer in terms of how you would like to see yourself or in terms of what you should be doing. Answer in terms of how you *typically behave*. The usefulness of the feedback from this inventory will depend on how honest you are with yourself about how frequently you actually engage in each of these behaviors.

For example, the first statement is "I look for opportunities that challenge my skills and abilities." If you believe you do this "once in a while," circle 2. If you believe you look for challenging opportunities "fairly often," circle 4.

When you have responded to all thirty statements, please transfer your responses as instructed. Thank you.

STUDENT LEADERSHIP PRACTICES INVENTORY-SELF

How frequently do you typically engage in the following behaviors and actions? *Circle* the number that applies to each statement.

1 SELDOM OR RARELY	2 ONCE IN A WHILE	3 SOMETIMES	4 FAIRLY OFTEN	5 VERY FREQUENTLY

1. I look for opportunities that challenge my skills and abilities.	1	2	3	4	5
2. I describe to others in our organization what we should be capable of accomplishing.	1	2	3	4	5
3. I include others in planning the activities and programs of our organization.	1	2	3	4	5
4. I share my beliefs about how things can be run most effectively within our organization.	1	2	3	4	5
5. I encourage others as they work on activities and programs in our organization.	1	2	3	4	5
6. I keep current on events and activities that might affect our organization.	1	2	3	4	5
7. I look ahead and communicate about what I believe will affect us in the future.	1	2	3	4	5
8. I treat others with dignity and respect.	1	2	3	4	5
9. I break our organization's projects down into manageable steps.	1	2	3	4	5
10. I make sure that people in our organization are recognized for their contributions.	1	2	3	4	5
11. I take initiative in experimenting with the way we do things in our organization.	1	2	3	4	5
12. I am upbeat and positive when talking about what our organization is doing.	1	2	3	4	5
13. I support the decisions that other people in our organization make on their own.	1	2	3	4	5
14. I set a personal example of what I expect from other people.	1	2	3	4	5
15. I praise people for a job well done.	1	2	3	4	5
16. I look for ways to improve whatever project or task I am involved in.	1	2	3	4	5

(continued)

17. I talk with others about how their own interests can be met by working toward a common goal.	1	2	3	4	5
18. I foster cooperative rather than competitive relationships among people I work with.	1	2	3	4	5
19. I talk about the values and principles that guide my actions.	1	2	3	4	5
20. I give people in our organization support and express appreciation for their contributions.	1	2	3	4	5
21. I ask, "What can we learn from this experience?" when things do not go as we expected.	1	2	3	4	5
22. I speak with conviction about the higher purpose and meaning of what we are doing.	1	2	3	4	5
23. I give others a great deal of freedom and choice in deciding how to do their work.	1	2	3	4	5
24. I follow through on the promises and commitments I make in this organization.	1	2	3	4	5
25. I find ways for us to celebrate our accomplishments publicly.	1	2	3	4	5
26. I let others experiment and take risks even when outcomes are uncertain.	1	2	3	4	5
27. I show my enthusiasm and excitement about what our organization is doing.	1	2	3	4	5
28. I provide opportunities for others to take on leadership responsibilities.	1	2	3	4	5
29. I make sure that we set goals and make specific plans for the projects we undertake.	1	2	3	4	5
30. I make it a point to tell others about the good work done by our organization.	1	2	3	4	5

Transferring the Scores

After you have responded to the thirty statements on the previous two pages, please transfer your responses to the blanks. This will make it easier to record and score your responses. Notice that the numbers of the statements are listed *horizontally*. Make sure that the number you assigned to each statement is transferred to the appropriate blank. Fill in a response for every item.

1. _____   2. _____   3. _____   4. _____   5. _____
6. _____   7. _____   8. _____   9. _____   10. _____
11. _____   12. _____   13. _____   14. _____   15. _____
16. _____   17. _____   18. _____   19. _____   20. _____
21. _____   22. _____   23. _____   24. _____   25. _____
26. _____   27. _____   28. _____   29. _____   30. _____

Further Instructions

Please write your name here: _____

Please bring this form with you to the workshop (seminar or class) or return this form to:

_____

_____

_____

If you are interested in feedback from other people, ask them to complete the Student LPI-Observer, which provides you with perspectives on your leadership behaviors as perceived by others.

STUDENT LEADERSHIP PRACTICES INVENTORY — OBSERVER

Name of Leader: _____

Instructions

What follows are thirty descriptive statements about various leadership behaviors. Please read each statement carefully. Then rate *the person who asked you to complete this form* in terms of *how frequently* he or she typically engages in the described behavior. *This is not a test* (there are no right or wrong answers).

Consider each statement in the context of the student organization (e.g., club, team, chapter, group, unit, hall, program, project) with which that person is most involved or with which you have had the greatest opportunity to observe him or her. The rating scale provides five choices:

(1) If this person RARELY or SELDOM does what is described in the statement, circle 1.
(2) If this person does what is described ONCE IN A WHILE, circle 2.
(3) If this person SOMETIMES does what is described, circle 3.
(4) If this person does what is described FAIRLY OFTEN, circle 4.
(5) If this person does what is described VERY FREQUENTLY or ALMOST ALWAYS, circle 5.

Please respond to every statement.

In selecting the response, be realistic about the extent to which this person *actually* engages in the behavior. Do *not* answer in terms of how you would like to see this person behaving or in terms of what this person should be doing. Answer in terms of how he or she *typically behaves*. The usefulness of the feedback from this inventory will depend on how honest you are about how frequently you observe this person actually engaging in each of these behaviors.

For example, the first statement is, "He or she looks for opportunities that challenge his or her skills and abilities." If you believe this person does this "once in a while," circle 2. If you believe he or she looks for challenging opportunities "fairly often," circle 4.

When you have responded to all thirty statements, please transfer your responses as instructed. Thank you.

STUDENT LEADERSHIP PRACTICES INVENTORY — OBSERVER

How frequently does this person typically engage in the following behaviors and actions? *Circle* the number that applies to each statement:

1	2	3	4	5
SELDOM OR RARELY	**ONCE IN A WHILE**	**SOMETIMES**	**FAIRLY OFTEN**	**VERY FREQUENTLY**

He or she:

1. looks for opportunities that challenge his or her skills and abilities.	1	2	3	4	5
2. describes to others in our organization what we should be capable of accomplishing.	1	2	3	4	5
3. includes others in planning the activities and programs of our organization.	1	2	3	4	5
4. shares his or her beliefs about how things can be run most effectively within our organization.	1	2	3	4	5
5. encourages others as they work on activities and programs in our organization.	1	2	3	4	5
6. keeps current on events and activities that might affect our organization.	1	2	3	4	5
7. looks ahead and communicates about what he or she believes will affect us in the future.	1	2	3	4	5
8. treats others with dignity and respect.	1	2	3	4	5
9. breaks our organization's projects down into manageable steps.	1	2	3	4	5
10. makes sure that people in our organization are recognized for their contributions.	1	2	3	4	5
11. takes initiative in experimenting with the way we do things in our organization.	1	2	3	4	5
12. is upbeat and positive when talking about what our organization is doing.	1	2	3	4	5
13. supports the decisions that other people in our organization make on their own.	1	2	3	4	5
14. sets a personal example of what he or she expects from other people.	1	2	3	4	5
15. praises people for a job well done.	1	2	3	4	5
16. looks for ways to improve whatever project or task he or she is involved in.	1	2	3	4	5
17. talks with others about how their own interests can be met by working toward a common goal.	1	2	3	4	5
18. fosters cooperative rather than competitive relationships among people he or she works with.	1	2	3	4	5
19. talks about the values and principles that guide his or her actions.	1	2	3	4	5
20. gives people in our organization support and expresses appreciation for their contributions.	1	2	3	4	5
21. asks "What can we learn from this experience?" when things do not go as we expected.	1	2	3	4	5
22. speaks with conviction about the higher purpose and meaning of what we are doing.	1	2	3	4	5
23. gives others a great deal of freedom and choice in deciding how to do their work.	1	2	3	4	5
24. follows through on the promises and commitments he or she makes in this organization.	1	2	3	4	5
25. finds ways for us to celebrate our accomplishments publicly.	1	2	3	4	5
26. lets others experiment and take risks even when outcomes are uncertain.	1	2	3	4	5
27. shows his or her enthusiasm and excitement about what our organization is doing.	1	2	3	4	5
28. provides opportunities for others to take on leadership responsibilities.	1	2	3	4	5
29. makes sure that we set goals and make specific plans for the projects we undertake.	1	2	3	4	5
30. makes it a point to tell others about the good work done by our organization.	1	2	3	4	5

Transferring the Scores

After you have responded to the thirty statements, please transfer your responses to the blanks below. This will make it easier to record and score your responses. Notice that the numbers of the statements are listed *horizontally*. Make sure that the number you assigned to each statement is transferred to the appropriate blank. Fill in a response for every item.

1. _____   2. _____   3. _____   4. _____   5. _____
6. _____   7. _____   8. _____   9. _____   10. _____
11. _____   12. _____   13. _____   14. _____   15. _____
16. _____   17. _____   18. _____   19. _____   20. _____
21. _____   22. _____   23. _____   24. _____   25. _____
26. _____   27. _____   28. _____   29. _____   30. _____

Further Instructions

The preceding scores are for (name of person): _____

Please bring this form with you to the workshop (seminar or class) or return this form to:

_____

_____

_____

ISBN: 0-7879-4427-0

All rights reserved. No part of this publication may be reproduced, stored in a retrieval system, or transmitted, in any form or by any means, electronic, mechanical, photocopying, recording, or otherwise, without the prior written permission of the publisher.

Jossey-Bass Publishers
350 Sansome Street
San Francisco, California 94104
(888) 378-2537
Fax (800) 605-2665

www.josseybass.com

LEARNING STYLE INVENTORY

This is a Wiley resource (www.wiley.com/college/schermerhorn).

Step 1.

Take the Learning Style Instrument at www.wiley.com/college/schermerhorn.

Step 2.

The instrument will give you scores on seven learning styles:

1. Visual learner—focus on visual depictions such as pictures and graphs
2. Print learner—focus on seeing written words
3. Auditory learner—focus on listening and hearing
4. Interactive learner—focus on conversation and verbalization
5. Haptic learner—focus on sense of touch or grasp
6. Kinesthetic learner—focus on physical involvement
7. Olfactory learner—focus on smell and taste

Step 3.

Consider your top four rankings among the learning styles. They suggest your most preferred methods of learning.

Step 4.

Read the following study tips for the learning styles. Think about how you can take best advantage of your preferred learning styles.

WHAT ARE LEARNING STYLES?

Have you ever repeated something to yourself over and over to help remember it? Or does your best friend ask you to draw a map to someplace where the two of you are planning to meet, rather than just tell her the directions? If so, then you already have an intuitive sense that people learn in different ways. Researchers in learning theory have developed various categories of learning styles. Some people, for example, learn best by reading or writing. Others learn best by using various senses: seeing, hearing, feeling, tasting, or even smelling. When you understand how you learn best, you can make use of learning strategies that will optimize the time you spend studying. To find out what your particular learning style is, go to www.wiley.com/college/boone and take the learning styles quiz you find there. The quiz will help you determine your primary learning style:

| Visual Learner | Auditory Learner | Haptic Learner | Olfactory Learner |
| Print Learner | Interactive Learner | Kinesthetic Learner | |

Then consult the following information as well as the following pages for study tips for each learning style. This information will help you better understand your learning style and how to apply it to the study of business.

Study Tips for Visual Learners

If you are a Visual Learner, you prefer to work with images and diagrams. It is important that you see information.

Visual Learning
- Draw charts/diagrams during lecture.
- Examine textbook figures and graphs.
- Look at images and videos on WileyPLUS and other Web sites.
- Pay close attention to the charts, drawings, and handouts your instructor uses.
- Underline; use different colors.
- Use symbols, flowcharts, graphs, different arrangements on the page, white spaces.

Visual Reinforcement
- Make flash cards by drawing tables/charts on one side and definition or description on the other side.
- Use art-based worksheets; cover labels on images in text and then rewrite the labels.

Study Tips for Visual Learners (Continued)

- Use colored pencils/markers and colored paper to organize information into types.
- Convert your lecture notes into "page pictures." To do this:
  - Use the visual learning strategies outlined above.
  - Reconstruct images in different ways.
  - Redraw pages from memory.
  - Replace words with symbols and initials.
  - Draw diagrams where appropriate.
  - Practice turning your visuals back into words.

If visual learning is your weakness: If you are not a Visual Learner but want to improve your visual learning, try re-keying tables/charts from the textbook.

Study Tips for Print Learners

If you are a Print Learner, reading will be important, but writing will be much more important.

Print Learning
- Write text lecture notes during lecture.
- Read relevant topics in textbook, especially textbook tables.
- Look at text descriptions in animations and Web sites.
- Use lists and headings.
- Use dictionaries, glossaries, and definitions.
- Read handouts, textbooks, and supplementary library readings.
- Use lecture notes.

Print Reinforcement
- Rewrite your notes from class, and copy classroom handouts in your own handwriting.
- Make your own flash cards.
- Write out essays summarizing lecture notes or textbook topics.
- Develop mnemonics.
- Identify word relationships.
- Create tables with information extracted from textbook or lecture notes.
- Use text-based worksheets or crossword puzzles.
- Write out words again and again.
- Reread notes silently.
- Rewrite ideas and principles into other words.
- Turn charts, diagrams, and other illustrations into statements.
- Practice writing exam answers.
- Practice with multiple choice questions.
- Write paragraphs, especially beginnings and endings.
- Write your lists in outline form.
- Arrange your words into hierarchies and points.

If print learning is your weakness: If you are not a Print Learner but want to improve your print learning, try covering labels of figures from the textbook and writing in the labels.

Study Tips for Auditory Learners

If you are an Auditory Learner, then you prefer listening as a way to learn information. Hearing will be very important, and sound helps you focus.

Auditory Learning
- Make audio recordings during lecture. Do not skip class; hearing the lecture is essential to understanding.
- Play audio files provided by your instructor and textbook.
- Listen to narration of animations.
- Attend lecture and tutorials.
- Discuss topics with students and instructors.
- Explain new ideas to other people.
- Leave spaces in your lecture notes for later recall.
- Describe overheads, pictures, and visuals to somebody who was not in class.

Auditory Reinforcement
- Record yourself reading the notes and listen to the recording.
- Write out transcripts of the audio files.
- Summarize information that you have read, speaking out loud.
- Use a recorder to create self-tests.
- Compose "songs" about information.
- Play music during studying to help focus.
- Expand your notes by talking with others and with information from your textbook.
- Read summarized notes out loud.
- Explain your notes to another auditory learner.
- Talk with the instructor.
- Spend time in quiet places recalling the ideas.
- Say your answers out loud.

If auditory learning is your weakness: If you are not an Auditory Learner but want to improve your auditory learning, try writing out the scripts from pre-recorded lectures.

Study Tips for Interactive Learners

If you are an Interactive Learner, you will want to share your information. A study group will be important.

Interactive Learning
- Ask a lot of questions during lecture or TA review sessions.
- Contact other students, via e-mail or discussion forums, and ask them to explain what they learned.

Interactive Reinforcement
- "Teach" the content to a group of other students.
- Talking to an empty room may seem odd, but it will be effective for you.
- Discuss information with others, making sure that you ask as well as answer questions.
- Work in small group discussions, making a verbal and written discussion of what others say.

If interactive learning is your weakness: If you are not an Interactive Learner but want to improve your interactive learning, try asking your study partner questions and then repeating them to the instructor.

Study Tips for Haptic Learners

If you are a Haptic Learner, you prefer to work with your hands. It is important to physically manipulate material.

Haptic Learning
- Take blank paper to lecture to draw charts/tables/diagrams.
- Using the textbook, run your fingers along the figures and graphs to get a "feel" for shapes and relationships.

Haptic Reinforcement
- Trace words and pictures on flash cards.
- Perform electronic exercises that involve drag-and-drop activities.
- Alternate between speaking and writing information.
- Observe someone performing a task that you would like to learn.
- Make sure you have freedom of movement while studying.

If haptic learning is your weakness: If you are not a Haptic Learner but want to improve your haptic learning, try spending more time in class working with graphs and tables while speaking or writing down information.

Study Tips for Kinesthetic Learners

If you are a Kinesthetic Learner, it will be important that you involve your body during studying.

Kinesthetic Learning
- Ask permission to get up and move during lecture.
- Participate in role-playing activities in the classroom.
- Use all your senses.
- Go to labs; take field trips.
- Listen to real-life examples.
- Pay attention to applications.
- Use trial-and-error methods.
- Use hands-on approaches.

Kinesthetic Reinforcement
- Make flash cards; place them on the floor, and move your body around them.
- Move while you are teaching the material to others.
- Put examples in your summaries.
- Use case studies and applications to help with principles and abstract concepts.
- Talk about your notes with another kinesthetic person.
- Use pictures and photographs that illustrate an idea.
- Write practice answers.
- Role-play the exam situation.

If kinesthetic learning is your weakness: If you are not a Kinesthetic Learner but want to improve your kinesthetic learning, try moving flash cards to reconstruct graphs, tables, and the like.

Study Tips for Olfactory Learners

If you are an Olfactory Learner, you will prefer to use the senses of smell and taste to reinforce learning. This is a rare learning modality.

Olfactory Learning
- During lecture, use different scented markers to identify different types of information.

Olfactory Reinforcement
- Rewrite notes with scented markers.
- If possible, go back to the computer lab to do your studying.
- Burn aromatic candles while studying.
- Try to associate the material that you're studying with a pleasant taste or smell.

If olfactory learning is your weakness: If you are not an Olfactory Learner but want to improve your olfactory learning, try burning an aromatic candle or incense while you study, or eating cookies during study sessions.

SELF-ASSESSMENT PORTFOLIO

Find online versions of many assessments at www.wiley.com/college/schermerhorn.

ASSESSMENT 1

Managerial Assumptions

Instructions
Read the following statements. Write "Yes" if you agree with the statement, or "No" if you disagree with it. Force yourself to take a "yes" or "no" position for every statement.

1. Are good pay and a secure job enough to satisfy most workers?
2. Should a manager help and coach subordinates in their work?
3. Do most people like real responsibility in their jobs?
4. Are most people afraid to learn new things in their jobs?
5. Should managers let subordinates control the quality of their work?
6. Do most people dislike work?
7. Are most people creative?
8. Should a manager closely supervise and direct work of subordinates?
9. Do most people tend to resist change?
10. Do most people work only as hard as they have to?
11. Should workers be allowed to set their own job goals?
12. Are most people happiest off the job?
13. Do most workers really care about the organization they work for?
14. Should a manager help subordinates advance and grow in their jobs?

Scoring
Count the number of "yes" responses to items 1, 4, 6, 8, 9, 10, 12; write that number here as [X = ____]. Count the number of "yes" responses to items 2, 3, 5, 7, 11, 13, 14; write that score here [Y = ____].

Interpretation
This assessment gives insight into your orientation toward Douglas McGregor's Theory X (your "X" score) and Theory Y (your "Y" score) assumptions. It's an opportunity to consider the ways in which you are likely to behave toward other people at work. Think, in particular, about the types of self-fulfilling prophecies you are likely to create.

Source: John R. Schermerhorn, *Management,* 5th ed. (New York, John Wiley & Sons, Inc., 1996), p. 51. By permission.

ASSESSMENT 2

A Twenty-First-Century Manager

Instructions
Rate yourself on the following personal characteristics. Use this scale.

> S = Strong. I am very confident with this one.
> G = Good. But I still have room to grow.
> W = Weak. I really need work on this one.
> ? = Unsure. I just don't know.

1. *Resistance to stress:* The ability to get work done even under stressful conditions.
2. *Tolerance for uncertainty:* The ability to get work done even under ambiguous and uncertain conditions.
3. *Social objectivity:* The ability to act free of racial, ethnic, gender, and other prejudices or biases.
4. *Inner work standards:* The ability to personally set and work to high-performance standards.
5. *Stamina:* The ability to sustain long work hours.
6. *Adaptability:* The ability to be flexible and adapt to changes.
7. *Self-confidence:* The ability to be consistently decisive and display one's personal presence.
8. *Self-objectivity:* The ability to evaluate personal strengths and weaknesses and to understand one's motives and skills relative to a job.
9. *Introspection:* The ability to learn from experience, awareness, and self-study.
10. *Entrepreneurism:* The ability to address problems and take advantage of opportunities for constructive change.

Scoring
Give yourself 1 point for each S, and ½ point for each G. Do not give yourself points for W and ? responses. Total your points and enter the result here [PMF = ____].

Interpretation
This assessment offers a self-described *profile of your management foundations* (*PMF*). Are you a perfect 10, or is your PMF score something less than that? There shouldn't be too many 10s around. Ask someone who knows you to assess you on this instrument. You may be surprised at the differences between your PMF score as self-described and your PMF score as described by someone else. Most of us, realistically speaking, must work hard to grow and develop continually in these and related management foundations. This list is a good starting point as you consider where and how to further pursue the development of your managerial skills and competencies. The items on the list are recommended by the American Assembly of Collegiate Schools of Business (AACSB) as skills and personal characteristics that should be nurtured in college and university students of business administration. Their success—and yours—as twenty-first-century managers may well rest on (1) an initial awareness of the importance of these basic management foundations and (2) a willingness to strive continually to strengthen them throughout your work career.

Source: See *Outcome Management Project,* Phase I and Phase II Reports (St. Louis: American Assembly of Collegiate Schools of Business, 1986 & 1987).

ASSESSMENT 3

Turbulence Tolerance Test

Instructions

The following statements were made by a thirty-seven-year-old manager in a large, successful corporation. How would you like to have a job with these characteristics? Using the following scale, write your response to the left of each statement.

> 4 = I would enjoy this very much; it's completely acceptable.
> 3 = This would be enjoyable and acceptable most of the time.
> 2 = I'd have no reaction to this feature one way or another, or it would be about equally enjoyable and unpleasant.
> 1 = This feature would be somewhat unpleasant for me.
> 0 = This feature would be very unpleasant for me.

_____ 1. I regularly spend 30 to 40 percent of my time in meetings.

_____ 2. Eighteen months ago my job did not exist, and I have been essentially inventing it as I go along.

_____ 3. The responsibilities I either assume or am assigned consistently exceed the authority I have for discharging them.

_____ 4. At any given moment in my job, I have on average about a dozen phone calls to be returned.

_____ 5. There seems to be very little relation between the quality of my job performance and my actual pay and fringe benefits.

_____ 6. About two weeks a year of formal management training is needed in my job just to stay current.

_____ 7. Because we have very effective equal employment opportunity (EEO) in my company and because it is thoroughly multinational, my job consistently brings me into close working contact at a professional level with people of many races, ethnic groups and nationalities, and of both sexes.

_____ 8. There is no objective way to measure my effectiveness.

_____ 9. I report to three different bosses for different aspects of my job, and each has an equal say in my performance appraisal.

_____ 10. On average, about a third of my time is spent dealing with unexpected emergencies that force all scheduled work to be postponed.

_____ 11. When I have to have a meeting of the people who report to me, it takes my secretary most of a day to find a time when we are all available; and even then I have yet to have a meeting where everyone is present for the entire meeting.

_____ 12. The college degree I earned in preparation for this type of work is now obsolete, and I probably should go back for another degree.

_____ 13. My job requires that I absorb 100 to 200 pages of technical materials per week.

_____ 14. I am out of town overnight at least one night per week.

_____ 15. My department is so interdependent with several other departments in the company that all distinctions about which departments are responsible for which tasks are quite arbitrary.

Source: Peter B. Vail, *Managing as a Performance Art: New Ideas for a World of Chaotic Change* (San Francisco: Jossey-Bass, 1989), pp. 8–9. Used by permission.

___ 16. In about a year I will probably get a promotion to a job in another division that has most of these same characteristics.

___ 17. During the period of my employment here, either the entire company or the division I worked in has been reorganized every year or so.

___ 18. While there are several possible promotions I can see ahead of me, I have no real career path in an objective sense.

___ 19. While there are several possible promotions I can see ahead of me, I think I have no realistic chance of getting to the top levels of the company.

___ 20. While I have many ideas about how to make things work better, I have no direct influence on either the business policies or the personnel policies that govern my division.

___ 21. My company has recently put in an "assessment center" where I and all other managers will be required to go through an extensive battery of psychological tests to assess our potential.

___ 22. My company is a defendant in an antitrust suit, and if the case comes to trial, I will probably have to testify about some decisions that were made a few years ago.

___ 23. Advanced computer and other electronic office technology is continually being introduced into my division, necessitating constant learning on my part.

___ 24. The computer terminal and screen I have in my office can be monitored in my bosses' offices without my knowledge.

Scoring
Total your responses and divide the sum by 24; enter the score here [TTT = ____].

Interpretation
This instrument gives an impression of your tolerance for managing in turbulent times—something likely to characterize the world of work well into the future. In general, the higher your TTT score, the more comfortable you seem to be with turbulence and change—a positive sign. For comparison purposes, the average scores for some 500 MBA students and young managers was 1.5–1.6. The test's author suggests the TTT scores may be interpreted much like a grade point average in which 4.0 is a perfect A. On this basis, a 1.5 is below a C! How did you do?

ASSESSMENT 4

Global Readiness Index

Instructions
Use the scale to rate yourself on each of the following items to establish a baseline measurement of your readiness to participate in the global work environment.

Rating Scale
1 = Very Poor
2 = Poor
3 = Acceptable
4 = Good
5 = Very Good

Source: Developed from "Is Your Company Really Global," *Business Week* (December 1, 1997).

___ 1. I understand my own culture in terms of its expectations, values, and influence on communication and relationships.

___ 2. When someone presents me with a different point of view, I try to understand it rather than attack it.

___ 3. I am comfortable dealing with situations where the available information is incomplete and the outcomes unpredictable.

___ 4. I am open to new situations and am always looking for new information and learning opportunities.

___ 5. I have a good understanding of the attitudes and perceptions toward my culture as they are held by people from other cultures.

___ 6. I am always gathering information about other countries and cultures and trying to learn from them.
___ 7. I am well informed regarding the major differences in government, political systems, and economic policies around the world.
___ 8. I work hard to increase my understanding of people from other cultures.
___ 9. I am able to adjust my communication style to work effectively with people from different cultures.
___ 10. I can recognize when cultural differences are influencing working relationships and adjust my attitudes and behavior accordingly.

Interpretation

To be successful in the twenty-first-century work environment, you must be comfortable with the global economy and the cultural diversity that it holds. This requires a *global mind-set* that is receptive to and respectful of cultural differences, *global knowledge* that includes the continuing quest to know and learn more about other nations and cultures, and *global work skills* that allow you to work effectively across cultures.

Scoring

The goal is to score as close to a perfect 5 as possible on each of the three dimensions of global readiness. Develop your scores as follows.

Items $(1 + 2 + 3 + 4)/4$
 = ___ Global Mind-Set Score

Items $(5 + 6 + 7)/3$
 = ___ Global Knowledge Score

Items $(8 + 9 + 10)/3$
 = ___ Global Work Skills Score

ASSESSMENT 5

Personal Values

Instructions

For the following 16 items, rate how important each one is to you on a scale of 0 (not important) to 100 (very important). Write the numbers 0 to 100 on the line to the left of each item.

Not important			Somewhat important				Very important			
0	10	20	30	40	50	60	70	80	90	100

___ 1. An enjoyable, satisfying job
___ 2. A high-paying job
___ 3. A good marriage
___ 4. Meeting new people; social events
___ 5. Involvement in community activities
___ 6. My religion
___ 7. Exercising, playing sports
___ 8. Intellectual development
___ 9. A career with challenging opportunities
___ 10. Nice cars, clothes, home, etc.
___ 11. Spending time with family
___ 12. Having several close friends
___ 13. Volunteer work for not-for-profit organizations, such as a cancer society

Source: Robert N. Lussier, *Human Relations in Organizations,* 2nd ed. (Homewood, IL: Richard D. Irwin, 1993). By permission.

___ 14. Meditation, quiet time to think, pray, etc.
___ 15. A healthy, balanced diet
___ 16. Educational reading, TV, self-improvement programs, etc.

Scoring
Transfer the numbers for each of the 16 items to the appropriate column below, then add the two numbers in each column.

	Professional	Financial	Family	Social
	1. ____	2. ____	3. ____	4. ____
	9. ____	10. ____	11. ____	12. ____
Totals	____	____	____	____
	Community	**Spiritual**	**Physical**	**Intellectual**
	5. ____	6. ____	7. ____	8. ____
	13. ____	14. ____	15. ____	16. ____
Totals	____	____	____	____

Interpretation
The higher the total in any area, the higher the value you place on that particular area. The closer the numbers are in all eight areas, the more well-rounded you are. Think about the time and effort you put forth in your top three values. Is it sufficient to allow you to achieve the level of success you want in each area? If not, what can you do to change? Is there any area in which you feel you should have a higher value total? If yes, which, and what can you do to change?

ASSESSMENT 6

Intolerance for Ambiguity

Instructions
To determine your level of tolerance (intolerance) for ambiguity, respond to the following items. PLEASE RATE EVERY ITEM; DO NOT LEAVE ANY ITEM BLANK. Rate each item on the following seven-point scale:

1	2	3	4	5	6	7
strongly disagree	moderately disagree	slightly disagree		slightly agree	moderately agree	strongly agree

Rating
___ 1. An expert who doesn't come up with a definite answer probably doesn't know too much.
___ 2. There is really no such thing as a problem that can't be solved.
___ 3. I would like to live in a foreign country for a while.
___ 4. People who fit their lives to a schedule probably miss the joy of living.
___ 5. A good job is one where what is to be done and how it is to be done are always clear.

Source: Based on S. Budner, "Intolerance of Ambiguity as a Personality Variable," *Journal of Personality,* 30:1 (1962), pp. 29–50.

____ 6. In the long run it is possible to get more done by tackling small, simple problems rather than large, complicated ones.
____ 7. It is more fun to tackle a complicated problem than it is to solve a simple one.
____ 8. Often the most interesting and stimulating people are those who don't mind being different and original.
____ 9. What we are used to is always preferable to what is unfamiliar.
____ 10. A person who leads an even, regular life in which few surprises or unexpected happenings arise really has a lot to be grateful for.
____ 11. People who insist upon a yes or no answer just don't know how complicated things really are.
____ 12. Many of our most important decisions are based on insufficient information.
____ 13. I like parties where I know most of the people more than ones where most of the people are complete strangers.
____ 14. The sooner we all acquire ideals, the better.
____ 15. Teachers or supervisors who hand out vague assignments give a chance for one to show initiative and originality.
____ 16. A good teacher is one who makes you wonder about your way of looking at things.
____ Total

Scoring

The scale was developed by S. Budner. Budner reports test–retest correlations of .85 with a variety of samples (mostly students and health care workers). Data, however, are more than 30 years old, so mean shifts may have occurred. Maximum ranges are 16–112, and score ranges were from 25 to 79, with a grand mean of approximately 49.

The test was designed to measure several different components of possible reactions to perceived threat in situations which are new, complex, or insoluble. Half of the items have been reversed.

To obtain a score, first *reverse* the scale score for the eight "reverse" items, 3, 4, 7, 8, 11, 12, 15, and 16 (i.e., a rating of 1 = 7, 2 = 6, 3 = 5, etc.), then add up the rating scores for all 16 items.

Interpretation

Empirically, low tolerance for ambiguity (high intolerance) has been positively correlated with:

- Conventionality of religious beliefs
- High attendance at religious services
- More intense religious beliefs
- More positive views of censorship
- Higher authoritarianism
- Lower Machiavellianism

The application of this concept to management in the 1990s is clear and relatively self-evident. The world of work and many organizations are full of ambiguity and change. Individuals with a *higher* tolerance for ambiguity are far more likely to be able to function effectively in organizations and contexts in which there is a high turbulence, a high rate of change, and less certainty about expectations, performance standards, what needs to be done, and so on. In contrast, individuals with a lower tolerance for ambiguity are far more likely to be unable to adapt or adjust quickly in turbulence, uncertainty, and change. These individuals are likely to become rigid, angry, stressed, and frustrated when there is a high level of uncertainty and ambiguity in the environment. High levels of tolerance for ambiguity, therefore, are associated with an ability to "roll with the punches" as organizations, environmental conditions, and demands change rapidly.

ASSESSMENT 7

Two-Factor Profile

Instructions
On each of the following dimensions, distribute a total of 10 points between the two options. For example:

Summer weather (_7_) ....(_3_) Winter weather

1. Very responsible job (____) ....(____) Job security

2. Recognition for work accomplishments (____) ....(____) Good relations with co-workers

3. Advancement opportunities at work (____) ....(____) A boss who knows his/her job well

4. Opportunities to grow and learn on the job (____) ....(____) Good working conditions

5. A job that I can do well (____) ....(____) Supportive rules, policies of employer

6. A prestigious or high-status job (____) ....(____) A high base wage or salary

Scoring
Summarize your total scores for all items in the *left-hand column* and write it here: MF = ____.
Summarize your total scores for all items in the *right-hand column* and write it here: HF = ____.

Interpretation
The "MF" score indicates the relative importance that you place on motivating or satisfier factors in Herzberg's two-factor theory. This shows how important job content is to you. The "HF" score indicates the relative importance that you place on hygiene or dissatisfier factors in Herzberg's two-factor theory. This shows how important job context is to you.

ASSESSMENT 8

Are You Cosmopolitan?

Instructions
Answer the questions using a scale of 1 to 5: 1 representing "strongly disagree"; 2, "somewhat disagree"; 3, "neutral"; 4, "somewhat agree"; and 5, "strongly agree."

____ 1. You believe it is the right of the professional to make his or her own decisions about what is to be done on the job.

Source: Developed from Joseph A. Raelin, *The Clash of Cultures, Managers and Professionals* (Harvard Business School Press, 1986).

____ 2. You believe a professional should stay in an individual staff role regardless of the income sacrifice.
____ 3. You have no interest in moving up to a top administrative post.
____ 4. You believe that professionals are better evaluated by professional colleagues than by management.
____ 5. Your friends tend to be members of your profession.
____ 6. You would rather be known or get credit for your work outside rather than inside the company.
____ 7. You would feel better making a contribution to society than to your organization.
____ 8. Managers have no right to place time and cost schedules on professional contributors.

Scoring and Interpretation

A "cosmopolitan" identifies with the career profession, and a "local" identifies with the employing organization. Total your scores. A score of 30–40 suggests a cosmopolitan work orientation, 10–20 a "local" orientation, and 20–30 a mixed orientation.

ASSESSMENT 9

Group Effectiveness

Instructions

For this assessment, select a specific group you work with or have worked with; it can be a college or work group. For each of the eight statements, select how often each statement describes the group's behavior. Place the number 1, 2, 3, or 4 on the line next to each of the 8 numbers.

Usually	Frequently	Occasionally	Seldom
1	2	3	4

____ 1. The members are loyal to one another and to the group leader.
____ 2. The members and leader have a high degree of confidence and trust in each other.
____ 3. Group values and goals express relevant values and needs of members.
____ 4. Activities of the group occur in a supportive atmosphere.
____ 5. The group is eager to help members develop to their full potential.
____ 6. The group knows the value of constructive conformity and knows when to use it and for what purpose.
____ 7. The members communicate all information relevant to the group's activity fully and frankly.
____ 8. The members feel secure in making decisions that seem appropriate to them.

Scoring

____ Total. Add up the eight numbers and place an X on the continuum below that represents the score.

Effective group   8 . . . 16 . . . 24 . . . 32   Ineffective group

Interpretation

The lower the score, the more effective the group. What can you do to help the group become more effective? What can the group do to become more effective?

ASSESSMENT 10

Least Preferred Co-worker Scale

Instructions
Think of all the different people with whom you have ever worked—in jobs, in social clubs, in student projects, or whatever. Next, think of the *one person* with whom you could work *least* well—that is, the person with whom you had the most difficulty getting a job done. This is the one person—a peer, boss, or subordinate—with whom you would least want to work. Describe this person by circling numbers at the appropriate points on each of the following pairs of bipolar adjectives. Work rapidly. There are no right or wrong answers.

Pleasant	8 7 6 5 4 3 2 1	Unpleasant
Friendly	8 7 6 5 4 3 2 1	Unfriendly
Rejecting	1 2 3 4 5 6 7 8	Accepting
Tense	1 2 3 4 5 6 7 8	Relaxed
Distant	1 2 3 4 5 6 7 8	Close
Cold	1 2 3 4 5 6 7 8	Warm
Supportive	8 7 6 5 4 3 2 1	Hostile
Boring	1 2 3 4 5 6 7 8	Interesting
Quarrelsome	1 2 3 4 5 6 7 8	Harmonious
Gloomy	1 2 3 4 5 6 7 8	Cheerful
Open	8 7 6 5 4 3 2 1	Guarded
Backbiting	1 2 3 4 5 6 7 8	Loyal
Untrustworthy	1 2 3 4 5 6 7 8	Trustworthy
Considerate	8 7 6 5 4 3 2 1	Inconsiderate
Nasty	1 2 3 4 5 6 7 8	Nice
Agreeable	8 7 6 5 4 3 2 1	Disagreeable
Insincere	1 2 3 4 5 6 7 8	Sincere
Kind	8 7 6 5 4 3 2 1	Unkind

Scoring
This is called the "least preferred co-worker (LPC) scale." Compute your LPC score by totaling all the numbers you circled; enter that score here [LPC = ____].

Interpretation
The LPC scale is used by Fred Fiedler to identify a person's dominant leadership style. Fiedler believes that this style is a relatively fixed part of one's personality and is therefore difficult to change. This leads Fiedler to his contingency views, which suggest that the key to leadership success is finding (or creating) good "matches" between style and situation. If your score is 73 or above, Fiedler considers you a "relationship-motivated" leader; if your score is 64 and below, he considers you a "task-motivated" leader. If your score is between 65 and 72, Fiedler leaves it up to you to determine which leadership style is most like yours.

Source: Fred E. Fiedler and Martin M. Chemers, *Improving Leadership Effectiveness: The Leader Match Concept,* 2nd ed. (New York: John Wiley & Sons, Inc., 1984). Used by permission.

ASSESSMENT 11

Leadership Style

Instructions
The following statements describe leadership acts. Indicate the way you would most likely act if you were leader of a workgroup, by circling whether you would most likely behave in this way:

> always (A); frequently (F); occasionally (O); seldom (S); or never (N)

A F O S N 1. Act as group spokesperson.
A F O S N 2. Encourage overtime work.
A F O S N 3. Allow members complete freedom in their work.
A F O S N 4. Encourage the use of uniform procedures.
A F O S N 5. Permit members to solve their own problems.
A F O S N 6. Stress being ahead of competing groups.
A F O S N 7. Speak as a representative of the group.
A F O S N 8. Push members for greater effort.
A F O S N 9. Try out ideas in the group.
A F O S N 10. Let the members work the way they think best.
A F O S N 11. Work hard for a personal promotion.
A F O S N 12. Tolerate postponement and uncertainty.
A F O S N 13. Speak for the group when visitors are present.
A F O S N 14. Keep the work moving at a rapid pace.
A F O S N 15. Turn members loose on a job.
A F O S N 16. Settle conflicts in the group.
A F O S N 17. Focus on work details.
A F O S N 18. Represent the group at outside meetings.
A F O S N 19. Avoid giving the members too much freedom.
A F O S N 20. Decide what should be done and how it should be done.
A F O S N 21. Push for increased production.
A F O S N 22. Give some members authority to act.
A F O S N 23. Expect things to turn out as predicted.
A F O S N 24. Allow the group to take initiative.
A F O S N 25. Assign group members to particular tasks.
A F O S N 26. Be willing to make changes.
A F O S N 27. Ask members to work harder.
A F O S N 28. Trust members to exercise good judgment.
A F O S N 29. Schedule the work to be done.
A F O S N 30. Refuse to explain my actions.
A F O S N 31. Persuade others that my ideas are best.
A F O S N 32. Permit the group to set its own pace.
A F O S N 33. Urge the group to beat its previous record.
A F O S N 34. Act without consulting the group.
A F O S N 35. Ask members to follow standard rules.

T _____   P _____

Scoring
1. Circle items 8, 12, 17, 18, 19, 30, 34, and 35.
2. Write the number 1 in front of a *circled item number* if you responded S (seldom) or N (never) to that item.

3. Write a number 1 in front of *item numbers not circled* if you responded A (always) or F (frequently).
4. Circle the number 1's which you have written in front of items 3, 5, 8, 10, 15, 18, 19, 22, 24, 26, 28, 30, 32, 34, and 35.
5. *Count the circled number 1's.* This is your score for leadership *concern for people.* Record the score in the blank following the letter P at the end of the questionnaire.
6. *Count the uncircled number 1's.* This is your score for leadership *concern for task.* Record this number in the blank following the letter T.

ASSESSMENT 12

"TT" Leadership Style

Instructions

For each of the following 10 pairs of statements, divide 5 points between the two elements of each pair according to your beliefs, perceptions of yourself, or which of the two statements characterizes you better. The 5 points may be divided between the a and b statements in any one of the following ways: 5 for a, 0 for b; 4 for a, 1 for b; 3 for a, 2 for b; 1 for a, 4 for b; 0 for a, 5 for b, but not equally (2.5) between the two. Weigh your choices between the two according to the one that characterizes you or your beliefs better.

1. (a) As leader I have a primary mission of maintaining stability.
   (b) As leader I have a primary mission of change.
2. (a) As leader I must cause events.
   (b) As leader I must facilitate events.
3. (a) I am concerned that my followers are rewarded equitably for their work.
   (b) I am concerned about what my followers want in life.
4. (a) My preference is to think long range: what might be.
   (b) My preference is to think short range: what is realistic.
5. (a) As a leader I spend considerable energy in managing separate but related goals.
   (b) As a leader I spend considerable energy in arousing hopes, expectations, and aspirations among my followers.

6. (a) Although not in a formal classroom sense, I believe that a significant part of my leadership is that of teacher.
   (b) I believe that a significant part of my leadership is that of facilitator.
7. (a) As leader I must engage with followers at an equal level of morality.
   (b) As leader I must represent a higher morality.
8. (a) I enjoy stimulating followers to want to do more.
   (b) I enjoy rewarding followers for a job well done.
9. (a) Leadership should be practical.
   (b) Leadership should be inspirational.
10. (a) What power I have to influence others comes primarily from my ability to get people to identify with me and my ideas.
    (b) What power I have to influence others comes primarily from my status and position.

Scoring

Circle your points for items 1b, 2a, 3b, 4a, 5b, 6a, 7b, 8a, 9b, 10a and add up the total points you allocated to these items; enter the score here [T = ____]. Next, add up the total points given to the uncircled items 1a, 2b, 3a, 4b, 5a, 6b, 7a, 8b, 9a, 10b; enter the score here [T = ____].

Interpretation

This instrument gives an impression of your tendencies toward "transformational" leadership (your T score) and "transactional" leadership (your T score). Today, a lot of attention is being given to the transformational aspects of leadership: those personal qualities that inspire a sense of vision and desire for extraordinary accomplishment in followers. The most successful leaders of the future will most likely be strong in both T's.

Source: Questionnaire by W. Warner Burke, Ph.D. Used by permission.

ASSESSMENT 13

Empowering Others

Instructions
Think of times when you have been in charge of a group—this could be a full-time or part-time work situation, a student workgroup, or whatever. Complete the following questionnaire by recording how you feel about each statement according to this scale.

> 1 = Strongly disagree
> 2 = Disagree
> 3 = Neutral
> 4 = Agree
> 5 = Strongly agree

When in charge of a group I find:

____ 1. Most of the time other people are too inexperienced to do things, so I prefer to do them myself.

____ 2. It often takes more time to explain things to others than just to do them myself.

____ 3. Mistakes made by others are costly, so I don't assign much work to them.

____ 4. Some things simply should not be delegated to others.

____ 5. I often get quicker action by doing a job myself.

____ 6. Many people are good only at very specific tasks, and thus can't be assigned additional responsibilities.

____ 7. Many people are too busy to take on additional work.

____ 8. Most people just aren't ready to handle additional responsibilities.

____ 9. In my position, I should be entitled to make my own decisions.

Scoring
Total your responses; enter the score here [____].

Interpretation
This instrument gives an impression of your *willingness to delegate*. Possible scores range from 9 to 45. The higher your score, the more willing you appear to be to delegate to others. Willingness to delegate is an important managerial characteristic. It is essential if you—as a manager—are to "empower" others and give them opportunities to assume responsibility and exercise self-control in their work. With the growing importance of empowerment in the new workplace, your willingness to delegate is well worth thinking about seriously.

Source: Questionnaire adapted from L. Steinmetz and R. Todd, *First Line Management,* 4th ed. (Homewood, IL: BPI/Irwin, 1986), pp. 64–67. Used by permission.

ASSESSMENT 14

Machiavellianism

Instructions

For each of the following statements, circle the number that most closely resembles your attitude.

Statement	Disagree A Lot	Disagree A Little	Neutral	Agree A Little	Agree A Lot
1. The best way to handle people is to tell them what they want to hear.	1	2	3	4	5
2. When you ask someone to do something for you, it is best to give the real reason for wanting it rather than reasons that might carry more weight.	1	2	3	4	5
3. Anyone who completely trusts someone else is asking for trouble.	1	2	3	4	5
4. It is hard to get ahead without cutting corners here and there.	1	2	3	4	5
5. It is safest to assume that all people have a vicious streak, and it will come out when they are given a chance.	1	2	3	4	5
6. One should take action only when it is morally right.	1	2	3	4	5
7. Most people are basically good and kind.	1	2	3	4	5
8. There is no excuse for lying to someone else.	1	2	3	4	5
9. Most people forget more easily the death of their father than the loss of their property.	1	2	3	4	5
10. Generally speaking, people won't work hard unless forced to do so.	1	2	3	4	5

Scoring and Interpretation

This assessment is designed to compute your Machiavellianism (Mach) score. Mach is a personality characteristic that taps people's power orientation. The high-Mach personality is pragmatic, maintains emotional distance from others, and believes that ends can justify means. To obtain your Mach score, add up the numbers you checked for questions 1, 3, 4, 5, 9, and 10. For the other four questions, reverse the numbers you have checked, so that 5 becomes 1; 4 is 2; and 1 is 5. Then total both sets of numbers to find your score. A random sample of adults found the national average to be 25. Students in business and management typically score higher.

The results of research using the Mach test have found that (1) men are generally more Machiavellian than women; (2) older adults tend to have lower Mach scores than younger adults; (3) there is no significant difference between high Machs and low Machs on measures of intelligence or ability; (4) Machiavellianism is not significantly related to demographic characteristics such as educational level or marital status; and (5) high Machs tend to be in professions that emphasize the control and manipulation of people—for example, managers, lawyers, psychiatrists, and behavioral scientists.

Source: From R. Christie and F. L. Geis, *Studies in Machiavellianism* (New York: Academic Press, 1970). By permission.

ASSESSMENT 15

Personal Power Profile

Contributed by Marcus Maier, Chapman University

Instructions

Following is a list of statements that may be used in describing behaviors that supervisors (leaders) in work organizations can direct toward their subordinates (followers). First, carefully read each descriptive statement, thinking in terms of *how you prefer to influence others*. Mark the number that most closely represents how you feel. Use the following numbers for your answers.

5 = Strongly agree
4 = Agree
3 = Neither agree nor disagree
2 = Disagree
1 = Strongly disagree

To influence others, I would prefer to:	Strongly Disagree	Disagree	Neither Agree nor Disagree	Agree	Strongly Agree
1. Increase their pay level	1	2	3	4	5
2. Make them feel valued	1	2	3	4	5
3. Give undesirable job assignments	1	2	3	4	5
4. Make them feel like I approve of them	1	2	3	4	5
5. Make them feel that they have commitments to meet	1	2	3	4	5
6. Make them feel personally accepted	1	2	3	4	5
7. Make them feel important	1	2	3	4	5
8. Give them good technical suggestions	1	2	3	4	5
9. Make the work difficult for them	1	2	3	4	5
10. Share my experience and/or training	1	2	3	4	5
11. Make things unpleasant here	1	2	3	4	5
12. Make being at work distasteful	1	2	3	4	5
13. Influence their getting a pay increase	1	2	3	4	5
14. Make them feel like they should satisfy their job requirements	1	2	3	4	5
15. Provide them with sound job-related advice	1	2	3	4	5
16. Provide them with special benefits	1	2	3	4	5
17. Influence their getting a promotion	1	2	3	4	5
18. Give them the feeling that they have responsibilities to fulfill	1	2	3	4	5
19. Provide them with needed technical knowledge	1	2	3	4	5
20. Make them recognize that they have tasks to accomplish	1	2	3	4	5

Source: Modified version of T. R. Hinken and C. A. Schriesheim, "Development and Application of New Scales to Measure the French and Raven (1959) Bases of Social Power," *Journal of Applied Psychology,* Vol. 74 (1989), pp. 561–567.

Scoring

Using the following grid, insert your scores from the 20 questions and proceed as follows: *Reward power*—sum your response to items 1, 13, 16, and 17 and divide by 4. *Coercive power*—sum your response to items 3, 9, 11, and 12 and divide by 4. *Legitimate power*—sum your response to questions 5, 14, 18, and 20 and divide by 4. *Referent power*—sum your response to questions 2, 4, 6, and 7 and divide by 4. *Expert power*—sum your response to questions 8, 10, 15, and 19 and divide by 4.

Reward	Coercive	Legitimate	Referent	Expert
1 ___	3 ___	5 ___	2 ___	8 ___
13 ___	9 ___	14 ___	4 ___	10 ___
16 ___	11 ___	18 ___	6 ___	15 ___
17 ___	12 ___	20 ___	7 ___	19 ___
Total ___	___	___	___	___
Divide by 4 ___	___	___	___	___

Interpretation

A high score (4 and greater) on any of the five dimensions of power implies that you prefer to influence others by employing that particular form of power. A low score (2 or less) implies that you prefer not to employ this particular form of power to influence others. This represents your power profile. Your overall power position is not reflected by the simple sum of the power derived from each of the five sources. Instead, some combinations of power are synergistic in nature—they are greater than the simple sum of their parts. For example, referent power tends to magnify the impact of other power sources because these other influence attempts are coming from a "respected" person. Reward power often increases the impact of referent power, because people generally tend to like those who give them things that they desire. Some power combinations tend to produce the opposite of synergistic effects, such that the total is less than the sum of the parts. Power dilution frequently accompanies the use of (or threatened use of) coercive power.

ASSESSMENT 16

Intuitive Ability

Instructions

Complete this survey as quickly as you can. Be honest with yourself. For each question, select the response that most appeals to you.

1. When working on a project, do you prefer to:
   (a) Be told what the problem is but be left free to decide how to solve it?
   (b) Get very clear instructions about how to go about solving the problem before you start?
2. When working on a project, do you prefer to work with colleagues who are:
   (a) Realistic?
   (b) Imaginative?

3. Do you most admire people who are:
   (a) Creative?
   (b) Careful?
4. Do the friends you choose tend to be:
   (a) Serious and hard working?
   (b) Exciting and often emotional?
5. When you ask a colleague for advice on a problem you have, do you:
   (a) Seldom or never get upset if he or she questions your basic assumptions?
   (b) Often get upset if he or she questions your basic assumptions?
6. When you start your day, do you:
   (a) Seldom make or follow a specific plan?
   (b) Usually first make a plan to follow?

Source: AIM Survey (El Paso, TX: ENFP Enterprises, 1989). Copyright © 1989 by Weston H. Agor. Used by permission.

7. When working with numbers do you find that you:
   (a) Seldom or never make factual errors?
   (b) Often make factual errors?
8. Do you find that you:
   (a) Seldom daydream during the day and really don't enjoy doing so when you do it?
   (b) Frequently daydream during the day and enjoy doing so?
9. When working on a problem, do you:
   (a) Prefer to follow the instructions or rules when they are given to you?
   (b) Often enjoy circumventing the instructions or rules when they are given to you?
10. When you are trying to put something together, do you prefer to have:
    (a) Step-by-step written instructions on how to assemble the item?
    (b) A picture of how the item is supposed to look once assembled?
11. Do you find that the person who irritates you *the most* is the one who appears to be:
    (a) Disorganized?
    (b) Organized?
12. When an expected crisis comes up that you have to deal with, do you:
    (a) Feel anxious about the situation?
    (b) Feel excited by the challenge of the situation?

Scoring

Total the number of "a" responses circled for questions 1, 3, 5, 6, 11; enter the score here [A = ____]. Total the number of "b" responses for questions 2, 4, 7, 8, 9, 10, 12; enter the score here [B = ____]. Add your "a" and "b" scores and enter the sum here [A + B = ____]. This is your *intuitive score*. The highest possible intuitive score is 12; the lowest is 0.

Interpretation

In his book *Intuition in Organizations* (Newbury Park, CA: Sage, 1989), pp. 10–11, Weston H. Agor states, "Traditional analytical techniques . . . are not as useful as they once were for guiding major decisions. . . . If you hope to be better prepared for tomorrow, then it only seems logical to pay some attention to the use and development of intuitive skills for decision making." Agor developed the prior survey to help people assess their tendencies to use intuition in decision making. Your score offers a general impression of your strength in this area. It may also suggest a need to further develop your skill and comfort with more intuitive decision approaches.

ASSESSMENT 17

Decision-Making Biases

Instructions

How good are you at avoiding potential decision-making biases? Test yourself by answering the following questions:

1. Which is riskier:
   (a) driving a car on a 400-mile trip?
   (b) flying on a 400-mile commercial airline flight?
2. Are there more words in the English language:
   (a) that begin with "r"?
   (b) that have "r" as the third letter?
3. Mark is finishing his MBA at a prestigious university. He is very interested in the arts and at one time considered a career as a musician. Is Mark more likely to take a job:
   (a) in the management of the arts?
   (b) with a management consulting firm?
4. You are about to hire a new central-region sales director for the fifth time this year. You predict that the next director should work out reasonably well since the last four were "lemons" and the odds favor hiring at least one good sales director in five tries. Is this thinking
   (a) correct?
   (b) incorrect?
5. A newly hired engineer for a computer firm in the Boston metropolitan area has four years' experience and good all-around qualifications. When asked to estimate the starting salary for this employee, a chemist with very little knowledge about the profession or industry guessed an annual salary of $35,000. What is your estimate?
   $____ per year

Source: Incidents from Max H. Bazerman, *Judgment in Managerial Decision Making*, 3rd ed. (New York: John Wiley & Sons, Inc., 1994), pp. 13–14. Used by permission.

Scoring

Your instructor will provide answers and explanations for the assessment questions.

Interpretation

Each of the preceding questions examines your tendency to use a different judgmental heuristic. In his book *Judgment in Managerial Decision Making,* 3rd ed. (New York: John Wiley & Sons, 1994), pp. 6–7, Max Bazerman calls these heuristics "simplifying strategies, or rules of thumb" used in making decisions. He states, "In general, heuristics are helpful, but their use can sometimes lead to severe errors. . . . If we can make managers aware of the potential adverse impacts of using heuristics, they can then decide when and where to use them." This assessment offers an initial insight into your use of such heuristics. An informed decision maker understands the heuristics, is able to recognize when they appear, and eliminates any that may inappropriately bias decision making.

Test yourself further. Before hearing from your instructor, go back and write next to each item the name of the judgmental heuristic that you think applies.

Then write down a situation that you have experienced and in which some decision-making bias may have occurred. Be prepared to share and discuss this incident with the class.

ASSESSMENT 18

Conflict Management Strategies

Instructions

Think of how you behave in conflict situations in which your wishes differ from those of others. In the space to the left, rate each of the following statements on a scale of "1/not at all" to "5/very much."

When I have a conflict at work, school, or in my personal life, I do the following:

____ 1. I give in to the wishes of the other party.
____ 2. I try to realize a middle-of-the-road solution.
____ 3. I push my own point of view.
____ 4. I examine issues until I find a solution that really satisfies me and the other party.
____ 5. I avoid a confrontation about our differences.
____ 6. I concur with the other party.
____ 7. I emphasize that we have to find a compromise solution.
____ 8. I search for gains.
____ 9. I stand for my own and the other's goals.
____ 10. I avoid differences of opinion as much as possible.
____ 11. I try to accommodate the other party.
____ 12. I insist we both give in a little.
____ 13. I fight for a good outcome for myself.
____ 14. I examine ideas from both sides to find a mutually optimal solution.
____ 15. I try to make differences seem less severe.
____ 16. I adapt to the other party's goals and interests.
____ 17. I strive whenever possible towards a fifty-fifty compromise.
____ 18. I do everything to win.
____ 19. I work out a solution that serves my own as well as others' interests as much as possible.
____ 20. I try to avoid a confrontation with the other person.

Scoring

Total your scores for items as follows.
Yielding tendency: 1 + 6 + 11 + 16 = ____.

Source: This instrument is described in Carsten K. W. De Drew, Arne Evers, Bianca Beersma, Esther S. Kluwer, and Aukje Nauta, "A Theory-Based Measure of Conflict Management Strategies in the Workplace," *Journal of Organizational Behavior* 22 (2001), pp. 645–668. Used by permission.

Compromising tendency: 2 + 7 + 12 + 17 = ____.
Forcing tendency: 3 + 8 + 13 + 18 = ____.
Problem-solving tendency: 4 + 9 + 14 + 19 = ____.
Avoiding tendency: 5 + 10 + 15 + 20 = ____.

Interpretation

Each of the scores approximates one of the conflict management styles discussed in the chapter. Although each style is part of management, only collaboration or problem solving leads to true conflict resolution. You should consider any patterns that may be evident in your scores and think about how to best handle the conflict situations in which you become involved.

ASSESSMENT 19
Your Personality Type

Instructions
How true is each statement for you?

	Not True at All		Not True or Untrue		Very True
1. I hate giving up before I'm absolutely sure that I'm licked.	1	2	3	4	5
2. Sometimes I feel that I should not be working so hard, but something drives me on.	1	2	3	4	5
3. I thrive on challenging situations. The more challenges I have, the better.	1	2	3	4	5
4. In comparison to most people I know, I'm very involved in my work.	1	2	3	4	5
5. It seems as if I need 30 hours a day to finish all the things I'm faced with.	1	2	3	4	5
6. In general, I approach my work more seriously than most people I know.	1	2	3	4	5
7. I guess there are some people who can be nonchalant about their work, but I'm not one of them.	1	2	3	4	5
8. My achievements are considered to be significantly higher than those of most people I know.	1	2	3	4	5
9. I've often been asked to be an officer of some group or groups.	1	2	3	4	5

Scoring
Add all your scores to create a total score = ____.

Interpretation
Type A personalities (hurried and competitive) tend to score 36 and above. Type B personalities (relaxed) tend to score 22 and below. Scores of 23–35 indicate a balance or mix of Type A and Type B.

Source: From *Job Demands and Worker Health* (HEW Publication No. [NIOSH] 75–160) (Washington, DC: US Department of Health, Education and Welfare, 1975), pp. 253–254.

ASSESSMENT 20

Time Management Profile

Instructions
Complete the following questionnaire by indicating "Y" (yes) or "N" (no) for each item. Be frank and allow your responses to create an accurate picture of how you tend to respond to these kinds of situations.

____ 1. When confronted with several items of similar urgency and importance, I tend to do the easiest one first.

____ 2. I do the most important things during that part of the day when I know I perform best.

____ 3. Most of the time I don't do things someone else can do; I delegate this type of work to others.

____ 4. Even though meetings without a clear and useful purpose upset me, I put up with them.

____ 5. I skim documents before reading them and don't complete any that offer a low return on my time investment.

____ 6. I don't worry much if I don't accomplish at least one significant task each day.

____ 7. I save the most trivial tasks for that time of day when my creative energy is lowest.

____ 8. My workspace is neat and organized.

____ 9. My office door is always "open"; I never work in complete privacy.

____ 10. I schedule my time completely from start to finish every workday.

____ 11. I don't like "to do" lists, preferring to respond to daily events as they occur.

____ 12. I "block" a certain amount of time each day or week that is dedicated to high-priority activities.

Scoring
Count the number of "Y" responses to items 2, 3, 5, 7, 8, 12. [Enter that score here ____.] Count the number of "N" responses to items 1, 4, 6, 9, 10, 11. [Enter that score here ____.] Add together the two scores.

Interpretation
The higher the total score, the closer your behavior matches recommended time management guidelines. Reread those items where your response did not match the desired one. Why don't they match? Do you have reasons why your behavior in this instance should be different from the recommended time management guideline? Think about what you can do (and how easily it can be done) to adjust your behavior to be more consistent with these guidelines.

For further reading, see Alan Lakein, *How to Control Your Time and Your Life* (New York: David McKay), and William Oncken, *Managing Management Time* (Englewood Cliffs, NJ: Prentice Hall, 1984).

Source: Suggested by a discussion in Robert E. Quinn, Sue R. Faerman, Michael P. Thompson, and Michael R. McGrath, *Becoming a Master Manager: A Contemporary Framework* (New York: John Wiley & Sons, Inc., 1990), pp. 75–76.

ASSESSMENT 21

Organizational Design Preference

Instructions
To the left of each item, write the number from the following scale that shows the extent to which the statement accurately describes your views.

> 5 = strongly agree
> 4 = agree somewhat
> 3 = undecided
> 2 = disagree somewhat
> 1 = strongly disagree

I prefer to work in an organization where:

1. Goals are defined by those in higher levels.
2. Work methods and procedures are specified.
3. Top management makes important decisions.
4. My loyalty counts as much as my ability to do the job.

Source: John F. Veiga and John N. Yanouzas, *The Dynamics of Organization Theory: Gaining a Macro Perspective* (St. Paul, MN: West, 1979), pp. 158–160. Used by permission.

5. Clear lines of authority and responsibility are established.
6. Top management is decisive and firm.
7. My career is pretty well planned out for me.
8. I can specialize.
9. My length of service is almost as important as my level of performance.
10. Management is able to provide the information I need to do my job well.
11. A chain of command is well established.
12. Rules and procedures are adhered to equally by everyone.
13. People accept authority of a leader's position.
14. People are loyal to their boss.
15. People do as they have been instructed.
16. People clear things with their boss before going over his or her head.

Scoring
Total your scores for all questions. Enter the score here [____].

Interpretation
This assessment measures your preference for working in an organization designed along "organic" or "mechanistic" lines. The higher your score (above 64), the more comfortable you are with a mechanistic design; the lower your score (below 48), the more comfortable you are with an organic design. Scores between 48 and 64 can go either way. This organizational design preference represents an important issue in the new workplace. Indications are that today's organizations are taking on more and more organic characteristics. Presumably, those of us who work in them will need to be comfortable with such designs.

ASSESSMENT 22

Which Culture Fits You?

Instructions
Check one of the following organization "cultures" in which you feel most comfortable working.

1. A culture that values talent, entrepreneurial activity, and performance over commitment; one that offers large financial rewards and individual recognition.
2. A culture that stresses loyalty, working for the good of the group, and getting to know the right people; one that believes in "generalists" and step-by-step career progress.
3. A culture that offers little job security; one that operates with a survival mentality, stresses that every individual can make a difference, and focuses attention on "turnaround" opportunities.
4. A culture that values long-term relationships; one that emphasizes systematic career development, regular training, and advancement based on gaining of functional expertise.

Scoring
These labels identify the four different cultures: 1 = "the baseball team," 2 = "the club," 3 = "the fortress," and 4 = "the academy."

Interpretation
To some extent, your future career success may depend on working for an organization in which there is a good fit between you and the prevailing corporate culture. This assessment can help you learn how to recognize various cultures, evaluate how well they can serve your needs, and recognize how they may change with time. A risk taker, for example, may be out of place in a "club" but fit right in with a "baseball team." Someone who wants to seek opportunities wherever they may occur may be out of place in an "academy" but fit right in with a "fortress."

Source: Developed from Carol Hymowitz, "Which Corporate Culture Fits You?" *Wall Street Journal* (July 17, 1989), p. B1.

TEAM AND EXPERIENTIAL EXERCISES

EXERCISE 1

My Best Manager

Instructions

1. Make a list of the attributes that describe the best manager you ever worked for. If you have trouble identifying an actual manager, make a list of attributes you would like the manager in your next job to have.
2. Form a group of four or five persons and share your lists.
3. Create one list that combines all the unique attributes of the "best" managers represented in your group. Make sure that you have all attributes listed, but list each only once. Place a check mark next to those that were reported by two or more members. Have one of your members prepared to present the list in general class discussion.
4. After all groups have finished Step 3, spokespersons should report to the whole class. The instructor will make a running list of the "best" manager attributes as viewed by the class.
5. Feel free to ask questions and discuss the results.

EXERCISE 2

Graffiti Needs Assessment: Involving Students in the First Class Session

Contributed by Barbara K. Goza, Visiting Associate Professor, University of California at Santa Cruz, and Associate Professor, California State Polytechnic University, Pomona. From *Journal of Management Education*, 1993.

Instructions

1. Complete the following sentences with as many endings as possible.
    1. When I first came to this class, I thought . . .
    2. My greatest concern this term is . . .
    3. In 3 years I will be . . .
    4. The greatest challenge facing the world today is . . .
    5. Organizational behavior specialists do . . .
    6. Human resources are . . .
    7. Organizational research is . . .
    8. The most useful question I've been asked is . . .
    9. The most important phenomenon in organizations is . . .
    10. I learn the most when . . .
2. Your instructor will guide you in a class discussion about your responses. Pay careful attention to similarities and differences among various students' answers.

EXERCISE 3

My Best Job

Procedure

1. Make a list of the top five things you expect from your first (or next) full-time job.
2. Exchange lists with a nearby partner. Assign probabilities (or odds) to each goal on your partner's list to indicate how likely you feel it is that the goal can be accomplished. (*Note:* Your instructor may ask that everyone use the same probabilities format.)
3. Discuss your evaluations with your partner. Try to delete superficial goals or modify them to become more substantial. Try to restate any unrealistic goals to make them more realistic. Help your partner do the same.
4. Form a group of four to six persons. Within the group, have everyone share what they now consider to be the most "realistic" goals on their lists. Elect a spokesperson to share a sample of these items with the entire class.
5. Discuss what group members have individually learned from the exercise. Await further class discussion led by your instructor.

EXERCISE 4

What Do You Value in Work?

Instructions

1. The following nine items are from a survey conducted by Nicholas J. Beutell and O. C. Brenner ("Sex Differences in Work Values," *Journal of Vocational Behavior,* 28, pp. 29–41, 1986). Rank the nine items in terms of how important (9 = most important) they would be to you in a job.

    How important is it to you to have a job that:
    ____ Is respected by other people?
    ____ Encourages continued development of knowledge and skills?
    ____ Provides job security?
    ____ Provides a feeling of accomplishment?
    ____ Provides the opportunity to earn a high income?
    ____ Is intellectually stimulating?
    ____ Rewards good performance with recognition?
    ____ Provides comfortable working conditions?
    ____ Permits advancement to high administrative responsibility?

2. Form into groups as designated by your instructor. Within each group, the *men in the group* will meet to develop a consensus ranking of the items as they think the *women* in the Beutell and Brenner survey ranked them. The reasons for the rankings should be shared and discussed so they are clear to everyone. The *women in the group* should not participate in this ranking task. They should listen to the discussion and be prepared to comment later in class discussion. A spokesperson for the men in the group should share the group's rankings with the class.

3. (*Optional*) Form into groups as designated by your instructor, but with each group consisting entirely of men or women. Each group should meet and decide which of the work values members of the *opposite* sex ranked first in the Beutell and Brenner survey. Do this again for the work value ranked last. The reasons should be discussed, along with reasons that each of the other values probably was not ranked first—or last. A spokesperson for each group should share group results with the rest of the class.

Source: Adapted from Roy J. Lewicki, Donald D. Bowen, Douglas T. Hall, and Francine S. Hall, *Experiences in Management and Organizational Behavior,* 3rd ed. (New York: John Wiley & Sons, Inc., 1988), pp. 23–26. Used by permission.

EXERCISE 5

My Asset Base

A business has an asset base or set of resources that it uses to produce a good or service of value to others. For a business, these are the assets or resources it uses to achieve results, including capital, land, patented products or processes, buildings and equipment, raw materials, and the human resources or employees, among others.

Each of us has an asset base that supports our ability to accomplish the things we set out to do. We refer to our personal assets as *talents, strengths,* or *abilities*. We probably inherit our talents from our parents, but we acquire many of our abilities and strengths through learning. One thing is certain: We feel very proud of the talents and abilities we have.

Instructions

1. Printed here is a T chart that you are to fill out. On the right-hand side of the T, list four or five of your accomplishments—*things you have done of which you are most proud.* Your accomplishments should only include those things for which you can take credit, those *things for which you are primarily responsible.* If you are proud of the sorority to which you belong, you may be justifiably proud, but don't list it unless you can argue that the sorority's excellence is due primarily to your efforts. However, if you feel that having been invited to join the sorority is a major accomplishment for you, then you may include it.

   When you have completed the right-hand side of the chart, fill in the left-hand side by listing *talents, strengths,* and *abilities* that you have that have enabled you to accomplish the outcomes listed on the right-hand side.

My Asset Base

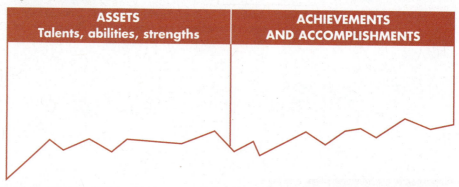

2. Share your lists with other team members. As each member shares his or her list, pay close attention to your own perceptions and feelings. Notice the effect this has on your attitudes toward the other team members.
3. Discuss these questions in your group:
   a. How did your attitudes and feelings toward other members of the team change as you pursued the activity? What does this tell you about the process whereby we come to get to know and care about people?
   b. How did you feel about the instructions the instructor provided? What did you expect to happen? Were your expectations accurate?

Source: Adapted from Donald D. Bowen et al., *Experiences in Management and Organizational Behavior,* 4th ed. (New York: John Wiley & Sons, Inc., 1997).

EXERCISE 6

Expatriate Assignments

Contributed by Robert E. Ledman, Morehouse College

This exercise focuses on issues related to workers facing international assignments. It illustrates that those workers face a multitude of issues. It further demonstrates that managers who want employees to realize the maximum benefits of international assignments should be aware of, and prepared to deal with, those issues. Some of the topics that are easily addressed with this exercise include the need for culture and language training for the employees and their families and the impact that international assignments may have on an employee's family and how that may affect an employee's willingness to seek such assignments.

Instructions

1. Form into "families" of four or five. Since many students today have only one parent at home, it is helpful if some groups do not have students to fill both parental roles in the exercise. Each student is assigned to play a family member and given a description of that person.
2. Enter into a 20-minute discussion to explore how a proposed overseas assignment will affect the family members. Your goal is to try to reach a decision about whether the assignment should be taken. You must also decide whether the entire family or only the family member being offered the assignment will relocate. The assignment is for a minimum of two years, with possible annual extensions resulting in a total of four years, and your family, or the member offered the assignment, will be provided, at company expense, one trip back to the states each year for a maximum period of fifteen days. The member offered the assignment will not receive any additional housing or cost-of-living supplements described in the role assignment if he or she chooses to go overseas alone and can expect his or her living expenses to exceed substantially the living allowance being provided by the company. In your discussion, address the following questions:

   a. What are the most important concerns your family has about relocating to a foreign country?
   b. What information should you seek about the proposed host country to be able to make a more informed decision?
   c. What can the member offered the assignment do to make the transition easier if he or she goes overseas alone? If the whole family relocates?
   d. What should the member offered the assignment do to ensure that this proposed assignment will not create unnecessary stress for him or her and the rest of the family?
   e. What lessons for managers of expatriate assignees are presented by the situation in this exercise?

   Try to reach some "family" consensus. If a consensus is not possible, however, resolve any differences in the manner you think the family in the role descriptions would ultimately resolve any differences.

3. Share your answers with the rest of the class. Explain the rationale for your answers and answer questions from the remainder of the class.
4. (*Optional*) After each group has reported on a given question, the instructor may query the class about how their answers are consistent, or inconsistent, with common practices of managers as described in the available literature.

Descriptions of Family Members
Person Being Offered Overseas Assignment

This person is a middle- to upper-level executive who is on a fast track to senior management. He or she has been offered the opportunity to manage an overseas operation, with the assurance of a promotion to a vice presidency upon return to the states. The company will pay all relocation expenses, including selling costs for the family home and the costs associated with finding a new home upon return. The employer will also provide language training for the employee and cultural awareness training for the entire family. The employee will receive a living allowance equal to 20 percent of his or her salary. This should be adequate to provide the family a comparable standard of living to that which is possible on the employee's current salary.

Spouse of the Person Offered an Overseas Assignment (Optional)

This person is also a professional with highly transferable skills and experience for the domestic market. It is unknown how easily he or she may be able to find

Source: Robert E. Ledman, Gannon University. Presented in the Experiential Exercise Track of the 1996 ABSEL Conference and published in the *Proceedings* of that conference.

employment in the foreign country. This person's income, though less than his or her spouse's, is necessary if the couple is to continue paying for their child's college tuition and to prepare for the next child to enter college in two years. This person has spent fifteen years developing a career, including completing a degree at night.

Oldest Child

This child is a second-semester junior in college and is on track to graduate in 16 months. Transferring at this time would probably mean adding at least one semester to complete the degree. He or she has been dating the same person for over a year; they have talked about getting married immediately after graduation, although they are not yet formally engaged.

Middle Child

This child is a junior in high school. He or she has already begun visiting college campuses in preparation for applying in the fall. This child is involved in a number of school activities; he or she is a photographer for the yearbook and plays a varsity sport. This child has a learning disability for which services are being provided by the school system.

Youngest Child

This child is a middle school student, age 13. He or she is actively involved in Scouting and takes piano lessons. This child has a history of medical conditions that have required regular visits to the family physician and specialists. This child has several very close friends who have attended the same school for several years.

EXERCISE 7

Cultural Cues

Contributed by Susan Rawson Zacur and W. Alan Randolph, University of Baltimore

Introduction

In the business context, culture involves shared beliefs and expectations that govern the behavior of people. In this exercise, *foreign culture* refers to a set of beliefs and expectations different from those of the participant's home culture (which has been invented by the participants).

Instructions

1. (10–15 minutes) Divide into two groups, each with color-coded badges. For example, the blue group could receive blue Sticky notes and the yellow group could receive yellow Sticky notes. Print your first name in bold letters on the badge and wear it throughout the exercise.

   Work with your group members to invent your own cultural cues. Think about the kinds of behaviors and words that will signify to all members that they belong together in one culture. For each of the following categories, identify and record at least one important attribute for your culture.

Cultural Cues:	Your Culture:
Facial expression:	
Eye contact (note: you must have some eye contact in order to observe others):	
Handshake:	
Body language (note: must be evident while standing):	
Key words or phrases:	

Source: Adapted by Susan Rawson Zacur and W. Alan Randolph from *Journal of Management Education,* 17:4 (November 1993), pp. 510–516.

Once you have identified desirable cultural aspects for your group, practice them. It is best to stand with your group and to engage one another in conversations involving two or three people at a time. Your aim in talking with one another is to learn as much as possible about each other—hobbies, interests, where you live, what your family is like, what courses you are taking, and so on, all the while practicing the behaviors and words on the previous page. It is not necessary for participants to answer questions of a personal nature truthfully. Invention is permissible because the conversation is only a means to the end of cultural observation. Your aim at this point is to become comfortable with the indicators of your particular culture. Practice until the indicators are second nature to you.

2. Now assume that you work for a business that has decided to explore the potential for doing business with companies in a different culture. You are to learn as much as possible about another culture. To do so, you will send from one to three representatives from your group on a "business trip" to the other culture. These representatives must, insofar as possible, behave in a manner that is consistent with your culture. At the same time, each representative must endeavor to learn as much as possible about the people in the other culture, while keeping eyes and ears open to cultural attributes that will be useful in future negotiations with foreign businesses. (*Note:* At no time will it be considered ethical behavior for the representative to ask direct questions about the foreign culture's attributes. These must be gleaned from firsthand experience.)

   While your representatives are away, you will receive one or more exchange visitors from the other culture, who will engage in conversation as they attempt to learn more about your organizational culture. You must strictly adhere to the cultural aspects of your own culture while you converse with the visitors.

3. (5–10 minutes) All travelers return to your home cultures. As a group, discuss and record what you have learned about the foreign culture based on the exchange of visitors. This information will serve as the basis for orienting the next representatives who will make a business trip.

4. (5–10 minutes) Select one to three different group members to make another trip to the other culture to check out the assumptions your group has made about the other culture. This "checking out" process will consist of actually practicing the other culture's cues to see whether they work.

5. (5–10 minutes) Once the traveler(s) have returned and reported on findings, as a group prepare to report to the class what you have learned about the other culture.

EXERCISE 8

Prejudice in Our Lives

Contributed by Susan Schor of Pace University and Annie McKee of The Wharton School, University of Pennsylvania, with the assistance of Ariel Fishman of The Wharton School

Instructions

1. As a large class group, generate a list of groups that tend to be targets of prejudice and stereotypes in our culture—such groups can be based on gender, race, ethnicity, sexual orientation, region, religion, and so on. After generating a list, either as a class or in small groups, identify a few common positive and negative stereotypes associated with each group. Also consider relationships or patterns that exist among some of the lists. Discuss the implications for groups that have stereotypes that are valued in organizations versus groups whose stereotypes are viewed negatively in organizations.

2. As an individual, think about the lists you have now generated, and list those groups with which you identify. Write about an experience in which you

were stereotyped as a member of a group. Ask yourself the following questions and write down your thoughts:
   a. What group do I identify with?
   b. What was the stereotype?
   c. What happened? When and where did the incident occur? Who said what to whom?
   d. What were my reactions? How did I feel? What did I think? What did I do?
   e. What were the consequences? How did the incident affect myself and others?
3. Now, in small groups, discuss your experiences. Briefly describe the incident and focus on how the incident made you feel. Select one incident from the ones shared in your group to role-play for the class. Then, as a class, discuss your reactions to each role-play. Identify the prejudice or stereotype portrayed, the feelings the situation evoked, and the consequences that might result from such a situation.
4. Think about the prejudices and stereotypes you hold about other people. Ask yourself, "What groups do I feel prejudice toward? What stereotypes do I hold about members of each of these groups?" How may such a prejudice have developed—did a family member or close friend or television influence you to stereotype a particular group in a certain way?
5. Now try to identify implications of prejudice in the workplace. How do prejudice and stereotypes affect workers, managers, relationships between people, and the organization as a whole? Consider how you might want to change erroneous beliefs as well as how you would encourage other people to change their own erroneous beliefs.

EXERCISE 9

How We View Differences

Contributed by Barbara Walker

Introduction
Clearly, the workplace of the future will be much more diverse than it is today: more women, more people of color, more international representation, more diverse lifestyles and ability profiles, and the like. Managing a diverse workforce and working across a range of differences is quickly becoming a "core competency" for effective managers.

Furthermore, it is also becoming clear that diversity in a work team can significantly enhance the creativity and quality of the team's output. In today's turbulent business environment, utilizing employee diversity will give the manager and the organization a competitive edge in tapping all of the available human resources more effectively. This exercise is an initial step in the examination of how we work with people whom we perceive as different from us. It is fairly simple, straightforward, and safe, but its implications are profound.

Instructions
1. Read the following:

   Imagine that you are traveling in a rental car in a city you have never visited before. You have a one-hour drive on an uncrowded highway before you reach your destination. You decide that you would like to spend the time listening to some of your favorite kind of music on the car radio.

   The rental car has four selection buttons available, each with a preset station that plays a different type of music. One plays *country music,* one plays *rock,* one plays *classical,* and one plays *jazz.* Which type of music would you choose to listen to for the next hour as you drive along? (Assume you want to relax and just stick with one station; you don't want to bother switching around between stations.)

2. Form into groups based on the type of music that you have chosen. All who have chosen country will meet in an area designated by the instructor. Those who chose rock will meet in another area, and so on. In your groups, answer the following question. Appoint one member to be the spokesperson to report your answers back to the total group.

Source: Exercise developed by Barbara Walker, a pioneer on work on valuing differences. Adapted for this volume by Douglas T. Hall. Used by permission of Barbara Walker.

Question

For each of the other groups, what words would you use to describe people who like to listen to that type of music?

3. Have each spokesperson report the responses of her or his group to the question in step 2. Follow with class discussion of these additional questions:
   a. What do you think is the purpose or value of this exercise?
   b. What did you notice about the words used to describe the other groups? Were there any *surprises* in this exercise for you?
   c. Upon what sorts of data do you think these images were based?
   d. What term do we normally use to describe these generalized perceptions of another group?
   e. What could some of the consequences be?
   f. How do the perceptual processes here relate to other kinds of intergroup differences, such as race, gender, culture, ability, ethnicity, health, age, nationality, and so on?
   g. What does this exercise suggest about the ease with which intergroup stereotypes form?
   h. What might be ways an organization might facilitate the valuing and utilizing of differences between people?

EXERCISE 10

Alligator River Story

The Alligator River Story

There lived a woman named Abigail who was in love with a man named Gregory. Gregory lived on the shore of a river. Abigail lived on the opposite shore of the same river. The river that separated the two lovers was teeming with dangerous alligators. Abigail wanted to cross the river to be with Gregory. Unfortunately, the bridge had been washed out by a heavy flood the previous week. So she went to ask Sinbad, a riverboat captain, to take her across. He said he would be glad to if she would consent to go to bed with him prior to the voyage. She promptly refused and went to a friend named Ivan to explain her plight. Ivan did not want to get involved at all in the situation. Abigail felt her only alternative was to accept Sinbad's terms. Sinbad fulfilled his promise to Abigail and delivered her into the arms of Gregory. When Abigail told Gregory about her amorous escapade in order to cross the river, Gregory cast her aside with disdain. Heartsick and rejected, Abigail turned to Slug with her tail of woe. Slug, feeling compassion for Abigail, sought out Gregory and beat him brutally. Abigail was overjoyed at the sight of Gregory getting his due. As the sun set on the horizon, people heard Abigail laughing at Gregory.

Instructions

1. Read "The Alligator River Story."
2. After reading the story, rank the five characters in the story beginning with the one whom you consider the most offensive and end with the one whom you consider the least objectionable. That is, the character who seems to be the most reprehensible to you should be entered first in the list following the story, then the second most reprehensible, and so on, with the least reprehensible or objectionable being entered fifth. Of course, you will have your own reasons as to why you rank them in the order that you do. Very briefly note these too.
3. Form groups as assigned by your instructor (at least four persons per group with gender mixed).
4. Each group should:
   a. Elect a spokesperson for the group
   b. Compare how the group members have ranked the characters
   c. Examine the reasons used by each of the members for their rankings
   d. Seek consensus on a final group ranking
5. Following your group discussions, you will be asked to share your outcomes and reasons for agreement or nonagreement. A general class discussion will then be held.

Source: From Sidney B. Simon, Howard Kirschenbaum, and Leland Howe, *Values Clarification, The Handbook*, rev. ed. (Sutherland, MA: Values Press, 1991).

EXERCISE 11

Teamwork and Motivation

Contributed by Dr. Barbara McCain, Oklahoma City University

Instructions

1. Read the following situation:

   You are the *owner* of a small manufacturing corporation. Your company manufactures widgets—a commodity. Your widget is a clone of nationally known widgets. Your widget, WooWoo, is less expensive and more readily available than the nationally known brand. Presently, the sales are high. However, there are many rejects, which increases your cost and delays the delivery. You have 50 employees in the following departments: sales, assembly, technology, and administration.

2. In groups, discuss methods to motivate all of the employees in the organization—rank them in terms of preference.
3. Design an organization motivation plan that encourages high job satisfaction, low turnover, high productivity, and high-quality work.
4. Is there anything special you can do about the minimum-wage service worker? How do you motivate this individual? On what motivation theory do you base your decision?
5. Report to the class your motivation plan. Record your ideas on the board and allow all groups to build on the first plan. Discuss additions and corrections as the discussion proceeds.

Worksheet

Individual Worker	Team Member
Talks	
Me oriented	
Department focused	
Competitive	
Logical	
Written messages	
Image	
Secrecy	
Short-term sighted	
Immediate results	
Critical	
Tenure	

Directions: Fill in the right-hand column with descriptive terms. These terms should suggest a change in behavior from individual work to teamwork.

EXERCISE 12

The Downside of Punishment

Contributed by Dr. Barbara McCain, Oklahoma City University

Instructions
There are numerous problems associated with using punishment or discipline to change behavior. Punishment creates negative effects in the workplace. To better understand this, work in your group to give an example of each of the following situations:

1. Punishment may not be applied to the person whose behavior you want to change.

2. Punishment applied over time may suppress the occurrence of socially desirable behaviors.

3. Punishment creates a dislike of the person who is implementing the punishment.

4. Punishment results in undesirable emotions such as anxiety and aggressiveness.

5. Punishment increases the desire to avoid punishment.

6. Punishing one behavior does not guarantee that the desired behavior will occur.

7. Punishment follow-up requires allocation of additional resources.

8. Punishment may create a communication barrier and inhibit the flow of information.

Source: Adapted from class notes: Dr. Larry Michaelson, Oklahoma University.

EXERCISE 13

Tinkertoys

Contributed by Bonnie McNeely, Murray State University

Materials Needed
Tinkertoy sets.

Instructions
1. Form groups as assigned by the instructor. The mission of each group or temporary organization is to build the tallest possible Tinkertoy tower. Each group should determine worker roles: at least four students will be builders, some will be consultants who offer suggestions, and the remaining students will be observers who remain silent and complete the observation sheet provided below.

Source: Adapted from Bonnie McNeely, "Using the Tinkertoy Exercise to Teach the Four Functions of Management," *Journal of Management Education,* 18: 4 (November 1994), pp. 468–472.

2. Rules for the exercise:
   1. 15 minutes allowed to plan the tower, but *only 60 seconds* to build.
   2. No more than two Tinkertoy pieces can be put together during the planning.
   3. All pieces must be put back in the box before the competition begins.
   4. Completed tower must stand alone.

Observation Sheet

1. What planning activities were observed?

   Did the group members adhere to the rules?

2. What organizing activities were observed?

   Was the task divided into subtasks? Division of labor?

3. Was the group motivated to succeed? Why or why not?

4. Were any control techniques observed?

   Was a timekeeper assigned?

   Were backup plans discussed?

5. Did a clear leader emerge from the group?

   What behaviors indicated that this person was the leader?

   How did the leader establish credibility with the group?

6. Did any conflicts within the group appear?

   Was there a power struggle for the leadership position?

EXERCISE 14

Job Design Preferences

Instructions

1. Use the left column to rank the following job characteristics in the order most important *to you* (1—highest to 10—lowest). Then use the right column to rank them in the order you think they are most important *to others*.

   ____ Variety of tasks ____
   ____ Performance feedback ____
   ____ Autonomy/freedom in work ____
   ____ Working on a team ____
   ____ Having responsibility ____
   ____ Making friends on the job ____
   ____ Doing all of a job, not part ____
   ____ Importance of job to others ____
   ____ Having resources to do well ____
   ____ Flexible work schedule ____

2. Form workgroups as assigned by your instructor. Share your rankings with other group members. Discuss where you have different individual preferences and where your impressions differ from the preferences of others. Are there any major patterns in your group—for either the "personal" or the "other" rankings? Develop group consensus rankings for each column. Designate a spokesperson to share the group rankings and results of any discussion with the rest of the class.

EXERCISE 15

My Fantasy Job

Contributed by Lady Hanson, California State Polytechnic University, Pomona

Instructions

1. Think about a possible job that represents what you consider to be your ideal or "fantasy" job. For discussion purposes, try to envision it as a job you would hold within a year of finishing your current studies. Write down a brief description of that job in the following space below. Start the description with the following words: *My fantasy job would be . . .*

   _____
   _____
   _____
   _____

2. Review the description of the Hackman/Oldham model of Job Characteristics Theory offered in the textbook. Note in particular the descriptions of the core characteristics. Consider how each of them could be maximized in your fantasy job. Indicate in the spaces that follow how specific parts of your fantasy job will fit into or relate to each of the core characteristics.

   1. Skill variety: _____
   2. Task identity: _____
   3. Task significance: _____
   4. Autonomy: _____
   5. Job feedback: _____

3. Form into groups as assigned by your instructor. In the group have each person share his or her fantasy job and the descriptions of its core characteristics. Select one person from your group to tell the class as a whole about her or his fantasy job. Be prepared to participate in a general discussion regarding the core characteristics and how they may or may not relate to job performance and job satisfaction. Consider also the likelihood that the fantasy jobs of class members are really attainable—in other words, Can "fantasy" become fact?

EXERCISE 16

Motivation by Job Enrichment

Contributed by Diana Page, University of West Florida

Instructions

1. Form groups of five to seven members. Each group is assigned one of the following categories:
   a. Bank teller
   b. Retail sales clerk
   c. Manager, fast-food service (e.g., McDonald's)
   d. Wait person
   e. Receptionist
   f. Restaurant manager
   g. Clerical worker (or bookkeeper)
   h. Janitor
2. As a group, develop a short description of job duties for the job your group has been assigned. The list should contain approximately four to six items.
3. Next, using job characteristics theory, enrich the job using the specific elements described in the theory. Develop a new list of job duties that incorporate any or all of the core job characteristics suggested by Richard Hackman and Greg Oldham, such as skill variety, task identity, and so on. Indicate for each of the new job duties which job characteristic(s) was/were used.
4. One member of each group should act as the spokesperson and will present the group's ideas to the class. Specifically describe one or two of the old job tasks. Describe the modified job tasks. Finally, relate the new job tasks the group has developed to specific job core characteristics such as skill variety, skill identity, and so on.
5. The group should also be prepared to discuss these and other follow-up questions:
   1. How would a manager go about enlarging but not enriching this job?
   2. Why was this job easy or hard?
   3. What are the possible constraints on actually accomplishing this enrichment in the workplace?
   4. What possible reasons are there that a worker would *not* like to have this newly enriched job?

EXERCISE 17

Annual Pay Raises

Instructions

1. Read the following job descriptions and decide on a percentage pay increase for each of the eight employees.
2. Make salary increase recommendations for each of the eight managers that you supervise. There are no formal company restrictions on the size of raises you give, but the total for everyone should not exceed the $10,900 (a 4 percent increase in the salary pool) that has been budgeted for this purpose. You have a variety of information on which to base the decisions, including a "productivity index" (PI), which

Industrial Engineering computes as a quantitative measure of operating efficiency for each manager's work unit. This index ranges from a high of 10 to a low of 1. Indicate the percentage increase *you* would give each manager in the blank space next to each manager's name. Be prepared to explain why.

____ *A. Alvarez* Alvarez is new this year and has a tough workgroup whose task is dirty and difficult. This is a hard position to fill, but you don't feel Alvarez is particularly good. The word around is that the other managers agree with you. PI = 3. Salary = $33,000.

____ *B. J. Cook* Cook is single and a "swinger" who enjoys leisure time. Everyone laughs at the problems Cook has getting the work out, and you feel it certainly is lacking. Cook has been in the job two years. PI = 3. Salary = $34,500.

____ *Z. Davis* In the position three years, Davis is one of your best people, even though some of the other managers don't agree. With a spouse who is independently wealthy, Davis doesn't need money but likes to work. PI = 7. Salary = $36,600.

____ *M. Frame* Frame has personal problems and is hurting financially. Others gossip about Frame's performance, but you are quite satisfied with this second-year employee. PI = 7. Salary = $34,700.

____ *C. M. Liu* Liu is just finishing a fine first year in a tough job. Highly respected by the others, Liu has a job offer in another company at a 15 percent increase in salary. You are impressed, and the word is that the money is important. PI = 9. Salary = $34,000.

____ *B. Ratin* Ratin is a first-year manager whom you and the others think is doing a good job. This is a bit surprising since Ratin turned out to be a "free spirit" who doesn't seem to care much about money or status. PI = 9. Salary = $33,800.

____ *H. Smith* Smith is a first-year manager recently divorced and with two children to support as a single parent. The others like Smith a lot, but your evaluation is not very high. Smith could certainly use extra money. PI = 5. Salary = $33,000.

____ *G. White* White is a big spender who always has the latest clothes and a new car. In the first year on what you would call an easy job, White doesn't seem to be doing very well. For some reason, though, the others talk about White as the "cream of the new crop." PI = 5. Salary = $33,000.

3. Convene in a group of four to seven persons and share your raise decisions.
4. As a group, decide on a new set of raises and be prepared to report them to the rest of the class. Make sure that the group spokesperson can provide the rationale for each person's raise.
5. The instructor will call on each group to report its raise decisions. After discussion, an "expert's" decision will be given.

EXERCISE 18

Serving on the Boundary

Contributed by Joseph A. Raelin, Boston College

Instructions

The objective of this exercise is to experience what it is like being on the boundary of your team or organization and to experience the boundary person's divided loyalties.

1. As a full class, decide on a stake you are willing to wager on this exercise. Perhaps it will be 5 cents or 10 cents per person, or even more.

2. Form into teams. Select or elect one member from your team to be an expert. The expert will be the person most competent in the field of international geography.
3. The experts will then form into a team of their own.
4. The teams, including the expert team, are going to be given a straightforward question to work on. Whichever team comes closest to deriving the correct answer will win the pool from the stakes already collected. The question is any one of the following as assigned by the instructor: (a) What is the airline distance between Beijing and Moscow (in miles)? (b) What is the highest point in Texas (in feet)? (c) What was the number of American battle deaths in the Revolutionary War?
5. Each team should now work on the question, including the expert team. However, after all the teams come up with a verdict, the experts will be allowed to return to their "home" team to inform the team of the expert team's deliberations.
6. The expert team members are now asked to reconvene as an expert team. They should determine their final answer to the question. Then they are to face a decision. The instructor will announce that for a period of up to two minutes, any expert may either return to their home team (to sink or swim with the answer of the home team) or remain with the expert team. As long as two members remain in the expert team, it will be considered a group and may vie for the pool. Home teams, during the two-minute decision period, can do whatever they would like to do—within bounds of normal decorum—to try to persuade their expert member to return.
7. After the two minutes are up, teams will hand in their responses to the question, and the team with the closest answer (up or down) will be awarded the pool.
8. Class members should be prepared to discuss the following questions:
    a. What did it feel like to be a boundary person (the expert)?
    b. What could the teams have done to corral any of the boundary persons who chose not to return home?

EXERCISE 19

Eggsperiential Exercise

Contributed by Dr. Barbara McCain, Oklahoma City University

Materials Needed
Chairs
1 raw egg per group
6 plastic straws per group
1 yard of plastic tape
1 large plastic jar

Instructions
1. Form into equal groups of five to seven people.
2. The task is to drop an egg from the chair onto the plastic without breaking the egg. Groups can evaluate the materials and plan their task for 10 minutes. During this period the materials may not be handled.
3. Groups have 10 minutes for construction.
4. One group member will drop the egg while standing on top of a chair in front of the class. One by one, a representative from each group will drop his or her group's eggs.
5. Optional: Each group will name their egg.
6. Each group discusses their individual/group behaviors during this activity.

Optional: This analysis may be summarized in written form. The following questions may be utilized in the analysis:
a. What kind of group is it? Explain.
b. Was the group cohesive? Explain.
c. How did the cohesiveness relate to performance? Explain.
d. Was there evidence of groupthink? Explain.
e. Were group norms established? Explain.
f. Was there evidence of conflict? Explain.
g. Was there any evidence of social loafing? Explain.

EXERCISE 20

Scavenger Hunt—Team Building

Contributed by Michael R. Manning and Paula J. Schmidt, New Mexico State University

Introduction
Think about what it means to be part of a team—a successful team. What makes one team more successful than another? What does each team member need to do in order for their team to be successful? What are the characteristics of an effective team?

Instructions
1. Form teams as assigned by your instructor. Locate the listed items while following these important rules:
   a. Your team *must stay together at all times*—that is, you cannot go in separate directions.
   b. Your team must return to the classroom within the time allotted by the instructor.

   The team with the most items on the list will be declared the most successful team.
2. Next, reflect on your team's experience. What did each team member do? What was your team's strategy? What made your team effective? Make a list of the most important things your team did to be successful. Nominate a spokesperson to summarize your team's discussion for the class. What items were similar between teams? That is, what helped each team to be effective?

Source: Adapted from Michael R. Manning and Paula J. Schmidt, *Journal of Management Education*, "Building Effective Work Teams: A Quick Exercise Based on a Scavenger Hunt" (Thousand Oaks, CA: Sage Publications, 1995), pp. 392–398. Used by permission. Reference for list of items for scavenger hunt from C. E. Larson and F. M. Lafas, *Team Work: What Must Go Right/What Can Go Wrong* (Newbury Park, CA: Sage Publications, 1989).

Items for Scavenger Hunt
Each item is to be identified and brought back to the classroom.

1. A book with the word *Team* in the title.
2. A joke about teams that you share with the class.
3. A blade of grass from the university football field.
4. A souvenir from the state.
5. A picture of a team or group.
6. A newspaper article about a team.
7. A team song to be composed and performed for the class.
8. A leaf from an oak tree.
9. Stationery from the dean's office.
10. A cup of sand.
11. A pine cone.
12. A live reptile. (*Note:* Sometimes a team member has one for a pet or the students are ingenious enough to visit a local pet store.)
13. A definition of group "cohesion" that you share with the class.
14. A set of chopsticks.
15. Three cans of vegetables.
16. A branch of an elm tree.
17. Three unusual items.
18. A ball of cotton.
19. The ear from a prickly pear cactus.
20. A group name.

(*Note:* Items may be substituted as appropriate for your locale.)

EXERCISE 21

Work Team Dynamics

Introduction
Think about your course work team, a work team you are involved in for another course, or any other team suggested by the instructor. Indicate how often each of the following statements accurately reflects your experience in the team. Use this scale:

Source: Adapted from William Dyer, *Team Building,* 2nd ed. (Reading, MA: Addison-Wesley, 1987), pp. 123–125.

1 = Always   2 = Frequently   3 = Sometimes   4 = Never

____ 1. My ideas get a fair hearing.
____ 2. I am encouraged for innovative ideas and risk taking.
____ 3. Diverse opinions within the team are encouraged.
____ 4. I have all the responsibility I want.
____ 5. There is a lot of favoritism shown in the team.
____ 6. Members trust one another to do their assigned work.
____ 7. The team sets high standards of performance excellence.
____ 8. People share and change jobs a lot in the team.
____ 9. You can make mistakes and learn from them on this team.
____ 10. This team has good operating rules.

Instructions

Form groups as assigned by your instructor. Ideally, this will be the team you have just rated. Have all team members share their ratings, and make one master rating for the team as a whole. Circle the items on which there are the biggest differences of opinion. Discuss those items and try to find out why they exist. In general, the better a team scores on this instrument, the higher its creative potential. If everyone has rated the same team, make a list of the five most important things members can do to improve its operations in the future. Nominate a spokesperson to summarize the team discussion for the class as a whole.

EXERCISE 22

Identifying Team Norms

Instructions

1. Choose an organization you know quite a bit about.
2. Complete the following questionnaire, indicating your responses using one of the following:

   1. Strongly agree or encourage it.
   2. Agree with it or encourage it.
   3. Consider it unimportant.
   4. Disagree with or discourage it.
   5. Strongly disagree with or discourage it.

If an employee in this organization were to _____, *most other employees would:*

1. show genuine concern for the problems that face the organization and make suggestions about solving them ____
2. set very high personal standards of performance ____
3. try to make the workgroup operate more like a team when dealing with issues or problems ____
4. think of going to a supervisor with a problem ____
5. evaluate expenditures in terms of the benefits they will provide for the organization ____

6. express concern for the well-being of other members of the organization ____
7. keep a customer or client waiting while looking after matters of personal convenience ____
8. criticize a fellow employee who is trying to improve things in the work situation ____
9. actively look for ways to expand his or her knowledge to be able to do a better job ____
10. be perfectly honest in answering this questionnaire ____

Scoring

$$A = +2, B = +1, C = 0, D = -1, E = -2$$

1. Organizational/Personal Pride Score ____
2. Performance/Excellence Score ____
3. Teamwork/Communication Score ____
4. Leadership/Supervision Score ____
5. Profitability/Cost-Effectiveness Score ____
6. Colleague/Associate Relations Score ____
7. Customer/Client Relations Score ____
8. Innovativeness/Creativity Score ____
9. Training/Development Score ____
10. Candor/Openness Score ____

EXERCISE 23

Workgroup Culture

Contributed by Conrad N. Jackson, MPC Inc.

Instructions

The bipolar scales on this instrument can be used to evaluate a group's process in a number of useful ways. Use it to measure where you see the group to be at present. To do this, *circle* the number that best represents *how you see the culture of the group*. You can also indicate how you think the group *should* function by using a different symbol, such as an asterisk (**), to indicate how you saw the group at some time in the past.

1. If you are assessing your own group, have everyone fill in the instrument, summarize the scores, then discuss their bases (what members say and do that has led to these interpretations) and implications. This is often an extremely productive intervention to improve group or team functioning.

2. If you are assessing another group, use the scores as the basis for your feedback. Be sure to provide specific feedback on behavior *you have observed* in addition to the subjective interpretations of your ratings on the scales in this instrument.

3. The instrument can also be used to compare a group's self-assessment with the assessment provided by another group.

1. Trusting	1 : 2 : 3 : 4 : 5	Suspicious
2. Helping	1 : 2 : 3 : 4 : 5	Ignoring, blocking
3. Expressing feelings	1 : 2 : 3 : 4 : 5	Suppressing feelings
4. Risk taking	1 : 2 : 3 : 4 : 5	Cautious
5. Authenticity	1 : 2 : 3 : 4 : 5	Game playing
6. Confronting	1 : 2 : 3 : 4 : 5	Avoiding
7. Open	1 : 2 : 3 : 4 : 5	Hidden, diplomatic

Source: Adapted from Donald D. Bowen et al., *Experiences in Management and Organizational Behavior,* 4th ed. (New York: John Wiley & Sons, Inc., 1997.)

EXERCISE 24

The Hot Seat

Contributed by Barry R. Armandi, SUNY–Old Westbury

Instructions
1. Form into groups as assigned by your instructor.
2. Read the following situation.

A number of years ago, Professor Stevens was asked to attend a departmental meeting at a university. He had been on leave from the department, but a junior faculty member discreetly requested that he attend to protect the rights of the junior faculty. The Chair, or head of the department, was a typical Machiavellian, whose only concerns were self-serving. Professor Stevens had had a number of previous disagreements with the Chair. The heart of the disagreements centered around the Chair's abrupt and domineering style and his poor relations with the junior faculty, many of whom felt mistreated and scared.

The department was a conglomeration of different professorial types. Included in the mix were behavioralists, generalists, computer scientists, and quantitative analysts. The department was embedded in the school of business, which included three other departments. There was much confusion and concern among the faculty, since this was a new organizational design. Many of the faculty were at odds with each other over the direction the school was now taking.

At the meeting, a number of proposals were to be presented that would seriously affect the performance and future of certain junior faculty, particularly those who were behavioral scientists. The Chair, a computer scientist, disliked the behaviorists, who he felt were "always analyzing the motives of people." Professor Stevens, who was a tenured full professor and a behaviorist, had an objective to protect the interests of the junior faculty and to counter the efforts of the Chair.

Including Professor Stevens, there were nine faculty present. The following diagram shows the seating

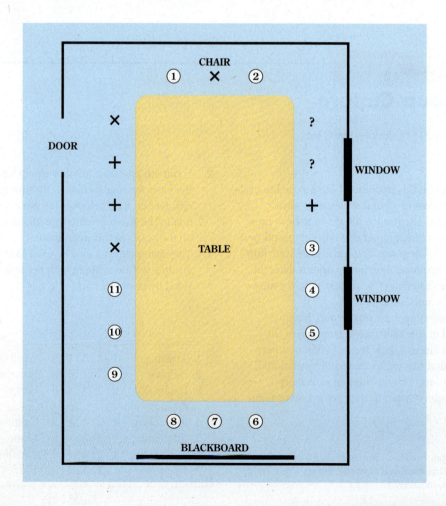

arrangement and the layout of the room. The ×s signify those faculty who were allies of the Chair. The +s are those opposed to the Chair and supportive of Professor Stevens, and the ?s were undecided and could be swayed either way. The circled numbers represent empty seats. Both ?s were behavioralists, and the + next to them was a quantitative analyst. Near the door, the first × was a generalist, the two +s were behavioralists, and the second × was a quantitative analyst. The diagram shows the seating of everyone but Professor Stevens, who was the last one to enter the room. Standing at the door, Professor Stevens surveyed the room and within 10 seconds knew which seat was the most effective to achieve his objective.

3. Answer the following questions in your group:
    1. Which seat did Professor Stevens select and why?
    2. What is the likely pattern of communication and interaction in this group?
    3. What can be done to get this group to work harmoniously?

EXERCISE 25

Interview a Leader

Contributed by Bonnie McNeely, Murray State University

Instructions

1. Make an appointment to interview a leader. It can be a leader working in a business or nonprofit organization, such as a government agency, school, and so on. Base the interview on the form provided here, but feel free to add your own questions.
2. Bring the results of your interview to class. Form into groups as assigned by your instructor. Share the responses from your interview with your group and compare answers. What issues were similar? Different? Were the stress levels of leaders working in nonprofit organizations as high as those working in for-profit firms? Were you surprised at the number of hours per week worked by leaders?
3. Be prepared to summarize the interviews done by your group as a formal written report if asked to do so by the instructor.

Interview Questionnaire

Student's Name ____ Date ____

1. Position in the organization (title):
2. Number of years in current position:
   Number of years of managerial experience:
3. Number of people directly supervised:
4. Average number of hours worked a week:
5. How did you get into leadership?
6. What is the most rewarding part of being a leader?
7. What is the most difficult part of your job?
8. What would you say are the *keys to success* for leaders?
9. What advice do you have for an aspiring leader?
10. What type of ethical issues have you faced as a leader?
11. If you were to enroll in a leadership seminar, what topics or issues would you want to learn more about?
12. (Student question)

Gender: M ____ F ____ Years of formal education ____
Level of job stress: Very high ____ High ____ Average ____ Low ____
Profit organization ____ Nonprofit organization ____
Additional information/Comments:

_____

Source: Adapted from Bonnie McNeely, "Make Your Principles of Management Class Come Alive," *Journal of Management Education,* 18:2 (May 1994), pp. 246–249.

EXERCISE 26

Leadership Skills Inventories

Instructions

1. Look over the following skills and ask your instructor to clarify those you do not understand.
2. Complete each category by checking either the "Strong" or "Needs Development" category in relation to your own level with each skill.
3. After completing each category, briefly describe a situation in which each of the listed skills has been utilized.
4. Meet in your groups to share and discuss inventories. Prepare a report summarizing major development needs in your group.

Instrument

	Strong	Needs Development	Situation
Communication			
Conflict management			
Delegation			
Ethical behavior			
Listening			
Motivation			
Negotiation			
Performance appraisal and feedback			
Planning and goal setting			
Power and influence			
Presentation and persuasion			
Problem solving and decision making			
Stress management			
Team building			
Time management			

EXERCISE 27

Leadership and Participation in Decision Making

Instructions

1. For the ten situations described here, decide which of the three styles you would use for that unique situation. Place the letter A, P, or L on the line before each situation's number.

    A—authority; make the decision alone without additional inputs.
    P—consultative; make the decision based on group inputs.
    L—group; allow the group to which you belong to make the decision.

Decision Situations

_____ i. You have developed a new work procedure that will increase productivity. Your boss likes the idea and wants you to try it within a few weeks. You view your employees as fairly capable and believe that they will be receptive to the change.

_____ ii. The industry of your product has new competition. Your organization's revenues have been dropping. You have been told to lay off three of your ten employees in two weeks. You have been the supervisor for over one year. Normally, your employees are very capable.

_____ iii. Your department has been facing a problem for several months. Many solutions have been tried and have failed. You finally thought of a solution, but you are not sure of the possible consequences of the change required or its acceptance by the highly capable employees.

_____ iv. Flextime has become popular in your organization. Some departments let each employee start and end work whenever they choose. However, because of the cooperative effort of your employees, they must all work the same eight hours. You are not sure of the level of interest in changing the hours. Your employees are a very capable group and like to make decisions.

_____ v. The technology in your industry is changing faster than the members of your organization can keep up. Top management hired a consultant who has given the recommended decision. You have two weeks to make your decision. Your employees are capable, and they enjoy participating in the decision-making process.

_____ vi. Your boss called you on the telephone to tell you that someone has requested an order for your department's product with a very short delivery date. She asked that you call her back in 15 minutes with the decision about taking the order. Looking over the work schedule, you realize that it will be very difficult to deliver the order on time. Your employees will have to push hard to make it. They are cooperative, capable, and enjoy being involved in decision making.

_____ vii. A change has been handed down from top management. How you implement it is your decision. The change takes effect in one month. It will personally affect everyone in your department. The acceptance of the department members is critical to the success of the change. Your employees are usually not too interested in being involved in making decisions.

_____ viii. You believe that productivity in your department could be increased. You have thought of some ways that may work, but you're not sure of them. Your employees are very experienced; almost all of them have been in the department longer than you have.

_____ ix. Top management has decided to make a change that will affect all of your employees. You know that they will be upset because it will cause them hardship. One or two may even quit. The change goes into effect in thirty days. Your employees are very capable.

_____ x. A customer has offered you a contract for your product with a quick delivery date. The offer is open for two days. Meeting the contract deadline would require employees to work nights and weekends for six weeks. You cannot require them to work overtime. Filling this profitable contract could help get you the raise you want and feel you deserve. However, if you take the contract and don't deliver on time, it will hurt your chances of getting a big raise. Your employees are very capable.

2. Form groups as assigned by your instructor. Share and compare your choices for each decision situation. Reconcile any differences and be prepared to defend your decision preferences in general class discussion.

EXERCISE 28

My Best Manager: Revisited

Contributed by J. Marcus Maier, Chapman University

Instructions

1. Refer to the list of qualities—or profiles—the class generated earlier in the course for the "Best Manager."
2. Looking first at your Typical Managers profile, suppose you took this list to 100 average people on the street (or at the local mall) and asked them whether ____ (Trait X, Quality Y) was "more typical of men or of women in our culture." What do you think *most* of them would say? That ____ (X, Y etc.) is more typical of *women?* or of *men?* or of neither/both?[1] Do this for every trait on your list(s). (5 min.)
3. Now do the same for the qualities we generated in our Best Manager profile. (5 min.)
4. A straw vote is taken, one quality at a time, to determine the class's overall gender identification of each trait, focusing on the Typical Managers profile (10–15 min.). Then this is repeated for the Best Manager profile (10–15 min.).[2]
5. Discussion. What do you see in the data this group has generated? How might you interpret these results? (15–20 min.)

Source: Based on J. Marcus Maier, "The Gender Prism," *Journal of Management Education* 17(3), pp. 285–314. 1994 Fritz Roethlisberger Award Recipient for Best Paper (Updated, 1996).

[1] This gets the participants to move outside of their *own* conceptions to their awareness of *societal* definitions of masculinity and femininity.

[2] This is done by a rapid show of hands, looking for a clear majority vote. An "f" (for "feminine") is placed next to those qualities that a clear majority indicate are more typical of women, and an "m" (for "masculine") is placed next to those qualities a clear majority indicate would be more typical of men. (This procedure parallels the median-split method used in determining Bem Sex Role Inventory classifications.) If no clear majority emerges (i.e., if the vote is close), the trait or quality is classified as "both" (f/m). The designations "masculine" or "feminine" are used (rather than "men" or "women") to underscore the socially constructed nature of each dimension.

EXERCISE 29

Active Listening

Contributed by Robert Ledman, Morehouse College

Instructions

1. Review active listening skills and behaviors as described in the textbook and in class.
2. Form into groups of three. Each group will have a listener, a talker, and an observer (if the number of students is not evenly divisible by three, two observers are used for one or two groups).
3. The "talkers" should talk about any subject they wish, but only *if* they are being actively listened to. Talkers should stop speaking as soon as they sense active listening has stopped.
4. The "listeners" should use a list of active listening skills and behaviors as their guide, and practice as many of them as possible to be sure the talker is kept

Source: Adapted from the presentation entitled "An Experiential Exercise to Teach Active Listening," presented at the Organizational Behavior Teaching Conference, Macomb, IL, 1995.

talking. Listeners should contribute nothing more than "active listening" to the communication.
5. The "observer" should note the behaviors and skills used by the listener and the effects they seemed to have on the communication process.
6. These roles are rotated until each student has played every role.
7. The instructor will lead a discussion of what the observers saw and what happened with the talkers and listeners. The discussion focuses on what behaviors from the posted list have been present, which have been absent, and how the communication has been affected by the listener's actions.

EXERCISE 30

Upward Appraisal

Instructions

1. Form workgroups as assigned by your instructor.
2. The instructor will leave the room.
3. Convene in your assigned workgroups for a period of 10 minutes. Create a list of comments, problems, issues, and concerns you would like to have communicated to the instructor in regard to the course experience to date. *Remember,* your interest in the exercise is twofold: (a) to communicate your feelings to the instructor and (b) to learn more about the process of giving and receiving feedback.
4. Select one person from the group to act as spokesperson in communicating the group's feelings to the instructor.
5. The spokespersons should briefly convene to decide on what physical arrangement of chairs, tables, and so forth is most appropriate to conduct the feedback session. The classroom should then be rearranged to fit the desired specifications.
6. While the spokespersons convene, persons in the remaining groups should discuss how they expect the forthcoming communications event to develop. Will it be a good experience for all parties concerned? Be prepared to critically observe the actual communication process.
7. The instructor should be invited to return, and the feedback session will begin. Observers should make notes so that they may make constructive comments at the conclusion of the exercise.
8. Once the feedback session is complete, the instructor will call on the observers for comments, ask the spokespersons for reactions, and open the session to discussion.

EXERCISE 31

360° Feedback

Contributed by Timothy J. Serey, Northern Kentucky University

Introduction
The time of performance reviews is often a time of genuine anxiety for many organizational members. On the one hand, it is an important organizational ritual and a key part of the human resources function. Organizations usually codify the process and provide a mechanism to appraise performance. On the other hand, it is rare for managers to feel comfortable with this process. Often, they feel discomfort over "playing God." One possible reason

for this is that managers rarely receive formal training about how to provide feedback. From the manager's point of view, if done properly, giving feedback is at the very heart of his or her job as "coach" and "teacher." It is an investment in the professional development of another person, rather than the punitive element we so often associate with hearing from "the boss." From the subordinate's perspective, most people want to know where they stand, but this is usually tempered by a fear of "getting it in the neck." In many organizations, it is rare to receive straight, non-sugar-coated feedback about where you stand.

Instructions
1. Review the section of the book dealing with feedback before you come to class. It is also helpful if individuals make notes about their perceptions and feelings about the course *before* they come to class.
2. Groups of students should discuss their experiences, both positive and negative, in this class. Each group should determine the dimensions of evaluating the class itself *and* the instructor. For example, students might select criteria that include the practicality of the course, the way the material is structured and presented (e.g., lecture or exercises), and the instructor's style (e.g., enthusiasm, fairness).
3. Groups select a member to represent them in a subgroup that next provides feedback to the instructor before the entire class.
4. The student audience then provides the subgroup with feedback about their effectiveness in this exercise. That is, the larger class provides feedback to the subgroup about the extent to which students actually put the principles of effective feedback into practice (e.g., descriptive, not evaluative; specific, not general).

Source: Adapted from Timothy J. Serey, *Journal of Management Education* 17:2 (May 1993). © 1993 by Sage Publications, Inc. Reprinted by permission of Sage Publications.

EXERCISE 32

Role Analysis Negotiation

Contributed by Paul Lyons, Frostburg State University

Introduction
A role is the set of various behaviors people expect from a person (or group) in a particular position. These role expectations occur in all types of organizations, such as one's place of work, school, family, clubs, and the like. Role ambiguity takes place when a person is confused about the expectations of the role. And sometimes, a role will have expectations that are contradictory—for example, being loyal to the company when the company is breaking the law.

The Role Analysis Technique, or RAT, is a method for improving the effectiveness of a team or group. RAT helps to clarify role expectations, and all organization members have responsibilities that translate to expectations. Determination of role requirements, by consensus—involving all concerned—will ultimately result in more effective and mutually satisfactory behavior. Participation and collaboration in the definition and

Source: Adapted from Paul Lyons, "Developing Expectations with the Role Analysis Technique," *Journal of Management Education* 17:3 (August 1993), pp. 386–389. © Sage Publications.

analysis of roles by group members should result in clarification regarding who is to do what as well as increase the level of commitment to the decisions made.

Instructions
Working alone, carefully read the course syllabus that your instructor has given you. Make a note of any questions you have about anything for which you need clarification or understanding. Pay particular attention to the performance requirements of the course. Make a list of any questions you have regarding what, specifically, is expected of you in order for you to be successful in the course. You will be sharing this information with others in small groups.

EXERCISE 33

Lost at Sea

Introduction
Consider this situation. You are adrift on a private yacht in the South Pacific when a fire of unknown origin destroys the yacht and most of its contents. You and a small group of survivors are now in a large raft with oars. Your location is unclear, but you estimate being about 1,000 miles south–southwest of the nearest land. One person has just found in her pockets five $1 bills and a packet of matches. Everyone else's pockets are empty. The following items are available to you on the raft.

	A	B	C
Sextant	___	___	
Shaving mirror	___	___	
5 gallons of water	___	___	
Mosquito netting	___	___	
1 survival meal	___	___	
Maps of Pacific Ocean	___	___	
Floatable seat cushion	___	___	
2 gallons oil–gas mix	___	___	
Small transistor radio	___	___	
Shark repellent	___	___	
20 square feet black plastic	___	___	
1 quart of 20-proof rum	___	___	
15 feet of nylon rope	___	___	
24 chocolate bars	___	___	
Fishing kit	___	___	

Source: Adapted from "Lost at Sea: A Consensus-Seeking Task," in J. William Pfeiffer and John E. Jones (eds.), *The 1975 Handbook for Group Facilitators*. Used with permission of University Associates, Inc., La Jolla, CA.

Instructions

1. *Working alone,* rank in Column A the 15 items in order of their importance to your survival ("1" is most important, and "15" is least important).
2. *Working in an assigned group,* arrive at a "team" ranking of the 15 items and record this ranking in Column B. Appoint one person as group spokesperson to report your group rankings to the class.
3. *Do not write in Column C* until further instructions are provided by your instructor.

EXERCISE 34

Entering the Unknown

Contributed by Michael R. Manning, New Mexico State University; Conrad N. Jackson, MPC Inc., Huntsville, Alabama; and Paula S. Weber, New Mexico Highlands University

Instructions

1. Form into groups of four or five members. In each group spend a few minutes reflecting on members' typical entry behaviors in new situations and their behaviors when they are in comfortable settings.
2. According to the instructor's directions, students count off to form new groups of four or five members each.
3. The new groups spend the next 15 to 20 minutes getting to know each other. There is no right or wrong way to proceed, but all members should become more aware of their entry behaviors. They should act in ways that can help them realize a goal of achieving comfortable behaviors with their group.
4. Students review what has occurred in the new groups, giving specific attention to the following questions:
   a. What topics did your group discuss (content)? Did these topics involve the "here and now" or were they focused on "there and then"?
   b. What approach did you and your group members take to the task (process)? Did you try to initiate or follow? How? Did you ask questions? Listen? Respond to others? Did you bring up topics?
   c. Were you more concerned with how you came across or with how others came across to you? Did you play it safe? Were you open? Did you share things even though it seemed uncomfortable or risky? How was humor used in your group? Did it add or detract?
   d. How do you feel about the approach you took or the behaviors you exhibited? Was this hard or easy? Did others respond the way you had anticipated? Is there some behavior you would like to do more of, do better, or do less of?
   e. Were your behaviors the ones you had intended (goals)?
5. Responses to these questions are next discussed by the class as a whole. (*Note:* Responses will tend to be mixed within a group, but between groups there should be more similarity.) This discussion helps individuals become aware of and understand their entry behaviors.
6. Optional individuals have identified their entry behaviors; each group can then spend 5 to 10 minutes discussing members' perceptions of each other:
   a. What behaviors did they like or find particularly useful? What did they dislike?

b. What were your reactions to others? What ways did they intend to come across? Did you see others in the way they had intended to come across?
(Alternatively, if there is concern about the personal nature of this discussion, ask the groups to discuss what they liked/didn't like without referring to specific individuals.)

EXERCISE 35

Vacation Puzzle

Contributed by Barbara G. McCain and Mary Khalili, Oklahoma City University

Instructions

Can you solve this puzzle? Give it a try and then compare your answers with those of classmates. Remember your communicative skills!

Puzzle

Khalili, McCain, Middleton, Porter, and Quintaro teach at Oklahoma City University. Each gets two weeks of vacation a year. Last year, each took his or her first week in the first five months of the year and his or her second week in the last five months. If each professor took each of his or her weeks in a different month from the other professors, in which months did each professor take his or her first and second week?

Here are the facts:

1. McCain took her first week before Khalili, who took *hers* before Porter; for their second week, the order was reversed.
2. The professor who vacationed in March also vacationed in September.
3. Quintaro did not take her first week in March or April.
4. Neither Quintaro nor the professor who took his or her first week in January took his or her second week in August or December.
5. Middleton took her second week before McCain but after Quintaro.

Month	Professor
January	
February	
March	
April	
May	
June	
July	
August	
September	
October	
November	
December	

Source: Adapted to classroom activity by Dr. Mary Khalili.

EXERCISE 36

The Ugli Orange

Introduction
In most work settings, people need other people to do their job, benefit the organization, and forward their career. Getting things done in organizations requires us to work together in cooperation, even though the ultimate objectives of those other people may be different from our own. Your task in the present exercise is learning how to achieve this cooperation more effectively.

Instructions
1. The class will be divided into pairs. One student in each pair will read and prepare the role of Dr. Roland, and one will play the role of Dr. Jones (role descriptions to be distributed by instructor). Students should read their respective role descriptions and prepare to meet with their counterpart (see steps 2 and 3).
2. At this point the group leader will read a statement. The instructor will indicate that he or she is playing the role of Mr. Cardoza, who owns the commodity in question. The instructor will tell you:
   a. How long you have to meet with the other
   b. What information the instructor will require at the end of your meeting

   After the instructor has given you this information, you may meet with the other firm's representative and determine whether you have issues you can agree to.
3. Following the meetings (negotiations), the spokesperson for each pair will report any agreements reached to the entire class. The observer for any pair will report on negotiation dynamics and the process by which agreement was reached.
4. Questions to consider:
   a. Did you reach a solution? If so, what was critical to reaching that agreement?
   b. Did you and the other negotiator trust one another? Why or why not?
   c. Was there full disclosure by both sides in each group? How much information was shared?
   d. How creative and/or complex were the solutions? If solutions were very complex, why do you think this occurred?
   e. What was the impact of having an "audience" on your behavior? Did it make the problem harder or easier to solve?

Source: Adapted from Douglas T. Hall et al., *Experiences in Management and Organizational Behavior,* 3rd ed. (New York: John Wiley and Sons, Inc., 1988). Originally developed by Robert J. House. Adapted by D. T. Hall and R. J. Lewicki, with suggested modifications by H. Kolodny and T. Ruble.

EXERCISE 37

Conflict Dialogues

Contributed by Edward G. Wertheim, Northeastern University

Instructions
1. Think of a conflict situation at work or at school and try to re-create a segment of the dialogue that gets to the heart of the conflict.
2. Write notes on the conflict dialogue using the following format.

Introduction
- Background
- My goals and objectives

- My strategy
- Assumptions I am making

Dialogue (re-create part of the following dialogue and try to put what you were really thinking in parentheses).
- *Me:*
- *Other:*
- *Me:*
- *Other,*
- etc.

3. Share your situation with members of your group. Read the dialogue to them, perhaps asking someone to play the role of "other."
4. Discuss with the group:
    a. The style of conflict resolution you used (confrontation, collaboration, avoidance, etc.)
    b. The triggers to the conflict, that is, what really set you off and why
    c. Whether or not you were effective
    d. Possible ways of handling this differently
5. Choose one dialogue from within the group to share with the class. Be prepared to discuss your analysis and also possible alternative approaches and resolutions for the situation described.

EXERCISE 38

Force-Field Analysis

Instructions

1. Choose a situation in which you have high personal stakes (for example, how to get a better grade in course X; how to get a promotion; how to obtain a position).
2. Using a version of the Sample Force-Field Analysis Form provided, apply the technique to your situation.
    a. Describe the situation as it now exists.
    b. Describe the situation as you would like it to be.
    c. Identify those "driving forces"—the factors that are presently helping to move things in the desired direction.
    d. Identify those "restraining forces"—the factors that are presently holding things back from moving in the desired direction.
3. Try to be as specific as possible in yours answers in relation to your situation. You should attempt to be exhaustive in your listing of these forces. List them all!
4. Now go back and classify the strength of each force as weak, medium, or strong. Do this for both the driving and the restraining forces.
5. At this point you should rank the forces regarding their ability to influence or control the situation.
6. In small groups, share your analyses. Discuss the usefulness and drawbacks to using this method for personal situations and its application to organizations.
7. Be prepared to share the results of your group's discussion with the rest of the class.

Sample Force-Field Analysis Form

Current Situation:	Situation as You Would Like It to Be:
Driving Forces:	**Restraining Forces:**

EXERCISE 39

Organizations Alive!

Contributed by Bonnie L. McNeely, Murray State University

Instructions

1. Find a copy of the following items from actual organizations. These items can be obtained from the company where you now work, a parent's workplace, or the university. Universities have mission statements, codes of conduct for students and faculty, organizational charts, job descriptions, performance appraisal forms, and control devices. Some student organizations also have these documents. All the items do not have to come from the same organization. *Bring these items to class.*
   a. Mission statement
   b. Code of ethics
   c. Organizational chart
   d. Job description
   e. Performance appraisal form
   f. Control device
2. Form groups in class as assigned by your instructor. Share your items with the group, as well as what you learned while collecting these items. For example, did you find that some firms have a mission, but it is not written down? Did you find that job descriptions existed, but they were not really used or had not been updated in years?

Source: Adapted from Bonnie L. McNeely, "Make Your Principles of Management Class Come Alive," *Journal of Management Education,* 18:2 (May 1994), pp. 246–249.

EXERCISE 40

Fast-Food Technology

Contributed by D. T. Hall, Boston University, and F. S. Hall, University of New Hampshire

Introduction

A critical first step in improving or changing any organization is *diagnosing* or analyzing its present functioning. Many change and organization development efforts fall short of their objectives because this important step was not taken or was conducted superficially. To illustrate this, imagine how you would feel if you went to your doctor complaining of stomach pains and he recommended surgery without conducting any tests, without obtaining any further information, and without a careful physical examination. You would probably switch doctors! Yet managers often attempt major changes with correspondingly little diagnostic work in advance. (It could be said that they undertake vast projects with half-vast ideas.)

In this exercise, you will be asked to conduct a group diagnosis of two different organizations in the fast-food business. The exercise will provide an opportunity to integrate much of the knowledge you have gained in other exercises and in studying other topics. Your task will be to describe the organizations as carefully as you can in terms of several key organizational concepts. Although the organizations are probably very familiar to you, try to step back and look at them as though you were seeing them for the first time.

Instructions

1. In groups of four or six people, your assignment is described here.

One experience most people in this country have shared is that of dining in the hamburger establishment known as McDonald's. In fact, someone has claimed that twenty-fifth-century archeologists may dig into the ruins of our present civilization and conclude that twentieth-century religion was devoted to the worship of golden arches.

Your group, Fastalk Consultants, is known as the shrewdest, most insightful, and most overpaid management consulting firm in the country. You have been hired by the president of McDonald's to make recommendations for improving the motivation and performance of personnel in its franchise operations. Let us assume that the key job activities in franchise operations are food preparation, order taking and dealing with customers, and routine cleanup operations.

Recently the president of McDonald's has come to suspect that his company's competitors—such as Burger King, Wendy's, Jack-in-the-Box, Dunkin' Donuts, various pizza establishments, and others—are making heavy inroads into McDonald's market share. He has also hired a market research firm to investigate and compare the relative merits of the sandwiches, french fries, and drinks served in McDonald's and the competitors, and has asked the market research firm to assess the advertising campaigns of the two organizations. Hence, you will not need to be concerned with marketing issues, except as they may have an impact on employee behavior. The president wants *you* to look into the *organization* of the franchises to determine the strengths and weaknesses of each. Select a competitor that gives McDonald's a good "run for its money" in your area.

The president has established an unusual contract with you. *He wants you to make your recommendations based upon your observations as a customer.* He does not want you to do a complete diagnosis with interviews, surveys, or behind-the-scenes observations. He wants your report in two parts. Remember, the president wants concrete, specific, and practical recommendations. Avoid vague generalizations such as "improve communications" or "increase trust." Say very clearly *how* management can improve organizational performance. Substantiate your recommendations by reference to one or more theories of motivation, leadership, small groups, or job design.

Part I

Given his organization's goals of profitability, sales volume, fast and courteous service, and cleanliness, the president of McDonald's wants an analysis that will *compare and contrast McDonald's and the competitor* in terms of the following concepts:
- Organizational goals
- Organizational structure
- Technology
- Environment
- Employee motivation
- Communication
- Leadership style
- Policies/procedures/rules/standards
- Job design
- Organizational climate

Part II

Given the corporate goals listed under Part I, what specific actions might McDonald's management and franchise owners take in the following areas to achieve these goals (profitability, sales volume, fast and courteous service, and cleanliness)?
- Job design and workflow
- Organizational structure (at the individual restaurant level)
- Employee incentives
- Leadership
- Employee selection

How do McDonald's and the competition differ in these aspects? Which company has the best approach?

2. Complete the assignment by going as a group to one McDonald's and one competitor's restaurant. If possible, have a meal in each place. To get a more valid comparison, visit a McDonald's and a competitor located in the same area. After observing each restaurant, meet with your group and prepare your 10-minute report to the executive committee.

3. In class, each group will present its report to the rest of the class, who will act as the executive committee. The group leader will appoint a timekeeper to be sure

that each group sticks to its 10-minute time limit. Possible discussion questions include:
a. What similarities are there between the two organizations?
b. What differences are there between the organizations?
c. Do you have any "hunches" about the reasons for the particular organizational characteristics you found? For example, can you try to explain why one organization might have a particular type of structure? Incentive system? Climate?
d. Can you try to explain one set of characteristics in terms of some other characteristics you found? For example, do the goals account for structure? Does the environment explain the structure?

EXERCISE 41

Alien Invasion

Instructions

This is an exercise in organizational culture. You will be assigned to a team (if you are not already in one) and instructed to visit an organization by your instructor.

1. Visit the assigned site as a team working under conditions set forth in the "situation" below.
2. Take detailed notes on the cultural forms that you observe.
3. Prepare a presentation for the class that describes these forms and draw any inferences you can about the nature of the culture of the organization—its ideologies, values, and norms of behavior.
4. Be sure to explain the basis of your inferences in terms of the cultural forms observed.

You will have 20 minutes to report your findings, so plan your presentation carefully. Use visual aids to help your audience understand what you have found.

Situation

You are Martians who have just arrived on Earth in the first spaceship from your planet. Your superiors have ordered you to learn as much about Earthlings and the way they behave as you can without doing anything to make them aware that you are Martians. It is vital for the future plans of your superiors that you do nothing to disturb the Earthlings. Unfortunately, Martians communicate by emitting electromagnetic waves and are incapable of speech, so you cannot talk to the natives. Even if you did, it is reported by the usually reliable Bureau of Interplanetary Intelligence that Earthlings may become cannibalistic if annoyed. However, the crash course in Earth languages taught by the bureau has enabled you to read the language.

Remember, these instructions limit your data collection to observation and request that you *not* talk to the "natives." There are two reasons for this instruction. First, your objective is to learn what the organization does when it is simply going about its normal business and not responding to a group of students asking questions. Second, you are likely to be surprised at how much you can learn by simply observing if you put your mind to it. Many skilled managers employ this ability in sensing what is going on as they walk through their plant or office area.

Since you cannot talk to people, some of the cultural forms (legends, sagas, etc.) will be difficult to spot unless you are able to pick up copies of the organization's promotional literature (brochures, company reports, advertisements) during your visit. Do not be discouraged, because the visible forms such as artifacts, setting, symbols, and (sometimes) rituals can convey a great deal about the culture. Just keep your eyes, ears, and antennae open!

Source: Adapted from Donald D. Bowen et al., *Experiences in Management and Organizational Behavior,* 4th ed. (New York: John Wiley & Sons, Inc., 1997).

EXERCISE 42

Power Circles

Contributed by Marian C. Schultz, University of West Florida

Introduction

This exercise is designed to examine power and influence in the classroom setting. Specifically, it allows you to identify the combination of power bases used by your instructor in accomplishing his or her objectives for the course.

Instructions

1. Recall that the instructor's power includes the following major bases: (a) the authority that comes from the instructor's position (position power), (b) the knowledge, skill, and expertise of the instructor in the subject area (expert power), and (c) the regard in which you personally hold the instructor (referent power).
2. Indicate the configuration of power that is most evident in the way the instructor behaves in the course overall and according to the following "power circle." This circle can be filled in to represent the relative emphasis on the three power bases (e.g., 60 percent position, 30 percent expert, and 10 percent referent). Use the key to the right of the circle as a guide and draw/fill in the circle to show the profile of instructor's power. The instructor will also complete a self-perceived power circle profile.

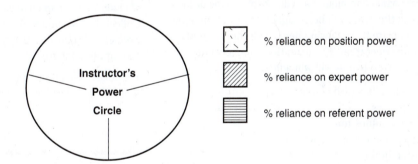

3. Consider also some possible special situations in which the instructor would have to use his or her power in the classroom context. Draw one power circle for each of the following situations, showing for each the power profile most likely to be used by the instructor to accomplish his or her goal. (The instructor will also complete a self-perceived power circle profile for each situation.)
   o Instructor wants to change the format of the final examination.
   o Instructor wants to add an additional group assignment to course requirements.
   o Instructor wants to have students attend a special two-hour guest lecture on a Saturday morning.
   o Instructor wants students to come to class better prepared for discussions of assigned material.
4. Share your power circles with members of your assigned group who will also share theirs. As a group, discuss the profiles and the reasons behind them. Appoint one group member as spokesperson to share results in general class discussion. Discuss with the group the best way to communicate this feedback effectively to the instructor in the presence of all class members, and help prepare the spokesperson for the feedback session.

5. Have the instructor share his or her power profiles with the class. Ask the instructor to comment on any differences between the self-perceptions and the views of the class. Comment as a class on the potential significance to leaders and managers of differences in the way they perceive themselves and the ways they are perceived by others.
6. Discuss with the instructor and class how people may tend to favor one or more of the power bases (i.e., to develop a somewhat predictable power circle profile). Discuss as well how effective leaders and managers need to use power contingently, and modify their use of different power bases and power circle profiles to best fit the needs of specific influence situations.

Class Activity Selections from The Pfeiffer Training Annuals

A. SWEET TOOTH: BONDING STRANGERS INTO A TEAM

Procedure:

The general idea is just to relax, have fun, and get to know one another while completing a task. Form groups of five. All groups in the room will be competing to see which one can first complete the following items with the name of a candy bar or sweet treat. The team that completes the most items correctly first will win a prize.

1. Pee Wee . . . baseball player
2. Dried up cows
3. Kids' game minus toes
4. Not bad and more than some
5. Explosion in the sky
6. Polka . . .
7. Rhymes with Bert's, dirts, hurts
8. Happy place to drink
9. Drowning prevention device
10. Belongs to a mechanic from Mayberry's cousin
11. They're not "lesses"; they're . . .
12. Two names for a purring pet
13. Takes 114 licks to get to the center of these
14. Sounds like asteroids
15. A military weapon
16. A young flavoring
17. Top of mountains in winter
18. To catch fish you need to . . .
19. Sounds like riddles and fiddles

Questions for discussion:
- What lessons about effective teamwork can be learned from this activity?
- What caused each subgroup to be successful?
- What might be learned about effective teamwork from what happened during this activity?
- What might be done next time to increase the chances of success?

Variation
- Have the individual subgroups create their own lists of clues for the names of candies/candy bars/sweets. Collect the lists and make a grand list using one or two from each group's contribution. Then hold a competition among the total group.

Source: Robert Allan Black, The 2002 Annual Volume 1, Training/© 2002 John Wiley & Sons, Inc.

B. INTERROGATORIES: IDENTIFYING ISSUES AND NEEDS

Procedure:

This activity is an opportunity to discover what issues and questions people have brought to the class. The instructor will select from the topic list below. Once a topic is raised, participants should ask any questions they have related to that topic. No one is to *answer* a question at this time. The goal is to come up with as many questions as possible in the time allowed. Feel free to build on a question already asked, or to share a completely different question.

Interrogatorics Starter Topic List

- Class requirements
- Social activities
- Performance appraisal
- Mission
- Coaching
- Success

- Communication
- Task uncertainty
- Priorities
- Instant messaging
- Time
- Quality
- Leadership
- Values
- Service
- Meetings
- Personality
- Customers
- Teamwork
- Project priorities
- Job demands
- Training
- Rules
- Management
- Work styles

Questions for discussion:
- How did you feel about this process?
- What common themes did you hear?
- What questions would you most like to have answered?

Source: Cher Holton, *The 2002 Annual: Volume 1, Training/* © 2002 John Wiley & Sons, Inc.

C. DECODE: WORKING WITH DIFFERENT INSTRUCTIONS

Procedure:

1. You are probably familiar with codes and cryptograms from your childhood days. In a cryptogram, each letter in the message is replaced by another letter of the alphabet. For example, LET THE GAMES BEGIN! may become this cryptogram:

    YZF FOZ JUKZH CZJVQ!

    In the cryptogram Y replaces L, Z replaces E, F replaces T, and so on. Notice that the same letter substitutions are used throughout this cryptogram: Every E in the sentence is replaced by a Z, and every T is replaced by an F.

    Here's some information to help you solve cryptograms:

    Letter Frequency

    The most commonly used letters of the English language are *e, t, a, i, o, n, s, h,* and *r*.

    The letters that are most commonly found at the beginning of words are *t, a, o, d,* and *w*.

    The letters that are most commonly found at the end of words are *e, s, d,* and *t*.

    Word Frequency

    One-letter words are either *a* or *I*.

    The most common two-letter words are *to, of, in, it, is, as, at, be, we, he, so, on, an, or, do, if, up, by,* and *my*.

    The most common three-letter words are *the, and, are, for, not, but, had, has, was, all, any, one, man, out, you, his, her,* and *can*.

    The most common four-letter words are *that, with, have, this, will, your, from, they, want, been, good, much, some,* and *very*.

2. The goal of the activity is to learn to work together more effectively in teams. Form into groups of four to seven members each. Have members briefly share their knowledge of solving cryptogram puzzles.

3. In this exercise all groups will be asked to solve the same cryptogram. If a team correctly and completely solves the cryptogram within two minutes, it will earn two hundred points. If it takes more than two minutes but fewer than three minutes, the team will earn fifty points.

4. Before working on the cryptogram, each participant will receive an Instruction Sheet with on how to solve cryptograms. Participants can study this sheet for two minutes only. They may not mark up the Instruction Sheet but they may take notes on an index card or a blank piece of paper. The Instruction Sheets will be taken back after two minutes.

5. At any time a group can send one of its members to ask for help from the instructor. The instruc-tor will decode any *one* of the words in the cryptogram selected by the group member.

6. After the points are tallied, the instructor will lead class discussion.

DECODE CRYPTOGRAM

ISV'B   JZZXYH   BPJB   BPH   SVQE

_____

UJE   BS   UCV   CZ   BS   FSYTHBH

_____

ZSYHBCYHZ   BPH   AHZB   UJE   BS

_____

UCV   CZ   BS   FSSTHWJBH   UCBP

_____

SBPHWZ—Z. BPCJMJWJOJV

_____

Source: Sivasailam "Thiagi" Thiagarajan, *The 2003 Annual: Volume 1, Training/*© 2003 John Wiley & Sons, Inc.

D. CHOICES: LEARNING EFFECTIVE CONFLICT MANAGEMENT STRATEGIES

Procedure: Form teams of three.

Assume you are a group of top managers who are responsible for an organization of seven departments. Working as a team, choose an appropriate strategy to intervene in the situations below when the conflict must be managed in some way. Your choices are *withdrawal, suppression, integration, compromise,* and *authority.* Refer to the list below for some characteristics of each strategy. Write your team's choice following each situation number. Engage in discussion led by the instructor.

CHOICES: STRATEGIES AND CONTINGENCIES

Withdrawal Strategy

Use When (Advantages)
Be Aware (Disadvantages)
- Choosing sides is to be avoided
- Legitimate action ceases
- Critical information is missing
- Direct information stops
- The issue is outside the group
- Failure can be perceived
- Others are competent and delegation is appropriate
- Cannot be used in a crisis
- You are powerless

Suppression (and Diffusion) Strategy

Use When (Advantages)
Be Aware (Disadvantages)
- A cooling down period is needed
- The issue may intensify
- The issue is unimportant
- You may appear weak and ineffective
- A relationship is important

Integration Strategy

Use When (Advantages)
Be Aware (Disadvantages)
- Group problem solving is needed
- Group goals must be put first
- New alternatives are helpful
- More time is required for dialogue
- Group commitment is required
- It doesn't work with rigid, dull people
- Promoting openness and trust

Compromise Strategy

Use When (Advantages)
Be Aware (Disadvantages)
- Power is equal
- Action (a third choice) can be weakened
- Resources are limited
- Inflation is encouraged
- A win-win settlement is desired
- A third party may be needed for negotiation

Authority Strategy

Use When (Advantages)
Be Aware (Disadvantages)
- A deadlock persists
- Emotions intensify quickly
- Others are incompetent
- Dependency is promoted
- Time is limited (crisis)
- Winners and losers are created
- An unpopular decision must be made
- Survival of the organization is critical

Situation #1

Two employees of the support staff have requested the same two-week vacation period. They are the only two trained to carry out an essential task using a complex computer software program that cannot be mastered quickly. You have encouraged others to learn this process so there is more backup for the position, but heavy workloads have prevented this from occurring.

Situation #2

A sales manager has requested a raise because there are now two salespeople on commission earning higher salaries. The work perfor-mance of this individual currently does not merit a raise of the amount requested, mostly due to the person turning in critical reports late and missing a number of days of work. The person's sales group is one of the highest rated in the organization, but this may be the result of having superior individuals assigned to the team, rather than to the effectiveness of the manager.

Situation #3

It has become obvious that the copy machine located in a customer service area is being used for a variety of personal purposes, including reproducing obscene jokes. A few copies have sometimes been found lying on or near the machine at the close of the business day. You have mentioned the matter briefly in the organization's employee newsletter, but recently you have noticed an increase in the activity. Most of the office staff seems to be involved.

Situation #4
Three complaints have filtered upward to you from long-term employees concerning a newly hired individual. This person has a pierced nose and a visible tattoo. The work performance of the individual is ade-quate and the person does not have to see customers; however, the employees who have complained allege that the professional appearance of the office area has been compromised.

Situation #5
The organization has a flex-time schedule format that requires all employees to work the core hours of 10 A.M. to 3 P.M., Monday through Friday. Two department managers have complained that another department does not always maintain that policy. The manager of the department in question has responded by citing recent layoffs and additional work responsibilities as reasons for making exceptions to policy.

Situation #6
As a result of a recent downsizing, an office in a coveted location is now available. Three individuals have made a request to the department manager for the office. The manager has recommended that the office be given to one of the three. This individual has the highest performance rating, but was aided in obtaining employment with the company by the department manager, who is a good friend of the person's family. Colleagues prefer not to work with this individual, as there is seldom any evidence of teamwork.

Situation #7
Two department managers have requested a budget increase in the areas of travel and computer equipment. Each asks that your group support this request. The CEO, not your group, will make the final decision. You are aware that increasing funds for one department will result in a decrease for others, as the total budget figures for all of these categories are set.

Situation #8
Few of the management staff attended the Fourth of July picnic held at a department manager's country home last year. This particular man-ager, who has been a loyal team player for the past twenty-one years, has indicated that he/she plans to host the event again this year. Many of you have personally found the event to be boring, with little to do but talk and eat. Already a few of the other managers have suggested that the event be held at a different location with a new format or else be cancelled.

Situation #9
It has come to your attention that a manager and a subordinate in the same department are having a romantic affair openly in the building. Both are married to other people. They have been taking extended lunch periods, yet both remain beyond quitting time to complete their work. Colleagues have begun to complain that neither is readily available mid-day and that they do not return messages in a timely manner.

Situation #10
Two loyal department managers are concerned that a newly hired manager who is wheelchair-bound has been given too much in the way of accommodations beyond what is required by the Americans with Disabilities Act. They have requested similar changes to make their own work lives easier. Specifically, they cite office size and location on the building's main floor as points of contention.

Source: Chuck Kormanski, Sr., and Chuck Kormanski, Jr., *The 2003 Annual: Volume 1, Training/*© 2003 John Wiley & Sons, Inc.

E. INTERNAL/EXTERNAL MOTIVATORS: ENCOURAGING CREATIVITY

Procedure:

1. This interactive, experience-based activity is designed to increase participants' awareness of creativity and creative processes. Begin by thinking of a job that you now hold or have held. Then complete Questions 1 and 2 from the Internal/External Motivators Questionnaire (see below).
2. Form into groups. Share your questionnaire results and make a list of responses to Question 1.
3. Discuss and compare rankings of major work activities listed for Question 2. Make a list with at least two responses from each participant.
4. Individually record your answers to Questions 3 and 4 below. Then share your answers and again list member responses within your group.
5. Individually, compare your responses to Questions 1 and 2 with your responses to Questions 3 and 4. Then answer Question 5. Again, share with the group and make a group list of answers to Question 5 for the recorder, who is to record these answers on the flip chart. (10 minutes.)

Questions for discussion:

- What was the most important part of this activity for you?
- What have you learned about motivation?
- What impact will having done this activity have for you back in the workplace?
- How will what you have learned change your leadership style or future participation in a group?
- What will you do differently based on what you have learned?

INTRINSIC/EXTRINSIC MOTIVATORS QUESTIONNAIRE

1. How could you do your job in a more creative manner? List some ways in the space below:

2. List four or five major work activities or jobs you perform on a regular basis in the left-hand boxes on the following chart. Use a seven-point scale that ranges from 1 (low) to 7 (high) to rate each work activity on three separate dimensions: (a) level of difficulty, (b) potential to motivate you, and (c) opportunity to add value to the organization.

Major Work Activity	Level of Difficulty	Potential to Motivate	Opportunity to Add Value
a.			
b.			
c.			
d.			
e.			

3. List five motivators or types of rewards that would encourage you to do your job in a more creative manner.

4. List three motivators or types of rewards from Question 3 above that you believe would *definitely increase your creativity*. Indicate whether these motivators are realistic or unrealistic in terms of your job or work setting. Indicate whether each is intrinsic or extrinsic.

Motivators	Realistic/ Unrealistic	Intrinsic	Extrinsic
1.			
2.			
3.			

5. List three types of work activities you like to perform and the motivators or rewards that would stimulate and reinforce your creativity.

Work Activity	Rewards That Reinforce Creativity
1.	
2.	
3.	

Source: Elizabeth A. Smith, *The 2003 Annual: Volume 1, Training/© 2003 John Wiley & Sons, Inc.*

F. QUICK HITTER: FOSTERING THE CREATIVE SPIRIT

Part A Procedure:
1. Write the Roman numeral nine (IX) on a sheet of paper.
2. Add one line to make six. After you have one response, try for others.

Questions for discussion:
- What does solving this puzzle show us about seeing things differently?
- Why don't some people consider alternatives easily?
- What skills or behaviors would be useful for us to develop our ability to see different points of view?

Part B Procedure:
1. Rent the video or DVD of "Patch Adams." In this video Patch (Robin Williams) is studying to become a doctor, but he does not look, act, or think like a traditional doctor. For Patch, humor is the best medicine. He is always willing to do unusual things to make his patients laugh. Scenes from this video can be revealing to an OB class.
2. Show the first Patch Adams scene (five minutes)—this is in the psychiatric hospital where Patch has admitted himself after a failed suicide attempt. He meets Arthur in the hospital. Arthur is obsessed with showing people four fingers of his hand and asking them: "How many fingers can you see?" Everybody says four. The scene shows Patch visiting Arthur to find out the solution. Arthur's answer is: "If you only focus on the problem, you will never see the solution. Look further. You have to see what other people do not see."
3. Engage the class in discussion of these questions and more:
   - How does this film clip relate to Part A of this exercise?
   - What restricts our abilities to look beyond what we see?
   - How can we achieve the goal of seeing what others do not see?
4. Show the second *Patch Adams* scene (five minutes)—this is when Patch has left the hospital and is studying medicine. Patch and his new friend Truman are having breakfast. Truman is reflecting on the human mind and on the changing of behavioral patterns (the adoption of programmed answers) as a person grows older. Patch proposes to carry out the Hello Experiment. The objective of the experiment is "to change the programmed answer by changing the usual parameters."
5. Engage the class in discussion of these questions and more:
   - What is a programmed answer?
   - What is the link between our programmed answers and our abilities to exhibit creativity?
   - How can we "deprogram" ourselves?
6. Summarize the session with a wrap-up discussion of creativity, including barriers and ways to encourage it.

Source: Mila Gascó Hernández and Teresa Torres Coronas, *The 2003 Annual: Volume 1, Training*/© 2003 John Wiley & Sons, Inc.

Today's problems and opportunities—career and personal—are often complex and unstructured. It takes lots of wisdom and good analytic skills to master them. How about it: Are you developing the critical thinking skills needed for future success?

CASES FOR CRITICAL THINKING

CASE 1A
Trader Joe's Keeps Things Fresh

The average Trader Joe's stocks only a small percentage of the products of local supermarkets in a space little larger than a corner store. How did this neighborhood market grow to earnings of $9 billion, garner superior ratings, and become a model of management? Take a walk down the aisles of Trader Joe's and learn how sharp attention to the fundamentals of retail management made this chain more than the average Joe.

From Corner Store to Foodie Mecca

In more than 365 stores across the United States, hundreds of thousands of customers are treasure hunting.[1] Driven by gourmet tastes but hungering for deals, they are led by cheerful guides in Hawaiian shirts who point them to culinary discoveries such as ahi jerky, ginger granola, and baked jalapeño cheese crunchies.

It's just an average day at Trader Joe's, the gourmet, specialty, and natural-foods store that offers staples such as milk and eggs along with curious, one-of-a-kind foods at below average prices in thirty-odd states.[2] With their plethora of kosher, vegan, and gluten-free fare, Trader Joe's has products to suit every dietary need.[3] Foodies, hipsters, and recessionistas alike are attracted to the chain's charming blend of low prices, tasty treats, and laid-back but enthusiastic customer service. Shopping at Trader Joe's is less a chore than it is immersion into another culture. In keeping with its whimsical faux-nautical theme, crew members and managers wear loud tropical-print shirts. Chalkboards around every corner unabashedly announce slogans, such as "You don't have to join a club, carry a card, or clip coupons to get a good deal."

"When you look at food retailers," says Richard George, professor of food marketing at St. Joseph's University, "there is the low end, the big middle, and then there is the cool edge—that's Trader Joe's."[4] But how does Trader Joe's compare with other stores with an edge, such as Whole Foods? Both obtain products locally and from all over the world. Each values employees and strives to offer the highest quality. However, there's no mistaking that Trader Joe's is cozy and intimate, whereas the spacious stores of Whole Foods offer an abundance of choices. By limiting its stock and selling quality products at low prices, Trader Joe's sells twice as much per square foot as other supermarkets.[5] Most retail megamarkets, such as Whole Foods, carry between 25,000 and 45,000 products; Trader Joe's stores carry only 4,000.[6] But this scarcity benefits both Trader Joe's and its customers. According to Swarthmore professor Barry Schwartz, author of *The Paradox of Choice: Why Less Is More*, "Giving people too much choice can result in paralysis. . . . [R]esearch shows that the more options you offer, the less likely people are to choose any."[7]

David Rogers of DSR Marketing Systems expects other supermarkets to follow the Trader Joe's model toward a smaller store size. He cites several reasons, including excessive competitive floor space, development costs, and the aging population.[8]

Named by *Fast Company* as one of this year's 50 Most Influential Companies, Trader Joe's didn't always stand for brie and baguettes at peanut butter and jelly prices.[9] In 1958, the company began life in Los Angeles as a chain of 7-Eleven–style corner stores called Pronto Markets. Striving to differentiate his stores from those of his competitors in order to survive in a crowded marketplace, founder "Trader" Joe Coulombe, vacationing in the Caribbean, reasoned that consumers are more likely to try new things while on vacation. In 1967 the first Trader Joe's store opened in Pasadena, California. Mr. Coulombe had transformed his stores into oases of value by replacing

W-97

humdrum sundries with exotic, one-of-a-kind foods priced persuasively below those of any reasonable competitor.[10] In 1979, he sold his chain to the Albrecht family, German billionaires and owners of an estimated 8,700 Aldi markets in the United States, Europe, and Australia.[11]

The Albrechts shared Coulombe's relentless pursuit of value—a trait inseparable from Trader Joe's success. Recent annual sales are estimated at $9 billion, landing Trader Joe's in the top third of *Supermarket News's* Top 75 Retailers.[12] Because it's not easy competing with such giants as Whole Foods and Dean & DeLuca, the company applies its pursuit of value to every facet of management. By keeping stores comparatively small—they average about 10,000 to 15,000 square feet—and shying away from prime locations, Trader Joe's keeps real estate costs down.[13] The chain prides itself on its thriftiness and cost-saving measures, proclaiming "Every penny we save is a penny you save" and "Our CEO doesn't even have a secretary."[14]

Trader Giotto, Trader José, Trader Ming, and Trader Darwin

Trader Joe's strongest weapon in the fight to keep costs low may also be its greatest appeal to customers: its stock. The company follows a deliciously simple approach to stocking stores: (1) search out tasty, unusual foods from all around the world; (2) contract directly with manufacturers; (3) label each product under one of several catchy house brands; and (4) maintain a small stock, making each product fight for its place on the shelf. This common-sense, low-overhead approach to retail serves Trader Joe's well, embodying its commitment to aggressive cost cutting.

Most Trader Joe's products are sold under a variant of its house brand—dried pasta under the "Trader Giotto's" moniker, frozen enchiladas under the "Trader Jose's" label, vitamins under "Trader Darwin's," and so on. But these store brands don't sacrifice quality—readers of *Consumer Reports* awarded Trader Joe's house brands top marks.[15] The house brand success is no accident. According to Trader Joe's President Doug Rauch, "the company pursued the strategy to put our destiny in our own hands."[16]

But playing a role in this destiny is no easy feat. Ten to fifteen new products debut each week at Trader Joe's—and the company maintains a strict "one in, one out" policy. Items that sell poorly or whose costs rise get the heave-ho in favor of new blood, something the company calls the "gangway factor."[17] If the company hears that customers don't like something about a product, out it goes. In just such a move, Trader Joe's phased out single-ingredient products (such as spinach and garlic) from China. "Our customers have voiced their concerns about products from this region and we have listened," the company said in a statement, noting that items would be replaced with "products from other regions until our customers feel as confident as we do about the quality and safety of Chinese products."[18]

Conversely, discontinued items may be brought back if customers are vocal enough, making Trader Joe's the model of an open system. "We feel really close to our customers," says Audrey O'Connell, vice president of marketing for Trader Joe's East. "When we want to know what's on their minds, we don't need to put them in a sterile room with a swinging bulb. We like to think of Trader Joe's as an economic food democracy."[19] In return, customers keep talking, and they recruit new converts. Word-of-mouth advertising has lowered the corporation's advertising budget to approximately 0.2 percent of sales, a fraction of the 4 percent spent by supermarkets.[20]

Customer Connection

Trader Joe's connects with its customers because of the culture of product knowledge and customer involvement that its management cultivates among store employees. Each employee is encouraged to taste and learn about the products and to engage customers to share what they've experienced. Most shoppers recall instances when helpful crew members took the time to locate or recommend particular items. Despite the lighthearted tone suggested by marketing materials and in-store ads, Trader Joe's aggressively courts friendly, customer-oriented employees by writing job descriptions highlighting desired soft skills ("ambitious and adventurous, enjoy smiling and have a strong sense of values") as much as actual retail experience.[21]

A responsible, knowledgeable, and friendly "crew" is critical to Trader Joe's success. Therefore, it nurtures its employees with a promote-from-within philosophy, and its employees earn more than their counterparts at other chain grocers. In California, Trader Joe's employees can earn almost 20 percent more than counterparts at supermarket giants Albertsons or Safeway.[22] Starting benefits include medical, dental, and vision insurance; company-paid retirement; paid vacation; and a 10 percent employee discount.[23] Assistant store managers earn a compensation package averaging $94,000 a year, and store managers' packages average $132,000. One analyst estimates that a Walmart store manager earning that much would need to run an outlet grossing six or seven times that of an average Trader Joe's.[24]

Outlet managers are highly compensated, partly because they know the Trader Joe's system inside and out (managers are hired only from within the company). Future leaders enroll in training programs such as Trader

Joe's University that foster in them the loyalty necessary to run stores according to both company and customer expectations, teaching managers to imbue their part-timers with the customer-focused attitude shoppers have come to expect.[25]

For all of its positive buzz, Trader Joe's narrowly avoided a boycott recently when it became embroiled in a controversy over its opposition to the Campaign for Fair Food, an initiative organized by the Coalition of Immokalee Workers (CIW) to push for better wages and working conditions in Florida's produce fields.[26] Trader Joe's insisted that it already followed the guidelines stipulated by the Fair Food campaign, but the CIW demanded increased transparency. Trader Joe's finally signed an agreement with the CIW in February 2012, mere days before the nationally organized boycott of its stores was scheduled to begin.[27]

If Trader Joe's has any puzzling trait, it's that the company is more than a bit media shy. Executives have granted no interviews since the Aldi group took over. Company statements and spokespersons have been known to be terse—the company's leases even stipulate that no store opening may be formally announced until a month before the outlet opens![28]

The future looks bright for Trader Joe's. In 2012, between twenty-five and thirty locations are slated to open, and the company continues to break into markets hungry for reasonably priced gourmet goodies. But will Trader Joe's struggle to sustain its international flavor in the face of rising fuel costs and shrinking discretionary income, or will the allure of cosmopolitan food at provincial prices continue to tempt consumers?

Review Questions

1. Does Trader Joe's seem to be basing its management practices on a solid understanding of human behavior in organizations? Is the company on track for valuing employees in a way that is good for them and for organizational performance over the long term? What weaknesses can you spot in the current approach that might cause problems in the future?
2. In what ways does this description of Trader Joe's show attention to each responsibility in the management process: planning, organizing, leading, and controlling?
3. *New employee situation*. At the age of twenty-two and newly graduated from college, Hazel has just accepted a job with Trader Joe's as a shift leader. She'll be supervising four team members who fill part-time jobs in the produce section. Given Trader Joe's casual and nontraditional work environment, what should she do and avoid doing in the first few days of work to establish herself as a skillful manager of this team?
4. *Global Economy Situation*. Trader Joe's is owned by a German company operating in America. What are the biggest risks that international ownership poses for the people who make a career commitment to Trader Joe's as their employer?

Discussion Questions

1. How does Trader Joe's design jobs for increased job satisfaction and higher performance?
2. In what ways does Trader Joe's demonstrate the importance of each responsibility in the management process: planning, organizing, leading, and controlling?
3. Describe the methods that show Trader Joe's knows the importance of human capital.
4. Does Trader Joe's utilize contingency thinking? Why or why not?
5. *Research Question*. What do the blogs and current news reports say? Is Trader Joe's a management benchmark for others to follow? In what areas relevant to Organizational Behavior does the firm have an edge on the competition? ∎

CASE 1B
Getting the Evidence: Leadership Training Dilemma

Developed by John R. Schermerhorn, Jr., Ohio University

Shane Alexander is the human resource director of the Central State Medical Center. One of her responsibilities is to oversee the hospital's leadership training programs. Recently Shane attended a professional conference during which a special "packaged" training program was advertised for sale. The package includes a set of videotaped lectures by a distinguished management consultant plus a workbook containing readings, exercises, cases, tests, and other instructional aids. The subjects covered in the program include motivation, group dynamics, communication skills, leadership styles, performance appraisal, and the dynamics of planned change.

In the past Shane felt that the hospital had not lived up to its training goals. One of the reasons for this was the high cost of hiring external consultants to do the actual instruction. This packaged program was designed, presumably, so that persons from within the hospital could act as session coordinators. The structure of the program provided through the videotapes and workbook agenda was supposed to substitute for a consultant's expertise. Because of this, Shane felt that use of the packaged program could substantially improve supervisory training in the hospital.

The cost of the program was $3,500 for an initial purchase of the videotapes plus fifty workbooks. Additional workbooks were then available at $8 per copy. Before purchasing the program, Shane needed the approval of the senior administrative staff.

At the next staff meeting, Shane proposed purchasing the training program. She was surprised at the response. The hospital president was noncommittal; the vice president for operations was openly hostile; and the three associate vice presidents were varied in their enthusiasm. It was the vice president's opinion that dominated the discussion. He argued that to invest in such a program on the assumption that it would lead to improved leadership practices was unwise. "This is especially true in respect to the proposed program," he said. "How could such a package possibly substitute for the training skills of an expert consultant?"

Shane argued her case and was left with the following challenge. The executives would allow $1,000 to be spent to rent the program with thirty workbooks. It would be up to Shane to demonstrate through a trial program, or pilot test, that an eventual purchase of the full program would be worthwhile.

There are 160 supervisors, team leaders, department and division heads, and executives in the hospital. The program was designed to be delivered in eight 2.5-hour sessions. It was preferred to schedule one session per week, with no more than fifteen participants per session. Shane knew that she would have to present very strong evidence to gain needed support for the continued use of the program. Given the opportunity, she wondered just how she could get evidence that would be conclusive one way or the other.

Review Questions

1. If you were Shane, what type of research design would you use to test this program? Why?
2. How would the design actually be implemented in this hospital setting?
3. What would be your research hypothesis? What variables would you need to measure to provide data that could test this hypothesis? How would you gather these data?
4. Do you think the administrator's request for "proof before purchase" was reasonable? Why or why not? ■

CASE 2
Diversity Leads the Way

At Xerox, Diversity equals Success. The equation certainly has worked for the company! According to *Fortune* magazine's annual reputation survey, Xerox is the world's most admired company in the computer industry. According to Anne Mulcahy, Xerox former Chairman and CEO, the firm's focus on diversity is based on an environment of inclusion within which each person can achieve to their highest potential. Xerox knows that employees with different ways of thinking, and different ways of perceiving the world, are employees who create innovative solutions. In a business like Xerox, whose lifeblood is fresh ideas, this variety of perspectives is a priceless resource—and a key to achieving critical business results.[1]

With recent annual revenue of $23+ billion, Xerox is the world's largest technology-and-services company specializing in document management.[2] Xerox provides the document industry's broadest portfolio of offerings. Digital systems include color and black-and-white printing and publishing systems, digital presses and "book factories," advanced and basic multifunction systems, laser and solid ink network printers, copiers, and fax machines. No competitor can match Xerox's services expertise, which includes helping businesses develop online document archives, analyzing how employees can most efficiently share documents and knowledge in the office, operating in-house print shops or mailrooms, and building Web-based processes for personalizing direct mail, invoices, brochures, and more. Xerox also offers associated software, support, and even supplies such as toner, paper, and ink.[3]

By recognizing and respecting diversity and empowering individuality, Xerox creates productive people and an innovative company. This corporate culture of inclusion with its commitment to diversity can be traced back to its very first chairman, Joseph C. Wilson. Chairman Wilson took proactive steps to create a more diverse workforce in response to race riots in the 1960s. With then Xerox President C. Peter McCullough, Wilson called for increased hiring of African Americans in an effort to achieve equality among its workforce. Starting in the 1970s, Xerox established an internal affirmative action office and began to hire a significant number of minority employees.[4]

Xerox placed emphasis on the advancement of minorities and females in the 1980s. It was during this time that Barry Rand, an African American, was named the first minority president of a division. Xerox's Balanced

Workforce Strategy (BWF) aimed to achieve unbiased representation for women and minorities throughout the organization at all times, including throughout times of restructuring. During the influx of women into its workforce Xerox recognized women's struggle to balance work and family commitments. In response, Xerox Human Resources (HR) initiated "flex time" and other HR policies to maintain a high level of productivity and satisfaction among its workforce.[5]

In the 1990s sexual orientation was included in the company's Equal Opportunity/Affirmative Action and Non-discrimination policy; GALAXe Pride at Work (a caucus group for gay, lesbian, bisexual, and transgender employees) was established; and Xerox began to provide domestic partner benefits for gay, lesbian, bisexual, and transgender employees. Annual diversity employee roundtables with senior managers were initiated, providing employees the opportunity to engage in unfiltered communication with management about the best practices, strengths, and weaknesses of Xerox's diversity initiatives.[6]

Xerox's view on a diverse workforce is most eloquently expressed by former Chairman Anne M. Mulcahy:

I'm convinced diversity is a key to success. Experience tells us that the most diverse companies—companies ruled by a hierarchy of imagination and filled with people of all ages, races, and backgrounds—are the most successful over time. Somehow, diversity breeds creativity. Maybe it's because people with different backgrounds challenge each other's underlying assumptions, freeing everybody from convention and orthodoxy. We provide a shining proof point that diversity in all its wonderful manifestations is good for business . . . good for our country . . . and good for people.[7]

Xerox is proud to say that women and minorities make up more than 50 percent of its workforce. About 48.2 percent of Xerox senior executives are women, people of color, or both. The employee roster is made up of roughly 30 percent African Americans, Latinos, Asians, and Native Americans. In fact, Xerox has been rated by *Fortune, Forbes, Working Mother, Latino Style*, and *Enable* magazines as one of the top ten companies in hiring minorities, women, disabled, and gay and lesbian employees. It is among *Working Mother*'s top 100 family-friendly companies for women—and has been for the past fifteen years.[8]

In 2007 Ursula Burns was named the first African-American female president of Xerox Corporation. In July 2009 she succeeded Anne M. Mulcahy as CEO, the first female-to-female hand-off in Fortune 500 history. In May 2010 Burns was also named chairman, heading a company of over 140,000 employees. Her philosophy is consistent with the company culture and history. She says:

The power of our people development model is that it recognizes the value of diversity from entry-level positions to the top seats. When you've been at it as long as we have, the bench gets pretty strong of next generation leaders who represent the real world: black, white, male, female, Hispanic, Asian from different religions and with different beliefs. What they all have in common is strong skills, a solid work ethic, commitment and a will to win.[9]

With Ursula Burns at the helm, and a 100 percent rating on the Human Rights Campaign Foundation's Corporate Equality Index *and* its Best Places to Work survey, there's no doubt about it: Xerox's commitment to diversity is still going strong.[10] In a difficult global environment and highly competitive industry, Burns's leadership will surely be tested to the fullest in the days ahead.

Review Questions

1. How would Xerox define diversity? How has its definition changed over the years?
2. What are the seven reasons why Xerox should be motivated to diversify its workforce? Illustrate how Xerox shows it values workplace diversity.
3. Does Xerox embody or defy the "leaking pipeline" phenomenon? Why?
4. *Research Question.* Compare Xerox to other Fortune 500 companies. How are women and minorities represented at the highest levels of each organization? How can these statistics be improved upon? ∎

CASE 3
OB Classic: The Jim Donovan Case

This classic case is by Allan R. Cohen and Michael Merenda, University of New Hampshire[1]

Jim Donovan, age thirty-seven, the new president and chief executive officer of Famous Products, was suddenly in the toughest spot in his life. He had just been selected by Omega Corporation, a huge conglomerate, to take over as president of its latest acquisition! And Jim had been feeling very good about himself.

Having grown up on "the wrong side of the tracks," worked his way through engineering college, earned an MBA from Harvard Business School, worked for ten years as a management consultant and two years as a successful president of a small company, Jim felt that he had arrived. The company he was going to manage was known throughout the world, had a good reputation, and would provide a good opportunity for visibility in the parent company.

The pay would be the highest he had ever earned, and while the money itself was not that important (though he'd be able to ensure financial security for his wife and four children), he enjoyed the indicator of success that a high salary provided. Jim also was eager to manage a company with over a thousand employees; the power to get things done on such a large scale was very attractive to him.

When Omega selected him, Jim had been told that Don Bird, the current president of Famous Products, was close to retirement and would be moved upstairs to chairman of the board. Bird had been president of Famous for twenty-two years and had done reasonably well, building sales steadily and guarding quality.

The top management group was highly experienced, closely knit, very loyal to the company, and its members had been in their jobs for a long time. As long-term employees, they all were reported to be good friends of Don Bird. They were almost all in their early sixties and quite proud of the record of their moderate-size but successful company.

Famous had not, however, grown in profits as rapidly as Omega expected of its operating companies, and Omega's president had told Jim that we wanted Jim to "grab a hold of Famous and make it take off."

With this challenge ringing in his ears, Jim flew out to Milwaukee for his first visit to Famous Products. He had talked briefly with Don Bird to say that he'd be arriving Thursday for half a day, then would be back for good after ten days in New York at Omega. Bird had been cordial but rather distant on the phone, and Jim wondered how Bird was taking Jim's appointment. "I've only got a few hours here," thought Jim. "I wonder how I should play it."

When Jim pulled up to Famous Products headquarters in his rented car, he noticed the neat grounds and immaculate landscaping. To his surprise, Don Bird met him at the door.

Bird had on a very conservative blue business suit, black tie, black shoes, and white shirt. He peered out at Jim through old-fashioned steel-rimmed glasses and said, "Welcome to our plant. You're just in time for our usual Thursday morning executive meeting. Would you like to sit in on that and meet our people?" Jim thought that the meeting would give him a chance to observe the management group in action, and he readily agreed, planning to sit back and watch for as long as he could.

Jim was ushered into the most formal meeting room he could remember ever having seen. The dark-paneled room was dominated by a long, heavy table, with twelve high-backed chairs around it. Seven of the chairs were filled with unsmiling executives in dark suits.

Bird led Jim to the front of the room, indicated an empty chair to the left of the seat at the head of the table, then sat down in the place that was obviously his. Turning to the group, he said:

Gentlemen, I want you to meet Mr. Donovan, but before I turn the meeting over to him, I want you to know that I do not believe he should be here; I do not believe he's qualified, and I will give him no support. Mr. Donovan. . . .

Review Questions

1. How well did Jim Donovan "play" things in terms of his new appointment? What mistakes did he make, and why did he make them?
2. Now that Jim Donovan is in the meeting and on the spot, what should he do (a) immediately, (b) right after the meeting ends, and (c) within the first few days of taking over?
3. How have perceptions influenced behavior in this situation? How could those perceptions have been better managed? ■

CASE 4
Tough Situation at MacRec, Inc.

Developed by Mary McGarry, Empire State College, and Barry R. Armandi, SUNY-Old Westbury

Background

MagRec, Incorporated was started by Mr. Leed, a brilliant engineer (he has several engineering patents) who was a group manager at Fairchild Republic. The company's product was magnetic recording heads, a crucial device used for reading, writing, and erasing data on tapes and disks.

Like any other start-up, MagRec had a humble beginning. It struggled during the early years, facing cash-flow and technical problems. After a slow start, it grew rapidly and gained 35 percent of the tape head market, making it the second-largest supplier in North America. Financially, the company suffered heavily because of price erosions caused by Far East competition. Unlike all its competitors, the company resisted moving its manufacturing operations offshore. But the company accumulated losses to a point of bankruptcy. Finally

MagRec entered a major international joint venture and received many new sales orders. Things looked good again. But....

Pat's Dilemma

When Fred Marsh promoted me to sales manager, I was in seventh heaven. Now, six months later, I feel I am in hell. This is the first time in my life that I am really on my own. I have been working with other people all my life. I tried my best and what I could not solve, I took upstairs. Now it's different because I am the boss (or am I?). Fred has taught me a lot. He was my mentor and gave me this job when he became vice president. I have always respected him and listened to his judgment. Now, thinking back, I wonder whether I should have listened to him at all on this problem.

It started late one Friday evening. I had planned to call my West Coast customer, Partco, to discuss certain contract clauses. I wanted to nail this one fast (Partco had just been acquired by Volks, Inc.). Partco was an old customer. In fact, through good and bad, it had always stayed with us. It was also a *major* customer. I was about to call Partco when Dinah Coates walked in, clutching a file. I had worked with Dinah for three years. She was good. I knew that my call to Partco would have to wait. Dinah had been cleaning out old files and came across a report about design and manufacturing defects in Partco heads. The report had been written nine years ago. The cover memo read as follows:

To: Ken Smith, Director of Marketing
From: Rich Grillo, V.P. Operations
Sub: Partco Head Schedule

This is to inform you that due to pole-depth problems in design, the Partco heads (all 514 in test) have failed. They can't reliably meet the reading requirements. The problem is basically a design error in calculations. It can be corrected. However, the fix will take at least six months. Meanwhile, Ron Scott in production informs me that the entire 5,000 heads (the year's production) have already been pole-slotted, thus they face the same problem.

Ken, I don't have to tell you how serious this is, but how can we OK and ship them to Partco knowing that they'll cause read error problems in the field? My engineering and manufacturing people realize this is the number-one priority. By pushing the Systems Tech job back we will be back on track in less than six months. In the interim I can modify Global Widgets heads. This will enable us to at least continue shipping some product to Partco. As a possible alternate I would like to get six Partco drives. Michaels and his team feel that with quick and easy changes in the drives tape path, they can get the head to work. If this is true we should be back on track within six to eight weeks.

A separate section of the report reads as follows:

Confidential
(Notes from meeting with Don Updyke and Rich Grillo)

Solution to Partco heads problem
All Partco heads can be reworked (.8 hrs. ea.—cost insignificant) to solve Partco's read problems by grinding an extra three-thousandths of an inch off the top of the head. This will reduce the overall pole depth to a point where no read errors occur. The heads will fully meet specifications in all respects except one, namely life. Don estimates that due to the reduced chrome layer (used for wear) the heads' useful life will be 2500 hours instead of 6000 hours of actual usage.

Our experience is that no customer keeps accurate records to tell actual usage and life. Moreover, the cost is removed since Partco sells drives to MegaComputer, who sells systems to end-users. The user at the site hardly knows or rarely complains about extra costs such as the replacement of a head 12 to 18 months down the line instead of the normal 2 years. Besides, the service technicians always innovatively believe in and offer plausible explanations—such as the temperature must be higher than average—or they really must be using the computer a lot.

I have directed that the heads be reworked and shipped to Partco. I also instructed John to tell Partco that due to inclement weather this week's shipment will be combined with next week's shipment.

Dinah was flabbergasted. The company planned to sell products deliberately that it knew would not meet life requirements—"risking our reputation as a quality supplier," she said. "Partco and others buy our heads thinking they are the best. Didn't we commit fraud through outright misrepresentation?"

Dinah insisted I had to do something. I told her I would look into the matter and get back to her by the end of next week.

Over the weekend I kept thinking about the Partco issue. We had no customer complaints. Partco had always been extremely pleased with our products and technical support. In fact, we were its sole suppliers. MegaComputer had us placed on the preferred, approved ship to stock, vendors list. It was a fact that other vendors were judged against our standards. MegaComputer's Quality Control never saw our product or checked it.

Monday morning I showed the report to Fred. He immediately recollected it and began to explain the situation to me.

MagRec had been under tremendous pressure and was growing rapidly at the time. "That year we had moved into a new 50,000-square-foot building and went from 50 or 60 employees to over 300. Our sales were increasing dramatically." Fred was head of purchasing at the time, and every week the requirements for raw materials would change. "We'd started using B.O.A.s (Broad Order Agreements, used as annual purchasing contracts) guaranteeing us the right to increase our numbers by 100 percent each quarter. The goal was to maintain the numbers. If we had lost Partco then, it could have had a domino effect and we could have ended up having no customers left to worry about."

Fred went on to explain that it had only been a short-term problem that was corrected within the year and no one ever knew it existed. He told me to forget it and to move the file into the back storage room. I conceded. I thought of all the possible hassles. The thing was ancient history anyway. Why should I be concerned about it? I wasn't even here when it happened.

The next Friday Dinah asked me what I had found out. I told her Fred's feelings on the matter and that I felt he had some pretty good arguments regarding the matter. Dinah became angry. She said I had changed since my promotion and that I was just as guilty as the crooks who had cheated the customers by selling low-life heads as long-life heads. I told her to calm down. The decision was made years ago. No one got hurt, and the heads weren't defective. They weren't causing any errors.

I felt bad but figured there wasn't much to do. The matter was closed as far as I was concerned, so I returned to my afternoon chores. Little was I to know the matter was not really closed.

That night Fred called me at 10:00. He wanted me to come over to the office right away. I quickly changed, wondering what the emergency was. I walked into Fred's office. The coffee was going. Charlie (Personnel Manager) was there. Rich Grillo (V. P. Operations) was sitting on the far side of Fred's conference table. I instinctively headed there for that was the designated smoking corner.

Ken (Director of Marketing) arrived fifteen minutes later. We settled in. Fred began the meeting by thanking everyone for coming. He then told them about the discovery of the Partco file and filled them in on the background. The problem now was that Dinah had called Partco and gotten through to their new vice president, Tim Rand. Rand had called Fred at 8:00 p.m. at home and said he was personally taking a red-eye flight to find out what this was all about. He would be here in the morning. We spent a grueling night followed by an extremely tense few weeks. Partco had a team of people going through our tests, quality control, and manufacturing records. Our production slipped, and overall morale was affected.

Mr. Leed personally spent a week in California assuring Partco that this would never happen again. Though we weathered the storm, we had certain losses. We were never to be Partco's sole source again. We still retained 60 percent of its business but had to agree to lower prices. The price reduction had a severe impact. Although Partco never disclosed to anyone what the issues were (since both companies had blanket nondisclosure agreements), word got around that Partco was paying a lower price. We were unable to explain to our other customers why Partco was paying this amount. Actually I felt the price word got out through Joe Byrne (an engineer who came to Partco from Systems Tech and told his colleagues back at Systems Tech that Partco really knew how to negotiate prices down). He was unaware, however, of the real issues. Faced with customers who perceived they were being treated inequitably, we experienced problems. Lowering prices meant incurring losses; not lowering them meant losing customers. The next two financial quarters saw sales revenue decline by 40 percent. As the sales manager, I felt pretty rotten presenting my figures to Fred.

With regard to Dinah, I now faced a monumental problem. The internal feeling was that she should be avoided at all costs. Because of price erosions, we faced cutbacks. Employees blamed her for production layoffs. The internal friction kept mounting. Dinah's ability to interface effectively with her colleagues and other departments plummeted to a point where normal functioning was impossible.

Fred called me into his office two months after the Partco episode and suggested that I fire Dinah. He told me that he was worried about results. Although he had nothing personally against her, he felt that she must go because she was seriously affecting my department's overall performance. I defended Dinah by stating that the Partco matter would blow over and given time I could smooth things out. I pointed out Dinah's accomplishments and stated I really wanted her to stay. Fred dropped the issue, but my problem persisted.

Things went from bad to worse. Finally, I decided to try to solve the problem myself. I had known Dinah well for many years and had a good relationship with her before the incident. I took her to lunch to address the issue. Over lunch, I acknowledged the stress the Partco situation had put on her and suggested that she move away for a while to the West Coast, where she could handle that area independently.

Dinah was hurt and asked why I didn't just fire her already. I responded by accusing her of causing the problem in the first place by going to Partco.

Dinah came back at me, calling me a lackey for having taken her story to Fred and having brought his management message back. She said I hadn't even attempted a solution and that I didn't have the guts to stand up for what was right. I was only interested in protecting my backside and keeping Fred happy. As her manager, I should have protected her and taken some of the heat off her back. Dinah refused to transfer or to quit. She told me to go ahead and fire her, and she walked out.

I sat in a daze as I watched Dinah leave the restaurant. What the heck went wrong? Had Dinah done the morally right thing? Was I right in defending MagRec's position? Should I have taken a stand with Fred? Should I have gone over Fred's head to Mr. Leed? Am I doing the right thing? Should I listen to Fred and fire Dinah? If not, how do I get my department back on track? What am I saying? If Dinah is right, shouldn't I be defending her rather than MagRec?

Review Questions

1. Place yourself in the role of the manager. What should you do now? After considering what happened, would you change any of your behaviors?
2. Do you think Dinah was right? Why or why not? If you were she and had it to do all over again, would you do anything differently? If so, what and why?
3. Using cognitive dissonance theory, explain the actions of Pat, Dinah, and Fred. ■

CASE 5
"It Isn't Fair . . ."

Developed by Barry R. Armandi, SUNY–Old Westbury

Mary Jones was in her senior year at Central University and interviewing for jobs. Mary was in the top 1 percent of her class, active in numerous extracurricular activities, and highly respected by her professors. After the interviews, Mary was offered positions with every company with which she interviewed. After much thought, she decided to take the offer from Universal Products, a multinational company. She felt that the salary was superb ($40,000), the benefits were excellent, and potential for promotion was good.

Mary started work a few weeks after graduation and learned her job assignments and responsibilities thoroughly and quickly. Mary was asked on many occasions to work late because report deadlines were often moved forward. Without hesitation she said, "Of course!" even though as an exempt employee she would receive no overtime.

Frequently she would take work home with her and use her personal computer to do further analyses. At other times she would come into the office on weekends to monitor the progress of her projects or just to catch up on the ever-growing mountain of correspondence.

On one occasion, her manager asked her to take on a difficult assignment. It seemed that the company's manufacturing facility in Costa Rica was having production problems. The quality of one of the products was highly questionable, and the reports on the matter were confusing. Mary was asked to be part of a team to investigate the quality and reporting problems. The team stayed in poor accommodations for the entire three weeks they were there. This was because of the plant's location near its resources, which happened to be in the heart of the jungle. Within the three-week period, the team had located the source of the quality problem, corrected it, and altered the reporting documents and processes. The head of the team, a quality engineer, wrote a note to Mary's manager stating the following: "Just wanted to inform you of the superb job Mary Jones did down in Costa Rica. Her suggestions and insights into the reporting system were invaluable. Without her help we would have been down there for another three weeks, and I was getting tired of the mosquitoes. Thanks for sending her."

Universal Products, like most companies, has a yearly performance review system. Since Mary had been with the company for a little over one year, it was time for her review. Mary entered her manager's office nervous, since this was her first review ever and she didn't know what to expect. After closing the door and exchanging the usual pleasantries, her manager, Tom, got right to the point.

Tom: Well, Mary, as I told you last week this meeting would be for your annual review. As you are aware, your performance and compensation are tied together. Since the philosophy of the company is to reward those who perform, we take these reviews very seriously. I have spent a great deal of time thinking about your performance over the past year, but before I begin I would like to know your impressions of the company, your assignments, and me as a manager.

Mary: Honestly, Tom, I have no complaints. The company and my job are everything I was led to believe. I enjoy working here. The staff are all very helpful. I like the team atmosphere, and my job is very challenging. I really feel appreciated and that I'm making a contribution. You have been very helpful and patient with me. You got me involved right from the start and listened to my opinions. You taught me a lot, and I'm very grateful. All in all I'm happy being here.

Tom: Great, Mary. I was hoping that's the way you felt because from my vantage point, most of the people you worked with feel the same. But before I give you the qualitative side of the review, allow me to go through the quantitative appraisal first. As you know, the rankings go from one (lowest) to five (highest). Let's go down each category, and I'll explain my reasoning for each.

Tom starts with category one (Quantity of Work) and ends with category ten (Teamwork). In each of the categories, Tom has either given Mary a 5 or a 4. Indeed, only two categories have a 4, and Tom explains these are normal areas for improvement for most employees.

Tom: As you can see, Mary, I was very happy with your performance. You have received the highest rating I have ever given any of my subordinates. Your attitude, desire, and help are truly appreciated. The other people on the Costa Rica team gave you glowing reports, and speaking with the plant manager, she felt that you helped her understand the reporting system better than anyone else. Since your performance has been stellar, I'm delighted to give you a 10 percent increase effective immediately!

Mary: (mouth agape, and eyes wide) Tom, frankly I'm flabbergasted! I don't know what to say, but thank you very much. I hope I can continue to do as fine a job as I have this last year. Thanks once again.

After exchanging some parting remarks and some more thank-yous, Mary left Tom's office with a smile from ear to ear. She was floating on air! Not only did she feel the performance review process was uplifting, but her review was outstanding and so was her raise. She knew from other employees that the company was only giving out a 5 percent average increase. She figured that if she got that, or perhaps 6 or 7 percent, she would be happy. But to get 10 percent. Wow!! Imagine. . . .

Sue: Hi, Mary! Lost in thought? My, you look great. Looks like you got some great news. What's up?

Susan Stevens was a recent hire, working for Tom. She had graduated from Central University also, but a year after Mary. Sue had excelled while at Central, graduating in the top 1 percent of her class. She had laudatory letters of recommendation from her professors and was into many after-school clubs and activities.

Mary: Oh, hi, Sue! Sorry, but I was just thinking about Universal and the opportunities here.
Sue: Yes, it truly is. . . .
Mary: Sue, I just came from my performance review, and let me tell you, the process isn't that bad. As a matter of fact I found it quite rewarding, if you get my drift. I got a wonderful review, and can't wait till next year's. What a great company!
Sue: You can say that again! I couldn't believe them hiring me right out of college at such a good salary. Between you and me, Mary, they started me at $45,000. Imagine that? Wow, was I impressed. I just couldn't believe that they would . . . Where are you going, Mary? Mary?

What's that you say? "It isn't fair?" What do you mean? Mary? Mary. . . .

Review Questions

1. Indicate Mary's attitudes before and after meeting Sue. If there was a change, why?
2. What do you think Mary will do now? Later?
3. What motivation theory applies best to this scenario? Explain. ■

CASE 6A
Perfect Pizzeria, or Not?

Perfect Pizzeria in Southville, in deep southern Illinois, is the second-largest franchise of the chain in the United States. The headquarters is located in Phoenix, Arizona. Although the business is prospering, employee and managerial problems exist.

Each operation has one manager, an assistant manager, and from two to five night managers. The managers of each pizzeria work under an area supervisor. There are no systematic criteria for being a manager or becoming a manager trainee. The franchise has no formalized training period for the manager. No college education is required. The managers for whom the case observer worked during a four-year period were relatively young (ages twenty-four to twenty-seven), and only one had completed college. They came from the ranks of night managers or assistant managers, or both. The night managers were chosen for their ability to perform the duties of the regular employees. The assistant managers worked a two-hour shift during the luncheon period five days a week to gain knowledge about bookkeeping and management. Those becoming managers remained at that level unless they expressed interest in investing in the business.

The employees were mostly college students, with a few high school students performing the less-challenging jobs. Since Perfect Pizzeria was located in an area with few job opportunities, it had a relatively easy task of filling its employee quotas. All the employees, with the exception of the manager, were employed part time and were paid the minimum wage.

The Perfect Pizzeria system is devised so that food and beverage costs and profits are computed according to a percentage. If the percentage of food unsold or damaged in any way is very low, the manager gets a bonus. If the percentage is high, the manager does not receive a bonus; rather, he or she receives only his or her normal salary.

There are many ways in which the percentage can fluctuate. Since the manager cannot be in the store twenty-four hours a day, some employees make up for their smaller paychecks by helping themselves to the food. When a friend comes in to order a pizza, extra ingredients are put on the friend's pizza. Occasional nibbles by eighteen to twenty employees throughout the day at the meal table also raise the percentage figure. An occasional bucket of sauce may be spilled or a pizza accidentally burned.

In the event of an employee mistake, the expense is supposed to come from the individual. Because of peer pressure, the night manager seldom writes up a bill for the erring employee. Instead, the establishment takes the loss and the error goes unnoticed until the end of the month when the inventory is taken. That's when the manager finds out that the percentage is high and that there will be no bonus.

In the present instance, the manager took retaliatory measures. Previously, each employee was entitled to a free pizza, salad, and all the soft drinks he or she could drink for every six hours of work. The manager raised this figure from six to twelve hours of work. However, the employees had received these six-hour benefits for a long time. Therefore, they simply took advantage of the situation whenever the manager or the assistant was not in the building. Although the night manager theoretically had complete control of the operation in the evenings, he did not command the respect that the manager or assistant manager did. This was because he received the same pay as the regular employees, he could not reprimand other employees, and he was basically the same age or sometimes even younger than the other employees.

Thus, apathy grew within the pizzeria. There seemed to be a further separation between the manager and his workers, who started out as a closely knit group. The manager made no attempt to alleviate the problem because he felt it would iron itself out. Either the employees that were dissatisfied would quit or they would be content to put up with the new regulations. As it turned out, a rash of employee dismissals occurred. The manager had no problem filling the vacancies with new workers, but the loss of key personnel was costly to the business.

With the large turnover, the manager found that he had to spend more time in the building, supervising and sometimes taking the place of inexperienced workers. This was in direct violation of the franchise regulation, which stated that a manager would act as a supervisor and at no time take part in the actual food preparation.

Employees were not placed under strict supervision with the manager working alongside them. The operation no longer worked smoothly because of differences between the remaining experienced workers and the manager concerning the way in which a particular function should be performed.

After a two-month period, the manager was again free to go back to his office and leave his subordinates in charge of the entire operation. During this two-month period, the percentage had returned to the previous low level, and the manager received a bonus each month. The manager felt that his problems had been resolved and that conditions would remain the same, since the new personnel had been properly trained.

It didn't take long for the new employees to become influenced by the other employees. Immediately after the manager returned to his supervisory role, the percentage began to rise. This time the manager took a bolder step. He cut out any benefits that the employees had—no free pizzas, salads, or drinks. With the job market at an even lower ebb than usual, most employees were forced to stay. The appointment of a new area supervisor made it impossible for the manager to "work behind the counter," since the supervisor was centrally located in Southville.

The manager tried still another approach to alleviate the rising percentage problem and maintain his bonus. He placed a notice on the bulletin board stating that if the percentage remained at a high level, a lie detector test would be given to all employees. All those found guilty of taking or purposefully wasting food or drinks would be immediately terminated. This did not have the desired effect on the employees because they knew if they were all subjected to the test, all would be found guilty and the manager would have to dismiss all of them. This would leave him in a worse situation than ever.

Even before the following month's percentage was calculated, the manager knew it would be high. He had evidently received information from one of the night managers about the employees' feelings about the notice. What he did not expect was that the percentage would reach an all-time high. That is the state of affairs at the present time.

Review Questions

1. Consider the situation where the manager changed the time period required to receive free food and drink from six to twelve hours of work. Try to apply each of the motivational approaches to explain what happened. Which of the approaches offers the most appropriate explanation? Why?

2. Repeat question 1 for the situation in which the manager worked beside the employees for a time and then later returned to his office.
3. Repeat question 1 for the situation as it exists at the end of the case.
4. Establish and justify a motivational program based on one or a combination of motivation theories to deal with the situation as it exists at the end of the case. ■

CASE 6B
OB Classic: Hovey and Beard Company

Written by James G. (Jerry) Hunt, Southern Illinois University at Carbondale

The Hovey and Beard Company manufactures a variety of wooden toys, including animals, pull toys, and the like.[1] The toys were manufactured by a transformation process that began in the wood room. There, toys were cut, sanded, and partially assembled. Then the toys were dipped into shellac and sent to the painting room.

In years past, the painting had been done by hand, with each employee working with a given toy until its painting was completed. The toys were predominantly painted with two colors, although a few required more colors. Now, in response to increased demand for the toys, the painting operation was changed so that the painters sat in a line by an endless chain of hooks. These hooks moved continuously in front of the painters and passed into a long horizontal oven. Each painter sat in a booth designed to carry away fumes and to backstop excess paint. The painters would take a toy from a nearby tray, position it in a jig inside the painting cubicle, spray on the color according to a pattern, and then hang the toy on a passing hook. The rate at which the hooks moved was calculated by the engineers so that each painter, when fully trained, could hang a painted toy on each hook before it passed beyond reach.

The painters were paid on a group bonus plan. Since the operation was new to them, they received a learning bonus that decreased by regular amounts each month. The learning bonus was scheduled to vanish in six months, by which time it was expected that they would be on their own—that is, able to meet the production standard and earn a group bonus when they exceeded it.

By the second month of the training period, trouble developed. The painters learned more slowly than had been anticipated, and it began to look as though their production would stabilize far below what was planned. Many of the hooks were going by empty. The painters complained that the hooks moved too fast and that the engineer had set the rates wrong. A few painters quit and had to be replaced with new ones. This further aggravated the learning problem. The team spirit that the management had expected to develop through the group bonus was not in evidence except as an expression of what the engineers called "resistance." One painter, whom the group regarded as its leader (and the management regarded as the ringleader), was outspoken in taking the complaints of the group to the supervisor. These complaints were that the job was messy, the hooks moved too fast, the incentive pay was not correctly calculated, and it was too hot working so close to the drying oven.

A consultant was hired to work with the supervisor. She recommended that the painters be brought together for a general discussion of the working conditions. Although hesitant, the supervisor agreed to this plan.

The first meeting was held immediately after the shift was over at 4:00 p.m. It was attended by all eight painters. They voiced the same complaints again: The hooks went by too fast, the job was too dirty, and the room was hot and poorly ventilated. For some reason, it was this last item that seemed to bother them most. The supervisor promised to discuss the problems of ventilation and temperature with the engineers, and a second meeting was scheduled. Over the next few days, the supervisor had several talks with the engineers. They, along with the plant superintendent, felt that this was really a trumped-up complaint and that the expense of corrective measures would be prohibitively high.

The supervisor came to the second meeting with some apprehension. The painters, however, did not seem to be much put out. Rather, they had a proposal of their own to make. They felt that if several large fans were set up to circulate the air around their feet, they would be much more comfortable. After some discussion, the supervisor agreed to pursue the idea. The supervisor and the consultant discussed the idea of fans with the superintendent. Three large propeller-type fans were purchased and installed.

The painters were jubilant. For several days the fans were moved about in various positions until they were placed to the satisfaction of the group. The painters seemed completely satisfied with the results, and the relations between them and the supervisor improved visibly.

The supervisor, after this encouraging episode, decided that further meetings might also prove profitable. The painters were asked if they would like to meet and discuss other aspects of the work situation. They were eager to do this. Another meeting was held, and the discussion quickly centered on the speed of the hooks. The painters maintained that the engineer had set them at an unreasonably fast speed and that they would never be able to fill enough of them to make a bonus.

The discussion reached a turning point when the group's leader explained that it wasn't that the painters couldn't work fast enough to keep up with the hooks but that they couldn't work at that pace all day long. The supervisor explored the point. The painters were unanimous in their opinion that they could keep up with the belt for short periods if they wanted. But they didn't want to because, if they showed they could do this for short periods, then they would be expected to do it all day long. The meeting ended with an unprecedented request by the painters: "Let us adjust the speed of the belt faster or slower depending on how we feel." The supervisor agreed to discuss this with the superintendent and the engineers.

The engineers reacted negatively to the suggestion. However, after several meetings it was granted that there was some latitude within which variations in the speed of the hooks would not affect the finished product. After considerable argument with the engineers, it was agreed to try out the painters' idea.

With misgivings, the supervisor had a control with a dial marked "Low, Medium, Fast" installed at the booth of the group leader. The speed of the belt could now be adjusted anywhere between the lower and upper limits that the engineers had set.

The painters were delighted and spent many lunch hours deciding how the speed of the belt should be varied from hour to hour throughout the day. Within a week the pattern had settled down to one in which the first half hour of the shift was run on a medium speed (a dial setting slightly above the point marked "Medium"). The next two and a half hours were run at high speed, and the half hour before lunch and the half hour after lunch were run at low speed. The rest of the afternoon was run at high speed with the exception of the last forty-five minutes of the shift, which was run at medium.

The constant speed at which the engineers had originally set the belt was actually slightly below the "Medium" mark on the control dial; the average speed at which the painters were running the belt was on the high side of the dial. Few, if any, empty hooks entered the oven, and inspection showed no increase of rejects from the paint room.

Production increased, and within three weeks (some two months before the scheduled ending of the learning bonus) the painters were operating at 30 to 50 percent above the level that had been expected under the original arrangement. Naturally, their earnings were correspondingly higher than anticipated. They were collecting their base pay, earning a considerable piece-rate bonus, and still benefiting from the learning bonus. They were earning more now than many skilled workers in other parts of the plant.

Management was besieged by demands that the inequity between the earnings of the painters and those of other workers in the plant be rectified. With growing irritation between the superintendent and the supervisor, the engineers and supervisor, and the superintendent and engineers, the situation came to a head when the superintendent revoked the learning bonus and returned the painting operation to its original status: The hooks moved again at their constant, time-studied, designated speed. Production dropped again, and within a month all but two of the eight painters had quit. The supervisor stayed on for several months, but, feeling aggrieved, left for another job.

Review Questions

1. How does the painters' job score on the core job characteristics before and after the changes were made? How can the positive impact of the job redesign be explained?
2. Was the learning bonus handled properly in this case? How can its motivational impact be explained? What alternative approaches could have been taken with similar motivational results?
3. How do you explain the situation described in the last paragraph of the case? How could this outcome have been avoided by appropriate managerial actions? ■

CASE 7
The Forgotten Group Member

Developed by Franklin Ramsoomair, Wilfred Laurier University

The OB course for the semester appeared to promise the opportunity to learn, enjoy, and practice some of the theories and principles in the textbook and class discussions. Christine Spencer was a devoted, hard-working student who had been maintaining an A– average to date. Although the skills and knowledge she had acquired through her courses were important, she was also very concerned about her grades. She felt that grades were paramount in giving her a competitive edge when looking for a job and, as a third-year student, she realized that she'd soon be doing just that.

Sunday afternoon. Two o'clock. Christine was working on an accounting assignment but didn't seem to be able to concentrate. Her courses were working out very well this semester, all but the OB. Much of the mark in that course was to be based on the quality of groupwork, and so she felt somewhat out of control. She recollected the events of the past five weeks. Professor Sandra Thiel had divided the class into groups of five people and had given them a major group assignment worth 30 percent of the final grade. The task was to analyze a seven-page case and to come up with a written analysis. In addition, Sandra had asked the groups to present the case in class, with the idea that the rest of the class members would be "members of the board of directors of the company" who would be listening to how the manager and her team dealt with the problem at hand.

Christine was elected team coordinator at the first group meeting. The other members of the group were Diane, Janet, Steve, and Mike. Diane was quiet and never volunteered suggestions, but when directly asked she would come up with high-quality ideas. Mike was the clown. Christine remembered that she had suggested that the group should get together before every class to discuss the day's case. Mike had balked, saying "No way!! This is an eight-thirty class, and I barely make it on time anyway! Besides, I'll miss my *Happy Harry* show on television!" The group couldn't help but laugh at his indignation. Steve was the businesslike individual, always wanting to ensure that group meetings were guided by an agenda and noting the tangible results achieved or not achieved at the end of every meeting. Janet was the reliable one who would always have more for the group than was expected of her. Christine saw herself as meticulous and organized and as a person who tried to give her best in whatever she did.

It was now week five into the semester, and Christine was deep in thought about the OB assignment. She had called everyone to arrange a meeting for a time that would suit them all, but she seemed to be running into a roadblock. Mike couldn't make it, saying that he was working that night as a member of the campus security force. In fact, he seemed to miss most meetings and would send in brief notes to Christine, which she was supposed to discuss for him at the group meetings. She wondered how to deal with this. She also remembered the incident last week. Just before class started, Diane, Janet, Steve, and she were joking with one another before class. They were laughing and enjoying themselves before Sandra came in. No one noticed that Mike had slipped in very quietly and taken his seat unobtrusively.

She recalled the cafeteria incident. Two weeks ago, she had gone to the cafeteria to grab something to eat. She had rushed to her accounting class and had skipped breakfast. When she got her club sandwich and headed to the tables, she saw her OB group and joined them. The discussion was light and enjoyable as it always was when they met informally. Mike had come in. He'd approached their table. "You guys didn't say you were having a group meeting," he blurted. Christine was taken aback.

We just happened to run into each other. Why not join us?"

Mike looked at them noncommittally. "Yeah . . . right," he muttered, and walked away.

Sandra Thiel had frequently told them that if there were problems in the group, the members should make an effort to deal with them first. If the problems could not be resolved, she had said that they should come to her. Mike seemed so distant, despite the apparent camaraderie of the first meeting.

An hour had passed, bringing the time to 3:00 p.m., and Christine found herself biting the tip of her pencil. The written case analysis was due next week. All the others had done their designated sections, but Mike had just handed in some rough handwritten notes. He had called Christine the week before, telling her that in addition to his course and his job, he was having problems with his girlfriend. Christine empathized with him. Yet, this was a group project! Besides, the final mark would be peer evaluated. This meant that whatever mark Sandra gave them could be lowered or raised, depending on the group's opinion about the value of the contribution of each member. She was definitely worried. She knew that Mike had creative ideas that could help to raise the overall mark. She was also concerned for him. As she listened to the music in the background, she wondered what she should do.

Review Questions

1. How could an understanding of the stages of group development assist Christine in leadership situations such as this one?
2. What should Christine understand about individual membership in groups in order to build group processes that are supportive of her work group's performance?
3. Is Christine an effective group leader in this case? Why or why not? ■

CASE 8
Teams Drive the Fast Cars

When you think of auto racing, do you think of teamwork? Watch any televised race, and the better majority of the camera time is dedicated to the drivers and their cars. But in each of the three major forms of auto racing, the driver is simply one member of a larger team that works together to achieve maximum performance. And when the driver wins, the team wins as well.

In the world of competitive auto racing, the drivers are the sport's rock stars. They're courted by sponsors, adored by fans, and portrayed as the subject of interview upon interview by the racing press. It goes without saying that drivers are absolutely essential to earning a trophy, but racing enthusiasts, teammates, and especially drivers will tell you that they can't win the race by themselves—it takes a successful team to win a race.

Furthermore, while the driver is the most visible member of the team and certainly the one responsible for guiding the car, he's not always calling the shots. The most successful teams rely on multiple sets of eyes to assess track conditions and identify opportunities to advance that drivers themselves can't see from the cockpit.

Ray Evernham, crew chief and team manager for Hendrick Motorsports's DuPont car, describes teamwork this way: "We're all spark plugs. If one doesn't fire just right, we can't win the race. So no matter whether you are the guy that's doing the fabricating or changing tires on Sundays and that's the only job responsibility you have, if you don't do your job then we're not going to win. And no one is more or less important than you."[1] Although three of the major forms of professional auto racing—NASCAR, Formula One, and rally car racing—each utilizes different vehicles, rules, and team structures, teamwork is the common denominator among them.

What are the qualities of successful racing teams? Let's take a look.

Nascar

NASCAR is the most widely known and watched racing sport in the United States, and the popularity and success of Jeff Gordon has more than a little to do with that. Gordon has the most wins in NASCAR's modern era, has the third-most all-time wins, and has become a spokesperson for the importance of teamwork in NASCAR racing.[2] NASCAR has come a long way since its origins in the late 1940s in racing stock cars purchased directly from auto dealerships. Today's NASCAR vehicles are custom fabricated from the ground up, although their thin metal bodies are molded in the shape of popular American sedans to reflect the sport's heritage. While most fans would be quick to point out the driver, manager, and pit crew as racing team members, shop mechanics, parts fabricators, and even aerodynamics experts are just as essential to a team's performance.

It's impossible for a car to complete a NASCAR race without multiple visits to the pit, and these pit stops are often the best example of teamwork in the sport. Pit crew members practice routine maintenance tasks like tire changes and refueling until they can execute them with lightning speed and the utmost precision. Aside from the skill and muscle memory of the pit crew members, other teammates contribute by modifying parts and equipment so they can be changed out in less time. Pit stops that would take mechanics twenty minutes or more to complete happen in less than twenty seconds.

Two-time Sprint Cup winner Jimmie Johnson cites the importance of cohesive teamwork even before a car is assembled and tested on the track. "If you really get inside each other's heads, as the car is developed, you're looking to split hairs," Johnson said. "If you really know each other, then you know what each other is looking for, you've built that foundation and belief on the teammates [and] the engineers, you can split those hairs and get it right."[3]

Formula One

Formula One drivers, team members, and fans have one quality that sets them apart from other racing participants: the need for speed. Formula One vehicles are the fastest circuit racing cars in the world, screaming down the track at top speeds as high as 225 miles per hour.

But there's another buzzword that equally defines Formula One racing: *performance*. Because of the high speeds racers achieve and the intense G-forces drivers and cars are subjected to, ensuring that Formula One cars perform efficiently and successfully throughout a race is literally a life-and-death matter.

The term *formula* refers to a strict set of regulations teams must abide by when building their cars in order to keep the races competitive. Unlike in other racing sports, Formula One teams have been required to build their own chassis since 1981, so although teams procure specialized engines from specific manufacturers, they are primarily responsible for building their cars from the ground up.

Each formula has its own set of rules that eligible cars must meet (*Formula One* being the highest and fastest of these designations), the idea being that these limitations will produce cars that are roughly equivalent in performance. Of course, that won't always be the case, as teams work furiously to seek out every last bit of efficiency and performance while adhering to sport guidelines.[4] Team members often lean heavily on aerodynamics, racing suspensions, and tires to achieve maximum performance.

The McLaren team is one of the most successful Formula One teams, and engineering director Paddy Lowe understands the behind-the-scenes dynamics that help great racing teams succeed. Speaking on the challenge of incorporating a new component into an existing car, he noted, "There weren't actually that many issues, but we kept experiencing a variety of failures with our new exhaust system. We'd come into the circuit each morning thinking we'd fixed the problems of the previous day, only to be met with a fresh series of trials the next day. Those days were very difficult for the team.

"You have to factor in the skill of the team to work together in a very short period of time to push in a completely different direction; to understand all the different issues. The reliability, the performance, the skills of the team, all the tools they've created over the years—they all came through to our profit. In those instances, there's not a big discussion about who's going to do what; there are very few instructions. Everybody moves seamlessly. They know what they've got to do."[5]

BMW Motorsport Director Mario Theissen put it simply: "Teamwork is the key to success," he said. "Of course the basis is formed by a competitive technical package, but without a well-integrated, highly motivated team, even the best car will not achieve prolonged success."[6]

Rally Car Racing

Whereas NASCAR and Formula One racers speed around a paved track, rally car racing frequently heads off the circuit and into territory that would make Dale Earnhardt step on the brakes: Finnish rallies feature long, treacherous stretches of ice and snow. The famed French *Méditerranée-le Cap* ran 10,000 miles from the Mediterranean to South Africa. The reputed Baja 1000 Rally ran the length of the Baja California peninsula, largely over deserts without a road in sight.

In rally car racing, drivers race against the clock instead of each other. Races generally consist of several stages that the driver must compete as quickly as possible, and the winning driver completes all stages in the least amount of time.[7]

You could argue that of all racing sports, rally drivers are the most reliant on teamwork to win. Unlike other forms of circuit racing, not only is the driver not racing on a fixed track, but he does not get to see the course before the race begins. Instead, he is wholly reliant on a teammate, the navigator, for information on upcoming terrain.

Part coach and part co-pilot, the navigator relies on page notes (detailed information on the sharpness of turns and the steepness of gradients) to keep the driver on course from his place in the car's passenger seat.[8]

Turkish driver Burcu Çetinkaya had already made a name for herself as a successful snowboarder before she decided to take up rally car racing at the age of twenty-four. "I grew up with cars," she said. "After visiting my first rally when I was twelve, I made up my mind to be a rally driver."[9]

"The thing that hooked me about rally driving was working together with a team for a common goal with nature working against you," she said. "I love cars, first of all—I grew up with them and I love every part of them. And I love competition. I have been competing all my life. In a rally, these things come together: nature, competition, teamwork and cars."[10]

You Can't Have One Without the Other

Though they may receive the lion's share of the notoriety and adulation, racing drivers are only one member of a larger team, wherein every team member's performance contributes to the team's success. The best drivers don't let the fame go to their heads. As Jeff Gordon—who knows a thing or two about success—put it, "The only way I can do my job correctly is to be totally clear in my mind and have 100 percent confidence in every person's job that went into this team so that they can have 100 percent confidence in what I'm doing as a driver."[11]

Review Questions

1. What types of formal and informal groups would you expect to find in a racing team? What roles could each play in helping the team toward a winning season?
2. Racing teams and their leaders have to make lots of decisions—from the pressures of race day to the routines of everyday team management. When and in what situations would you see teams making decisions by authority rule, minority rule, majority rule, consensus, or unanimity? Are all of these decision approaches acceptable at some times and situations, or are some unacceptable at any time? Defend your answer.
3. Assume you have been retained as a team-building consultant by a famous and successful racing team whose performance fell badly during the prior season. Design a series of team-building activities you will lead the team in performing to strengthen their trust in each other and to improve their individual and collective efforts.

4. Choose a racing team of interest to you. Research the team, its personnel, and its performance in the most recent racing season. Try to answer this question: What accounts for this team's success or lack of success—driver talent, technology, teamwork, or all three? Can you find lessons in the racing team that might apply to teams and organizations in any setting? If so, list at least three that you believe are valuable and transferable insights. ■

CASE 9
Decisions, Decisions, Decisions

Developed by John R. Schermerhorn, Jr., Ohio University

The Case of the Diamond Ring

Setting—A woman is preparing for a job interview.

Dilemma—She wants the job desperately and is worried that her marital status might adversely affect the interview.

Decision—Should she or should she not wear her diamond engagement ring?

Considerations—When queried for a column in the *Wall Street Journal*, some women claimed that they would try to hide their marital status during a job interview.[1] One said, "Although I will never remove my wedding band, I don't want anyone to look at my engagement ring and think, she doesn't need this job, what is she doing working?" Even the writer remembers that she considered removing her engagement ring some years back when applying for a job. "I had no idea about the office culture," she said. "I didn't want anyone making assumptions, however unreasonable, about my commitment to work."

Wellness or Invasive Coercion?

Setting—Scotts Miracle-Gro Company, Marysville, Ohio.

Dilemma—Corporate executives are concerned about rising health-care costs. CEO Jim Hagedorn backs an aggressive wellness program and anti-smoking campaign to improve health of employees and reduce healthcare costs for the firm. Scott employees are asked to take extensive health-risk assessments; failure to do so increases their health insurance premiums by $40 a month. Employees found to have "moderate to high" health risks are assigned health coaches and given action plans; failure to comply adds another $67 per month. In states where the practice is legal, the firm will not hire a smoker and tests new employees for nicotine use. In response to complaints that the policy is intrusive, Hagedorn says, "If people understand the facts and still choose to smoke, it's suicidal. And we can't encourage suicidal behavior."

Decision—Is Hagedorn doing the right thing by leading Scotts's human resource policies in this direction?

Considerations—Joe Pellegrini's life was probably saved by his employer. After urging from one of Scotts's health coaches, he saw his doctor about weight and cholesterol concerns. This led to a visit with a heart specialist who inserted two stents, correcting a 95 percent blockage. Scott Rodrigues's life was changed by his employer; he is suing Scotts for wrongful dismissal. A smoker, he claims that he was fired after failing a drug test for nicotine even though he wasn't informed about the test and had been told the company would help him stop smoking. CEO Hagedorn says, "This is an area where CEOs are afraid to go. A lot of people are watching to see how badly we get sued."[2]

Super Saleswoman Won't Ask for Raise

Setting—A woman is described as a "productive star" and "super-successful" member of an eighteen-person sales force.[3]

Dilemma—She finds out that both she and the other female salesperson are being paid 20 percent less than the men. Her sister wants her to talk with her boss and ask for more pay. She says, "No, I'm satisfied with my present pay, and I don't want to 'rock the boat'." The sister can't understand how and why she puts up with this situation, allowing herself to be paid less than a man for at least equal and quite possibly better performance.

Considerations—Women still earn only about 75 cents on the average for each dollar earned by a man. Some claim that one explanation for the wage gap and its growing size is that women tolerate the situation and allow it to continue, rather than confronting the gap in their personal circumstances and trying to change it.

Firm Goes Public with Annual Bonuses

Setting—Executives released to the public information on the annual bonuses paid to store employees.

Dilemma—The bonus program has been in place for a number of years. The goal is to link employee motivation and performance with the firm's financial success. In the past each person's bonus was considered a private matter and no bonuses were made public within the firm. However, recently the firm has released to the news media data on bonuses paid to lower-level employees. Coincidentally, the firm has been receiving negative publicity about the low wages paid to employees and the minimal benefits they are eligible to receive. A company spokesperson says that going public with the bonuses was not a response to such criticism.

Considerations—One employee said she received over $1,000 as a bonus, more than the prior year. But a critic stated that the firm "gives executives millions in bonuses and the mere crumbs to the workers."

Review Questions

1. Critique the decisions being made in these situations. Identify how, where, and why different decisions might be made.
2. What are the issues involved in these situations? How are they best addressed by the decision makers?
3. Find other decision-making examples that raise similar issues and quandaries. Share them with classmates and analyze the possible decisions. ■

CASE 10
The Case of the Missing Raise

Prepared by John R. Schermerhorn, Jr., Ohio University

It was late February, and Marsha Lloyd had just completed an important long-distance telephone call with Professor Fred Massie, head of the Department of Management at Central University. During the conversation Marsha accepted an offer to move from her present position at Private University, located in the East, to Central in the Midwest as an assistant professor. Marsha and her husband, John, then shared the following thoughts.

Marsha: "Well, it's final."
John: "It's been a difficult decision, but I know it will work out for the best."
Marsha: "Yes, however, we are leaving many things we like here."
John: "I know, but remember, Professor Massie is someone you respect a great deal, and he is offering you a challenge to come and introduce new courses at Central. Besides, he will surely be a pleasure to work for."

Marsha: "John we're young, eager, and a little adventurous. There's no reason we shouldn't go."
John: "We're going, dear."

Marsha Lloyd began the fall semester eagerly. The points discussed in her earlier conversations with Fred were now real challenges, and she was teaching new undergraduate and graduate courses in Central's curriculum. Overall, the transition to Central had been pleasant. The nine faculty members were warm in welcoming her, and Marsha felt it would be good working with them. She also felt comfortable with the performance standards that appeared to exist in the department. Although it was certainly not a "publish or perish" situation, Fred had indicated during the recruiting process that research and publications would be given increasing weight along with teaching and service in future departmental decisions. This was consistent with Marsha's personal belief that a professor should live up to each of these responsibilities. Although there was some conflict evident among the faculty over what weighting and standards should apply to these performance areas, she sensed some consensus that the multiple responsibilities should be respected.

It was April, and spring vacation time. Marsha was sitting at home reflecting upon her experiences to date at Central. She was pleased. Both she and John had adjusted very well to Midwestern life. Although there were things they both missed from their prior location, she was in an interesting new job and they found the rural environment of Central very satisfying. Marsha had also received positive student feedback on her fall semester courses, had presented two papers at a recent professional meeting, and had just been informed that two of her papers would be published by a journal. This was a good record, and she felt satisfied. She had been working hard, and it was paying off.

The spring semester ended, and Marsha was preoccupied. It was time, she thought, for an end-of-the-year performance review by Fred Massie. This anticipation had been stimulated, in part, by a recent meeting of the College faculty in which the dean indicated that a 7 percent pay raise pool was now available for the coming year. He was encouraging department chairpersons to distribute this money differentially based on performance merit. Marsha had listened closely to the dean and liked what she heard. She felt this meant that Central was really trying to establish a performance-oriented reward system. Such a system was consistent with her personal philosophy and, indeed, she taught such reasoning in her courses.

Throughout May, Marsha kept expecting to have a conversation with Fred Massie on these topics. One day, the following memo appeared in her faculty mailbox.

MEMORANDUM
TO: Fellow Faculty
FROM: Fred
RE: Raises for Next Year

The Dean has been most open about the finances of the College as evidenced by his detail and candor regarding the budget at the last faculty meeting. Consistent with that philosophy I want to provide a perspective on raises and clarify a point or two.

The actual dollars available to our department exclusive of the chairman total 7.03 percent. In allocating those funds I have attempted to reward people on the basis of their contribution to the life of the Department and the University, as well as professional growth and development. In addition, it was essential this year to adjust a couple of inequities which had developed over a period of time. The distribution of increments was the following:

5 percent or less	3
5+ percent to 7 percent	2
7+ percent to 9 percent	3
More than 9 percent	2

Marsha read the memo with mixed emotions. Initially, she was upset that Fred had obviously made the pay raise decisions without having spoken first with her about her performance. Still, she felt good because she was sure to be one of those receiving a 9+ percent increase. "Now," she mused to herself, "it will be good to sit down with Fred and discuss not only this past year's efforts, but my plans for next year's as well."

Marsha was disappointed when Fred did not contact her for such a discussion. Furthermore, she found herself frequently involved in informal conversations with other faculty members who were speculating over who received the various pay increments.

One day Carla Block, a faculty colleague, came into Marsha's office and said she had asked Fred about Marsha's raise. She said that Marsha received a 7+ percent increase and also learned that the two 9+ percent increases had been given to senior faculty members. Marsha was incredulous. "It can't be," she thought. "I was a top performer this past year. My teaching and publications records are strong, and I feel I've been a positive force in the department." She felt Carla could be mistaken and waited to talk the matter out with Fred.

A few days later another colleague reported to Marsha the results of a similar conversation with Fred. This time Marsha exploded internally. She felt she deserved just reward.

The next day Marsha received a computerized notice on her pay increment from the Accounting Office. Her raise was 7.2 percent. That night, after airing her feelings with John, Marsha telephoned Fred at home and arranged to meet with him the next day.

Fred Massie knocked on the door to Marsha's office and entered. The greetings were cordial. Marsha began the conversation. "Fred, we've always been frank with one another, and now I'm concerned about my raise," she said. "I thought I had a good year, but I understand that I've received just an average raise." Fred Massie was a person who talked openly, and Marsha could trust him. He responded to Marsha in this way.

"Yes, Marsha, you are a top performer. I feel you have made great contributions to the department. The two nine-plus percent raises went to correct 'inequities' that had built up over a period of time for two senior people. I felt that since the money was available this year, I had a responsibility to make the adjustments. If we don't consider them, you received one of the three top raises, and I consider any percentage differences between these three very superficial. I suppose I could have been more discriminating at the lower end of the distribution, but I can't give zero increments. I know you had a good year. It's what I expected when I hired you. You haven't let me down. From your perspective I know you feel you earned an 'A,' and I agree. I gave you a 'B-plus.' I hope you understand why."

Marsha sympathized with Fred's logic and felt good having spoken with him. Although she wasn't happy, she understood Fred's position. Her final comment to Fred was this: "You know, it's not the absolute dollar value of the raise that hurts. It's the sense of letdown. Recently, for example, I turned down an extensive consulting job that would have paid far more than the missing raise. I did so because I felt it would require too many days away from the office. I'm not sure my colleagues would make that choice."

In the course of a casual summer conversation, Carla mentioned to Marsha that she had heard two of the faculty who had received 4+ percent raises had complained to Fred and the dean. After lodging the complaints, they had received additional salary increments. "Oh, great," Marsha responded to herself, "I thought I had put this thing to rest."

About three weeks later, Marsha, Fred, Carla, and another colleague were in a meeting with the dean. Although the meeting was on a separate matter, something was said which implied that Carla had also received an additional pay increment. Marsha confronted the dean and learned that this was the case. Carla had protested to Fred and the dean, and they had raised her pay on the justification that an historical salary inequity had been overlooked. Fred was visibly uncomfortable as a discussion ensued on how salary increments should be awarded and what had transpired in the department on this matter.

Fred eventually excused himself to attend another meeting. Marsha and the others continued to discuss the matter with the dean, and the conversation became increasingly heated. Finally, they each rose to terminate the meeting. Marsha felt compelled to say one more thing: "It's not that I'm not making enough money," she said to the dean, "but I just don't feel I received my fair share, especially in terms of your own stated policy of rewarding faculty on the basis of performance merit."

With that remark, Marsha left the meeting. As she walked down the hall to her office, she said to herself, "Next year there will be no turning down consulting jobs because of a misguided sense of departmental responsibility."

Review Questions

1. What is Marsha's conflict management style, and how has it influenced events in this case? What were Marsha's goals, and what conflict management style would have worked best in helping her achieve them?
2. What is Fred's conflict management style, and how has it influenced events in this case?
3. Once Marsha found out what her raise was to be, how could she have used the notion and elements of distributive negotiation to create a situation in which Fred would make a raise adjustment that was favorable and motivating for her? ∎

CASE 11
The Poorly Informed Walrus

Developed by Barbara McCain, Oklahoma City University

"How's it going down there?" barked the big walrus from his perch on the highest rock near the shore. He waited for the good word.

Down below, the smaller walruses conferred hastily among themselves. Things weren't going well at all, but none of them wanted to break the news to the Old Man. He was the biggest and wisest walrus in the herd, and he knew his business, but he had such a terrible temper that every walrus in the herd was terrified of his ferocious bark.

"What will we tell him?" whispered Basil, the second-ranking walrus. He well remembered how the Old Man had raved and ranted at him the last time the herd had caught less than its quota of herring, and he had no desire to go through that experience again. Nevertheless, the walrus noticed for several weeks that the water level in the nearby Arctic bay had been falling constantly, and it had become necessary to travel much farther to catch the dwindling supply of herring. Someone should tell the Old Man; he would probably know what to do. But who? and how?

Finally Basil spoke up: "Things are going pretty well, Chief," he said. The thought of the receding water line made his heart grow heavy, but he went on: "As a matter of fact, the beach seems to be getting larger."

The Old Man grunted. "Fine, fine," he said. "That will give us a bit more elbow room." He closed his eyes and continued basking in the sun.

The next day brought more trouble. A new herd of walruses moved in down the beach and, with the supply of herring dwindling, this invasion could be dangerous. No one wanted to tell the Old Man, though only he could take the steps necessary to meet this new competition.

Reluctantly, Basil approached the big walrus, who was still sunning himself on the large rock. After some small talk, he said, "Oh, by the way, Chief, a new herd of walruses seems to have moved into our territory." The Old Man's eyes snapped open, and he filled his great lungs in preparation for a mighty bellow. But Basil added quickly, "Of course, we don't anticipate any trouble. They don't look like herring eaters to me. More likely interested in minnows. And as you know, we don't bother with minnows ourselves."

The Old Man let out the air with a long sigh. "Good, good," he said. "No point in our getting excited over nothing then, is there?"

Things didn't get any better in the weeks that followed. One day, peering down from the large rock, the Old Man noticed that part of the herd seemed to be missing. Summoning Basil, he grunted peevishly. "What's going on, Basil? Where is everyone?" Poor Basil didn't have the courage to tell the Old Man that many of the younger walruses were leaving every day to join the new herd. Clearing his throat nervously, he said, "Well Chief, we've been tightening up things a bit. You know, getting rid of some of the dead wood. After all, a herd is only as good as the walruses in it."

"Run a tight ship, I always say," the Old Man grunted. "Glad to hear that all is going so well."

Before long, everyone but Basil had left to join the new herd, and Basil realized that the time had come to tell the Old Man the facts. Terrified but determined, he flopped up to the large rock. "Chief," he said, "I have bad news. The rest of the herd has left you." The old walrus was so astonished that he couldn't even work up a good bellow. "Left me?" he cried. "All of them? But why? How could this happen?"

Basil didn't have the heart to tell him, so he merely shrugged helplessly.

"I can't understand it," the old walrus said. "And just when everything was going so well."

Review Questions

1. What barriers to communication are evident in this fable?
2. What communication "lessons" does this fable offer to those who are serious about careers in the new workplace?

CASE 12
Political Behavior Analysis

Developed by John R. Schermerhorn, Jr., Ohio University

Read the following incidents and answer the following questions for each:

1. To what extent are power and politics already at play in this situation?
2. How might one of the actors in the incident use power and politics to achieve advantage in the situation described?

Incident 1: New Product Development

Two research scientists are competing for an internal new product development award worth $300,000 and a nice résumé boost. Scientist A is technically the stronger of the two. She is also relatively quiet, reserved, and modest in her dealings with co-workers and higher management. Scientist B is technically good and is considered a good candidate for a management position sometime in the future. He is outgoing, networks widely, and is a real self-promoter. After the proposals were submitted, Scientist A went back to work to await final word on the winner. Scientist B began an aggressive campaign to win the award by making sure that those in charge of the decision and others knew why his proposal should be considered the best one.

Incident 2: Career Advancement

A young woman has been with the financial services firm for two years. She is happy with the work, pleased with her responsibilities, and looking forward to career advancement within the firm. During a casual conversation over coffee she has just learned that a male colleague with less time at the firm has gone to higher management and negotiated a special off-cycle pay raise. The colleague is now earning more, in fact quite a bit more, than she is. The firm's CEO has made many public statements supporting career advancement for women. The culture is one in which no one is supposed to talk about their pay with others inside or outside the firm. The young woman wants more pay and is now unhappy in a situation that she had previously found very satisfying.

Incident 3: Headphones On in the Office

Saul, aged twenty-five, has just started a new job where everyone works in an open-plan office. He's been there about three weeks and is content. A music lover, he has been wearing headphones during the day while working on the computer. Yesterday a colleague who Saul guesses to be about forty to forty-five years old, offered him some "advice." "You should take off the headphones in the office," she said, "that's not the way we do things here. People are starting to say that you aren't friendly and tend to be a loner." This caught Saul by surprise since he has the headphones on most of his free time as well, and he thinks the music helps him stay relaxed and focused while doing detailed computer work. Nobody said anything about such things when he interviewed, and he can't find any company policy or rule that forbids wearing headphones at work. He likes the job, even likes the people, but he doesn't like being told to take the headphones off.

CASE 13
Selecting a New Vice President

Note: Please read only those parts identified by your instructor. Do not read ahead.

Part A

When the new president at Mid-West U took over, it was only a short time before the incumbent vice president announced his resignation. Unfortunately, there was no one waiting in the wings, and a hiring freeze prevented a national search from commencing.

Many faculty leaders and former administrators suggested that the president appoint Jennifer Treeholm, Associate Vice President for Academic Affairs, as interim.

She was an extremely popular person on campus and had ten years of experience in the role of associate vice president. She knew everyone and everything about the campus. Treeholm, they assured him, was the natural choice. Besides, she *deserved* the job. Her devotion to the school was unparalleled, and her energy knew no bounds. The new president, acting on advice from many campus leaders, appointed Treeholm as interim vice president for a term of up to three years. He also agreed that she could be a candidate for the permanent position when the hiring freeze was lifted.

Treeholm and her friends were ecstatic. It was high time more women moved into important positions on campus. They went out for dinner to their every-Friday-night watering hole to celebrate and reflect on Treeholm's career.

Except for a brief stint outside of academe, Treeholm's entire career had been at Mid-West U. She started out teaching introductory history, then, realizing she wanted to get on the tenure track, went back to school and earned her Ph.D. at Metropolitan U while continuing to teach at Mid-West. Upon completion of her degree, she was appointed as an assistant professor and eventually earned the rank of associate based on her popularity and excellent teaching.

Treeholm was well liked, and she devoted her entire life, it seemed, to Mid-West, helping to form the first union, getting grants, writing skits for the faculty club's annual follies, and going out of her way to befriend everyone who needed support.

Eventually, Treeholm was elected president of the faculty senate. After serving for two years, she was offered the position of associate vice president. During her ten years as associate vice president, she handled most of the academic complaints, oversaw several committees, wrote almost all of the letters and reports for the vice president, and was even known to run personal errands for the president. People just knew they could count on her.

Review Questions

1. At this point, what are your predictions about Treeholm as the interim vice president?
2. What do you predict will be her management/leadership style?
3. What are her strengths? Her weaknesses? What is the basis for your assessment?

After you have discussed Part A, please read Part B.

Part B

Treeholm's appointment as interim vice president was met with great enthusiasm. Finally the school was getting someone who was "one of their own," a person who understood the culture, knew the faculty, and could get things done.

It was not long before the campus realized that things were not moving and that Treeholm, despite her long-standing popularity, had difficulty making tough decisions. Her desire to please people and to try to take care of everyone made it difficult for her to choose opposing alternatives. (To make matters worse, she had trouble planning, organizing, and managing her time.)

The biggest problem was that she did not understand her role as the number-two person at the top of the organization. The president expected her to support him and his decisions without question. Over time the president also expected her to implement some of his decisions—to do his dirty work. This became particularly problematic when it involved firing people or saying "no" to longtime faculty cronies. Treeholm also found herself uncomfortable with the other members of the president's senior staff. Although she was not the only woman (the general counsel, a very bright, analytical woman was part of the group), she found the behavior and decision-making style to be different from what she was used to handling.

Most of the men took their lead from the president and discussed very little in the meetings. Instead, they tried to influence decisions privately. Often, a decision arrived in a meeting as a fait accompli. Treeholm felt excluded and wondered why, as vice president, she felt so powerless.

In time, she and the president spent less and less time together talking and discussing how to move the campus along. Although her relations with the men on the senior staff were cordial, she talked mostly to her female friends.

Treeholm's friends, especially her close-knit group of longtime female colleagues, all assured her that it was because she was "interim." "Just stay out of trouble," they told her. Of course this just added to her hesitancy when it came to making tough choices.

As the president's own image on campus shifted after his "honeymoon year," Treeholm decided to listen to her friends rather than follow the president's lead. After all, her reputation on campus was at stake.

Review Questions

1. What is the major problem facing Treeholm?
2. What would you do if you were in her position?
3. Would a man have the same experience as Treeholm?
4. Are any of your predictions about her management style holding up?

Part C

When the hiring freeze was lifted and Treeholm's position could be filled, the president insisted on a national search. Treeholm and her friends felt this was silly, given that she was going into her third year in the job. Nonetheless, she entered the search process.

After a year-long search, the search committee met with the president. The external candidates were not acceptable to the campus. Treeholm, they recommended, should only be appointed on a permanent basis if she agreed to change her management style.

The president mulled over his dilemma, then decided to give Treeholm the benefit of the doubt and the opportunity. He appointed her permanent provost, while making the following private agreement with her.

1. She would organize her office and staff and begin delegating more work to others.
2. She would "play" her number-two position, backing the president and echoing his position on the university's vision statement.
3. She would provide greater direction for the deans who report to her.

Treeholm agreed to take the position. She was now the university's first female vice president and presided over a council of eleven deans, three of whom were her best female friends. Once again, they sought out their every-Friday-night watering hole for an evening of dinner and celebration.

Review Questions

1. If you were Treeholm, would you have accepted the job?
2. What would you do as the new and permanent vice president?
3. Will Treeholm change her management style? If so, in what ways?
4. What are your predictions for the future?

Part D

Although people had predicted that things would be better once Treeholm was permanently in the job, things in fact became more problematic. People now expected Treeholm to be able to take decisive action. She did not feel she could.

Every time an issue came up, Treeholm would spend weeks, sometimes months, trying to get a sense of the campus. Nothing moved once it hit her office. After a while, people began referring to the vice president's office as "the black hole" where things just went in and disappeared.

Her immediate staff members were concerned and frustrated. Not only did she not delegate effectively, but her desire to make things better led her to try to do more and more herself.

The vice president's job also carried social obligations and requests. Here again, she tried to please everyone and often ran from one evening obligation to another, trying to show her support and concern for every constituency on campus. She was exhausted, overwhelmed, and, knowing the mandate under which she was appointed, anxious about the president's evaluation of her behavior.

The greatest deterioration occurred within her dean's council. Several of the male deans, weary of waiting for direction from Treeholm regarding where she was taking some of the academic proposals of the president, had started making decisions without Treeholm's approval.

"Loose cannons," was how she described a couple of them. "They don't listen. They just march out there on their own."

One of the big problems with two of the deans was that they just didn't take "no" for an answer when it came from Treeholm. Privately, each conceded that her "no" sounded like a "maybe"—she always left room to renegotiate.

Whatever the problem—and there were several by now—Treeholm's ability to lead was being questioned. Although her popularity was as high as ever, more and more people on campus were expressing their frustrations with what sometimes appeared as mixed signals from her and the president and sometimes was seen as virtually no direction. People wanted priorities. Instead, crisis management reigned.

Review Questions

1. If you were president, what would you do?
2. If you were Treeholm, what would you do?

Conclusion

Treeholm had a few retreats with her senior staff. Each time, she committed herself to delegate more, prioritize, and work on time management issues, but within ten days or so, everything was back to business as usual.

The president decided to hire a person with extensive corporate experience to fill the vacant position of vice president of finance and administration. The new man was an experienced team player who had survived mergers, been fired and bounced back, and spent years in the number-two position in several companies. Within a few months he had earned the respect of the campus as well as the president and was in fact emerging as the person who really ran the place. Meanwhile, the president concentrated on external affairs and fund-raising.

Treeholm felt relieved. Her role felt clearer. She could devote herself to academic and faculty issues and she was out from under the pressure to play "hatchet man."

As she neared the magic age for early retirement, Treeholm began to talk more and more about what she wanted to do next.

CASE 14
Zappos Does It with Humor

Zappos.com customers are known for their fierce loyalty, and it's easy to see why. CEO Tony Hsieh has built a billion-dollar business providing happiness to his customers, employees, and even fellow businesspeople seeking to learn more about the company's unique blend of humor, compassion, and high-quality customer service. How does Zappos do it?

Unusual Leader Faces Unusual Circumstances

No stranger to high-pressure conversations, Zappos CEO Tony Hsieh recently found himself discussing a very familiar topic under unusual circumstances.

Hsieh was the featured guest on *The Colbert Report*, where host Stephen Colbert grilled Hsieh to learn the secrets of Zappos's phenomenal success and rabid customer loyalty. Hsieh simply replied that it's Zappos's goal to deliver *WOW* in every shoe or clothing box. When Colbert pressed him to explain, Hsieh elaborated that, among other tactics, loyal Zappos customers are sometimes treated to a complementary upgrade to overnight shipping. "A lot of people order as late as midnight Eastern, and the shoes show up on their doorstep eight hours later," he explained.

Seemingly speechless, Colbert peered over his glasses and only said, "Wow."[1]

From Start-up to One of *Fortune's* Best Places to Work

The brainchild of Hsieh and founder Nick Swinmurn, Zappos.com launched in 1999, selling only shoes complemented with the unique premise to deliver happiness with every customer interaction. By 2001, gross sales had reached $8.6 million. That number nearly quadrupled to $32 million in 2002. A few years later, Zappos caught the eye of Amazon's Jeff Bezos. He liked what he saw and spent $928 million to buy the firm for Amazon's business stable in 2009.

Today, the company is one of *Fortune's* 15 Best Companies to Work For and continues to earn more than $1 billion annually. Zappos fulfillment centers currently stock more than three million shoes, handbags, clothing items, and accessories from over 1,130 brands.[2]

Zappos Grows, Amazon Buys In

Zappos sees a lot of potential in continuing to expand beyond shoes. While footwear still constituted 80 percent to 85 percent of Zappos's business last year, Hsieh wants Zappos's clothing lineup to be another billion-dollar business, and he's working hard to attain that goal within the next three years. "Hopefully, ten years from now, people won't even realize that we started selling shoes," he said.[3]

Under Amazon, Zappos has maintained its focus on customer service. For Hsieh, the Zappos brand is less about a particular type of product and more about providing good customer service. He remarked that he could see the Zappos name on things as large as airlines or hotels, as long as the service was up to his exacting standards. "We could be in any industry that we can differentiate ourselves through better customer service and better customer experience," he said.[4] This customer-first strategy is working out in a big way for the company: At last count, over 75 percent of its customers are repeat customers.[5]

Customers Get Special Handling

The blog search engine *Land* calls Zappos "the poster child for how to connect with customers online." It uses Facebook and Twitter to connect with their customers, distributors, employees, and other businesses.

The company's relentless pursuit of the ultimate customer experience is the stuff of legend. Zappos offers extremely fast shipping at no cost and will cover the return shipping if you are dissatisfied for any reason at any time.

Hsieh, who was unsurprisingly named "The Smartest Dude in Town" by business magazine *Vegas Inc.*, feels employees have to be free to be themselves. That means no-call times or scripts for customer service representatives, regular costume parties, and parades and decorations in each department. Customer service reps are given a lot of leeway to make sure every customer is an enthusiastic customer.

A Culture to Thrive In

Zappos's past success comes down to the company's culture and the unusual amount of openness Hsieh encourages employees, vendors, and other businesses. "If we get the culture right," he says, "most of the other stuff, like the brand and the customer service will just happen. With most companies, as they grow, the culture goes downhill. We want the culture to grow stronger and stronger as we grow."

Like other CEOs in it for the long haul, Hsieh is forecasting Zappos's success and the brand experience he intends to deliver years into the future. "Many companies think only one quarter ahead, or one year ahead," he said. "We like to think about what we want our brand and culture to be like ten or even twenty years down the line. In general, with a ten- to twenty-year timeline versus a three- to five-year timeline, relationships are much more important. What you do after taking someone's money, such as customer service, matters much more than what you do to get their money, such as marketing."[6]

A Culture to Share

In fact, Hsieh believes so strongly in the organizational culture that encompasses Zappos's desire to satisfy that he's on a mission to share it with anyone who will listen via tours of their headquarters, leadership retreats, and even two new books.

It comes together in a program called Zappos Insights. The core experience is a tour of Zappos's Las Vegas headquarters. "Company Evangelists" lead groups of twenty around the cubicles, which often overflow with kitschy action figures and brightly colored balloons, giving participants a glimpse of a workplace that prizes individuality and fun as much as satisfied customers. Staffers blow horns and ring cowbells to greet participants in the sixteen weekly tours, and each department tries to offer a more outlandish welcome than the last. "The original idea was to add a little fun," Hsieh says, but it grew into a friendly competition "as the next aisle said, 'We can do it better.'"[7]

The tours are free, but many visitors actually come for paid one- and two-day seminars that immerse participants in the Zappos culture. Want to learn how to recruit employees who are committed to your company culture? You'll get face time with Zappos HR staff. Yearn to learn what keeps customers coming back? Ask their Customer Loyalty Team. Hungry for a home-cooked meal? The capstone of the two-day boot camp is dinner at Tony Hsieh's house, with ample time to talk customer service with the CEO himself. Seminars range from $497 to $3,997.

"There are management consulting firms that charge really high rates," says Hsieh. "We wanted to come up with something that's accessible to almost any business."[8]

Those who want to learn Zappos's secrets without venturing to Las Vegas have a few options. For $39 a month, you can subscribe to a members-only community that grants access to video interviews and chats with Zappos management. Ask nicely, and the company will send you a free copy of its *Zappos Family Culture Book*, an annual compilation of every employee's ideas about Zappos's mission and core values. Hsieh has his own tome, too—*Delivering Happiness*.

They may be giving away hard-earned knowledge, but Zappos definitely isn't losing money on the Insights project—profits from the seminars pay for the entire program, and Hsieh hopes it will someday represent 10 percent of Zappos's operating profit.

"There's a huge open market," says Robert Richman, co-leader of Zappos Insights. "We were afraid that we've been talking about this for free for so long. 'Are people going to be upset we are charging for it?' Instead, the reaction is opposite."[9] Now that Zappos is part of Amazon, will it still prosper and grow? Will the company continue to put customers first?

Review Questions

1. What traits of effective leadership does Tony Hsieh demonstrate at Zappos? What aspects of his leadership can you criticize, if any? Is his approach transferable to other leaders and other organizations, or is it person and situation specific?
2. Can you find examples of where any of the contingency theories of leadership can be confirmed or disconfirmed in the Zappos setting? Explain your answer.
3. Tony Hsieh is a big thinker, and Zappos is clearly his baby. But he's also into philanthropy and community development activities that are taking up more of his time. Perhaps he'll come up with other new business ideas as well. As a leadership coach, what steps would you recommend that he take now to ensure that his leadership approach and vision lives on at Zappos long after his departure? What can a strong and secure leader like him do to ensure a positive leadership legacy in any situation?

CASE 15
Never on a Sunday

Developed by Anne C. Cowden, California State University, Sacramento

McCoy's Building Supply Centers of San Marcos, Texas, have been in continuous successful operation for over seventy years in an increasingly competitive retail business. McCoy's is one of the nation's largest family-owned and family-managed building-supply companies, serving 10 million customers a year in a regional area currently covering New Mexico, Texas, Oklahoma, Arkansas, Mississippi, and Louisiana. McCoy's strategy has been to occupy a niche in the market of small and medium-size cities.

McCoy's grounding principle is acquiring and selling the finest-quality products that can be found and providing quality service to customers. As an operations-oriented company. McCoy's has always managed without many layers of management. Managers are asked to concentrate on service-related issues in their stores: get the merchandise on the floor, price it, sell it, and help the customer carry it out. The majority of the administrative workload is handled through headquarters so that store employees can concentrate on customer service. The top management team (Emmett McCoy and his two sons, Brian and Mike, who serve as co-presidents) has established eleven teams of managers drawn from the different regions that McCoy's stores cover. The teams meet regularly to discuss new products, better ways for product delivery, and a host of items integral to maintaining customer satisfaction. Team leadership is rotated among the managers.

McCoy's has a workforce of 70 percent full-time and 30 percent part-time employees. The firm has a long-standing reputation of fair dealing that is a source of pride for all employees. McCoy's philosophy values loyal, adaptable, skilled employees as the most essential element of its overall success.

In order to implement this philosophy, the company offers extensive on-the-job training. The path to management involves starting at the store level and learning all facets of operations before advancing into a management program. All management trainees are required to relocate to a number of stores. Most promotions come from within. Managers are rarely recruited from the outside. This may begin to change as the business implements more technology requiring greater reliance on college-educated personnel.

A strong religious belief and a strong commitment to community permeate all that McCoy's does. Many McCoy family members are Evangelical Christians who believe in their faith through letting their "feet do it"—that is, showing their commitment to God through action, not just talk. Although their beliefs and values permeate the company's culture in countless ways, one very concrete way is reflected in the title of this case: "Never on a Sunday." Even though it's a busy business day for retailers, all 103 McCoy's stores are closed on Sunday.

Review Questions

1. How have the personal beliefs of the McCoy family influenced the organizational culture of their firm?
2. What difference do being "family founded" and "family owned" make when it comes to establishing and maintaining an organizational culture?
3. What lessons for developing organizational cultures can this case provide for other firms that aren't family run?

CASE 16
First Community Financial

Developed by Marcus Osborn, Kutak Rock LLP

First Community Financial is a small business lender that specializes in asset-based lending and factoring for a primarily small-business clientele. First Community's business is generated by high-growth companies in diverse industries, whose capital needs will not be met by traditional banking institutions. First Community Financial will lend in amounts up to $1 million, so its focus is on small business. Since many of the loans that it administers are viewed by many banks as high-risk loans, it is important that the sales staff and loan processors have a solid working relationship. Since the loans and factoring deals that First Community finances are risky, the interest that it charges is at prime plus 6 percent and sometimes higher.

First Community is a credible player in the market because of its history and the human resource policies of the company. The company invests in its employees and works to ensure that turnover is low. The goal of this strategy is to develop a consistent, professional team that has more expertise than its competitors.

Whereas Jim Adamany, president and CEO, has a strong history in the industry and is a recognized expert in asset-based lending and factoring, First Community has one of the youngest staff and management teams in the finance industry. In the banking industry, promotions are slow in coming, because many banks employ conservative personnel programs. First Community, however, has recruited young, ambitious people who are specifically looking to grow with the company. As the company grows, so will the responsibility and rewards for these young executives. In his early thirties, for example, Matt Vincent is a vice president; at only twenty-eight, Brian Zcray is director of marketing.

Since First Community has a diverse product line, it must compete in distinct markets. Its factoring products compete with small specialized factoring companies. Factoring is a way for businesses to improve their cash flow by selling their invoices at a discount. Factoring clients are traditionally the smallest clients finance companies must serve. Education about the nature of the product is crucial if the company is to be successful, since this is often a new approach to financing for many companies. First Community's sales staff is well trained in understanding its product lines and acts as the client's representative as they work through the approval process.

To ensure that the loans or factoring deals fit within the risk profile of the company, First Community must ask many complex financial questions. Many small businesses are intimidated by credit officers, so First Community handles all of these inquiries through the business development officers. The business development officers, in turn, must understand the needs of their credit officers, who are attempting to minimize risk to the company while maintaining a friendly rapport with the client. By centralizing the client contract through educated sales representatives, First Community is able to ask the hard financial questions and still keep the clients interested in the process. A potential customer can be easily discouraged by a credit administrator's strong questioning about financial background. Utilizing the business development officers as an intermediary reduces the fear of many applicants about the credit approval process. Thus, a sales focus is maintained throughout the recruitment and loan application process.

Internally at First Community Financial, one finds continual pressure between the business development staff and the credit committee. The business development staff is focused on bringing in new clients. Their compensation is in large part dependent on how many deals they can execute for the company. Like sales staff in any industry, they are aggressive and always look for new markets for business. The sales staff sells products from both the finance department and the factoring department, so they must interact with credit officers from each division. In each of these groups are credit administrators specifically responsible for ensuring that potential deals meet the lending criteria of the organization. While the business development officer's orientation is to bring in more and more deals, the credit administrator's primary goal is to limit bad loans.

The pressure develops when business development officers bring in potential loans that are rejected by the credit administrators. Since the business development officers have some experience understanding the credit risks of their clients, they often understand the policy reasoning for denying or approving a loan. The business development officers have additional concerns that their loans that have potential to be financed are approved because many of the referral sources of the sales staff will only refer deals to companies that are lending. If First Community fails to help many of a bank's referral clients, that source of business may dry up, as bankers refer deals to other lending institutions.

These structural differences are handled by focused attempts at improving communication. As noted, the First Community staff experiences an extremely low turnover rate. This allows for the development of a cohesive team. With a cohesive staff, the opportunity to maintain frank and open communication helps bridge the different orientations of the sales staff and the administration divisions. A simple philosophy that the opinions of all staff are to be respected is continually implemented.

Since approving a loan is often a policy decision, the sales staff and the loan administrators can have an open forum to discuss whether a loan will be approved. CEO Jim Adamany approves all loans, but since he values the opinions of all of his staff, he provides them all an opportunity to communicate. Issues such as the loan history for an applicant's industry, current bank loan policies, and other factors can be openly discussed from multiple perspectives.

Review Questions

1. What coordinative mechanisms does First Community use to manage the potential conflict between its sales and finance/auditing functions?
2. What qualities should First Community emphasize in hiring new staff to ensure that its functional organizational structure will not yield too many problems?
3. What are the key types of information transfer that First Community needs to emphasize, and how is this transmitted throughout the firm?
4. Why might a small finance company have such a simple structure while a larger firm might find this structure inappropriate?

NOTES

Case 1 References

[1] "Trader Joe's." *Hoover's Company Records*. Posted February 14, 2013. 2/14/12.

[2] "Where in the Dickens Can You Find a Trader Joe's?" *Trader Joe's*. www.traderjoes.com/pdf/locations/all-llocations.pdf (accessed July 17, 2013).

[3] "Product & Guides," *Trader Joe's*. www.traderjoes.com/products.asp (accessed July 17, 2013).

[4] Deborah Orr, "The Cheap Gourmet," *Forbes* (April 10, 2006), www.forbes.com/forbes/2006/0410/076.html (accessed July 17, 2013).

[5] *BusinessWeek Online*. February 21, 2008.

[6] "11: Trader Joe's: For vaulting past Whole Foods to become America's favorite organic grocer." *Fast Company*. www.fastcompany.com/most-innovative-companies/2011/profile/trader-joes.php (accessed July 17, 2013).

[7] Marianne Wilson, "When Less Is More," *Chain Store Age* (November 2006).

[8] Mark Hamstra and Elliot Zwiebach, "Food Retailing 2020: SN examines how the food retailing landscape might evolve during the next 10 years" (March 1, 2010), supermarketnews.com/retail_financial/food-retailing-0301/index3.html (accessed July 17, 2013).

[9] "11: Trader Joe's," op. cit.

[10] Orr, "The Cheap Gourmet" (2006), op. cit.

[11] "Aldi." *Wikipedia*. http://en.wikipedia.org/wiki/Aldi#Geographic_distribution (accessed July 17, 2013).

[12] "Trader Joe's Co. 2012." *Supermarket News*. http://supermarketnews.com/trader-joe-s-co-2012 (accessed February 2, 2013). *Supermarket News's* Top 75 Retailers January 12, 2009.

[13] Shan Li, "Trader Joe's Tries to Keep Quirky Vibe as It Expands Quickly," *Los Angeles Times* (October 26, 2011), http://articles.latimes.com/2011/oct/26/business/la-fi-trader-joes-20111027 (accessed July 17, 2013).

[14] www.traderjoes.com/value.html

[15] www.traderjoes.com/how_we_do_biz.html

[16] "Win at the Grocery Game," *Consumer Reports* (October 2006), p. 10.

[17] Orr, "The Cheap Gourmet" (2006), op. cit.

[18] www.traderjoes.com/tjs_faqs.asp#DiscontinueProducts

[19] Jerry Hirsch, "Trader Joe's Halting Some Chinese Imports," *Los Angeles Times* (February 12, 2008), www.latimes.com/business/la-fi-tj12feb12,1,1079460.story (accessed July 17, 2013).

[20] Jena McGregor, "2004 Customer 1st," *Fast Company* (October 2004).

[21] Irwin Speizer, "The Grocery Chain That Shouldn't Be," *Fast Company* (February 2004).

[22] Heidi Brown, "Buy German," *Forbes* (January 12, 2004).

[23] "Trader Joe's Careers: Benefits," *Trader Joe's* (n.d.), www.traderjoes.com/careers/benefits.asp

[24] Irwin Speizer, "Shopper's Special," *Workforce Management* (September 2004).

[25] Ibid.

[26] Tom Broderick. "Why We Picketed Trader Joe's," *OakPark.com,* (November 29, 2011), www.oakpark.com/News/Articles/11-29-2011/Why_we_picketed_Trader_Joe%27s (accessed July 13, 2013).

[27] "Welcome Aboard . . . Trader Joe's and CIW Sign Fair Food Agreement!" *CIW Online* (February 9, 2012), http://ciw-online.org/TJ_agreement.html (accessed July 17, 2013).

[28] "Retailer Spotlight," *Gourmet Retailer* (June 2006).

Case 2 References

[1] "How Xerox Diversity Breeds Business Success," http://a1851.g.akamaitech.net/f/1851/2996/24h/cacheB.xerox.com/downloads/usa/en/d/Diversity_Brochure_2006.pdf2 (accessed July 17, 2013).

[2] "Xerox Reports Fourth-Quarter 2010 Earnings," *Wall Street Journal Online* (January 26, 2011), http://online.wsj.com/article/PR-CO-20110126-903779.html (accessed March 1, 2011).

[3] www.xerox.com/go/xrx/template/019d.jsp?view=Factbook&id=Overview&Xcntry=USA&Xlang=en_US&Xseg=xnet (accessed July 7, 2009).

[4] www.xerox.com/downloads/usa/en/n/nr_Xerox_Diversity_Timeline_2008.pdf (accessed July 7, 2009).

[5] Ibid.

[6] Ibid.

[7] www.xeroxcareers.com/working-xerox/diversity.aspx (accessed July 7, 2009).

[8] "Diversity, Inclusion and Opportunity," *Xerox 2010 Report on Global Citizenship*. www.xerox.com/corporate-citizenship-2010/employee-engagement/diversity.html, accessed March 1, 2011.

[9] "How Xerox Diversity Breeds Business Success," op. cit.

[10] "Corporate Equality Index: A Report Card on Lesbian, Gay, Bisexual and Transgender Equality in Corporate America," Human Rights Campaign Foundation (2008), www.hrc.org/files/assets/resources/CorporateEqualityIndex_2009.pdf (accessed July 8, 2009).

Case 3 References

[1] This case is adapted from Jim Donovan (A) and (B) written by Allan R. Cohen and Michael Merenda, University of New Hampshire, for purpose of classroom discussion. Copyright © 1979, Whittemore School of Business and Economics, University of New Hampshire. Reproduced with permission.

Case 6B References

[1] Abridged and adapted from George Strauss and Alex Bavelas, "Group Dynamics and Intergroup Relations" (under the title "The Hovey and Beard Case"), in *Money and Motivation*, William F. Whyte (ed.), New York: Harper & Row, 1955.

Case 8 References

[1] Robert M. Williamson, "NASCAR Racing: A Model for Equipment Reliability & Teamwork," *Strategic Work Systems* (1999), www.swspitcrew.com/articles/NASCAR%200999.pdf (accessed July 17, 2013).

[2] "Modern Era Race Winners," *NASCAR.com* (n.d.), www.nascar.com/kyn/nbtn/cup/data/race_winners.html (accessed February 13, 2013); and Mike Hembree, "CUP: Gordon's Ride Has Been One of Sport's Grandest," *Speed TV* (September 6, 2011), http://nascar.speedtv.com/article/cup-jeff-gordons-ride-has-been-one-of-nascars-grandest (accessed July 17, 2013).

[3] Dave Rodman, "Teamwork More Important with COT Going Full Time," *NASCAR.com* (January 14, 2008), www.nascar.com/2008/news/headlines/cup/01/14/cot.teamwork.kbusch.rnewman.jjohnson/index.html (accessed February 13, 2013).

[4] "Formula Racing," *Bethelame Indy*, www.bethelame-indy.org/formula-racing.php (accessed July 17, 2013).

[5] Adam Cooper, "F1: Lowe Credits McLaren Teamwork for Success," *Speed TV* (April 27, 2011), http://formula-one.speedtv.com/article/f1-lowe-credits-mclaren-teamwork-for-success (accessed July 17, 2013).

[6] "Teamwork Is the Key to Success—Theissen," *F1 Technical*, www.f1technical.net/news/8632 (accessed July 17, 2013).

[7] "Rallying," *Bethelame Indy*, www.bethelame-indy.org/rallying.php (accessed July 17, 2013).

[8] Ibid.

[9] Biser3a, "Turkish Ladies Take on the Men in Dubai Rally," *Biser3a*, http://biser3a.com/rally/turkish-ladies-take-on-the-men-in-dubai-rally, (accessed July 17, 2013).

[10] Nick Hardy, "The Fastest Woman on Four Wheels?" *Gulf News* (November 18, 2011), http://gulfnews.com/life-style/motoring/the-fastest-woman-on-four-wheels-1.930540 (accessed July 17, 2013).

[11] Williamson (1999), op. cit.

Case 9 References

[1] Information from Sara Schaefer Munoz, "Is Hiding Your Wedding Band Necessary at a Job Interview?" *Wall Street Journal* (March 15, 2007), p. D3.

[2] Information and quotes from "Get Healthy—Or Else," *Business Week* (February 26, 2007), cover story; and, "Wellness—or Orwellness?" *Business Week* (March 19, 2007), cover story.

Case 14 References

[1] Kimberly Schaefer, "Zappos.com CEO Tony Hsieh Named the 'Smartest' in Town," *Vegas Inc.* (September 5, 2011), www.vegasinc.com/news/2011/sep/05/tony-hsieh/#/0 (accessed July 17, 2013).

[2] "Looking Ahead—Let There Be Anything and Everything," *Zappos* (n.d.), http://about.zappos.com/zappos-story/looking-ahead-let-there-be-anything-and-everything (accessed July 17, 2013).

[3] Jeremy Twitchell, "From Upstart to $1 Billion Behemoth, Zappos Marks 10 Years" *Las Vegas Sun* (June 16, 2009), www.lasvegassun.com/news/2009/jun/16/upstart-1-billion-behemoth-zappos-marks-10-year-an (accessed July 17, 2013).

[4] Andria Cheng, "Zappos, Under Amazon, Keeps its Independent Streak," *MarketWatch* (June 11, 2010), www.marketwatch.com/story/zappos-under-amazon-keeps-its-independent-streak-2010-06-11 (accessed July 18, 2013).

[5] Jeff Cerny, "10 Questions on Customer Service and 'Delivering Happiness': An Interview with Zappos CEO Tony Hsieh," *TechRepublic* (October 1, 2009), www.techrepublic.com/blog/10things/10-questions-on-customer-service-and-delivering-happiness-an-interview-with-zappos-ceo-tony-hsieh/1067 (accessed July 18, 2013).

[6] Ibid.

[7] Christopher Palmeri, "Zappos Retails Its Culture," *BloombergBusinessWeek* (December 30, 2009), www.businessweek.com/magazine/content/10_02/b4162057120453.htm (accessed July 18, 2013).

[8] Brian Morrissey, "Zappos Launches Insights Service," *AdWeek* (December 15, 2008), www.adweek.com/aw/content_display/news/digital/e3i1ccc5c91366de3d-9c9a65c32df3b5cdc (accessed July 18, 2013).

[9] Andria Cheng, "Zappos's Grand Mission Doesn't Involve Selling Shoes," *MarketWatch* (September 13, 2010), www.marketwatch.com/story/zapposs-grand-mission-goes-beyond-selling-shoes-2010-09-13 (accessed July 17, 2013).

Glossary

360⁰ evaluation gathers evaluations from a jobholder's bosses, peers, and subordinates, as well as internal and external customers and self-ratings.
Absorptive capacity is the ability to learn.
Accommodation, or **smoothing**, involves playing down differences and finding areas of agreement.
Achievement-oriented leadership emphasizes setting goals, stressing excellence, and showing confidence in people's ability to achieve high standards of performance.
Active listening encourages people to say what they really mean.
Activity measures of performance assess inputs in terms of work efforts.
Adaptive capacity refers to the ability to change.
Adhocracy emphasizes shared, decentralized decision making; extreme horizontal specialization; few levels of management; the virtual absence of formal controls; and few rules, policies, and procedures.
Adjourning stage is where teams disband when their work is finished.
Affect is the range of feelings in the forms of emotions and moods that people experience.
Agency theory suggests that public corporations can function effectively even though their managers are self-interested and do not always automatically bear the full consequences of their managerial actions.
Americans with Disabilities Act is a federal civil rights statute that protects the rights of people with disabilities.
Amoral managers fail to consider the ethics of a decision or behavior.
Anchoring and adjustment heuristic bases a decision on incremental adjustments to an initial value determined by historical precedent or some reference point.
Attitude is a predisposition to respond positively or negatively to someone or something.
Attribution is the process of creating explanations for events.
Authoritarianism is a tendency to adhere rigidly to conventional values and to obey recognized authority.
Authoritative command uses formal authority to end conflict.
Availability heuristic bases a decision on recent events relating to the situation at hand.
Avoidance involves pretending a conflict does not really exist.
Awareness of others is being aware of the behaviors, preferences, styles, biases, and personalities of others.

Bargaining zone is the range between one party's minimum reservation point and the other party's maximum.
Behavioral complexity is the possession of a repertoire of roles and the ability to selectively apply them.
Behavioral decision model views decision makers as acting only in terms of what they perceive about a given situation.
Behavioral perspective assumes that leadership is central to performance and other outcomes.
Behaviorally anchored rating scale links performance ratings to specific and observable job-relevant behaviors.
Bonuses are extra pay awards for special performance accomplishments.
Brainstorming involves generating ideas through "free-wheeling" and without criticism.
Bureaucracy is an ideal form of organizations, the characteristics of which were defined by the German sociologist Max Weber.

Centralization is the degree to which the authority to make decisions is restricted to higher levels of management.
Centralized communication networks link group members through a central control point.
Certain environments provide full information on the expected results for decision-making alternatives.
Channel richness indicates the capacity of a channel to convey information.
Charisma provides vision and a sense of mission, and it instills pride along with follower respect and trust.
Charismatic leaders are those leaders who are capable of having a profound and extraordinary effect on followers.
Classical decision model views decision makers as acting in a world of complete certainty.
Coalition power is the ability to control another's behavior indirectly because the individual owes an obligation to you or another as part of a larger collective interest.
Coercive power is the extent to which a manager can deny desired rewards or administer punishment to control other people.
Cognitive complexity is the degree to which individuals perceive nuances and subtle differences.
Cognitive dissonance is experienced inconsistency between one's attitudes and/or between attitudes and behavior.

Cohesiveness is the degree to which members are attracted to a group and motivated to remain a part of it.

Collaboration and problem solving involves recognition that something is wrong and needs attention through problem solving.

Collective intelligence is the ability of a team to perform well across a range of tasks.

Communication is the process of sending and receiving symbols with attached meanings.

Communication channels are the pathways through which messages are communicated.

Commutative justice is the degree to which exchanges and transactions are considered fair.

Competition seeks victory by force, superior skill, or domination.

Complex adaptive systems interact and adapt with their environments to survive.

Compressed workweek allows a full-time job to be completed in fewer than the standard five days.

Compromise occurs when each party gives up something of value to the other.

Conceptual skill is the ability to analyze and solve complex problems.

Confirmation error is the tendency to seek confirmation for what is already thought to be true and not search for disconfirming information.

Conflict occurs when parties disagree over substantive issues or when emotional antagonisms create friction between them.

Conflict resolution occurs when the reasons for a conflict are eliminated.

Conglomerates are firms that own several different unrelated businesses.

Consensus is a group decision that has the expressed support of most members.

Consideration is sensitive to people's feelings.

Consultative decisions are made by one individual after seeking input from or consulting with members of a group.

Content theories profile different needs that may motivate individual behavior.

Context is the collection of opportunities and constraints that affect the occurrence and meaning of behavior and the relationships among variables.

Contingency thinking seeks ways to meet the needs of different management situations.

Continuous reinforcement administers a reward each time a desired behavior occurs.

Contrast effect occurs when the meaning of something that takes place is based on a contrast with another recent event or situation.

Control is the set of mechanisms used to keep actions and outputs within predetermined limits.

Controlling monitors performance and takes any needed corrective action.

Coordination is the set of mechanisms used in an organization to link the actions of its subunits into a consistent pattern.

Coping is a response or reaction to distress that has occurred or is threatened.

Countercultures are groups in which the patterns of values and philosophies outwardly reject those of the organization or social system.

Counterproductive work behaviors are behaviors that intentionally disrupt relationships or performance at work.

Creativity generates unique and novel responses to problems.

Crisis decision occurs when an unexpected problem can lead to disaster if not resolved quickly and appropriately.

Criteria questions assess a decision in terms of utility, rights, justice, and caring.

Critical incident diaries record actual examples of positive and negative work behaviors and results.

Cross-functional team has members from different functions or work units.

Cultural symbol is any object, act, or event that serves to transmit cultural meaning.

Culturally endorsed leadership dimension is one that members of a culture expect from effective leaders.

Culture is the learned and shared way of thinking and acting among a group of people or society.

Decentralization is the degree to which the authority to make decisions is given to lower levels in an organization's hierarchy.

Decentralized communication networks allow members to communicate directly with one another.

Decision making is the process of choosing among alternative courses of action.

Deep-level diversity involves individual differences in things like personality and values.

Defensiveness occurs when individuals feel they are being attacked and need to protect themselves.

Delphi technique involves generating decision-making alternatives through a series of survey questionnaires.

Dependent variables are outcomes of practical value and interest that are influenced by independent variables.

Directive leadership spells out the what and how of subordinates' tasks.

Disconfirmation occurs when an individual feels his or her self-worth is being questioned.

Discrimination actively denies minority members the full benefits of organizational membership.

Display rules govern the degree to which it is appropriate to display emotions.

Disruptive behaviors in teams harm the group process and limit team effectiveness.

Distress is a negative impact on both attitudes and performance.

Distributed leadership shares responsibility among members for meeting team task and maintenance needs.

Distributive justice is the degree to which all people are treated the same under a policy.

Distributive negotiation focuses on positions staked out or declared by the parties involved, each of whom is trying to claim certain portions of the available pie.

Diversity–consensus dilemma is the tendency for diversity in groups to create process difficulties even as it offers improved potential for problem solving.

Divisional departmentation groups individuals and resources by products, territories, services, clients, or legal entities.

Dogmatism leads a person to see the world as a threatening place and to regard authority as absolute.

Downward communication follows the chain of command from top to bottom.

Dysfunctional conflict works to the group's or organization's disadvantage.

Ecological fallacy acting with the mistaken assumption that a generalized cultural value applies always and equally to all members of the culture.

Effective leaders are individuals who use influence to create change that benefits the mission and vision of the organization.

Effective manager helps others achieve high levels of both performance and satisfaction.

Effective negotiation occurs when substance issues are resolved and working relationships are maintained or improved.

Effective team is one that achieves high levels of task performance, member satisfaction, and team viability.

Emotion and mood contagion is the spillover of one's emotions and mood onto others.

Emotion-focused coping are mechanisms that regulate emotions or distress.

Emotional adjustment traits are traits related to how much an individual experiences emotional distress or displays unacceptable acts.

Emotional conflict involves interpersonal difficulties that arise over feelings of anger, mistrust, dislike, fear, resentment, and the like.

Emotional dissonance is inconsistency between emotions we feel and those we try to project.

Emotional intelligence is an ability to understand emotions and manage relationships effectively.

Emotional labor is a situation in which a person displays organizationally desired emotions in a job.

Emotions are strong positive or negative feelings directed toward someone or something.

Employee engagement is a strong sense of connection with the organization and passion for one's job.

Employee involvement team meets regularly to address workplace issues.

Employee stock ownership plans give stock to employees or allow them to purchase stock at special prices.

Empowerment is the process by which managers help others to acquire and use the power needed to make decisions affecting themselves and their work.

Encoding is the process of translating an idea or thought into a message consisting of verbal, written, or nonverbal symbols (such as gestures), or some combination of them.

Environmental complexity is the magnitude of the problems and opportunities in the organization's environment as evidenced by the degree of richness, interdependence, and uncertainty.

Equity theory posits that people will act to eliminate any felt inequity in the rewards received for their work in comparison with others.

ERG theory identifies existence, relatedness, and growth needs.

Ethics is the philosophical study of morality.

Ethics mindfulness is an enriched awareness that causes one to consistently behave with ethical consciousness.

Ethnocentrism is the tendency to believe one's culture and its values are superior to those of others.

Eustress is a stress that has a positive impact on both attitudes and performance.

Evidence-based management uses hard facts and empirical evidence to make decisions.

Existence needs are desires for physiological and material well-being.

Expectancy is the probability that work effort will be followed by performance accomplishment.

Expectancy theory argues that work motivation is determined by individual beliefs regarding effort–performance relationships and work outcomes.

Expert power is the ability to control another's behavior because of the possession of knowledge, experience, or judgment that the other person does not have but needs.

Exploitation focuses on refinement and reuse of existing products and processes.

Exploration calls for the organization and its managers to stress freedom and radical thinking and therefore opens the firm to big changes—or what some call radical innovations.

External adaptation deals with reaching goals, the tasks to be accomplished, the methods used to achieve the goals, and the methods of coping with success and failure.

Extinction discourages a behavior by making the removal of a desirable consequence contingent on its occurrence.

Extrinsic rewards are valued outcomes given by some other person.

Feedback communicates how one feels about something another person has done or said.

Filter limits information by conveying only certain parts that are relevant.

FIRO-B theory examines differences in how people relate to one another based on their needs to express and receive feelings of inclusion, control, and affection.

Flaming is expressing rudeness when using e-mail or other forms of electronic communication.

Flexible working hours gives individuals some amount of choice in scheduling their daily work hours.

Followership is defined as the behaviors of individuals acting in relation to leaders.

Force–coercion strategy uses authority, rewards, and punishments to create change.

Forced distribution in performance appraisal forces a set percentage of persons into predetermined rating categories.

Formal channels follow the official chain of command.

Formal teams are official and designated to serve a specific purpose.

Formalization is written documentation of work rules, policies, and procedures.

Forming stage focuses around the initial entry of members to a team.

Framing means tailoring communication in ways to encourage certain interpretations and discourage others.

Framing error is solving a problem in the context perceived.

Functional conflict results in positive benefits to the group.

Functional departmentation is grouping individuals by skill, knowledge, and action.

Functional silos problem occurs when members of one functional team fail to interact with others from other functional teams.

Fundamental attribution error overestimates internal factors and underestimates external factors as influences on someone's behavior.

Gain sharing rewards employees in some proportion to productivity gains.

General environment is the set of cultural, economic, legal–political, and educational conditions found in the areas in which the organization operates.

Glass ceiling effect is an invisible barrier limiting career advancement of women and minorities.

Goal setting is the process of setting performance targets.

Grafting is the process of acquiring individuals, units, or firms to bring in useful knowledge.

Grapevine transfers information through networks of friendships and acquaintances.

Graphic rating scales in performance appraisal assigns scores to specific performance dimensions.

Group or team dynamics are the forces operating in teams that affect the ways members work together.

Groupthink is the tendency of cohesive group members to lose their critical evaluative capabilities.

Growth needs are desires for continued personal growth and development.

Halo effect uses one attribute to develop an overall impression of a person or situation.

Heterogeneous team members differ in many characteristics.

Heuristics are simplifying strategies or "rules of thumb" used to make decisions.

Hierarchy of needs theory offers a pyramid of physiological, safety, social, esteem, and self-actualization needs.

High-context cultures use words to convey only part of a message, while the rest of the message must be inferred from body language and additional contextual cues.

Higher-order needs in Maslow's hierarchy are esteem and self-actualization.

Hindsight trap is a tendency to overestimate the degree to which an event that has already taken place could have been predicted.

Homogeneous team members share many similar characteristics.

Hope is the tendency to look for alternative pathways to reach a desired goal.

Horizontal specialization is a division of labor through the formation of work units or groups within an organization.

Human skill is the ability to work well with other people.

Hygiene factors in the job context are sources of job dissatisfaction.

Immoral manager chooses to behave unethically; an **amoral manager** fails to consider the ethics of a decision or behavior.

Implicit followership theories are preconceived notions about prototypical and antiprototypical followership behaviors and characteristics.

Implicit leadership theories are preconceived notions about the attributes associated with leaders that reflect the structure and content of "cognitive categories" used to distinguish leaders from nonleaders.

Impression management is the systematic attempt to influence how others perceive us.

In-group is a state that occurs when individuals feel part of a group and experience favorable status and a sense of belonging.

Inclusion is the degree to which an organization's culture respects and values diversity.

Incremental change builds on the existing ways of operating to enhance or extend them in new directions.

Independent variables are presumed causes that influence dependent variables.

Individual decisions (or authority decisions) are made by one person on behalf of the team.

Individual differences are the ways in which people are similar and how they vary in their thinking, feeling, and behavior.

Individualism–collectivism is the tendency of members of a culture to emphasize individual self-interests or group relationships.

Individualized consideration provides personal attention, treats each employee individually, and coaches and advises.

Influence is a behavioral response to the exercise of power.

Informal channels do not follow the chain of command.

Informal groups are unofficial and emerge to serve special interests.

Information power is the access to and/or the control of information.

Information technology is the combination of machines, artifacts, procedures, and systems used to gather, store, analyze, and disseminate information for translating it into knowledge.

Initiating structure is concerned with spelling out the task requirements and clarifying aspects of the work agenda.

Innovation is the process of creating new ideas and putting them into practice.

Inspiration communicates high expectations, uses symbols to focus efforts, and expresses important purposes in simple ways.

Instrumental values reflect a person's beliefs about the means to achieve desired ends.

Instrumentality is the probability that performance will lead to various work outcomes.

Integrative negotiation focuses on the merits of the issues; the parties involved try to enlarge the available pie rather than stake claims to certain portions of it.

Intellectual stimulation promotes intelligence, rationality, and careful problem solving by, for example, encouraging looking at a very difficult problem in a new way.

Inter-team dynamics occur as groups cooperate and compete with one another.

Interactional justice is the degree to which people are treated with dignity and respect in decisions affecting them.

Interactional transparency is the open and honest sharing of information.

Interfirm alliances are announced cooperative agreements or joint ventures between two independent firms.

Intergroup conflict occurs among groups in an organization.

Intermittent reinforcement rewards behavior only periodically.

Internal integration deals with the creation of a collective identity and with ways of working and living together.

Interorganizational conflict occurs between organizations.

Interpersonal barriers occur when individuals are not able to listen objectively to the sender due to considerations such as lack of trust, personality clashes, a bad reputation, or stereotypes/prejudices.

Interpersonal conflict occurs between two or more individuals in opposition to each other.

Intrapersonal conflict occurs within the individual because of actual or perceived pressures from incompatible goals or expectations.

Intrinsic rewards are valued outcomes received directly through task performance.

Intuitive thinking approaches problems in a flexible and spontaneous fashion.

Job burnout is a loss of interest in or satisfaction with a job due to stressful working conditions.

Job design is the process of specifying job tasks and work arrangements.

Job enlargement increases task variety by combining into one job two or more tasks that were previously assigned to separate workers.

Job enrichment builds high-content jobs that involve planning and evaluating duties normally done by supervisors.

Job involvement is the extent to which an individual is dedicated to a job.

Job rotation increases task variety by periodically shifting workers among jobs involving different tasks.

Job satisfaction is the degree to which an individual feels positive or negative about a job.

Job sharing is where one full-time job is split between two or more persons who divide the work according to agreed-upon hours.

Job simplification standardizes work to create clearly defined and highly specialized tasks.

Lack-of-participation error occurs when important people are excluded from the decision-making process.

Lateral communication is the flow of messages at the same levels across organizations.

Law of contingent reinforcement states a reward should only be given when the desired behavior occurs.

Law of effect states that behavior followed by pleasant consequences is likely to be repeated; behavior followed by unpleasant consequences is not.

Law of immediate reinforcement states a reward should be given as soon as possible after the desired behavior occurs.

Law of reciprocity says that if someone does something for someone else it will invoke a sense of obligation to return the favor.

Leader match training is when leaders are trained to diagnose the situation to match their high and low LPC scores with situational control.

Leader–member exchange (LMX) theory emphasizes the quality of the working relationship between leaders and followers.

Leadership is the process of influencing others and the process of facilitating individual and collective efforts to accomplish shared objectives.

Leadership grid is an approach that uses a grid that places concern for production on the horizontal axis and concern for people on the vertical axis.

Leadership process involves individuals (followers) being influenced by others (leaders).

Leading creates enthusiasm to work hard to accomplish tasks successfully.

Leaking pipeline is a phrase coined to describe how women have not reached the highest levels of organizations.

Learning is an enduring change in behavior that results from experience.

Least-preferred co-worker (LPC) scale is a measure of a person's leadership style based on a description of the person with whom respondents have been able to work least well.

Legitimate power or formal authority is the extent to which a manager can use the "right of command" to control other people.

Lifelong learning is continuous learning from everyday experiences.

Line units are workgroups that conduct the major business of the organization.

Locus of control is the extent a person feels able to control his or her own life and is concerned with a person's internal–external orientation.

Long-term/short-term orientation is the degree to which a culture emphasizes long-term or short-term thinking.

Low-context cultures express messages mainly by the spoken and written word.

Lower-order needs in Maslow's hierarchy are physiological, safety, and social.

Machiavellianism causes someone to view and manipulate others purely for personal gain.

Maintenance activities support the emotional life of the team as an ongoing social system.

Management by objectives is a process of joint goal setting between a supervisor and a subordinate.

Management philosophy links key goal-related issues with key collaboration issues to come up with general ways by which the firm will manage its affairs.

Management process involves fulfilling the four responsibilities of planning, organizing, leading, and controlling.

Managerial script is a series of well-known routines for problem identification and alternative generation and analysis common to managers within a firm.

Managerial wisdom is the ability to perceive variations in the environment and understand the social actors and their relationships.

Managers are persons who support the work efforts of other people.

Masculinity–femininity is the degree to which a society values assertiveness or relationships.

Matrix departmentation is a combination of functional and divisional patterns wherein an individual is assigned to more than one type of unit.

Mechanistic type or machine bureaucracy emphasizes vertical specialization with impersonal coordination and a heavy reliance on standardization, formalization, rules, policies, and procedures.

Merit pay links an individual's salary or wage increase directly to measures of performance accomplishment.

Mimicry is the copying of the successful practices of others.

Mission statements are written statements of organizational purpose.

Models are simplified views of reality that attempt to explain real-world phenomena.

Moods are generalized positive and negative feelings or states of mind.

Moral dilemma involves a choice between two or more ethically uncomfortable alternatives.

Moral manager makes ethical behavior a personal goal.

Moral problem poses major ethical consequences for the decision maker or others.

Motivation refers to forces within an individual that account for the level, direction, and persistence of effort expended at work.

Motivator factors in the job content are sources of job satisfaction.

Multicultural organization is a firm that values diversity but systematically works to block the transfer of societally based subcultures into the fabric of the organization.

Multiculturalism refers to pluralism and respect for diversity in the workplace.

Multiskilling is a state in which team members are each capable of performing many different jobs.

Mum effect occurs when people are reluctant to communicate bad news.

Need for achievement (nAch) is the desire to do better, solve problems, or master complex tasks.

Need for affiliation (nAff) is the desire for friendly and warm relations with others.

Need for power (nPower) is the desire to control others and influence their behavior.

Negative reinforcement strengthens a behavior by making the avoidance of an undesirable consequence contingent on its occurrence.

Negotiation is the process of making joint decisions when the parties involved have different preferences.

Noise is anything that interferes with the effectiveness of communication.

Nominal group technique involves structured rules for generating and prioritizing ideas.

Nonprogrammed decisions are created to deal specifically with a problem at hand.

Nonverbal communication occurs through facial expressions, body motions, eye contact, and other physical gestures.

Norming stage is when members work together as a coordinated team.

Norms are rules or standards for the behavior of group members.

Observable culture is the way things are done in an organization.

Open systems transform human and material resource inputs into finished goods and services.

Operant conditioning is the control of behavior by manipulating its consequences.

Operations technology is the combination of resources, knowledge, and techniques that creates a product or service output for an organization.

Optimism is the expectation of positive outcomes.

Optimizing decisions give the absolute best solution to a problem.

Organic type or professional bureaucracy emphasizes horizontal specialization, extensive use of personal coordination, and loose rules, policies, and procedures.

Organizational behavior is the study of individuals and groups in organizations.

Organizational behavior modification is the use of extrinsic rewards to systematically reinforce desirable work behavior and discourage undesirable behavior.

Organizational charts are diagrams that depict the formal structures of organizations.

Organizational citizenship behaviors are the extras people do to go the additional distance in their work.

Organizational climate represents shared perceptions of members regarding what the organization is like in terms of management policies and practices.

Organizational commitment is the loyalty of an individual to the organization.

Organizational cultural lag is a condition in which dominant cultural patterns are inconsistent with new emerging innovations.

Organizational culture is a shared set of beliefs and values within an organization.

Organizational design is the process of choosing and implementing a structural configuration for an organization.

Organizational governance is the pattern of authority, influence, and acceptable managerial behavior established at the top of the organization.

Organizational justice concerns the degree to which people view workplace practices as fair and equitable.

Organizational learning is the process of knowledge acquisition, information distribution, information interpretation, and organizational retention.

Organizational myth is a commonly held cause–effect relationship or assertion that cannot be supported empirically.

Organizational or corporate culture is the system of shared actions, values, and beliefs that develops within an organization and guides the behavior of its members.

Organizational politics is the management of influence to obtain ends not sanctioned by the organization or to obtain sanctioned ends through nonsanctioned means and the art of creative compromise among competing interests.

Organizations are collections of people working together to achieve a common purpose.

Organizing divides up tasks and arranges resources to accomplish them.

Out-group occurs when one does not feel part of a group and experiences discomfort and low belongingness.

Output controls are controls that focus on desired targets and allow managers to use their own methods for reaching defined targets.

Output goals are the goals that define the type of business an organization is in.

Output measures of performance assess achievements in terms of actual work results.

Paired comparison in performance appraisal compares each person with every other.

Parochialism assumes the ways of your culture are the only ways of doing things.

Participative leadership focuses on consulting with subordinates and seeking and taking their suggestions into account before making decisions.

Passive followership beliefs are beliefs that followers should be passive, deferent, and obedient to authority.

Path-goal view of managerial leadership assumes that a leader's key function is to adjust his or her behaviors to complement situational contingencies.

Patterning of attention involves isolating and communicating what information is important and what is given attention from a potentially endless stream of events, actions, and outcome.

Perceived inequity is feeling under-rewarded or over-rewarded in comparison with others.

Perception is the process through which people receive and interpret information from the environment.

Performance gap is a discrepancy between the desired and the actual conditions.

Performance norm sets expectations for how hard members work and what the team should accomplish.

Performance-contingent pay is based on earning more when you produce more and earning less when you produce less.

Performing stage marks the emergence of a mature and well-functioning team.

Personal conception traits represent individuals' major beliefs and personal orientation concerning a range of issues involving social and physical setting.

Personal wellness involves the pursuit of one's job and career goals with the support of a personal health promotion program.

Personality is the overall combination of characteristics that capture the unique nature of a person as that person reacts to and interacts with others.

Personality traits are enduring characteristics describing an individual's behavior.

Physical distractions include interruptions from noises, visitors, and the like that interfere with communication.

Planned change is a response to someone's perception of a performance gap—a discrepancy between the desired and actual state of affairs.

Planning sets objectives and identifies the actions needed to achieve them.

Political savvy is knowing how to negotiate, persuade, and deal with people regarding goals they will accept.

Positive reinforcement strengthens a behavior by making a desirable consequence contingent on its occurrence.

Power is the ability to get someone else to do something you want done, or the ability to make things happen or get things done the way you want.

Power distance is a culture's acceptance of the status and power differences among its members.

Power-oriented behavior is action directed primarily at developing or using relationships in which other people are willing to defer to one's wishes.

Prejudice is the display of negative, irrational, and superior opinions and attitudes toward persons who are different from ourselves.

Presence is the act of speaking without using words.

Presence-aware tools are software programs that allow a user to view others' real-time availability status and readiness to communicate.

Proactive followership beliefs are beliefs that followers should express opinions, take initiative, and constructively question and challenge leaders.

Proactive personality is the disposition that identifies whether or not individuals act to influence their environments.

Problem-focused coping mechanisms manage the problem that is causing the distress.

Problem-solving style reflects the way a person gathers and evaluates information when solving problems and making decisions.

Problem-solving team is set up to deal with a specific problem or opportunity.

Procedural justice is the degree to which rules are always properly followed to implement policies.

Process controls are controls that attempt to specify the manner in which tasks are to be accomplished.

Process innovations introduce into operations new and better ways of doing things.

Process power is the control over methods of production and analysis.

Process theories examine the thought processes that motivate individual behavior.

Product innovations introduce new goods or services to better meet customer needs.

Profit sharing rewards employees in some proportion to changes in organizational profits.

Programmed decisions simply implement solutions that have already been determined by past experience as appropriate for the problem at hand.

Projection assigns personal attributes to other individuals.

Prosocial power motivation is power oriented toward benefiting others.

Prototypes are mental images of the characteristics that comprise an implicit theory.

Proxemics involves the use of space as people interact.

Psychological contract is an unwritten set of expectations about a person's exchange of inducements and contributions with an organization.

Psychological empowerment is a sense of personal fulfillment and purpose that arouses one's feelings of competency and commitment to work.

Punishment discourages a behavior by making an unpleasant consequence contingent on its occurrence.

Quality circle is a team that meets regularly to address quality issues.

Ranking in performance appraisal orders each person from best to worst.

Rational persuasion is the ability to control another's behavior because, through the individual's efforts, the person accepts the desirability of an offered goal and a reasonable way of achieving it.

Rational persuasion strategy uses facts, special knowledge, and rational argument to create change.

Receiver is the individual or group of individuals to whom a message is directed.

Referent power is the ability to control another's behavior because of the individual's desire to identify with the power source.

Reinforcement is the delivery of a consequence as a result of behavior.

Relatedness needs are desires for satisfying interpersonal relationships.

Relationship management is the ability to establish rapport with others to build good relationships.

Reliability means a performance measure gives consistent results.

Representative power is the formal right conferred by the firm to speak for and to a potentially important group.

Representativeness heuristic bases a decision on similarities between the situation at hand and stereotypes of similar occurrences.

Resilience is the ability to bounce back from failure and keep forging ahead.

Resistance to change is any attitude or behavior that indicates unwillingness to make or support a desired change.

Restricted communication networks link subgroups that disagree with one another's positions.

Reward power is the extent to which a manager can use extrinsic and intrinsic rewards to control other people.

Risk environments provide probabilities regarding expected results for decision-making alternatives.

Risk management involves anticipating risks and factoring them into decision making.

Rites are standardized and recurring activities used at special times to influence the behaviors and understanding of organizational members.

Rituals are systems of rites.

Role is a set of expectations for a team member or person in a job.

Role ambiguity occurs when someone is uncertain about what is expected of him or her.

Role conflict occurs when someone is unable to respond to role expectations that conflict with one another.

Role negotiation is a process for discussing and agreeing upon what team members expect of one another.

Role overload occurs when too much work is expected of the individual.

Role underload occurs when too little work is expected of the individual.

Romance of leadership involves people attributing romantic, almost magical, qualities to leadership.

Rule of conformity states that the greater the cohesiveness, the greater the conformity of members to team norms.

Saga is an embellished heroic account of accomplishments.

Satisficing decisions choose the first alternative that appears to give an acceptable or satisfactory resolution of the problem.

Scanning involves looking outside the firm and bringing back useful solutions.

Schemas are cognitive frameworks that represent organized knowledge developed through experience about people, objects, or events.

Scientific management uses systematic study of job components to develop practices to increase people's efficiency at work.

Selective listening is when individuals block out information or only hear things that match preconceived notions.

Selective perception is the tendency to define problems from one's own point of view.

Selective screening allows only a portion of available information to enter our perceptions.

Self-awareness is the ability to understand our emotions and their impact on us and others.

Self-concept is the view individuals have of themselves as physical, social, spiritual, or moral beings.

Self-conscious emotions arise from internal sources, and **social emotions** derive from external sources.

Self-efficacy is an individual's belief about the likelihood of successfully completing a specific task.

Self-esteem is a belief about one's own worth based on an overall self-evaluation.

Self-fulfilling prophecy is creating or finding in a situation that which one expected to find in the first place.

Self-management is the ability to think before acting and control disruptive impulses.

Self-managing teams are empowered to make decisions to manage themselves in day-to-day work.

Self-monitoring is a person's ability to adjust his or her behavior to external situational (environmental) factors.

Self-serving bias underestimates internal factors and overestimates external factors as influences on someone's behavior.

Semantic barriers involve a poor choice or use of words and mixed messages.

Sender is a person or group trying to communicate with someone else.

Shaping is positive reinforcement of successive approximations to the desired behavior.

Shared leadership is a dynamic, interactive influence process through which individuals in teams lead one another.

Shared-power strategy uses participatory methods and emphasizes common values to create change.

Simple design is a configuration involving one or two ways of specializing individuals and units.

Situational control is the extent to which leaders can determine what their groups are going to do and what the outcomes of their actions are going to be.

Situational leadership model focuses on the situational contingency of maturity or "readiness" of followers.

Skill is an ability to turn knowledge into effective action.

Skill-based pay rewards people for acquiring and developing job-relevant skills.

Smart workforces work in shifting communities of action where knowledge and skills are shared to solve real and complex problems.

Social awareness is the ability to empathize and understand the emotions of others.

Social capital is a capacity to get things done due to relationships with other people.

Social construction approaches describe individual behavior as "constructed" in context, as people act and interact in situations.

Social exchange means that people build human relationships and trust through exchanges of favors based on reciprocity.

Social facilitation is the tendency for one's behavior to be influenced by the presence of others in a group.

Social identity theory is a theory developed to understand the psychological basis of discrimination.

Social learning theory describes how learning occurs through interactions among people, behavior, and environment.

Social loafing occurs when people work less hard in groups than they would individually.

Social network analysis identifies the informal structures and their embedded social relationships that are active in an organization.

Social traits are surface-level traits that reflect the way a person appears to others when interacting in social settings.

Societal goals reflect the intended contributions of an organization to the broader society.

Span of control refers to the number of individuals reporting to a supervisor.

Specific environment is the set of owners, suppliers, distributors, government agencies, and competitors with which an organization must interact to grow and survive.

Spotlight questions expose a decision to public scrutiny and full transparency.

Staff units assist the line units by performing specialized services to the organization.

Stakeholders are people and groups with an interest or "stake" in the performance of the organization.

Standardization is the degree to which the range of actions in a job or series of jobs is limited.

Status congruence involves consistency between a person's status within and outside a group.

Status differences are differences between persons of higher and lower ranks.

Stereotype assigns attributes commonly associated with a group to an individual.

Stereotyping occurs when people make a generalization, usually exaggerated or oversimplified (and potentially offensive), that is used to describe or distinguish a group.

Stigma is a phenomenon whereby an individual is rejected as a result of an attribute that is deeply discredited by his or her society.

Stock options give the right to purchase shares at a fixed price in the future.

Storming stage is one of high emotionality and tension among team members.

Strategic leadership is leadership of a quasi-independent unit, department, or organization.

Strategy positions the organization in the competitive environment and implements actions to compete successfully.

Stress is tension from extraordinary demands, constraints, or opportunities.

Subcultures are groups exhibiting unique patterns of values and philosophies not consistent with the dominant culture of the larger organization or system.

Substantive conflict involves fundamental disagreement over ends or goals to be pursued and the means for their accomplishment.

Substitutes for leadership make a leader's influence either unnecessary or redundant in that they replace a leader's influence.

Supportive communication principles are a set of tools focused on joint problem solving.

Supportive leadership focuses on subordinate needs, well-being, and promotion of a friendly work climate.

Surface-level diversity involves individual differences in visible attributes such as race, sex, age, and physical abilities.

Synergy is the creation of a whole greater than the sum of its parts.

Systematic thinking approaches problems in a rational and analytical fashion.

Systems goals are concerned with the conditions within the organization that are expected to increase its survival potential.

Task activities directly contribute to the performance of important tasks.

Task performance consists of the quantity and quality of work produced.

Team is a group of people holding themselves collectively accountable for using complementary skills to achieve a common purpose.

Team building is a collaborative way to gather and analyze data to improve teamwork.

Team composition is the mix of abilities, skills, personalities, and experiences that the members bring to the team.

Team decisions are made by all members of the team.

Teamwork occurs when team members live up to their collective accountability for goal accomplishment.

Technical skill is an ability to perform specialized tasks.

Telecommuting is working at home or from a remote location using computers and advanced telecommunications.

Terminal values reflect a person's preferences concerning the "ends" to be achieved.

Title VII of the Civil Rights Act of 1964 protects individuals against employment discrimination on the basis of race and color, as well as national origin, sex, and religion.

Trait perspectives assume that traits play a central role in differentiating between leaders and nonleaders or in predicting leader or organizational outcomes.

Transactional leadership involves leader–follower exchanges necessary for achieving routine performance agreed upon between leaders and followers.

Transformational change radically shifts the fundamental character of an organization.

Transformational leadership occurs when leaders broaden and elevate followers' interests and stir followers to look beyond their own interests to the good of others.

Two-factor theory identifies job context as the source of job dissatisfaction and job content as the source of job satisfaction.

Type A orientations are characterized by impatience, desire for achievement, and a more competitive nature than Type B.

Type B orientations are characterized by an easygoing and less competitive nature than Type A.

Uncertain environments provide no information to predict expected results for decision-making alternatives.

Uncertainty avoidance is the cultural tendency to be uncomfortable with uncertainty and risk in everyday life.

Universal design is the practice of designing products, buildings, public spaces, and programs to be usable by the greatest number of people.

Unplanned change occurs spontaneously or randomly.

Upward communication is the flow of messages from lower to higher organizational levels.

Upward delegation means passing problems or responsibilities upward in the hierarchy.

Valence is the value to the individual of various work outcomes.

Validity means a performance measure addresses job-relevant dimensions.

Value chain is a sequence of activities that creates valued goods and services for customers.

Value congruence occurs when individuals express positive feelings upon encountering others who exhibit values similar to their own.

Values are broad preferences concerning appropriate courses of action or outcomes.

Vertical specialization is a hierarchical division of labor that distributes formal authority.

Vicarious learning involves capturing the lessons of others' experiences.

Virtual communication networks link team members through electronic communication.

Virtual organization is an ever-shifting constellation of firms, with a lead corporation, that pools skills, resources, and experiences to thrive jointly.

Virtual teams work together through computer mediation.

Work sharing is when employees agree to work fewer hours to avoid layoffs.

Workforce diversity is a mix of people within a workforce who are considered to be, in some way, different from those in the prevailing constituency.

Zone of indifference is the range of authoritative requests to which a subordinate is willing to respond without subjecting the directives to critical evaluation or judgment.

Self-Test Answers

Self-Test Answers 1

Multiple Choice
1. b 2. d 3. c 4. c 5. c 6. b 7. c 8. a 9. d 10. d 11. a 12. c 13. c 14. c 15. a

Short Response

16. OB as a scientific discipline has the following characteristics: (a) It is an interdisciplinary body of knowledge, drawing upon insights from such allied social sciences as sociology and psychology. (b) OB researchers use scientific methods to develop and test models and theories about human behavior in organizations. (c) OB focuses on application, trying to develop from science practical insights that can improve organizations. (d) OB uses contingency thinking, trying to fit explanations to situations rather than trying to find "one best" answer that fits all situations.

17. The term valuing diversity is used to describe behavior that respects individual differences. In the workplace this means respecting the talents and potential contributions of people from different races and of different genders, ethnicities, and ages, for example.

18. Emotional intelligence is an ability to understand and manage emotions well, both personally and in interactions with others. Self-regulation is an important emotional intelligence competency. It is the capacity to think before taking action, and thus make sure that actions are functional rather than dysfunctional. It is the capacity to quickly spot tendencies to behave in disruptive or unhelpful ways due to an emotional reaction to a person or situation, and then control those tendencies to avoid bad behavior.

19. Just being a manager—having the job title, doesn't guarantee that a person will be an effective leader. A true leader is someone who interacts with and influences others to do things that are good for the team or organization. This person uses influence to attract followers not due to the authority of a position—such as being designated the manager, supervisor, or team leader—but by virtue of what he or she knows, values, and can accomplish. Indeed, leaders don't have to be managers, and they don't have to be formally designated. A "leader" can emerge in a team without authority but still end up being highly influential in bringing about change and moving others to do things that support team accomplishments.

Applications Essay

20. Carla is about to lead an important discussion since the world of work will certainly be different by the time these sixth-graders are ready to enter the workforce. As they look ahead, she should encourage them to consider the following points:

    - Commitment to ethical behavior
    - Importance of knowledge and experience in the form of "human capital"
    - Less emphasis on boss-centered "command and control"
    - Emphasis on teamwork

- Emphasis on use of computers and information technology
- Respect for people and their work expectations
- More people working for themselves and more job/employer shifting by people; fewer people working an entire lifetime for one organization

Of course, one of Carla's greatest challenges will be to express these concepts in words and examples that sixth-graders will understand. Your answer should reflect that use of language and examples.

Self-Test Answers 2

Multiple Choice

1. d 2. c 3. b 4. a 5. b 6. c 7. d 8. b 9. a 10. c 11. b 12. d 13. c 14. a 15. d

Short Response

16. Individual differences reflect the ways in which people are similar and how they vary in their thinking, feeling, and behavior. They are important in organizational behavior because by categorizing behavioral tendencies of different types of people, and then identifying groups to which individuals (including ourselves) belong, we can more accurately predict why and how people behave as they do.

17. Both nature and nurture are important, and research isn't conclusive as to whether one is more influential than the other. Some studies show there is a 50–50 split, and the twin studies show that about 32 percent of variance in leadership is related to nurture. What is clear is that who we are is affected by *both* the genes we inherit and the environments in which we are raised.

18. Meglino and colleagues found that the most common values held by people in the workplace are those related to achievement, helping and concern for others, honesty, and fairness. When individuals in organizations share values with those around them, they experience greater satisfaction; when their values differ from those around them, they may experience conflict over such things as goals and how to achieve them.

19. Environments that are most conducive to diversity are those that appreciate differences, create a setting where everyone feels valued and accepted, and recognize the benefits diversity brings to workplace and organizational functioning. Such environments offer commitment to inclusion from the highest levels, opportunities for networking and mentoring, and role models and exposure to high-visibility assignments for diverse groups.

Applications Essay

20. The first step would be to identify the source of the stress. It is important at this stage to gather data from multiple perspectives (e.g., employees, managers, HR) and to create a safe environment for people to provide input to ensure accurate information. Factors you should consider are these: Is the stress due to personal issues of employees, or workplace issues? Are some employees more stressed than others, and if so why? How do individual differences come into play, if at all? What workplace or organizational factors are causing the stress? How much agreement is there about the causes of the stress? What are the effects of the stress, and who is most affected? Once you have gathered enough information that you are satisfied you have a complete picture of the situation, develop an action plan. This plan should (a) address the appropriate source, (b) be realistic and impactful, and (c) not cause more stress. Typically many stress issues can be resolved with good communication and support, and by working with individuals to find ways they can manage the factors causing their stress. Managers must be careful to

avoid environments that are highly stressful and lead to burnout, such as fear climates, environments that are too individually competitive (pitting employees against one another), not dealing with poor performers, overly stressful change situations, and bad communication. The most promising plan of action would be one that helps both employees and managers understand specific steps and techniques for reducing stress.

Self-Test Answers 3

Multiple Choice

1. b 2. d 3. b 4. c 5. d 6. c 7. c 8. a 9. a 10. d 11. c 12. c 13. c 14. a 15. a

Short Response

16. A model should be constructed to show information flowing in from the environment and eventually resulting in some individual response—feeling, thinking, or acting. In between the input and the response influences such as the characteristics of the perceiver, the setting, and what is being perceived should be identified. Your answer should include for four stages of information processing: attention and selection, organization, interpretation, and retrieval.

17. There are six perceptual distortions listed and discussed in this chapter: stereotype, halo effect, selective perception, projection, contrast, and self-fulfilling prophecies. Select any two and briefly note how they distort the perceptual process.

18. The law of effect states that a behavior followed by a pleasant consequence is likely to be repeated and a behavior followed by an unpleasant consequence is unlikely to be repeated. Managers and people at work deal regularly with others who exhibit desirable and undesirable behaviors. By understanding the law of effect, they should be able to strengthen the desired behaviors and weaken the undesired ones by manipulating consequences.

19. Reinforcement learning focuses on behavior as a function of its consequences, whereas social learning theory emphasizes observational learning and the importance of perception and attribution. Thus, people respond to how their perceptions and attributions help define consequences, and not to the objective consequences as emphasized in reinforcement learning.

Applications Essay

20. A good example to illustrate attribution is the fundamental attribution error as opposed to the self-serving bias. You should explain the fundamental attribution error as the tendency to underestimate the influence of situational factors and to overestimate the influence of personal factors in evaluating someone else's behaviors. In contrast, the self-serving bias is the tendency to deny personal responsibility for performance problems but accept personal responsibility for performance success. Then follow up with an example of each and implications for managing the department.

Self-Test Answers 4

Multiple Choice

1. d 2. b 3. a 4. d 5. a 6. b 7. a 8. c 9. a 10. d 11. a 12. d 13. d 14. c 15. c

▶ Short Response

16. Emotions and moods are both part of what is called affect, or the range of feelings that people experience in their life context. An emotion is a strong positive or negative feeling directed toward someone or something. It is usually intense, not long lasting, and always associated with a source: someone or something that makes you feel the way you do. An example is the positive emotion of elation a student feels when congratulated by an instructor. A mood is a more generalized positive and negative feeling or state of mind that may persist for some time. An example is someone who wakes up and feels grouchy that day.

17. The three components of an attitude are cognition, affect, and behavior. Cognition might occur as the belief that "I think being a management major is important to my future career." Affect might occur as "I feel really good about taking this organizational behavior course." Behavior might occur in responses to the intention "I am going to study hard and earn an A in the course." The cognition influences affect, which influences intended behavior. But the behavior is only an intention. As we well know, lots of things happen during a semester that might lead an otherwise well-intentioned management major who likes his or her OB course to not study hard enough to earn an A grade.

18. Five aspects of job satisfaction that are commonly measured are (1) work itself: responsibility, interest, and growth; (2) quality of supervision: technical and social support; (3) relationships with co-workers: social harmony and respect; (4) promotion opportunities: chances for further advancement; (5) pay: adequacy and perceived equity vis-á-vis others. Although it depends on the individual and the context, in general each of these can be considered equally important.

19. Cognitive dissonance describes a state of inconsistency between an individual's attitudes and his or her behavior. Such inconsistency can result in changing attitudes, changing future behavior, or developing new ways to explain the inconsistency. The amount of control an individual has over the situation and the magnitude of the reward tend to influence which of these actions will be chosen.

▶ Applications Essay

20. The heart of the issue rests with the satisfaction–performance relationship as discussed in this chapter. Does satisfaction cause performance? It appears that satisfaction alone is no guarantee of high-level job performance. Although a satisfied worker is likely not to quit and to have good attendance, his or her performance still remains uncertain. In the integrated model of motivation, performance is a function of motivation and effort as well as individual attributes and organizational support. Thus I would be cautious in focusing only on creating satisfied and high-performing workers. I would try to make sure that the rewards for performance create satisfaction. I would also try to make sure that the satisfied worker has the right abilities, training, and other support needed to perform a job really well. Assuming that satisfaction alone will always lead to high performance seems risky at best; it leaves too many other important considerations left untouched, an example of which is described in the study of satisfaction in groups across time.

Self-Test Answers 5

▶ Multiple Choice

1. a 2. d 3. b 4. b 5. d 6. d 7. d 8. c 9. a 10. a 11. c 12. a 13. d 14. a 15. b

Short Response

16. Basically, the frustration–regression principle in Alderfer's ERG theory states that when one level of need is unsatisfied (or frustrated) the individual can revert back (or regress) to seek further satisfaction of a lower level need. For example, if a need for psychological growth in one's job is frustrated, the person may regress back to place more emphasis on satisfying relatedness needs.

17. According to Herzberg, the job content or satisfier factors are what really motivate people to work hard. They include such things as feelings of responsibility, opportunities for advancement and growth, and job challenges. To build these things into jobs and make them more motivational, Herzberg recommends job enrichment—that is, adding job content factors by moving into a job things traditionally done by higher levels, such as planning and controlling responsibilities.

18. Distributive justice is when everyone is treated by the same rules with no one getting special favors or exceptions; procedural justice is when all rules and procedures are properly followed.

19. Expectancy theory states that Motivation = Expectancy × Instrumentality × Valence. The presence of multiplication signs creates the multiplier effect. This means that a zero in expectancy or instrumentality or valence creates a zero for motivation. In other words, the multiplier effect is that all three factors—expectancy, instrumentality, valence—must be positive in order for motivation to be positive.

Applications Essay

20. The issue in this case boils down to motivation to work hard. A job might provide lots of satisfaction for someone—relationships, good pay, and so on—and they may not work hard because there is no link between receiving the need satisfaction and doing a really good job every day. To apply the needs theories of motivation, managers need to link opportunities for need satisfaction with tasks and activities that are important to getting the job done well. In other words, hard work on things important to the organization are viewed as pathways toward individual need satisfaction. In this case, as perhaps Person B would be suggesting, individuals will work hard because they are satisfying important needs by doing important job-relevant things.

Self-Test Answers 6

Multiple Choice

1. d 2. c 3. b 4. b 5. a 6. c 7. b 8. d 9. c 10. d 11. c 12. d
13. d 14. a 15. a

Short Response

16. In a traditional evaluation, the employee's performance is evaluated by the supervisor. In the 360° evaluation the employee's performance is evaluated by those with whom he or she works, including supervisor, peers, subordinates, and perhaps even customers. The 360° evaluation also typically includes a self-evaluation. When the results of all evaluations are analyzed and compared, the employee has a good sense of his or her accomplishments and areas for improvement. This evaluation can then be discussed with the supervisor.

17. A halo error in performance appraisal occurs when one attribute or behavior inappropriately influences the overall appraisal. For example, an individual may have a unique style of dress but be a very high performer. If the evaluator lets his or her distaste for the dress style negatively bias the overall performance evaluation, a halo error has occurred. A recency error occurs when a performance appraisal is biased due to the influence of recent events. In other words, the performance appraisal is based on most recent performance and may not be an accurate reflection of performance for a full evaluation period. For example, just prior to an evaluation I might have had a very bad week due to family problems. If my supervisor uses that week's performance to negatively bias the evaluation even though for the prior six months I had been a very strong performer, recency error would have occurred.

18. Growth-need strength is a moderator variable in the job characteristics model. In other words, it sets the condition under which an individual will or will not respond positively to the job characteristics. When an individual is high in growth-need strength, the prediction is that he or she will respond positively to a job high in the core characteristics and therefore largely enriched. However, when the individual has low-growth-need strength, the prediction is that he or she will not respond positively to high core characteristics and may be dissatisfied and less productive in such enriched job conditions.

19. The compressed workweek, or 4/40 schedule, offers employees the advantage of a three-day weekend. However, it can cause problems for the employer in terms of ensuring that operations are covered adequately during the normal five-day workweek. Also, the compressed workweek will entail more complicated work scheduling. In addition, some employees find that the schedule is tiring and can cause family adjustment problems.

▶ Applications Essay

20. Many things can be done to use rewards and performance management well in the context of student organizations. On the reward side, the most appropriate thing is to make sure that those who get the benefits from the organization are the ones who do the work. For example, if there is a fund-raiser to support a student trip, only those who actively raise the money should get financial support for the trip. Possibly, the financial support should be proportionate to the amount of time and effort each person contributed toward raising the funds. Also, it is probably quite common that little or no evaluation is done of how people perform in offices and special assignments in the student organizations. Many possible ways of creating and using more formal evaluation systems could be established. For example, officers could be rated on a BARS scale developed by the membership to reflect the desirable officer behaviors. These ratings could take place every month or two, and individuals who perform poorly can be counseled or removed, whereas those who perform well can be praised and continued.

Self-Test Answers 7

▶ Multiple Choice

1. a 2. b 3. d 4. c 5. b 6. d 7. b 8. d 9. d 10. c 11. b 12. c 13. d 14. c 15. c

▶ Short Response

16. Teams are potentially good for organizations for several reasons: They are good for people, they can improve creativity, they sometimes make the best decisions, they gain commitment to decisions, they help control the behavior of their members, and they can help to counterbalance the effects of large organization size.

17. Permanent formal groups appear on organization charts and serve an ongoing purpose. These groups may include departments, divisions, teams, and the like. Temporary groups are created to solve a specific problem or perform a defined task and are then disbanded. Examples are committees, cross-functional task forces, and project teams.

18. Self-managing teams take different forms. A common pattern, however, involves empowering team members to make decisions about the division of labor and scheduling, to develop and maintain the skills needed to perform several different jobs for the team, to help train one another to learn those jobs, and to help select new team members.

19. The diversity–consensus dilemma occurs when a team with high membership diversity gets caught between diversity advantages and disadvantages. On the one hand, the team has the potential advantages of many viewpoints, perspectives, and enriched information. On the other hand, it suffers the potential pitfalls of members having a hard time learning how to work well with one another; this can make it hard to reach consensus.

Applications Essay

20. "Saw your message and wanted to respond. Don't worry. There is no reason at all that a great design engineer can't run a high-performance project team. Go into the job with confidence, but try to follow some basic guidelines as you build and work with the team. First off, remember that a "team" isn't just a "group." You have to make sure that the members—and that includes you—identify highly with the goals and will hold themselves collectively accountable for results. I suggest that you communicate high-performance standards right from the beginning. Set the tone in the first team meeting and even create a sense of urgency to get things going. Be sure that the members have the right skills, and find ways to create some early "successes" for them. Don't let them drift apart; make sure they spend a lot of time together. Give lots of positive feedback as the project develops and, perhaps most important, model the expected behaviors yourself. Go for it!"

Self-Test Answers 8

Multiple Choice

1. d 2. a 3. a 4. b 5. b 6. c 7. c 8. a 9. b 10. b 11. a 12. d 13. a 14. a 15. c

Short Response

16. Team building usually begins when someone notices that a problem exists or may develop in the group. Members then work collaboratively to gather data, analyze the situation, plan for improvements, and implement the plan. Everyone is expected to participate in each step, and the group as a whole is expected to benefit from continuous improvement.

17. To help build positive norms, a team leader must first act as a positive role model. She or he should carefully select members for the team and be sure to reinforce and reward members for performing as desired. She or he should also hold meetings to review performance, provide feedback, and discuss and agree on goals.

18. A basic rule of team dynamics is that members of highly cohesive groups tend to conform to group norms. Thus, when group norms are positive for performance, the conformity is likely to create high-performance outcomes. When the norms are negative, however, the conformity is likely to create low-performance outcomes.

19. Inter-team competition can create problems in the way groups work with one another. Ideally, an organization is a cooperative system in which groups are well integrated and help one another out as needed. When groups get competitive, however, there is a potential dysfunctional side. Instead of communicating with one another, they decrease communication. Instead of viewing one another positively, they develop negative stereotypes of one another. Instead of viewing each other as mutual partners in the organization, they become hostile and view one another more as enemies. Although inter-team competition can be good by adding creative tension and encouraging more focused efforts, this potential negative side should not be forgotten.

■ Applications Essay

20. I would tell Alejandro that consensus and unanimity are different, but related. Consensus results from extensive discussion and lots of give and take during which group members share ideas and listen carefully to one another. Eventually, one alternative emerges that is preferred by most. Those who disagree, however, know that they have been listened to and have had a fair chance to influence the decision outcome. Consensus, therefore, does not require unanimity. What it does require is the opportunity for any dissenting members to feel they have been able to speak and be listened to sincerely. A decision by unanimity that generates 100 percent agreement on an issue may be the ideal state of affairs, but it is not always possible to achieve. Thus, Alejandro should always try to help members work together intensively, communicate well with one another, and sincerely share ideas and listen. However, he should not be concerned for complete unanimity on every issue. Rather, consensus should be the agreed-on goal in most cases.

Self-Test Answers 9

■ Multiple Choice

1. c 2. b 3. a 4. c 5. b 6. a 7. a 8. c 9. a 10. c 11. b 12. a 13. b 14. c 15. d

■ Short Response

16. Heuristics are simplifying strategies, or "rules of thumb," that people use to make decisions. They make it easier for individuals to deal with uncertainty and limited information, but they can also lead to biased results. Common heuristics include availability-making decisions based on recent events; representativeness-making decisions based on similar events; and anchoring and adjustment-making decisions based on historical precedents.

17. Individual, or authority, decisions are made by the manager or team leader acting alone based on information that he or she possesses. Consultative decisions are made by the manager or team leader after soliciting input from other persons. Group decisions are made when the manager or team leader asks others to participate in problem solving. The ideal form of the group decision is true consensus.

18. Escalating commitment is the tendency to continue with a previously chosen course of action even though feedback indicates that it is not working. This can lead to a waste of time, money, and other resources, in addition to the sacrificing of the opportunity to pursue a course of action offering more valuable results. Escalating commitment is encouraged by the popular adage "If at first you don't succeed, try, try, again." Another way to look at it is "throwing good money after bad."

19. Most people are too busy to respond personally to every problem that comes their way. The effective manager and team leader knows when to delegate decisions to others,

how to set priorities, and when to abstain from acting altogether. Questions to ask include these: Is the problem easy to deal with? Might the problem resolve itself? Is this my decision to make? Is this a solvable problem within the context of the organization?

Applications Essay

20. This is what I would say in the mentoring situation: First, teams can be great for creativity but they have to be set up and then led so that their creative potential is fully realized. To start with, the team needs to have at least some highly creative members. They bring to the team context valuable insights, new ideas, and enthusiasm for finding new ways of doing things. These are people who already have strong creativity skills such as high energy, resourcefulness, intuition, and lateral thinking. With people like this as part of the team it will have a strong baseline of team creativity skills in place. Then it is important to give this team management and organizational support to harness this creativity potential. The team leader has to believe in and want team creativity, he or she has to be patient and allow time for creative processes to work, and he or she also needs to make sure the team has all the resources it needs to do creative work. An organizational culture in which creativity is valued is also an asset since it provides a broader context of support for what the team is trying to accomplish. When people throughout the organization value creativity, it tends to pull others along and also support their creative efforts. When creativity is expected and even evaluated as part of performance appraisals, it is also further encouraged by the surrounding organizational context.

Self-Test Answers 10

Multiple Choice

1. c 2. a 3. b 4. b 5. d 6. c 7. b 8. c 9. d 10. c 11. a 12. c
13. c 14. a 15. b

Short Response

16. Managers can be faced with the following conflict situations: vertical conflict—conflict that occurs between hierarchical levels; horizontal conflict—conflict that occurs between those at the same hierarchical level; line–staff conflict—conflict that occurs between line and staff representatives; role conflict—conflict that occurs when the communication of task expectations is inadequate or upsetting.

17. The major indirect conflict management approaches include the following: appeals to common goals—involves focusing the attention of potentially conflicting parties on one mutually desirable conclusion; hierarchical referral—using the chain of command for conflict resolution; organizational redesign—including decoupling, buffering, linking pins, and liaison groups; use of myths and scripts—managing superficially through behavioral routines (scripts) or to hide conflict by denying the necessity to make a trade-off in conflict resolution.

18. You should acknowledge that different styles may be appropriate under different conditions. Avoidance is the extreme form of nonattention and is most commonly used when the issue is trivial, when more important issues are pressing, or when individuals need to cool off. An accommodation strategy is used when an issue is more important to the other party than it is to you, or to build social credits.

19. Distributive negotiation focuses on staking out positions and claiming portions of the available "pie." It usually takes the form of hard negotiation—the parties maximize their self-interests and hold out to get their own way—or soft negotiation—one party is willing to make concessions in order to reach an agreement. Distributive

negotiation can lead to competition, compromise, or accommodation, but it tends to be win–lose oriented in all cases. Integrative negotiation focuses on the merits of an issue and attempts to enlarge the available "pie." It may lead to avoidance, compromise, or collaboration. It tends to be more win–win oriented and seeks to satisfy the needs and interests of all parties.

Applications Essay

20. When negotiating the salary for your first job, you should attempt to avoid the common pitfalls of negotiation. These include falling prey to the myth of the fixed "pie"; nonrational escalation of conflict, such as trying to compare the proposed salary to the highest offer you have heard; overconfidence; and ignoring other's needs (the personnel officer probably has a fixed limit). The initial salary may be very important to you, but you should also recognize that it may not be as significant as what type of job you will have and whether you will have an opportunity to move up in the firm.

Self-Test Answers 11

Multiple Choice

1. d 2. c 3. a 4. b 5. a 6. a 7. c 8. d 9. a 10. d 11. b 12. a
13. c 14. d 15. a

Short Response

16. Channel richness is a useful concept for managers because it describes the capacity of a communication channel to convey and move information. For example, if a manager wants to convey basic and routine information to a lot of people, a lean channel such as the electronic bulletin or written memorandum may be sufficient. However, if the manager needs to convey a complicated message and one that may involve some uncertainty, a richer channel such as the face-to-face meeting may be necessary. Simply put, the choice of channel may have a lot of impact on the effectiveness of a communication attempt.

17. Informal communication channels are very important in today's organizations. Modern work environments place great emphasis on cross-functional relationships and communication. Employee involvement and participation in decision making are very important. This requires that people know and talk with one another, often across departmental lines. Progressive organizations make it easy for people to interact and meet outside of formal work assignments and relationships. When people know one another, they can more easily and frequently communicate with one another.

18. Status effects can interfere with the effectiveness of communication between lower and higher levels in an organization. Lower-level members are concerned about how the higher-level members will respond, especially if the information being communicated is negative or unfavorable. In such cases, a tendency exists to filter or modify the information to make it as attractive as possible to the recipient. The result is that high-level decision makers in organizations sometimes act on inaccurate or incomplete information. Although their intentions are good, they just aren't getting good information from their subordinates.

19. Active listening works by increasing the flow of information to help the communicator analyze the issue being processed. In active listening, the focus should be on the communicator, not the listener. At the beginning of the conversation the listener helps increase information flow to open up communication by listening for content

and feelings. The listener also uses reinforcing statements to support those feelings and create a safe environment. Once the information has been processed, the listener helps the communicator identify a course of action by turning to reflecting and advising statements that help represent what the communicator expressed.

■ Applications Essay

20. Organizations depend on communication flowing upward, downward, and laterally. Rapid developments in technology have led to a heavy reliance on computers to assist in the movement of this information. E-mail is one part of an electronic organizational communication system. Research suggests that people may fall prey to the "impersonality" of computer-based operations and that the personal or face-to-face side of communication may suffer. Rather than eliminate e-mail and other forms of computermediated communication, however, the managing director should work hard to establish proper e-mail protocols and provide many other avenues for communication. The managing director can serve as a role model in his or her use of e-mail, in being regularly available for face-to-face interactions, by holding regular meetings, and by "wandering around" frequently to meet and talk with people from all levels. In addition, the director can make sure that facility designs and office arrangements support interaction and make it less easy for people to disappear behind computer screens. Finally, the director must actively encourage communication of all types without getting trapped into serving as a classic example of the "e-mail boss."

Self-Test Answers 12

■ Multiple Choice

1. b 2. d 3. c 4. a 5. d 6. c 7. a 8. b 9. c 10. b 11. d 12. a
13. c 14. b 15. d

■ Short Response

16. An individual's power is directly proportional to the dependence others have on him or her. If a dependency can be easily removed, an individual has power only as long as the other is willing to give it to him or her. If a dependency cannot be easily removed, an individual has little choice but to go along.

17. Powerlessness is a problem in organizations because it can create spirals of helplessness and alienation. When people feel powerless, they try to regain some sense of control over themselves and their work environment. The resulting behaviors can be extremely detrimental to organizations (e.g., absenteeism, tardiness, theft, vandalism, grievances, shoddy workmanship, and counterproductive behavior).

18. Position power comes from the formal hierarchy or authority vested in a particular role, whereas personal power is generated in relationships with others. You can tell if the power one holds is position or personal because personal power goes with the individual when he or she leaves a position.

19. Organizational politics involve efforts by organizational members to seek resources and achieve desired goals through informal systems and structures. Most politics involve workarounds, which means working around the system to accomplish a task or goal when the normal process or method isn't producing the desired result. In less political environments, actions are more direct and straightforward (more rational); in more political environments, individuals need to interpret and watch out for behaviors happening behind the scenes.

Applications Essay

20. Cristos should be careful not to get sucked into any negative political behaviors of others and build his power bases so they are available for him to use when needed. He should work to be in the know and connected but not become part of a political coalition that uses power and politics negatively, in ways that are self-interested and disadvantage others and the organization.

    Cristos can build his power bases by establishing competence and value added to the organization (position and personal power) and developing organizational and professional networks (information and connection power). He should make himself non-substitutable.

    He should also develop his political savvy, which is skill and adroitness at reading political environments and understanding how to influence effectively in these environments. One of the best ways to do this is by finding a mentor or sponsor who can provide him with developmental feedback and coaching in how to interpret and respond to the political environment in the organization.

Self-Test Answers 13

Multiple Choice

1. a 2. c 3. d 4. b 5. a 6. b 7. d 8. c 9. d 10. b 11. a 12. b 13. d 14. c 15. c

Short Response

16. Social construction describes leadership as generated in relational interactions among people and in context. As a result leadership is dynamic, developing, and changing over time. This means there is no one-size-fits-all solution in leadership, and leaders need to be flexible and adaptive to be able to adjust to the needs of the context and the actors.

17. Findings show that some followers hold *passive beliefs*, viewing their roles in the classic sense of following—that is, passive, deferential, and obedient to authority. These individuals have a power distance orientation. Others hold *proactive beliefs*, viewing their role as expressing opinions, taking initiative, and constructively questioning and challenging leaders. These individuals have constructive follower orientations. Because social construction is dependent on context, however, individuals are not always able to act according to their beliefs.

18. According to social exchange theory, relationships develop through *exchanges*, or actions contingent upon rewarding reactions. When exchanges are one-sided or not satisfactory, relationships will not develop effectively.

    The norm of reciprocity helps us understand that when one party does something for another an obligation is generated, and that party is now indebted to the other until the obligation is repaid. Therefore, effective relationship development means meeting obligations in accordance with expected norms of reciprocity.

19. Scholars are paying more attention to collective leadership to increase understanding that leadership is about more than one person's behaviors. It is a social phenomenon constructed in interaction. Therefore, collective leadership helps us to consider not only individuals' traits and characteristics but, also, the shared activities and collective processes that more accurately describe how leadership works in practice.

Applications Essay

20. Your roommate is externalizing blame and probably assuming that he is a leader because he has the title of student government president. But to be a leader, you need to have willing followership. So, a key step is to help your friend think about how others see him, and why they don't see him as a leader. If not, what can he do to better tap into others' implicit theories and get them to grant his leadership claims? He can also consider the kinds of followers they are and how he can better meet their identities as followers. Finally, what are aspects of the context that he can tap into to help him meet the needs of the situation and generate collective processes that help advance more positive outcomes for the organization?

Self-Test Answers 14

Multiple Choice

1. d 2. c 3. b 4. c 5. a 6. b 7. d 8. c 9. b 10. a 11. d 12. a 13. c 14. b 15. a

Short Response

16. The early trait approaches fell out of favor because researchers failed to find any traits that were significantly associated with leadership. A primary reason was the failure to consider mediating variables. Researchers looked instead for significant correlations between traits and leadership outcomes, which were not found.

17. The problems with contingency approaches is that they can't tell us much beyond common sense because so many variables are involved in leadership that it is practically impossible to construct models that accurately reflect leadership practice.

18. Complexity approaches are being developed to bring our understanding of leadership more in line with today's complex environments. Predominant views are grounded in bureaucratic organizing principles that are more than a hundred years old. Not only are these bureaucratic views less relevant; they may actually be doing harm by stifling adaptive dynamics needed for productive emergence in complex environments.

19. Challenges come primarily from the hierarchical nature of the leader role. Personality characteristics (such as narcissism and achievement orientation) and social biases (prejudices and norms) can also complicate ethical behavior in leadership. Perhaps the greatest challenge, however, comes from the tension between self-interest and collective good.

Applications Essay

20. Charisma is a powerful force that can be a dangerous one. Because charismatic leadership arouses strong emotions among followers, it can produce radical behaviors even if a leader did not intend it. Psychological needs of followers can cause them to want and need hero figures that make them feel secure and special. If Jonathan does not live up to the raised expectations of his followers, therefore, they may feel let down. This might affect his personal power as well as create morale and motivation problems for those working with and for him.

Jonathan should be careful not to get caught up in the allure and self-inflating effects others' admiration can have on him. He should make sure to analyze his own intentions to avoid becoming a personalized charismatic. Perhaps most important, he should work to reduce power distance and not allow others to put him on a pedestal. He should redirect others' energies onto the collective rather than onto himself, and he should empower others to think critically, openly question him, push back on him with concerns, and share credit for innovations and successes.

Self-Test Answers 15

▶ Multiple Choice

1. c 2. a 3. b 4. a 5. d 6. d 7. a 8. a 9. b 10. c 11. b 12. a
13. d 14. d 15. a

▶ Short Response

16. Cox's theory is designed for organizations that are located in the United States. His ideas may not be easily expanded to multinational corporations headquartered in other cultures. Cox believes that it is important for culturally divergent groups within an organization to communicate and educate one another. This helps subgroups become more tolerant and interactive with other portions of the organization. Second, the organization needs to make sure that one type of cultural group is not segregated into one type of position. When cultural subgroups are spread throughout the organization, the levels of interaction increase as the stereotyping decreases. The company also needs to help restructure many of its informal lines of communication. By encouraging the integration of the informal communication, subgroups become more involved with one another. The organization must also ensure that no one group is associated with the company's outside image. A company that is perceived to be uniform in its culture attracts individuals who are from a similar culture. Finally, Cox states that interpersonal conflict that is based on group identity needs to be controlled.

17. Groups first need to define who is in the group and who is not. Criteria for both formal and informal groups need to be established to provide a framework for membership. Second, the group needs to set standards of behavior. These standards should consist of a series of informal rules that describe proper behavior and activities for the members. Finally, group members need to identify the friends and adversaries of the group. The identification process helps the group build alliances throughout the organization when they attempt to get projects and ideas completed.

18. If you have not had full-time employment, think seriously about this question because it is designed to help you appreciate the importance of organizational rules and roles. Formal rules should be covered to show that they help dictate procedures individuals use. Informal interaction should be discussed as well. Such questions as, "How are subgroups treated?" "Do different instructors have different rules?" and "Are Seniors treated differently from Sophomores in this system?" could all be potential subtopics.

19. The first element is the need for a widely shared philosophy. Although this first element seems vague, an effective company philosophy is anything but abstract. An organization member needs to be exposed to what the firm stands for. The firm's mission needs to be articulated often and throughout the organization. Organizations should put people ahead of rules and general policy mandates. When staffers feel included and important in a system they feel more loyal and accepting of the culture. Every company has heroes or individuals who have succeeded beyond expectations. Companies with strong company cultures allow the stories of these individuals to become well known throughout the organization. Through these

stories, workers need to make sure that they understand the rituals and ceremonies that are important to the company's identity. Maintaining and enhancing these rituals helps many organizations keep a strong corporate culture. Informal rules and expectations must be evident so that workers understand what is expected of them and the organization. Finally, employees need to realize that their work is important; their work and knowledge should be networked throughout the company. The better the communication system in the company, the better the company's culture.

■ Applications Essay

20. An overemphasis on exploration is likely to yield a great number of new ideas, programs, and initiatives, but comparatively little effective commercialization. In contrast, an overemphasis on exploitation often results in small incremental changes to existing products in existing markets and does not yield the changes often dictated by environmental and technological change. Thus, most OB researchers stress the need for some type of balance. There are a variety of ways to do this. The most ambitious is to develop an ambidextrous organization that stresses both. Often, however, senior managers ask some parts to stress exploration and others exploitation. Here they recognize the tension and are prepared to reconcile opposing views.

Self-Test Answers 16

■ Multiple Choice

1. b 2. b 3. e 4. a 5. a 6. d 7. d 8. b 9. b 10. c 11. b 12. c 13. b 14. b 15. a

■ Short Response

16. Output goals are designed to help an organization define its overall mission and to help define the kind of business it is in. Output goals can often help define the types of products and the relationships that the company has with its consumers. Output goals often help demonstrate how a company fits into society. The second kind of organizational goal is the systems goal. A systems goal helps the company realize what behaviors it needs to maintain for its survival. The systems goal provides the means for the ends. It is important to recognize the importance of systems goals for day-to-day operations.

17. Control is the set of mechanisms used to keep action and/or outputs within predetermined limits. Two types of controls are often found in organizations. Output controls focus on desired targets to allow managers discretion in using different methods for reaching these targets. Process controls attempt to specify the manner in which tasks are accomplished. Policies, procedures, and rules as well as formalization and standardization can be seen as types of process controls. Total Quality Management can be seen as a systemic way of managing processes within the firm and thus be viewed as a control mechanism.

18. There are a number of ways to answer this question. Actually, a very large firm could use a simple structure but its chances of reaching its goals and surviving would be small. As the firm grows so does the complexity inside and individuals become overwhelmed if the firm does not evolve into a bureaucracy. Recall that a bureaucracy involved labor that is divided so that each worker was specialized. Every worker would have well-defined responsibilities and authorities. To complement this specialization, the organization should be arranged hierarchically. Authority should be arranged from the bottom up. A worker should be promoted

only on the basis of merit and technical competence. Most importantly, employees are to work under rules and guidelines that were impersonal and applied to all staffers equally.

19. James Thompson believed that technology could be divided into three categories—intensive, mediating, or long linked. An intensive technology occurs when uncertainty exists as to how to produce the desired outcomes. Teams of specialists are brought together to pool knowledge and resources to solve the problem. An interdependence among specialists develops because all parties need one another to fulfill the project successfully. This technology often occurs in the research and development portion of organizations. A mediating technology allows various parties to become interdependent. For example, the ATM network that most banks utilize allows customers to bank at other institutions and still be tied to their home bank, automatically. Without this technology, the banking industry would not be so well linked. The technology helps determine the nature of the banks' relationships with one another. Finally, Thompson believed that long-linked technologies had a unique effect on organizations as well. Long-linked technology is more commonly known as industrial technology. This type of knowledge allows organizations to produce goods in mass quantities. The assembly line designed by Henry Ford is one of the early examples of long-linked technology. Thompson uses these distinctions to highlight the various impacts that technology has on organizations. His approach differs greatly from Joan Woodward's approach, which focuses more on the mode of production. Woodward divides technology into three areas: small-batch manufacturing, mass production, and continuous process custom goods. Crafts persons are often characterized as small producers who must alter production to fit the needs of each client. Mass production technology deals with production of uniform goods for a mass market. The production design is altered to maximize speed while limiting product styles. The last type of technology deals with continuous-process technology. Oil refineries and chemical plants are classic examples of this type of technology. These industries are intensely automated and produce the same products without variation.

▶ Applications Essay

20. The notion that the Postal Service is a mechanistic bureaucracy is important because it suggests that there are already many controls built into the system by the division of labor. You should recognize several primary side effects that are exhibited when control mechanisms are placed on an individual in an organization such as the Postal Service. There is often a difficulty in balancing organizational controls. As one control is emphasized, others may be neglected. Controls often force managers to emphasize the "quick fix" instead of long-term planning. Often, controls lead to solutions that are not customized to specific problems (i.e., "across the board cuts"). Planning and documentation can become burdensome and limit the amount of action that actually occurs. Managers often become more concerned with internal paperwork than with problem solving or customers. And there are far too many supervisors and managers. Controls that are vaguely designed are often ineffective and unrealistic. As a result, the manager may interpret the control as he or she wants. The "do the best you can" goal that is commonly given to managers in the Postal Service is an example of this concept. Controls that are inserted drastically and harshly often cause panic among managers and administrators. A swift change in the territories of postal delivery clerks is an example. Finally, many goals and controls are inserted without the appropriate resources. This practice can make the attainment of goals difficult, if not impossible.

Notes

CHAPTER 1
ENDNOTES

[1] "Unlock the Potential in All Your People," *Bloomberg BusinessWeek* (January 28–February 3, 2013), p. 63.

[2] "The Rise of Social Business," *Wall Street Journal* (January 30, 2013), p. A14.

[3] For historical foundations see Jay A. Conger, *Winning 'Em Over: A New Model for Managing in the Age of Persuasion* (New York: Simon & Schuster, 1998), pp. 180–181; Stewart D. Friedman, Perry Christensen, and Jessica DeGroot, "Work and Life: The End of the Zero-Sum Game," *Harvard Business Review* (November/December 1998), pp. 119–129; and C. Argyris, "Empowerment: The Emperor's New Clothes," *Harvard Business Review* (May/June 1998), pp. 98–105.

[4] For a general overview see Jay W. Lorsch (ed.), *Handbook of Organizational Behavior* (Englewood Cliffs, NJ: Prentice Hall, 1987); and Julian Barling, Cary Li Cooper, and Stewart Clegg (eds.), *The Sage Handbook of Organizational Behavior*, Volumes 1 and 2 (San Francisco: Sage, 2009).

[5] Jeffrey Pfeffer and Robert I. Sutton, *Hard Facts, Dangerous Half-Truths, and Total Nonsense: Profiting from Evidence-Based Management* (Boston: Harvard Business School Press, 2006). See also Jeffrey Pfeffer and Robert I. Sutton, "Management Half-Truths and Nonsense," *California Management Review* 48.3 (2006), pp. 77–100; and Jeffrey Pfeffer and Robert I. Sutton, "Evidence-Based-Management," *Harvard Business Review* (January 2006), R0601E.

[6] Geert Hofstede, "Cultural Constraints in Management Theories," *Academy of Management Executive* 7 (1993), pp. 81–94.

[7] For a discussion of experiential learning, see D. Christopher Kayes, "Experiential Learning and Its Critics: Preserving the Role of Experience in Management Learning and Education," *Academy of Management Learning and Education* 1.2 (2002), pp. 137–149.

[8] "Leading through Connections," IBM Institute for Business Value, accessed June 5, 2013, at www-01.ibm.com/software/solutions/soa/newsletter/june12/leading_connections.html.

[9] Rajiv Dutta, "eBay's Meg Whitman on Building a Company's Culture," *Business Week* (March 27, 2009), accessed June 5, 2013, at www.businessweek.com/managing/content/mar2009/ca20090327_626373.htm.

[10] R. Roosevelt Thomas Jr., *Beyond Race and Gender* (New York: AMACOM, 1992), p. 10. See also R. Roosevelt Thomas Jr., "From 'Affirmative Action' to 'Affirming Diversity,'" *Harvard Business Review* (November/December 1990), pp. 107–117; and R. Roosevelt Thomas Jr., with Marjorie I. Woodruff, *Building a House for Diversity: A Fable About a Giraffe & an Elephant Offers New Strategies for Today's Workforce* (New York: AMACOM, 1999).

[11] A baseline report on diversity in the American workplace is *Workforce 2000: Work and Workers in the 21st Century* (Indianapolis, IN: Hudson Institute, 1987). For comprehensive discussions, see Martin M. Chemers, Stuart Oskamp, and Mark A. Costanzo, *Diversity in Organization: New Perspectives for a Changing Workplace* (Beverly Hills, CA: Sage, 1995); and Robert T. Golembiewski, *Managing Diversity in Organizations* (Tuscaloosa: University of Alabama Press, 1995).

[12] See Taylor Cox Jr., "The Multicultural Organization," *Academy of Management Executive* 5 (1991), pp. 34–47; *Cultural Diversity in Organizations: Theory, Research and Practice* (San Francisco: Berrett-Koehler, 1993).

[13] "In CEO Pay, Another Gender Gap." *BusinessWeek* (November 24, 2008), p. 22; "The View from the Kitchen Table," *Newsweek* (January 26, 2009), p. 29; Del Jones, "Women Slowly Gain on Men," *USA Today* (January 2, 2009), p. 6B; Catalyst research reports at www.catalyst.org; and "Nicking the Glass Ceiling," *BusinessWeek* (June 9, 2009), p. 18.

[14] "We're Getting Old," *Wall Street Journal* (March 26, 2009), p. D2; and Les Christie, "Hispanic Population Boom Fuels Rising U.S. Diversity," accessed June 5, 2013, at www.cnn.com/2009/US/05/14/money.census.diversity; and Betsy Towner, "The New Face of 501 America," *AARP Bulletin* (June 2009), p. 31. "Los U.S.A.: Latino Population Grows Faster, Spreads Wider," *Wall Street Journal* (March 25, 2011), p. A1; and, Laura Meckler, "Hispanic Future in the Cards," *Wall Street Journal* (December 13, 2012), p. A3. See also U.S. Census Bureau reports at www.factfinder.census.gov.

[15] Thomas and Woodruff, *Building a House for Diversity* (1999).

[16] Conor Dougherty, "Strides by Women, Still a Wage Gap," *Wall Street Journal* (March 1, 2011), p. A3; Jones, op. cit.; Catalyst research reports, op. cit.; Women in Top Jobs; Information from Del Jones, "Women Slowly Gain on Corporate America," *USA Today* (January 2, 2009), p. 6B; "Catalyst 2008 Census of the Fortune 500 Reveals Women Gained Little Ground Advancing to Business Leadership Positions," *Catalyst Press Release* (December 8, 2008).

[17] William M. Bulkeley, "Xerox Names Burns Chief as Mulcahy Retires Early," *Wall Street Journal* (May 22, 2009), pp. B1, B2.

[18] Henry Mintzberg, The Nature of Managerial Work (New York: Harper & Row, 1973). See also Henry Mintzberg, *Mintzberg on Management* (New York: Free Press, 1989); and Henry

Mintzberg, "Rounding Out the Manager's Job," *Sloan Management Review* (Fall 1994), pp. 11–26.

[19] Robert L. Katz, "Skills of an Effective Administrator, *Harvard Business Review* 52 (September/October 1974), p. 94. See also Richard E. Royatzis, *The Competent Manager: A Model for Effective Performance* (New York: Wiley, 1982).

[20] Daniel Goleman, *Emotional Intelligence* (New York: Bantam, 1995); Daniel Goleman, *Working with Emotional Intelligence* (New York: Bantam, 1998). See also Daniel Goleman, "What Makes a Leader," *Harvard Business Review* (November/December 1998), pp. 93–102; and Daniel Goleman, "Leadership That Gets Results," *Harvard Business Review* (March/April 2000), pp. 79–90, quote from p. 80.

[21] John P. Kotter, "What Effective General Managers Really Do," *Harvard Business Review* 60 (November/December 1982), p. 161.

[22] Herminia Ibarra, "Managerial Networks," Teaching Note: 9-495-039, Boston: Harvard Business School Publishing.

[23] Archie B. Carroll, "In Search of the Moral Manager," *Business Horizons* (March/April 2001), pp. 7–15.

[24] See Mahzarin R. Banagji, Max H. Bazerman, and Dolly Chugh, "How (Un)ethical Are You?" *Harvard Business Review* (December 2003), pp. 56–64.

[25] Terry Thomas, John R. Schermerhorn Jr., and John W. Dinehart, "Strategic Leadership of Ethical Behavior in Business," *Academy of Management Executive* (2004), pp. 56–66.

FEATURES AND PHOTO ESSAYS

Bringing OB to Life—Information and quotes from Sally Blount, "The Collaboration Economy," *Kellogg* (Fall, 2012), pp. 4–7; and Jacob Morgan, "The New Role of HR in Collaboration," Chess Media Group: www.slideshare.net/JacobMorgan8 (accessed: January 21, 2013). See also Jacob Morgan, *The Collaborative Organization* (New York: McGraw-Hill, 2012).

Worth Considering . . . or Best Avoided?—Information from The Undercover Economist, "Home Workers Aren't Always Shirkers," *Financial Times*, Kindle Edition (September 1, 2012); and, Nicholas Bloom, James Liang, John Roberts and Zhichun Jenny Ying, "Does Working from Home Work? Evidence from a Chinese Experiment," www.stanford.edu/~nbloom/WFH.pdf (accessed September 14, 2012).

Checking Ethics in OB—Rakesh Khuran and Nitin Noria, "It's Time to Make Management a True Profession," *Harvard Business Review* (October 2008), pp. 70–77; and, mbaoath.org.

Finding the Leader in You—Information and quotes from Joe Higgins, "Athens Business Owner Presented State Award," *Athens Messenger* (November 18, 2009), p. 3; and Samantha Pirc, "A Local Success Story: Q&A with Michelle Greenfield of Third Sun," *OHIO Today* (Fall/Winter, 2009), pp. 14, 15.

OB in Popular Culture—*John Q.* Dir. Nick Cassavetes. Perf. Denzel Washington, Robert Duvall, Gabriela Oltean, and Daniel Smith. New Line Cinema, 2002. Film.

Photo Essays—Generation F—Information from Gary Hamel, "The Facebook Generation vs. the Fortune 500," blogs.wsj.com/management/2009/03/24. *Crowdsourcing Grades*—Information and quote from Adam F. Falk, "In Defense of the Living, Breathing Professor," Wall Street Journal, Kindle Edition (August 29, 2012). *Recommended Reading*—Lynda Gratton—*The Shift: The Future of Work is Already Here* (London: Harper-Business UK, 2011).

CHAPTER 2

ENDNOTES

[1] See, for example, S. E. Jackson, K. E. May, and K. Whitney, "Understanding the Dynamics of Diversity in Decision-Making Teams, " pp. 204–261, in Richard A. Guzzo and Eduardo Salas (eds.) *Team Decision-Making Effectiveness in Organizations* (San Francisco: Jossey-Bass, 2005); Kenneth H. Price, and Myrtle P. Bell, "Beyond Relational Demography: Time and the Effects of Surface- and Deep-Level Diversity on Work Group Cohesion," *Academy of Management Journal*. 41 (1998), pp. 96–107; and Kenneth H. Price, Joanne H. Gavin, and Anna T. Florey, "Time, Teams, and Task Performance: Changing Effects of Surface- and Deep-Level Diversity on Group Functioning," *Academy of Management Journal* 45 (2002), pp. 1029–1045.

[2] Information from "Women and Work: We Did It!" *Economist* (December 31, 2009).

[3] Information from Eric Shurenberg, "Salary Gap: Men vs. Women," March 10, 2010, accessed June 10, 2013, at www.cbsnews.com/video/watch/?id=10397821n.

[4] Information from "Racism in Hiring Remains, Study Says," *The Columbus Dispatch* (January 17, 2003), p. B2.

[5] Viktor Gecas, "The Self-Concept," in *Annual Review of Sociology* 8, Ralph H. Turner and James F. Short Jr. (eds.), (Palo Alto, CA: Annual Review, 1982), p. 3. Also see Arthur P. Brief and Ramon J. Aldag, "The Self in Work Organizations: A Conceptual Review," *Academy of Management Review* (January 1981), pp. 75–88; and Jerry J. Sullivan, "Self Theories and Employee Motivation," *Journal of Management* (June 1989), pp. 345–363.

[6] Based in part on a definition in Gecas, 1982, p. 3.

[7] See N. Brody, *Personality: In Search of Individuality* (San Diego, CA: Academic Press, 1988), pp. 68–101; and C. Holden, "The Genetics of Personality," *Science* (August 7, 1987), pp. 598–601.

[8] Laura B. Shrestha and Elayne J. Heisler, *The Changing Demographic Profile of the United States*, CRS Report for Congress (Washington, DC: Congressional Research Service 7-5700, March 31, 2011); "Los USA: Latin Population Grows Faster, Spreads Wider," *Wall Street Journal* (March 25, 2011), p. A1; and, Laura Melcker, "Hispanic Future in the Cards," *Wall Street Journal* (December 13, 2012), p. A3.

[9] Rob McInnes, "Workforce Diversity: Changing the Way You Do Business," (1999), accessed June 10, 2013, at www.diversityworld.com/Diversity/workforce_diversity.htm.

[10] Ibid.

[11] See for example Judith B. Rosener, "Women Make Good Managers. So What?" *BusinessWeek* (December 11, 2000), p. 24. Also see P. E. Jacob, J. J. Flink, and H. L. Schuchman, "Values and Their Function in Decision Making," *American Behavioral Scientist* 5, suppl. 9 (1962), pp. 6–38.

[12] "Racism in Hiring Remains, Study Says," op. cit., 2003.

[13] See Lois Joy, "Advancing Women Leaders: The Connection Between Women Corporate Board Directors and Women Corporate Officers." Catalyst.org (July 15, 2008), accessed June 10,

2013, at www.catalyst.org/knowledge/advancing-women-leaders-connection-between-women-board-directors-and-women-corporate.

[14] See Lynda Gratton, Elisabeth Kelan, and Lamia Walker, "Inspiring Women: Corporate Best Practice in Europe," London: London Business School, The Lehman Brothers Centre for Women in Business (2007), accessed June 10, 2013, at http://communications.london.edu/aem/clients/LBS001/docs/lehman/May_2007_Corporate_Best_Practice.pdf.

[15] See "The Double-Bind Dilemma for Women in Leadership: Damned if You Do, Doomed if You Don't" (July 15, 2007), accessed June 10, 2013, at http://www.catalyst.org/knowledge/double-bind-dilemma-women-leadership-damned-if-you-do-doomed-if-you-dont-0.

[16] Ibid.

[17] Ibid. Also see Global Human Capital Gender Advisory Council, "The Leaking Pipeline: Where Are Our Female Leaders? 79 Women Share Their Stories," PricewaterhouseCoopers (March 2008), accessed June 10, 2013, at www.pwc.com/en_GX/gx/women-at-pwc/assets/leaking_pipeline.pdf.

[18] See "The Workplace Improves for Gay Americans," GFN News (December 17, 2007), accessed May 5, 2009 from www.gfn.com/recordDetails.php?page_id=19&section_id=22&pcontent_id=18.

[19] www.eeoc.gov/facts/fs-orientation_parent_marital_political.html.

[20] See "The Workplace Improves for Gay Americans," op. cit.

[21] "Same-Sex Marriage, Gay Rights," Polling report.com (2013), accessed June 10, 2013, at www.pollingreport.com/civil.htm.

[22] See Carol Mithers, "Workplace Wars," in *Ladies' Home Journal* (May 2009), pp. 104–109.

[23] Ibid.

[24] "The Americans with Disabilities Act," The Center for an Accessible Society (n.d.), accessed June 11, 2013, at www.accessiblesociety.org/topics/ada/index.htm.

[25] Patricia Digh, "Finding New Talent in a Tight Market," *Mosaics* 4.3 (March–April, 1998), pp. 1, 4–6.

[26] "The Americans with Disabilities Act," op. cit.

[27] www.shrm.org/.../Diversity_CLA_Definitions_of_Diversity_Inclusion.ppt.

[28] "The Americans with Disabilities Act," op. cit.

[29] See Katharine Esty, "From Diversity to Inclusion," Northeast Human Resources Association (April 30, 2007), accessed June 11, 2013, at www.boston.com/jobs/nehra/043007.shtml

[30] See Henri Tajfel and John Turner, "An Integrative Theory of Intergroup Conflict," in G. William Austin and Stephen Worchel, *The Social Psychology of Intergroup Relations*, Monterey, CA: Brooks-Cole (1979), pp. 94–109.

[31] www.catalystwomen.org/press_room/factsheets/factwoc3.htm. Accessed May 4, 2009.

[32] M. R. Barrick and M. K. Mount, "The Big Five Personality Dimensions and Job Performance: A Meta Analysis," *Personnel Psychology* 44 (1991), pp. 1–26; and M. R. Barrick and M. K. Mount, "Autonomy as a Moderator of the Relationships Between the Big Five Personality Dimensions and Job Performance," *Journal of Applied Psychology* (February 1993), pp. 111–118.

[33] "The Big Five Personality Dimensions and Job Performance: A Meta-Analysis," op. cit.

[34] Some examples of firms using the Myers-Briggs Type Indicators are given in J. M. Kunimerow and L. W. McAllister, "Team Building with the Myers-Briggs Type Indicator: Case Studies," *Journal of Psychological Type* 15 (1988), pp. 26–32; G. H. Rice Jr. and D. P. Lindecamps, "Personality Types and Business Success of Small Retailers," *Journal of Occupational Psychology* 62 (1989), pp. 177–182; and B. Roach, *Strategy Styles and Management Types: A Resource Book for Organizational Management Consultants* (Stanford, CA: Balestrand, 1989).

[35] Raymond G. Hunt, Frank J. Kryzstofiak, James R. Meindl, and Abdalla M. Yousry, "Cognitive Style and Decision Making," *Organizational Behavior and Human Decision Processes* 44.3 (1989), pp. 436–453. For additional work on problem-solving styles, see Ferdinand A. Gul, "The Joint and Moderating Role of Personality and Cognitive Style on Decision Making," *Accounting Review* (April 1984), pp. 264–277; Brian H. Kleiner, "The Interrelationship of Jungian Modes of Mental Functioning with Organizational Factors: Implications for Management Development," *Human Relations* (November 1983), pp. 997–1012; and James L. McKenney and Peter G. W. Keen, "How Managers' Minds Work," *Harvard Business Review* (May–June 1974), pp. 79–90.

[36] J. B. Rotter, "Generalized Expectancies for Internal versus External Control of Reinforcement," *Psychological Monographs* 80 (1966), pp. 1–28.

[37] See J. Michael Crant, "Proactive Behavior in Organizations," *Journal of Management* 26 (2000), pp. 435–462. See also T. S. Bateman, and J. M. Crant, "The Proactive Component of Organizational Behavior," *Journal of Organizational Behavior* 14 (1993), pp. 103–118.

[38] Don Hellriegel, John W. Slocum Jr., and Richard W. Woodman, *Organizational Behavior*, 5th ed. (St. Paul, MN: West, 1989), p. 46.

[39] Niccolo Machiavelli, *The Prince*, trans. George Bull (Middlesex, UK: Penguin, 1961).

[40] Richard Christie and Florence L. Geis, *Studies in Machiavellianism* (New York: Academic Press, 1970).

[41] See M. Snyder, *Public Appearances/Private Realities: The Psychology of Self-Monitoring* (New York: Freeman, 1987).

[42] Ibid.

[43] Adapted from R. W. Bonner, "A Short Scale: A Potential Measure of Pattern A Behavior," *Journal of Chronic Diseases* 22 (1969). Used by permission.

[44] See Meyer Friedman and Ray Roseman, *Type A Behavior and Your Heart* (New York: Knopf, 1974). For another view, see Walter Kiechel III, "Attack of the Obsessive Managers," *Fortune* (February 16, 1987), pp. 127–128.

[45] Data from Michael Mandel, "The Real Reasons You're Working So Hard," *BusinessWeek* (October 3, 2005), pp. 60–70; "Many U.S. Employees Have Negative Attitudes to Their Jobs, Employers and Top Managers," The Harris Poll #38 (May 6, 2005), accessed June 11, 2013, at www.thefreelibrary.com/PR+Newswire/2005/May/6-p51926.

[46] Arthur P. Brief, Randall S. Schuler, and Mary Van Sell, *Managing Job Stress* (Boston: Little, Brown, 1981).

⁴⁷ The classic work is Meyer Friedman and Ray Roseman, *Type A Behavior and Your Heart*, op. cit.

⁴⁸ See H. Selye, *The Stress of Life*, rev. ed. (New York: McGraw-Hill, 1976).

⁴⁹ See John D. Adams, "Health, Stress and the Manager's Life Style," *Group and Organization Studies* 6 (1981), pp. 291–301.

⁵⁰ See Susan Folkman "Personal Control and Stress and Coping Processes: A Theoretical Analysis," *Journal of Personality and Social Psychology* 46(4) (1984), p. 844.

⁵¹ See Mayo Clinic, "Stress Relief: When and How to Say No" (July 23, 2010), accessed June 11, 2013, at www.riversideonline.com/health_reference/Stress/SR00039.cfm.

⁵² See P. E. Jacob, J. J. Flink, and H. L. Schuchman, "Values and Their Function in Decision Making," *American Behavioral Scientist* 5, suppl. 9 (1962), pp. 6–38.

⁵³ See M. Rokeach and S. J. Ball Rokeach, "Stability and Change in American Value Priorities, 1968–1981," *American Psychologist* (May 1989), pp. 775–784.

⁵⁴ Milton Rokeach, *The Nature of Human Values* (New York: Free Press, 1973).

⁵⁵ Bruce M. Meglino and Elizabeth C. Ravlin, "Individual Values in Organizations: Concepts, Controversies and Research," *Journal of Management* 24 (1998), pp. 351–389.

⁵⁶ Ibid.

⁵⁷ Geert Hofstede, *Culture's Consequences: International Differences in Work-Related Values*, 2nd ed. (Beverly Hills, CA: Sage, 2001). See also Peter B. Smith and Michael Harris Bond, "Culture: The Neglected Concept," in *Social Psychology Across Cultures*, 2nd ed. (Boston: Allyn & Bacon, 1998); Michael H. Hoppe, "An Interview with Geert Hofstede," *Academy of Management Executive* 18 (2004), pp. 75–79; and Harry C. Triandis, "The Many Dimensions of Culture," *Academy of Management Executive* 18 (2004), pp. 88–93.

⁵⁸ Geert Hofstede, *Culture and Organizations: Software of the Mind* (London: McGraw-Hill, 1991).

⁵⁹ Hofstede, *Culture's Consequences*, op. cit.; Geert Hofstede and Michael H. Bond, "The Confucius Connection: From Culture Roots to Economic Growth," *Organizational Dynamics* 16 (1988), pp. 4–21.

⁶⁰ Hofstede, *Culture's Consequences*, op. cit.

⁶¹ Chinese Culture Connection, "Chinese Values and the Search for Culture-Free Dimensions of Culture," *Journal of Cross-Cultural Psychology* 18 (1987), pp. 143–164.

⁶² Hofstede and Bond, "The Confucius Connection," op. cit.; Geert Hofstede, "Cultural Constraints in Management Theories," *Academy of Management Executive* 7 (1993), pp. 81–94. For a further discussion of Asian and Confucian values, see also Jim Rohwer, *Asia Rising: Why America Will Prosper as Asia's Economies Boom* (New York: Simon & Schuster, 1995).

⁶³ For an example, see John R. Schermerhorn Jr. and Michael H. Bond, "Cross-Cultural Leadership Dynamics in Collectivism 1 High Power Distance Settings," *Leadership and Organization Development Journal* 18 (1997), pp. 187–193.

⁶⁴ Hofstede, *Culture and Organizations*, op. cit.

⁶⁵ See, for example, Edward T. Hall, *The Silent Language* (New York: Anchor Books, 1959); Fons Trompenaars, *Riding the Waves of Culture: Understanding Cultural Diversity in Business* (London: Nicholas Brealey Publishing, 1993); Steven H. Schwartz, "A Theory of Cultural Values and Some Implications for Work," *Applied Psychology: An International Review* 48 (1999), pp. 23–47; Robert J. House, Paul J. Hanges, Mansour Javidan, Peter W. Dorfman, and Vipin Gupta (eds.), *Culture, Leadership and Organizations: The GLOBE Study of 62 Societies* (Thousand Oaks, CA: Sage, 2004); and Michele J. Gelfand et al. (42 co-authors), "Differences Between Tight and Loose Cultures: A 33 Nation Study," *Science* 332 (May 2011), pp. 100–1104.

FEATURES AND PHOTO ESSAYS

Bringing OB to Life—Information and quotes from Iris Bohnet, Alexandra van Geen, and Max H. Bazerman, "When Performance Trumps Gender Bias: Joint versus Separate Evaluation," working paper 12-083 (March 16, 2012), Harvard Business School; Maggie Starvish, "Better by the Bunch: Evaluating Job Candidates in Groups," *Working Knowledge* (June 18, 2012), Harvard Business School; and Rachel Emma Silverman, "Study Suggests Fix for Gender Bias on the Job," *Wall Street Journal* (January 9, 2013), p. D4.

Worth Considering . . . or Best Avoided?—Information from Leslie Kwoh, "More Firms Bow to Generation Y's Demands," *Wall Street Journal* (August 22, 2012), Kindle Edition.

Checking Ethics in OB—Information from Victoria Knight, "Personality Tests as Hiring Tools," *Wall Street Journal* (March 15, 2006), p. B3C.

Finding the Leader in You—"Stephen Hawking: Brief Biography," www.hawking.org.uk/index.php/about-stephen/questionsandanswers.

OB in Popular Culture—Eric Ditzian, "The Social Network: The Reviews Are In!" mtv.com (October 1, 2010); and Ethan Smith, "'Social Network' Opens at No. 1," *Wall Street Journal* (October 4, 2010), p. B5.

Photo Essays—Attractiveness—"Physical Attractiveness and Careers," *The Economist, Kindle Edition* (March 30, 2012). *Vacation Habits*—Information and quotes from Peter Coy, "The Leisure Gap," *Bloomberg BusinessWeek* (July 23–29, 2012), pp. 8–9; Sue Shellenbarger, "If You Need to Work Better, Maybe Try Working Less," *Wall Street Journal* (September 23, 2009), p. D1; and Steve Stephens, "All Work and No Play a Growing Trend in the U.S.," *The Columbus Dispatch* (December 7, 2012), p. A1.

CHAPTER 3

ENDNOTES

¹ H. R. Schiffmann, *Sensation and Perception: An Integrated Approach*, 3rd ed. (New York: Wiley, 1990).

² See Georgia T. Chao and Steve W. J. Kozlowski, "Employee Perceptions on the Implementation of Robotic Manufacturing Technology," *Journal of Applied Psychology* 71 (1986), pp. 70–76; Steven F. Cronshaw and Robert G. Lord, "Effects of Categorization, Attribution, and Encoding Processes in Leadership Perceptions," *Journal of Applied Psychology* 72 (1987), pp. 97–106.

³ See Robert G. Lord, "An Information Processing Approach to Social Perceptions, Leadership, and Behavioral Measurement in Organizations," in *Research in Organizational Behavior* 7, ed. B. M. Staw and L. L. Cummings (Greenwich, CT: JAI Press, 1985),

pp. 87–128; T. K. Srull and R. S. Wyer, *Advances in Social Cognition* (Hillsdale, NJ: Erlbaum, 1988); and U. Neisser, *Cognition and Reality* (San Francisco: Freeman, 1976), p. 112.

[4] See J. G. Hunt, *Leadership: A New Synthesis* (Newbury Park, CA: Sage, 1991), ch. 7; R. G. Lord and R. J. Foti, "Schema Theories, Information Processing, and Organizational Behavior," in *Thinking Organization*, ed. H. P. Simms Jr. and D. A. Gioia (San Francisco: Jossey-Bass, 1986), pp. 20–48; and S. T. Fiske and S. E. Taylor, *Social Cognition* (Reading, MA: Addison-Wesley, 1984).

[5] See William L. Gardner and Mark J. Martinko, "Impression Management in Organizations," *Journal of Management* (June 1988), p. 332.

[6] Quotation from Sheila O'Flanagan, "Underestimate Casual Dressers at Your Peril," *Irish Times* (July 22, 2005).

[7] See B. R. Schlenker, *Impression Management: The Self-Concept, Social Identity, and Interpersonal Relations* (Monterey, CA: Brooks/Cole, 1980); W. L. Gardner and M. J. Martinko, "Impression Management in Organizations," *Journal of Management* (June 1988), p. 332; R. B. Cialdini, "Indirect Tactics of Image Management: Beyond Banking" in *Impression Management in the Organization*, ed. R. A. Giacolini and P. Rosenfeld (Hillsdale, NJ: Erlbaum, 1989), pp. 45–71; and Sandy Wayne and Robert Liden, "Effects of Impression Management on Performance Ratings," *Academy of Management Journal* 38:1 (1995), pp. 232–260.

[8] See, for example, Stephan Thernstrom and Abigail Thernstrom, *America in Black and White* (New York: Simon & Schuster, 1997); and David A. Thomas and Suzy Wetlaufer, "A Question of Color: A Debate on Race in the U.S. Workspace," *Harvard Business Review* 2 (September–October 1997), pp. 118–132.

[9] Information from "Misconceptions about Women in the Global Arena Keep Their Number Low," accessed June 24, 2013, at www.catalyst.org/media/misconceptions-about-women-global-arena-keep-their-numbers-low.

[10] These examples are from Natasha Josefowitz, *Paths to Power* (Reading, MA: Addison-Wesley, 1980), p. 60. For more on gender issues, see Gray N. Powell (ed.), *Handbook of Gender and Work* (Thousand Oaks, CA: Sage, 1999).

[11] For a recent report on age discrimination, see Joseph C. Santora and William J. Seaton, "Age Discrimination: Alive and Well in the Workplace?" *The Academy of Management Perspectives* 22 (May 2008), pp. 103–104.

[12] Survey reported in Kelly Greene, "Age Is Still More Than a Number," *Wall Street Journal* (April 10, 2003), p. D2.

[13] "Facebook Gets Down to Business," *BusinessWeek* (April 20, 2009), p. 30.

[14] Dewitt C. Dearborn and Herbert A. Simon, "Selective Perception: A Note on the Departmental Identification of Executives," *Sociometry* 21 (1958), pp. 140–144.

[15] J. Sterling Livingston, "Pygmalion in Management," *Harvard Business Review* (July–August 1969), pp. 81–89.

[16] D. Eden and A. B. Shani, "Pygmalion Goes to Boot Camp," *Journal of Applied Psychology* 67 (1982), pp. 194–199.

[17] See H. H. Kelley, "Attribution in Social Interaction," in E. Jones et al. (eds.), *Attribution: Perceiving the Causes of Behavior* (Morristown, NJ: General Learning Press, 1972).

[18] See Terence R. Mitchell, S. G. Green, and R. E. Wood, "An Attribution Model of Leadership and the Poor Performing Subordinate," in *Research in Organizational Behavior*, ed. Barry Staw and Larry L. Cummings (New York: JAI Press, 1981), pp. 197–234; and John H. Harvey and Gifford Weary, "Current Issues in Attribution Theory and Research," *Annual Review of Psychology* 35 (1984), pp. 427–459.

[19] See F. Fosterling, "Attributional Retraining: A Review," *Psychological Bulletin* (November 1985), pp. 496–512.

[20] Albert Bandura, *Social Learning Theory* (Englewood Cliffs, NJ: Prentice-Hall, 1977); and Albert Bandura, *Self-Efficacy: The Exercise of Control* (New York: W. H. Freeman, 1997).

[21] See, for example, A. M. Morrison, R. P. White, and E. Van Velsor, *Breaking the Glass Ceiling* (Reading, MA: Addison-Wesley, 1987); J. D. Zalesny and J. K. Ford, "Extending the Social Information Processing Perspective: New Links to Attitudes, Behaviors and Perceptions," *Organizational Behavior and Human Decision Processes* 47 (1990), pp. 205–246; M. E. Gist, C. Schwoerer, and B. Rosen, "Effects of Alternative Training Methods of Self-Efficacy and Performance in Computer Software Training," *Journal of Applied Psychology* 74 (1989), pp. 884–891; D. D. Sutton and R. W. Woodman, "Pygmalion Goes to Work: The Effects of Supervisor Expectations in a Retail Setting," *Journal of Applied Psychology* 74 (1989), pp. 943–950; and M. E. Gist, "The Influence of Training Method on Self-Efficacy and Idea Generation among Managers," *Personnel Psychology* 42 (1989), pp. 787–805.

[22] Bandura (1977 and 1997), op. cit.

[23] See M. E. Gist, "Self Efficacy: Implications in Organizational Behavior and Human Resource Management," *Academy of Management Review* 12 (1987), pp. 472–485; and A. Bandura, "Self-Efficacy Mechanisms in Human Agency," *American Psychologist* 37 (1987), pp. 122–147.

[24] For good overviews of reinforcement-based views, see W. E. Scott Jr. and P. M. Podsakoff, *Behavioral Principles in the Practice of Management* (New York: Wiley, 1985); and Fred Luthans and Robert Kreitner, *Organizational Behavior Modification and Beyond* (Glenview, IL: Scott Foresman, 1985).

[25] For some of B. F. Skinner's work, see *Walden Two* (New York: Macmillan, 1948); *Science and Human Behavior* (New York: Macmillan, 1953); and *Contingencies of Reinforcement* (New York: Appleton-Century-Crofts, 1969).

[26] Fred Luthans and Robert Kreitner, *Organizational Behavior Modification* (Glenview, IL: Scott Foresman, 1975); Fred Luthans and Robert Kreitner (1985), op cit.; and Fred Luthans and Alexander D. Stajkovic, "Reinforce for Performance: The Need to Go Beyond Pay and Even Rewards," *Academy of Management Executive* 13 (1999), pp. 49–57.

[27] E. L. Thorndike, *Animal Intelligence* (New York: Macmillan, 1911), p. 244.

[28] Example adapted from Luthans and Kreitner (1985), op. cit.

[29] Luthans and Kreitner (1985), op. cit.

[30] Both laws are stated in Keith L. Miller, *Principles of Everyday Behavior Analysis* (Monterey, CA: Brooks/Cole, 1975), p. 122.

[31] This example is based on a study by Barbara Price and Richard Osborn, "Shaping the Training of Skilled Workers," working paper (Detroit: Department of Management, Wayne State University, 1999).

[32] A. R. Korukonda and James G. Hunt, "Pat on the Back versus Kick in the Pants: An Application of Cognitive Inference to

the Study of Leader Reward and Punishment Behavior," *Group and Organization Studies* 14 (1989), pp. 199–234.

[33] Edwin A. Locke, "The Myths of Behavior Mod in Organizations," *Academy of Management Review* 2 (October 1977), pp. 543–553. For a counterpoint, see Jerry L. Gray, "The Myths of the Myths about Behavior Mod in Organizations: A Reply to Locke's Criticisms of Behavior Modification," *Academy of Management Review* 4 (January 1979), pp. 121–129.

[34] Robert Kreitner, "Controversy in OBM: History, Misconceptions, and Ethics," in Lee Frederiksen (ed.), *Handbook of Organizational Behavior Management* (New York: Wiley, 1982), pp. 71–91.

[35] W. E. Scott Jr. and P. M. Podsakoff, *Behavioral Principles in the Practice of Management* (New York: Wiley, 1985); also see W. Clay Hamner, "Reinforcement Theory and Contingency Management in Organizational Settings," in Richard M. Steers and Lyman W. Porters (eds.), *Motivation and Work Behavior*, 4th ed. (New York: McGraw-Hill, 1987), pp. 139–165; Luthans and Kreitner (1985), op. cit.; and Charles C. Manz and Henry P. Sims Jr., *Superleadership* (New York: Berkeley, 1990).

FEATURES AND PHOTO ESSAYS

Bringing OB to Life—Information and quote from Dan Ariely, "Coming to Grips with Chips and Dips," *Wall Street Journal* (January 19–20, 2013), p. C12.

Worth Considering . . . or Best Avoided?—Information from Joseph Schumpeter, "The mommy track," *The Economist, Kindle Edition* (August 25, 2012); Jill Parkin, "Women at Director Level Help to Make a Marque, *Financial Times,* Kindle Edition (May 22, 2012); "Gender Politics," The Economist, Kindle Edition (September 7, 2012); Joann S. Lublin, "Europe's Boards Recruit U.S. Women," *The Wall Street Journal* (September 12, 2012), p. B8; James Fontanella-Khan, "EU Scraps Board Quotas for Women," *Financial Times,* Kindle Edition (October 24, 2012); and, Jeff Green, "The Boardroom's Still the Boys' Room," *Bloomberg BusinessWeek* (October 29–November 4, 2012), pp. 25–26.

Checking Ethics in OB—Information from Deloitte LLP, "Leadership Counts: 2007 Deloitte & Touche USA Ethics & Workplace Survey Results," *Kiplinger Business Resource Center* (June 2007).

Finding the Leader in You—Information and quotes from the corporate Web sites and from The Entrepreneur's Hall of Fame, www.1tbn.com/halloffame.html; Knowledge@Wharton, "The Importance of Being Richard Branson," Wharton School Publishing (June 3, 2005), www.whartonsp.com.

OB in Popular Culture—"The Gothowitz Deviation." *The Big Bang Theory.* CBS. WBNS, Columbus, OH. 5 Oct. 2009. Television.

Photo Essay—Football Quarterbacks—Andrew M. Carton and Ashleigh Shelby Rosette, "Explaining Bias Against Black Leaders: Integrating Theory on Information Processing and Goal-Based Stereotyping," *Academy of Management Journal*, Vol. 54, No. 6 (2011), pp. 1141–1158.

CHAPTER 4

ENDNOTES

[1] These concept definitions and discussions are based in J. M. George, "Trait and State Affect," in K. R. Murphy (ed.), *Individual Differences in Behavior in Organizations,* (San Francisco: Jossey-Bass, 1996), p. 45; N. H. Frijda, "Moods, Emotion Episodes and Emotions," in M. Lewis and J. M. Haviland (eds.), *Handbook of Emotions* (New York: Guilford Press, 1993), pp. 381–403; H. M. Weiss and R. Cropanzano, "Affective Events Theory: A Theoretical Discussion of the Structure, Causes, and Consequences of Affective Experiences at Work," in B. M. Staw and L. L. Cummings (eds.), *Research in Organizational Behavior,* 18 (Greenwich, CT: JAI Press, 1996), pp. 17–19; and P. Ekman and R. J. Davidson (eds.), *The Nature of Emotions: Fundamental Questions* (Oxford, UK: Oxford University Press, 1994).

[2] For an example, see Mary Ann Hazen, "Grief and the Workplace," *Academy of Management Perspective* 22 (August 2008), pp. 78–86.

[3] J. A. Fuller, J. M. Stanton, G. G. Fisher, C. Spitzmuller, S. S. Russell, and P. C. Smith, "A Lengthy Look at the Daily Grind: Time Series Analysis of Events, Mood, Stress, and Satisfaction," *Journal of Applied Psychology* 88 (2003), pp. 1019–1033; C. J. Thoreson, S. A. Kaplan, A. P. Barsky, C. R. Warren, and K. de Chermont, "The Affective Underpinnings of Job Perceptions and Attitudes: A Meta-Analytic Review and Integration," *Psychological Bulletin* 129 (2003), pp. 914–925.

[4] Daniel Goleman, "Leadership That Gets Results," *Harvard Business Review* (March–April 2000), pp. 78–90. See also his books *Emotional Intelligence* (New York: Bantam Books, 1995) and *Working with Emotional Intelligence* (New York: Bantam Books, 1998).

[5] See Davies L. Stankow and R. D. Roberts, "Emotion and Intelligence: In Search of an Elusive Construct," *Journal of Personality and Social Psychology* 75 (1998), pp. 989–1015; and I. Greenstein, *The Presidential Difference: Leadership Style from FDR to Clinton* (Princeton, NJ: Princeton University Press, 2001); Goleman (2000), op. cit.

[6] Goleman (1998), op. cit.

[7] J. P. Tangney and K. W. Fischer (eds.), "*Self-Conscious Emotions: The Psychology of Shame, Guilt, Embarrassment and Price* (New York: Guilford Press, 1995); J. L. Tracy and R. W. Robbins, "Putting the Self into Self-Conscious Emotions: A Theoretical Model," *Psychological Inquiry* 15 (2004), pp. 103–125; D. Keltner and C. Anderson, "Saving Face for Darwin: The Functions and Uses of Embarrassment," *Current Directions in Psychological Science* 9 (2000), pp. 187–192; J. S. Beer, E. A. Heery, D. Keltner, D. Scabini, and R. T. Knight, "The Regulatory Function of Self-Conscious Emotion: Insights from Patients with Orbitofrontal Damage," *Journal of Personality and Social Psychology* 85 (2003), pp. 594–604; R. P. Vecchio, "Explorations of Employee Envy: Feeling Envious and Feeling Envied," *Cognition and Emotion* 19 (2005), pp. 69–81; and C. F. Poulson II, "Shame and Work," in N. M. Ashkanasy, W. Zerby, and C. E. J. Hartel (eds.), *Emotions in the Workplace: Research, Theory, and Practice* (Westport, CT: Quorum Books), pp. 490–541.

[8] Diane Brady, "Charm Offensive," *BusinessWeek* (June 26, 2006), pp. 76–80.

[9] Lewis and Haviland (1993), op. cit.

[10] R. E. Lucas, A. E. Clark, Y. Georgellis, and E. Deiner, "Unemployment Alters the Set Points for Life Satisfaction," *Psychological Science* 15 (2004), pp. 8–13; C. Graham, A. Eggers, and S. Sukhtaner, "Does Happiness Pay? An Exploration Based on Panel Data from Russia," *Journal of Economic Behavior and*

Organization 55 (November 2004), pp. 319–342; G. L. Clore, N. Schwartz, and M. Conway, "Affective Causes and Consequences of Social Information Processing," in R. S. Wyer Jr. and T. K. Srull (eds.), *Handbook of Social Cognition*, Vol. 1, (Hillsdale, NJ: Erlbaum, 1994), pp. 323–417; K. D. Vohs, R. F. Baumeister, and G. Lowenstein, *Do Emotions Help or Hurt Decision Making?* (New York: Russell Sage Foundation Press, 2007; H. M. Weiss, J. P. Nicholas, and C. S. Daus, "An Examination of the Joint Effects of Affective Experiences and Job Beliefs on Job Satisfaction and Variations in Affective Experiences over Time," *Organizational Behavior and Human Decision Processes* 78 (1999), pp. 1–24; and N. M. Ashkanasy, "Emotion and Performance," *Human Performance* 17 (2004), pp. 137–144.

[11] See Robert G. Lord, Richard J. Klimoski, and Ruth Knafer (eds.), *Emotions in the Workplace: Understanding the Structure and Role of Emotions in Organizational Behavior* (San Francisco: Jossey-Bass, 2002); Roy L. Payne and Cary L. Cooper (eds.), *Emotions at Work: Theory Research and Applications for Management* (Chichester, UK: John Wiley & Sons, 2004); and Daniel Goleman and Richard Boyatzis, "Social Intelligence and the Biology of Leadership," *Harvard Business Review* (September 2008), Reprint R0809E.

[12] Daniel Goleman, Richard Boyatzis, and Annie McKie, *Primal Leadership: Realizing the Power of Emotional Intelligence* (Boston: Harvard Business School Publishing, 2002); quote from "Managing the Mood Is Crucial When Times Are Tough," *Financial Times* (March 24, 2009).

[13] Joyce K. Bono and Remus Ilies, "Charisma, Positive Emotions and Mood Contagion," *Leadership Quarterly* 17 (2006), pp. 317–334; Goleman and Boyatzis (2008), op. cit.

[14] Caroline Bartel and Richard Saavedra, "The Collective Construction of Work Group Moods," *Administrative Science Quarterly* 45 (June 2000), pp. 197–231.

[15] S. M. Kruml and D. Geddes, "Catching Fire Without Burning Out: Is There an Ideal Way to Perform Emotional Labor?" in N. M. Ashkanasy, C. E. J. Hartel, and W. J. Zerby, *Emotions in the Workplace* (New York: Quorum, 2000), pp. 177–188.

[16] A. Grandey, "Emotional Regulation in the Workplace: A New Way to Conceptualize Emotional Labor," *Journal of Occupational Health Psychology* 5.1 (2000), pp. 95–110; and R. Cropanzano, D. E. Rupp, and Z. S. Byrne, "The Relationship of Emotional Exhaustion to Work Attitudes, Job Performance and Organizational Citizenship Behavior," *Journal of Applied Psychology* (2003), pp. 160–169.

[17] W. Tasi and Y. Huang, "Mechanisms Linking Employee Affective Delivery and Customer Behavioral Intentions," *Journal of Applied Psychology* 87 (2002), pp. 1001–1008.

[18] See Adam Smith, "Cognitive Empathy and Emotional Empathy in Human Behavior and Evolution," *The Psychological Record*, Vol. 56 (2006), pp. 3–21.

[19] Daniel Goleman, "Are Women More Emotionally Intelligent than Men?" accessed June 26, 2013, at www.psychologytoday.com/blog/the-brain-and-emotional-intelligence/201104/are-women-more-emotionally-intelligent-men.

[20] Shiri Cohen, Marc S. Shulz, Emily Weiss, and Robert J. Waldinger, "Eye of the Beholder: The Individual and Dyadic Contributions of Empathic Accuracy and Perceived Effort to Relationship Satisfaction," *Journal of Family Psychology* 26 (2012), pp. 236–245.

[21] Michele Williams, "Building Genuine Trust Through Interpersonal Emotion Management: A Threat Regulation Model of Trust and Collaboration across Boundaries," *Academy of Management Review* 32 (2007), pp. 595–621.

[22] Goleman (2011), op. cit.

[23] M. Eid and E. Diener, "Norms for Experiencing Emotions in Different Cultures: Inter- and Intranational Differences," *Journal of Personality and Social Psychology* 81.5 (2001), pp. 869–885.

[24] Ibid.

[25] B. Mesquita, "Emotions in Collectivist and Individualist Contexts," *Journal of Personality and Social Psychology* 80.1 (2001), pp. 68–74.

[26] D. Rubin, "Grumpy German Shoppers Distrust the Wal-Mart Style," *Seattle Times* (December 30, 2001), p. a15; and A. Rafaeli, "When Cashiers Meet Customers: An Analysis of Supermarket Cashiers," *Academy of Management Journal* (1989), pp. 245–273.

[27] H. M. Weiss and R. Cropanzano, "An Affective Events Approach to Job Satisfaction," in B. M. Staw and L. L. Cummings (eds.), *Research in Organizational Behavior*, vol. 18 (Greenwich, CT: JAI Press, 1996), pp. 1–74; and N. M. Ashkanasy and C. S. Daus, "Emotion in the Workplace: New Challenges for Managers," *Academy of Management Executive* 16 (2002), pp. 76–86.

[28] A. G. Miner and C. L. Hulin, *Affective Experience at Work: A Test of Affective Events Theory*. Poster presented at the 15th annual conference of the Society for Industrial and Organizational Psychology (2000).

[29] Information and quote from Joann S. Lublin, "How One Black Woman Lands Her Top Jobs: Risks and Networking," *Wall Street Journal* (March 4, 2003), p. B1.

[30] Compare Martin Fishbein and Icek Ajzen, *Belief, Attitude, Intention and Behavior: An Introduction to Theory and Research* (Reading, MA: Addison-Wesley, 1973).

[31] See A. W. Wicker, "Attitude Versus Action: The Relationship of Verbal and Overt Behavioral Responses to Attitude Objects," *Journal of Social Issues* (Autumn 1969), pp. 41–78.

[32] L. Festinger, *A Theory of Cognitive Dissonance* (Palo Alto, CA: Stanford University Press, 1957).

[33] See "The Things They Do for Love," *Harvard Business Review* (December 2004), pp. 19–20.

[34] See Henry Tajfel and John C. Turner, "The Social Identity Theory of Intergroup Behavior," in S. Worchel and W. Austin (eds.), *Psychology of Intergroup Relations* (Chicago: Nelson, 1986).

[35] See for example, Blake E. Ashforth, Spencer H. Harrison, and Kevin G. Corely, "Identification in Organizations: An Examination of Four Fundamental Questions," *Journal of Management* 34 (2008), pp. 325–274.

[36] Ibid.

[37] Glen E. Kreiner and Blake E. Ashforth, "Evidence Toward an Expanded Model of Organizational Identification," *Journal of Organizational Behavior* 25 (2004), pp. 1–27.

[38] Tony DiRomualdo, "The High Cost of Employee Disengagement" (2004, July 7), accessed June 26, 2013, at http://wtnnews.com/articles/983.

[39] Jeffrey Pfeffer, "Building Sustainable Organizations: The Human Factor," *Academy of Management Perspectives* 24 (2010, February), pp. 34–45.

⁴⁰ Jim Harter, "Mondays Not So 'Blue' for Engaged Employees," Gallup Wellbeing (2012, July 23), accessed June 26, 2013, at www.gallup.com/poll/155924/mondays-not-blue-engaged-employees.aspx.

⁴¹ Information from Sue Shellenbarger, "Employers Are Finding It Doesn't Cost Much to Make a Staff Happy," *Wall Street Journal* (November 19, 1977), p. B1; see also "Special Consumer Survey Report: Job Satisfaction on the Decline," *The Conference Board* (July 2002).

⁴² "Majority of American Workers Not Engaged in Their Jobs," Gallup news release (Washington, DC: October 28, 2011): gallup.com (accessed January 24, 2013); Melissa Korn, "Employed, but Not Engaged on the Job," *The Wall Street Journal* (June 11, 2013): www.wsj.com (accessed July 3, 2013).

⁴³ See, for example, Remus Ilies, Kelly Schwind Wilson, and David T. Wagner, "The Spillover of Daily Job Satisfaction onto Employees' Family Lives: The Facilitating Role of Work-Family Integration," *Academy of Management Journal* 52 (February 2009), pp. 87–102.

⁴⁴ See W. E. Wymer and J. M. Carsten, "Alternative Ways to Gather Opinions," *HR Magazine* 37.4 (April 1992), pp. 71–78.

⁴⁵ The Job Descriptive Index (JDI) is available from Dr. Patricia C. Smith, Department of Psychology, Bowling Green State University; the Minnesota Satisfaction Questionnaire (MSQ) is available from the Industrial Relations Center and Vocational Psychology Research Center, University of Minnesota.

⁴⁶ See Ibid.; Timothy A. Judge, "Promote Job Satisfaction through Mental Challenge," Chapter 6 in Edwin A. Locke (ed.), *The Blackwell Handbook of Principles of Organizational Behavior* (Malden, MA: Blackwell, 2004); "U.S. Employees More Dissatisfied with Their Jobs," *Associated Press* (February 28, 2005), www.msnbc.com; "U.S. Job Satisfaction Keeps Falling, The Conference Board Reports Today," *The Conference Board* (February 28, 2005), www.conference-board.org; and Salary.com, "Survey Shows Impact of Downturn on Job Satisfaction," *OH&S: Occupational Health and Safety* (February 7, 2009), www.ohsonline.com.

⁴⁷ Data reported in Jeannine Aversa, "Happy Workers Harder to Find," *Columbus Dispatch* (January 5, 2010), pp. A1, A4. Data from "U.S. Job Satisfaction the Lowest in Two Decades," press release, The Conference Board (January 5, 2010), accessed January 6, 2010 at www.conference-board.org.

⁴⁸ Accenture, "Despite Low Job Satisfaction, Employees Unlikely to Seek New Jobs, Accenture Research Reports, Prefer to Focus on Creating Opportunities with Current Employers" (2011, March 4), accessed June 26, 2013, at newsroom.accenture.com/article_display.cfm?article_id=5163.

⁴⁹ The Conference Board (2005), op. cit.

⁵⁰ For historical research, see B. M. Staw, "The Consequences of Turnover," *Journal of Occupational Behavior* 1 (1980), pp. 253–273; and J. P. Wanous, *Organizational Entry* (Reading, MA: Addison-Wesley, 1980).

⁵¹ C. N. Greene, "The Satisfaction-Performance Controversy," *Business Horizons* 15 (1972), pp. 31–41; M. T. Iaffaldano and P. M. Muchinsky, "Job Satisfaction and Job Performance: A Meta-Analysis," *Psychological Bulletin* 97 (1985), pp. 251–273; D. Organ, "A Reappraisal and Reinterpretation of the Satisfaction-Causes-Performance Hypothesis," *Academy of Management Review* 2 (1977), pp. 46–53; and P. Lorenzi, "A Comment on Organ's Reappraisal of the Satisfaction-Causes-Performance Hypothesis," *Academy of Management Review* 3 (1978), pp. 380–382.

⁵² Salary.com (2009), op. cit.

⁵³ Tony DiRomualdo, "The High Cost of Employee Disengagement" (July 7, 2004), www.wistechnology.com.

⁵⁴ Dennis W. Organ, *Organizational Citizenship Behavior: The Good Soldier Syndrome* (Lexington, MA: Lexington Books, 1988); and Dennis W. Organ, "Organizational Citizenship Behavior: It's Constructive Cleanup Time," *Human Performance* 10 (1997), pp. 85–97.

⁵⁵ See Mark C. Bolino and William H. Turnley, "Going the Extra Mile: Cultivating and Managing Employee Citizenship Behavior," *Academy of Management Executive* 17 (August 2003), pp. 60–67.

⁵⁶ See Venetta I. Coleman and Walter C. Borman, "Investigating the Underlying Structure of the Citizenship Performance Domain," *Human Resource Management Review* 10 (2000), pp. 115–126.

⁵⁷ Sandra L. Robinson and Rebecca J. Bennett, "A Typology of Deviant Workplace Behaviors: A Multidimensional Scaling Study," *Academy of Management Journal* 38 (1995), pp. 555–572.

⁵⁸ Reeshad S. Dalal, "A Meta-Analysis of the Relationship Among Organizational Citizenship Behavior and Counterproductive Work Behavior," *Journal of Applied Psychology* 90 (2005), pp. 1241–1255.

⁵⁹ HealthForceOntario, *Bullying in the Workplace: A Handbook for the Workplace* (Toronto: Ontario Safety Association for Community and Health Care, 2009).

⁶⁰ Timothy A. Judge and Remus Ilies, "Affect and Job Satisfaction: A Study of Their Relationship at Work and at Home," *Journal of Applied Psychology* 89 (2004), pp. 661–673.

⁶¹ Ilies et al. (2009), op. cit.

⁶² See Benjamin Schneider, Paul J. Hanges, D. Brent Smith, and Amy Salvaggio, "Which Comes First: Employee Attitudes or Organizational, Financial, and Market Performance?" *Journal of Applied Psychology* 88.5 (2003), pp. 836–851.

⁶³ L. W. Porter and E. E. Lawler III, *Managerial Attitudes and Work Performance* (Homewood, IL: Irwin, 1968).

⁶⁴ Schneider, Hanges, Smith, and Salvaggio (2003), op. cit.

⁶⁵ Ibid.

FEATURES AND PHOTO ESSAYS

Bringing OB to Life—Information from Christine Porath and Christine Pearson, "The Price of Incivility: Lack of Respect Hurts Morale and the Bottom Line," *Harvard Business Review*, Vol. 91 (January–February, 2013), pp. 114–121.

Worth Considering . . . or Best Avoided?—Information from David Gelles, "The Mind Business," *Financial Times*, U.S. Kindle Edition (August 25, 2012).

Checking Ethics in OB—Information from Joe O'Shea, "How a Facebook Update Can Cost You Your Job," *Irish Independent* (September 1, 2010), p. 34.

Finding the Leader in You—Don Thompson: Information from Julie Bennett, "McGolden Opportunity," *Franchise Times* (February, 2008), www.franchisetimes.com; www.mcdonalds.com.

OB in Popular Culture—Crash. Dir. Paul Haggis. Perf. Don Cheadle, Sandra Bullock, and Thandie Newton. Lions Gate Films, 2005. Film.

Photo Essays—Video Games—Information from Robert Lee Hotz, "When Gaming Is Good for You," *Wall Street Journal* (March 6, 2012), pp. D1, D2. *Cheating*—Pamela Engel, "Students Don't Cheat; They Collaborate?" *The Columbus Dispatch* (September 10, 2012), dispatch.com.

CHAPTER 5
ENDNOTES

[1] Adaped from Dale McConkey, "The 'Jackass Effect' in Management Compensation," *Business Horizons* 17 (June, 1974), pp. 81–91.

[2] See John P. Campbell, Marvin D. Dunnette, Edward E. Lawler III, and Karl E. Weick Jr., *Managerial Behavior Performance and Effectiveness* (New York: McGraw-Hill, 1970), ch. 15.

[3] Abraham Maslow, *Eupsychian Management* (Homewood, IL: Irwin, 1965); Abraham Maslow, *Motivation and Personality*, 2nd ed. (New York: Harper & Row, 1970).

[4] Lyman W. Porter, "Job Attitudes in Management: Perceived Importance of Needs as a Function of Job Level," *Journal of Applied Psychology* 47 (April 1963), pp. 141–148.

[5] Douglas T. Hall and Khalil E. Nougaim, "An Examination of Maslow's Need Hierarchy in an Organizational Setting," *Organizational Behavior and Human Performance* 3 (1968), pp. 12–35; and John M. Ivancevich, "Perceived Need Satisfactions of Domestic versus Overseas Managers," *Journal of Applied Psychology* 54 (August 1969), pp. 274–278.

[6] Mahmoud A. Wahba and Lawrence G. Bridwell, "Maslow Reconsidered: A Review of Research on the Need Hierarchy Theory," *Academy of Management Proceedings* (1974), pp. 514–520; and Edward E. Lawler III and J. Lloyd Shuttle, "A Causal Correlation Test of the Need Hierarchy Concept," *Organizational Behavior and Human Performance* 7 (1973), pp. 265–287.

[7] Nancy J. Adler, *International Dimensions of Organizational Behavior*, 2nd ed. (Boston: PWS-Kent, 1991), p. 153; and Richard M. Hodgetts and Fred Luthans, *International Management* (New York: McGraw-Hill, 1991), ch. 11.

[8] Clayton P. Alderfer, "An Empirical Test of a New Theory of Human Needs," *Organizational Behavior and Human Performance* 4 (1969), pp. 142–175; Clayton P. Alderfer, *Existence, Relatedness, and Growth* (New York: Free Press, 1972); and Benjamin Schneider and Clayton P. Alderfer, "Three Studies of Need Satisfaction in Organizations," *Administrative Science Quarterly* 18 (1973), pp. 489–505.

[9] Lane Tracy, "A Dynamic Living Systems Model of Work Motivation," *Systems Research* 1 (1984), pp. 191–203; and John Rauschenberger, Neal Schmidt, and John E. Hunter, "A Test of the Need Hierarchy Concept by a Markov Model of Change in Need Strength," *Administrative Science Quarterly* 25 (1980), pp. 654–670.

[10] Sources pertinent to this discussion are David C. McClelland, *The Achieving Society* (New York: Van Nostrand, 1961); David C. McClelland, "Business, Drive and National Achievement," *Harvard Business Review* 40 (July/August 1962), pp. 99–112; David C. McClelland, "That Urge to Achieve," *Think* (November/December 1966), pp. 19–32; and G. H. Litwin and R. A. Stringer, *Motivation and Organizational Climate* (Boston: Division of Research, Harvard Business School, 1966), pp. 18–25.

[11] George Harris, "To Know Why Men Do What They Do: A Conversation with David C. McClelland," *Psychology Today* 4 (January 1971), pp. 35–39.

[12] David C. McClelland and David H. Burnham, "Power Is the Great Motivator," *Harvard Business Review* 54 (March/April 1976), pp. 100–110; and David C. McClelland and Richard E. Boyatzis, "Leadership Motive Pattern and Long-Term Success in Management," *Journal of Applied Psychology* 67 (1982), pp. 737–743.

[13] The complete two-factor theory is well explained by Herzberg and his associates in Frederick Herzberg, Bernard Mausner, and Barbara Bloch Synderman, *The Motivation to Work*, 2nd ed. (New York: Wiley, 1967); and Frederick Herzberg, "One More Time: How Do You Motivate Employees?" *Harvard Business Review* 46 (January/February 1968), pp. 53–62.

[14] From Herzberg (1968), op. cit.

[15] See Robert J. House and Lawrence A. Wigdor, "Herzberg's Dual-Factor Theory of Job Satisfaction and Motivation: A Review of the Evidence and a Criticism," *Personnel Psychology* 20 (Winter 1967), pp. 369–389.

[16] Adler (1991), op. cit.; Nancy J. Adler and J. T. Graham, "Cross Cultural Interaction: The International Comparison Fallacy," *Journal of International Business Studies* (Fall 1989), pp. 515–537; and Frederick Herzberg, "Workers' Needs: The Same Around the World," *Industry Week* (September 27, 1987), pp. 29–32.

[17] Paul R. Lawrence and Nitin Nohria, *Drive: How Human Nature Shapes Our Choices* (San Francisco: Jossey-Bass, 2002); and Nitin Nohria, Bors Groysberg, and Linda-Eling Lee, "Employee Motivation: A Powerful New Model," *Harvard Business Review* (July–August, 2008), pp. 78–84.

[18] Nohria et al. (2008), op. cit.

[19] Ibid, p. 83.

[20] See, for example, J. Stacy Adams, "Toward an Understanding of Inequality," *Journal of Abnormal and Social Psychology* 67 (1963), pp. 422–436; and J. Stacy Adams, "Inequity in Social Exchange," in L. Berkowitz (ed.), *Advances in Experimental Social Psychology* 2 (New York: Academic Press, 1965), pp. 267–300.

[21] Adams (1965), op. cit.

[22] These issues are discussed in C. Kagitcibasi and J. W. Berry, "Cross-Cultural Psychology: Current Research and Trends," *Annual Review of Psychology* 40 (1989), pp. 493–531.

[23] See Blair Sheppard, Roy J. Lewicki, and John Minton, *Organizational Justice: The Search for Fairness in the Workplace* (New York: Lexington Books, 1992); Jerald Greenberg, *The Quest for Justice on the Job: Essays and Experiments* (Thousand Oaks, CA: Sage, 1995); Robert Folger and Russell Cropanzano, *Organizational Justice and Human Resource Management* (Thousand Oaks, CA: Sage, 1998); and Mary A. Konovsky, "Understanding Procedural Justice and Its Impact on Business Organizations," *Journal of Management* 26 (2000), pp. 489–511.

[24] Interactional justice is described by Robert J. Bies, "The Predicament of Injustice: The Management of Moral Outrage," in L. L. Cummings and B. M. Staw (eds.), *Research in Organizational*

Behavior 9 (Greenwich, CT: JAI Press, 1987), pp. 289–319. The example is from Carol T. Kulik and Robert L. Holbrook, "Demographics in Service Encounters: Effects of Racial and Gender Congruence on Perceived Fairness," *Social Justice Research* 13 (2000), pp. 375–402. On commutative justice see Marion Fortin and Martin Fellenz, "Hypocrisies of Fairness: Towards a More Reflexive Ethical Base in Organizational Justice Research and Practice," *Journal of Business Ethics*, vol. 78 (2008), pp. 415–433.

[25] Victor H. Vroom, *Work and Motivation* (New York: Wiley, 1964).

[26] Ibid.

[27] See Terence R. Mitchell, "Expectancy Models of Job Satisfaction, Occupational Preference and Effort: A Theoretical, Methodological, and Empirical Appraisal," *Psychological Bulletin* 81 (1974), pp. 1053–1077; Mahmoud A. Wahba and Robert J. House, "Expectancy Theory in Work and Motivation: Some Logical and Methodological Issues," *Human Relations* 27 (January 1974), pp. 121–147; Terry Connolly, "Some Conceptual and Methodological Issues in Expectancy Models of Work Performance Motivation," *Academy of Management Review* 1 (October 1976), pp. 37–47; and Terrence Mitchell, "Expectancy-Value Models in Organizational Psychology," in N. Feather (ed.), *Expectancy, Incentive and Action* (New York: Erlbaum & Associates, 1980).

[28] See Adler (1991), op. cit.

[29] Edwin A. Locke, Karyll N. Shaw, Lise M. Saari, and Gary P. Latham, "Goal Setting and Task Performance: 1969–1980," *Psychological Bulletin* 90 (July/November 1981), pp. 125–152; Edwin A. Locke and Gary P. Latham, "Work Motivation and Satisfaction: Light at the End of the Tunnel," *Psychological Science* 1.4 (July 1990), pp. 240–246; and Edwin A. Locke and Gary Latham, *A Theory of Goal-Setting and Task Performance* (Englewood Cliffs, NJ: Prentice Hall, 1990).

[30] Edwin A. Locke and Gary P. Latham, "Has Goal Setting Gone Wild, or Have Its Attackers Abandoned Good Scholarship?" *The Academy of Management Perspective* 23 (February 2009), pp. 17–23.

[31] For recent debate on goal setting, see Lisa D. Ordóñez, Maurice E. Schwitzer, Adam D. Galinsky, and Max H. Bazerman, "Goals Gone Wild: The Systematic Side Effects of Overprescribing Goal Setting," *The Academy of Management Perspective* 23 (February 2009), pp. 6–16; Locke and Latham (2009), op. cit.

[32] Ibid.

[33] For a good review of MBO, see Anthony P. Raia, *Managing by Objectives* (Glenview, IL: Scott Foresman, 1974).

[34] Ibid. Steven Kerr summarizes the criticisms well in "Overcoming the Dysfunctions of MBO," *Management by Objectives* 5.1 (1976).

FEATURES AND PHOTO ESSAYS

Bringing OB to Life—Information from Lauren Weber, "Go Ahead, Hit the Snooze Button," *Wall Street Journal* (January 23, 2013), pp. B1, B8.

Worth Considering . . . or Best Avoided?—Information from Henry Blodgett, "Whole Foods CEO: Here's Why We Pay Our Employees More than We Have To," *The Daily Ticker*, Yahoo! Finance: yahoo.com/finance (September 14, 2012).

Checking Ethics in OB—Information on this situation from Jared Sandberg, "Why You May Regret Looking at Papers Left on the Office Copier," *Wall Street Journal* (June 20, 2006), p. B1.

Finding the Leader in You—Information and quotes from Lorraine Monroe, "Leadership Is About Making Vision Happen—What I Call 'Vision Acts,'" *Fast Company* (March 2001), p. 98; See also Lorraine Monroe, *Nothing's Impossible: Leadership Lessons from Inside and Outside The Classroom* (New York: PublicAffairs Books, 1999) and *The Monroe Doctrine: An ABC Guide to What Great Bosses Do* (New York: PublicAffairs Books, 2003).

OB in Popular Culture—Ally Bank. "Would you like a pony?" Advertisement. May 2009. Television.

Photo Essays—Something to Read—Drive: The Surprising Truth About What Motivates Us—Daniel Pink, *Drive: The Surprising Truth about What Motivates Us* (New York: Riverhead Trade, 2011).

CHAPTER 6

ENDNOTES

[1] For a good overview see Adrienne Fox, "Make a 'Deal,'" *HR Magazine* (January, 2012), pp. 37–42.

[2] Information from Adam Lashinsky, "Zappos: Life After Acquisition," tech.fortune.cnn.com (November 24, 2010); and Nicholas Boothman, "Will You Be My Friend?" *Bloomberg-BusinessWeek* (January 7–January 13, 2013), pp. 63–65.

[3] Steve Hamm, "A Passion for the Plan," *BusinessWeek* (August 21, 2B 2006), pp. 92–94. See also Yvon Chouinard, *Let My People Go Surfing: The Education of a Reluctant Businessman* (New York: Penguin, 2006).

[4] For complete reviews of theory, research, and practice see Edward E. Lawler III, *Pay and Organizational Effectiveness* (New York: McGraw-Hill, 1971); Edward E. Lawler III, *Pay and Organizational Development* (Reading, MA: Addison-Wesley, 1981); and Edward E. Lawler III, "The Design of Effective Reward Systems," in Jay W. Lorsch (ed.), *Handbook of Organizational Behavior* (Englewood Cliffs, NJ: Prentice-Hall, 1987), pp. 255–271.

[5] "Reasons for Pay Raises," *BusinessWeek* (May 29, 2006), p. 11.

[6] As an example, see D. B. Balkin and L. R. Gómez-Mejia (eds.), *New Perspectives on Compensation* (Englewood Cliffs, NJ: Prentice-Hall, 1987).

[7] Erin White, "How to Reduce Turnover," *Wall Street Journal* (November 21, 2005), p. B5.

[8] S. E. Markham, K. D. Scott, and B. L. Little, "National Gainsharing Study: The Importance of Industry Differences," *Compensation and Benefits Review* (January/February 1992), pp. 34–45.

[9] See Brian Graham-Moore, "Review of the Literature," in Brian Graham-Moore and Timothy L. Ross (eds.), *Gainsharing* (Washington, DC: Bureau of National Affairs, 1990), p. 20.

[10] Jeffrey Pfeffer and John F. Veiga, "Putting People First for Organizational Success," *Academy of Management Executive* 13 (May 1999), pp. 37–48.

[11] L. R. Gómez-Mejia, D. B. Balkin, and R. L. Cardy, *Managing Human Resources* (Englewood Cliffs, NJ: Prentice-Hall, 1995), pp. 410–411.

[12] N. Gupta, G. E. Ledford, G. D. Jenkins, and D. H. Doty, "Survey Based Prescriptions for Skill-Based Pay," *American Compensation Association Journal* 1.1 (1992), pp. 48–59; and L. W. Ledford, "The Effectiveness of Skill-Based Pay," *Perspectives in Total Compensation* 1.1 (1991), pp. 1–4.

¹³ Mina Kines, "P&G's Leadership Machine," *Fortune* (April 14, 2009).

¹⁴ For discussion of many of these errors, see David L. Devries, Ann M. Morrison, Sandra L. Shullman, and Michael P. Gerlach, *Performance Appraisal on the Line* (Greensboro, NC: Center for Creative Leadership, 1986), ch. 3.

¹⁵ For more details, see G. P. Latham and K. N. Wexley, *Increasing Productivity through Performance Appraisal* (2nd ed.); and Stephen J. Carroll and Craig E. Schneier, *Performance Appraisal and Review Systems* (Glenview, IL: Scott Foresman, 1982).

¹⁶ See George T. Milkovich and John W. Boudreau, *Personnel/Human Resource Management: A Diagnostic Approach*, 5th ed. (Plano, TX: Business Publications, 1988).

¹⁷ Examples are from Jena McGregor, "Job Review in 140 Keystrokes," *Business Week* (March 23 and 30, 2009), p. 58.

¹⁸ For an overall discussion see Greg R. Oldham and J. Richard Hackman, "Not What It Was and Not What It Will Be: The Future of Job Design Research," *Journal of Organizational Behavior* 31 (2010), pp. 463–479.

¹⁹ Frederick W. Taylor, *The Principles of Scientific Management* (New York: Norton, 1967).

²⁰ Frederick Herzberg, "One More Time: How Do You Motivate Employees?" *Harvard Business Review* 46 (January/February 1968), pp. 53–62.

²¹ For a complete description, see J. Richard Hackman and Greg R. Oldham, *Work Redesign* (Reading, MA: Addison-Wesley, 1980).

²² See J. Richard Hackman and Greg Oldham, "Development of the Job Diagnostic Survey," *Journal of Applied Psychology* 60 (1975), pp. 159–170.

²³ See, for example, Kenneth D. Thomas and Betty A. Velthouse, "Cognitive Elements of Empowerment: An 'Interpretive' Model of Intrinsic Task Motivation," *Academy of Management Review*, 15.4 (1990), pp. 666–681.

²⁴ For forerunner research, see Charles L. Hulin and Milton R. Blood, "Job Enlargement, Individual Differences, and Worker Responses," *Psychological Bulletin* 69 (1968), pp. 41–55; and Milton R. Blood and Charles L. Hulin, "Alienation, Environmental Characteristics and Worker Responses," *Journal of Applied Psychology* 51 (1967), pp. 284–290.

²⁵ Gerald Salancik and Jeffrey Pfeffer, "An Examination of Need-Satisfaction Models of Job Attitudes," *Administrative Science Quarterly* 22 (1977), pp. 427–456; Gerald Salancik and Jeffrey Pfeffer, "A Social Information Processing Approach to Job Attitude and Task Design," *Administrative Science Quarterly* 23 (1978), pp. 224–253.

²⁶ For overviews, see Allan R. Cohen and Herman Gadon, *Alternative Work Schedules: Integrating Individual and Organizational Needs* (Reading, MA: Addison-Wesley, 1978); and Jon L. Pearce, John W. Newstrom, Randall B. Dunham, and Alison E. Barber, *Alternative Work Schedules* (Boston: Allyn & Bacon, 1989). See also Sharon Parker and Toby Wall, *Job and Work Design* (Thousand Oaks, CA: Sage, 1998).

²⁷ Data reported in "A Saner Workplace," *BusinessWeek* (June 1, 2009), pp. 66–69, and based on excerpt from Claire Shipman and Katty Kay, *Womenomics: Write Your Own Rules for Success* (New York: Harper Business, 2009); and "A to Z of Generation Y Attitudes," *Financial Times* (June 18, 2009).

²⁸ See Sue Shellenbarger, "What Makes a Company a Great Place to Work," *Wall Street Journal* (October 4, 2007), p. D1.

²⁹ Olga Kharif, "Chopping Hours, Not Heads," *BusinessWeek* (January 5, 2009), p. 85.

³⁰ See Wayne F. Cascio, "Managing a Virtual Workplace," *Academy of Management Executive* 14 (2000), pp. 81–90.

³¹ Claire Suddath, "Work-from-Home Truths, Half-Truths, and Myths," *BloombergBusinessWeek* (March 4–March 10, 2013), p. 75.

³² Quote from Phil Porter, "Telecommuting Mom Is Part of a National Trend," *Columbus Dispatch* (November 29, 2000), pp. H1, H2.

³³ Ibid.

³⁴ *Times*, opinionator.blogs.nytimes.com (January 26, 2013): (accessed August 8, 2013).

³⁵ Heesun Wee, "Why More Millennials Go Part Time for Full Time Pay" (October 1, 2013), accessed June 29, 2013, at www.cnbc.com/id/49181054.

FEATURES AND PHOTO ESSAYS

Worth Considering . . . or Best Avoided?—Information from Reed Hastings, "How to Set Your Employees Free," *BloombergBusinessWeek* (April 12, 2012); and, Leslie Kwoh, "Go Ahead and Take Off, for as Long as You Like," *Wall Street Journal* (October 29, 2012), p. B7.

Checking Ethics in OB—Information from Reuters, "Coming to Work Sick Affects Biz," *Economic Times Bangalore* (January 28, 2007), p. 14; www.webmd.com.

Finding the Leader in You—Information from Andrew Ward, "Spanx Queen Firms Up the Bottom Line," *Financial Times* (November 30, 2006), p. 7; and Simona Covel, "A Dated Industry Gets a Modern Makeover," *Wall Street Journal* (August 7, 2008), p. B9.

OB in Popular Culture—Information and quotes from Manohla Dargis, "Orphan's Lifeline Out of Hell Could Be a Game Show in Mumbai," *New York Times* (November 12, 2008): movies.nytimes.com; and James Christopher, "Slumdog Millionaire," *The Times* (January 8, 2009): entertainment.timesonline.co.uk.

Photo Essays—Bosses—Information from Leslie Kwoh, "Difficult Bosses Hurt Workers' Motivation," *Wall Street Journal* (February 29, 2012), p. B8. *Job Satisfaction*—Information from PewResearch, "Take This Job and Love It," pewresearch.org/databank (accessed October 2, 2012). *Luck and Hard Work*—Information from Lauren Weber, "Luck Is Hard Work," *Wall Street Journal* (March 14, 2012), p. B8.

CHAPTER 7

ENDNOTES

¹ Information from Scott Thurm, "Teamwork Raises Everyone's Game," *Wall Street Journal* (November 7, 2005), p. B7.

² Ibid.

³ See, for example, Jon R. Katzenbach and Douglas K. Smith, "The Discipline of Teams," *Harvard Business Review* (March/April 1993a), pp. 111–120; and Jon R. Katzenbach and Douglas K. Smith, *The Wisdom of Teams: Creating the High-Performance Organization* (Boston: Harvard Business School Press, 1993b).

[4] For a good overview, see Greg L. Stewart, Charles C. Manz, and Henry P. Sims, *Team Work and Group Dynamics* (New York: Wiley, 1999).

[5] Katzenbach and Smith (1993a, 1993b), op. cit.

[6] Katzenbach and Smith (1993a), op. cit., p. 112.

[7] Katzenbach and Smith (1993a, 1993b), op. cit.

[8] See Jon R. Katzenbach, "The Myth of the Top Management Team," *Harvard Business Review* 75 (November/December 1997), pp. 83–91.

[9] See Stewart, Manz, and Sims (1999), pp. 43–44.

[10] Rensis Likert, *New Patterns of Management* (New York: McGraw-Hill, 1961).

[11] See Jay R. Galbraith, *Designing Organizations* (San Francisco: Jossey-Bass, 1998).

[12] Robert P. Steel, Anthony J. Mento, Benjamin L. Dilla, Nestor Ovalle, and Russell F. Lloyd, "Factors Influencing the Success and Failure of Two Quality Circles Programs," *Journal of Management* 11.1 (1985), pp. 99–119; and Edward E. Lawler III and Susan A. Mohrman, "Quality Circles: After the Honeymoon," *Organizational Dynamics* 15.4 (1987), pp. 42–54.

[13] See, for example, Paul S. Goodman, Rukmini Devadas, and Terri L. Griffith Hughson, "Groups and Productivity: Analyzing the Effectiveness of Self-Managing Teams," ch. 11, in John R. Campbell and Richard J. Campbell (eds.), *Productivity in Organizations* (San Francisco: Jossey-Bass, 1988); Jack Orsrbrun, Linda Moran, Ed Musslewhite, and John H. Zenger, with Craig Perrin, *Self-Directed Work Teams: The New American Challenge* (Homewood, IL: Business One Irwin, 1990); and Dale E. Yeatts and Cloyd Hyten, *High Performing Self-Managed Work Teams* (Thousand Oaks, CA: Sage, 1997).

[14] See D. Duarte and N. Snyder, *Mastering Virtual Teams: Strategies, Tools, and Techniques that Succeed* (San Francisco: Jossey-Bass, 1999); and Jessica Lipnack and Jeffrey Stamps, *Virtual Teams: Reaching Across Space, Time, and Organizations with Technology* (New York: Wiley, 1997).

[15] For reviews see Wayne F. Cascio, "Managing a Virtual Workplace," *Academy of Management Executive* 14 (2000), pp. 81–90; and Sheila Simsarian Webber, "Virtual Teams: A Meta-Analysis" (2002), paper presented at the Academy of Management Conference, Denver, CO.

[16] Stacie A. Furst, Martha Reeves, Benson Rosen, and Richard S. Blackburn, "Managing the Life Cycle of Virtual Teams," *Academy of Management Executive* 18.2 (2004), pp. 6–11; Ibid.; Duarte and Schneider (1999), op. cit.; Lipnack and Stamps (1997), op. cit.; and J. Richard Hackman by Diane Coutu, "Why Teams Don't Work," *Harvard Business Review* (May 2009), pp. 99–105.

[17] See, for example, J. Richard Hackman and Nancy Katz, "Group Behavior and Performance," ch. 32, pp. 1208–1251, in Susan T. Fiske, Daniel T. Gilbert, and Gardner Lindzey (eds.), *Handbook of Social Psychology*, 5th ed. (Hoboken, NJ: Wiley, 2010).

[18] Marvin E. Shaw, *Group Dynamics: The Psychology of Small Group Behavior*, 2nd ed. (New York: McGraw-Hill, 1976).

[19] Bib Latané, Kipling Williams, and Stephen Harkins, "Many Hands Make Light the Work: The Causes and Consequences of Social Loafing," *Journal of Personality and Social Psychology* 37 (1978), pp. 822–832; E. Weklon and G. M. Gargano, "Cognitive Effort in Additive Task Groups: The Effects of Shared Responsibility on the Quality of Multi-Attribute Judgments," *Organizational Behavior and Human Decision Processes* 36 (1985), pp. 348–361; John M. George, "Extrinsic and Intrinsic Origins of Perceived Social Loafing in Organizations," *Academy of Management Journal* (March 1992), pp. 191–202; and W. Jack Duncan, "Why Some People Loaf in Groups While Others Loaf Alone," *Academy of Management Executive* 8 (1994), pp. 79–80.

[20] D. A. Kravitz and B. Martin, "Ringelmann Rediscovered," *Journal of Personality and Social Psychology* 50 (1986), pp. 936–941.

[21] John M. George (1992), op. cit.; and W. Jack Duncan (1994), op. cit.

[22] A classic article by Richard B. Zajonc, "Social Facilitation," *Science* 149 (1965), pp. 269–274.

[23] See, for example, Leland P. Bradford, *Group Development*, 2nd ed. (San Francisco: Jossey-Bass, 1997).

[24] J. Steven Heinen and Eugene Jacobson, "A Model of Task Group Development in Complex Organizations and a Strategy of Implementation," *Academy of Management Review* 1 (October 1976), pp. 98–111; Bruce W. Tuckman, "Developmental Sequence in Small Groups," *Psychological Bulletin* 63 (1965), pp. 384–399; and Bruce W. Tuckman and Mary Ann C. Jensen, "Stages of Small Group Development Revisited," *Group & Organization Studies* 2 (1977), pp. 419–427.

[25] Quote from Alex Markels, "Money & Business," usnews.com (October 22, 2006).

[26] Ibid.

[27] Example from Jessica Sung, "Designed for Interaction," *Fortune* (January 8, 2001), p. 150.

[28] David M. Herold, "The Effectiveness of Work Groups," in Steven Kerr (ed.), *Organizational Behavior* (New York: Wiley, 1979), p. 95. See also the discussion of group tasks in Stewart, Manz, and Sims (1999), op. cit., pp. 142–143.

[29] F. J. Thomas and C. F. Fink, "Effects of Group Size," in Larry L. Cummings and William E. Scott (eds.), *Readings in Organizational and Human Performance* (Homewood, IL: Irwin, 1969), pp. 394–408.

[30] Thomas and Fink (1969), op. cit.

[31] Robert D. Hof, "Amazon's Risky Bet," *BusinessWeek* (November 13, 2006), p. 52.

[32] Shaw (1976), op. cit.

[33] William C. Schultz, *FIRO: A Three-Dimensional Theory of Interpersonal Behavior* (New York: Rinehart, 1958).

[34] William C. Schultz, "The Interpersonal Underworld," *Harvard Business Review* 36 (July/August 1958), p. 130.

[35] See Daniel, R. Ilgen, Jeffrey A. LePiner, and John R. Hollenbeck, "Effective Decision Making in Multinational Teams," in P. Christopher Earley and Miriam Erez (eds.), *New Perspectives on International Industrial/Organizational Psychology* (San Francisco: New Lexington Press, 1997), pp. 377–409.

[36] Matt Golosinski, "Teamwork Takes Center Stage," *Northwestern* (Winter 2005), p. 39.

[37] Ilgen, LePine, and Hollenbeck (1997), op. cit.; and Warren Watson, "Cultural Diversity's Impact on Interaction Process and Performance," *Academy of Management Journal* 16 (1993).

[38] L. Argote and J. E. McGrath, "Group Processes in Organizations: Continuity and Change," in C. L. Cooper and I. T. Robertson (eds.), *International Review of Industrial and Organizational Psychology* (New York: Wiley, 1993), pp. 333–389.

[39] See Ilgen, LePiner, and Hollenbeck (1997), op. cit.

[40] Golosinski (2005), op. cit., p. 39.

[41] "Dream Teams," *Northwestern* (Winter 2005), p. 10; and Golosinski (2005), op. cit.

[42] Anita Williams Woolley, Christopher F. Chabris, Alex Pentland, Nada Hasmi, and Thomas W. Malone, "Evidence for a Collective Intelligence Factor in the Performance of Human Groups," *Science* 330 (October 29, 2010), pp. 686–688.

FEATURES AND PHOTO ESSAYS

Bringing OB to Life—Information from "Do Headphones in the Office Suggest I Lack Team Spirit," *Financial Times*, Kindle Edition (January 16, 2013).

Worth Considering . . . or Best Avoided?—Information from Mark Milian, "It's Not You, It's Meetings," *BloombergBusinessWeek* (June 11–17, 2012), pp. 51–52.

Checking Ethics in OB—Information from "MBAs 'Cheat Most,'" *Financial Times* (September 21, 2006), p. 1; "The Devil Made Me Do It," *BusinessWeek* (July 24, 2006), p. 10; Karen Richardson, "Buffett Advises on Scandals: Avoid Temptations," *Wall Street Journal* (October 10, 2006), p. A9; Alma Acevedo, "Of Fallacies and Curricula: A Case of Business Ethics," *Teaching Business Ethics* 5 (2001), pp. 157–170.

Finding the Leader in You—Information and quotes from Allen St. John, "Racing's Fastest Pit Crew," *Wall Street Journal* (May 9, 2008), p. W4; see also "High-Octane Business Training," *BizEd* (July/August 2008), p. 72.

OB in Popular Culture—"Season 10." *Survivor*. CBS. WBNS, Columbus, OH. 2005. Television.

Photo Essays—Worker Cooperatives—April Dembosky, "When the Workers Run the Show," *Financial Times, Kindle Edition* (August 28, 2012). *Officeless Companies*—Rachel Emma Silverman, "Step Into the Office-Less Company, *Wall Street Journal*, Kindle Edition (September 5, 2012).

CHAPTER 8

ENDNOTES

[1] See Owen Linzmeyer and Owen W. Linzmeyer, *Apple Confidential 2.0: The Definitive History of the World's Most Colorful Company* (San Francisco: No Starch Press, 2004); and Jeffrey L. Cruikshank, *The Apple Way* (New York: McGraw-Hill, 2005).

[2] Diane Coutu, "Why Teams Don't Work," *Harvard Business Review* (May 2009), pp. 99–105.

[3] Ibid.

[4] Steven Levy, "Insanely Great," *Wired* (February 1994), accessed July 1, 2013, at www.wired.com/wired/archive/2.02/macintosh_pr.html.

[5] Ibid.

[6] Anita Williams Woolley, Christopher F. Chabris, Alex Pentland, Nada Hasmi, and Thomas W. Malone, "Evidence for a Collective Intelligence Factor in the Performance of Human Groups," *Science* 330 (October) 29, 2010), pp. 686–688.

[7] For an interesting discussion of sports teams, see Ellen Fagenson-Eland, "The National Football League's Bill Parcells on Winning, Leading, and Turning around Teams," *Academy of Management Executive* 15 (August 2001), pp. 48–57; and Nancy Katz, "Sport Teams as a Model for Workplace Teams: Lessons and Liabilities," *Academy of Management Executive* 15 (August 2002), pp. 56–69.

[8] See William D. Dyer, *Team Building*, 3rd ed. (Reading, MA: Addison-Wesley, 1995).

[9] Dennis Berman, "Zap! Pow! Splat!" *BusinessWeek*, Enterprise Issue (February 9, 1998), p. ENT22.

[10] The classic work in this area is George Homans, *The Human Group* (New York: Harcourt Brace, 1950).

[11] Developed from a discussion by Edgar H. Schein, *Process Consultation* (Reading, MA: Addison-Wesley, 1969), pp. 32–37; and Edgar H. Schein, *Process Consultation*, Vol. 1 (Reading, MA: Addison-Wesley, 1988), pp. 40–49.

[12] The classic work is Robert F. Bales, "Task Roles and Social Roles in Problem-Solving Groups," in Eleanor E. Maccoby, Theodore M. Newcomb, and E. L. Hartley (eds.), *Readings in Social Psychology* (New York: Holt, Rinehart & Winston, 1958).

[13] For a good description of task and maintenance functions, see John J. Gabarro and Anne Harlan, "Note on Process Observation," Note 9-477-029 (Harvard Business School, 1976).

[14] Christine Porath and Christine Pearson, "How Toxic Colleagues Corrode Performance," *Harvard Business Review* (April 2009), p. 24.

[15] See Daniel C. Feldman, "The Development and Enforcement of Group Norms," *Academy of Management Review* 9 (1984), pp. 47–53.

[16] See Robert F. Allen and Saul Pilnick, "Confronting the Shadow Organization: How to Select and Defeat Negative Norms," *Organizational Dynamics* (Spring 1973), pp. 13–17; and Alvin Zander, *Making Groups Effective* (San Francisco: Jossey-Bass, 1982), ch. 4; Feldman (1984), op. cit.

[17] For a summary of research on group cohesiveness, see Marvin E. Shaw, *Group Dynamics* (New York: McGraw-Hill, 1971), pp. 110–112, 192.

[18] See Jay R. Galbraith, *Designing Organizations* (San Francisco: Jossey-Bass, 1998).

[19] Jerry Yoram Wind and Jeremy Main, *Driving Change: How the Best Companies Are Preparing for the 21st Century* (New York: Free Press, 1998), p. 135.

[20] The concept of interacting, coaching, and counteracting groups is presented in Fred E. Fiedler, *A Theory of Leadership Productivity* (New York: McGraw-Hill, 1967).

[21] Research on communication networks is found in Alex Bavelas, "Communication Patterns in Task-Oriented Groups," *Journal of the Acoustical Society of America* 22 (1950), pp. 725–730. See also "Research on Communication Networks," as summarized in Shaw (1971), op. cit., pp. 137–153.

[22] A classic work on proxemics is Edward T. Hall's book, *The Hidden Dimension* (Garden City, NY: Doubleday, 1986).

[23] Mirand Wewll, "Alternative Spaces Spawning Desk-Free Zones," *Columbus Dispatch* (May 18, 1998), pp. 10–11.

[24] "Tread: Rethinking the Workplace," *BusinessWeek* (September 25, 2006), p. IN.

25 Michelle Conlin and Douglas MacMillan, "Managing the Tweets," *BusinessWeek* (June 1, 2009), pp. 20–21.

26 See Wayne F. Cascio, "Managing a Virtual Workplace," *Academy of Management Executive* 14 (2000), pp. 81–90; Sheila Simsarian Webber, "Virtual Teams: A Meta-Analysis," www.shrm.org/foundation/findings.asp; and Stacie A. Furst, Martha Reeves, Benson Rosen, and Richard S. Blackburn, "Managing the Life Cycle of Virtual Teams," *Academy of Management Executive* 18 (2004), pp. 6–20.

27 The discussion is developed from Schein (1988), op. cit., pp. 69–75.

28 Developed from guidelines presented in the classic article by Jay Hall, "Decisions, Decisions, Decisions," *Psychology Today* (November 1971), pp. 55–56.

29 Norman R. F. Maier, "Assets and Liabilities in Group Problem Solving," *Psychological Review* 74 (1967), pp. 239–249.

30 Irving L. Janis, "Groupthink," *Psychology Today* (November 1971), pp. 33–36; and Irving L. Janis. *Groupthink*, 2nd ed. (Boston: Houghton Mifflin, 1982). See also J. Longley and D. G. Pruitt, "Groupthink: A Critique of Janis' Theory," in L. Wheeler (ed.), *Review of Personality and Social Psychology* (Beverly Hills, CA: Sage, 1980); and Carrie R. Leana, "A Partial Test of Janis's Groupthink Model: The Effects of Group Cohesiveness and Leader Behavior on Decision Processes," *Journal of Management* 1.1 (1985), pp. 5–18. See also Jerry Harvey, "Managing Agreement in Organizations: The Abilene Paradox," *Organizational Dynamics* (Summer 1974), pp. 63–80.

31 See Janis (1971, 1982), op. cit.

32 Gayle W. Hill, "Group versus Individual Performance: Are Two Leads Better Than One?" *Psychological Bulletin* 91 (1982), pp. 517–539.

33 These techniques are well described in George P. Huber, *Managerial Decision Making* (Glenview, IL: Scott, Foresman, 1980); Andre L. Delbecq, Andrew L. Van de Ven, and David H. Gustafson, *Group Techniques for Program Planning: A Guide to Nominal Groups and Delphi Techniques* (Glenview, IL: Scott, Foresman. 1975); and William M. Fox, "Anonymity and Other Keys to a Successful Problem-Solving Meeting," *National Productivity Review* 8 (Spring 1989), pp. 145–156.

34 Anne Stein, "On Track," *Kellogg* (Winter, 2012), pp. 14–27. See also Leigh Thompson, *The Creative Conspiracy: The New Rules of Breakthrough Collaboration* (Cambridge, MA: Harvard Business Review Press, 2013).

35 Delbecq et al. (1975), op. cit.

FEATURES AND PHOTO ESSAYS

Bringing OB to Life—Information from Claire Suddath, "Inside the Elephant Room," *BloombergBusinessWeek* (December 10–December 16, 2012), pp. 83–85.

Worth Considering . . . or Best Avoided?—Information and quotes from Rachel Emma Silverman, "My Colleague, My Paymaster," *Wall Street Journal* (April 3, 2012): wsj.com (accessed April 3, 2012).

Checking Ethics in OB—Information from Ken Gordon, "Tressel's Way Transforms OSU into 'Model Program,'" *Columbus Dispatch* (January 5, 2007), pp. A1, A4.

Finding the Leader in You—Information and quotes from Robert D. Hof, "Amazon's Risky Bet," *Business Week* (November 13, 2006), p. 52; Jon Neale, "Jeff Bezos," *BusinessWings* (February 16, 2007): www.businesswings.com.uk; Alan Deutschman, "Inside the Mind of Jeff Bezos," *Fast Company* (December 19, 2007); www.fastcompany.com/magazine/85; and http://en.wikipedia.org/wiki/Jeff_Bezos.

OB in Popular Culture—Madagascar. Dir. Eric Darnell and Tom McGrath. Perf. Chris Rock, Ben Stiller, David Schwimmer. Dreamworks, 2005. Film.

Photo Essays—Boot Camp—Information from "Boot Camps for Start-ups," *Financial Times*, Kindle Edition (September 7, 2012). *Stand Up Meetings*—Information and quote from Rachael Emma Silverman, "No More Angling for the Best Seat: More Meetings Are Stand-Up Jobs," *Wall Street Journal* (February 2, 2012), pp. A9, A10.

CHAPTER 9

ENDNOTES

1 "Skills Stakeholders Want," *Biz-Ed* (May/June 2009), p. 11.

2 For concise overviews, see Susan J. Miller, David J. Hickson, and David C. Wilson, "Decision-Making in Organizations" in Steward R. Clegg, Cynthia Hardy, and Walter Nord (eds.), *Handbook of Organizational Studies* (London: Sage, 1996); and George P. Huber, *Managerial Decision Making* (Glenview, IL: Scott Foresman, 1980), pp. 293–312.

3 This figure and the related discussion are developed from conversations with Dr. Alma Acevedo of the University of Puerto Rico at Rio Piedras and from her articles "Of Fallacies and Curricula: A Case of Business Ethics," *Teaching Business Ethics* 5 (2001), pp. 157–170, and "Business Ethics: An Introduction," working paper (2009).

4 Acevedo (2009), op. cit.

5 Stephen Fineman, "Emotion and Organizing," in Clegg, Hardy, and Nord (eds.) (1996) op. cit., pp. 542–580.

6 For discussion of ethical frameworks for decision making, see Joseph R. Desjardins, *Business, Ethics and the Environment* (Upper Saddle River, NJ: Pearson Education, 2007); Linda A. Trevino and Katherine A. Nelson, *Managing Business Ethics* (New York: Wiley, 1995); Saul W. Gellerman, "Why 'Good' Managers Make Bad Ethical Choices," *Harvard Business Review* 64 (July/August 1986), pp. 85–90; and Barbara Ley Toffler, *Tough Choices: Managers Talk Ethics* (New York: Wiley, 1986).

7 Based on Gerald F. Cavanagh, *American Business Values*, 4th ed. (Upper Saddle River, NJ: Prentice-Hall, 1998).

8 The Josephson Institute, www.josephsoninstitute.org.

9 This section stems from the classic work on decision making found in Michael D. Cohen, James G. March, and Johan P. Olsen, "The Garbage Can Model of Organizational Choice," *Administrative Science Quarterly* 17 (1972), pp. 1–25; and James G. March and Herbert A. Simon, *Organizations* (New York: Wiley, 1958), pp. 137–142.

10 See, for example, Jonathan Rosenoer and William Scherlis, "Risk Gone Wild," *Harvard Business Review* (May 2009), p. 26.

11 See KPMG, "Enterprise Risk Management," www.kpmg.com/global/en/topics/climate-change-sustainability-services/pages/enterprise-risk-management.aspx, accessed July 3, 2013.

[12] For scholarly reviews, see Dean Tjosvold, "Effects of Crisis Orientation on Managers' Approach to Controversy in Decision Making," *Academy of Management Journal* 27 (1984), pp. 130–138; and Ian I. Mitroff, Paul Shrivastava, and Firdaus E. Udwadia, "Effective Crisis Management," *Academy of Management Executive* 1 (1987), pp. 283–292.

[13] Ibid.

[14] Mitroff et. al (1987), op. cit.

[15] This traditional distinction is often attributed to Herbert Simon, *Administrative Behavior* (New York: Free Press, 1945); see also Herbert Simon, *The New Science of Management Decision* (New York: Harper and Row, 1960).

[16] For a historical review, see Leight Buchanan and Andrew O'Connell, "Thinking Machines," *Harvard Business Review* 84.1 (2006), pp. 38–49. For recent applications, see Jiju Antony, Raj Anand, Maneesh Kumar, and M. K. Tiwari, "Multiple Response Optimization Using Taguchi Methodology and Nero-Fuzzy Based Model," *Journal of Manufacturing Technology Management* 17.7 (2006), pp. 908–112; and Craig Boutilier, "The Influence of Influence Diagrams on Artificial Intelligence," *Decision Analysis* 2.4 (2005), pp. 229–232.

[17] Simon, *Administrative Behavior* (1945), op. cit. See also Mary Zey (ed.), *Decision Making: Alternatives to Rational Choice Models* (Thousand Oaks, CA: Sage, 1992).

[18] March and Simo (1958), op. cit.

[19] For a comprehensive discussion see Daniel Kahneman, *Thinking, Fast and Slow* (New York: Random House), 2011.

[20] For a good discussion, see Watson H. Agor, *Intuition in Organizations: Leading and Managing Productively* (Newbury Park, CA: Sage, 1989); Herbert A. Simon, "Making Management Decisions: The Role of Intuition and Emotion," *Academy of Management Executive* 1 (1987), pp. 57–64; Orlando Behling and Norman L. Eckel, "Making Sense Out of Intuition," *Academy of Management Executive* 1 (1987), pp. 57–64; and Orlando Behling and Norman L. Eckel, "Making Sense Out of Intuition," *Academy of Management Executive* 5 (1991), pp. 46–54.

[21] Agor (1989), op. cit.

[22] Quote from Susan Carey, "Pilot 'in Shock' as He Landed Jet in River," *Wall Street Journal* (February 9, 2009), p. A6.

[23] The classic work in this area is found in a series of articles by D. Kahneman and A. Tversky, "Subjective Probability: A Judgment of Representativeness," *Cognitive Psychology* 3 (1972), pp. 430–454; "On the Psychology of Prediction," *Psychological Review* 80 (1973), pp. 237–251; "Prospect Theory: An Analysis of Decision under Risk," *Econometrica* 47 (1979), pp. 263–291; "Psychology of Preferences," *Scientific American* (1982), pp. 161–173; and "Choices, Values, Frames," *American Psychologist* 39 (1984), pp. 341–350. Alsop see Kahneman (2011), op. cit.

[24] See Max H. Bazerman, *Judgment in Managerial Decision Making*, 6th ed. (New York: Wiley, 2005).

[25] Barry M. Staw, "The Escalation of Commitment to a Course of Action," *Academy of Management Review* 6 (1981), pp. 577–587; Barry M. Staw and Jerry Ross, "Knowing When to Pull the Plug," *Harvard Business Review* 65 (March/April 1987), pp. 68–74. See also Glen Whyte, "Escalating Commitment to a Course of Action: A Reinterpretation," *Academy of Management Review* 11 (1986), pp. 311–321; Joel Brockner, "The Escalation of Commitment to a Failing Course of Action: Toward Theoretical Progress," *Academy of Management Review* 17 (1992), pp. 39–61; and J. Ross and B. M. Staw, "Organizational Escalation and Exit: Lessons from the Shoreham Nuclear Power Plant," *Academy of Management Journal* 36 (1993), pp. 701–732.

[26] Joel Brockner, "The Escalation of Commitment to a Failing Course of Action: Toward Theoretical Progress," *Academy of Management Review* 17 (1992), pp. 39–61; and Ross and Staw (1993), op. cit.

[27] They may also try to include too many others, as shown by Phillip G. Clampitt and M. Lee Williams in "Decision Downsizing," *MIT Sloan Management Review* 48.2 (2007), pp. 77–89.

[28] Victor H. Vroom and Arthur G. Jago, *The New Leadership: Managing Participation in Organizations* (Englewood Cliffs, NJ: Prentice-Hall, 1988). This is based on earlier work by Victor H. Vroom, "A New Look in Managerial Decision-Making," *Organizational Dynamics* (Spring 1973), pp. 66–80; and Victor H. Vroom and Phillip Yetton, *Leadership and Decision-Making* (Pittsburgh, PA: University of Pittsburgh Press, 1973).

[29] Vroom and Yetton (1973), op. cit.; and Vroom and Jago (1988), op. cit.

[30] See the discussion by Victor H. Vroom, "Leadership and the Decision Making Process," *Organizational Dynamics* 28 (2000), pp. 82–94.

[31] See, for example, Roger von Oech's books, *A Whack on the Side of the Head* (New York: Warner Books, 1983) and *A Kick in the Seat of the Pants* (New York: Harper & Row, 1986).

[32] See Cameron M. Ford and Dennis A. Gioia, *Creative Action in Organizations* (Thousand Oaks, CA: Sage, 1995).

[33] Teresa M. Amabile, "Motivating Creativity in Organizations," *California Management Review* 40 (Fall 1997), pp. 39–58.

[34] Developed from discussions by Edward DeBono, *Lateral Thinking: Creativity Step-by-Step* (New York: HarperCollins, 1970); John S. Dacey and Kathleen H. Lennon, *Understanding Creativity* (San Francisco: Jossey-Bass, 1998); and Bettina von Stamm, *Managing Innovation, Design and Creativity* (Chichester, UK: Wiley, 2003).

[35] R. Drazen, M. Glenn, and R. Kazanijan, "Multilevel Theorizing about Creativity in Organizations: A Sensemaking Perspective," *Academy of Management Review* 21 (1999), pp. 286–307.

[36] Developed from discussions by DeBono (1970), op. cit.; Dacey and Lennon (1998), op. cit.; and von Stamm (2003), op. cit.

[37] See "Mosh Pits for Creativity," *BusinessWeek* (November 7, 2005), pp. 98–99.

FEATURES AND PHOTO ESSAYS

Bringing OB to Life—Information from Lauren Weber, "At Work," *Wall Street Journal* (December 12, 2013), p. B6.

Worth Considering . . . or Best Avoided?—Information and quotes from Leslie Kwoh, "More Firms Swap Cash for Time," *Wall Street Journal* (September 26, 2012), p. B. 8.

Checking Ethics in OB—Information and quotes from "Life and Death at the iPad Factory," *Bloomberg BusinessWeek* (June 7–13, 2010), pp. 35–36.

Finding the Leader in You—www.sfgate.com/business/prweb/article/Bodacious-Young-Entrepreneur-Makes-Case-for-4080789.php#ixzz2FKrY3eId and www.news.yahoo.com/bodacious-young-entrepreneur-makes-case-kickstarter; www.prweb.com/releases/2012/11/prweb10183554.htm; and www.bodaciouscases.com

OB in Popular Culture—Quote from Chesley Sullenberger III from Robert I. Sutton, "In Praise of Simple Competence," *BusinessWeek* (April 13, 2009), p. 67.

Photo Essays—Something to Read—John Kay, "A Checklist Will Save You from Getting Ticked Off on Holiday," *Irish Times* (August 29, 2012), p. 6; and Atoll Gawande, *The Checklist Manifesto: How to Get Things Right* (New York: Picador, 2011). *Computer Programs*—Information from Joseph Walker, "Meet the New Boss: Big Data," *Wall Street Journal* (September 20, 2012), pp. B1, B2; and Rachel Emma Silverman, "Big Data Upends the Way Workers Are Paid," *Wall Street Journal* (September 20, 2012), pp. B1, B2.

CHAPTER 10
ENDNOTES

[1] See, for example, Henry Mintzberg, *The Nature of Managerial Work* (New York: Harper & Row, 1973); and John R. P. Kotter, *The General Managers* (New York: Free Press, 1982).

[2] One of the classic discussions is by Richard E. Walton, *Interpersonal Peacemaking: Confrontations and Third-Party Consultation* (Reading, MA: Addison-Wesley, 1969).

[3] Kenneth W. Thomas and Warren H. Schmidt, "A Survey of Managerial Interests with Respect to Conflict," *Academy of Management Journal* 19 (1976), pp. 315–318.

[4] For a good overview, see Richard E. Walton, *Managing Conflict: Interpersonal Dialogue and Third Party Roles*, 2nd ed. (Reading, MA: Addison-Wesley, 1987); and Dean Tjosvold, *The Conflict-Positive Organization: Stimulate Diversity and Create Unity* (Reading, MA: Addison-Wesley, 1991).

[5] Walton (1969), op. cit.

[6] Ibid.

[7] Richard E. Walton and John M. Dutton, "The Management of Interdepartmental Conflict: A Model and Review," *Administrative Science Quarterly* 14 (1969), pp. 73–84.

[8] Geert Hofstede, *Culture's Consequences: International Differences in Work-Related Values* (Beverly Hills, CA: Sage, 1980); and Geert Hofstede, "Cultural Constraints in Management Theories," *Academy of Management Executive* 7 (1993), pp. 81–94.

[9] Information from "Capitalizing on Diversity: Navigating the Seas of the Multicultural Workforce and Workplace," *BusinessWeek*, Special Advertising Section (December 4, 1998).

[10] These stages are consistent with the conflict models described by Alan C. Filley, *Interpersonal Conflict Resolution* (Glenview, IL: Scott Foresman, 1975); and Louis R. Pondy, "Organizational Conflict: Concepts and Models," *Administrative Science Quarterly* (September 1967), pp. 269–320.

[11] Information from Ken Brown and Gee L. Lee. "Lucent Fires Top China Executives," *Wall Street Journal* (April 7, 2004), p. A8.

[12] Walton and Dutton (1969), op. cit.

[13] Rensis Likert and Jane B. Likert, *New Ways of Managing Conflict* (New York: McGraw-Hill, 1976).

[14] See Jay Galbraith, *Designing Complex Organizations* (Reading, MA: Addison-Wesley, 1973); and David Nadler and Michael Tushman, *Strategic Organizational Design* (Glenview, IL: Scott Foresman, 1988).

[15] E. M. Eisenberg and M. G. Witten, "Reconsidering Openness in Organizational Communication," *Academy of Management Review* 12 (1987), pp. 418–426.

[16] R. G. Lord and M. C. Kernan, "Scripts as Determinants of Purposeful Behavior in Organizations," *Academy of Management Review* 12 (1987), pp. 265–277.

[17] See Filley (1975), op. cit.; and L. David Brown, *Managing Conflict at Organizational Interfaces* (Reading, MA: Addison-Wesley, 1983).

[18] Ibid., pp. 27, 29.

[19] For discussions, see Robert R. Blake and Jane Strygley Mouton, "The Fifth Achievement," *Journal of Applied Behavioral Science* 6 (1970), pp. 413–427; Kenneth Thomas, "Conflict and Conflict Management," in M. D. Dunnett (ed.), *Handbook of Industrial and Organizational Behavior* (Chicago: Rand McNally, 1976), pp. 889–935; and Kenneth W. Thomas, "Toward Multi-Dimensional Values in Teaching: The Examples of Conflict Behaviors," *Academy of Management Review* 2 (1977), pp. 484–490.

[20] See Roger Fisher and William Ury, *Getting to Yes: Negotiating Agreement Without Giving In* (New York: Penguin, 1983). See also James A. Wall Jr., *Negotiation: Theory and Practice* (Glenview, IL: Scott Foresman, 1985).

[21] Roy J. Lewicki and Joseph A. Litterer, *Negotiation* (Homewood, IL: Irwin, 1985), pp. 315–319.

[22] Ibid., pp. 328–329.

[23] The following discussion is based on Fisher and Ury (1983), op. cit.; and Lewicki and Litterer (1985), op. cit.

[24] This example is developed from Max H. Bazerman, *Judgment in Managerial Decision Making*, 2nd ed. (New York: Wiley, 1991), pp. 106–108.

[25] For a detailed discussion, see Fisher and Ury (1983), op. cit.; and Lewicki and Litterer (1985), op. cit.

[26] Developed from Bazerman (1991), pp. 127–141.

[27] Fisher and Ury (1983), p. 33.

[28] Lewicki and Litterer (1985), pp. 177–181.

FEATURES AND PHOTO ESSAYS

Bringing OB to Life—Information from Susan Gregory Thomas, "When the Wife Has a Fatter Paycheck," *Wall Street Journal* (July 21–22, 2012), p. C2.

Worth Considering…or Best Avoided?—Information from Amanda Ripley, "Training Teachers to Embrace Reform," *Wall Street Journal* (September 15–16, 2012), p. C2; Stephanie Banchero and Melanie Trottman, "Chicago Teachers, City Reach Tentative Deal," *Wall Street Journal* (September 15–16, 2012), p. A3; and, "Chicago Teachers Strike Continues, Rahm Emanuel Turns to Courts," *Fox News Latino*, latino.foxnews.com (accessed September 18, 2012).

Checking Ethics in OB—Information from Bridget Jones, "Blogger Fire Fury," CNN.com (July 19, 2006); and Bobbie Johnson, "Briton Sacked for Writing Paris Blog Wins Tribunal Case," *The Guardian* (March 29, 2007): www.guardian.co.uk/technology/2007/mar/30/news.france?INTCMP=SRCH (accessed July 2, 2013).

Finding the Leader in You—Information and quotes from David Kiley, "Ford's Savior?" *BusinessWeek* (March 16, 2009), pp. 31–34; and Alex Taylor III, "Fixing up Ford," *Fortune* (May 14, 2009).

OB in Popular Culture—W. C. Byham, "Start Networking Right Away (Even if You Hate It)," *Harvard Business Review* 87 (January, 2009), p. 22.

Photo Essays—Two-Tier Wages—See Bill Vlasic, "Equal Work, Unequal Pay at U.S. Auto Plants," *New York Times*, Global Edition (September 14, 2011), p. 15.

CHAPTER 11

ENDNOTES

[1] Edward T. Hall, *The Hidden Dimension* (Garden City, NY: Doubleday, 1966).

[2] See D. E. Campbell, "Interior Office Design and Visitor Response," *Journal of Applied Psychology* 64 (1979), pp. 648–653; P. C. Morrow and J. C. McElroy, "Interior Office Design and Visitor Response: A Constructive Replication," *Journal of Applied Psychology* 66 (1981), pp. 646–650.

[3] Information from "Chapter 2.2," *Kellogg* (Winter 2004), p. 6; "Room to Read," *Northwestern* (Spring 2007), pp. 32–33.

[4] The statements are from *BusinessWeek* (July 6, 1981), p. 107.

[5] See C. Bamum and N. Woliansky, "Taking Cues from Body Language," *Management Review* (78) 1989, p. 59; S. Bochner (ed.), *Cultures in Contact: Studies in Cross-Cultural Interaction* (London: Pergamon, 1982); A. Furnham and S. Bochner, *Culture Shock: Psychological Reactions to Unfamiliar Environments* (London: Methuen, 1986); "How Not to Do International Business," *BusinessWeek* (April 12, 1999); Yon Kagegama, "Tokyo Auto Show Highlights," *Associated Press* (October 24, 2001).

[6] Edward T. Hall, *Beyond Culture* (New York: Doubleday, 1976).

[7] Quotes from "Lost in Translation," *The Wall Street Journal* (May 18, 2004), pp. B1, B6.

[8] F. Lee, "Being Polite and Keeping Mum: How Bad News Is Communicated in Organizational Hierarchies," *Journal of Applied Social Psychology* 23 (1983), pp. 1124–1149.

[9] See Elizabeth W. Morrison, "Employee Voice Behavior: Integration and Directions for Future Research," *The Academy of Management Annals* 5 (2011), pp. 373–412.

[10] Ibid.

[11] See Elizabeth W. Morrison and Frances Milliken, "Organizational Silence: A Barrier to Change and Development in a Pluralistic World," *Academy of Management Review* 25 (2000), pp. 706–725, and Elizabeth W. Morrison and Frances Milliken, "Speaking Up, Remaining Silent: The Dynamics of Voice and Silence in Organizations, 40 (2003), pp. 1353–1358; Elizabeth W. Morrison, "Employee Voice Behavior: Integration and Directions for Future Research," *The Academy of Management Annals* 5 (2011), pp. 373–412.

[12] Ibid.

[13] Ibid.

[14] D. A. Whetten and K. S. Cameron, *Developing Management Skills* (New York: Prentice Hall, 2006).

[15] Variation on Epictetus.

[16] Scott D. Williams, "Listening Effectively." Accessed June 1, 2013, at www.wright.edu/~scott.williams/LeaderLetter/listening.htm

[17] Ibid.

[18] "Giving Feedback: Keeping Team Member Performance High, and Well Integrated." Accessed June 2, 2013, at www.mindtools.com/pages/article/newTMM_98.htm

[19] See Susan Ashford, Ruth Blatt, and Don VandeWalle, "Reflections on the Looking Glass: A Review of Research on Feedback-Seeking Behavior in Organizations," *Journal of Management* 29 (2003), pp. 773–799.

[20] Ibid.

[21] See Susan Ashford and Anne Tsui, "Self-Regulation for Managerial Effectiveness: The Role of Active Feedback Seeking," *Academy of Management Journal* 34 (1991), pp. 251–280.

[22] See Jason J. Dahling, Samantha L. Chau, and Alison O'Malley, "Correlates and Consequences of Feedback Orientation in Organizations" *Journal of Management* 38 (2012), pp. 531–546.

[23] B. G. Linderbaum and P. E. Levy, "The Development and Validation of the Feedback Orientation Scale (FOS), *Journal of Management* 36 (2010), pp. 1372–1405; M. London and J. W. Smither, "Feedback Orientation, Feedback Culture, and the Longitudinal Performance Management Process," *Human Resource Management Review* 12 (2002), pp. 81–100.

[24] See Jason J. Dahling, Samantha L. Chau, and Alison O'Malley, "Correlates and Consequences of Feedback Orientation in Organizations," *Journal of Management* 38 (2012), pp. 531–546.

FEATURES AND PHOTO ESSAYS

Bringing OB to Life—Information from Rachel Emma Silverman, "Psst . . . This Is What Your Co-Worker Is Paid," *The Wall Street Journal* (January 30, 2013), p. B6.

Worth Considering . . . or Best Avoided?—Information from Ravi Mattu, "Be a Good Sport and You Might Be a Better Manager," *Financial Times*, Kindle Edition (October 11, 2012); and Andrew Hill, "The Right Number of Stars for a Team," *Financial Times*, Kindle Edition (August 12, 2012). See also Mark de Rond, *There Is an I in Team: What Elite Athletes and Coaches Really Know about High Performance* (Cambridge, MA: Harvard Business Review Press, 2012).

Checking Ethics in OB—"Request Puts Employees in a Tough Spot," *Columbus Dispatch* (May 28, 2006), p. B3.

Finding the Leader in You—Description of design thinking found on IDEO Web page, accessed February 22, 2009, at www.ideo.com. Information taken from Web site at www.ideo.com. Quotes can be found in Harvard Business School Case 9-600-143, "IDEO Product Development," April 26, 2007, written by Stefan Thomke and Ashok Nimgade, pp. 5–6. See also T. Peters, "The Peters Principles," *Forbes ASAP*, September 13, 1993, p. 180.

OB in Popular Culture—"Season 6." *The Amazing Race*. CBS. WBNS, Columbus, OH. 2004. Television.

Photo Essays—Perception Alert!—Pew Research Center, "Trends in American Values: 1987–2012," www.people-press.org/values (accessed October 2, 2012). *Tough Talk from Bosses a Real Turnoff for Workers*—Information from Leslie Kwoh, "Difficult Bosses Hurt Workers' Motivation," *Wall Street Journal* (February 29, 2012), p. B8.

CHAPTER 12

ENDNOTES

[1] See Ahmad N. Azim and F. Glenn Boseman, "An Empirical Assessment of Etzioni's Topology of Power and Involvement within a University Setting," *Academy of Management Journal* 18:4 (December 1975); Herbert C. Kelman, "Compliance, Identification, and Internalization: Three Processes of Attitude Change," *The Journal of Conflict Resolution* 2:1 (March 1958): pp. 51–60; and Cameron Anderson, Oliver John, and Dacher Keltner, "The Personal Sense of Power," *Journal of Personality* 80:2 (April 2012).

[2] See Richard M. Emerson, "Power-Dependence Relations," *American Sociological Review* 27:1 (1962); see also David Mechanic, "Sources of Power of Lower Participants in Complex Organizations," *Administrative Science Quarterly* 7:3 (December 1962).

[3] See Mechanic (1962), op. cit.

[4] See Emerson (1962), op. cit. see also Lisa A. Mainiero, "Coping with Powerlessness: The Relationship of Gender and Job Dependency to Empowerment-Strategy Usage," *Administrative Science Quarterly* 31 (1986); Blake E. Ashforth, "The Experience of Powerlessness in Organizations," *Organizational Behavior and Human Decision Processes* 43 (1989); and R. Blauner, *Alienation and Freedom: The Factory Worker and His Industry* (Chicago: University of Chicago Press, 1964).

[5] Cameron Anderson and Jennifer L. Berdahl, "The Experience of Power: Examining the Effects of Power on Approach and Inhibition Tendencies," *Journal of Personality and Social Psychology* 83 (2002), pp. 1362–1377.

[6] See Ashforth (1989), op. cit.

[7] Jack W. Brehm, *A Theory of Psychological Reactance* (New York: Academic Press, 1966).

[8] See Mary Parker Follett, "The Basis of Authority," in L. Urwick (ed.), *Freedom and Coordination: Lectures in Business Organisation by Mary Parker Follett* (London: Management Publications Trust, Ltd., 1949) pp. 34–46.

[9] See John R. P. French, Jr., and Bertram Raven, "The Bases of Social Power," in D. Cartwright (ed.), *Studies in Social Power* (Ann Arbor, MI: Institute for Social Research, 1959), pp. 259–269.

[10] See Bertram H. Raven, "The Bases of Power: Origins and Recent Developments," *Journal of Social Issues* 49:4 (1993), p. 233.

[11] See French and Raven (1959), op. cit.

[12] See Chester Barnard, *The Functions of the Executive* (Cambridge, MA: Harvard University Press, 1938).

[13] See Bill McKelvey, "Emergent Strategy via Complexity Leadership: Using Complexity Science and Adaptive Tension to Build Distributed Intelligence," in Mary Uhl-Bien and Russ Marion (eds.), *Complexity Leadership, Volume I: Conceptual Foundations* (Charlotte, NC: Information Age Publishing, 2008), pp. 225–268.

[14] See Bernard M. Bass, *Leadership, Psychology, and Organizational Behavior* (New York: Harper, 1960). See also French and Raven (1959), op. cit.; Erin Landells and Simon L. Albrecht, "Organizational Political Climate: Shared Perceptions about the Building and Use of Power Bases," *Human Resource Management Review* (2012), doi:10.1016/j.hrmr.2012.06.014.

[15] See Richard M. Emerson, "Power-Dependence Relations," *American Sociological Review* 27:1 (1962).

[16] See Paul Hersey, Kenneth H. Blanchard, and Walter E. Natemeyer, "Situational Leadership, Perception, and the Impact of Power," *Group and Organization Studies* 4 (1979); see also Bertram Raven, "Social Influence and Power," in I. D. Steiner and M. Fishbein (eds.), *Current Studies in Social Psychology* (New York: Holt, Rinehart, Winston, 1965), pp. 371–381.

[17] See L. E. Greiner and V. E. Schein, *Power and Organization Development: Mobilizing Power to Implement Change* (Reading, MA: Addison-Wesley Publishing Company 1988). See also Hersey, Blanchard, and Natemeyer (1979), op. cit.; and Landells and Albrecht (2012), op. cit.

[18] See Rob Cross, "A Smarter Way to Network," *Harvard Business Review* (July–August 2011).

[19] See Herbert C. Kelman, "Compliance, Identification, and Internalization: Three Processes of Attitude Change," *Journal of Conflict Resolution* 2:1 (March 1958), p. 53.

[20] See Bennett J. Tepper, Michelle K. Duffy, and Jason D. Shaw, "Personality Moderators of the Relationship between Abusive Supervision and Subordinates' Resistance," *Journal of Applied Psychology* 86:5 (2001), pp. 974–983.

[21] See Bennett J. Tepper, Mary Uhl-Bien, Gary Kohut, Steven Rogelberg, Daniel Lockhart, and Michael Ensley, "Subordinates' Resistance and Managers' Evaluations of Subordinates' Performance," *Journal of Management* 32:2 (2006), pp. 185–209.

[22] Ibid.

[23] See Tepper, Duffy, and Shaw (2001), op. cit.

[24] See B. J. Tepper, C. A. Schriesheim, D. Nehring, R. J. Nelson, E. C. Taylor, and R. J. Eisenbach, "The Multi-Dimensionality and Multi-Functionality of Subordinates' Resistance to Downward Influence Attempts," paper presented at the annual meeting of the Academy of Management, San Diego, CA (1998).

[25] See Dean C. Ludwig and Clinton O. Longenecker, "The Bathsheba Syndrome: The Ethical Failure of Successful Leaders," *Journal of Business Ethics* 12:4 (1993), pp. 265–273.

[26] Useful reviews include a chapter in Robert H. Miles, *Macro Organizational Behavior* (Santa Monica, CA: Goodyear, 1980); Bronston T. Mayes and Robert W. Allen, "Toward a Definition of Organizational Politics," *Academy of Management Review* 2 (1977), pp. 672–677; Dan Farrell and James C. Petersen, "Patterns of Political Behavior in Organizations," *Academy of Management Review* 7 (1982), pp. 403–412; and D. L. Madison, R. W. Allen, L. W. Porter, and B. T. Mayes, "Organizational Politics: An Exploration of Managers' Perceptions," *Human Relations* 33 (1980), pp. 92–107.

[27] See Philip Selznick, "Foundations of the Theory of Organizations," *American Sociological Review* 13 (1948), pp. 25–35; and Philip Selznick, *Leadership in Administration* (New York: Harper and Row, 1957).

[28] See Chu-Hsiang Chang (2009), op. cit.

[29] See Landells and Albrecht (2012), op. cit.

[30] Ibid.

[31] Ibid.

[32] See A. Drory, "Perceived Political Climate and Job Attitudes," *Organization Studies* 14 (1993), pp. 59–71. See also G. R. Ferris, Darren C. Treadway, Pamela L. Perrewe, Robyn L. Brouer, Ceasar Douglas, and Sean Lux, "Political Skill in Organizations," *Journal of Management* 33 (2007). See also Chu-Hsiang Chang (2009), op. cit.

[33] See Landells and Albrecht (2012), op. cit.

[34] See Daniel J. Brass, "Taking Stock of Networks and Organizations: A Multilevel Perspective," *Academy of Management Journal* 47:6 (2004).

[35] See Gerald R. Ferris, Sherry L. Davidson, and Pamela L. Perrewe, *Political Skill at Work* (Palo Alto, CA: Davies-Black Publishing, 2005).

[36] See J. Nahapiet and S. Ghoshal, "Social Capital, Intellectual Capital, and the Organizational Advantage," *Academy of Management Review*, 23:2 (1998), p. 243.

37 See Daniel J. Brass, "Taking Stock of Networks and Organizations: A Multilevel Perspective," *Academy of Management Journal* 47:6 (2004); E. Bueno, P. Salmador, and O. Rodriguez, "The Role of Social Capital in Today's Economy, *Journal of Intellectual Capital* 5 (2004), pp. 556–574; and H. C. Sozen, "Social Networks and Power in Organizations: A Research on the Roles and Positions of Junior Level Secretaries in an Organizational Network, *Personnel Review* 41 (2012), pp. 487–512.

38 See R. S. Burt, *Structural Holes: The Social Structure of Competition* (Cambridge, MA: Harvard University Press, 1992).

FEATURES AND PHOTO ESSAYS

Bringing OB to Life—Information from Lisa Quast, "To Flirt or Not to Flirt at Work," www.forbes.com/sites/lisaquast/2013/02/11/to-flirt-or-not-to-flirt-at-work (accessed July 7, 2013). See also J. Bradley, S. Chan-Serafin, A. Brief, and M. Watkins, "Sex as a Tool: Does Utilizing Sexuality at Work Work? Paper presented at the 2005 Annual Meeting of the Academy of Management, Honolulu (2005); and Laura Kray, Connson C. Locke, and Alex B. Van Zant, "Feminine Charm: An Experimental Analysis of Its Costs and Benefits in Negotiations," *Personality and Social Psychology Bulletin* 38 (2012), pp. 1343–1357.

Worth Considering . . . or Best Avoided?—Information and quotes from Parminder Bahra, "The Science Behind Persuading People," *Wall Street Journal* (December 27, 2012), p. D5.

Checking Ethics in OB—Information from Clif Boutelle, "Psychological Impact of Job Furloughs," Society for Industrial & Organizational Psychology, Inc. www.siop.org/Media/News/furlough.aspx (accessed July 7, 2013).

Finding the Leader in You—See John F. Burns and Alan Cowell, "Report Depicts Horrific Pattern of Child Sexual Abuse by BBC Celebrity," *New York Times*, January 11, 2013; John F. Burns and Ravi Somaiya, "A Shield of Celebrity Let a BBC Host Escape Legal Scrutiny for Decades," November 1, 2012; and Sarah Lyall, "Internal Documents Portray BBC as Top-Heavy, Bickering and Dysfunctional," *New York Times*, February 22, 2013.

OB in Popular Culture—*Spanglish*. Dir. James L. Brooks. Perf. Adam Sandler, Tea Leoni, Paz Vega, Phil Rosenthal, and Angela Goethals. Columbia Pictures Corporation, 2004. Film.

Photo Essays—*Whistleblowing*—See Michael Rehg, Marcia Miceli, Janet Near, and James Van Scotter, "Antecedents and Outcomes of Retaliation Against Whistleblowers: Gender Differences and Power Relationships," *Organization Science* 19 (2008) pp. 221–240. *What You Know*—See Auren Hoffman, "It's Now What You Know that Matters, Not Who You Know," *Forbes* (October 1, 2012), www.forbes.com/sites/ericsavitz/2012/10/01/its-now-what-you-know-that-matters-not-who-you-know (accessed July 7, 2013).

CHAPTER 13

ENDNOTES

1 See Edwin P. Hollander and James W. Julian, "Contemporary Trends in the Analysis of Leadership Processes," *Psychological Bulletin* 71 (1969), pp. 387–397. See also Gary Yukl, *Leadership in Organizations,* 8th ed. (Boston: Pearson, 2013).

2 See Edwin P. Hollander, "Emergent Leadership and Social Influence," in L. Petrullo and B.M. Bass (eds.), *Leadership and Interpersonal Behavior* (New York: Holt, Rinehart & Winston, 1961), pp. 30–47; see also Edwin P. Hollander, "Processes of Leadership Emergence," *Journal of Contemporary Business* 3 (1974), pp. 19–33.

3 See Gail Fairhurst and Mary Uhl-Bien, "Organizational Discourse Analysis (ODA): Examining Leadership as a Relational Process," *The Leadership Quarterly* 23:6 (2012), pp. 1043–1062.

4 See D. Scott DeRue and Susan J. Ashford, "Who Will Lead and Who Will Follow? A Social Process of Leadership Identity Construction in Organizations," *Academy of Management Review* 35 (2010), pp. 627–647.

5 Ibid.

6 See K. Y. Chan and F. Drasgow, "Toward a Theory of Individual Differences and Leadership: Understanding the Motivation to Lead," *Journal of Applied Psychology* 86 (2001), pp. 481–498; and R. Kark and D. van Dijk, "Motivation to Lead, Motivation to Follow: The Role of the Self-Regulatory Focus in Leadership Processes," *Academy of Management Review* 32 (2007), pp. 500–528.

7 D. Eden and U. Leviatan. "Implicit Leadership Theory as a Determinant of the Factor Structure Underlying Supervisory Behavior Scales," *Journal of Applied Psychology* 60 (1975), pp. 736–741; and R. Lord and C. Emrich, "Thinking Outside the Box by Looking Inside the Box: Extending the Cognitive Revolution in Leadership Research," *The Leadership Quarterly* 11 (2001), pp. 551–579.

8 Based on L. R. Offermann, John K. Kennedy, Jr., and P. W. Wirtz. "Implicit Leadership Theories: Content, Structure, and Generalizability, *The Leadership Quarterly* 5 (1994), pp. 43–58.

9 J. Meindl, S. Erlich, and J. Dukerich, "The Romance of Leadership," *Administrative Science Quarterly* 30 (1985), pp. 78–102.

10 M. Uhl-Bien and R. Pillai, "The Romance of Leadership and the Social Construction of Followership," in B. Shamir, R. Pillai, M. Bligh, and M. Uhl-Bien (eds.), *Follower-Centered Perspectives on Leadership: A Tribute to the Memory of James R. Meindl* (Charlotte, NC: Information Age Publishers, 2007, pp. 187–209).

11 M. Carsten, M. Uhl-Bien, B. West, J. Patera, and R. McGregor, "Exploring Social Constructions of Followership, *The Leadership Quarterly 21*:3, (2010), pp. 543–562.

12 M. Carsten, M. Uhl-Bien, and L. Huang, "How Followers See Their Role in Relation to Leaders: An Investigation of Follower Role Orientation," working paper, University of Nebraska (2013).

13 See Bradley Kirkman, Gilad Chen, Jiing-Lih Harh, Zhen Xiong Chen, and Kevin Lowe, "Individual Power Distance Orientation and Follower Reactions to Transformational Leaders: A Cross-Cultural Examination," *Academy of Management Journal* 52 (2009), pp. 744–764.

14 Carsten et al. (2013), op. cit.

15 T. Sy, "What Do You Think of Followers? Examining the Content, Structure, and Consequences of Implicit Followership Theories," *Organizational Behavior and Human Decision Processes 113*:2 (2010), pp. 73–84.

16 Based on T. Sy, "What Do You Think of Followers? Examining the Content, Structure, and Consequences of Implicit Followership Theories," *Organizational Behavior and Human Decision Processes* 113:2 (2010), pp. 73–84.

17 G. B. Graen and M. Uhl-Bien, "Relationship-Based Approach to Leadership: Development of Leader-Member Exchange (LMX) Theory of Leadership over 25 Years: Applying a Multi-Level

Multi-Domain Perspective," *The Leadership Quarterly* 6 (1995), pp. 219–247.

[18] See B. Tepper, "Abusive Supervision in Work Organizations: Review, Synthesis and Research Agenda," *Journal of Management* 33 (2007), pp. 261–289.

[19] G. C. Homans, "Social Behavior as Exchange," *American Journal of Sociology* 63 (1958), pp. 597–606.

[20] A. W. Gouldner, "The Norm of Reciprocity: A Preliminary Statement," *American Sociological Review* 25 (1960), pp. 161–177.

[21] E. P. Hollander, "Conformity, Status, and Idiosyncrasy Credit," *Psychological Review* 65 (1958), pp. 117–127.

[22] C. A. Gibb, "The Sociometry of Leadership in Temporary Groups," *Sociometry* 13:3, pp. 226–243; and C. A. Gibb, "Leadership," in G. Lindzay (ed.), *Handbook of Social Psychology*, Vol. 2, (Reading, MA: Addison-Wesley, 1954), pp. 877–917.

[23] R. Bolden, "Distributed Leadership in Organizations: A Review of Theory and Research," *International Journal of Management Reviews* 13:3 (2011), pp. 251–269; and R. Bolden, G. Petrov, and J. Gosling, "Distributed Leadership in Higher Education: Rhetoric and Reality," *Educational Management Administration & Leadership* 37:2 (2009), pp. 257–277.

[24] See Mary Uhl-Bien, Russ Marion, and Bill McKelvey, "Complexity Leadership Theory: Shifting Leadership from the Industrial Age to the Knowledge Era," *The Leadership Quarterly* 18:4 (2007), pp. 298–318.

[25] See J.L. Denis, A. Langley, and V. Sergi, "Leadership in the Plural," *The Academy of Management Annals* 6 (2012), pp. 211–283.

[26] Ibid.

[27] C. L. Pearce, "The Future of Leadership: Combining Vertical and Shared Leadership to Transform Knowledge Work," *Academy of Management Executive* 18:1 (2004), pp. 47–59; and C. L. Pearce and J. A. Conger (eds.), *Shared Leadership: Reframing the Hows and Whys of Leadership* (Thousand Oaks, CA: Sage Publications, 2003).

[28] C. Pearce and C. Manz, "The New Silver Bullets of Leadership: The Importance of Self- and Shared Leadership in Knowledge Work," *Organizational Dynamics* 34:2 (2005), pp. 130–140.

FEATURES AND PHOTO ESSAYS

Bringing OB to Life—Information from John Antonakis, Marika Fenley, and Sue Liechti, "Learning Charisma," *Harvard Business Review* 90 (June 2012), pp. 127–130; and Alicia Clegg, "The Subtle Secrets of Charisma," *Financial Times*, Kindle Edition (January 3, 2013).

Worth Considering . . . or Best Avoided?—Information and quotes from Julian Sancton, "Milgram at McDonald's," *Bloomberg BusinessWeek* (August 27–September 2, 2012), pp. 74–75.

Checking Ethics in OB—Lauren Weber and Rachel Emma Silverman, "Workers Share Their Salary Secrets," *Wall Street Journal* (April 16, 2013), http://online.wsj.com/article/SB10001424127887324345804578426744168583824.html?mod=djem_jiewr_BE_domainid (accessed July 21, 2013); Jayne O'Donnell, "Gen Y Can Guide Their Offices with Tech Savvy," *USA Today* (June 10, 2013), www.usatoday.com/story/money/business/2013/06/10/millennials-boomers-workplace-challenges/2398403 (accessed July 21, 2013); and Edward E Lawler III, "Pay Secrecy: Why Bother?" *Forbes* (September 12, 2013), www.forbes.com/sites/edwardlawler/2012/09/12/pay-secrecy-why-bother (accessed July 21, 2013).

Finding the Leader in You—James Temple, "Google's Larry Page must prove he has CEO skills," SFGate.com, Sun. Jan. 23, 2011. "Meet the New Boss: Google Cofounder Larry Page is ready to show the world he's all grown up," Newsweek.com, Jan. 23, 2011.

OB in Popular Culture—*Forrest Gump*. Dir. Robert Zemeckis. Perf. Tom Hanks, Robin Wright, and Gary Sinise. Paramount Pictures, 1994. Film.

Photo Essays—*Pay Gaps*—Information from "Closing the Gap," *Bloomberg BusinessWeek* (September 17–23, 2012), p. 103. *Value Divide*—PewResearch, "The American-European Values Gap," pewresearch.org/databank (accessed October 2, 2012).

CHAPTER 14

ENDNOTES

[1] See Gary Yukl, *Leadership in Organizations*, 8th ed. (New York: Pearson, 2013).

[2] See Timothy Judge, Joyce Bono, Remus Ilies, and Megan Gerhardt, "Personality and Leadership: A Qualitative and Quantitative Review," *Journal of Applied Psychology* 87 (2002), pp. 765–780.

[3] See Mark Van Vugt, Robert Hogan, and Robert Kaiser, "Leadership, Follower and Evolution: Some Lessons from the Past," *American Psychologist* 63 (2008), pp. 182–196. See also Timothy Judge and Ronald Piccolo, "The Bright and Dark Sides of Leader Traits: A Review and Theoretical Extension," *Leadership Quarterly* 20 (2009), pp. 855–875.

[4] See Edward Fleishman, "The Description of Supervisory Behavior Fleishman," *Personnel Psychology* 37 (1953), pp. 1–6. See also A. Halpin and B. Winer, "A Factorial Study of the Leader Behavior Descriptions," in R. Stogdill and A. E. Coons (eds.), *Leader Behavior: Its Description and Measurement* (Columbus, OH: Bureau of Business Research, Ohio State University, 1957); J. K. Hemphill and A. E. Coons, "Development of the Leader Behavior Description Questionnaire," in R. Stogdill and A.E. Coons, (eds.), *Leader Behavior: Its Description and Measurement* (Columbus, OH: Bureau of Business Research, Ohio State University, 1957), pp. 6–38.

[5] See Yukl (2013), op. cit.

[6] Ibid.

[7] See R. Arvey, Z. Zhang, B. Avolio, and R. Krueger, "Developmental and Genetic Determinants of Leadership Role Occupancy among Women." *Journal of Applied Psychology* 92 (2007), pp. 693–706.

[8] See Martin Evans, "The Effects of Supervisory Behavior on the Path-Goal Relationship," *Organizational Behavior and Human Performance* 5 (1970), pp. 277–298. See also Robert House, "Path Goal Theory of Leadership: Lessons, Legacy and a Reformulated Theory," *Leadership Quarterly* 7 (1996), pp. 323–352; R. J. House and T. R. Mitchell, "Path-Goal Theory of Leadership," *Contemporary Business* 3 (1974), pp. 81–98.

[9] For documentation, see Fred E. Fiedler and Linda Mahar, "The Effectiveness of Contingency Model Training: A Review of the Validation of Leader Match," *Personnel Psychology* 32 (Spring

1979), pp. 45–62; Fred E. Garcia, Cecil H. Bell, Martin M. Chemers, and Dennis Patrick, "Increasing Mine Productivity and Safety Through Management Training and Organization Development: A Comparative Study," *Basic and Applied Social Psychology* 5.1 (March 1984), pp. 1–18; Arthur G. Jago and James W. Ragan, "The Trouble with Leader Match Is That It Doesn't Match Fiedler's Contingency Model," *Journal of Applied Psychology* 71 (November 1986), pp. 555–559; and R. Ayman, M. M. Chemers, and F. E. Fiedler, "The Contingency Model of Leadership Effectiveness: Its Levels of Analysis," *The Leadership Quarterly* 6.2 (Summer 1995), pp. 147–168.

[10] See Jerry Hunt, "Transformational/Charismatic Leadership's Transformation of the Field: An Historical Essay," *Leadership Quarterly* 10 (1999), pp. 129–144; and Russ Marion and Mary Uhl-Bien, "Leadership in Complex Organizations," *Leadership Quarterly* 12 (2001), pp. 389–418.

[11] See Max Weber, *The Theory of Social and Economic Organizations* (New York: Free Press, 1947).

[12] See Katherine Klein and Robert House, "On Fire: Charismatic Leadership and Levels of Analysis," *Leadership Quarterly* 6 (1995), pp. 183–198.

[13] Ibid.

[14] See B. Angle, J. Nagarajan, J. Sonnenfeld, and D. Srinivisan, "Does CEO Charisma Matter? An Empirical Analysis of the Relationships Among Organizational Performance, Environmental Uncertainty and Top Management Team Perceptions of CEO Charisma," *Academy of Management Journal* 49 (2006), pp. 161–174; Yukl (2013), op. cit.; H. Tosi, V. Misangyi, A. Fanelli, D. Waldman, and F. Yammarino, "CEO Charisma, Compensation and Firm Performance," *Leadership Quarterly* 15 (2004), pp. 405–420.

[15] See Jean Lipman-Blumen, *The Allure of Toxic Leaders* (Oxford, UK: Oxford University Press, 2005).

[16] See G. Hofstede, *Culture's Consequences: Comparing Values, Behaviors, Institutions, and Organizations Across Nations* (Thousand Oaks, CA: Sage, 2001); and B. Kirkman, G. Chen, J-L. Fahr, Z. Chen, and K. Lowe, "Individual Power Distance Orientation and Follower Reactions to Transformational Leaders: A Cross-Level, Cross-Cultural Examination," *Academy of Management Journal* 52 (2009), pp. 744–764.

[17] See James MacGregor Burns, *Leadership* (New York: Harper & Row, 1978).

[18] See Ram de la Rosa, "Book Synopsis: Leadership—James McGregory Burns" (January 23, 2012), http://ramdelarosa.blogspot.com/2012/01/book-synopsis-leadership-james.html (accessed January 14, 2013).

[19] See J. Ciulla, "Leadership Ethics: Mapping the Territory," *The Business Ethics Quarterly* 5 (1995), pp. 5–24; and J. Ciulla, "Introduction to Volume I: Theoretical Aspects of Leadership Ethics," in J. Ciulla, M. Uhl-Bien, and P. Werhane (eds.), *Leadership Ethics* (London: Sage, 2013).

[20] See Scott London, "Book Review: Leadership" (2008), www.scottlondon.com/reviews/burns.html (accessed January 12, 2013).

[21] See Yukl (2013), op. cit.; and Bernard M. Bass, *Leadership and Performance Beyond Expectations* (New York: Free Press).

[22] B. Bass, "Two Decades of Research and Development in Transformational Leadership," *European Journal of Work and Organizational Psychology* 8 (1999), pp. 9–32.

[23] This sentence taken from Bradley Kirkman, Gilad Chen, Jiing-Lih Harh, Zhen Xiong Chen, and Kevin Lowe, "Individual Power Distance Orientation and Follower Reactions to Transformational Leaders: A Cross-Cultural Examination," *Academy of Management Journal* 52 (2009), pp. 744–745.

[24] See B. Bass and B. Avolio, "Multifactor Leadership Questionnaire, Form 5x," www.mindgarden.com/products/mlq.htm (accessed July 12, 2013).

[25] Ibid.

[26] See K. Dirks and D. Ferrin, "Trust in Leadership: Meta-Analytic Findings and Implications for Research and Practice," (2002), pp. 611–628; T. Judge and R. Piccolo, "Transformational and Transactional Leadership: A Meta-Analytic Test of Their Relative Validity," *Journal of Applied Psychology*, 89 (2004), pp. 755–768; K. Lowe, K. G. Kroeck, and N. Sivasubramaniam, "Effectiveness of Correlates of Transformational and Transactional Leadership: A Meta-Analytic Review of the MLQ Literature," *Leadership Quarterly* 7 (1996), pp. 385–425; and G. Wang, I-S. Oh, S. Courtright, and A. Colbert, "Transformational Leadership and Performance Across Criteria and Levels: A Meta-Analytic Review of 25 Years of Research," *Group and Organization Management* 36 (2011), pp. 223–270.

[27] See M. Kets de Vries and D. Miller, "Narcissism and Leadership: An Object Relations Perspective," *Human Relations* 38 (1985), pp. 583–601; Dirk Van Dierendonck, "Servant Leadership: A Review and Synthesis," *Journal of Management* 37 (2011), pp. 1228–1261; and J. Ciulla, "Leadership Ethics: Mapping the Territory," *The Business Ethics Quarterly* 5 (1995), pp. 5–24.

[28] See Warren Bennis, *On Becoming a Leader* (Reading, MA: Addison-Wesley, 2009).

[29] See Richard Osborn, Jerry Hunt, and Larry Jauch, "Toward a Contextual Theory of Leadership," *The Leadership Quarterly* 13 (2002), pp. 797–837.

[30] See Melanie Mitchell, *Complexity: A Guided Tour* (Oxford, UK: Oxford University Press, 2009).

[31] See Yasmin Merali and Peter Allen, "Complexity and Systems Thinking," in Peter Allen, Steve Maguire, and Bill McKelvey (eds.), *The Sage Handbook* of *Complexity and Management* (London: Sage, 2011), p. 41.

[32] See Gary Hamel, "Moon Shots for Management," *Harvard Business Review* (February 2009), pp. 91–98.

[33] See Charles C. Heckscher, "Defining the Post-Bureaucratic Type," in Charles Heckscher and Anne Donnellon (eds.), *The Post-Bureaucratic Organization: New Perspectives on Organizational Change* (Thousand Oaks, CA: Sage, 1994), pp. 14–62.

[34] See Edwin Olson and Glenda Eoyang, Facilitating Organizational *Change: Lessons from Complexity Science*. (SanFrancisco: Jossey-Bass/Pfeiffer, 2001).

[35] See Mary Uhl-Bien, Russ Marion, and Bill McKelvey, "Complexity Leadership Theory: Shifting Leadership from the Industrial Age to the Knowledge Era," *The Leadership Quarterly* 18 (2007), pp. 298–318.

[36] See Mary Uhl-Bien and Russ Marion, "Complexity Leadership in Bureaucratic Forms of Organizing: A Meso Model," *The Leadership Quarterly* 20 (2009), pp. 631–650.

[37] See Uhl-Bien and Marion (2007), op. cit.; and Uhl-Bien and Marion (2009), op. cit.

[38] See Joanne Ciulla, Mary Uhl-Bien, and Patricia Werhane, *Leadership Ethics* (London: Sage, 2013); and Mary Uhl-Bien and Melissa Carsten, "How to Be Ethical When the Boss Is Not," *Organizational Dynamics* 36 (2007), pp. 187–201.

[39] See Joanne Ciulla, "Introduction to Volume I: Theoretical Aspects of Leadership Ethics," in Joanne Ciulla, Mary Uhl-Bien, and Patricia Werhane (eds.), *Leadership Ethics* (London: Sage, 2013); and Joanne Ciulla, "Leadership Ethics: Mapping the Territory," *The Business Ethics Quarterly* 5 (1995), pp. 5–24. See also J. Ciulla, "Leadership Ethics: Mapping the Territory," *The Business Ethics Quarterly* 5 (1995), pp. 5–24; and Joanne Ciulla, *Ethics: The Heart of Leadership* (New York: Praeger, 2004).

[40] See Milton Friedman, "The Social Responsibility of Business Is to Increase Its Profits," *New York Times Magazine* (Sept. 13, 1970).

[41] See M. Porter and M. Kramer, "Creating Shared Value," *Harvard Business Review* (Jan.–Feb. 2011), pp. 63–77. See also "Conscious Capitalism," www.consciouscapitalism.org (accessed July 13, 2013).

[42] Based on Louis W. Fry, "Toward a Paradigm of Spiritual Leadership," *The Leadership Quarterly* 16 (2005), pp. 619–622; and Louis W. Fry, Steve Vitucci, and Marie Cedillo, "Spiritual Leadership and Army Transformation: Theory, Measurement, and Establishing a Baseline," *The Leadership Quarterly* 16.5 (2005), pp. 835–862.

[43] See Dirk Van Dierendonck, "Servant Leadership: A Review and Synthesis," *Journal of Management* 37 (2011), pp. 1228–1261; and Dirk Van Dierendonck, "The Servant Leadership Survey: Development and Validation of a Multidimensional Measure," *Journal of Business and Psychology* 26 (2011), pp. 249–267.

[44] Ibid.

[45] Dirk Van Dierendonck, "The Role of the Follower in the Relationship Between Empowering Leadership and Empowerment: A Longitudinal Investigation," *Journal of Applied Social Psychology* 42 (2012), pp. E1–E20; J. Arnold, S. Arad, J. Rhoades, and F. Drasgow, "The Empowering Leadership Questionnaire: The Construction and Validation of a New Scale for Measuring Leader Behaviors," *Journal of Organizational Behavior* 21 (2000), pp. 249–269; B. Kirkman and B. Rosen, "A Model of Work Team Empowerment," in R. W. Woodman & W. A. Pasmore (eds.), *Research in Organizational Change and Development*, Vol. 10 (Greenwich, CT: JAI Press, 1997), pp. 131–167; and B. Kirkman and B. Rosen, "Beyond Self-Management: Antecedents and Consequences of Team Empowerment," *Academy of Management Journal* 42 (1999), pp. 58–74.

[46] See M. Ahearne, J. Mathieu, and A. Rapp, "To Empower or Not to Empower Your Sales Force? An Empirical Examination of the Influence of Leadership Empowerment Behavior on Customer Satisfaction and Performance," *Journal of Applied Psychology* 90 (2005), pp. 945–955; and X. Zhang and K. Bartol, "Linking Empowering Leadership and Employee Creativity: The Influence of Psychological Empowerment, Intrinsic Motivation, and Creative Process Engagement," *Academy of Management Journal* 53 (2010), pp. 107–128.

[47] See M. Brown, L. Trevino, and D. Harrison, "Ethical Leadership: A Social Learning Perspective for Construct Development and Testing," *Organizational Behavior and Human Decision Processes* 97 (2005), pp. 117–134.

[48] See M. Schminke, A. Arnaud, and M. Kuenzi, "The Power of Ethical Work Climates," *Organizational Dynamics* 36 (2007), pp. 171–186.

[49] See Brown, Trevino, and Harrison (2005), op. cit.

[50] See R. Piccolo, R. Greenbaum, D. Den Hartog, and R. Folger, "The Relationship Between Ethical Leadership and Core Job Characteristics," *Journal of Organizational Behavior* 31 (2010), pp. 259–278; D. Mayer, M. Kuenzi, and R. Greenbaum, "Examining the Link Between Ethical Leadership and Employee Misconduct: The Mediating Role of Ethical Climate," *Journal of Business Ethics* 95 (2010), pp. 7–16.

FEATURES AND PHOTO ESSAYS

Bringing OB to Life—Information from Leslie Kwoh, "Want to Be CEO? What About Your BMI?" *Wall Street Journal* (January 16, 2013), pp. B1, B6.

Worth Considering . . . or Best Avoided?—Information and quotes from Chris Serb, "Stop Overmanaging," *Kellogg* (Fall 2012), p. 24. See also J. Keith Murnighan, *Do Nothing: How to Stop Overmanaging and Become a Great Leader* (New York: Portfolio Hardcover, 2012).

Checking Ethics in OB—Stephen Howard, "Beyond Buzzwords: How to Make Values Matter," *Business in the Community* (June 10, 2013), www.bitc.org.uk/blog/post/beyond-buzzwords-how-make-values-matter; and "Unethical Practice 'Common in UK Workplaces' Finds ILM/BITC Study," *Ethical Performance*, http://ethicalperformance.com/news/article/7722 (2012).

Finding the Leader in You—Information and quotes from Stacy Perman, "Scones and Social Responsibility," *BusinessWeek* (August 21/28, 2006), p. 38; and Dancing Deer Baking Co., www.dancingdeer.com.

OB in Popular Culture—*Lincoln*. Dir. Steven Spielberg. Perf. Daniel Day-Lewis, Sally Field David Strathirn, and Tommy Lee Jones. *DreamWorks* SKG, 2012. Film.

Photo Essays—*New Venture Start-ups*—See Deborah Gage, "Study: Start-Ups Led by Females do Better," *Wall Street Journal* (October 5, 2012), p. B5. *Corruption*—Information and quote from Joe Palazzolo, "The Business of Bribery," *Wall Street Journal* (October 2, 2012), pp. B1, B.4; and Ashby Jones, "The Cost of Compliance Grows," *Wall Street Journal* (October 2, 2012), p. B4.

CHAPTER 15
ENDNOTES

[1] This treatment and many analyses of corporate culture are based on Edgar Schein, "Organizational Culture," *American Psychologist* 45 (1990), pp. 109–119; and E. Schein, *Organizational Culture and Leadership* (San Francisco: Jossey-Bass, 1985).

[2] For a recent treatment, see Ali Danisman, C. R. Hinnings, and Trevor Slack, "Integration and Differentiation in Institutional Values: An Empirical Investigation in the Field of Canadian National Sport Organizations," *Canadian Journal of Administrative Sciences* 23.4 (2006), pp. 301–315.

[3] Schein (1990).

[4] See www.dellapp.us.dell.com.

[5] This example was reported in an interview with Edgar Schein, "Corporate Culture Is the Real Key to Creativity," *Business Month* (May 1989), pp. 73–74.

6. Schein (1990).

7. Aetna. (2001–2013). "Culture." Accessed June 19, 2013, at http://qawww.aetna.com/working/why/culture.html.

8. Schein (1990).

9. For an extended discussion, see J. M. Beyer and H. M. Trice, "How an Organization's Rites Reveal Its Culture," *Organizational Dynamics* (Spring 1987), pp. 27–41.

10. A. Cooke and D. M. Rousseau, "Behavioral Norms and Expectations: A Quantitative Approach to the Assessment of Organizational Culture," *Group and Organizational Studies* 13 (1988), pp. 245–273.

11. Mary Trefry, "A Double-Edged Sword: Organizational Culture in Multicultural Organizations," *International Journal of Management* 23 (2006), pp. 563–576; and J. Martin and C. Siehl, "Organization Culture and Counterculture," *Organizational Dynamics* 12 (1983), pp. 52–64.

12. Accessed June 19, 2013, at www.apple-history.com.

13. See R. N. Osborn, "The Culture Clash at BofA," Working Paper, Department of Management, Wayne State University, 2008.

14. For a recent discussion of the clash of corporate cultures, see George Lodorfos and Agyenim Boateng, "The Role of Culture in the Merger and Acquisition Process: Evidence from the European Chemical Industry," *Management Decision* 44 (2006), pp. 1405–1410.

15. Jean Louis Barsoux, "Start Slow, End Fast—Jean Louis Barsoux Offers Advice on Working in Multicultural Teams," *Financial Times* (July 8, 1994), p. 12.

16. Osborn (2008); and Osawa Juro, "Japan Investors: Why No Women, Foreigners in the Board Room," *Wall Street Journal*, June 30, 2010, accessed June 19, 2013, at http://blogs.wsj.com/japanrealtime/2010/06/30/japan-investors-why-no-women-foreigners-in-the-boardroom.

17. Taylor Cox Jr., "The Multicultural Organization," *Academy of Management Executive* 2.2 (May 1991), pp. 34–47.

18. See Schein (1985), pp. 52–57, and Schein (1990).

19. For a discussion from a different perspective, see Anat Rafaeli and Michael G. Pratt (eds.), *Artifacts and Organizations: Beyond Mere Symbols* (Mahwah, NJ: Erlbaum, 2006).

20. For early work, see T. Deal and A. Kennedy, *Corporate Culture* (Reading, MA: Addison-Wesley, 1982); and T. Peters and R. Waterman, *In Search of Excellence* (New York: Harper & Row, 1982), whereas more recent studies are summarized in Joanne Martin and Peter Frost, "The Organizational Culture War Games: The Struggle for Intellectual Dominance," in Stewart R. Clegg, Cynthia Hardy, and Walter R. Nord (eds.), *Handbook of Organization Studies* (London: Sage, 1996), pp. 599–621.

21. Schein (1990).

22. See www.montereypasta.com for the original quotes; www.montereygourmetfoods.com for updated information; and www.fundinguniverse.com/company-histories/monterey-pasta-company for a more complete history until 2003.

23. H. Gertz, *The Interpretation of Culture* (New York: Basic Books, 1973).

24. See Rafaeli and Pratt (2006) and Beyer and Trice (1987).

25. H. M. Trice and J. M. Beyer, "Studying Organizational Cultures through Rites and Ceremonials," *Academy of Management Review* 3 (1984), pp. 633–669.

26. J. Martin, M. S. Feldman, M. J. Hatch, and S. B. Sitkin, "The Uniqueness Paradox in Organizational Stories," *Administrative Science Quarterly* 28 (1983), pp. 438–453.

27. For a recent study, see John Barnes, Donald W. Jackson, Michael D. Hutt, and Ajith Kumar, "The Role of Culture Strength in Shaping Sales Force Outcomes," *Journal of Personal Setting and Sales Management* 26.3 (2006), pp. 255–269. This tradition of strong cultures goes back to work by Deal and Kennedy (1982) and Peters and Waterman (1982).

28. Wikipedia.org (2013, June 15), "One World Trade Center," accessed June 20, 2013, at http://en.wikipedia.org/wiki/One_World_Trade_Center; and News24.com, "Twin Tower Replacement to Be Impressive" (2011, August 5), accessed June 20, 2013, at www.news24.com/World/News/Twin-Tower-replacement-to-be-impressive-20110805.

29. Trice and Beyer (1984).

30. J. Collins, *How Do the Mighty Fall* (New York: HarperCollins, 2009).

31. R. N. Osborn and D. Jackson, "Leaders, River Boat Gamblers or Purposeful Unintended Consequences," *Academy of Management Journal* 31 (1988), pp. 924–947.

32. For an interesting twist, see John Connolly, "High Performance Cultures," *Business Strategy Review* 17 (2006), pp. 19–32; a more conventional treatment may be found in Martin, Feldman, Hatch, and Sitkin (1983).

33. Martin and Frost (1996).

34. This section was originally based on R. N. Osborn and C. C. Baughn, *An Assessment of the State of the Field of Organizational Design* (Alexandria, VA: U.S. Army Research Institute, 1994).

35. For example, see Gerard J. Tellis, Jaideep C. Prabhu, and Rajesh K. Chandy, "Radical Innovation Across Nations: The Preeminence of Corporate Culture," *Journal of Marketing* 73.1 (2009), pp. 3–23.

36. Richard N. Osborn, James G. Hunt, and Lawrence R. Jauch, *Organization Theory: Integrated Text and Cases* (Melbourne, FL: Krieger, 1985).

37. Ibid. (1985); and W. Richard Scott and Gerald F. Davis, *Organizations and Organizing: Rational and Open Systems* (Englewood Cliffs, NJ: Prentice Hall, 2007).

38. H. Talcott Parsons, *Structure and Processes in Modern Societies* (New York: Free Press, 1960).

39. See B. Bartkus, M. Glassman, and B. McAfee, "Mission Statement Quality and Financial Performance," *European Management Journal* 24.1 (2006), pp. 66–79; J. Peyrefitte and F. R. David, "A Content Analysis of the Mission Statements of United States Firms in Four Industries," *International Journal of Management* 23.2 (2006), pp. 296–305; Terri Lammers, "The Effective and Indispensable Mission Statement," *Inc.* 7.1 (August 1992), p. 23; and I. C. MacMillan and A. Meshulack, "Replacement versus Expansion: Dilemma for Mature U.S. Businesses," *Academy of Management Journal* 26 (1983), pp. 708–726.

40. Osborn, Hunt, and Jauch (1985).

41. See Jeffery Pfeffer, "Barriers to the Advance of Organization Science," *Academy of Management Review* 18.4 (1994), pp. 599–620; and Richard M. Cyert and James G. March, *A Behavioral Theory of the Firm* (Englewood Cliffs, NJ: Prentice-Hall, 1963). A

historical view of organizational goals is also found in Charles Perrow, *Organizational Analysis: A Sociological View* (Belmont, CA: Wadsworth, 1970), and in Richard H. Hall, "Organizational Behavior: A Sociological Perspective," in Jay W. Lorsch (ed.), *Handbook of Organizational Behavior* (Englewood Cliffs, NJ: Prentice-Hall, 1987), pp. 84–95.

[42] W. Richard Scott and Gerald F. Davis, *Organizations and Organizing: Rational and Open Systems* (Englewood Cliffs, NJ: Prentice-Hall. 2007); Stewart R. Clegg and Cynthia Hardy, "Organizations, Organization and Organizing," in Clegg, Hardy, and Nord (eds.), *Handbook of Organizational Studies* (1996), pp. 1–28; and William H. Starbuck and Paul C. Nystrom, "Designing and Understanding Organizations," in P. C. Nystrom and W. H. Starbuck (eds.), *Handbook of Organizational Design: Adapting Organizations to Their Environments* (New York: Oxford University Press, 1981).

[43] See Osborn, Hunt, and Jauch (1985) for the historical rates, and for differences in survival rates by time of formation in the development of a technology, see R. Agarwal, M. Sarkar, and R. Echambadi, "The Conditioning Effect of Time on Firm Survival: An Industry Life Cycle Approach," *Academy of Management Journal* 25 (2002), pp. 971–985.

[44] J. Karpoff, D. S. Lee, and Gerald Martin, "A Company's Reputation Is What Gets Fried When Its Books Are Cooked" (2007). Accessed June 24, 2013, at www.washington.edu/news/2006/11/16/a-companys-reputation-is-what-gets-fried-when-its-books-get-cooked-2.

[45] J. Kerr and J. Slocum, "Managing Corporate Culture through Reward Systems," *Academy of Management Executive* 19.4 (2005), pp. 130–138.

[46] For the classic popular work, see Peter F. Drucker, *Innovation and Entrepreneurship* (New York: Harper, 1985). Edward B. Roberts, "Managing Invention and Innovation," *Research Technology Management* (January/February 1989), pp. 1–19 provides a practitioner perspective, whereas an interesting extended case study is provided by John Clark, *Managing Innovation and Change* (Thousand Oaks, CA: Sage, 1995).

[47] C. Miller, *Formalization and Innovation: An Ethnographic Study of Process Formalization* (Ann Arbor, MI: Proquest, 2008).

[48] P. Berrone, L. Gelabert, A. Fosfuri, and L. Gomez-Mejia, "Can Institutional Forces Create Competitive Advantage? An Empirical Examination of Environmental Innovation," *2008 Academy of Management Proceedings* (2008).

[49] U. Hulsher, N. Anderson, and J. Salgado, "Team-Level Predictors of Innovation at Work: A Comprehensive Meta-Analysis Spanning Three Decades of Research," *Journal of Applied Psychology* 94.5 (2009), pp. 1128–1145.

[50] D. Dougherty, "Organizing for Innovation," in Clegg, Hardy, and Nord (eds.), *Handbook of Organization Studies* (1996), pp. 424–439.

[51] For a discussion of product cannibalization, see S. Netessie and T. Taylor, "Product Line Design and Production Technology," *Marketing Science* 26.1 (2007), pp. 101–118.

[52] Tellis, Prabhu, and Chandy (2009).

[53] N. Clymer and S. Asaba, "A New Approach for Understanding Dominant Design: The Case of the Ink-jet Printer," *Journal of Engineering and Technology Management* 25.3 (2008), pp. 137–152.

[54] V. Acha, "Open by Design: The Role of Design in Open Innovation," *2008 Academy of Management Proceedings* (2008), pp. 1–6.

[55] One of the first to emphasize the role of lead uses was E. von Hipple, *The Sources of Innovation* (New York: Oxford University Press, 1988).

[56] See J. Birkinshaw, G. Hamel, and M. Mol, "Management Innovation," *Academy of Management Review* 33 (2008), pp. 825–845.

[57] The terms *exploration* and *exploitation* were popularized by James G. March. See James G. March, "Exploration and Exploitation in Organizational Learning," *Organization Science* 2.1 (1991), pp. 71–87. For a recent review, see Sung-Choon Kang, Shad S. Morris, and Scot A. Shell, "Relational Archetypes, Organizational Learning, and Value Creation: Extending the Human Resource Architecture," *Academy of Management Review* 32 (2007), pp. 236–256.

[58] Tellis, Prabhu, and Chandy (2009). For an extended discussion of radical innovation, see Osborn and Baughn (1994).

[59] See M. Tushman and P. Anderson, "Technological Discontinuities and Organizational Environments," *Administrative Science Quarterly* 31 (1986), pp. 439–465.

[60] M. Tushman and C. O. Reilly, "Ambidextrous Organizations: Managing Evolutionary and Revolutionary Change," *California Management Review* 38.4 (1996), pp. 8–30.

[61] M. Tokman, R. G. Richey, L. Marino, and K. M. Weaver, "Exploration, Exploitation and Satisfaction in Supply Chain Portfolio Strategy," *Journal of Business Logistics* 28 (2007), pp. 25–48.

[62] See C. Mirow, K. Hoelzle, and H. Gemueden, "The Ambidextrous Organization in Practice: Barriers to Innovation within Research and Development," *2008 Academy of Management Proceedings* (2008), pp. 1–6.

[63] For an excellent review, see Miller (2008).

[64] Ibid., p. 391.

[65] See K. Boal and P. Schultz, "Storytelling, Time and Evolution: The Role of Strategic Leadership in Complex Adaptive Systems," *The Leadership Quarterly* 18 (2007), pp. 411–428; and A. Grove, *Only the Paranoid Survive* (New York: Doubleday, 1996).

[66] Osborn and Jackson (1988).

[67] R. N. Osborn, "Purposeful Unintended Consequences and Systemic Financial Risk," Working Paper, Department of Management, Wayne State University (2009).

FEATURES AND PHOTO ESSAYS

Bringing OB to Life—Information from Alec Foege, "The Trouble with Tinkering Time," *Wall Street Journal* (January 19–20, 2013), p. C3.

Worth Considering . . . or Best Avoided?—Information and quote from Ashley Powers, "Quirky Culture Helps Online Store Zappos Sell," *Columbus Dispatch* (May 19, 2011), p. A12; and, Rhymer Rigby, "The Benefits of Workplace Levity," *Financial Times*, Kindle Edition (December 19, 2012).

Checking Ethics in OB—Information and quotes from Dana Mattioli. "With Jobs Scarce, Age Becomes an Issue," *Wall Street Journal* (May 19, 2009), p. D4.

Finding the Leader in You—Information derived from www.Cousinssubs.com; Carolyn Walkup, "Having Words With:

Christine Specht, President and Chief Operating Officer, Cousins Subs," *Nation's Restaurant News* 42:49 (2008, December 22), p. 78; and Alexis Mattera, "Christine Specht Continues Family Legacy at Cousins Subs," www.associatedcontent.com/article/972566/christine_specht_continues_family_legacy.html (2008, August 26).

OB in Popular Culture—The Firm, DVD, directed by Sydney Pollack (1993; Los Angeles: Paramount, 2000).

Photo Essays—Organizations with More Engaged Employees Perform Better—Information from "Employee Engagement: A Leading Indicator of Financial Performance," accessed June 19, 2013, at http://employeeengagement.com/gallup-employee-engagement-a-leading-indicator-of-financial-performance. *Clif Bar*—Information from Marnie Hanel, "Clif Bar's Offices Keep Employees Limber," *Bloomberg BusinessWeek* (November 21–27, 2011), pp. 104–105; and www.clifbar.com.

CHAPTER 16

ENDNOTES

[1] The bulk of this chapter was originally based on Richard N. Osborn, James G. Hunt, and Lawrence R. Jauch, *Organization Theory: Integrated Text and Cases* (Melbourne, FL: Krieger, 1985). For a more recent but consistent view, see Lex Donaldson, "The Normal Science of Structural Contingency Theory," in Stewart R. Clegg, Cynthia Hardy, and Walter R. Nord (eds.), *Handbook of Organizational Studies* (London: Sage Publications, 1996), pp. 57–76. For a more advanced treatment, see W. Richard Scott and Gerald F. Davis, *Organizations and Organizing: Rational and Open Systems* (Englewood Cliffs, NJ: Prentice-Hall. 2007).

[2] Osborn, Hunt, and Jauch (1985).

[3] For reviews, see Scott and Davis (2007); Osborn, Hunt, and Jauch (1985); Clegg, Hardy, and Nord (1996).

[4] William G. Ouchi and M. A. McGuire, "Organization Control: Two Functions," *Administrative Science Quarterly* 20 (1977), pp. 559–569.

[5] Ibid.

[6] Osborn, Hunt, and Jauch (1985).

[7] This discussion is adapted from W. Edwards Deming, "Improvement of Quality and Productivity Through Action by Management," *Productivity Review* (Winter 1982), pp. 12–22; W. Edwards Deming, *Quality, Productivity and Competitive Position* (Cambridge, MA: MIT Center for Advanced Engineering, 1982).

[8] For related reviews, see Scott and Davis (2007); Osborn, Hunt, and Jauch (1985); Clegg, Hardy, and Nord (1996).

[9] Rhys Andrews, George A. Boyne, Jennifer Law, and Richard M. Walker, "Centralization, Organization Strategy, and Public Service Performance," *Journal of Public Administration Research and Theory* 19.1 (2009), pp. 57–81.

[10] See C. Bradley, "Succeeding by (Organizational) Design," *Decision: Irelands Business Review* 11.1 (2006), pp. 24–29; and Osborn, Hunt, and Jauch (1985), pp. 273–303, for a discussion of centralization/decentralization.

[11] R. Durand, "Predicting a Firm's Forecasting Ability: The Roles of Organizational Illusion of Control and Organizational Attention," *Strategic Management Journal* 24 (September 2003), pp. 821–838.

[12] For reviews of structural tendencies and their influence on outcomes, also see Scott and Davis (2007); and Clegg, Hardy, and Nord (1996).

[13] See P. R. Lawrence and J. W. Lorsch, *Organization and Environment: Managing Differentiation and Integration* (Homewood, IL: Richard D. Irwin, 1967).

[14] Osborn, Hunt, and Jauch (1985).

[15] For a good discussion of the early use of matrix structures, see Stanley Davis, Paul Lawrence, Harvey Kolodny, and Michael Beer, *Matrix* (Reading, MA: Addison-Wesley, 1977).

[16] Lawrence and Lorsch (1967).

[17] See Osborn, Hunt, and Jauch (1985); and Scott and Davis (2007).

[18] Chris P. Long, Corinee Bendersky, and Calvin Morrill, "Fair Control: Complementarities Between Types of Managerial Controls and Employees' Fairness Evaluations," *2008 Academy of Management Proceedings* (2008), pp. 362–368.

[19] This discussion of organizational design was initially based on R. N. Osborn, J. G. Hunt, and L. Jauch, *Organization Theory Integrated Text and Cases* (Melbourne, FL: Krieger, 1984), pp. 123–215. For a more advanced treatment, see W. Richard Scott and Gerald F. Davis, *Organizations and Organizing: Rational and Open Systems* (Englewood Cliffs, NJ: Prentice-Hall, 2007).

[20] See Henry Mintzberg, *Structure in Fives: Designing Effective Organizations* (Englewood Cliffs, NJ: Prentice-Hall, 1983), pp. 76–83.

[21] See Scott and Davis (2007); and Osborn, Hunt, and Jauch (1984).

[22] See Peter M. Blau and Richard A. Schoenner, *The Structure of Organizations* (New York: Basic Books, 1971); and Joan Woodward, *Industrial Organization: Theory and Practice* (London: Oxford University Press, 1965).

[23] James D. Thompson, *Organization in Action* (New York: McGraw-Hill, 1967).

[24] Woodward (1965).

[25] For an updated review, see Scott and Davis (2007). This discussion also incorporates Osborn, Hunt, and Jauch (1984); and Louis Fry, "Technology-Structure Research: Three Critical Issues," *Academy of Management Journal* 25 (1982), pp. 532–552.

[26] Mintzberg (1983).

[27] See Henry Mintzberg and Alexandra McHugh, "Strategy Formulation in an Adhocracy," *Administrative Science Quarterly* 30.2 (1985), pp. 160–193.

[28] Halit Keskis, Ali E. Akgun, Ayse Gunsel, and Salih Imamoglu, "The Relationship between Adhocracy and Clan Cultures and Tacit Oriented KM Strategy," *Journal of Transnational Management* 10.3 (2005), pp. 39–51.

[29] Gerardine DeSanctis, "Information Technology," in Nigel Nicholson (ed.), *Blackwell Encyclopedic Dictionary of Organizational Behavior* (Cambridge, MA: Blackwell, 1995), pp. 232–233.

[30] Prashant C. Palvia, Shailendra C. Palvia, and Edward M. Roche, *Global Information Technology and Systems Management: Key Issues and Trends* (Nashua, NH: Ivy League Publishing, 1996).

[31] While this form is known under a variety of names, we emphasize the information technology base that makes it possible. See Peter Senge, Benjamin B. Lichtenstein, Katrin Kaeufer,

Hilary Bradbury, and John S. Carol, "Collaborating for Systematic Change," *MIT Sloan Management Review* 48.2 (2007), pp. 44–59; Josh Hyatt, "The Soul of a New Team," *Fortune* 153.11 (2006), pp. 134–145; M. L. Markus, B. Manville, and C. E. Agres, "What Makes a Virtual Organization Work," *MIT Sloan Management Review* 42 (2002), pp. 13–27; B. Hedgerg, G. Hahlgren, J. Hansson, and N. Olve, *Virtual Organizations and Beyond* (New York: Wiley, 2001); and Janice Beyer, Danti P. Ashmos, and R. N. Osborn, "Contrasts in Enacting TQM: Mechanistic vs. Organic Ideology and Implementation," *Journal of Quality Management* 1 (1997), pp. 13–29.

[32] Markus, Manville, and Agres (2002), pp. 13–27.

[33] Ibid.

[34] This section is based on R. N. Osborn, "The Evolution of Strategic Alliances in High Technology," Working Paper, Detroit: Department of Business, Wayne State University (2007); R. N. Osborn and J. G. Hunt, "The Environment and Organization Effectiveness," *Administrative Science Quarterly* 19 (1974), pp. 231–246; and Osborn, Hunt, and Jauch (1984). For a more extended discussion, see P. Kenis and D. Knoke, "How Organizational Field Networks Shape Interorganizational Information Rates," *Academy of Management Journal* 27 (2002), pp. 275–294.

[35] See R. N. Osborn and C. C. Baughn, "New Patterns in the Formation of U.S. Japanese Cooperative Ventures," *Columbia Journal of World Business* 22 (1988), pp. 57–65.

[36] This section is based on R. N. Osborn, "International Alliances: Going Beyond the Hype," *Mt Eliza Business Review* 6 (2003), pp. 37–44; S. Reddy, J. F. Hennart, and R. Osborn, "The Prevalence of Equity and Non-equity Cross-boarder Linkages: Japanese Investments in the U.S.," *Organization Studies* 23 (2002), pp. 759–780; and Wepin Tsai, "Knowledge Transfer in Interorganizational Networks: Effects of Network Position and Absorptive Capacity on Business Unit Innovation and Performance," *Academy of Management Journal* 44.5 (2001), pp. 996–1004.

[37] Osborn (2007).

[38] Max Weber, *The Theory of Social and Economic Organization*, translated by A. M. Henderson and H. T. Parsons (New York: Free Press, 1947).

[39] Stephen Cummings and Todd Bridgman, "The Strawman: The Reconfiguration of Max Weber in Management Textbooks and Why it Matters," *2008 Academy of Management Proceedings* (2008), pp. 243–249.

[40] Ibid.

[41] These relationships were initially outlined by Tom Burns and G. M. Stalker, *The Management of Innovation* (London: Tavistock, 1961).

[42] See Mintzberg (1983).

[43] Ibid.

[44] See Osborn, Hunt, and Jauch (1984) for an extended discussion.

[45] See Peter Clark and Ken Starkey, *Organization Transitions and Innovation—Design* (London: Pinter Publications, 1988).

FEATURES AND PHOTO ESSAYS

Bringing OB to Life—Information from Rachel Emma Silverman and Leslie Kwoh, "Peer Performance Reviews Take Off," *Wall Street Journal* (August 1, 2012), p. B6.

Worth Considering . . . or Best Avoided?—Information and quotes from James R. Hagerty, "Hog Maker Harley Gets Lean," *Wall Street Journal* (September 22–23, 2012), pp. B1, B3.

Finding the Leader in You—Information based on Lauren Canon, "Inc. 5000 Applicant of the Week," Inc., www.inc.com/articles/201102/applicant-of-the-week-desert-jet.html, February 22, 2011; and Desert Jet, www.desertjet.com.

OB in Popular Culture—Ratatouille. Dir. Brad Bird and Jan Pinkava. Perf. Brad Garrett, Lou Romano, Patton Oswalt. Pixar Animation Studios, Walt Disney Pictures, 2007. Film.

Photo Essays—Too Much Technology May Cause Airline Flight Crews to Lose Critical Skills—Information and quote from Brian Todd and Dugald McConnell, "Autopilots May Dull Skills of Pilots, Committee Says," CNN Washington, www.cnn.com/2011/TRAVEL/09/01/airlines.autopilot/index.html, September 1, 2011. *Millennials Are Warming Up to Part-time Employment for Full-time Pay*—Information from Hessun Wee, "Why More Millennials Go Part Time for Full Time Pay," CNBC, www.cnbc.com/id/49181054.

Name Index

A

Acevedo, Alma, 154
Adams, J. Stacy, 106
Akhmechet, Slava, 253
Alderfer, Clayton, 102
Amelio, Gil, 330
Anderson, Cameron, 229
Antonakis, John, 287
Ariely, Dan, 54
Arvey, Rich, 29
Atkinson, Dane, 253
Avery, Rich, 305

B

Bader, Brian, 289
Bandura, Albert, 62
Barlow, James, 166
Barnard, Chester, 264
Bass, Bernard, 312–313
Bazerman, Max H., 31
Bechky, Beth, 363
Berson, Yair, 339
Bezos, Jeff, 156, 176
Blair, Eden S., 113
Blakely, Sara, 122
Blount, Sally, 5
Boehnlein, Bob, 32
Bohnet, Iris, 31
Bond, Michael, 45
Branson, Richard, 56, 66, 310
Brett, Jeanne, 229
Brief, Arthur, 265
Brin, Sergey, 295
Bruno, Robert, 216
Buckley, M. Ronald, 128
Buffett, Warren, 154
Burns, James M., 311–312
Burns, Ursula, 14
Burris, Ethan, 245
Byham, William C., 221

C

Carroll, Archie B., 19
Carton, Andrew M., 62
Cavanagh, Gerald, 192–193
Chan-Serafin, Suzanne, 265
Cialdini, Robert B., 262
Collins, Jim, 337
Cook, Tim, 239
Cox, Taylor, 332

D

De Rond, Mark, 248
DeButts, John, 32
Deming, W. Edwards, 357–358
Detert, James, 245
DuBois, L. Z., 128
Dvir, Taly, 339

E

Eagley, Alice, 9
Emerson, Ralph Waldo, 239
Emmanuel, Rahm, 216
English, Paul, 173
Erickson, Gary, 336

F

Falk, Adam, 15
Ferguson, Merideth, 55
Festinger, Leon, 84
Fiedler, F. E., 307
Ford, J. K., 128
Ford, William Clay Jr., 225
Franco, Lynn, 89
French, John, 263
Friedman, Ray, 55

G

Gandhi, Mahatma, 309, 312
Garrity, Steve, 358
Gavin, Joanne H., 150
Gawande, Atul, 191
George, William, 59
Goates, Nathan, 229
Goldstein, Noah J., 262
Goleman, Daniel, 17, 76, 79, 81
Gorovsky, Brett, 135
Graham, Paul, 147
Gratton, Lynda, 31
Greenfield, Geoff, 21
Greenfield, Michelle, 21
Greenleaf, Robert K., 319

H

Hackman, Richard, 131–132, 164, 248
Hall, Edward T., 242
Hamel, Gary, 13
Harrison, David A., 150
Hastings, Reed, 124
Hawking, Stephen, 33
Hertzberg, Frederick, 104–105
Hitler, Adolf, 239, 312
Hofstede, Geert, 44–45, 46
Hollander, Edwin, 294
House, Robert, 309

I

Ilies, Remus, 93

J

Jago, Arthur, 204
Janis, Irving, 181
Jobs, Steve, 164, 239, 310, 329–330
Johnson, James, 146
Jordan, Michael, 248
Jung, Carl, 35–36

K

Kahneman, Daniel, 190, 201
Karter, Patricia, 311
Katz, Robert, 16, 18
Kay, Laura, 265
Kennedy, John F., 182, 309
King, Martin Luther, 310
Klein, Katherine, 309
Kraiger, K., 128

L

Langois, Marilyn, 146
Latham, Gary, 112
Lau, Dora, 169
Lawler, Edward, 122
Lawrence, Paul, 105
Lester, Cameron, 317
Levy, Steven, 164
Lincoln, Abraham, 314
Lisco, Cara Cherry, 229
Locke, Edwin, 112, 113
Longenecker, Clinton, 268

Lowe, Challis M., 83
Ludwig, Dean, 268

M
Maas, James, 103
MacGregor, James, 311
Machiavelli, Niccolo, 40
Mackey, John, 319
Mandela, Nelson, 309
Martin, Steve J., 262
Maslow, Abraham, 101–102
Mayer, Marissa, 136
McCabe, Donald, 154
McClelland, David L., 102–103
McNair, Tim, 303
Meglino, Bruce, 44
Milgram, Stanley, 291
Mines, Raymond, 88
Mintzberg, Henry, 16, 372
Mongello, Kimi, 253
Monroe, Lorraine, 105
Morgan, Jacob, 5
Mother Theresa, 309
Moye, Neta, 55
Mulally, Alan, 225
Murnighan, Keith, 169, 308

N
Neil, Becky, 171
Nohria, Nitin, 105

O
Obama, Barack, 310
Oldham, Greg, 131–132
Olekans, Marla, 229
Oreg, Shaul, 339

P
Page, Larry, 295
Pavlov, Ivan, 64
Pearson, Christine, 90
Peters, Tom, 239
Pfeffer, Jeffrey, 9, 86
Pink, Daniel, 100

Pope John Paul II, 269
Porath, Christine, 90
Porter, Michael, 319
Posner, Barry, 303
Price, Kenneth H., 150

Q
Queen Elizabeth, 269

R
Raven, Bertram, 263
Ringlemann, Max, 150
Robb, Walter, 111
Rokeach, Milton, 43–44
Rosedale, Philip, 171
Rosensweig, Dan, 32
Rosette, Ashleigh Shelby, 62
Russell, Arianna, 207
Russell, Bertrand, 260
Ryan, Nicole, 333

S
Sackett, P. R., 128
Sandberg, Sheryl, 58
Sanderson, Catherine, 217
Savile, Jimmy, 269
Schauer, David, 333
Schein, Edgar, 167, 179
Schmidt, Eric, 295
Schultz, William, 156
Schwind Wilson, Kelly, 93
Seidman, Dov, 124
Sheppard, Jim, 341
Simon, Herbert, 190, 197
Skinner, B. F., 64, 65
Skinner, Jim, 88
Snowden, Edward, 289
Snyder, Stacy, 244
Sozen, H. Cenk, 274
Specht, Bill, 341
Specht, Christine, 340, 341
Spreitzer, Gretchen, 283
Stajkovic, Alexander D., 113
Stauffer, Joseph M., 128

Stengel, Casey, 158
Stevens, Thaddeus, 314
Sullenberger, Chesley III, 199, 200
Sullivan, John, 358
Sutton, Robert, 9

T
Tajfel, Henri, 34
Taylor, Frederick, 129–130
Thomas, R. Roosevelt, 14
Thomas, Terry, 19
Thompson, Don, 88
Thompson, James D., 365
Thompson, Leigh, 182
Thorndike, E. L., 65
Tolstoy, Leo, 288
Turner, John, 34

V
Van Geen, Alexandra, 31
Van Susteren, Greta, 200
Vroom, Victor, 110, 204, 205

W
Wagner, David T., 93
Walkses, John, 329
Watson, Judith, 369
Weber, Max, 367, 370–371
West, Tim, 154
Whitman, Meg, 13
Wilson, Denise, 365
Winfrey, Oprah, 122, 309
Winklevoss, Cameron, 36
Winklevoss, Tyler, 36
Woodward, Joan, 366

Y
Yetton, Phillip, 204
Yukl, Gary, 313

Z
Zuckerberg, Mark, 36, 58

Organization Index

A
Accenture, 88–89, 134
Aetna, 59, 331
Airbus, 215
Allied Chemical, 369
Ally Bank, 108
Amazon.com, 156, 176
American Electric Power (AEP), 166
Apple, Inc., 164, 193, 239, 291, 312, 332–333
Applebee's, 123
Aprimo, 32
AT&T, 215
Atomic Object, 178
Automatitic, Inc., 157
Avon, 322

B
BBC, 269
Berkshire Hathaway, 154
BMW, 54
Bodacious Cases (Band-It Case), 207
Boeing, 215, 225, 332
Booz Allen Hamilton, 134
British Airways, 56

C
Catalyst, 31–32, 83
CCH, 135
Chegg, 32
Chi Générale de Radiologie, 334
Chrysler, 226
Cisco Systems, 90, 339
Clif Bar, 338
Coffee & Power, 171
Corning, 218
Cousins Subs, 342, 343

D
Dancing Deer Baking, 313
Dell, 193
Desert Jet, 367
Development Dimensions International, 126, 202
Dow Jones, 319
Dropbox, 147

E
EBay, 13, 229
Ernst & Young, 85

F
Facebook, 5, 36, 58, 78, 147, 178, 236, 291
Federal Express, 337
Fisher-Price, 207
Ford Motor Company, 91, 215, 225, 226, 242, 334
Foxconn, 193
Fusenet, 346

G
Gallup, 86, 87, 89, 332
General Electric, 178, 334, 375
General Mills, 59
General Motors, 226, 339
GitHub, 147
Glassdoor, 291
Goldman-Sachs, 297
Google, 58, 59, 178, 297, 346
Grouper, 147

H
Harley Davidson, 375
Harvard University, 321
Hearsay Social, Inc., 360
Heidrick & Struggles, 85
Hewlett-Packard, 193, 361
Hyundai, 215

I
IBM, 12, 28
IDEO, 239
Institute of Leadership and Management, 320

K
Kayak.com, 173
KPMG, 41, 195–196
Kraft, 28

L
LinkedIn, 5, 129
Living Social, 360
Lorraine Monroe Leadership Institute, 105

M
Macy's, 361
Mary Kay Cosmetics, 337
Mattel, Inc., 207
McDonald's, 88, 293
McKinsey & Company, 85
Medtronic, 59
MetLife, 178
Microsoft, 147, 336, 337, 369
Millward Brown Optimor, 85
Minnesota Twin Registry, 307
Monterey Gourmet Foods, 337
Monterey Pasta Company, 337
MySpace, 244

N
NASCAR, 144
NEC, 362
Neiman-Marcus, 122
Nestlé, 362
Netflix, 124
Nissan, 362

P
PepsiCo, 28
Pew Research Center, 129, 237
Philips, 362
Pittsburgh Pirates, 78
Pixar, 373
Proctor & Gamble (P&G), 125

R
Red Cross, 196
Red Frog Events, 124
RethinkDB, 253

S
Salary.com, 89
Sears, Roebuck and Co., 309
SEI Investments, 154
Skype, 178
Society for Human Resource Management, 198

OI-1

Sony, 362
Southwest Airlines, 80
Spanx, 122
Square, 147
Square Trade, 229
Stoke Mandeville Hospital, 269
Sun Microsystems, 178
SYSCO, 361

T
Target, 59
Tenmast Software, 253
Third Sun Solar Wind and Power Ltd., 21
3M, 330, 346, 369
Twitter, 178, 291

U
Union Carbide, 361
UPS, 337
US Airways, 199, 200
USAA, 198
USG, 198

V
Virgin Airlines, 56
Virgin Galactic, 66
Virgin Group, 56, 66, 312
Vodaphone, 215

W
Walmart, 81, 111, 322
WebMD, 135
Weight Watchers International, 305
What If? 331
Whole Foods, 111, 321
Williams-Sonoma, 313

X
Xerox, 14, 28, 195, 260

Y
Yahoo! 135, 236
Yelp, 5
YouTube, 199

Z
Zappos.com, 120, 331

Subject Index

A

Ability
   diversity, 33–34
   stereotypes, 58
Accommodation (smoothing), 223
Accountability, in feedback orientation, 253
Achievement, as workplace value, 44
Achievement-oriented leadership, 306, 307
Acquired needs theory, 102–104
Active listening
   advising and, 251
   defined, 250
   deflecting and, 251
   probing and, 250–251
   reflecting and, 250
   tips for, 250
Activity measures, 125
ADA (Americans with Disabilities Act), 33–34
Adaptive leadership, 317
Adhocracy, 366–367
Adjourning stage, teams, 152
Administrative leadership, 316–317
Advising, 251
Affect, 76
Affective events theory (AET), 82
Age
   diversity, 32–33
   in job layoffs, 333
   stereotypes, 58
Agreeableness, 35
Alliances
   for complex environments, 369–370
   interfirm, 370
Altering scripts and myths, 222
Alternative dispute resolution, 230
Ambition, *The Social Network* and, 36
Americans with Disabilities Act (ADA), 33–34
Amoral managers, 19
Analogies and metaphors, 207
Analytic approaches, 199
Anchoring and adjustment heuristic, 201
Appeals to common goals, 221

Applications, 8
Approach-approach conflict, 215
Approach-avoidance conflict, 215
Arbitration, 230
Association power, 266–267
Associative play, 206
At-home affect, 91
Attitudes
   affective component, 84
   as behavior influence, 83
   behavioral component, 84
   cognitive component, 83
   cognitive consistency and, 84
   components of, 83–84
   defined, 83
   as inferred, 83
   in the workplace, 84–87
Attractiveness, 28
Attribution
   defined, 61
   errors, 62
   importance of, 61
   social learning and, 62–63
   theory, 61
Authoritarian (autocratic) leadership, 320
Authoritarianism, 39
Authoritative command, 223
Authority decisions, 203
Authority rule, decision by, 179–180
Autonomy, 131
Availability heuristic, 201
Avoidance
   in interpersonal communication, 240
   lose-lose strategy, 223
Avoidance-avoidance conflict, 215
Awareness. *See also* Self-awareness
   cross-cultural, 9
   enriched, 19
   of others, 29
   social, 77

B

Baby Boomers, 33, 133
Bargaining zone, 227
BARS (behaviorally anchored rating scale), 126, 127

Bass's transactional leadership, 313
Bass's transformational leadership, 312–313
Bathsheba syndrome, 268–269
BATNA (best alternative to a negotiated agreement), 228
Behavioral approach
   defined, 304
   to leadership, 303–305
   relations-oriented behavior, 304–305
   task-oriented behavior, 305
Behavioral decision model, 97
Behaviorally anchored rating scale (BARS), 126, 127
Best alternative to a negotiated agreement (BATNA), 228
Bias
   against black leaders, 62
   decision, 201–202
   no risk, 346
   performance assessment, 31
   racial, 128
   self-serving, 62
Big Five Model, 35, 302
Blogging, 217
Bonuses, 123
Boot camps, 166
Brainstorming
   defined, 182
   in design thinking, 239
A Brief History of Time (Hawking), 33
Brokers, 276
Buffering, 220–221
Bureaucracies
   assumptions, 315
   defined, 370
   mechanistic (machine) type, 372
   organic (professional) type, 372

C

Career networks, 18
Careers, changing views of, 6
Cartels, 370
Central tendency error, 128
Centralization, 358
Centralized communication network, 177

CEO values, 339
Certain environments, 194
Channel richness, 243
Charisma
  consequences of, 310
  defined, 309
  as relational process, 309
  through polished rhetoric, 287
Charismatic leadership. *See also*
    Leadership
  characteristics of, 310
  dangers of, 310–311
  power distance and, 311
The Checklist Manifesto (Gawande), 191
Claiming
  defined, 285
  Forrest Gump and, 286
Classical conditioning, 64
Classical decision model, 97
Coercive power, 264
Cognitive consistency, 84
Cognitive empathy, 81
Cohesiveness. *See* Team cohesiveness
Co-leadership, 295
Collaboration
  economy, 5
  student's sharing of assignments
      and, 86
Collaboration and problem solving, 223
The Collaborative Organization
    (Morgan), 5
Collective intelligence, 157–158, 165
Collective leadership
  co-leadership, 295
  defined, 294
  distributed leadership, 294–295
  shared leadership, 296
Command-and-control, demise of, 6
Commitment, 268
Communication
  active listening and, 250–251
  biased, 244
  cross-cultural, 241
  defined, 236–237
  developmental feedback, 251–254
  downward, 243
  feedback, 237–238
  flows, 243–245
  importance of, 236
  lateral, 243
  nature of, 236–239
  noise and, 238
  nonverbal, 238–239
  in organizational contexts, 242–246
  owning, 249
  process, 236–238
  receiver, 237

  in relational contexts, 246–251
  relational development, 246–247
  relational maintenance, 247
  sender, 237
  supportive principles, 248–249
  team, 176–179
  technologies, 178–179
  upward, 243
  voice/silence and, 245–246
Communication barriers
  cultural, 241–242
  interpersonal, 239–240
  physical, 240
  semantic, 240–241
  types of, 239
Communication channels
  defined, 237, 242
  formal, 242
  informal, 242–243
  richness, 243
  types of, 237
Commutative justice, 109
Competition (win-lose strategy), 223
Complex adaptive systems, 12
Complexity leadership approaches
  adaptive leadership, 317
  administrative leadership, 316–317
  challenges of, 317–318
  complex adaptive systems, 315
  entrepreneurial leadership, 317
  environments, 315–316
Compliance
  defined, 267
  diversity and, 34
Compressed workweeks, 134
Compromise, 223
Conceptual skills, 18
Confirmation error, 201
Conflict management
  altering scripts and myths, 222
  appeal to common goals, 221
  direct, strategies, 222–223
  indirect, strategies, 220–222
  lose-lose strategies, 223
  managed interdependence, 220–221
  upward referral, 222
  win-lose strategies, 223
  win-win strategies, 223
Conflict resolution, 218
Conflicts
  antecedents, 218
  common causes in organizations, 219
  contextual causes of, 219
  culture and, 217–218
  defined, 214
  The Devil Wears Prada and, 221
  dysfunctional, 215, 216

  emotional, 214
  felt, 218
  functional, 215, 216
  hierarchical causes of, 218–219
  horizontal, 218–219
  intergroup, 215
  interorganizational, 215
  interpersonal, 214
  intrapersonal, 215
  levels of, 214–215
  life-staff, 219
  lose-lose, 223
  manifest, 218
  in organizations, 214–218
  perceived, 218
  role, 170
  role ambiguity, 219
  stages of, 218
  substantive, 214
  suppression, 218
  types of, 214
  vertical, 218
  win-lose, 223
  win-win, 223
Conformity to norms, 174
Confucian dynamism, 45–46
Conglomerates, 373
Connection power
  association, 266–267
  defined, 266
  reciprocal alliances, 267
  sources of, 274
Connections
  importance of, 5
  perceptions and, 271–272
Conscientiousness, 35
Consensus, 180
Consensus, decision by, 180
Consistency, in attribution theory, 61
Constituency negotiation, 224
Constructive conflict, 216
Constructive follower orientation, 290
Constructive resistance, 268
Consultative decisions
  defined, 203
  use recommendation, 205
  variants, 204–205
Content theories, 100–101
Context satisfaction moderator, 133
Contingency approaches, 306
Contingency model, 306–307
Contingency theories
  central argument of, 306
  contingency model, 306–307
  findings from, 307
  leader-match, 307
  leadership behaviors, 307

leadership effectiveness prediction, 306–307
problems with, 308–309
Contingency thinking, 8
Continuous improvement approach, 167
Continuous reinforcement, 67
Continuous-process technology, 366
Contrast effects, 59
Contrived rewards, 65
Control, 260
Controlling, 15
Controls
as basic feature, 356
defined, 356
output, 356
process, 356–357
Coordination
defined, 359
impersonal methods of, 364
personal methods of, 362–364
in temporary organizations, 363
Coping, 42
Corporate culture. See Organizational culture
Corruption, leadership and, 320
Countercultures, 330–331
Counterproductive behaviors
defined, 90
spotting, 91
CQ. See Cultural quotient
Creative membership, 206
Creativity
in decision making, 205–207
skills, 206
Crisis decisions, 196
Critical incident diaries, 126–127
Critical questions, ethics, 192–193
Cross pollination, 206
Cross-cultural awareness, 9
Cross-cultural communication, *The Amazing Race* and, 241
Cross-functional teams, 144
Crowdsourcing
grades, 15
peer evaluations, 358
Cultural barriers, 241–242
Cultural quotient (CQ), 45
Cultural symbols, 335
Cultural values
defined, 44
differences in, 45
dimensions, 45
Hofstede framework, 45–46
Culture managers, 338
Cultures
conflict and, 217–218

defined, 44
high-context, 242
low-context, 242

D

Decentralization
defined, 358
participation and, 359
Decentralized communication network, 177
Decision biases, 201–202
Decision making
biases, 201–202
creativity in, 205–207
defined, 179, 190
ethical reasoning and, 191–193
ideal, steps in, 190
judgmental heuristics, 201
perspectives, 197
process, 190–196
rational decision model, 190
risk management in, 195–196
traps and issues, 200–205
when to quit and, 202–203
who to involve and, 203–205
Decision techniques, 206
Decision to belong, 91
Decision to perform, 91
Decision tree, 205
Decisional roles, manager, 16
Decision-making models
behavioral, 197
classical, 197
systematic/intuitive thinking and, 198–199
Decisions. *See also* Decision making
combinations of environments and types of decisions, 193–195
consultative, 203
crisis, 196
individual, 203
nonprogrammed, 193, 194
optimizing, 197
programmed, 194–195
satisficing, 197
Decoupling, 220
Deep acting, 81
Deep-level diversity, 28
Defensiveness, 248–249
Deflecting, 251
Delegation, upward, 22
Denial of trade-offs, 346
Departments
divisional, 360
functional, 359–360
types of, 359
Dependence

defined, 260
increasing/reducing, 261
management, 261
in organizations, 261
power and, 260–261
Design thinking, 239
Destructive conflict, 216
Developmental feedback
defined, 251
feedback orientation, 252–253
feedback seeking, 252
Johari window, 251–252
techniques for giving, 251–252
Direct conflict management strategies, 222–223
Direction, in motivation, 100
Directive leadership, 306, 307
Disclosure, 246
Disconfirmation, 249
Discrimination, 30
Display rules, 81
Dispute resolution, 230
Disruptive behaviors, 168–169
Distinctiveness, in attribution theory, 61
Distress, 42
Distributed leadership, 168, 294–295
Distributive justice, 109
Distributive negotiation
approaches to, 226–227
bargaining zone, 227
defined, 226
hard, 226
soft, 226
Diversity
ability, 33–34
age, 32–33
compliance and, 34
deep-level, 28
discrimination and, 30
gender, 30–32
race and ethnicity, 30
sexual orientation, 32
social identity and, 34
surface-level, 28
team membership, 156–158
valuing, 30
workplace issues, 30–34
Diversity-consensus dilemma, 157
Divisional departments, 360
Divisional firms, 373
Do Nothing: How to Stop Overmanaging and Become a Great Leader (Murnighan), 308
Dogmatism, 39
Downward communication, 243
Drive to acquire, 106
Drive to bond, 106

Drive to defend, 106
Drivers
    of employee engagement, 87
    personal creativity, 205–206
    team creativity, 206–207
Dynamics
    inter-team, 175
    team, 167
Dysfunctional conflicts, 215, 216
Dysfunctional resistance, 268

E
Early trait approaches, 302
Ecological fallacy, 46
Effectance motive. *See* Self-efficacy
Effective followers, 22
Effective leaders. *See also* Leaders; Leadership
    defined, 20
    following, 21
    framing, 21
    in organizations, 20–21
    relationship building, 21
Effective managers. *See also* Managers
    defined, 14
    ten roles of, 16
Effective negotiation, 224
Effective teams. *See also* Teams
    criteria, 148
    defined, 148
    social facilitation, 148–149
    social loafing and, 149–151
    synergy, 148
Effort, 121
EI. *See* Emotional intelligence
Elephant in the room, 173
Emergence, 316
Emotion and mood contagion, 79–80
Emotional adjustment traits, 40–41
Emotional commitment, 85
Emotional conflicts, 214
Emotional dissonance, 81
Emotional drives or needs model, 105–106
Emotional empathy, 81
Emotional intelligence (EI)
    building blocks of, 17
    competencies, 77
    defined, 17, 76
    relationship management in, 77
    self-awareness in, 77
    self-management in, 77
    social awareness in, 77
Emotional labor, 80–81
Emotional stability, 35
Emotion-focused coping, 42
Emotions

as affective events, 82
cultural aspects of, 81
display rules, 81
in influencing behavior, 79–82
in leadership, 88
moods and, 79
nature of, 76
self-conscious, 77
social, 77–78
types of, 77–78
understanding, 76–78
Empathy
    cognitive, 81
    defined, 17
    emotional, 81
Employability, 261
Employee engagement
    defined, 86
    drivers of, 87
Employee involvement teams, 145
Employee stock ownership plans (ESOPs), 124
Employee value proposition, 120
Employees, engaged, 330
Empowering leadership, 320–321
Empowerment, 262–263
Encoding, 237
Engaged employees, 330
Enriched awareness, 19
Entrepreneurial leadership, 317
Environmental complexity, 368
Environmental interdependence, 369
Environmental richness, 369
Environmental uncertainty, 369
Environments
    certain, 194
    complex, networks and alliances for, 369–370
    complexity leadership approaches, 315–316
    external, 11–12
    general, 368
    internal, 13
    organizational design and, 368–370
    risk, 194–195
    specific, 368
    uncertain, 194
Equity. *See also* Inequity
    motivation and, 106–109
    perceived, 107
    social comparisons and, 106–107
Equity theory
    Ally Bank and, 108
    defined, 106
    organizational justice and, 108–109
    predictions and findings, 107
Equivalence, in social exchange, 293

ERG theory, 102
Escalating commitments, 203, 228
ESOPs (employee stock ownership plans), 124
Ethical behavior, commitment to, 5
Ethical climates, 321
Ethical leadership theory, 321
Ethical management, 19–20
Ethical standards, modifying, 340
Ethical workplace conduct, 60
Ethics
    critical questions, 192–193
    decision making and, 191–193
    defined, 191
    double-checks, 192–193
    leadership, 318–321
    in negotiation, 224–225
    spotlight questions, 193
Ethics center of gravity, 19
Ethics mindfulness, 19
Ethics team norms, 172
Ethnocentrism, 241
Eustress, 42
Evidence-based management, 9
Existence needs, 102
Expectancy
    defined, 110
    low, 111
    motivation and, 110–112
    terms and concepts, 110
Expectancy theory
    defined, 110
    in effort-performance-rewards linkage, 121
    implications and research, 111–112
    predictions, 110–111
Expectations, raising, 54
Expert power, 265
Exploitation, 345
Exploration, 345
External adaptation, 328–329
External environment, organizations and, 11–12
External support, 207
Externals, 38
Extinction, 69
Extraversion, 35
Extrinsic rewards, 65, 121

F
Fairness, as workplace value, 44
Feedback
    defined, 237
    developmental, 251–254
    giving, 251–252
    self-efficacy, 253
    techniques for giving, 251–252

Feedback orientation, 253–254
Feedback seeking, 252
Feeling-sensation individuals, 37
Feeling-type individuals, 36
Felt conflict, 218
Felt negative inequity, 107
Figure-ground separation, 53
Filtering, 240
FIRO-B theory, 156
Fixed-interval schedules, 68
Fixed-ratio schedules, 68
Flexible work hours, 134
Flirting, 267
Followers
  effective, 22
  leaders relationship, 292–294
  passive beliefs, 288
  proactive beliefs, 288–289
  readiness, 307
  role orientation, 290
  roles, leaders view of, 290–292
Followership
  defined, 288
  socially constructed, 288–289
  willing, 282, 283
Force, 260
Forced distribution, 126
Formal channels, 242
Formal leadership, 282
Formal retreat approach, 167
Formal systems, 270
Formal teams, 143
Formalization, 357
Forming stage, teams, 151
Framing
  defined, 21
  error, 201–202
Friendly helpers, 167–168
Friendship groups, 143
Frustration-regression, 102
Functional conflicts, 215, 216
Functional departmentation, 359–360
Functional silos (chimneys)
    problem, 144
Fundamental attribution error, 62
Furlough versus fire, 271

G

Gain sharing, 123
Gender. *See also* Women
  diversity, 30–32
  performance assessment and, 31
  stereotypes, 31, 57–58
General environments, 368
Generation F (Facebook Generation), 13
Generation X (Millennials), 33
Generation Y, 32, 133

Glass ceiling effect, 30
Goal setting
  defined, 112
  guidelines, 112–114
  management process and, 114
  using, 112
Goals
  appeals to common, 221
  challenging, 112
  conscious, 113
  feedback, 112, 113
  motivational properties of, 112
  negotiation, 224
  output, 339
  priorities, clarifying, 112
  relationship, 224
  shared, 338–340
  societal, 339
  specific, 112, 113
  subconscious, 113
  substance, 224
  system, 340
Granting
  defined, 285
  Forrest Gump and, 286
Grapevine, 243, 362
Graphic rating scales, 126
Group negotiation, 224
Groupthink
  defined, 181
  Madagascar and, 183
  remedies, 182
  symptoms, 181–182
Growth needs, 102
Growth-need strength, 132

H

Halo effects, 58
Halo error, 127
Headphones, 155
Hearing problem, negotiation, 229
Helping others, as workplace value, 44
Heroic leadership views, 314–315
Heuristics, 201
Hierarchical thinking, 264
Hierarchy, *Ratatouille* and, 371
Hierarchy of needs
  defined, 101–106
  higher order needs, 102
  illustrated, 101
  lower order needs, 102
High-context cultures, 242
Higher order needs, 102
High-performance teams. *See also* Team
    performance; Teams
  characteristics of, 164–165
  collective intelligence, 165

  team-building alternatives, 166–167
  team-building process, 165–166
Hindsight trap, 201
Homogeneous teams, 156–157
Honesty, as workplace value, 44
Horizontal conflict, 218–219
Horizontal loading, 130
Horizontal specialization, 359
How Do the Mighty Fall (Collins), 337
Human capital
  defined, 275
  emphasis on, 6
Human skills
  defined, 16
  emotional intelligence (EI), 17–18
  qualities of people with, 16–17
  social capital and, 18
  types of, 17–18
Hygiene factors, 104

I

Idealized influence, 312
Identification
  defined, 268
  organizational, 86
Idiosyncrasy credits, 294
Illusion of control, 359
Immediacy, in social exchange, 293
Immoral managers, 19
Implicit followership theories, 290–292
Implicit leadership theories
  defined, 285
  leaders/nonleaders classification, 285
  prototypes, 287
Impression management
  building brands through, 56
  defined, 56
  practice of, 56–57
  in social media, 56, 57
Improvement and change team
    norms, 172
Incivility, 90, 168–169
Inclusion, 14
Indirect conflict management
    strategies, 220–222
Individual attributes, 121
Individual decisions
  defined, 203
  use recommendation, 205
  variants, 204–205
Individual differences, 28
Individualism-collectivism, 45
Individualized consideration, 312
Inequity
  dilemma, 109
  felt negative, 107
  perceived, 107

Influence. *See also* Power
　gaining through persuasion, 262
　idealized, 312
　responses to, 267–269
　sources of, 263–267
Informal channels, 242
Informal combines, 370
Informal groups, 143
Informal leadership, 282
Informal systems, 270
Information power, 266, 273
Information technology (IT), 6, 367–368
Informational roles, manager, 16
In-group membership, 34
Innovation
　adhocracy and, 367
　cultural stability and, 345–347
　defined, 342
　exploration/exploitation balance, 345
　organizational culture lag, 345–346
　in organizations, 341–347
　process, 344
　process of, 342–343
　product, 343–344
　purposeful unintended consequences, 346–347
　raising ownership takes to boost, 344
　steps, 342
　success, 343
Inspiration, 105
Inspirational leadership, 312
Instrumental motivation, 267
Instrumental values, 43–44
Instrumentality
　defined, 110
　low, 111
Integrated model of motivation, 120–121
Integrative negotiation
　attitudinal foundations, 228
　behavioral foundations, 228
　defined, 226
　information foundations, 228
　use of, 227–228
Intellectual stimulation, 312
Intensive technology, 365
Interactional justice, 109
Interest, in social exchange, 293
Interest groups, 143
Interfirm alliances, 370
Intergroup conflicts, 215
Intergroup negotiation, 224
Intermittent reinforcement, 67–68
Internal environment, organizations, 13
Internal integration, 329–330
Internalization, 268

Internals, 38
Interorganizational conflicts, 215
Interpersonal barriers, 239–240
Interpersonal conflicts, 214
Interpersonal roles, manager, 16
Interpretation, in preception process, 56
Inter-role conflict, 170
Intersender role conflict, 170
Inter-team dynamics, 175
Intrapersonal conflicts, 215
Intrasender role conflict, 170
Intrinsic rewards, 121
Intuition
　defined, 198
　U.S. Air Flight 1549 and, 200
Intuitive approaches, 199
Intuitive thinking, 198
Intuitive-feeling individuals, 37
Intuitive-thinking individuals, 37
Intuitive-type individuals, 36
Involuntary part-timers, 136
Iron Law of Responsibility, 263
IT (information technology), 6, 367–368

J
Job burnout, 42
Job characteristics model
　core characteristics, 131
　defined, 131
　moderator variables, 132–133
　research concerns/questions, 133
Job Descriptive Index (JDI), 87
Job design
　defined, 129
　job characteristics model and, 131–133
　motivation and, 129–133
　scientific management and, 129–130
　strategy continuum, 129
Job enlargement, 130
Job enrichment, 104–105, 131
Job feedback, 131
Job involvement, 85
Job offers, decision to accept, 202
Job performance, job satisfaction link, 91–92
Job rotation, 130
Job satisfaction
　as attitude, 84
　components of, 87
　counterproductive behaviors and, 90
　defined, 14, 84
　influence in work behavior, 89–91
　issues, 87–93
　job performance link, 91–92
　organizational citizenship and, 89–90

　phycological withdrawal and, 89
　physical withdrawal and, 89
　self-employment and, 130
　spillover, 91, 93
　trends, 87–89
Job sharing, 134–135
Job simplification, 130
Johari window, 251, 252
Joint problem solving, 249
Judgmental heuristics, 201

K
Keiretsu, 370
Knowledge and skill moderator, 132

L
Lack of response, decision by, 179
Lack-of-participation error, 190
Later trait approaches, 302–303
Lateral communication, 243
Law of contingent reinforcement, 65
Law of effect, 65
Law of immediate reinforcement, 65
Law of reciprocity, 21
Layoffs, age and, 333
Leader position power, 307
Leader-follower relationship
　idiosyncrasy credits and, 294
　leader-member exchange (LMX) theory and, 292–293
　reciprocity and social exchange in, 293
　social exchange theory and, 293–294
Leader-match, 307
Leader-member exchange (LMX) theory, 292–293
Leaders
　born versus made question, 305
　collaborative, 239
　effective, 20–21, 302
　emergence, 302
　servant, 320
　success of, 21
　traits and behaviors, 302–305
Leadership
　achievement-oriented, 306, 307
　adaptive, 317
　administrative, 316–317
　authoritarian (autocratic), 320
　Bass's transactional, 313
　Bass's transformational, 312–313
　behavioral approaches, 303–305
　broad view of, 6
　charismatic, 287, 309–311
　co-leadership, 295
　collective, 294–296
　complexity views, 315–318

corruption and, 320
defined, 282
directive, 306, 307
distributed, 168, 294–295
do-nothing, 308
employee voice and, 245
empowering, 320–321
entrepreneurial, 317
formal, 282
heroic views, 314–315
as identity construction, 284–285
implicit theories, 285–287
informal, 282
inspirational, 312
Lincoln and, 314
in organizations, 20–22
participative, 306, 307
participatory, 283
physical appearance and, 303
process, 20, 281–296
romance of, 288
servant, 319–320
shared, 296
as social construction, 284
supportive, 306, 307
as talent, 305
trait approaches, 302–303
transactional, 312
transformational, 312
unethical, 318
upward, 282
women and, 9
Leadership ethics
defined, 319
empowering leadership and, 320–321
ethical climates and, 321
normative theory, 321
servant leadership and, 319–320
shared value view, 319
Leadership identity construction process, 284–285
Leading, 15
Leaking pipeline, 31
Learning
about organizational behavior, 9–10
defined, 9
experiential, in OB courses, 10
lifelong, 9
by reinforcement, 64–69
social, 62–63
Legitimate power, 263–264
Leniency error, 128
Life stressors, 41–42
Lifelong learning, 9
Life-staff conflict, 219
Line units, 356
Linking-pin roles, 221

Listening
active, 250–251
selective, 240
LMX (leader-member exchange) theory, 292–293
Locus of control, 37–38
Long-linked technology, 366
Long-term/short-term orientation, 45
Lose-lose strategies, 223
Low-context cultures, 242
Lower order needs, 102

M

Machiavellianism, 40
Maintenance activities, 168
Majority rule, decision by, 180
Managed interdependence, 223–224
Management
ethical, 19–20
evidence-based, 9
functions of, 14
moral, 11
open-book, 253
as profession, 18
scientific, 129–130
Management by objective (MBO), 114
Management philosophy, 338
Management process, 15
Managerial skills
conceptual, 18–19
defined, 16
human, 16–18
technical, 16
Managers
amoral, 19
decisional roles, 16
defined, 14
effective, 14–15, 16
with human skills, 17–18
immoral, 19
informational roles, 16
interpersonal roles, 16
moral, 19, 20
replacement terms for, 14
Masculinity-femininity, 45
Mass production, 366
Matrix departmentation, 361
MBA Oath, 18
MBO. *See* Management by objective
MBTI (Myers-Briggs Type Indicator), 35
Mechanistic (machine) type of bureaucracy, 372
Mediating technology, 365–366
Mediation, 230
Meditation, 59
Men, attractiveness in job hunting, 28
Merit pay, 122–123

Minnesota Satisfaction Questionnaire (MSQ), 87
Minority rule, decision by, 180
Mission statements, 339
"Mommy drain," 134
Moods
as affective events, 82
Crash and, 80
cultural aspects of, 81
defined, 78
emotions and, 79
in influencing behavior, 79–82
Moral dilemmas, 192
Moral management, 11
Moral managers, 19, 20
Moral problems, 191
Morale, 84–87
Motivation
acquired needs theory, 102–104
content theories, 100–101
defined, 17, 100, 120
direction and, 100
emotional drives or needs model, 105–106
equity and, 106–109
ERG theory, 102
expectancy and, 110–112
goals and, 112–114
hierarchy of needs theory, 101–102
human needs and, 101–106
instrumental, 267
integrated model of, 120–121
intrinsic, 101
job design and, 129–133
to lead, 285
performance and, 119–136
performance management and, 125–129
persistence and, 100
process theories, 101
theories, 100–101
two-factor theory, 104–105
Motivator factors, 104
Multiculturalism, 14
Multifactor Leadership Questionnaire (MLQ), 312
Multiskilling, 145
Mum effect, 245
Myers-Briggs Type Indicator (MBTI), 35
Myth of the fixed pie, 228
Myths, organizational, 337

N

National culture
corporate culture and, 332–333
diversity, building on, 332–333
Natural rewards, 65

Nature/nurture controversy, 29
Need for achievement (nAch), 102
Need for affiliation (nAff), 102–103
Need for power (nPower), 103
Negative reinforcement, 68
Negotiation
  common pitfalls, 228–229
  constituency, 224
  defined, 224
  distributive, 226–227
  effective, 224
  escalating commitments, 228
  ethical aspects of, 224–225
  goals and outcomes, 224
  group, 224
  hearing problem, 229
  integrative, 226, 227–228
  intergroup, 224
  labor-management, 226
  myth of the fixed pie, 228
  online dispute resolution, 229
  organizational settings for, 224
  overconfidence in, 229
  raise, 226
  strategies, 226–230
  telling problem, 229
  third-party roles in, 230
  two-party, 224
Networking, 275
Networks
  for complex environments, 369–370
  high performers and, 267
  importance of, 5
  sample scenarios for, 275
"No," learning to say, 43
No risk bias, 346
Noise, 238
Nominal group technique, 182–183
Nominal questions, 183
Nonprogrammed decisions
  crisis decision, 196
  defined, 194
  uncertain environments and, 194
Non-substitutable, 273
Nonverbal communication
  defined, 238
  furniture placement and, 238
  presence, 239
Norm of reciprocity, 293
Normative theory, 321
Norming stage, teams, 152
Norms, team, 170–173

O
OB. *See* Organizational behavior
OB Skills Workbook, 10
Objective thinkers, 168

Observable culture, 334
OCBs. *See* Organizational citizenship behaviors (OCBs)
Officeless companies, 157
Online dispute resolution, 229
Open systems, 12
Open-book management, 253
Openness to experience, 35
Operant conditioning
  defined, 64
  occurrence of, 65
Operational risks, 196
Operations technology, 365–366
Optimists, 79
Optimizing decisions, 197
Organic (professional) type of bureaucracy, 372
Organizational and personal pride team norms, 172
Organizational behavior modification, 65
Organizational behavior (OB)
  common scientific research methods in, 8
  context of, 11–14
  contingency thinking, 8
  cross-cultural awareness, 9
  defined, 4
  focus on applications, 8
  importance of, 4–6
  insights, 3
  as interdisciplinary body of knowledge, 6–7
  introduction to, 4–6
  learning about, 9–10
  quest for evidence, 8–9
  scientific foundations of, 6–9
Organizational charts, 354–355
Organizational citizenship behaviors (OCBs)
  defined, 89
  organizational, 89–90
  personal, 89
Organizational climate, 13
Organizational commitment, 85
Organizational cultural lag, 345–346
Organizational culture
  CEO values and, 339
  counterculture, 330–331
  defined, 13, 328
  external adaptation, 328–329
  The Firm and, 331
  fit, 13
  functioning of, 13
  functions of, 328–330
  importing societal subgroups, 332
  internal integration, 329–330

  layers of analysis, 334
  managing, 337–341
  mission statements and, 339
  national culture and, 332–333
  organizational myths, 337
  rules and roles, 237–238
  shared goals, 338–340
  shared meanings, 337
  shared values, 336–337
  stories, rites, rituals, and symbols, 334–335
  subcultures, 330
  understanding, 333–337
  visible aspects, modifying, 340–341
Organizational design
  defined, 364
  environment and, 368–370
  information technology and, 367–368
  operations technology and, 365–366
  simple, 364
  simplicity, 365
  technology and, 365–368
Organizational identification, 86
Organizational justice
  defined, 108
  types of, 109
Organizational myths, 337
Organizational politics
  defined, 270
  perceptions of, 272
  reasons for, 270
  self-interest role in, 270
  understanding, 270–272
Organizational silos, 243
Organizational structure
  controls, 356–359
  coordination, 362–364
  departments, 359–362
  formal, 354–359
  hierarchies, 354–356
  horizontal specialization, 359
  line and staff units, 356
  matrix structures, 360–362
  organization chart, 354–355
  span of control, 355–356
  vertical specialization, 354
Organizational support, 121
Organizations
  as complex adaptive systems, 12
  conflict in, 214–218
  defined, 11–12
  diversity and multiculturalism in, 14
  ethics center of gravity, 19
  external environment and, 11–12
  inclusion and, 14
  innovation in, 341–347
  internal environment of, 13

leadership in, 20–22
management in, 14–20
multicultural, 332
networks in, 275
as networks of teams, 143–144
as open systems, 12
teams in, 142–147
temporary, coordination in, 363
virtual, 367–368
Organizing, 15
Outdoor experience approach, 166
Out-group membership, 34
Output controls, 356
Output goals, 339
Output measures, 125
Overconfidence, negotiator, 228

P

Paired comparison, 126
Parochialism, 241
Participation, decentralization and, 359
Participative leadership, 306, 307
Participatory leadership, 283
Part-time work, 136
Pay
    merit, 122–123
    for performance, 121–124
    performance-contingent, 122
    secrecy, 289
    skill-based, 124
PechaKucha, 329
Peer evaluations, crowdsourcing, 358
Perceived conflict, 218
Perceived inequity, 107
Perceived legitimacy, 261
Perception
    attention and selection and, 53–54
    connections and, 271–272
    contrast example, 52
    defined, 52
    factors influencing, 52–53
    impression management and, 56–57
    information organization and, 54–56
    information processing and, 53–56
    interactional justice, 55
    interpretation and, 56
    perceived characteristics and, 53
    perceiver characteristics and, 53
    process, 52–57
    retrieval and, 56
    selective, 58
    setting characteristics and, 53
    wealth, 237
Perceptual distortions
    common, 57–61
    contrast effects, 59
    halo effects, 58
    projection, 58–59
    selective perception, 58
    self-fulfilling prophecies, 60–61
    stereotypes, 57–58
Performance
    motivation and, 119–136
    norms, 171
    pay for, 121–124
Performance assessment
    bias, 31
    comparative methods, 126
    critical incident diary, 126–127
    defined, 126
    methods, 126–127
    rating scales, 126
    360° review, 127
Performance contingency, 92
Performance management
    developmental purpose, 125
    evaluation purpose, 125
    motivation and, 125–129
    process, 125–126
Performance measurements
    activity, 125–126
    basis, 125
    errors, 127–128
    output, 125–126
    reliability test, 127
    validity test, 127
Performance Multiplier, 127
Performance-contingent pay, 122
Performing stage, teams, 152
Permanent part-time work, 136
Persistence, in motivation, 100
Person schemas, 55–56
Personal aggression, 91
Personal bias error, 128
Personal conception traits. *See also* Personality
    authoritarianism/dogmatism, 39
    defined, 37
    locus of control, 37–38
    Machiavellianism, 40
    proactive personality, 38
    self-monitoring, 40
Personal creativity drivers, 205–206
Personal leverage, 261
Personal power
    defined, 263
    expert, 265
    referent, 265–266
    sources of, 265–266
Personal values, 43–44
Personal wellness, 43
Personality
    Big Five Model, 35, 302
    defined, 34
    personal conception traits, 37–40
    social traits, 35–37
    stress and, 40–43
    in terms of emotional adjustment traits, 40–41
    traits, 35
    Type A orientation, 40–41
    Type B orientation, 40–41
Personality testing, 39
Personalized charismatics, 310
Person-job fit, 120
Person-organization fit, 120
Person-role conflict, 170
Person-to-situation schemas, 56
Persuading, 262
Pessimists, 79
Physical barriers, 240
Physical distractions, 240
Planning, 15
Political behavior, 273
Political climates, 270–272
Political deviance, 91
Political savvy, 274–275
Political skills
    defined, 274
    developing, 274–275
Politics
    navigating, 272–276
    organizational, 270–272
    role of self-interest in, 270
    self-interested, 270
    word connotation, 270
Porter-Lawler model, 92
Position power
    coercive, 264
    defined, 263
    legitimate, 263–264
    reward, 264
Positive reinforcement
    The Big Bang Theory, 67
    defined, 65
    leading with, 66
    scheduling, 67–68
    shaping, 66–67
    using, 69
Power
    of celebrity, corruptive, 269
    coercive, 264
    connection, 266–267, 274
    corruption and, 268–269
    defined, 260
    dependence and, 260–261
    as expanding pie, 262–263
    expert, 265
    force and, 260
    importance of, 260
    information, 266, 273

Power (*continued*)
  leader position, 307
  legitimate, 263–264
  navigating, 272–276
  in organizations, 274
  personal, 263, 265–266
  position, 263–264
  referent, 265–266
  responses to, 267–269
  reward, 264
  social, 260
  sources of, 263–267
  understanding, 260–263
  whistleblowing and, 261
Power bases
  building, 273–274
  defined, 273
Power distance
  defined, 45
  orientation, 290
  reducing, 311
Power or value asymmetries, 219
Power wielders, 311–312
Powerlessness, 261–262
Prejudice, 29
Presence, 239
Presenteeism, 135
Presumption of administrative competence, 346
The Prince (Machiavelli), 40
Privacy, social networking and, 244
Proactive personality, 38
Probing, 250–251
Problem-focused coping, 42
Problem-solving style
  defined, 35
  Jungian, 36–37
Problem-solving teams, 145
Procedural justice, 109
Process controls. *See also* Controls
  defined, 356
  formalization, 357
  rules and procedures, 357
  standardization, 357
Process innovations, 344
Process theories, 101
Product innovations, 343–344
Production deviance, 91
Profit motive, 319
Profit sharing, 123
Programmed decision
  certain environments and, 194
  defined, 194
  risk environments and, 194–195
Projection, 58–59
Property deviance, 91
Proxemics, 178

Psychological empowerment, 131
Psychological reactance theory, 263
Punishment, 68–69

Q
Quality circles, 145
Quit, knowing when to, 202–203

R
Race and ethnicity, 30
Racial and ethnic stereotypes, 57
Racial bias, 128
Ranking, 126
Rating scales, 126
Rational commitment, 85
Rational decision model, 190
Receivers, 237
Recency error, 128
Reciprocal alliances, 267
Referent power, 265–266
Reflecting, 250
Reinforcement
  continuous, 67
  defined, 64
  extinction and, 69
  intermittent, 67–68
  learning by, 64–69
  negative, 68
  operant conditioning and, 64–65
  positive, 65–68
  pros and cons, 69
  punishment and, 68–69
Relatedness needs, 102
Relational maintenance, 247–248
Relational repair, 247
Relational testing
  defined, 246
  disclosure and, 246
  process, 247
Relational violations, 247
Relationship goals, 224
Relationship management, 77
Relations-oriented behavior, 304, 305
Reliability, performance measurements, 127
Representativeness heuristic, 201
Reputation risks, 196
Resistance, 268
Resource scarcity, 219
Restricted communication network, 177–178
Retrieval, in perception process, 56
Reward power, 264
Rewards
  as cause of both satisfaction and performance, 92

  contrived, 65
  extrinsic, 65, 121
  intrinsic, 121
  motivational value of, 107
  natural, 65
  in performance causes satisfaction model, 92
  systems, modifying, 340–341
Ringlemann effect. *See* Social loafing
Risk environments, 194–195
Risk management
  in decision making, 195–196
  defined, 195
Rites, 335
Rituals, 335
Role ambiguity conflicts, 219
Roles. *See also* Team members; Teams
  ambiguity, 170
  conflict, 170
  defined, 169–170
  negotiation, 170
  overload, 170
  underload, 170
Romance of leadership, 288
Rule of conformity, 174

S
Sagas, 335
Satisficing decisions, 197
Scheduling positive reinforcement, 67–68
Schemas
  defined, 54
  person, 55–56
  person-to-situation, 56
  script, 54
  self, 54–55
Scientific management, 129–130
Script schemas, 54
Secrecy, 253
Secretaries, 274
Selective listening, 240
Selective perception, 58
Selective screening, 53
Self management, in emotional intelligence (EI), 77
Self schemas, 54–55
Self-awareness
  defined, 17, 28–29
  in emotional intelligence (EI), 77
Self-concept, 28
Self-conscious emotions, 77
Self-directed work teams, 145
Self-efficacy
  defined, 29, 63
  feedback, 253
  ways to build or enhance, 63

Self-esteem, 29
Self-fulfilling prophecies
    defined, 60
    negative outcomes, 60
    positive outcomes, 61
Self-interested politics, 270
Self-management
    in emotional intelligence (EI), 77
    Slumdog Millionaire and, 132
Self-managing teams, 145
Self-monitoring, 40
Self-regulation
    as core building block of EI, 17
    defined, 17
    self-management as form of, 77
Self-serving bias, 62
Semantic barriers, 240–241
Senders, 237
Sensation-thinking individuals, 37
Sensation-type individuals, 36
Servant leadership. *See also* Leadership
    characteristics of, 319
    defined, 319
    spiritual values, 320
Sexual orientation, 32
Shaping, 66–67
Shared leadership, 296
Shared meanings, 337
Shared value view, 319
Shared values, 336–337
Sickness, work and, 135
Silence, 245
Simple design, 364
Skills
    conceptual, 18–19
    creativity, 206
    defined, 16
    human, 16–18
    managerial, 16–19
    political, 274–275
    social, 17
    technical, 16
    variety of, 131
Sleep for Success (Maas), 103
Small-batch production, 366
Smart workforces, 4
Social awareness
    in emotional intelligence (EI), 77
    in feedback orientation, 253
Social capital
    benefits of, 275
    defined, 18, 275
Social construction
    context dependency, 289
    followership as, 288–289
    leadership as, 289
Social demands, team task, 155

Social emotions, 77–78
Social exchange
    defined, 21
    theory, 293–294
Social facilitation, 148–149
Social identity, 34
Social learning
    attribution and, 62–63
    model of, 63
    theory, 62–63
Social loafing
    defined, 149–150
    handling, 150
    influences on, 150
    Survivor and, 149
    as tendency within groups, 172
Social media, impression management in, 56, 57
Social network analysis, 143–144
Social networks
    human skills and, 18
    in organizations, 274
    privacy and, 244
Social power, 260
Social skills
    defined, 17
    in emotional intelligence (EI), 17
Social traits, 35. *See also* Personality
Socialized charismatic power orientation, 310
Socially constructed followership, 288–289
Socially constructed leadership, 284
Societal goals, 339
Span of control, 355–356
Specific environments, 368
Spillover effect, 41
Spotlight questions, ethics, 193
Staff units, 356
Stakeholders, 12
Standardization, 357
Star network, 177
Status congruence, 156
Status differences, 244
Stereotypes
    ability, 58
    age, 58
    defined, 55, 57
    gender, 31, 57–58
    racial and ethnic, 57
Stigmas, 34
Stock options, 124
Storming stage, teams, 151
Strategic risks, 196
Stress
    approaches to managing, 42–43
    coping mechanisms, 42

defined, 40
life stressors, 41–42
outcomes of, 42
personal wellness and, 43
personality and, 40–43
prevention, 42
Type A orientation and, 40–41
vacation habits and, 41
work stressors, 41
Strikes, 216
Structural differentiation, 219
Structural holes, 276
"Student Leadership Practices Inventory," 10
Subcultures, 330
Substance goals, 224
Substantive conflicts, 214
Success
    flirting and chatting up for, 267
    innovation, 343
    source of, 129
Support and helpfulness team norms, 172
Supportive communication principles. *See also* Communication
    defensiveness and, 248–249
    defined, 248
    disconfirmation and, 249
    joint problem solving, 249
    list of, 249
    owning communication and, 249
    problem focus, 249
    specificity and objectivity, 249
Supportive leadership, 306, 307
Surface-level diversity, 28
Surfacing acting, 81
Sustainability, 6
Synergy, 148
System goals, 340
Systematic thinking, 198

T

Task activities, 168
Task motivation, 205
Task networks, 17–18
Task performance, 14
Task structure, 307
Task-oriented behavior, 305
Tasks
    identity, 131
    significance, 131
    team, 154–155
TAT (Thematic Apperception Test), 102
Team building
    alternatives, 166–167
    boot camps, 166

Team building (*continued*)
    continuous improvement approach, 167
    defined, 165
    formal retreat approach, 167
    outdoor experience approach, 166
    process, 165–166
Team cohesiveness
    conformity to norms and, 174
    defined, 174
    increasing/decreasing, 175
    influencing, 174–175
Team communications
    centralized network, 177
    decentralized network, 177
    improving, 176–179
    interaction patterns, 177
    proxemics and use of space, 178
    restricted network, 177–178
    technologies, 178–179
Team composition, 156
Team creativity drivers, 206–207
Team decisions
    assets and liabilities of, 180–181
    by authority rule, 179–180
    brainstorming and, 182
    by consensus, 180
    defined, 203
    Delphi technique, 183
    groupthink and, 181–182
    improving, 179–183
    by lack of response, 179–180
    by majority rule, 180
    by minority rule, 180
    nominal group technique, 182–183
    techniques, 182–183
    by unanimity, 180
    use recommendation, 205
    variants, 204–205
    ways for making, 179–180
Team members
    friendly helper, 167–168
    high-performance teams, 164
    incivility, 168–169
    must-have contributions by, 142
    new, entry of, 167–168
    objective thinker, 168
    role ambiguity, 170
    role conflict, 170
    role negotiation, 170
    role overload/underload, 170
    roles, 169–170
    standing up, 178
    success at complex tasks, 154
    tough battler, 167
Team norms
    conformity to, 174
    defined, 170
    discussing, 173
    ethics, 172
    improvement and change, 172
    influencing, 173
    organizational and personal pride, 172
    performance, 171
    support and helpfulness, 172
    types of, 171–173
Team or group dynamics, 167
Team performance
    high, 164–167
    meetings to discuss, 173
    membership diversity and, 156–158
Teams
    adjourning stage, 152
    Amazon.com, 176
    challenges, 165
    collective intelligence, 157–158
    composition of, 156
    criteria for being effective, 148
    cross-functional, 144
    defined, 142
    demographic faultlines and, 169
    development stages, 151–152
    disruptions to, 150–151
    disruptive behaviors, 168–169
    distributed leadership, 168
    diversity-consensus dilemma, 157
    effectiveness, 147–151
    employee involvement, 145
    formal, 143
    forming stage, 151
    functions of, 142–143
    headphones and, 155
    heterogeneous, 157
    high-performance, 164–167
    homogeneous, 156–157
    inter-team dynamics, 175
    maintenance activities, 168
    maturity criteria, 152
    membership diversity, 156–158
    nature of, 141–158
    networks of, 143–144
    new members, 167–168
    norming stage, 152
    in organizations, 142–147
    performing stage, 152
    problem-solving, 145
    processes, improving, 167–176
    resources and setting, 153–154
    self-managing, 145
    size of, 155–156
    social facilitation, 148–149
    social loafing and, 149–151
    storming stage, 151
    synergy, 148
    task, 154–155
    task activities, 168
    that make or do things, 143
    that recommend things, 143
    that run things, 143
    virtual, 146–147
Teamwork
    defined, 142
    emphasis on, 6
    input foundations, 153–158
    NASCAR, 144
    worker-owner, 146
Technical demands, team task, 155
Technical skills
    defined, 16
    at entry levels, 18–19
Technology
    airline flight crews and, 367
    information, 367–368
    intensive, 365
    long-linked, 366
    mediating, 365–366
    operations, 365–366
    organizational design and, 365–368
Telecommuting
    benefits of, 135–136
    defined, 135
    work-life balance and, 136
Telling problem, negotiation, 229
Temporary part-time work, 136
Terminal values, 43, 44
Thematic Apperception Test (TAT), 102
There is an I in Team: What Elite Athletes and Coaches Really Know About High Performance (de Rond), 248
Thinking-type individuals, 36
360° review, 127
Title VII of the Civil Rights Act of 1964, 30, 31
Top-down management subculture, 338
Total quality management, 357–358
Tough battlers, 167
Tough talk, 250
Trait approaches to leadership
    defined, 302
    early, 302
    later, 302–303
Transactional leadership, 312
Transformational leadership, 312
Transforming leadership theory, 311–312
Transparency, 253
Trust, in social exchange, 293–294
Two-factor theory
    defined, 104
    hygiene factors, 104

job enrichment, 104–105
motivator factors, 104
Two-party negotiation, 224
Type A orientation
defined, 40
stress and, 40–41
stress prevention, 42
Type B orientation, 40

U

Unanimity, decision by, 180
Uncertain environments, 194
Uncertainty avoidance, 45
Universal design, 34
Upward communication, 243
Upward delegation, 22
Upward leadership, 282
Upward referral, 222
Utility, in feedback orientation, 253

V

Vacations
freedom and responsibility culture, 124
habits of, 41
Valence
defined, 110
low, 111
Validity, performance measurements, 127
Value congruence, 44
Values
asymmetries, 219
CEO, 339
cultural, 44–46
defined, 43
incongruent, 44
instrumental, 43–44
national, dimensions of, 44–45
personal, 43–44
shared, 336–337
shared view, 319
sources of, 43
spiritual, 320
terminal, 43, 44
workplace-important, 44
Variable schedules, 68
Variable-interval schedules, 68
Variable-ratio schedules, 68
Vertical conflict, 218
Vertical keiretsu, 370
Vertical loading, 131
Vertical specialization, 354
Video games, 82
Virtual communication networks, 178–179
Virtual organizations, 367–368
Virtual teams. *See also* Teams
advantages of, 146–147
defined, 146
downsides of, 147
meetings, 147
steps to success, 146
Voice, 245

W

Wheel network, 177
Whistleblowing, 261
Willing followership, 282, 283
Willingness to ask concrete questions, 228
Willingness to share, 228
Willingness to trust, 228
Win-lose strategies, 223
Win-win strategies, 223
Women
attractiveness, in job hunting, 28
as breadwinner, 220
European quotas for, 85
inclusion and, 14
as leaders, 9
leaking pipeline, 31
parity for, 284
venture start-ups led by, 317
Work from home, 17
Work schedules
alternative, 133–136
compressed workweeks, 134
flexible work hours, 134
job sharing, 134–135
part-time, 136
telecommuting, 135–136
Work sharing, 135
Work stressors, 41
Workarounds, 270–271
Workforce
diversity, 14
expectations, 6
smart, 4
Workgroups, 165
Work-home spillover, 91
Workplace
bullying, 90
as fun place, 329–330
Workplace-important values, 44

Y

Yoga, 59

Z

Zero sum game, 263
Zone of indifference, 264

Special Features

BRINGING OB TO LIFE

- Building Skills to Succeed in a Collaboration Economy
- Taking Steps to Curb Bias in Performance Assessment
- Managing Expectations and Getting Better Feedback
- Putting a Price Tag on Incivility at Work
- Hitting the Snooze Button and Gaining Motivation
- Paying, or Not Paying, for Kids' Grades
- Removing the Headphones to Show Team Spirit
- Spotting the Elephant in the Conference Room
- Getting Real to Make the Right Job Choice
- Keeping It All Together When Mom's The Breadwinner
- Removing Doubts by Embracing Open Information
- Flirting and Chatting Up For Success
- Building Charisma through Polished Rhetoric
- Staying Thin to Gain a Leadership Edge
- Raising the Ownership Stakes to Boost Innovation
- Flattening Structures by Crowdsourcing Peer Evaluations

WORTH CONSIDERING...OR BEST AVOIDED?

- Trouble Balancing Work and Home? Home Working May Be the Answer
- Would You Please Move Over? We're Making Room for Generation Y
- Not Enough Women on Board? Europe Turns to Quotas
- Got a Yoga Mat? Meditation Can Be Good for You and Your Job
- Paying More than the Minimum May Be Best Choice
- Want Vacation? No Problem, Take As Much As You Want
- Software Makes Online Meetings Easy. Is it Time to Kill Face-To-Face Sitdowns?
- Teammates May Know You Best. Should They Pay You As Well?
- Need a Break? Some Workers are Swapping Cash for Time
- Labor and Management Sides Disagree. Is a Strike the Answer?
- Everyone On the Team Seems Really Happy. Is It Time to Create Some Disharmony?
- Struggling to Gain Influence? Tap Into the Science of Persuading
- Bosses Are to Be Obeyed and My Job Is To Comply. Or Is It?
- Newly Promoted To Manager? "Do Nothing" May Be Your Key to Success
- Is It Time to Make the Workplace a Fun Place?
- Do Flexible Factories Have Staying Power?

CHECKING ETHICS IN OB

- Is Management a Profession?
- Personality Testing Required
- Workers Report Views on Ethical Workplace Conduct
- The Downside of Facebook Follies
- Information Goldmine Creates a Dilemma
- Sniffling At Work Hurts More Than the Nose
- Cheat Now . . . Cheat Later
- Social Loafing May Be Closer Than You Think
- Life and Death at Outsourcing Factory
- Blogging Can Be Fun, But Bloggers Beware
- Privacy in the Age of Social Networking
- Furlough or Fire? Weighing Alternative Interests
- Workers Share Their Salary Secrets
- Tackling Unethical Leadership in the Workplace
- Age Becomes an Issue in Job Layoffs
- Flattened into Exhaustion

FINDING THE LEADER IN YOU

- Michelle Greenfield Leads with a Sustainability Vision
- Stephen Hawking Inspires and Soars Despite Disability
- Richard Branson Leads with Personality and Positive Reinforcement
- Don Thompson Lets Emotions and Listening Take the Lead
- Lorraine Monroe Turns Leadership Vision into Inspiration
- Sara Blakely Leads Spanx from Idea to Bottom Line
- Teamwork Leads NASCAR's Race in the Fast Lane
- Amazon's Jeff Bezos Harnesses Teamwork to Drive Innovation
- Arianna Russell Leads with Intuition at the Bodacious Bandit
- Alan Mulally Leads by Transforming an Executive Team
- IDEO Selects for Collaborative Leaders
- Corruptive Power of Celebrity Turns Blind Eye to Pedophilia
- Google's Triumvirate Gives Way to New Leadership Structure
- Patricia Karter Uses Core Values as Her Guide
- Christine Specht Puts a Smile on Cousins Subs
- Denise Wilson Keeps Structure Simple at Desert Jet